Experimental Sociology
of Architecture

New Babylon

Studies in the Social Sciences
36

MOUTON PUBLISHERS · THE HAGUE · PARIS · NEW YORK

Experimental Sociology of Architecture

A Guide to Theory, Research and Literature

Guy Ankerl

MOUTON PUBLISHERS · THE HAGUE · PARIS · NEW YORK

Library of Congress Cataloging in Publication Data

Ankerl, Guy.
 Experimental sociology of architecture.

 (New Babylon, studies in the social sciences ; 36)
 Bibliography: p.
 Includes index.
 1. Architecture and society. 2. Architecture –
Human factors. I. Title. II. Series.
NA2543.S6A53   720'.1'03   81-11186
ISBN 90-279-3219-0

ISBN: 90-279-3219-0
Copyright © 1981, Guy Ankerl
Printed in Germany

There may, at the present time, be a lack of architectural taste: there is, unfortunately, no lack of architectural opinion. Architecture, it is said, must be 'expressive of its purpose', or 'expressive of its true constructions', or 'expressive of the materials it employs', or 'expressive of the material life', (whether noble or otherwise), or 'expressive of a noble life' (whether material or not); or 'expressive of the craftsman's temperament', or the owner's or the architect's, or, on the contrary, 'academic' and studiously indifferent to these factors.

   The Architecture of Humanism, by Geoffrey Scott

Preface

Readers can judge a book for themselves — critics feel enjoined to do so for others. In neither case are prefaces meant to plead for the book, or to obviate the need to read it. Prefaces exist to prevent misreading by indicating the scope and nature of the work. Indeed, the circle of readers must fit within the framework of the author's intentions.

Today a bound collection of printed sheets does not necessarily constitute a book. In reading through the special literature relevant to the experimental sociology of architecture, the author realized that more and more volumes are published that are nonbooks. This trend is present not only in the New World but also on the European Continent as well as in the British Isles. Often, reprinted articles are assembled and rushed into print as a volume without due concern for consistency or theoretical underpinnings (see for example recent publications of Dowden, Hutchinson and Ross, Inc.).

William H. Batchelder (1975) has reason to state that 'Essays reflect an unfortunate tendency . . . to encourage a *profusion* of book chapters that are largely rehashes of previous work' (see also Patterson 1977).

Other nonbooks stem from publishers who imagine that a class of works exists that can be truly useful for both specialists and the public at large (cf. Ankerl 1977). It must be said in no uncertain terms that this kind of work cannot exist unless the field involved, such as palmistry, has no true claim to being a science.

Authors must make their choice. The present author made his: to try to write a *book* that is a work of science. The author respects books as a vehicle of civilization for *lasting* knowledge. The distinctive attribute of a book is not the number of copies printed, the best sale in the first hour at the marketplace. As we know, the media launch names and faces; titles salute readers' eyes; hordes of barkers and critics laud works before publication. *Fashion* is created by design.

Books have to outlast a rotary press or computer tapes. Even if the circulation of the Sunday *Times* exceeds one million and even if *The How and Why of French Cooking* (1974) was published under the scholarly imprint of the University of Chicago Press, their sales will never have a significance comparable to that of Plato's *Republic* or Aristotle's *Politics*, which were transcribed again and again, and in later times printed and reprinted. If success is a reward for effort, such reading and rereading over generations is what has meaning.

Based on the title *Sociology of Architecture*, editors often expect an easy-to-read picture book aimed at a mass audience nurtured on television. The author believes that *like mathematicians, physicists, and engineers, architects as well as sociologists deserve scientific books*. (As explained in the 'Introduction', the author also had a specific reason to abstain from writing even an appropriate picture book: to emphasize the fact that architecture is not exclusively a matter of *optical* space creation.)

In political essay writing, consensus is often seen as the main test of truth, while in *belles-lettres* an attractive, good-humored presentation can gain easy acceptance. For scientific works, both consensus and polish distract attention from rigorous argumentation even if it is original and inventive. Valuable scientific works must be uncompromising and their exposition must be dry if scientific exactness requires it. Scientific material is not for skimming. It is not unusual that some sentences must be perused slowly and repeatedly for a complete assimilation of the content.

Science is the result of a cumulative process. Although this is the first work about the sociology of architecture, this fact does not excuse the reader from the requirement of already having some proficiency in the matter nor the author from synthesizing contributions in the literature, not only of sociology and architecture but also of experimental psychology, communication theory, linguistics, and even physics, insofar as these fields are relevant to the present concern. The author has done so, and in several languages. Today it is important in human sciences to employ a 'multilingual approach', particularly as regards conceptualization. This approach makes it possible to detach terms from their narrow context (cf. Whorf 1956) and lingual biases that can otherwise lead to a scientifically unfounded acceptance of a given proposition or an unjustified rejection of another.

The volume at hand is an attempt to evaluate and integrate previous findings in related fields and build a new conceptual framework for a sociological theory of architecture. As a first comprehensive work on the subject, instead of being overburdened with findings, this book represents a systematic foundation upon which innovative researchers in experimental sociology can build. The last section in particular is addressed to sociological experimenters, showing research methods and techniques as well as epistemological criteria to direct future research in directions promising solid results. Moreover, the book is also addressed to architects in search of a fresh conceptual basis to open up new potentialities for creation (see especially Part III).

In the course of writing a book one encounters other works that provide encouraging or discouraging examples. Translated into several languages, Gatz's *Color and Architecture,* with its direct, practical appeal, seems inspiring in some respects; however, as a picture book with a fragmentary, unsystematic approach and scientifically dubious recipes, it reduces itself to a deceptive cookbook. Engineer Giedion's *Space, Time and Architecture* (1963) considers fundamental issues and has inspired many debates in architecture over the last 40 years. It also stimulated the author to treat its issues systematically, with a more rigorous scientific approach, in which concepts with operational definitions allow the production of experimentally induced knowledge. Finally, Fitch's very comprehensive *American Buildings* (1972), published first without illustrations and later with, provided a good example of how a work can unfold itself in successive editions.

The present text is also a reference book composed of clearly differentiated chapters and sections that can be read continuously as well as separately (e.g., Chapter 13 on acoustical space).

The Experimental Sociology of Architecture has been realized after long preparation, including the contribution of three research teams, various editors, and numerous consultants. The considerable financial and material support (laboratory facilities, various services) has been assumed mainly by three institutions: the Massachusetts Institute of Technology, the Swiss National Science Foundation, and Montreal University.

It is an honorable and agreeable obligation to name those individuals who contributed to this task beyond considerations of financial reward. The author wishes to take this opportunity to express his thanks to them publicly.

In the research teams at work in Cambridge, Montreal, and Switzerland, important responsibility was assumed by the research assistants Dr. A. Chapuis and S. Deforges. Editorial assistance has been provided by a large number of collaborators. The generous and intelligent efforts of Mary Ellen Bushnell at MIT must be stressed; she took charge of virtually the entire, crucial third part. Prof. James J. M. Curry worked on the chapter on optic space. Jerry Ralya made a very valuable contribution to the fourth part, while the first two parts bear the imprint of several persons, among them the very conscientious Ruth Danis and Dr. M. Vaughan. Jacques Latour and Prof. Vera Lee worked on an earlier version of this manuscript. The author also received loyal assistance from Sylviane Pilot, who provided the line drawing for this book.

The multidisciplinary character of the research demanded preliminary studies as well as extensive consultation. Methodological questions involved in the application of linguistic categories in the social sciences had been clarified in the framework of previous, computer-aided research (Ankerl

x   *Preface*

1972b). The author also resorted extensively to comments and expert opinions in various specializations, garnered both informally and formally, orally and in writing. In fact, the author received very valuable aid in formulating the issues and focusing the presentation even from persons not intimately involved with the sociology of architecture.

Discussions with Prof. Harrison White led to accentuating the prolegomenous character of this text. Prof. Robert Gutman revealed how a 'pure' sociologist exposed also to frequent contacts with students of architecture perceived problems of this profession. Exchanges also took place with specialists in related fields, such as Prof. Robert Sommer, Prof. Raymond Studer, Prof. David Stea, and Prof. Walter Ruegg. Lively discussions took place with psychologists of very different orientations but all interested in questions of space perception, such as Prof. Richard Held, Prof. Rudolf Arnheim, and Prof. Sandra Howell. In mathematics the author is indebted to Prof. Georges Polya, Prof. Gian-Carlo Rota, and Dr. Claude Willard. In acoustics Prof. Robert Newman and Prof. Leslie Doelle provided expert advice.

The author is also grateful to architects and other gifted creators in the plastic arts for their enlightening and learned opinions, namely Prof. I. Halasz, Victor Vasarely, Prof. William R. Porter, Prof. Gyorgy Kepes, Dr. Michael Stettler, Anthony Hars, and Leslie Huszar.

Finally, a vivid memory remains of long discussions with Dr. Dirk Pereboom. These were very instrumental in clarifying fundamental epistemological questions.

This is meant to be an acknowledgement and in no way a distribution of responsibilities. The book is the author's creation: Ankerl's sociological theory of architecture. The author asks of the reader a careful examination of the text, as the effort expended in its writing deserves. In the course of the research the author was obliged to read several thousand publications; no matter how worthy or unworthy they seemed, he respected the deontological code: no opinion without a thorough perusal. Scholars and serious readers simply cannot do otherwise.

Professor Guy Ankerl

Massachusetts Institute of Technology
Cambridge, New England
June 1978

Contents

Preface vii

List of Figures xvii

Introduction: Why this Book? 1

PART I: PROLEGOMENON TO THE SCIENCE OF
ARCHITECTURAL SOCIOLOGY 9

1. Precursors 11

2. Conceptualization 15
   Architecture is a created space system 15
   The sociological theme of architecture: The face-to-face
      communication network 42
   Sociology of architecture: A privileged field for research in
      objective (external) sociology 49

3. Systematization 53
   The prolegomenous order: What will and will not be
      discussed, why, and in what order? 53
   1. Priorities and other potential subjects in the area of
      sociology of architecture 54
   2. The whole ambient context and the research in experimental
      sociology of architecture 57
   3. Presentation of the order of this work 61

PART II: SOCIAL SPACING AS A SOCIOLOGICAL THEME
OF ARCHITECTURE 65

4. The Face-to-Face Communication Network and Structure in General 67
   Telecommunication and face-to-face communication 68
   Face-to-face communication in the phenomenologist's perspective:
      A historical excursus 70

xii Contents

    Network and structure in communications theory and
       face-to-face communication   71
    Face-to-face communication network   72
    Face-to-face communication structure and transformation of
       the network: Kinesics and paralinguistics   75
    Introduction to the detailed study of the face-to-face message
       transmission processes by individual sensory sectors   77
    Determinants of the face-to-face communication network
       and its transformation   80
    Demography as a tool of communication network description:
       An enlarged view   88

5. Visible Communication   91
    Visual sensitivity   92
    Visible expression: Intervals of visibility   95
    Network position values and the visible component of the
       communication structure   98

6. Audible Communication   106
    Auditory sensitivity   107
    Audible expression   109
    Network position values and the audible component of the
       communication structure   112

7. Osmatic Communication   114
    Olfactory sensitivity   115
    Kinds of odor emission relevant to osmatic communication   116
    Network position values and the osmatic component of the
       communication structure   119
    Themes for future research and the aromatic detour   120

8. Haptic Communication   122
    Haptic sensitivity   122
    Palpable expression   124
    Network position values and the haptic component of the
       communication structure   128

9. Sapid Communication   134

10. Polysensory Communication   136
    Constitution of zones for the face-to-face
       communication network   138
    From polysensory network to polysensory
       communication structure   141

PART III: COMMUNICATION THROUGH ARCHITECTURE: WHAT IS ARCHITECTURE? A SOCIOLOGIST'S VIEW   147

11. Architecture as a Communication Medium:
    A General Discussion   149
    Architecture is neither monumental sculpture nor
        a designed environment in general   149
    Architecture and signs   150

12. The Geometry of Architectural Morphology: From
    'Free Form' to 'Open Region'   171
    Inventory number in the architectural repertory and
        the internal geometry   172
    Topological taxonomy for the enveloping surfaces of space   174
    The geometry of concave shapes   179

13. Acoustical Space   207
    Why begin the description of the architectural medium with
        acoustical space? Some conceptual considerations   207
    Physical conditions of the perceptible acoustical space   209
    The reverberation time as the most important variable of the
        acoustical space impression   213
    Resonance as another variable of the acoustical space impression   217
    Acoustically heterogeneous spaces and the impression
        of their shape   218
    Complex acoustical words of architecture   221
    Acoustical space impression and the existing varieties
        of polysensory spaces   222

14. Optical Space   225
    Physical conditions of the constitution of optical space   225
    The visual impression: Calibration of the repertory of
        optical architecture by experimental cataloguing   252
    Application of past findings to use of peripheral variables
        for space impression: Elements for hypotheses   262
    Interaction of the main variables in optical space
        impression and past research   274

15. Haptic Space   293
    Physics of haptic space   294
    Haptic space impression   300

16. 'Osmotic' and Hermetic Space   307
    Is there any such thing? Some conceptual considerations   307

xiv   Contents

      'Respired and ingested space'   308
      Air conditioning   308
      Summing up   310

17. Multiplicity of Sensory Spaces and the Multisensory Composition   311
      Physical composition of multisensory spaces   311
      Space impression and past findings   318
      Outlook for future experiments: Questions and hypotheses   329

18. Space Impression through Dynamic Exploration   335
      The morphological concept and the dynamic exploration of space   335
      The temporal aliases of a space   341
      New types of impression in dynamic exploration   345

19. Syntax of Space Systems and Subsystems   355
      From morphology to syntax: Morphemes, ultimate and immediate constituents, and their construction   355
      Infrastructures, syntagmatic arrangement, and syntactical construction: Basic questions   358
      Mathematical description of architectural space systems in general   371
      Architectural text, its graph and syntax   377
      Reading architecture: From network to factors   389
      Recognizable objective pattern in architectural texts: The use of descriptive tools   405

PART IV: STUDYING SPACE EFFECTS ON FACE-TO-FACE COMMUNICATION BY EXPERIMENTATION: EXPERIMENTAL SOCIOLOGY BEGINS WITH THE SOCIOLOGY OF ARCHITECTURE   441

20. Systematic Observation and Inferences: Epistemological Foundation   443
      Experimentation and etiological inference   444

21. Traceable Elements for a Model in Experimental Sociology of Architecture   455
      Communication pattern as the dependent or Y variable   456
      Architectural space as the independent or X variable   458
      Dimensions of variables to measure   459
      Recording variables, their relations, and techniques of recording   462

22. Prospects for Future Research   479
      Research strategy and past trends   480
      Opportunities for experiments and sampling: 'Normal' confinements as experimental field laboratories   483
      Circumstantial parameters of total institutions   485

23. Epistemological Qualifiers of Hardness (in Soft Sciences)	494
Epistemological modalities and etiological relations	497
Falsification procedures	499
Priority and hierarchical order in epistemological certainty: Criteriology	502

| Bibliography | 505 |

| Subject Index | 541 |

List of Figures

Figure		
1.1.	Life spans of various phenomena (Not true-to-scale scheme)	30
1.2.	Determinant aspects of the face-to-face communication other than the distance in a dyad	45
1.3.	Architectural communication in the ensemble of the social communication process and the possible subjects of the sociology of architecture (Schematic representation)	55
2.1.	Horizontal characteristics of a dyad	81
2.2.	Representation of elementary network relation by graph	82
2.3.	Leaders' positions	85
2.4.	Visual sensitivity (Schematic representation)	94
2.5.	Network and visual control	104
2.6.	Auditory autologous 'short-circuit' (Bodenheimer)	107
2.7.	Human sound emission and their audibility	109
2.8.	Haptic communication in groups	132
2.9.	Sapid sensibility of human tongue	134
2.10.	Pentagonal profile of polysensory sensitivity characterizing zones of face-to-face communication network	139
2.11.	Seating arrangement and communication structure	145
3.1.	Multisensory space composition without polysensory coextension	156
3.2.	Two possible cases of bound spaces	166
3.3.	Model of architectural communication	167
3.4.	Definition of the topological class of space envelope	173
3.5.	Dupinian surfaces	185
3.6.	Symmetrization	201
3.7.	Sound behavior at obstacle	212
3.8.	Special cases of acoustical space shapes	219
3.9.	The base of the trichromatic pyramid	239
3.10.	Luminous surfaces	240
3.11.	Graphic and picturial structures	251
3.12.	Distance estimation	257
3.13.	The retinal color field	264
3.14.	Space effects of graphic surface structures	272
3.15.	Roofs	281
3.16.	Observation point and errors in volume estimate	288
3.17.	Order of area overestimation according to different authors (Schematic representation)	291
3.18.	Notation of multisensory composition of a space and of the metric constraint implied	316

List of Figures

3.19.	*Cases of illusion of multisensory space identity*	319
3.20.	*Sensorilly homogeneous space parcels*	336
3.21.	*Morphological equivalence and paradigmatic valence of space*	337
3.22.	*The division of the floor in discrete elements for enumeration of possible paths*	344
3.23.	*The blind by dynamic exploration of the haptic space usually follow the wall*	350
3.24.	*Graph of an architectural text and other graphs used in analyses*	360
3.25.	*Notation of doors and paradigmatic valence for the network of accessibility*	363
3.26.	*Adjacencies and syntagmatic arrangements*	364
3.27.	*Aliases of pathtaking on the floor*	367
3.28.	*Equal morphemes and their identity in the syntactical arrangement*	369
3.29.	*Notation of a bisensory compound spaces and their unisensory space components by graph*	376
3.30.	*Further notation in network of accessibility*	380
3.31.	*Architectural text and its subdivision*	387
3.32.	*Isomorphism of a graph and its incidence matrix*	410
3.33.	*Kuratowski's pentagonal and hexagonal graphs*	413
3.34.	*Open planar graphs and the dual graph G**	414
3.35.	*Three-dimensional syntactic arrangements in cross sections*	416
3.36.	*Diagram of regular planar graphs and their duals*	422
3.37.	*Aligning rectangular parallelepipeds*	427
3.38.	*Bidimensional harmonic arrangement*	436
4.1.	*Etiological inferences*	447
4.2.	*Relevant logical relations in terms of Boolean albegra*	448
4.3.	*Schematic presentation of etiological relations*	498

Introduction: Why this Book?

Being not only a sociologist but also an engineering architect, the author was charged some ten years ago with teaching sociology to students in a school of architecture. It became clear that the sociology of architecture was situated on the confluence of two crisis-ridden professions. In reading the then-scarce special literature on the subject published in English, French, and German, it became obvious that more often than not architects and sociologists took pleasure in a somewhat relaxed epistemological attitude − reflected, for example, by their use of ambiguous terms unaccompanied by operational definitions. The 'progress' that results brings to mind the blind leading the blind.

However, in the course of analyzing the reasons for the existence of such a critical situation in these two professions, the author became aware of the fact that a more fundamental approach can turn the tide and even open up new perspectives for the development of sociology and architecture by producing knowledge which is − as compared with that produced in other fields of applied sociology − harder and more precise.

What this volume proposes, in fact, is an experimentally induced sociology of architecture as the most appropriate *prolegomenous* field of research − i.e., the first strategic step toward the constitution of a cumulative stock of testable knowledge for both disciplines, not only for sociology but also for what has already been designated as 'architecturology' (Friedman 1975; Boudon 1978), a discipline somewhat similar to medical science.

Before going further, however, it would be helpful to explain how the crisis in architectural competence was assessed (Ankerl 1973) in order to propose remedies.

Before the coming of our highly specialized modern age, the 'architect' and the 'builder' were the same person − the same *craftsman*. At that time the conception, creation, and construction of habitable structures were encompassed in one and the same field of knowledge called 'archi-tectural', which consequently included a very broad range of know-how. Since then, construction has become the task of civil engineers, removing a large portion of the applied physical sciences from the architect's domain.

2 *Introduction*

In a situation where justification for a profession is lacking — which in practical terms implies a lack of the protection afforded by a professional title in many countries — architects had two options: to define the concept of space creation as specifically an architectural act (Pelpel et al. 1978: 1-55) and draw together the sciences necessary to carry out that activity; or to seek magic formulas — in other words, substituting for the science of medicine the doctrines of quack doctors and faith healers.

Crisis does not result merely from problems but from the feeling of proceeding down a blind alley. New generations of architects lacked significant, systematic knowledge of *any* of the sciences prerequisite to learning how space ought to be devised in order to obtain desired space impressions and to accommodate the spaces' social use — in short, they lacked systematic knowledge concerning their own media. Such knowledge includes the human sciences as well as the natural ones, and embraces *physical* optics, acoustics, the sciences of sense-data, and communication theory. Like engineering, these sciences have theories composed of experimentally induced statements (in addition to heuristic principles), thereby promising cumulative, testable (i.e., refutable) knowledge.

Unfortunately the emerging architecturology, instead of being grounded on scientific theories, had been guided by doctrines, which certainly express very different systems of thought. Doctrines do not contain propositions which are formulated in operational terms; consequently they cannot be empirically verified, but only sanctioned by authority. The persuasiveness of these propositions is dependent on the verbal charm of the formulas themselves or the prodigious activities of those who gave utterance to them (cf. Mumford's doctrines [1963]). Generally these individuals have been architects of creative genius. They performed a disservice, however, when they would have had us take their intution as the result of a scientifically grounded investigation, thereby making their skill transmissible and thus their architectural creation reproducible. These pseudo-scientific doctrines in the arts have unfortunately always met with a certain gullible audience.

For example, Benedetto Croce stated that the literature on aesthetic measures and proportional systems represents an 'astrology of numbers'. (An appropriate refutation of some magic formulas can be found in Alexander 1959.) Issues such as the concept of the golden section, Modulor, how the anthropomorphic projection of the proportions of the human body in larger-than-natural size on building facades became mythified as a means of the 'humanization of architecture', will be discussed fully in appropriate sections of this work.

Builders who adhere to architectural science will remain unresponsive to the siren song of *architecture parlée,* a kind of verbal exhibitionism of famous architects such as that of the technician of Chaux-de-Fonds, Charles-Eduard Jeanneret, better known by his *nom de plume,* Le Corbusier.

The thorough study of the concept of created space as the medium of architectural communication designates a whole program of applied human sciences eminently suited to architectural application. In order to build architecturology, or architectural science, it is necessary to establish an epistemologically well founded strategy of investigation in which the more fundamental and harder results have a certain priority (e.g., physical optics versus perception).

As already stated, sociology is also in a crisis. Without presenting a history of sociology in a nutshell, it can be stated that sociology harbored for too prolonged a period of time too large a mass of thoughts heterogeneous in their substance as well as in their epistemological status (Ankerl 1972a). This led to the present 'formless state' (sometimes called 'formless interregnum') in sociological theory.

Within this heterogeneous mass of thoughts can be distinguished *grosso modo* two poles. At one is phenomenological and historical sociology, less eager to exclude ideological and subjective influences (in all such research, various subjective time concepts come to the fore, as in Hareven 1970). At the other pole is sociology concerned with communication facts as the empirical substratum of the science of society which apprehends its subjects by objective or 'definitive' (Blumer 1954) concepts and generates experimentally (directly or indirectly) induced statements (Burgess and Bushell 1969). The first tendency is more ambitious in the choice of subjects, and ready to supply rhetoric and justification for the action of political clients; but works of this type of sociology abound in empirically untestable, authoritarian arguments.

Rooted in demography and communication theory, the second tendency is less ambitious. It seems somewhat disenchanted; but by reverting to perceptible and objectively observable aspects of reality it is more exacting in its epistemological stance (Jonas 1968: 84).

Insofar as sociology will fully claim the status of science, sharing its prestige, instead of remaining in the wake of traditional erudition (in fact, how many historians and philosophers disguise themselves as sociologists in order to bridge the credibility gap of their disciplines and establish modern credentials?), it must have ideas, procedures, and goals similar to those of the so-called 'hard sciences' (see Ankerl 1977; Gove 1979). It is obvious that the present uneasy coexistence between 'humanists' and 'scientists,' which erodes the paradigmatic coherence of sociology, allows the first group willy-nilly to abuse the second's scientific authority by maintaining social philosophers under the guise of social scientists.

In order to bring sociology out of its present stagnation by hardening its paradigms and making its findings more reliable, some important procedures

4 Introduction

have already been proposed. According to Donald Ploch, former director of the National Science Foundation's sociological program an increased 'mathematicization of the field' must be considered first (quoted by Wiley 1979: 797). On the one hand, it forces the researcher to abstain from statements with double meaning — is it not a tradition of the humanities to promise 'deeper and deeper meaning' for the initiated? — by the requirement of precise formulation; and on the other hand, it precludes false inferences. Important contributions have already been made in this direction by the sociologist and physicist Harrison White and his school, particularly in applying the Markov process to the analysis of organizations (cf. also the S Theory of Stuart Dodd 1942).

By proposing the experimentally induced sociology of architecture as a field of investigation, the aim is not exclusivity; rather, it is a response to the following question: in the given state of our science, from an epistemological viewpoint, which priority in the strategy of investigation favors, and which does not favor, the hardening of sociology as a science?

Beyond any mathematical formalism the main reason for softness in sociology is its poorly grounded conceptualization (Gutman 1966: 105; Studer 1966: 32; Gray 1980). Concepts are too often imprecise, inconsistent, and, above all, not anchored objectively to identified aspects of reality and therefore exposed to ambiguous, subjective ideological interpretation. So it is a waste of effort to apply sophisticated mathematical tools to them.

However, of the two basic concepts through which we apprehend reality — time and space — the second shows particular qualities which make it separable from subjectivity (Whorf 1956; Bergson 1967), and therefore make its systematic introduction to sociological investigation particularly suitable for the renewal of sociology in a prolegomenous way. Among other authors, Konau (1977), in her short history of the sociological use of the space concept, underlines how it has been neglected in sociological theory building. In addition, it is clear that *space is the central concept of the sociology of architecture.*

What are the specific epistemological qualities of the space concept? Which space concept is that of the sociology of architecture? How does it relate architecture to sociology?

The space concept is treated in depth in the first part; here is an outline of the main ideas.

— Like life, time is irreversible. Spatiality, in contrast, exists in a reversible, objective environment.
— Insofar as banal (volumetric) space is concerned, Euclidean solid geometry can apprehend it. Geometry, in contrast to mathematics, is not only abstract but also *anschaulich* (J. Piaget in *L'Epistémologie de l'Espace* 1964: 4) and therefore relates two orders of realities, as does experimentation — namely, empirics and generalizable abstraction.

— From the viewpoint of genetic epistemology, concave, enveloping, volumetric space is the prime category of our environment. First fetal space surrounds us; later, various aerial spaces. Space is omnipresent and is also the general frame of reference for all perceived objects.

— Another epistemological 'privilege' of space stems from the fact that it can exist in a purely physical form, such as a cave; this makes it possible to analyze heuristically its effect as X variable without having to consider the effects of its being man-made, as with architectural space.

After having assessed the significance of sociology of architecture for research in sociology and architectural science in general, attention should now be briefly focused on the main themes of sociology of architecture itself.

Sociology of architecture can be experimentally induced and give cumulative results only if the concept of architectural space is a definitive one — i.e., if it is formulated in operational terms and without ambiguity. Without implying any rank order in the enumeration, the following are basic properties:

— Architectural space implies a created closed surface with human access into this concavity; therefore all tridimensional structures such as traffic networks cannot be classified as architectural space.
— The architectural envelope has at least one side defining an inside or interior (space can be underground, encased in the lithosphere).
— Architectural space has volumetric magnitude — i.e., it has finite boundaries.
— It also has a precise geometrical shape which must be clearly distinguished from 'form' (cf. urban form, good gestalt, etc. — Goldmeier 1972), a concept of scholastic inspiration.
— The closed surface as envelope has hylic characteristics, which means that the space (with its volume and shape) is perceptible by at least one sense organ of the beholder in the so-called interior.
— Due to the multitude of human sense organs, not only optical but also acoustical and haptic spaces can and ought to be conceived and designed by architects. Multisensory architectural space can be composed of physically and geometrically different unisensory spaces (in order to underline the multisensory intricacy of architectural spaces, this volume includes no photographs, still less photographs of facades).
— Architectural space ought to be described — at first — by the architect in terms of physical language, including all quantitative aspects relevant to its sensory impression (cf. etic description).
— Architectural space is not created for its own sake but to isolate a numerable set of individuals for certain activities and from interference from the broader physical and social environment.

6 *Introduction*

— The sensorily specified protection of smaller or larger groups' intimacy or privacy is a social function of architectural space.
— Insofar as communication is a specifically sociological fact, created multisensory space can influence most directly polysensory face-to-face communication by means of prefiguring a set of face-to-face communication networks. Although created space can express other contents, this network set is specifically its immediate sociological theme.
— Because it is perceptible, architectural space does not affect face-to-face communication only through the conditioning of the set of networks, but also directly stimulates the communicators — that is, it affects the face-to-face communication flow directly.
— Architecture is a multisensory medium which must also be apprehended in terms of sense-datum language (without reception there is no communication).
— It is the denotative image of the created space (the self-presentation of the space) which constitutes the repertory of the architectural media — that is, the enumeration of repertory items is generated by the thresholds of perceptible differences between spaces based on the estimated volume and shape.
— In order to well establish architectural competence, semantic study of the connotative significance of architecture cannot precede the constitution of the architectural repertory. Asking about the pleasantness of vaguely identified objects is without scientific value.

In Part III the architectural media are examined systematically, level by level; this is a *sine qua non* of any architecturology. In order to enumerate all potential items of a repertory — open-ended or not — for architects, it is necessary to know the rules of morphological construction. Questions such as the following must first be answered: what are the possible analogies and differences between the morphology of our media and that of spoken language as part of general linguistics? How can the concept 'word' be applied to architectural space? Which are the submorphic elements? How do 'bound spaces' constitute 'free forms'? How can the multisensory intricacy of the architectural morphemes be handled? How does the concept of 'compound word' apply?

After apprehending the subjects in physical language, how to design the experimentation appropriate to constituting a distinctive architectural repertory can be seen (space discrimination thresholds according to different sensory spaces, according to polysensory impression, according to topological, geometrical, volumetric, and hylic factors, and all of these in the cases of static, kinetic, and dynamic exploration).

The same section also treats the syntax — one of the three branches of Morris's semiotics (1938, 1946) — of the architectural media. Due to the finite nature of a space, it can exist simultaneously in multitude, even as several copies of one and the same repertory item, and can constitute space systems and subsystems. Such questions as the following are considered: to what extent can linguistic concepts be applied to syntactical construction in architecture? How can architectural text as an opus — as opposed to so-called contextual space — be delineated? Can rules for well formed architectural sentences, if identified, be established? Which are the immediate and which the ultimate constituents? How can the application of syntagmatic operations contrasted to paradigmatic ones (*in praesentia* opposed to *in absentia*) be heuristically justified? Finally, how can the various multisensory readings of architectural texts be experimentally studied?

In order to move in the presentation from the simple to the complex, the multisensory face-to-face communication process, identified as the sociological theme of architectural space creation in Part II, is dealt with. Part II treats the network and structure of multisensory face-to-face communication within the framework of pure sociology — i.e., the potential Y variable of sociology of architecture is identified where the network is still exclusively a function of the partners' relative spatial positions without any interference from the perceptible surrounding space. However, the focus is on aspects of face-to-face communication that can be significantly and directly influenced by architectural spaces, namely insofar as the communication process is shaped by the psychophysical substratum of the channeling of the message (the visibility, audibility, tangibility, and tasteability of signs as a function of network position).

In order to arrive at the analysis of polysensory face-to-face communication, basic conceptual questions will be clarified as early as Part I. These include application of the network and structure concepts (Flament 1965a; Bavelas et al. 1965) to face-to-face communication; integration of the concept of network transformation at the appropriate level of analysis; and consideration of telecommunication as a parameter which must be neutralized in the context.

The fourth and final part deals with epistemological, methodological, and 'instrumental' issues inherent to the application of experimental design in sociology of architecture. For instance, how can theoretical and practical problems resulting from the experimental study of effect of the X variable — architectural space, described in Part III — on the Y variable — polysensory face-to-face communication flow, described in Part II — be solved in order to accumulate hard findings in sociology of architecture in particular and in objective, experimental sociology in general?

Why does experimentation promise, by relating empirics and (abstract) universals in a constructive manner, generalizable nonidiosyncratic knowledge? Are laboratory and experimental design closely related to one another?

Why and how does the unique character of sociology of architecture give a privileged solution to the problem of experimentation in human sciences?

8   Introduction

For epistemological reasons, why cannot so-called ecological validity compensate for any loss in internal validity?

What criteriology can establish the relative hardness of each finding in order to systematically construct a consistent body of a science step by step (hypothesis, theory, law)?

This book treats issues specifically involved in the development of sociology of architecture as a specialization and suggests elements for a model and a more systematic use of total institutions as field laboratories for longitudinal experimentation in the future. These suggestions are for immediate and concrete use by those who do not look for slogans and rhetoric in selling architecture but are interested in improving their architectural competence.

The author does not hide an intention to infuse this work with a broader significance. Sociology conceived as an empirical science based on spatio-temporal aspects of communication processes has a chance to make a leapfrog advance, outstripping in exactness even experimental psychology and economics. Indeed, psychology, even behavioral psychology, always relies on the study of internal processes, especially psychophysiological processes; and economics always remains tied to values. Inspired by demography and communication theory, sociology can develop a field where men with their value systems remain truly in a black box. (Among the epistemological privileges of sociology of architecture are experimentation in a normal setting and volumetric space as X variable for the concrete study of the polysensory face-to-face communication flow.) Sociology of architecture seems predestined to write the first chapter in objective, experimental sociology.

The main significance of this approach is epistemological, bringing sociology closer to existing hard sciences. It is clear that some very interesting and exciting topics debated on the ideological and political scene remain outside the scope of sociology of architecture. But the choice is made deliberately and consistently: science and erudition must not be confused. In the end, other perhaps useful but not necessarily scientific thought can only profit from the fact that at least a modest body of knowledge exists within sociology that is as reliable as that which permitted man to leave his own atmospheric space to explore a larger one.

I

Prolegomenon to the Science
of Architectural Sociology

1

Precursors

Although undertaking this study places us in an enviable position, it is simultaneously somewhat peculiar. For, while few people today would question the practical or scientific relevance of the sociology of architecture, it has not been possible to find any bibliographical evidence of systematic study of this area. Further, we can find no chapters in sociology textbooks dealing with the sociology of architecture. To some extent, sociologists tend to confine themselves to urban sociology, an area lacking sufficient specificity for initiating a truly analytical approach to sociology of architecture. Or they deal with the sociology of the habitat, a concept which has lost its precise meaning since the separation of the dwelling place from the place of work.

It is true that the Series E of the *Annales Sociologiques* between 1935 and 1942, edited by Maurice Halbwachs, brought together under a single heading all areas of sociology pertinent to sociology of architecture: social morphology, language, technology, and esthetics. However, in spite of this, no integrated approach to sociology of architecture as such has been developed.

To our knowledge, the first to direct his attention to this topic was Franz Arens (1927-1928), a specialist in baroque art, in a series of articles in the periodical *Ethos*. But both his main references (Gurlitt, Rose, etc.) and the title of his first chapter ('History of the Art and that of the Culture') suggest that he approaches his subject strictly in his capacity as an art historian. He sketches an outline of the history of architectural ideas in which architectural art, both practical and universal, reflects, to his mind, the best of the whole of art history. Consistent with this approach, he rejects the idea that the history of architecture is an independent discipline. He proffered these general conclusions somewhat lightly, accepting the fashionable Jesuit idea that baroque architecture is an art which is both sacred and, in a missionary sense, efficient. Despite this somewhat biased assumption, Arens, who is a positivist like Lamprecht, gives priority to the analysis of objective facts in his investigation of culture. For this reason we consider his work more closely.

In his second chapter, Arens discusses the function of architectural art. To him, baroque art, with its spiritual efficiency, constitutes an appropriate paradigm for architecture. Whereas Frankl (1968) groups even the library

12 Prolegomenon to the science of architectural sociology

with sacred spaces, if Arens were to consider the habitat he would distinguish living spaces sharply from those whose primary purpose is productive (e.g., the kitchen).

Chapter 3 comes closest to our subject: 'The Influence of Social Factors on the Architectural Creation'. He defines three areas of investigation for sociology of architecture: (1) the social status of architects; (2) the social characteristics of the principal client classes in their national and historical context; and (3) representations of architects and client groups.

Notwithstanding his positive methodology, Arens has a spiritualist *weltanschauung*. This leads him to discuss point 3 before dealing with the physical milieu. He explains how the 16th and 18th century salons' predilection for architecture affected the architect's social status, and shows how the user's spatial norms prefigure architectural shapes. He also gives many instructive examples of how the three roles – the public, the developer, and the user – were sometimes played by different people, sometimes by a single person. According to the era, the client might be an anonymous agent, a vulgar profiteer, or a sophisticated individual.

Like Hugo Schmerber and Frankl, Arens demanded concrete and detailed studies of how living spaces influenced social life. Recall that late baroque architecture satisfied requirements other than the visual, such as the thermic, etc. Arens clearly recognized the existence of this influence and saw its possibilities for scientific investigation. But as an art historian of the spiritualist tradition, he refused to consider the architectural space system apart from the designer's creative intention, and so refused to take a purely structuralist approach, i.e., considering impression without stimultaneously considering expression. For Arens, any impression is interesting only in terms of decoding the creator's intention.

The fourth chapter deals with the effects of the spiritual life on architecture and has little bearing on the sociology of architecture.

The fifth chapter, however, discusses national differentiation in architecture. Although Arens reveals his own nationalistic biases, his heuristic premises are not without interest. He considers national differences in terms of a general theory of spatio-temporal localization, rather than limiting himself to a purely geographic and climatic determinism. With reference to Karl Mannheim, he defines a nation as a group of people sharing a culture. His concept of community is evidently influenced by that of Toennies (1969). According to Arens, the arts are determined by national invariants and epochal constants.

In the sixth and last chapter he treats continuity and periodicity, as well as the sociological and psychological integration of contemporary architecture. Here Arens rejects the Hegelian philosophy of history which sees any difference in national development as a simple relative advancement or underdevelopment on the road to the realization of one universal trend in history. In discussing contemporary architecture, he is more concerned with the *'architecture parlée'*, i.e., with what architects have said about their work, than with the works themselves. (On this point he reveals some ignorance in regard to certain facts, e.g., he calls Le Corbusier an architect of Geneva.)

Arens' historian's predilection gives more credence to written documents than to physical objects. However, we conclude that although Arens does not develop a systematic sociology of architecture, he does outline sociology of architecture, especially in the third chapter of his work.

While for Arens sociology of architecture is part of cultural history, for Simmel (1906, 1921, 1950) it is part of sociology. His contribution to sociology of architecture, through sketchy, is an integral part of his general sociology, and the influence of his contribution could be followed even to the work of Gurvitch (1964).

The ninth chapter of Simmel's 'Soziologie' treats the 'space and spatial order of the society'. Interestingly, he adds to his work a sociology of the senses, translated into English in 1921, which contains many inspiring hypotheses. Although Simmel's work is sometimes hasty, intuitive, and unverified, it is interesting to see how he brings together practically all aspects of sociology which are relevant to the sociology of architecture:

(1) Basic characteristics of space forms taken into account:
    (A) exclusiveness of the space;
    (B) partitioning of the space;
    (C) spatial fixation (sedentarism);
    (D) spatial distances between people;
    (E) communication, traffic.
(2) Spatial determination of a group through its sociological forms:
    (A) territorial sovereignty;
    (B) the residents;
    (C) social establishments;
    (D) the empty space.

Simmel holds the physical aspects of expression and sensory impressions to be relevant parts of the social communication process and indicates how one might establish a sociology of physical spatial relations. Later we will call this a 'face-to-face communication network'. He also considers light and other environmental factors which influence this communication process. Nevertheless, he is not specific about how this face-to-face communication network, and consequently the flow of communication itself, could be influenced by the architectural space system's enveloping and compartmentalizing function. Moreover, he is far from consistent in his use of the terms 'social distance' and

14 Prolegomenon to the science of architectural sociology

and 'social density', using them in both objective and metaphorical senses, as does Durkheim.

Gurvitch (1964) utilizes Simmel's concept of universal space, 'the Space', and even reproduces Simmel's examples, though he never mentions Simmel by name. He then takes advantage of the opportunity to express the well-known basic concepts of his general theory of sociology, which were deeply influenced by the German idealist philosopher Fichte. However, his study remains wholly programmatic, without indicating any operationalized concepts useful for future, empirically verifiable, investigations.

Gurvitch's discipline and successor at the Sorbonne, Jean Cazeneuve, followed his teacher's article with 'The Perception of the Extensions in the Archaic Societies' (1964). This contains a number of concrete, mainly ethnographic, findings. Its conceptualization is influenced not only by Gurvitch, Bergson, and the phenomenologists, but also by Jean Pieaget.

2

Conceptualization

ARCHITECTURE IS A CREATED SPACE SYSTEM

Many works start off by explaining the different meanings of a word; we will leave this task to the lexicographers. A scientist must begin his definition with a collection of objects having common attributes. Epistemologically, this means that his definition will be apodictic or indexical (cf. definition *quid rei* rather than *quid nominis*). This approach is useful, since it enables us to avoid a sterile debate concerning the 'true' definition of 'architecture'. Indeed, if necessary, we would rather renounce using the word altogether, and use the letter A instead. We will define A through characteristics which, when combined, belong *exclusively* to this category (A as a definitive definition).

A is a created system of spaces which are perceptible from their interior points. A space is a set of points within a closed orientable surface. This space has essential geometrical characteristics: a shape and a volume. The latter can be measured as volumetric magnitude. The space itself does not include its envelope, but only its interior points, or 'air space'. Mathematically, this is an 'open region'.

An architectural space is a created object and thus involves the designer's creative intention. However, its effect cannot be perceived unless the space has a large enough geometric dimension for it to be accessible to humans, such that it envelopes them and their group. In order for this enveloping to become efficient and the fact of being enveloped perceptible beyond the above-mentioned topological, geometrical, and metric requirements, it must also satisfy material or hylic requirements. In this way the envelope can affect our sensory organs. The architect, as we shall see later, can make as many types of sensory spaces as the reflected waves for any particular sensory modality allow the beholder to have a space impression of, to which he can attribute shape and volume. The full meaning of A can be conveyed to the beholder only if he is enclosed within a sensory space and has an impression of it.

Finally, the definition speaks about space *systems*. The architectural space is not a single space like the cosmological Space filled with 'aether' or 'quintessence' that we find in Aristotle's *Metaphysics*. It is a clearly delimited multiple and literal space where the geometrical concepts of shape and volumetric magnitude are operative. From the viewpoint of our present study, any other use of the word 'space' is considered metaphorical. To clearly express our conception of space, we will call it 'volumetric space' or, with reference to the German *Raum*, 'roomraum', which includes room as well as space. These delimited spaces can be connected to constitute a network, which we call a system of spaces. As a sentence can consist of one word, so an architectural space system can consist of one space (e.g., a hangar).

We see on the one hand, how architecture depends on the space concept, and on the other hand how easily spaces, Space, 'extension and spatiality', in opposition to 'time', tend to constitute a confused conglomerate, especially in works about the 'esthetics of architectural forms'. For this reason the concept of space will be closely scrutinized in the next few pages.

In more general terms, because space is a basic concept of all objective, experimental sciences, it would seem that, since creating space is the architect's exclusive task, we have a unique occasion to contribute to the clarification of this concept. Usually, if one knows how to reconstruct a space system, one has an insight into its nature which can have an 'exacting' effect on its definition, in the sense of genetic epistemology.

The Space and the Concept of Spaces as Roomraum: The Architect's Space Concept

Alexander Gosztonyi of Zurich has written the most complete study (1976) about the use of the word 'space in the history of philosophy and science'. Here, we take a somewhat different approach and ask: what collection of concrete phenomena make it necessary to have this category at all?

The three different terms, space, spatiality, and extension, are often used synonymously, as Gosztonyi's book tells us. But the reason for the existence of these three different terms is not clarified, even by him.

All three have in common opposition to the dimension of time, which is unidirectional, irreversible, and, as a category, not in the same relation to the observer as space is. Among the three other concepts, 'space' is the 'hardcore' concept which could be specified by shape and volumetric magnitude that it has on its own. As a matter of fact, like Cartesian coordinates, for us space effectively constitutes a framework of reference. During our individual lives, and in the history of our species, we have experienced the 'concavity' of an enveloping space: first the womb, the biofactual space; later the cave, the geofactual space; or the architectural space, the created one. As we learned to situate ourselves in it, all other spatial phenomena, such as so-called space curves, are also situated *in* this space.

Going further, contrary to deductive metaphysics, we see no reason to think that the cosmological, universal Space constitutes the true paradigm for the concrete space concept. We may theorize that the true genesis of the concept proceeded in the opposite direction: the concept of universal Space may be more easily understood and explained as an outgrowth or extrapolation of our first space experience, which occurred in the womb. Within this perspective of genetic epistemology we can conceive of cosmological Space as the limit or end value of a series of nested, finite spaces which, as cosmological Space, becomes infinite. The most determinant attribute of space — the volumetric magnitude — is thereby lost. An analogous situation arises at time in mathematics, where logical necessity dictates that certain operations become either ineffectual or undefined, e.g., for all x, $x^0 = 1$, and $1/0^1 = 0^{-1} = \infty$.

Recapitulating, we may say that our concrete space concept can be related to the fact that from prenatal existence to death we are always enveloped within a space. We will see later that this envelope need not be solid. It must only be different from what it encloses, so that it reflects waves, giving the beholder sensory impressions of a volume and shape which are at least partly concave. For example, in an aquarium, one has a sensory space impression even though one side, the ceiling of the envelope, is the air, which has lower viscosity than the filling medium, the water.

Recent research in visual space perception confirms the claim that the perception of any event is preceded by the perception of the space within which that event is situated. The space becomes a frame of reference. Thus, one may conclude that the specifically space-creating art, architecture, provides the prime framework for all other designs of the physical environment, a prerogative often denied it in our time.

Space Without Architects: The Prefiguration of the Roomraum

The perception, and, in more general terms, the reception of the created A depends upon one's preconceived notions of space and upon one's past space experiences. In this sense, A has two types of prehistory:

(1) Biofactual: the genetic epistemology of the space for each individual begins in the womb.
(2) Geofactual: the historical origin of the space for the human race began with the caves used by early men.

18 Prolegomenon to the science of architectural sociology

Space embryo: our biofactual space and its possible effects on our space concept

> All bits and pieces are transformed into good and useful things: the base of an egg shell formed the base of the earth. The top part gave us our sublime firmament, the yellow yolk became the radiant sun, the white the shining moon. And all the shell's stained debris formed stars in the sky, while deep grey speckles here and there were made into clouds on high.
>
> *The Song I. 231-244 of the Kalevala*

To have any sort of coherent knowledge of a volumetric space, the beholder must have, first, enough sensory data at his disposal to form an impression and, second, a conceptual framework derived from previous space experiences. This framework determines actual data collection and selection.

The first volumetric space in which an individual finds himself, the womb, plays a double role in forming his space perception faculty: (1) it gives him an impression of the enveloped state, *umraum*, inducing him to conceive of this impression as space; and (2) the particular geometrical and physical nature of the envelope gives him the first quantitative human scale, a kind of primary measure of the spaciousness of the space.

Information theory and cognitive psychology teach the particular importance of the *first* experience in forming a conceptual framework. The formation of categories, the crystallization of specific, concrete experiences into abstract concepts, is a complex process. Here we are concerned with the influence of the womb experience on the formation of the space concept. Because the research in the field of prenatal experience is still in an early stage, we will not adhere to any particular doctrine (e.g., nativistic), or make any assumption with regard to the relative importance of prenatal experience as compared to other sources, such as historically and educationally transmitted sources. We will simply describe the first experienced space objectively as a biofactual space in order to see what kind of sensory data *could* influence the prototypical space concept, and what kind of individual variety *could* emerge there. The discussion of these questions about possibilities does not involve any inadmissible projection in terms of the cognitive accountability of the embryo in the mother's womb.

The fetus is always within an enveloping space as '*umraum*'. This space has shape and volume, and is single. It is in fact a specific case of concrete spaces such as architectural spaces, which share with the womb shape and volume as characteristics. However, because the first space is single, this attribute is easily extrapolated to the conception of universal Space as a metaphorical (platonic) paradigm. And by extension, universal Space, being single, must then be limitless. In making the ungrounded assumption that space is single and limitless, the determinant attributes of space — volume and shape — go by the wayside. In fact, spaces as distinct from spatiality are multiple and not limitless.

In this connection, we do not accept the notion that the autic 'space' of skin is a space at all; since we perceive our body within it as a convex 'subject–object'.

As already noted, we do not attribute any 'obligatory process of conceptualization' realized in the womb by the embryo. Without adhering to an innate space concept in the literal sense of the term, it is incontestably established that before birth the embryo has visual, auditory, and tactual sensations. Thus, the sensory input for optical, auditory, and tactual spaces is present in the uterus. It is also a biological fact that not only do lighting and sound conditions change in the womb, but the volume and shape by contractions and dilations. This means that our first enveloping space can be perceived as a medium of communication, one that is nonverbal and 'represents' a subject, namely the mother. The mother communicates, we may say, by altering the intrauterine space of the fetus.

From this we can make some heuristic assumptions with far-reaching implications. The first space is an enveloping, volumetric and communicative space. This space is similar in specification to architectural space. If this biofactual space contributes to our conceptualization of space, the space multiplication made by the architect gives rise to the factual basis necessary for the conceptualization of space in the largest sense.

In order to learn more about the effective 'germination' of space perception after conception, we consider the marsupials, which give behavioral scientists a striking possibility for exploring the effects of postnatal biofactual space. The Australian red kangaroo is particularly interesting because the pouch provides an intermediary stage between intra- and extra-uterine life. After being born and spending one day under the sun, the newborn kangaroo experiences the enclosed space of the mother's pouch, which maintains the creature in an intimate state of opaqueness within a living trailer that runs at approximately 50 km. an hour. Unlike the so-called autic space, the marsupial pouch may be considered authentic space, since it is perceived from within the envelope.

Finally, while the communication between mother and fetus provides us with an embryonic form of architectural communication, multiple birth gives us an embryonic model for the study of sociology of architecture itself. The fetus is here not in isolation. The mother can have a social effect on the face-to-face communication between the twins, triplets, etc. This enveloping of the face-to-face communication of groups is precisely the sociological theme of architectural creation.

Twins, especially identical twins, have always been of interest to researchers, who have studied them in order to distinguish inherited from

20 *Prolegomenon to the science of architectural sociology*

acquired characteristics. To us, the communication between twins, which are in an interchangeable situation in the womb and in an exclusively mother-children situation, could be a valuable area of study.

We may summarize by saying that within the uterus we can experience our first space, a unique envelope that already has volume and shape. These dimensions vary between individuals, and so give rise to different gauges for later space experiences: the architectural roomraum. The mother's modifications of this uterus space is the archetype of architectural communication. And if the embryos are multiple, the womb provides an archetypal (exemplar) model for the sociology of architecture.

Space as geofact: the prehistory of architecture

> Caves having been among men's earliest shelters, may turn out to be his last ones.
>
> B. Rudofsky, *Architecture without Architects*, 1965

> Dig tunnel deep. Store grain everywhere.
>
> Mao Tse-Tung, 1969

Recent ethnographic discoveries in the Philippines gave new impulse to research about cave dwelling. Our interest in the subject is not historical. It does not consider the problem of where the history of architecture — with or without architects — truly began, namely the historical cyclic move from housing being earth-covered to its not being so covered. Important international literature exists on the subject of natural and constructed underground spaces. We do not look at this question from any particular interest, e.g., underground cities as a special case, but rather in order to grasp the essential aspects of architecture which are *prefigured* in caves.

Compared to the atmospheric space, the cavern already has a well-defined geometry with human scale.

A particularly important aspect of this natural space is that a cavern could be created with a closed surface having only one face, the interior. This must not be confounded with the so-called one-sided surface, well known in geometry, such as a Klein bottle. It is a created concavity without showing a convex face. Indeed, the whole sheltering function of the 'enclosure' could be realized without externality. If neither the concept of roomraum nor modern technology excludes filmy, nonhard walls, it is also not essential that another accessible side of the surface exist. Through considering geofactual spaces, we may surmise that the face of architecture which is the subject of most consideration and publicity, the facade, is only a contingency, not a necessity. The accessible (interior) volumetric space, 'the concave side', is the indispensible constituent of architecture. These considerations have far-reaching implications. There is no need to pass negative judgment upon *faux facades*, indeed, the formation of the other side of the enveloping surface can and must follow the requirements of the space that begins on that side. For example, the modern multilevel building's facade does not necessarily reflect the shape or size of the included spaces.

If the teaching of design in schools of architecture took into account this order of priority and began projects in terms of space systems without facades, like underground cities, the perspective of the new graduate would be different from that of the present ones in many ways (Ankerl 1971a, 1973).

Because architecture finds its true fulfillment in creating space systems which could be completely autarchic, the urbanism of our open-air cities, which transforms the atmospheric space but does not create (autarchic) spaces, adds to architecture but does not represent architecture's supreme integration. As a matter of fact, city planning comes from agriculture, or, more precisely, from horticulture (i.e., Howard's Garden-City and the park systems in the USA), which is fundamentally two-dimensional. Even the traffic engineering which completed this original goal of urbanism brought tri-dimensional arrangements (e.g., bypass bridges) which remain merely line systems. They do not form a large-scale space system as such. Conceptually, only the underground arctic or tropic cities realize the full integration of all the individual architectural spaces into a system, subordinating particular architectural space systems, such as so-called buildings as subsystems.

Within our first space, the womb, we were tied by the umbilical cord. Early man, however, *chose* his spaces, the geofactual spaces such as the cavern. This choice was limited at first. But just as agriculture increased the variety of foods·available to hunting and gathering societies, so architecture expanded the range of shelters available to early man. Thus, the architectural imagination enlarges the possibilities of choice. Why and how did the caveman choose his shelters?

Without shelter, man leaving the uterus space would find himself in the atmosphere, a space which is not clearly limited above. He would be exposed to daily, seasonal, and other incalculable changes. However, shelters are well-defined spaces within which the presence or absence of animate, as well as inanimate, objects may be easy to control. So in choosing an appropriate shelter, the user has two main components to consider: ecological or physical, and social. The former determines man's relationship to the physical environment, and the latter to his congeners, viz., fellow beings.

We have the habit of associating the ecological function with the roof of the shelter, and the social one with the wall. Homelessness, for example, is dramatized in our language by 'rooflessness'. This simplification must be

22 Prolegomenon to the science of architectural sociology

basically amended. On the one hand, certain windy cultures shelter the fire with walls and lack roofs. On the other hand, it is wrong to associate social control of face-to-face communication exclusively with wall construction. For example, in an urban situation the privacy of individuals and the intimacy of couples depend upon separation provided by floors and ceilings, as well as by walls. Here, too, the symbolism revolving around 'cryptic' and other social functions cannot be related only to the wall.

In summary, in multistory urban architecture bulwarks, walls, and the like, do not adequately symbolize the protective and cryptic social function of architecture: that function which opposes social accessibility.

Space, Artifact or Not, Perceived

A participant in the Calico conference in 1970, the geologist Vance Haynes (1973), wrote an article entitled: 'The Calico Site: Artifacts or Geofacts'. Without discussing here his geomorphological approach as compared with other approaches of archaelogists and anthropologists, for us it is an interesting fact that for a long time it can remain an open question as to whether an object is an artifact or a natural object. If we did not observe an object's creation, we may have difficulty knowing whether it was man-made or not. Yet this is a preliminary question for all perception.

Neither an object's usefulness nor the esthetic response it arouses is able to guarantee that it is man-made. An imaginative beholder can find a natural object useful, and there also exist geographic esthetics. What creation is is itself a complex question. Is the fact that an object has been touched or not by man the essential criterion? According to O'Brien, there can be 'creation by accident'. Is the intention of transformation the essential criterion? The Dadaist Jean Arp has expressed this dilemma well: 'Dadaism is the foundation of the arts. It is art without sense, but not nonsense. Data is without sense as nature is without sense'. F. Rapp (1974: 96) speaks about 'nature in the narrower sense of the natural course of things, without human interference'.

Concerning spaces, we also find a continuum from natural to created ones (e.g., grottoes have been transformed partially to become 'grotta'). We also find so-called architecture without architects where (tropical) habitats are covered by leaves from trees. In the Göreme valley, 'crevices and hollows that occur in the soft stone had only to be enlarged and smoothed in order to provide habitable space'. With reference to the expression 'construction industry', we can call this the 'agriculture of construction' (Rudofsky 1969).

The existence and activities of other animal species further complicate the question. A particular object might result from nobody's work, or from the work of a Pliopithecus, of a Proconsul, of a Dryopithecus, of an Oreopitecus, of a Ramapithecus, of an Australopithecus, advanced or not, of a Paranthropus, of a Homo erectus or even of an early Homo sapiens or a Rhodesian man.

How are these questions related to sociology of architecture?

All spaces, man-made, natural, animal, exert an influence on the beholder. This influence goes beyond the purely physical in that a sensory impression is formed. As a matter of fact, before any space can become behaviorally efficient (e.g., modulating social communication), the beholder must have some kind of space impression, the impression of being enveloped by a volumetric space with a certain geometry. This impression of the existence of a determined space is realized by comparing the present space to previously experienced ones. The attribution of an adjective, such as 'familiar' or 'pleasant' to a space, which is on the level of *vécu* and which determines ambience, could be apprehended by the researcher only *after* he knows what the beholder objectively perceives, in regard to a space; that is, what is the beholder's impression of volume and shape. This is a common precondition for studying the behavioral efficiency of *any* spaces, whether created or not.

And yet the space impressions of natural spaces are simpler than those of created ones, because the creator's intention has not been stamped upon them, so that the beholder can form an impression without having to decode the creative intention behind it. (When we think of a created thing, we could think of machines and design.) For this reason, in the perspective of setting out a 'flow chart' for programming an analytic approach, it seems appropriate to begin the experimentation by the study of volumetric estimation of natural spaces. The facts that natural space cannot be easily manipulated, and that its shape is often very difficult to apprehend, invite the experimenter to simulate natural space for research purposes.

We next consider the common conceptual conditions of space-impression processes, whether they involve natural or created spaces.

Space impression and the dimension of time

The temptation of some contemporary authors to tie architecture to time as closely as it is tied to space makes it necessary to specify more precisely how time is related to the architectural space impression.

Hegel, in his evolutionary theory, and later Sprengler, studied the opposition and symmetry between the spatial and the temporal. However, it was Bergson who most fundamentally deepened the distinction between these two categories. Gurvitch, Cazeneuve, and the school of Piaget in his *Epistemology of Space* realize Bergson's importance for this question and begin their discussion with his ideas, or else refer to them. Indeed, Bergson makes a very original distinction between these two categories, while, as a philosopher of the vitalistic school, manifesting a particular concern for the temporal. Here we will concentrate our attention on the distinction between these two without looking for a hierarchy of any kind between them.

The temporal is directed, or, in more particular and concrete terms, irreversible. Different points of time cannot be symmetrically related to each other. They are heterogeneous, nonadditive, and situated on a continuous line. Our life also has this irreversible characteristic. We can apprehend it intuitively in its immediacy as a *vécu*. This firsthand knowledge of the temporal is fundamentally subjective, in that we can know only ourselves in this immediate manner. For example, if I see myself in the mirror of my creation, this is only a shadow of my own: '*Le moi fantôme, l'ombre du moi, se projète dans l'espace*' (Bergson 1967: 124). In this order of ideas, we see other subjects, namely the social, only indirectly, in the 'second instance', in the space. If I denominate all that which exists outside myself as objective, all objectivity is related to space. We objectivize ourselves and relate ourselves socially by means of linguistic expressions, and the language itself is permeated more or less by 'spatialization' of feeling and ideas.

Specifically, how do these considerations relate to our subject?

(1) The spatial and social are intimately tied to all objective and quantitative data. Unlike time, both are deeply related to geometry, which, compared to mathematics, shows through the *anschaulichkeit* [descriptiveness] a special liaison between abstract and concrete, as well as between signifier and signified. Therefore, it is reasonable to expect that the sociology of architecture, the sociology of the art of space creation, would turn out to provide a useful foundation for an objective sociology.

(2) Although objective facts are spatial, their cognition is impossible without successive temporal processing. We just mentioned that we cannot add data without involving the homogeneity present in the side-by-side simultaneity of the spatial (Bergson means that all measurement of time, except numbering, distorts its true dimension). What is more interesting for us here is that despite this side-by-side nature of objective data, it is not possible to grasp them without ordering them in some chosen sequence. Otherwise the virtual existence present in them cannot be actualized. *On this second level, and only on this level, the temporal dimension intervenes in the perceived (volumetric) space; that is, not on the level of objective fact itself – namely- the constructed (created) space – but only on its sense impression.* In order to specify the space impression as such, this statement has numerous far-reaching implications.

The architect: the creator without muse To compare space impression with impressions of sequentially ordered phenomena, consider music, film, television, etc. These consist of completely ordered sequences of events. The speed and sequence are imposed on the beholder.

Space impressions also come from input arranged in sequential order, but this order is not imposed on the beholder. Thus, theoretically at least, space impressions allow the beholder more independence, because he is not obliged to receive the sensory input in a particular order or succession.

Let us be more explicit. First, all pathways, or sequences of observed points, are reversible. Moreover, unlike music, there could be more than one counterpoint, because not only could a direction be reversed, but the orientation itself could be changed in many ways. If the reversibility doubles of the number of possible explorations, the free orientation yields R^3 or, if the beholder is earthbound, R^2 alternative possibilities (see 4 in Figure 3.22). The freedom of space impressions from any contingent sequential inputs is further enlarged in two ways. The speed of space exploration is not imposed, and the data inputs are multisensorial. This means that in the case of space impressions, the beholder has a certain degree of freedom with regard to the specific processing sequence proper to sensory organs (indeed, e.g., in the case of acoustical space impressions, the change of the received wave characteristics per unit time are more involved than in the case of optical space impressions, and haptic space impressions are the most dependent upon the beholder's movements. Therefore, we can even differentiate our statement about the involvement of the temporal element in the formation of space impressions, according to various sensory modalities).

Aspects of sensory spaces Theoretically, any closed surface which prevents the entry and/or departure of a stimulus could generate its own perceptible space. If we consider all five 'classical' sense modalities, each could contribute something more or less toward forming a common polysensory space impression, but only certain ones could create space impressions on their own. We may hypothesize that these are optical, acoustical, and haptic envelopes which can give rise to autonomous space impressions. That is, in the absence of sensory input from any other sensory modality, a space impression could occur on the basis of this one sensory input. Since envelopes of the various autonomous sensory space do not necessarily coincide, we must treat each sensory space separately, as well as in combination with the others.

(1a) Let us first look at the traits common to all unisensory spaces. The minimum criterion for any space impression is that some stimuli of a specific kind must be reflected by the envelope. This minimal criterion allows some stimuli to enter the space from the envelope or some to leave it, but not both (see Figure 3.2). Of course, we always consider one and the same sensory modality. Such a space will be referred to as a 'minimal space' or bound form. Thus, minimal spaces are semidetached because they allow one-way communication with another minimal space. Those semidetached spaces such that a message (of the sensory modality under consideration) can neither enter nor leave constitute together complex space, which is a free form (Klaus 1968: 308-309).

26 *Prolegomenon to the science of architectural sociology*

(1b) Another variation of the same kind of sensory spaces is related to the manner in which the stimuli are reflected and how this reflection is distributed over the enveloping surface. Two spaces of the same sensory kind, even with equal geometry, could be perceived as different in shape or volume if they differed in reflecting characteristics. If an estimation has a systematic deviation attributable to this factor, one commonly speaks of a sensory 'illusion'.

All of these considerations assume that the beholder occupies an observation point that is fixed within the space. The impression gained in most unisensory spaces can be improved if the beholder moves, especially if the area is relatively large. This is particularly true of haptic spaces. Moreover, if the multisensory composition is such that the haptic space is smaller than the optic space, it is possible that 'corners' of the optic space will remain inaccessible and so imperceptible (see Figure 3.1). In the inverse case this handicap does not arise. The intimate relation between haptic space and active exploration also appears through kinesthesic sensory input present in haptic space impressions. This will be discussed in detail in the relevant section of the third part.

(2a) If the different unisensory spaces are not identical in their geometry, as, for example, when a space is enclosed by a glass wall, we speak of multisensory spaces in general. In this case the different but simultaneous space impressions do not add to knowledge of *one* space with a common and coinciding geometry. We call this kind of space composition 'space intricacy'. This is an important and very neglected area of research in sociology of architecture.

(2b) When the autonomous spaces of various sensory modalities are geometrically identical, that is, when they coincide completely, we call the space 'polysensorial'. This is a special case of multisensory space where the different sensory data can be used cumulatively, because they are all related to one space with a common geometry.

The preceding discussion suggests the following implications for the representation by architects of spaces and their systems:

— The space is volumetric — viz. in R^n — if n is neither greater nor less than three. Although ground plans and cross-sections can represent the space in technical terms, this sort of mapping is not sufficient to simulate the space for the future beholder, giving an immediate perception of the space (Banham 1967: 323).
— Even photographs of maquettes, usually taken from the convex side of space systems, only show the facade and are thus not sufficient. As a matter of fact, though the way chosen is easy, such photographs do not show the space system.
— Cinematographic representation of the enveloping spaces more closely simulates architecture than the previous two representations; but even this is

not satisfactory because of the multisensory nature of architecture. In the case of polysensorial space the haptic and acoustical components of the space system are lacking. Even in the case of space intricacy, it ignores all autonomous spaces other than the optical.

We must free ourselves from the simplification that spaces, architectural or natural, must be solidly constructed and that their impression can be completely represented visually.

Space as Artifact

When a space is constructed, rather than found, it gains a new element: the creator's purpose. One must have a reason for creating: one makes something for its own sake or in order for it to be instrumental in some other purpose. In order to find paradigms for the sociological treatment of architecture as a created object given from creator to beholder, and in order to use findings from analogous research, we must classify architecture among the artifacts.

Excursus: artificial artifact − a question of doctrinal opinion

La base de l'architecture est la Pâtisserie.

Marie-Antoine Carême (1784-1833)

We now discuss a point of doctrine in order to know what is involved if we attribute specific purposes to architecture.

Early man sought to leave atmospheric space for controllable and well-delimited air spaces and came upon geofactual ones, namely caverns. Space construction may be considered either (a) an imitation of these natural spaces or (b) an attempt to submit our whole environment to our desire by control realized through architecture. We may call the latter a 'culturalist' attitude, which seeks to have the whole environment become man-made. Not only do the number and choice of 'artificial caverns' increase, but as their shapes and volumes diversify, so does their level of sophistication: complex and intricate spaces are constructed. The conditioning of the air space will be perfectly commandable. The perfect isolation of space, realized by membranes, even without making the envelope thicker, permits people to be near each other without actually being together. The tridimensional compact urban space arrangement without open air-streets shows the achievement of the autarchic, man-made biosphere.

The epitome of a controlled framing of our physical and social environment would be the full-scale competition between atmospheric and architectural spaces. However, we must realize that the rich variety of the surface of atmospheric space – valleys, mountains, the sky itself – gives this space a monumental grandeur and permanence. To free the human mind from its dependence upon all-enveloping nature, architecture would then have to compete with and equal all this. In order to do this, architecture has two alternatives:

– It can divert our attention from the landscape as a permanent frame of reference by changing nature ceaselessly, making itself ephemeral. Silver (Jencks and Baird 1969) speaks about 'ephemora' and criticizes the Norberg-Schultz's position on permanence.
– The architect can also try to construct spaces which are immutable, indestructible, and colossal.

The first alternative, at least for those living today within the Earth's atmospheric space, is perhaps more science fiction than a realizable project. The second is within the scope of architecture. Let us examine how it is reflected in certain 'schools of construction' and what its sociological implications are.

Monumentality Fundamentally, the somewhat monumental nature of space derives from the fact that all perceived spaces must be accessible to human beings. This 'minimal monumentality' is present in a prototypical form in the womb. The architect may also create spaces which hold more than a hundred thousand people. Whether these spaces are full or empty, a single person within them seems insignificant. In such a space, he also loses 'touch' with the haptic space. But this effect of colossal spaces does not originate with the Coliseum, modern stadiums, or other major architectural spaces, but with the 'landscapic' ones (e.g., the Grand Canyon). As a matter of fact, the repeatedly mentioned 'architectural determinism' (Broady 1966) is here competing with the geographic one. Architecture is primarily a physical determinant. The fact that architecture may determine social organization, hinder its change, or even be used as a means of social manipulation, is a second effect. In the case of constructing major spaces, the sociological implications of architecture must be carefully and explicitly weighed, but this cannot be the *only* consideration, and often the sociological effect is largely exaggerated.

If for underground spaces the whole effect consists of that resulting from the architectural spaces, constructions which rise from the surface of the earth, such as skyscrapers, have an additional effect, that of sculptural relief or the pyramid effect. This constitutes a direct counterpoint to the effect of mountains and so transforms atmospheric space. From the surface of the earth, this monumentality appears vertical. Although in the past — as in the case of the Roman Coliseum, — the facade was proportional to the inner monumental effect, as previously noted, today this isomorphism no longer holds. The detachment of created spaces from their 'convex' effects in the forming of atmospheric space is closely related to contemporary construction technology: modern techniques make the core city possible. This arrangement, in which the horizontal dimension is hardly greater than the vertical, has the functional effect of mutual nearness without togetherness (Lynch 1960; Ankerl 1971, 1974). This detachment of the relief effect from the functional dimension of each space makes the manipulation of monumentality easier, an idea employed by the city planner.

The large number of spaces involved in this paradoxical arrangement means that a common decision must be made for a large number of individuals and that a considerable amount of capital must be fixed for a long term. Not only are many generations of users involved, but these expensive 'economic mountains', competing with the natural, ecological ones, are here to make an impression on the everyday spectator. Veblen spoke about 'conspicuous consumption' (Ankerl 1965: 187); many corporations and insurance companies use this effect as an advertisement (for example, the Hancock Building is higher than the Prudential Tower in Boston). The sociological interpretation of these phenomena must be a function of the socialization of the various publics and of the past and present decision-making processes involved in these constructions. This field of investigation awaits major considerations from a truly behavioral viewpoint.

Permanence and ferroconcrete In historical processes it is often found that different kinds of phenomena which interact follow different cycles, which may be more or less regular and so more or less predictable. This may cause tentions to surface, making difficult any clear-cut optimal choice. Architectural space creation is an attempt to replace geographic determinism by social responsibility in so far as that creation is a social act. While human decisions are not responsible for the size of a valley or for meteorological changes, they are responsible for the conditioning of architectural spaces, for their geometry and arrangement in systems and subsystems. While there could be contradictions between different synchronic requirements, between developer and present user, we examine here only the matter of contradiction existing within a diachronic perspective, especially as inherent in the durability of architecture.

The basic problem is shown in Figure 1.1.

Even in traditional construction, with renovation, architecture may last for centuries, which could be either too long or too short, depending upon the perspective. If architecture will truly replace natural spaces as a permanent

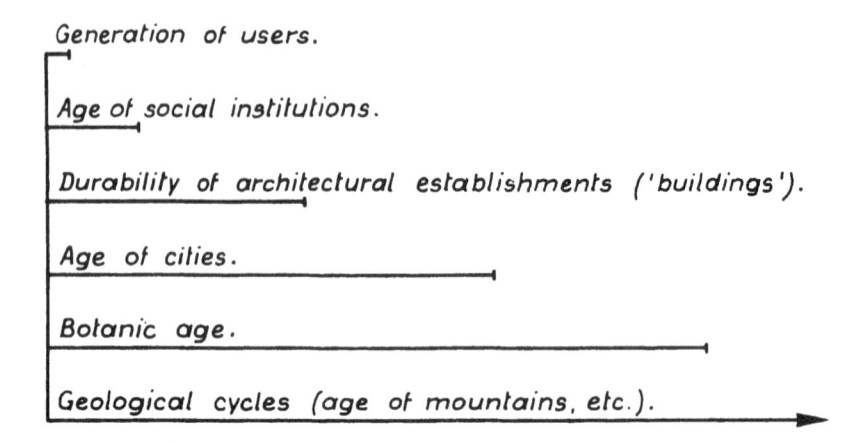

30 *Prolegomenon to the science of architectural sociology*

```
Generation of users.
├─┐
│ Age of social institutions.
├─────┐
│ Durability of architectural establishments ('buildings').
├──────────────┐
│ Age of cities.
├───────────────────┐
│ Botanic age.
├────────────────────────────────┐
│ Geological cycles (age of mountains, etc.).
└──────────────────────────────────────────→
```

Figure 1.1. *Life spans of various phenomena. (Not true-to-scale.)*

framework for reference, the architect must look for much more durable materials and construction techniques, since traditional techniques have created an architecture which last less time than valleys and grottoes. Traditional architecture lasts even less time than urban. For this reason, architectural art tends to be more heterogeneous than urban art.

In other respects, these same constructions often endure longer than the social institutions which called them into being. These time discrepancies give rise to the perception that architecture tends to conserve social institutions (Sennett 1980). The time discrepancy is even worse if we compare a construction's life with the much shorter one of a generation of users. Without admitting the Marxian–Hegelian teleological perspective that the sense of creation is to be avant garde — viz., what counts is not contemporary but future opinion — the architect must be a visionary to satisfy equally present as well as future users.

If a team which makes architectural decisions opts for ephemeral spaces, the architect runs the risk of failing to fulfill a very specific and important aspect of his mission, namely to counterbalance the atmospheric space by spaces which are as stable as nature, but more appropriate for human beings (see Ankerl 1971a). Otherwise, an architect may find himself a tailor of sorts, creating shelters which conform to people's momentary desires (e.g., clothes). In so doing, architecture loses all reference to the 'immemorial time' which natural spaces evoke.

On the other hand, 'architectural establishments' or buildings could, by this design philosophy, overstabilize social institutions and brake social change, which would otherwise appear desirable. In such a case demolition ensues. Without trying here to define how much stability is necessary in order to maintain or increase human societies' independence from the rigors of atmospheric spaces, we may mention that such implications are implicit in architectural decision making. Such decisions cannot be made by easy rhetoric, operating with dubious so-called evidence.

In many cases, the question of durability reduces to that of what material and what construction technique to employ. Today's large variety of possibilities implies a correspondingly large opportunity for human intervention. Indeed, in some cases, the same physical requirements could be realized by solutions of very different durabilities, and a choice is possible. For different reasons — such as the frequent unimaginative application of reinforced concrete surfaces without use of colored ballast — ferroconcrete becomes a scapegoat which some believe 'petrifies our society'.

However, the excellence of this material for durable artificial spaces is evident. If iron is necessary for high-rise buildings (cf. wind pressure), ferroconcrete is necessary for 'deep-rise' buildings. The underground verticality, the deep rooting of the modern cities is inconceivable without this material, which resists fire and corrosion by water, neither of which is the case with iron. Its resistance to stretching makes it more valuable than artificial stone. It is a truly plastic material, monolithic and versatile, and can be used to freely follow the designer's conception. For example, it is now possible to create large flat roofs, where formerly an arch would have been required. It is characteristic that very few American architects use ferroconcrete (Fitch 1972: 218). Frank Lloyd Wright is an exception to this rule. We may also mention the Field House, University of Virginia in Charlottesville, by the architects Baskerville & Son, and the Dallas Air Terminal by Eero Saarinen.

In the debate between 'permanentist' and 'ephemerist' there is no qualitative answer, a simple binary yes or no, but only a quantitative one: what should be the share of permanent and ephemeral man-made elements in our physical environment? In summing up, we can say that architects should be guided by the following considerations (Ankerl 1971a):

— Architects are not responsible for the whole man-made physical environment, but only for space creation; but the latter, as framing of all 'convex' and 'convex-concave' objects and subjects, has primacy and is in direct competition with the universal atmospheric spaces.
— The architect must not overdetermine his creation. Indeed, it may remain largely 'ambiguous' in the sense of a polyvalence or polyfunction (Venturi 1966: 40) for changing use. In general, if inserting a space into a system did not make it already unifunctional, equipping it with particular fixtures will do so (Fitch 1972: 189).
— Finally, permanent space systems could be fitted with instantly autoregulating features, analogous, for example, to a thermostat or pneutics. This is a

rapidly expanding field of automation which helps round out architecture as a 'living art'. Kendrick speaks of 'built-in change' (Michelson 1975: 27; Venturi 1966: 40). This is an extension of architecture, but not architecture itself.

The machine: architecture's paradigm?

It is not by chance that the technician Jeanneret-Gris from Chaux-de-Fonds, called Le Corbusier, wrote the sentence: 'The house is a machine for living in' (Le Corbusier 1927: 4). It was also he who wrote a letter to A. Sartori to 'invent' the word *funzionale* for characterizing the architecture of the 'first machine age' (Banham 1967: 321), a word which had replaced the original word of Sartori, which was *razionale* (this letter has been printed as a preface to Sartori 1932). Indeed, the precise sense of functionalism as a doctrine comes from the application of the mechanical analogy, as it is expressed in Le Corbusier's sentence, to architecture. Other interpretations either lack all historical specificity or else are implications of the mechanical analogy. It is true that all architects who called themselves functionalists did not follow a mechanomorph line, but in this case the word lost its specific sense. On the other hand, it is true that perennial Western rationalism, utilitarianism, biological organicism, and even 'naturalism', as sources of primitive rationalism (cf., Adam Smith), are involved in the construction of machines.

The question is: what is a machine? Has architecture been modeled on machines? Is modern architecture so modeled? Must it be?

What is a machine? It is an eingine which is mobile and has an internal movement following a precise and strict technological prescription. It functions like a robot in order to produce previously specified goods. We should understand that if certain machines, such as cars and domestic appliances, are in touch with human beings, and their design is 'engineered and styled' (e.g., a car), there are machines which have contact only with other machines: machine–machine vs. human–machine (cybernetic) symbioses. In the former case human beings are touched only by the end products and less by the machine's appearance. On the other hand, the production process is exactly prescribed and followed.

At first glance, an architect may have the idea that machines constitute a paradigm for architecture as a creation which functions better than architecture. Indeed, architects wish to promote specific behavior in the created spaces and their system. But upon further analysis it appears that the analogy overlooks essential aspects.

If we look at the main functions of architectural spaces, we see that these include the social function of face-to-face communication, the ergonomic function, and that of protecting individual privacy (e.g., sleep). With the exception of the protection of sleepers, these are performed by a 'functioning' of architecture on two levels: assuring the physical ambience by geometries of specifically isolated spaces, and stimulating an adequate impression by the appearance of this ambient space. The room must not only have an appropriate geometry for an activity, but it must also give the impression of being adequate, even, if necessary, by means of sensory illusions.

Of course we find, especially in the case of the machines which constitute our everyday environment, this stimulating aspect, but this is not the essential aspect as it is in the case of architecture. Why? A good machine handles physical raw materials or semifinished products and not human, or even living, beings. Even the titles of Negroponte's two books (1970, 1974) *The Architecture Machine* and *Soft Architecture Machines,* do not suggest this idea. Rather, it speaks about machines which produce architecture, in a previsible manner. The human intervention and so the stimulating component of the machine design is a marginal affair in this technology. This question should become clearer with the rise of automated factories. In a well-engineered machine, the active part is mechanical and the human intervention, and thus stimulation, is marginal. (There exist machines which control the control function itself, and so the machine-machine dialog will always be larger.) Therefore we cannot say that the stimulating process, not only the designed room but also its impression, can have any comparably important part in the mechanism which guides the technological process in a machine. In mechanical functioning the machine, instead of the man, has the active role.

— The designed space is enveloping, but in general the designed machine is not.
— If a machine can be multipurpose, this will mean here alternative functions but not any virtually as *Spielraum.* From the beginning the process is unequivocally fixed. Perhaps architectural space is a condition for some behaviors which had been foreseen by the architect, but this is done in a polyvalent manner. This kind of 'architectural indeterminacy' is inherent also in architecture because it is one and the same object, namely the space which operates on both levels: physically (e.g., a soundproof room), and through stimulation received by the room's impression. As we have seen, unifunctional specification of rooms comes for the most part only in terms of the equipment of the spaces, or in the context of a room given by its syntactical integration within a space system.

We can go further and see that criteria like unequivocal 'readability' (Lynch), as opposed to ambiguity and 'complexity' (Venturi), are based on the assumption that they are appropriate for evaluating a space, and that the most important human activities in all architectural spaces must be rationalized and uniformized; viz., there must be a best user's response to a space. On another level this kind of weakly founded reasoning finds backing in the hasty application of information theory analogies to architecture. In this case we try to assimilate architecture to a discourse which has as its unique *raison d'être* the transmitting of a maximum of unequivocal information with a minimum of time and effort.

The baroque theoretician Alberti was right to say that the ends of architecture are *commoditas* and *voluptas*. Indeed, all authors, including the present one, agree that there are spaces for which there is no interest in creating a space impression. These are spaces where human beings rarely have access, such as automatic machinery houses, transformer houses, tabernacles, and garages. These spaces are submitted quasi-exclusively to an unesthetic utility'. (We are now speaking about the inner space impression.) Even in a gradual way, these kinds of pure supply or convenience rooms could multiply in an age of extreme mechanization (e.g., a fully automated kitchen). But it would be incorrect to infer that spaces without a stimulating space effect will of necessity be the most significant spaces of tomorrow, and so the crowning of architecture.

(1) As an envelope, architecture would lose its specificity if its stimulating aspect lost its role. We suggest that even a room for songbirds brings together the specific tasks of an architect more than even the creation of large spaces which are useful but inaccessible by man. Architecture must be understood as framing not the inanimate, not even the vital, but more specifically the animate function, if one could consider writing a poem a function.

(2) Under the auspices of the idea of the industrial society or the technological or machine age, some functionalist theoreticians hold that copying the machine design forms, which is an obligation for machinery houses, must be generalized for all kinds of architectural space creations. This kind of extention from the most common of major constructions of an epoch to other contemporary constructions has operated at all times. We see religious forms in the Middle Ages transposed to other civil buildings, and chateau forms to other buildings in the Renaissance. This sort of unjustified transfer, such as the transposition of industrial, especially machinery-house, space forms, to spaces primarily for human activities (cf. Banham 1967: 326-330), has far-reaching consequences: namely, that the stimulating criteria be subordinated to a physical convenience. This 'econocratic ideology' (Ankerl 1965), the predominance of the productive over all creative, as well as recreative, activities, is implied by this kind of architectural design philosophy, and creates obstacles to broader potentialities.

Architecture and communication processes

We cannot consider any problem from a sociological perspective without seeing how it is related to the communication process. Indeed, we cannot conceive of any real social events not involving communication processes, and the latter constitute the best discriminable aspect of social phenomena as specifically social and empirical.

Indeed, as will be seen, architecture and the field of communication have more than one point of contact. The central point is that typically architecture must be considered as a one-way communication link between the architect and recipients. The contemporary client may perhaps give some feedback, but even he does not express himself in space systems as does the architect. And the one-way link becomes even more evident when we recall that architecture can be sold to new recipients and finally to future generations of users.

In order to consider architecture as a medium between designer and recipients, in all of its specific dimensions, we must clarify how architecture could be identified in the family of created objects or artifacts. The place of architecture among technical machine objects has already been considered. The question now is how architecture pertains to the arts.

We have identified the proper task of the architect as space creation: a space which, with its volume and shape, could make an impression on the 'recipient' who is enveloped there. So the product of architectural creation appears as multisensorially perceptible tridimensional space 'concavities' which, by their enveloping qualities, have a primacy over all other objects situated within them.

The repertory of conceivable and discriminable spaces and the mode of choice among them in order to fashion them into concrete connected systems constitutes the proper means of architectural creation. Of course, a medium does not necessarily determine for what purpose it will be exclusively used. For instance, we know the spoken and the pictographic language, but we can transmit a message – coded by convention (e.g., Morse code) – by any medium having enough combinable elements. In spite of current 'mentalistic' sociological traditions deriving from the humanities, we do not look at the matter of how architecture could fill the communication tasks which could be performed by any other media, namely language – and we mean here by language, as the word 'langage' in French expresses, a set of *arbitrarily* chosen signs. We can look only into the truly specific task of architecture and eventually into the message which could not be conveyed by any other art.

To make our concern more explicit, we must bear in mind onomatopoeia – a case of isomorphism between signifier and signified (Dorfles, in Jencks and Baird 1963: 40) – icons or pictograms (Alleton 1970: 8), and figurative art. In all these cases there is an intimate relation between the object and its representation (Pierce 1961).

It seems to us that in the case of architecture the relation between the purpose and its representation is still closer.

36 Prolegomenon to the science of architectural sociology

The purpose of architecture is not to be a simple communication medium. It is directly instrumental in the realization of certain human-life activities, even life as such. Architects create various spaces not primarily in order to create space impressions. (Otherwise it would be enough to stimulate space impressions by some tactile-audiovisual medium yet to be invented.) First of all, architecture is created, literal, banal space. If the impression is an integral part of the effect and purpose of architecture, the directly physical protecting, sheltering, and framing of vital functions are no less fundamental. These enveloped vital states are: (a) social behavior activities realized by communications; (b) activities which we may call ergonomic activities like object manipulations; and finally (c) inactive life functions (e.g., sleeping). Many environmental conditions relevant to these life functions could be maintained by alternative means. Architecture assures only those conditions which explicitly require an enveloping space. In this sense we can say that space presents the activities in their spatial virtuality.

The impression of a space, which we will identify as one aspect of architecture, provides stimulation. A space can also be connotative of attractiveness or unpleasantness for the recipient, but the first denotative message for the recipient concerns the 'estimated' physical character of the space in order to know what set of human activities − e.g., possibilities of face-to-face communication in a group − is possible. In this sense, on a very general level, architecture appears as a vehicle of possibilities. Indeed, e.g., the channeling of face-to-face communication in a space itself does not involve effective communication flows, but is itself a set of virtual communication structures. The 'roominess' of a space, which involves not only volumetric capaciousness, but also shape and isolation characteristics, gives the impression of a set of networks and provides a certain degree of freedom by means of its polyvalence. The first impression conveyed to the recipient is expressed by his answer to such questions as: have these rooms different volumes and/or shapes in terms of any sensory modality? Which set of potential activities is possible here or there? Only after this assimilation of information could the room, without name or any other verbal mediation, impress the recipient in such a way that he eventually feels stimulated himself by the room to carry out some particular activity (e.g., writing a poem).

The distinction concerning this first stage of space impression is very important for knowledge of the space consumption process's relevance for an efficient architectural communication. Indeed, the first type of question to which the space impression gives some answer could be experimentally explored, since the question is unambiguous and generally understandable, and the answer is on the denotative level, which allows one to expect a quite generalizable reply. Systematically asking these questions in the framework of a well-designed experiment, we can hope to find difference thresholds which allow us to transform the continuous field of spaces, which could differ, for example, by an infinitely small magnitude, into a list of discrete units which would be a repertory of meaningful architectural signs which we here call, for the sake of simplicity, the 'vocabulary of architecture' without implying that architecture would be a language in the proper sense.

Indeed, it would be a fatal error to skip this stage of research in order to advance more rapidly to 'more significant' findings, a strategy often proposed by semiologists and semanticists of architecture (Raymond 1968: 167-179).

In general, verbal replies given about connotative impressions lack consistency, and the reactions are idiosyncratic and seldom generalizable. But even if this evaluative attitude is measured by nonverbal behavior, we must study the language of architecture as such before the style (Eco 1971: 683, 2.1 and 2.3). In any case the inquiry about the 'denotative impression' must come first in the research strategy. This is a prolegomenon to the study of architectural art.

On the other hand, the architect also has objective means of manipulating the appearance of a space *without* changing the effective geometry of it. For this purpose it is enough that he simply modify the envelope's surface for pictorial acoustical, and/or tactual effects. The means for these effects could be borrowed from the fine arts. Does that mean that architecture itself is one of them?

Fine art and architecture: is architecture a habitable sculpture? As the pictogram does in a schematic manner, the painting can represent bidimensional phenomena or even copy them, and by virtue of the constitution of our visual system even simulate a three-dimensional phenomenon. But the written form of verbal language as its *relais* cannot realize such figurative representation.

Applied to the closed surface of an architectural envelope, either figurative representations of a three-dimensional space, or (proper) distribution of colors — called nonfigurative or 'abstract' painting — can modify the effect of a space impression (Gibson 1966: 240). On the other hand, if a painting is nonfigurative, it is confined to being expressive or connotative. If we disregard the use of paint as a protective layer, painting can serve only a communicative purpose. Apart from its two-dimensional nature, this makes it fundamentally different from architecture.

Much of what has been said is equally valid for sculpture as a tactile-visual art, but sometimes its differentiation from architecture seems more difficult because both are three-dimensional. Indeed, concerning painting, the difference between the literal space of architecture and the figurative space of painting is easily seen. Even if some authors refer to the Statue of Liberty in New York (Arnheim 1966: 4) or the sculptured uteri of Tingely and of Niki de Saint-Phalle as 'accessible', this does not in principle constitute a fundamental objection to what has been said. Such works cannot provide useful space, or else they would simply be architecture. Suzanne Langer and other authors also see clearly that arrangements *in* space, even if they are there to facilitate our perceiving the space, are instrumental in terms of space impressions but do not create spaces in the proper sense of the term.

Plastic art, such as sculpture and painting, appears similar to architecture. Spoken language imposes a temporary unilinear sequence, which is not the case with the spatial arts. But sculpture and painting are not composed of discursive utterances which, combined by discernible rules, can also communicate scientific knowledge. However, unifying such heterogeneous functions as literary expression and scientific knowledge, spoken language is similar to architecture: architecture accommodates various more-or-less rational human activities. Dorfles points out that architecture is a more exact art than is sculpture. But apart from the evident fact that the reading sequence of architecture is generally not irreversibly determined, its meaningful elements, the roomraum, are not purely conventional signs but inherently connected to their signification. There is an isomorphism between them (Dorfles 1969: 40–41), much like what we see in the phenomenon of 'body language', which will be the social theme of architecture. As communication, architecture is a epidictique phenomenon; it is not primarily representative, but presents itself. In relation to typical words, architectural space is even more 'excentric' than the presentive word (Pei), because the room is also the real thing, and if this presentation were destroyed, the space itself would also perish.

Linguistics, architectural semiologists, and eventual relevance of their contribution to the architectural communication theory: (attempts and temptations)

We have seen that all created things (a) involve the act of creation (b) and, if designed for someone, an act of reception (c).

Among creations, those that are linguistic materials — if we do not count verses — pretend to be contingent only accidentally on any 'physicalness' or hylic aspect. Indeed, language results from purely arbitrary conventions about signs and rules, conventions which do not establish any intrinsic link between signifier and signified. The material appearance of a sign is accidental and so substitutable (e.g., the written form of spoken language and the spoken *relais* of pictographic writing). The well-structured nature of this quite abstract vehicle, namely, language, allows a good scientific treatment, realized in linguistics. How may we apply such a treatment to architecture? Architecture presents its purpose itself, and this presentation, which is manifest in its appearance, bears an integral part of its purposefulness. This double (physical and perceptual) but inseparable articulation inherent in architecture also involves an isomorphism (Dorfles) between substance and 'image' (cf. Winkel's 'imageability': Ittelson 1973: 56).

Conceptualization   39

The first problem arises from this fundamental difference between language and architecture, if we hope to transfer any available linguistic knowledge to the treatment of architectural communication.

Any transfer of concepts and methods applied in studies of literary communication (which are even here applied only with more or less success) to the spatial fine arts and even to architecture is problematical. Indeed, for them to be applicable, we must accept the premise that some specific analogy exists both (a) between language and the structure of architectural creation, and also (b) between literary and architectural art.

In general, today we encounter numerous studies which relate architectural communication to linguistics, semiology, semiotics, semantics, and the New Criticism. First of all, following national schools and fashions, the use of these terms is quite arbitrary, but viewed from the origin of these approaches, the following specifications seem reasonable.

Semiology originates with the Genevan linguist F. de Saussure. If he enlarges the treatment of linguistic sign systems by considering the 'life of signs in the framework of social life' (1967: 33), it must not be forgotten that language is composed of *parole* and *langue* (1967: 33-35, 112). By the former is meant the individual use of words, and the latter is the object of linguistics, and so linguistic communication (cf. Tavolga) with its arbitrary but by convention well-established sign system remains his focus of interest. In this sense the study of other sign systems eventually less dependent on arbitrary sign conventions and strict systematic syntactic rules easily involves an undue extrapolation of his linguistic based paradigms. So any communication which, following the Jacobsonian distinction, is based less on rhetorical convention and fulfills a more poetic function (e.g., the plastic arts, mimics) comes off rather badly by this approach. Guiraud (1971: 81, 111) calls semiology an 'erratic discipline'.

Of course, the so-called New Criticism (Ogden, Richards), the *Literaturwissenschaft*, or the *Nouvelle Critique* is typically an approach to literature looking for archetypical symbolism (Northrop Frye), and the morphology of tales originated in the Russian formalism (cf. Propp's analyses of Russian folktales in 1928) and in the linguist circle of Prague (cf. Jacobson, Martinet). If the line followed by Greimas – and Bachelard – serves any purpose, it would be for the rhetoric of literary art.

All of these approaches belong to the field of semantics, in the sense that they cannot leave the meaning of signs out of consideration. Semantics studies precisely this meaning, especially of linguistic signs, the relationships of meanings among them in the semantic fields, and in relation to the referent, and their historical changes and other variations. De Saussure would speak of sign's value. Even though some authors such as Panofsky developed an iconology opposed to iconography, the elaborate structural method of content analysis remains within the field of linguistic messages. It is certainly this dimension of semiotics which shows the strongest vulnerability to ideological abuses. This holds even if an esoteric and overinflated vocabulary used by a single author and his followers, often composed of ill-defined pseudoterminology, is used to hide the true situation.

Indeed, semantics is only one of the three dimensions of semiotics, as it was defined by Charles Morris, and is perhaps not the dimension best suited for reliable scientific treatment. Indeed, semiotics, whose philosophical origin goes back to Peirce, finds in Morris's theory the best formulation which is capable of approaching any system of signs. This approach can generate objective as well as cumulative knowledge, without becoming submerged in a mechanistic model of communication theory (McCardle 1974: 3; McQuail 1975: 21) based on the Shannon–Weaver mathematical theory of information transmission, applicable especially to telephone engineering.

Morris's semiotics has three dimensions, orthogonally representable, which allows an independent consideration of (a) the syntactic aspects, (b) the semantic aspects, and (c) the pragmatic aspects of communication (Ankerl 1972b). The last relates locutor to receiver and is close to semiology. The first of the three semiotic fields deals with structural analysis of messages without any reference to meaning or locutor (cf. Harris) and is the most firmly grounded.

Apart from the fact that architectural communication is not directly related to linguistic communication, we have another reason to interest ourselves particularly in semiotics as a general theory of signs, namely the face-to-face communication network upon which will be built the 'sociological theme' of architecture, and which, like architectural communication, largely includes the field of nonlinguistic communication behavior.

Let us sum up what contributions could be expected from the different theoretical approaches to understanding architectural communication.

(1) In order to produce useful and cumulative knowledge, as a first step we must describe architecture as a specific medium. Parry (1967: 229) has written that a medium is 'any instrument or contribution of senses for transmitting information, whether a human sense or a natural or man-made vehicle of transmission; every medium is selective in respect to the materials it transmits so that "accounts" given by two media are never identical'. This task involves the systematic description of the composition of perceptible space systems with definite volumes and shapes. Before trying to attribute any intention or meaning to specific space creations, the message itself must be studied in order to convey to us the substance of the medium. (It is necessary to say that the 'physicalness' of an architectural construction is not its substance, but is rather the isolating character of the envelope and its

durability.) In the present stage of understanding architecture as a medium, we must avoid research which scrutinizes the (connotated) meaning of architecture: we should avoid studying, before architecture itself, 'para-architectural' phenomena, the great texts of famous architects, the *architecture parlée* (see Le Corbusier's lecture, the appendix in Boudon 1972). If the texts are not true legends and 'specifications' necessary for builders, these architects' commentaries and brochures are often simple 'eyewash'. In them architects try to attribute meaning to their works which was not there in the first place.

(2) We emphasize the description of the 'architectural substance' as a first stage, as opposed, on the one hand, to other manifestation of an architect's intentions, and on the other hand, to the meaning connotated by the object and readable on the structural register of the object as the code of 'a style'. On the contrary, the appearance of the substance as a source of illusion is an integral part of the actualization of the specific purpose of architecture in the first instance, which implies that the recipient's impression is involved. No repertory for architectural communication can be established as long as we do not know the threshold which makes it possible for a receiver to distinguish between spaces with various volumes, shapes, and multisensory compositions. This impression does not necessarily involve an interpreter who conveys the connotative meaning. This is a fundamental point for the denotation conveyed by a created space system. German authors such as Klaus and Bense speak about the *sigmatik* [signaling] function, as distinguished from the semantic one (indeed, the distinction between connotation and denotation is here that between value judgment about space and volumetric magnitude estimation).

The knowledge concerning the architectural medium generated by this kind of research promises to be solid and generalizable, without any reference to a particular school, epoch, or region of architecture.

(3) In order to understand the categories introduced in the systematic description of architecture as a medium, we allow ourselves to borrow terms used in linguistics. But before doing that we must say why architecture cannot be fully classed with language as present communication theory defines it (*langue*).

Even if by admitting ideographic sign systems without phonetic representation we detach language from its ordinary spoken background, language (cf. Chao 1968: 18) involves a lexicon of symbols possessing arbitrary, conventional meanings and systematic syntactic rules. The arbitrary and conventional character – and the marginal nature of onomatopoeia or iconic analogy of signs – is essential if language is to carry abstract ideas and concepts (ideogram versus pictogram). Here is a fundamental difference between language proper and architecture as media. Operating by connotation, the fine arts do not follow an arbitrary codification (Hjelmslev). On the other hand, as previously mentioned, architecture does not follow the fine arts because architecture consists of a system of discrete units having a specific denotation. If we speak about architectural morphology, we mean that which is composed of sensorily discernible spaces. We can list open-ended repertory which potentially includes all simple architectural elements which can stand on their own. Whereas the physical transition between one space size and another is continuous, the units of this list are discrete in two respects: (a) given two spaces which differ geometrically but not perceptibly, the rule is that they constitute one item in the list composing the architectural repertory; (b) on the concrete level, space systems are composed of a countable number of spaces, but may differ in the positioning of those spaces (so any occurrence of one and the same repertory item in the concrete syntactical context could be individualized, identified).

We refer to a perceptibly discernible architectural roomraum as a 'morpheme', implying that all of its constitutive elements are, from the viewpoint of architecture, on the submorphemic level (e.g., the face of an envelope such as a floor, or colors). Such elements are architecturally accountable only in their morphological context, which is a space.

(4) If an open-ended enumeration of units which may be properly denoted as architectural is possible (that is, a repertory of spaces), we can generate space systems with topologically and geometrically defined rules, precise rules such as are found in syntactic and syntagmatic operations. (Paradigmatic transformation relates to architectural morphology.) Indeed, by borrowing terms such as 'systematic syntax' from linguistics, which would be inappropriate in dealing with such media as sculpture or painting because of the asystematic nature of their codes, we do not imply that architecture can be classed as a language. Rather, we suggest that the construction of space systems follows a strict system of rules, and, on the other hand, that the imbedding of spaces in a space system adds new specifications to them on the level of denotation and on that of meaning. The space systems could be put in analogy with sentences because, like the latter, they utter a complete unit of meaning and as a whole attribute a specific purposefulness to each composing space.

THE SOCIOLOGICAL THEME OF ARCHITECTURE: THE FACE-TO-FACE COMMUNICATION NETWORK

We have seen that, in the first instance, sociology considers architecture as a particular medium of communication. We have also seen that architecture is not only a roof which protects us against the hazards of atmospheric space, but that it is also walls separating us from others. By means of the possibility of determining the presence of others, and so a virtual set of such presences (e.g., face-to-face communications), what we may call spatial sociology provides the sociological theme for architectural creation.

Let us develop this subject. Social relations are effectuated by means of communicative transmissions. If we consider the invariants which emerge from the mutual interactive effects of these communications without taking into account the influence of the physical environment, we are studying the pure sociological effect. On the other hand, it is ecosociology or socionomics (Drever 1968: 275) if we consider the effect of the physical environment on the communication network and structure. That is, if we consider territoriality as a rooting within a specific geographic area, we are making use of the ecosocial aspect, but if we consider only the mutual position or proximity of social partners as determining their communication network, we are working within pure sociology.

In the absence of architectural constraints, if somebody searched out exclusive communication with someone else, he transformed the communication network (as defined by the mutual position of him and his partner) by changing his relative position, viz, by moving near or turning to the other. In pure sociology, for which the endless flat sand of the desert is a good model (cf. Eco 1971: 683; Ankerl 1973), the intimacy involved in exclusive communication access for a group or dyad could be reached by situating themselves out of range of the others. Architectural space creates virtual intimacy, permitting certain communication flows or strcutures by means of a set of communication networks. Indeed, a well-defined space prefigures how many participants and which multisensorily defined communication networks are possible and which are excluded. This provides a synomorphy between architectural space and its communication network (Atteslander and Hamm 1974). If interiority is the essence of enveloping space, it is not fortuitous that 'intimacy' is generated from the superlative of 'interior'.

We must now address two frequent sources of confusion:

(1) First of all, if we speak in sociology about 'intimacy' or 'central figure', we must consider such terms in a behavioral, rather than in a figurative or an attitudinal, sense. Indeed, physical centrality or a superior situation are effectively determined by position within a communication network, in that those holding such positions have certain communication privileges. By means of creating such privileged network positions, architectural spaces generate sociological effects (e.g., speech delivered *ex cathedra*, speaking from stage, podium, estrade, platform, rostrum, etc.). One's position within a communication network simultaneously determines two questions: (a) how many people can be perceived without considerable movement (viz., reciprocity of partners), and (b) what multisensory composition will the communication

channel have? The modern development of architecture (cf. Fitch) has greatly enlarged its sociological efficiency because it is now possible to construct complex and complicated spaces (e.g., compound architectural words) from presently available material and construction techniques. While in fully closed, unsophisticated spaces the distance and direction of the mutual positions are the quasi-exclusive variables determining the network positions, if it happens that some wall can fulfill filtering functions the situation becomes more complicated and the 'architect's social responsibility' has been enlarged. He can now make some sensory access *uni*lateral (complex space), or he can separate one sensory channel from another (intricated space). For example, in the Figure 1.2.4 we see that a is nearer to c than to b but b is for him more multisensorily accessible than is c (indeed, this compound space is composed of one optical space and two composing acoustical spaces which are subsystems). We will see that this question can become very complicated if we consider all sensory modalities and admit that their hierarchical order, in its *poly*sensory composition, is not the same for 'space perception' as for 'social perception'. Indeed, one could be primarily optico-acoustical and the other audiovisual.

(2) We must introduce a clarification in connection with the appearance of elaborate systems of telecommunication now in existence. At present, telecommunication involves the elimination of certain sensory components, such as touch and olfaction. What is an essentially new element of telecommunication is its ubiquitous nature (Ankerl 1974): distance is no longer important in the determination of one's communication network position. The importance of transport facilities for human relations will be diminished with the multisensory extension of telecommunication networks.

Insofar as the sociological effect of architecture is to assure face-to-face communication, it constitutes an alternative to telecommunication. *Urban architectural space systems are characterized by closeness without togetherness* — e.g., a large number of neighboring but nonoverlapping intimacies. The advantage of this situation is that it allows one to easily and rapidly change rooms, so that the urban dweller can exchange his face-to-face communication network for another. With progress in multisensory transmission by telecommunication networks, this nearness, now only realized in the urban space system, will become more and more universal.

In the present stage of technical development we can say that as far as the multisensorial channeling of telecommunication is limited, face-to-face communication and the intimacy assured by modern refined architectural space creation remain necessary. Even the development of efficient, cheap, and rapid transportation systems works in the direction of more face-to-face communication. That is not the case with the urban space system, if we consider this space system not as a simple facility (for encounter) (Ankerl 1974) but as a settlement or habitation with dense permanent living quarters.

1.

I.
$a_I \qquad b_I$

Dyad without a third person.

II.
$a_{II} \qquad b_{II}$
$\qquad\qquad\qquad c_{II}$

Dyad in a triad.

2.

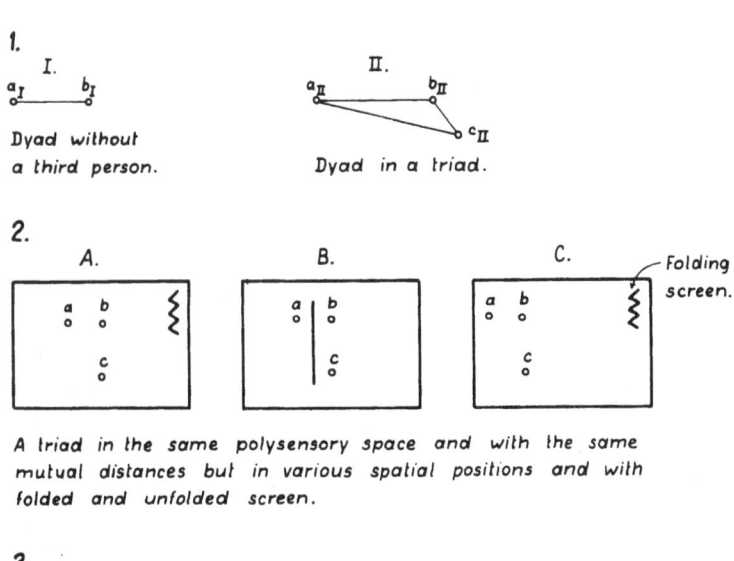

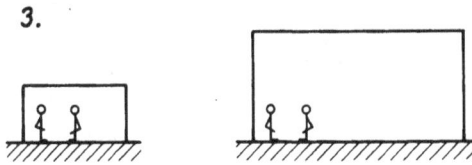

A. a b   c — Folding screen.

B. a | b   c

C. a b   c

A triad in the same polysensory space and with the same mutual distances but in various spatial positions and with folded and unfolded screen.

3.

Dyads with equal mutual distance but in very different polysensory spaces.

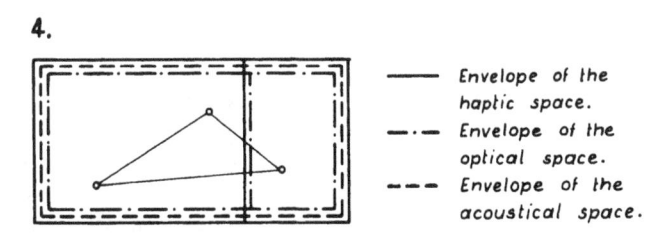

4.

——— Envelope of the haptic space.
—·— Envelope of the optical space.
— — — Envelope of the acoustical space.

Polysensory communication network determined by the multisensory intricacy of the architectural space composition.

Figure 1.2. *Determinant aspects of the face-to-face communication other than the distance in a dyad.*

Indeed, the development of transportation (helicopters, etc.) allows great mobility and the possibility for realizing large numbers of face-to-face encounters. In a desired composition it is enough to have the space system with appropriated rooms, but that will not necessarily involve a high residential density any more (e.g., convention center or marketplace as new city concept: Ankerl 1971a; recent tendency to move to the countryside; 'citified country').

In summary, we can say that traffic, as far as it facilitates encounter and face-to-face communication, promotes a kind of city, but the extensive and intensive (namely polysensory) development of telecommunication makes cities somewhat superceded (cf. M. Nilles in Pool 1977; Short et al. 1976, about audio-and-video teleconferencing in business.)

Architectural Rooms and the Application of Communication Network and Structure Concepts to Face-to-Face Communication

The relevance of created spaces for social behavior comes from the fact that all human and so social events are situated in a room with determined volume and shape (and with specific multisensory composition) which physically admit or exclude certain polysensory face-to-face communication networks; moreover, the impression of the space in question on the beholder mediates this effect by giving an idea of communication network possibilities, such as transforming one position into another (viz., one network into another) in order to realize in it effective communicative behavior.

In order to model these sociological effects of spaces, we make use of two basic concepts used by — among others — Bavelas and Flament in dealing with the communicative behavior of various groups which are basically limited to phone lines. We apply the terms 'communication network' (e.g., possibilities) and 'communication structure' (e.g., flow) in treating face-to-face communication. Indeed, mutual position of partners in a given space involves determined polysensory communication transmission possibilities with specific thresholds. This network is so determined by direct transmission lines and by the reflection of specific waves by the architectural envelope. Indeed, this face-to-face communication network is not necessarily centered on verbal communication, especially not on the transmissibility of meaning of linguistic signs, but on all kinds of communicative expression such that the transmissible polysensory compositions change by mutual position: what is perceptible in a polysensory composition from one position may not be from another. So the predominance of this or that sensory channel will be a function of the network position (cf. whispering, etc.). This differentiation of the transmissible polysensory message constitutes the network.

The transmissibility of polysensory messages is determined by the network position potentially present in a space. This transmissibility could be experimentally determined by means of perceptual threshold studies.

On another level, the impression that the participant has concerning this communication value of his position stimulates him partly to choose this or that polysensory composition of his message in order to use the network to

Conceptualization   47

let that message flow. If the effectively transmitted polysensory message that the recipient receives depends on the physical conditions, it is not the effective physical space which directly influences the polysensory organization of the emitted message but its impression.

If we state here that the impression of face-to-face communication possibilities influences the message emission, by that we do not mean that the architectural space is determinant in this emission. We will not specify a specific relative importance of architecture. We only state that *if* architecture can specifically affect, and insofar as it can affect, the communication structure, how it is that it can do so.

But before the space impression exerts any effect on the actual communication structure, it can have a more important specific effect on the communication structure by virtue of the fact that the space could be perceived as a set of network positions potentially inherent in a room. This potential use of the space impression will be reflected mainly in the movement which changes one's network position (displacement and turning). In spite of many wrong interpretations, these movements are not communications themselves, but transformations of network positions as conditions for future communications. Indeed the movement of some group members in a space could be understood as transformations of face-to-face communication networks, while the changing of rooms could be a transformation of a telecommunication network into a face-to-face communication network (come around and see; step across; pop over).

We see that communication structure as social exchange behavior could be affected by architecture on two levels. The physical nature of the rooms directly affects the reception of another's response, and the space impression already affects the original voice emission. If the former 'manipulates' the message physically, the latter directly affects the 'mind', and so even the mechanisms of the relation between independent and dependent variables themselves. In other words, if a specific sensory space can affect only the transmission of a message of the same sensory nature, the impression of different sensory rooms can also have cross-effects on the emission of any other sensory messages (see Figure 4.3.1).

We also see that we have an interest in considering the space impression on its own. In order to explain changing communication structures as a function of architectural enveloping spaces, and even to help architectural communication in establishing space repertories, it is appropriate to study space impressions.

If we map the whole image of a space in order to fully know the impression it creates, the knowledge will be phenomenological or idiosyncratic, which can certainly not establish a repertory for architectural communication in which schools and epochs can inscribe the 'idioms of their styles'. In order not to lose oneself in the morass of phenomenological psychology or introspection (or mentalism: Yasuo 1960: 17) and yet without making an arbitrary amputation of nonnegligible factors, we do not propose to study the space impression in its connotated image which bears the beholders' emotions projected onto it.

In order to study space impression on a more stable level which is intermediate between physical space and the *espace vécu*, we do not ask the beholder about the affective (verbal) adjectives which he associates with such or such a room but only about descriptive qualifications with precise denotation, related to the relative volumetric magnitude or geometrical shape of the room. Of course, these responses (in sense-datum language) are verbal too – i.e., if we use them not in their original phonetic nature but on the mental level. But we can expect that the meaning of these terms – related to relative volumetric magnitude and inequality or equality of geometrical shapes – is generally accepted and unequivocal and, on the other hand, that these estimations are only secondarily 'parasitized' by affection, and give more long-lasting and generalizable results.

In order to generate standard thresholds for relative space impression differences we can vary not only the volume and/or shape of each sensory space, but quantitatively and qualitatively the reflective characteristics of the envelopes. The reflective nature of the envelope does not, of course, change the geometrical form (volume and shape) of the space, but does change its physical reverberatory nature, which affects the physical transmission and what the observer can project in volume or shape in terms of over- or underestimation. A yet more sophisticated projection on the impression level – as opposed to the purely physical one – can come from the fact that two sensory spaces, which do not coincide but which are in a complicated spatial composition, affect the impression of one another without having any effect on the physical transmission.

We do not go into detail here, but only note which factors could be efficient and which factors must and could be investigated as part of our specific study. We see here in what 'heuristic context' the effect of physical space characteristics – effective through the communication network – on communicative behavior could be studied and also the effect of space impressions themselves mediated through the observer's 'denotation' of volume and shape differences. On the following pages we will show how the possibility of applying the requirements of an objective sociology (Leclercq 1963: 97, 105, 108; Piéron 1968: 353) make sociology of architecture a privileged field for the development of sociology itself, which can in turn show more and more cumulative knowledge.

SOCIOLOGY OF ARCHITECTURE: A PRIVILEGED FIELD FOR RESEARCH IN OBJECTIVE (EXTERNAL) SOCIOLOGY

'Why Is Literary Criticism Not an Exact Science?' is asked of us by Levin (1967). It appears easier than our question: how could the sociology of architecture become an exact and objective science?

An appropriate sociological approach to architecture gives rise to fundamental possibilities for developing such a science, for the benefit of both architecturology and sociology itself. But it is also true that the first encounters between architecture and sociology during this past decade show that this opportunity has been largely missed. Indeed, encounters are easily given over to accommodations. The architectural profession lost any scientific basis the moment structural engineering was separated from architecture. Architects did not look to perceptual psychology and spatial sociology for a scientific basis specific to that profession (Ankerl 1973). On the other hand, the German mentalistic (*verstehende,* i.e., interpretive) tradition (Max Weber) in sociology (Ankerl 1972a) — and Max Scheler's introspection — favored the attitudinal research on the basis of linguistic manifestations, research about an 'inner state' as the only legitimate subject of human science (Spiegel and Machotka 1974: 5), thus neglecting the properly (geo)metrical aspects of social phenomena, i.e., spacing and corporal manifestations. These two tendencies found each other's complaisance: the sociologist does not disturb the intuitive method of the architectural creation process — creation without 'architectural competence' — and provides only useful rhetoric for the interpretation of architecture on the symbolic level, facilitating the marketing of architecture after the designed *fait accompli.*

But what is the occasion that both sociologists and architects have missed by this kind of collaboration?

(1) The architectural art has been defined as space creation. The social theme of this art has been identified as the enveloping of a set of virtual spatial positions which implies a face-to-face communication network; therefore, spatial sociology, which is especially interested in spatial behavior — as network transformation and as communication process — is the field of sociology which is particularly related to sociology of architecture. Here architecture and sociology share a concern for geometrical measurements. However, architecture and spatial sociology show a homogeneity in terms of this measure on a single level — namely the geometrical one — which is privileged among all other measurable quantities. Especially as compared to linguistic units, geometrical ones relating physical variables to 'logico-arithmetic' abstraction are the archetype of all objectively measurable things. It is simultaneously real and abstract. Objectivity, and generalizability of this type of findings are predictable.

50 Prolegomenon to the science of architectural sociology

From the point of view of sociological tradition, an objection of principle could emerge insofar as we measure spatial behavior or other non-linguistic manifestations which we find in the whole ethological field, since this is said to constitute a 'zoological perspective in the social sciences' (Tiger and Fox 1966: 80). Will these data have any unequivocal semiological (viz., symptomatic) relevance in revealing men's attitudes? Is it not necessary to intervene with an interpretation, and, in this case, is not spatial — and other directly measured — behavior easily measured but in fact a more indirect revelator than linguistic manifestations?

The answer to these arguments is double: first, it is spatial behavior, which is for the architect of final relevancy. And as concerns sociology itself, it is possible to consider this science also in an analytical and objective — or behavioral (Burgess, Park) — perspective. Although some intuition concerning motives may inspire choice and articulation of a particular hypothesis, the scientifically valid answer to the problem of the subjects' preference coming from present and previous experience can only be given in terms of frequentation and other similar variables. Indeed the motives remain in a black box. Just as a producer determines preference based on buying statistics, the architect's expectation would also be formulated in behavioral terms — i.e., the relatively great frequentation by users of space. This is a restrictive perspective, but promises to open progress in sociology through analytical and objective ways and means.

(2) As far as sociology separated itself from speculative social philosophy and the introspective and empathic method applied to history (Bénézé 1967: 56) and employed in the *verstehende* sociology, it made an epistemological decision to submit its findings to inductive and empirical verification. The precise verification of a single fact renders it necessary to have measured under unimpeachible conditions. If we hope to go further than knowing single historical events (Ankerl 1972a: 15) and look for etiological relations between specific factors (Pagès 1974: 274), it is necessary for the events to repeat themselves in their specified aspects and for this to occur under the same good recording conditions. In order to generalize the results of an investigation, one must relate abstract and general concepts — including so-called universals — to systematically observed or rather registered empirical facts. It is especially true that fundamental research capable of leading to scientific theories is not possible without the use of controlled registration of systematically chosen sets of events identified in the framework of a model. We called this 'experimental design', and it is necessary for the perpetuation of the cumulation of knowledge in any science. Rejecting as impractical the uneconomic, unreasonable patience of a birdwatcher shows, the investigator must try under controlled observational conditions to manipulate

the variable under study. This calls for an experimental setup (Déribéré 1959: 13), which in its conventional form is a laboratory.

With a surprising easiness, some authors conclude *a priori* that this kind of 'ambush' for scientific research on humans — especially sociological research — is, if not immoral, methodologically irrelevant (cf. von Cranach 1977). Thus, sociology does not lend itself to experimentation, chiefly for two reasons: first, man anticipates the intervention of the investigator, which fundamentally alters his reaction — this is called obtrusive and reactive data (cf. Webb), operator- or, briefly, O-data (Barker 1965: 3) in oppostioh to T-data, which involves the investigator only, as transducer. Second, human events are 'historical' — personal and social history are irreversible — (Bénézé quotes Bergson: 1967: 72) — and the minimal requirement for their study, namely longitudinal experimentation, is unrealizable within a laboratory.

Without discussing in detail objections of principles here, we will only state that at least some of these objections can be countered by the very nature of the created space as independent variable. We consider this a second privilege of sociology of architecture in sociological theory construction.

Indeed, if an experiment is to be carried out in pure sociology — and not in ecosociology — in order to provoke a behavioral reaction the investigator must make the 'first step', introducing an accomplice as the human stimulus on which the response depends. The investigator must lure the subject into a bugged space (laboratory) in order to precisely register the reaction. However, the investigator himself as well as the independent variable (the human stimulus) will be unnatural, and so the reaction not 'accountable'. In addition, the anticipating of the bugged space will also alter the reaction. But if the independent variable is a created space, the experimenter's situation is far more favorable.

At any given time man is *in* a space, so it is not necessary to lure him into one. It is enough to construct the planned series of spaces for the experimentation, so that among them it will be possible to choose those for the experimental group and those for the control group. Experimentees *expect* that architectural spaces are constructed. If the space as a first eco-stimulus could be accepted by the group of experimentees without suspicion, at the same time it would be possible to multiply rooms with shape and volume continuously variable, along with the modifications wished for in the experiment. This flexibility and authentic nature of the independent variable would by its very nature — being a space — make the bugging needed for the controlled recording simple. If laboratories are unusual or abnormal artifacts, architecture as such is a normal — i.e., sociologically accepted as such — artifact.

In addition to this specific methodological — resp. 'heuristic' — advantage inherent in sociology of architecture for developing experimental sociology

52 *Prolegomenon to the science of architectural sociology*

comes the possibility that if the study is carried out in a closed institution — e.g., a penitentiary, an arctic city — longitudinal experimentation is possible.

This book about experimental sociology of architecture will reveal in its pages how this field contributes particularly well to an objective (behavioral) and experimental sociology as a parergon.

3

Systematization

THE PROLEGOMENOUS ORDER: WHAT WILL AND WILL NOT BE DISCUSSED, WHY, AND IN WHAT ORDER?

If we now contrast the subject discussed in the first historical chapter — for example, Arens's article on the sociology of architecture — and Panofsky's *Gothic Architecture and Scholasticism* (recommended by the Marxist sociologist Bordieu [1970]) with our conceptualization of the sociology of architecture on the previous pages, it seems necessary to discuss what motivates us to choose this particular approach in our construction of an experimental sociology of architecture.

We first need to delimit the subject as a whole which we can consider within the scope of the sociology of architecture. Following that, we must determinate the various priorities. Finally, we must decide how to present the different questions which are pertinent to this subject.

There is a lack of generally accepted paradigms in 'architecturology' and in sociology itself. Indeed, concerning architecture, some authors follow more the tradition of the application of the term 'architecture' itself, instead of looking for some clear-cut denotation. As we have seen, in order to consider a systematically specified object, we take the latter way. Concerning the sociological treatment guiding research toward cumulative and empirically verifiable findings, a very serious *a priori* epistemological 'censorship' has been imposed. The same considerations prevent us from precipitating an order in the design of scientific investigations which follows logical requirements and gives priority to prolegomenous considerations — deduced by the need of founding a science rather than by the imperative of practical urgency. As a matter of fact, this urgency has the tendency to imply, in our opinion, some sweeping statement which has only illusory news value and rarely any solid scientific significance (Ankerl 1972b). Let us illustrate our thinking on this point.

Some authors demand that sociology of architecture be devoted to the study of the meanings of architectural styles in the framework of the sociology of arts — a kind of auxiliary science of architectural criticism and of its history. As phonetics is necessary for morphemics and scientific linguistics before the scientific study of literature is possible, the application of some kind of connotative semantics or semiology of meaning (Greimas) to architecture cannot give even the modest results that this approach gives in the field of the study of literature before the descriptive morphology of architecture is well enough developed. It is a *sine qua non* substrate, a fact that Eco clearly sees (1971: 683).

Even within morphosociology, some temptation to 'leapfrog' approaches is current. Blinded by the rapid and omnipresent urbanization process, many authors think that the postulate according to which the sum total of architectural spaces constituting an urban architectural space system is less than the city as such authorizes them to study urban architectural space systems before or without the study of the sociology of individual architectural spaces. It is a reduction of sociology of architecture to the sociology of (urban) settlement and housing without passing through the microsociology of architectural spaces (Atteslander and Hamm 1974: 23).

1. PRIORITIES AND OTHER POTENTIAL SUBJECTS IN THE AREA OF SOCIOLOGY OF ARCHITECTURE

We reiterate that sociology of architecture is primarily devoted to the study of the originally one-way communication using a created space system as a proper medium and also to the study of such a system's denoted sociological meaning, the structuring of face-to-face communication processes. This structuring occurs through the shaping of the network of these communications by means of both physics and the impression of the created spaces. Indeed, the subject under study, architectural communication, is a one-way communication because it takes place as a professional communication by means of space creation, and the client does not reciprocate in turn by means of his own space creations.

The delivered architecture as a 'morphemic' system — its morphology — is first of all 'at stake'. If consideration of the specific subject of our study were not sufficient reason for giving priority to morphology, the need for a well-founded theory in sociology points in the same direction. Epistemological principles dictate that achieving more solid, durable findings — even if 'only' descriptive ones — must be the first consideration. But, on the other hand, in order to look for sociological variables which can affect the structural regularities of these morphological constants or how sociological formations and processes are affected by architecture, we must indicate here the entire outline for a larger sociological framework, even if the 'epistemological censorship' does not allow us to reach out to this subject yet in this book.

Systematization 55

Within a proper sociological perspective — viz., without enlarging its perspective to a science of culture — this more comprehensive question would be asked as follows: specifically, how do other communication structures precede space creation, and in general what place does architecture find in the entire social communication process, with its multiple feedback mechanisms. In this latter context we must consider those aspects of architectural communication which could be replaced by alternative media.

Indeed, there is the 'reception process' of the successive, alternative, and simultaneous (e.g., client and officer) user's groups which make architecture efficient by means of the face-to-face communications carried out by the receivers in these space systems. We can relate the reception expressed in behavioral reactions — by behavior we can only know frequentation and not preferences, if we understand by the latter a simple verbal reaction — to sociological characteristics of the particular user's group which, through personal histories brings determinant expectations and so on.

But architecture is a created 'artisan's' work — both artistic and technological — and so the process of creation itself involves broader social communication processes prior to architecture itself (fixed by design and construction). Consistent with the designer's anticipation, the user's expectation itself is prefigured by the created architecture (a designer's decision-making process goes from information to creation).

In order to get a better picture of the whole potential panorama of the sociology of architecture, consider the Figure 1.3.

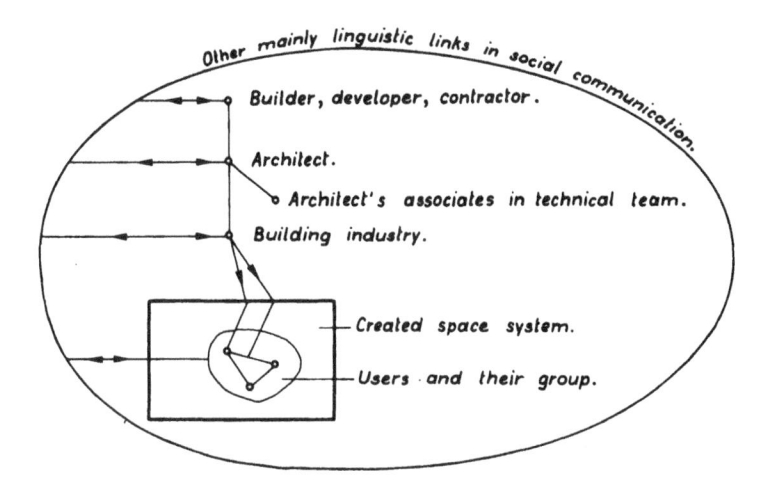

Figure 1.3. *Architectural communication in the ensemble of the social communication process and the possible subjects of the sociology of architecture. (Schematic representation.)*

Looking at the process of creating space systems as a sociological decision-making process, the builder-developer, who has financial responsibility and allocates resources, the architect, who conceives the space systems with his team, associates and cooperating professionals — various engineers — and finally the building industry all enter into a relation which gives rise to the delivery. The communication and control links among developers, architect, engineers, and contractors could vary, even within one institutional network. The organizational links vary according to the type of decision that must be made — large urban development or a less extensive space system called an individual building — and according to the construction speed determined by technology — one or two years or one, two, or even more generations (e.g., a cathedral). In addition, changes which are not specifically related to the construction process, reforms and reorganizations in the sociological framework of the whole society, can have repercussions on this creation process. If the use (lease and frequentation) of the created space systems is subject to competition among alternatives offered on the market, the efficiency could be studied in the long term through the demands of a whole range of user generations, and so general schemes of organizational links — e.g., team of architects, and engineers under the aegis of the building industry or the developer as responsible for the formulation of the recipient's expectations — as well as actual communication structures could be made employing critical analysis for its organization (cf. Turner and Richter 1973).

We have now seen an area whose efficiency can be increased by means of the application of sociological considerations. If we in turn look at the place of architecture among all means of social communication in the light of its specificity, the investigation will contribute to general sociological theory. But in this case the considerations must be made in long-range perspective — of history and of civilization — and definitely must take place on the macrosociological level. Yet we can see immediately how the characterization of architecture as a medium is also a precondition for this future study. Indeed it is vocabulary and syntax which reveal change in use, and further reveal how styles and new architectural schools — like the Bauhaus — integrate other arts into their opus. If forms (sensorily perceptible geometric shapes and volumes), and systems of such forms, are the specific structural characteristics of architecture which can be objectively apprehended (Dorfles in Jencks and Baird 1969 on structuralism; Tafuri 1971) the relative permanence of architecture, viz., its relation to the features of atmospheric space, its more or less easy transformation, and its possible completion by furniture and equipment — is a particularly relevant aspect to consider in this respect. In this way, we learn how communication patterns are reinforced by the 'architectural heritage': e.g. large mass meetings rather than the use of telemedia.

As already mentioned, at present, sociology of architecture as a speciality is nonexistent. Works in this field of research are difficult to find, being dispersed within various chapters of the sociological literature. We have found materials about experimental sociology of architecture in the sociology of communication through art, in that of habitat and of housing, and in urban sociology, as well as in studies on related fields, such as social psychology of architecture.

In the light of this state, in our contribution to the construction of the sociology of architecture, we attempt to conform to the following principles:

– All research on sociology of architecture must stay within its scope: studying created and perceptible spaces as a primary framework for all spatial activities. Restricting or enlarging the field of investigation would bring about a loss of speciality. On the practical level, the enlargement of architecture to the study of the symbolic meaning of all monuments or the arbitrary identification of architecture with buildings or with the whole environment as such (illumination, all mobile objects, signals, etc.) allowed one to make 'architectural determinism' the scapegoat for failures in every other quarter of the social fabric (Ankerl 1974).

– The investigation must also be limited strictly to the sociological aspect and must not, for example, try to construct a kind of structural phenomenology of architecture as a cultural institution (cultural history). We must first look at created space systems as a proper communication medium, and after describing it structurally, look at those of its characteristics which both affect and are affected by other social communication structures.

– Finally, in order to systematically construct a theory in this field, in the design of the investigation of this field, for epistemological reasons priority must be given as a prolegomenon to all regularities found under experimental conditions and stated in objective terms, concerning the repertory of architecture itself. Without that stipulation the scientific study of any medium is impossible, and in particular, it would be impossible to relate the effect of specific spaces on face-to-face communication structures in it, an effect exerting its influence through both the virtual (face-to-face) communication network and the set of network transformations.

On the following pages we will make an outline of all the 'objectal contexts', namely the whole range of objects and barriers which could be 'interposed' between human groups and the enveloping architectural spaces. After that we will briefly discuss the order of presentation of the subject treated in this book.

2. THE WHOLE AMBIENT CONTEXT AND THE RESEARCH IN EXPERIMENTAL SOCIOLOGY OF ARCHITECTURE

We identified as the proper and central subject of sociology of architecture, on the one hand, the 'calibration' of perceptible spaces as discriminable morphemic units of architectural creation and, on the other hand, the study of the sociological effect produced on the regularities of the face-to-face communication network and communication flow among the partners within the room. This constitutes a discrete field of investigation for the sociology of architecture. By studying the effects of spaces — the prime aspect of the physical environment — as architectural communication on the communication process of those 'enveloped' within a space, we learn how one sociological event affects another. We also stated that the sociology of architecture is a privileged field in terms of applying experimental methods and making unobtrusive objective measurements. The advantages of experimental sociology of architecture can be realized only if the experimental contexts are perceived by the experimentees as normal space conditions. However, if we consider the fact that human communication often occurs in connection with work on material objects or machines, for example, we see that it is necessary to be able to take into account the other objects present in the space in order to see how they could affect the etiological relation between architectural space and the communication of a group.

First of all, the architectural space as such needs to be further specified: as a starting point we can state that a roomraum is at every moment defined by the whole (enveloping) closed surface, which has propagation characteristics that differ from the enveloped volume. This means that the surfaces of the furniture also constitute elements of the space envelope. Indeed, we will see that in order to calculate reverbation time — a fundamental characteristic of acoustical space — we must take into account the whole surface including furniture, and even the clothes of those present.

Movables

In order to clarify architectural space as an independent variable, we must take into account *all* features of the envelope — including protrusions and outgrowths like barriers — if they have fixed and so permanent status, in the sense that the user cannot quickly remove them for the sake of reshaping the potential face-to-face communication network without depending on the professional service of an architect (this issue relates to the protection of historical monuments). The question of doors and windows is of another nature. In accordance with these distinctions, furniture — but not fittings — as movable elements influences the impression of an architectural space but is not part of it, not even as submorphemic elements.

Indeed, all movable elements, for example, folding or draft screens, without permanent localization, are interfering variables. The participants can use them for transforming their positions in the network without changing either the absolute distance from the others on their own location in the architectural space. Consider the example in Figure 1.2.2. The face-to-face communication networks linking the people *a, b,* and *c* are different in the cases *A, B,* and *C,* although the architectural space is the same, as are the beeline distances among the three people in all three cases. Comparing the cases *A* and *C,* the reflecting effects of the space are not equal. The cases *A* and *B* differ also, because the relatively distant *b* and *c* have better mutual sensory accessibility between themselves. This is namely because in the case *B,* there is a separator, and for the face-to-face communication network the sensory accessibility is determinant (the separator can be a removable folding screen, a table, a simple umbrella, or a more sophisticated object — if we consider the multisensory nature of communication).

If this point is accepted, we have introduced into the model two kinds of elements: the architectural space as a predetermined fundamental, immovable by anyone other than the architect; and the users present, who constitute a present 'We' (Ankerl 1972a: 98) understood here in the sense that they are provided with a face-to-face communication capability and can choose any position in the face-to-face communication network. The set of network transformations as a virtuality is fixed by the architectural space.

To these two elements now under study we add movable physical objects, which can have two types of effects on the etiological relation between architectural space and the face-to-face communication structure:

(1) The face-to-face communication network that was essentially determined by the space as a virtual network set and the transformation of positions actually undertaken by the group participants through their displacement, could now be modified by the more or less instantaneous interposing of physical objects as hiding or veiling elements.

(2) A second effect of these objects — which are here considered only with reference to their purely physical properties — is that they could directly affect the face-to-face communication structure without affecting the network. Indeed, if in the absence of all 'third' elements the face-to-face communication flow is chiefly a result of the communication possibilities inherent in the face-to-face communication network and of the mutual communicative interest of the present participants, the physical objects present could attract interest on their own and so divert the participants from communication.

Representationals

The drunken tatooed sailor who enters a bar in London's East End, even if he comes without any belongings, brings with him a message of his faraway lover.

In an art gallery or a sanctuary, people do not move solely in order to come near to the guardian or to someone else but also in order to 'hear' the painter's or God's message represented on the icon.

These strange examples have been chosen in order to focus on their common point: the 'excess of presence' (Baudrillard 1968) which an object with representational value bears. In the case of tatooing, the subject does not even need a physical object as support.

Equipment, machines, and other man-made objects bear in a space this quality of an excess of 'physical' presence. We now concern ourselves with two types of representational objects particularly relevant to the model of our research design.

— Telecommunication: epistolary communication was once telecommunication, but the competition between telecommunication and communication realized in the framework of a face-to-face communication network becomes compelling only given the modern development of instantaneous media, such as television, telex, and telephone. They have a pressing immediacy, an intruding manner, soliciting immediate attention.

— Traffic signals: this is a subject of considerable confusion. In a very superficial manner, some authors hold that markers create the 'explicit truly sociological spaces' (Atteslander and Hamm 1974: 29-30). These symbolic markers are not constituents of architectural space in any way, even as submorphemic elements. (In reality, they cannot physically affect the face-to-face communication network; they are only *thesei* and not *physei*. Truly architectural spaces have both physical and perceptual effects.)

How can these representational objects present in an architectural space interfere with the etiological relation under study?

The physical elements as such have the possibility to act as modifiers of the face-to-face communication network itself. On the other hand, the representational elements do not modify the face-to-face communication network among the participants actually present. Even the symbolic space delimitation does not affect the face-to-face communication channels among them. And telecommunication, permitting and inviting the 'outsiders' to communicate to those present, completes the face-to-face communication by simulating presence, and so completing the *whole* communication network but not the face-to-face communication network as such. The representational elements exert their 'parasitizing' effect on the studied relations by means which directly affect the face-to-face communication structure insofar as they make apparently 'attractive' offers for alternative communication by enlarging the circle of potential partners in a figurative way (bringing in simulated or partial partners). From this follows that the 'parasitizing' effect of representational objects does not run in line with that of architectural spaces.

3. PRESENTATION OF THE ORDER OF THIS WORK

On the preceeding pages we have discussed at length the scope of this work. Until this time, research in the field related to the sociology of architecture has advanced in a very disparate order, producing noncumulative and, in most intances, epistemologically incommensurable findings. On the other hand, the history of science and humanities teaches us that only exact and empirical sciences give true paradigms for cumulative investigation. Therefore, we must treat our present subject on a prolegomenous level, i.e., we must lay the foundation for theory construction and systematic investigation, hereby delineating the field of the experimental sociology of architecture.

We recall that this field is the study of both architectural communication and its effects on the face-to-face communication process occurring within the spaces created by architects. Writing, of course, necessarily compels us to present our thought in a linear order. This linear order of presentation will be fundamentally composed of three parts:

(1) In order for the presentation to go from more primitive sociological problems to more complex ones, following this introductory part, Part II will be devoted to the dependent or Y variable of the sociology of architecture, the face-to-face communication network — referred to by some as a 'channel' — and structure — also called 'flow'. Of course, considering the subject from the viewpoint of (architectural) creation — as we have seen — the matter in question is the sociological theme of architectural design.

After a general discussion clarifying our approach and the basic concepts which will be used, we will study how the transmissible message depends on the position of the group participants in the face-to-face communication network. First we investigate each sensory channel in the order of its hypothesized predominance in the face-to-face communication structure — i.e., the visible, audible, osmatic, palpable, and sapid communications. After this analysis of each channel, we look at the whole problem of polysensory composition and its reception as a function of the face-to-face communication network, as well as the transformation of this latter.

(2) In Part III we discuss the independent or X variable. We try to find out what knowledge of the medium, which is architecture, must be covered by professionals who claim 'architectural competence'. After a general discussion we begin with the morphology of this medium: in a manner appropriate to this specific field, we first consider the geometrical level, since it is a common characteristic for all sensory spaces. Then we discuss which sensory modalities could produce autonomous space impressions on their own. We treat the acoustical space, the optical space, and the haptic space, and the complementary problems resulting from subsidiary

contributions of the osmatic senses to space impressions, namely the hermetic space. Once the autonomy of these space impressions is established, we search for methods which allow us to constitute a repertory of architectural entities, which we refer to as 'morphemes' or 'free forms', a repertory where each item will be a discrete entity, distinguishable one from another by a normal observer. Corresponding to the field of architecture, volumetric magnitude and the shapes of enveloping surfaces will be the subject of discrimination, specifically for each sense modality of standardized observers.

The standardization of observation conditions themselves enlarges the field of investigation by introducing the 'vector' of dynamic exploration. Already within the framework of morphologic considerations we must deal with the possible variations in the multisensory composition of the architectural spaces with all their complexity.

In order to complete the entire grammar of architectural competence, we discuss the syntax of the construction of space systems and subsystems.

(3) The fourth and last part of this book treats the question of testing, by experiment, hypotheses concerning the various effects of architectural spaces on the face-to-face communication structure within them. Epistemological and methodological questions will be discussed, as well as that of measurement.

On the technical level, broadly speaking, temporal sequences of face-to-face communication structure components and their synchronization must be made, together with those of the transformation occurring in the face-to-face communication network. Problems of unobtrusively making videotapes, audiotapes, and mechanical facsimiles occur at the point of emission as well as of reception of the communication flow. In order not to fail by arbitrarily choosing relations for study, the extremely large number of possible connections necessitates considering computer applications for automatic recording of data as well as for the automatic analysis of the regularities of these data.

The status of the measured magnitudes will be determined in the general model by the epistemological rule which accords fundamental priority to variables denoted by behavior patterns, without our interpreting these data as symptoms of attitudes (in fact, the concept of attitude refer to 'private events' and can hardly be detached from subjective connotations).

In order to choose the heuristically most rewarding methods and research strategy (e.g., choice of experimental situations), we will raise the question of what particular opportunity the field of experimentally induced sociology of architecture offers for the development of an objective experimental sociology, and ask in which directions future investigation could be considered as particularly productive.

Finally, systematic theory construction cannot be without explicit epistemological criteria which establish the relative scientific 'hardness' of various findings in order to qualify past and often contradictory statements, thus preventing the coherence of the theory as a whole from being jeopardized.

II

Social Spacing as a Sociological Theme of Architecture

4

The Face-to-Face Communication Network and Structure in General

In the first part we discussed the historical foundations of the sociology of architecture, its conceptualization problems, and the system of questions treated in this work. Let us now develop more fully the analytical methods necessary for the construction of a sociology of architecture as a scientific discipline.

As we have seen, the central problem of the sociology of architecture is the understanding of architecture as a medium of communication. (This communication process begins with the designer's decision and continues through to the response of the recipient.) While the properties of architecture as a specific means of transmission will be treated in the next part, here we intend to focus our attention on the sociological theme itself: what messages can the architect actually transmit by the specific means that are at his disposal (i.e., by the creation of space systems)?

Generally speaking, we can say that sociology deals with the various multitudes of human animals by identifying networks and structures of communication which characterize various social formations on an empirical level. Thus, while the architect obviously cannot hope to influence all aspects of the human communication process, he can influence some aspects of the social communication process which may, in fact, be influenced by 'scenic' or more generally geographic situations. In reality, it is of prime sociological concern to the architect to take into consideration the fact that architectural spaces can serve as substitutes for various 'geographical situations' and can therefore influence the communication process. Some authors would argue that if one considers the social communication process in all its diverse aspects and at all possible levels, any influence exerted by architectural spaces on the message transmission process would have to be of relative insignificance. Regardless, however, of any hypothetical arguments as to the extent of the architect's possibilities for social influence, we must, in the sociology of architecture, consider only sociological phenomena that the architect can affect by the specific means within the range of his own professional competence. In fact, the sets of face-to-face communication networks can be seen to be the major sociological denotation of the architecture. (Somewhat freely speaking, we can say that architectural communication — namely the created space system — is related to the set of the face-to-face communication network allowed in these spaces in a manner analogous to metalanguage's relationship to its object language.)

As noted in the previous chapter, prior to the advent of artificial or architectural spaces, persons seeking privacy for intimate encounters were obliged to await nightfall, to find natural shelters, or to retreat to a satisfactory distance from other humans. Architecture spares us these inconveniences.

TELECOMMUNICATION AND FACE-TO-FACE COMMUNICATION

If we disregard all alleged telepathic phenomena and devices such as the smoke or drum signals used for ages by the Africans, we can say that, until recently, communication, this prototype of all social activities, necessarily involved, at least in its instantaneous form, physical presence on the part of the participants. The relatively recent development of the field of telecommunications — and also of the new communication conservation techniques (such as videocassettes) — opened new horizons for certain types of communication, more specifically for self-representation, even in deferred form. Here we must think of 'representation' as opposed to 'presentation', or of proximity without proxy (Drever 1968: 221; Spiegel and Machotka 1974: 24). The rapid development of this technical panoply, often paralleled by the expansion of transportation facilities ('le reseau des voies de communication': Hagget and Chorley 1970: 90) has captivated our attention almost to the exclusion of face-to-face communication. It is time, therefore, to reassess in the light of new development the value of human presence for the communication process. The sociology of architecture gives an excellent opportunity.

As a matter of fact, while architecture can have little impact on the telecommunication process, if new possibilities for telecommunications affect architecture, this may be in a negative manner: where architecture is concerned, the physical presence of human beings is the pertinent aspect of social life. For this reason, it is a mistake to maintain, as would some authors, that developments in transportation and telecommunications have *similar* effects on architecture, especially in the case of urban architecture. Indeed, whereas transportation can facilitate rapid and dense physical togetherness, telecommunications can render such togetherness virtually superfluous (Ankerl 1974). Architecture provides a setting for face-to-face — or direct — communication, and thus assumes some physical accessibility. In contrast, one of the most essential aspects of telecommunications, and one of its inherent strengths, is that it allows us to simulate a ubiquitous presence: John can whisper in Mary's ear absolutely independently of his distance from her. To date, however, these telecommunication facilities have had one very serious drawback: they have decimated our senses as communication channels.

The continued appreciation for polysensory communication is evidenced, nonetheless, by such intense diplomatic shuttles as those of Henry Kissinger in the mid-1970's, or by such furnishings for executive conferences as the 700-gallon water bed installed at the direction of Tom H. Wattson in the McDonald's Headquarters in Oak Brook, Illinois (interior with bed designed by Associate Space Design of Atlanta; building by Salvatore Balfano of Chicago). Indeed, the tactile component of polysensory communication on a water bed is virtually instantaneous; it could also be considered as a form of telecommunication, although the transmission is not quite independent of the partners' physical distance from one another.

By way of contrast, in speculating as to the fate of face-to-face communication in the future, biologist Jean Rostand goes even one step further than science-fiction writer Isaac Asimov, in whose *Naked Sun* (1957) mutual physical presence remains necessary for human procreation, to foresee a different manner of insemination involving no mutual physical presence at all. Here we can only say that if face-to-face communication were of no importance to sociology, then neither would architecture be.

Where face-to-face communication is concerned, the partners' physical distance and, more precisely, their mutual positions, play essential roles in determining the polysensory composition of the communication. Here emerge the outlines of a spatial sociology in which objective (external) geometrical variables are pertinent factors and therefore relevant to the sociology of architecture.

This is where the architect can come in. It is enough to think that the measurable volume and shape of multisensory space define the presence situation. Present-day technology and materials make it possible for a simple membrane to completely isolate one person from another, even though physically they are in immediate proximity. As creator of spaces, the architect can indeed have a significant effect on the face-to-face communication process by determining the set of transmission possibilities. Moreover, since both space impression and face-to-face communication are multisensory phenomena (architecture is not, after all, exclusively a visual art), various autonomous spaces can form a complex and complicated composition realizing a differentiated, sophisticated filtration of the 'multisensorily coded' message that is transmitted.

In the light of these considerations, we can see how and why face-to-face communication provides the 'sociological denotation' for architectural communication, and why spatial sociology is not only a relevant chapter of sociology for the architect but actually a prerequisite for the entire field of the sociology of architecture, if architecture is to be considered a medium of communication.

FACE-TO-FACE COMMUNICATION IN THE PHENOMENOLOGIST'S PERSPECTIVE: A HISTORICAL EXCURSUS

Within the framework of the sociology of architecture we must give special consideration to the study of face-to-face communication, that social-relational field where communication may take place without any technical mediation (Laver and Hutcheson; Key). Relevant findings in the field of tele-relations (Ankerl 1972a: 291) will serve only as a background to this study.

In the phenomenologist's tradition, sociology has tended to approach such questions with a certain literary bias, using words, instead of things, as a starting point of fact finding (Furth 1966). As Stuart Chase emphasized in his *Tyranny of Words,* any concept that was neither linguistic nor verbal, but rather geometrical or spatial, was customarily treated in such a way as to evoke only its figurative sense (e.g., concepts such as 'distance' and 'superior'). Authors espousing this school of thought focused their attention almost exclusively on those social phenomena which appeared to them as being uniquely human. If, then, they favored conversational and visual communication as the preferred channel for conveying messages with discursive and cognitive content, it was because this form of communication could be associated with man's so-called 'phylogenetic superiority', with all its metaphysical implications.

The beginnings of spatial sociology preceed those of experimental sociology. Georg Simmel (1950) states that 'space in general is an activity of the soul', but he understood, too, that the sociology of space and the sociology of the sense organs belong to the same chapter of sociology, and that mutual sensory accessibility — the nexus, the neighbor — has sociological relevance on its own. Unfortunately, Simmel's conceptualization of 'spatial forms' as they relate to social behavior did not extend beyond the intuitive level, and thus cannot serve as a basis for analytical studies. Sharing the bias of the mainstream of sociological literature. Simmel's work reveals a strong preference for 'worded facts' over spatial and other physical realities. At the same time, his ambitions were not only scientific but literary (Ankerl 1972a: 107). He is thus hindered from establishing a kernel of objective knowledge in this field.

In Simmel's work it is not uncommon to find 'telescoping' of ideas, confusion of different levels of considerations. He tries, for example, to relate concepts such as 'state' and 'incest' to spatial situations, but he fails to make adequate distinction between the sociological effect of a geographic situation — a problem belonging to geographic sociology, a part of ecosociology — and the sociological significance of a particular place (*lieu*), such as a *rendez-vous*, which may have sociological significance because of memories associated with it (Simmel 1906: 635). He also fails to differentiate between the sociological effect of a geographic situation and that of the partners' mutual positions in a communicative situation, the first problem again belonging to ecosociology and the second to pure spatial sociology.

Durkheim, another founder of our discipline, discusses the *substrat social* in social morphology. He does not, however, use social morphology as a solid, objective foundation for sociology. Instead of relating physical factors such as the dirt pathways formed between dwellings through constant use — observable, lasting evidence of regular human movements — to other hard facts of social life, he relegates them, along with geographic and other exogenous factors, to the category of 'material conditions', aspects which he prefers to consider as being merely peripheral to sociology, which, for him, is a moral science (e.g., he opposes 'physical density' to 'moral density', where today we would say 'density versus crowding' [Ankerl 1974: 574, 586]).

Finally, a superficial reader could expect to find Kurt Lewin's topology a particularly relevant contribution to the field of spatial sociology. Indeed, his 'psychological topology' could offer some logical clarification, and it could have mnemotechnical and pedagogical value. It cannot, however, be related to spatial metrics in any way. As Lewin himself acknowledged, his topology is not homogeneous with 'empirical space'. Moreover, his work as a whole is not experimental. His 'action research' might be said to approach what today we would call 'clinical social psychology'.

NETWORK AND STRUCTURE IN COMMUNICATIONS THEORY AND FACE-TO-FACE COMMUNICATION

The communication theory originated in the laboratories of Bell Telephone. It was conceived by mathematicians and electrical engineers Shannon and Weaver (1949), whose goal was to compare the relative merits of various information teletransmission systems. We must keep this background in mind when using their conceptualizations, because otherwise the entire accompanying information theory may well suffer from 'telephonomorphism' or 'mechanomorphism'.

We accept the assumption that 'all social interaction is necessarily communicative' and that 'any social process presumes a communication process' (McQuail 1975: 1, 7-8). In attempting, however, to describe the process of face-to-face communication as a social fact relevant to the sociology of architecture, one has a delicate task in applying concepts which originated in

72 *Social spacing as a sociological theme of architecture*

the context of telephone communications engineering, a field so remote from the study of face-to-face communication and from that of interactive human behavior, to the characterizations of social formation patterns. We acknowledge, too, that there are many other communication models which have been constructed by different schools and on different conceptual levels. We believe, nonetheless, that the attempts made by Bavelas and Flament at characterizing the functioning of various small group structures in empirical and objective terms via the concepts of communication network and communication structure were sufficiently conclusive as to apply to the field of face-to-face communication.

Briefly, the communication network, which we also call the 'chain' or 'set of channels' (McQuail 1975: 23, 27), is a physical system of channels permitting and also limiting communication possibilities among a number (n) of subjects. When a person chooses to use this physical asset by transmitting through it an actual message, he generates a communication structure or flow.

If a sociologist were to trace a selective and discontinuous flow of communication (as it takes place in partial actualization of the communication possibilities inherent in the network), the resulting record could be regarded as a significant datum for reconstructing a pattern of social formations. Representing this idea in terms of graph theory: whether the graph of the original communication network is directed, partially directed, or not directed at all, any graph representing an instant of communication structure could never be longer than the original graph of the network in which it is inscribed (it could be the same length as the network graph, or it could be its 'partial graph' or its 'subgraph', but it could never be longer). Because the choice of channel is very characteristic, significant data may also be found in the 'anti-graph', defined by the edges of the network graphs which remain unused after the actual flow of communication has been recorded. The methodological aspects of graph theory as a tool for characterization will be discussed in more detail in the next part.

Bavelas and Flament applied these concepts in describing small-group communication patterns in a system which did not allow for face-to-face contact but in which communication was channeled through a 'domestic telephone system', each participant being in a separate booth. How then might one apply these same concepts to a situation involving actual face-to-face communication?

FACE-TO-FACE COMMUNICATION NETWORK

Our communication network in the presence situation (face-to-face communication network) is characteristically independent of any technical means;

it is an exclusive function of the mutual positions of the interlocutors. Now if we consider as constants any physical factors perhaps necessary for the transmission (i.e., any space-filling medium, such as air, or other possible sources of stimulation, such as lighting conditions), the only way the network could be altered would be if the participants themselves were to vary their positions. Again we must emphasize that any such change in position does not constitute an act of communication (does not 'inscribe' in the network a structure) but is instead a transformation of the network itself.

The communicative value of each relative position in the network consists in the possibilities it holds for multisensory transmission. Indeed, as we are 'prisoners of our senses' (Kaufmann 1967: 127), each relative position we may assume offers a gradual utilization of the different sensory communication channels that define the face-to-face communication network. By using these channels over and over again, the participants inscribe in the network a face-to-face communication structure. When we describe the participants' mutual positions in terms of the communication-relevant aspects (e.g., 'out of earshot', or 'out of sight'), we specify the spatial-relational order between or among them — relational human density — as a face-to-face communication network. We can deal with this continuous network in analytical terms by relating a given human expression (e.g., a smile, a wink) with a set of relative positions (a discrete number of zones) where a set of receptors can receive the expression as message. A particularly significant characteristic of these zones is the multisensory composition of the receivable message. Because of the fact that with different sensory organs not only the absolute and relative 'thresholds' for acuities change but also the mechanisms of the receptors, we must discuss multisensory composition in more specific terms later in the text — in the forthcoming chapters devoted to the various individual sensory channels, and in the last chapter of this part, which treats the topic from a more synthetical perspective.

In describing the network we must be mindful of the fact that mutuality — binary relation — does not necessarily imply reciprocity. Within this two-way graph there are many symmetrical and asymmetrical possibilities, including simultaneous message exchange, alternating exchange, and absence of exchange altogether.

Over the past few decades numerous authors have distinguished themselves through their studies of face-to-face communication. Their works have yielded a considerable amount of detailed information, but also a good deal of confusion. The shortcomings of their efforts lay primarily in the fact that before undertaking their research, most authors had not settled on a sound conceptual framework which would serve for all aspects of the topic at hand.

Within their conceptualizations, two problems are particularly prevalent: (1) a tendency to confuse communication network with structure; and (2) failure to distinguish between the artist's intended expression and the receptor's actual impression when categorizing various communication modes. (For example, since modes of expression such as dance and architecture are visible, there has been a tendency to forget that they are not necessarily purely visual in their effects.)

The first problem we hope to clarify via a discussion of 'proxemics' versus 'kinesics'. The second will be relieved somewhat if we can detach our study of polysensory communication from that arbitrary linguistic focus which has grouped all nonverbal communication lines, shared by humans and other animals alike, under the category of paralinguistics. Our conceptual framework must, after all, allow us to consider the face-to-face communication process even in those situations where communication is neither oral nor visual in its manifestation.

Proxemics

Proxemics, which comprises relative mutual positions among present parties (adding to distance the concepts of direction and orientation), defines the face-to-face communication network as a relational field with identifiable two-way links. Here two points of confusion must be avoided: we must make a distinction between posture and position; the first is an expression and, as such, is part of the communication structure; the second term will be reserved for the network description. Of course, in some situations, network and structure could represent two relevant aspects of one reality. We have already made a distinction between (a) the type of movement which changes the receptor's position and thus transforms the network, and (b) other body movements which do not change the actor's position as message receiver. If one could record all relative positions of the parties present, one would be describing the face-to-face communication network. It is a three-dimensional 'web' which may contain many parallel, intersecting, or nonintersecting 'skew' lines. The degree of immediacy (Wiener and Mehrabian 1968) or the relative proximity (Heider 1958) could be established between or among individuals or groups of individuals.

While the face-to-face communication network itself may be defined by the components of all of the two-way relationships it contains, the communicative value of these relationships (viz. the communication possibilities inherent in the network) may be assessed in analytical terms only by relating these positions to the zones determined by the grossly uniform sensory reception of all individual senses within each zone. Each zone is characterized by a multisensory profile determining 'social perceptibility'. (See Figure 2.10.)

Depending upon the specific thresholds of each sensory organ, every time a change in position results in a significant difference in the perceptible signal magnitude for a given human expression, the new position will constitute a new zone which, in turn, will have its own profile. We can see that the number of senses considered increases the number of possible zones. A final count of these zones can be made only when all sensory channels have been taken individually into consideration. Here we should also mention that relative immediacy of position in the face-to-face communication network is not a unique function of relative distance, nor does minimal distance between communication partners assure maximum acuity for all senses. And even where for a particular sense there is a broad tendency in the passage from zone to zone toward an increase (or decrease) in the magnitude of the signal perceived, this tendency does not necessarily follow through in a monotonic way.

FACE-TO-FACE COMMUNICATION STRUCTURE AND TRANSFORMATION OF THE NETWORK: KINESICS AND PARALINGUISTICS

The face-to-face communication network is defined chiefly by the message-reception capability inherent in a normal receiver's position relative to that of the transmitter. For the face-to-face communication structure what is relevant is not the potential for communication but rather the actual message as it is effectively expressed and received. An Indian warrior can paint his 'attitude' on his face, and other makeup can intervene in the communication process, but the actual face-to-face communication consists not in the intentions of the transmitter but rather in the reception of the expressive performance or 'performing art' (Goffman 1963: 'presentation of self') as the communication takes place in time.

Because self-presentation in the face-to-face communication process involves a sequence of various movements, some authors have tended to reduce the entire question of face-to-face communication structure to a matter of kinesics. Others, as mentioned earlier, have tended to view the phenomenon almost exclusively from the perspective of linguistic communication, and have considered the whole face-to-face communication process as essentially a paralinguistic prolongation of the linguistic communication which occurs in oral form (viz. verbal communication). Both perspectives arbitrarily limit the potential scope for research on the subject, as we shall see.

With respect to kinesics, Birdwhistell is the preeminent researcher in this field. The thorough bibliography compiled by Davis (1972) shows (as previously mentioned) that there have been two major pitfalls for the researchers in this field. The first has been in assuming that all movements represent

76   *Social spacing as a sociological theme of architecture*

expressive behavior and may therefore be directly introduced into the register of the face-to-face communication structure (von Cranach and Vine (1973). The second problem consists in the erroneous assumption that the entire field of face-to-face communication is a matter of kinesics.

It is true that movement can be expressive. Birdwhistell reserves the word 'kinesics' to denote body-motion communication. He studies the sequential structures and the hierarchical order of different kinds and magnitudes of body motions. Nevertheless, gross body movements, displacements, or various turns and inclinations can have other functions than those which are directly expressive; they are capable, as we have stated, of altering the relative position of the receiver's sensory receptor and therefore of transforming the face-to-face communication network. While this transforming movement can be expressive, e.g., the series of maneuvers which have been called the 'waltz of social positioning' (Webb et al. 1971: 124), as seen at a cocktail party, can signify a preference in attention for a certain individual.

Two main types of communication network transformations can be distinguished:

(1) If an individual leaves his telephone in order to visit his communication partner 'in person', he transforms by his displacement a telecommunication network into a face-to-face network, thus increasing the number of senses that may be involved in the communication.
(2) A less radical type of transformation occurs when someone moves within a given room in order to pass from one determined zone of the face-to-face communication network to another, relative to the position of a specified interlocutor.

In making a distinction in this social ballet between "communicative' and 'network-transforming' movements, the latter can be referred to as 'kinetic movement' (Chao 1968: 19, 23 n.6), while Birdwhistell's 'kinesics' applies to the former.

An attempt to explain the whole nonlexical part of the face-to-face communication process with kinesics would constitute a false perspective. It would be equally fallacious to reduce kinesics to a complement of linguistic communication, as implied by the terms 'paralinguistics' (Trager 1958: 1-12) and 'silent language'. Looking at the body of literature on the subject to date, it is relatively easy to recognize when these assumptions have distorted a researcher's perspective. Some investigators have tried to impose linguistic categories on the study of body movement. (This is well exemplified by Schefflen's application of the lexical system in his studies of 'body languages'.) Others have manifested their preference for verbal and cephalic communication through their choice of movement to be studied namely, those gestures (called 'kinemes') which accompany the oral message (Cf. Duncan Fiske 1977). Still others have biased their investigations through their choice of situation to be studied. For example, many psychiatrists study face-to-face communication structures only in traditional interview situations; such sedentary positions for conversation are quite convenient for observation, but limit the possibilities for consideration of larger body movements. Ekman is a notable exception to this pattern. He examines a wide variety of communicative corporal movements, from the positioning of an eyebrow, which can be an extremely subtle, fine-grained stimulus, to entire body movements, which require a more coarse-grained approach.

To sum up what has been said, in order to preserve the whole 'picture' of the communication that may take place in a face-to-face situation, the researcher must consider *all* message transmissions, intentional or not, linguistically articulated (by humans) or not — including such spontaneous expressions as crying, flushing, or pheromonic signals related to emotional states — which humans share in common with other primates and, more generally, with other animals. For this reason, we shall attempt in this study to avoid any bias toward linguistic communication, especially in the establishment of categories for the recording of face-to-face communication structure. Applying this nonlinguistically biased approach to communication in general, we shall see that the consideration of communication as a particular type of interaction has the advantage of allowing us to deal with those expressions which are not informative in a discursive way (here, linguistic or other written formulations with well-structured syntax are admittedly the most appropriate means), but which are emotive or imperative (e.g., pointing) in nature.

INTRODUCTION TO THE DETAILED STUDY OF THE FACE-TO-FACE MESSAGE TRANSMISSION PROCESSES BY INDIVIDUAL SENSORY SECTORS

In speaking of communication in general, we have stated that at the juncture of expression and impression is an ensuing message transmission which is a communicative event (McQuail 1975: 20: no communication without effect). In this chapter we are studying *only* that transmission which occurs in a situation where individuals are present — face-to-face communication — preferably in a controlled experimental setting where *only* the actually present communicators and receivers can affect the transaction. The subjects must, of course, be persons who have the ability to communicate with one another and who can therefore take part in a face-to-face communication network.

We will discuss the tools employed to describe the face-to-face communication structure in empirical, objective terms, as it results only from 'intersubjective forces' (Cuvillier 1970: 169 n.1). This means that, for the moment, we will not include in our considerations 'socionomic force' (Drever 1968: 275), which falls within the scope of ecosociology and therefore acts as 'noise' in the interplay of the 'social forces' actually present.

As we attempt to study the juncture of expression and impression in an analytical way (a task which presupposes the study of the transmission by each individual sensory sector), two problems arise: (1) an emission in a face-to-face communication seldom addresses itself exclusively to one sensory modality; and (2) each sensory organ may function in a different way. The counting and enumeration of all sensory modalities thus cannot be done without considerable difficulty.

These problems are reflected in our inability to classify satisfactorily the arts in general and the performing arts in particular. Certain performing arts address more than one sensory organ; hence it becomes ambiguous to speak about 'visual art', 'auditory art', and so forth. (An additional difficulty in attempts at such classification arises from the fact that some performing arts elicit public response, while others do not.) For this reason, we think that the best analytical approach for treating the complex polysensory face-to-face communication process is to begin by examining the 'impressive moment,' (i.e., the registration of the expression on each isolated sector of sensory reception).

In this chapter, therefore, we will first discuss communication in its receptive aspect, independently of any consideration of the communicator's intention in formulating the polysensory message. We will further simplify our studies by examining not the polysensory reconstruction (decoding) of the message but rather the impression on each sense, modality by modality. Here we can speak of visible communication rather than visual, and so on. Some useful materials for this approach are found in studies by certain psychologists and psychiatrists (e.g., Bodenheimer) who have addressed themselves to specific communication problems among individuals who are sensorily deprived, as discussed below.

For heuristic reasons, we must accept at least on a hypothetical basis the following enumeration of autonomous sources of communicative input by sensory sectors (subject to subsequent revision): visible, audible, 'olfactable', palpable, and tasteable. Each of these senses could be treated independently in order to explain its autonomous role as a register of sensory information, or discussed as a component in polysensory reconstruction. In this framework, one could question the order of priority of the individual sense organs in the communication process.

Unfortunately, many authors' presentation orders of the different senses reflect their unquestioning acceptance of prevailing ideological opinions about man in the phylogenic order, man as a speaking and rational living being. The pernicious nature of this doctrine resides in the fact that it remains largely implicit and is not supported by scientific evidence. Even the nature of the 'priority' and 'superiority' of the organs remains unspecified. This kind of 'metaphysical bias' has often contaminated otherwise sound empirical studies.

We will see how the senses which are most often involved in linguistic message transfer (both in conversational and written form) are referred to as the 'intelligent' senses, and therefore as 'superior' and 'predominant', without justification and without specification as to whether this 'superiority' and 'predominance' is thought to occur in the organization (encoding) of the polysensory message or in its reception (decoding), *or* on the level of the sensory system or on that of the perceptual system, where the verbal formation (c.f. Whorf) — and hence the visualistic bias inherent in the language (object and pattern recognition being related to names) — can exert an effect on the pattern recognition by the act of labeling.

The following questions could be asked separately without yielding the same response: in the expression or reception of a message, what sensory organ can function autonomously? Which sense can, on its own, give the most complete information regarding various types of information? And which sensory modality is predominant in the polysensory organization of the message expression, and which is predominant in the polysensory message reception (encoding vs. decoding)? (As an extension to this last question, we should be prepared to accept the possibility that the organization of the polysensory input data may not necessarily be the same for all kinds of messages received.)

More specifically relevant for our present investigation: should our order of presentation of the senses in describing the reception aspect of face-to-face communication (as in this part) be the same as the order we use in describing the impression of various sensory spaces (in the next part)? For example, if one were to learn about auditory space by studying the echo of one's own voice, so that communicator and receiver would be one and the same person (Tavolga 1974: 66), the conclusions drawn might be quite different from those drawn if one were to consider face-to-face communication where one's voice goes to another.

In an attempt to counteract the effects of this implicit bias that has been prevalent in the literature, we shall order our presentation of senses differently in this part and the next. While in neither case is the order we have chosen entirely arbitrary, we do intend to point out the arbitrariness and resultant methodological shortcoming of the tradition that has preceded us.

DETERMINANTS OF THE FACE-TO-FACE COMMUNICATION NETWORK AND ITS TRANSFORMATION

Pure Spatial Topology: Spatiality As It Relates to the Communication Network

In *pure* spatial sociology, the face-to-face communication network is an exclusive function of the participants' mutual positions and of their kinetic state. Unlike ecosociology, pure spatial sociology does not take into account 'territoriality' or other 'geographic' references, artificial or natural. In this study, therefore, nothing will be localizable or rooted (Kaminsky and Osterkamp 1962). Instead of territorial space, only aerial space will be valid for our considerations; more precisely, we will examine only the purely relational field of the participants' network.

As was the case with Einstein's special chamber, in which the occupant was in a state of weightlessness and therefore incapable of distinguishing total immobility from rectilinear motion with constant speed, if we can study the (social) relational field in a similar manner, in a situation devised, at least for the sake of 'mental experiment' (Hempel), such that environmental factors are eliminated, we can focus upon pure spatial sociology without the interference of those factors which will not be considered here. This experimental situation could very well be approached in reality e.g., the communication process can take place on an infinite sand beach, where at least one of the two-dimensional motions is completely independent of geographical situation (Ankerl 1973; Alexander 1964: 72), on a large grassy lawn (cf. Gibson 1966: 188-189), or on a very large dance floor.

A face-to-face communication network could be composed of any number of participants, but if the network is represented by a graph, all edges can be seen as binary elements of the network, or paired interactions (Klaus 1968: 240), which do not necessarily imply reciprocity. We can also say that the dyad comprising these two-way (mutual but not necessarily symmetrical) relations is the most elementary part of the network, and that this characteristic is present in all face-to-face communication networks, either directly or indirectly (as in the case of a dyad of two subgroups).

With this in mind, we can present the characteristics of the network in three stages:

(1) First, there is the dyad, which is a 'minimal social situation' (Kelley and Thibaut 1978) revealing all elementary relations in biunivocal terms (Ankerl 1972a: 55). Indeed, it is composed of two directed edges between two vertices; while these two opposite edges of graph bear as value the same

absolute distance, but perhaps the value describing the partners' mutual orientation and direction could be different (mutuality versus reciprocity).
(2) Second, we have the triad, which brings a new aspect into consideration: here, the distance between the partners will be 'relativized'.
(3) If we now consider subsets of groups constituted in function of the ('local') variation of the 'demographic density' (as the distribution index), and if we apply concepts to subsets of *larger* groups analogous to those we applied in microsociology to individuals, we can use these network concepts to deal with relationships among macrosociological units as well.

Face-to-Face Elementary Relation

The network, as a potential field of communication, is determined on the static level by the station and position of the participants, on the kinetic level by the capacity for change of the given static coordinates, and on the temporal level by the stationary or dynamic state of the network transformation. If we disregard geocentric considerations (i.e., a subject's position in the earth's gravitational field), the dyad's elementary relation is not localized but is instead 'free-floating', and only the absolute distance between partners and their mutual orientation and direction can determine their network (see Figure 2.1).

For the sake of consistency, we must agree that between two 'protagonists' there is to be only one absolute distance, expressed in measure of length

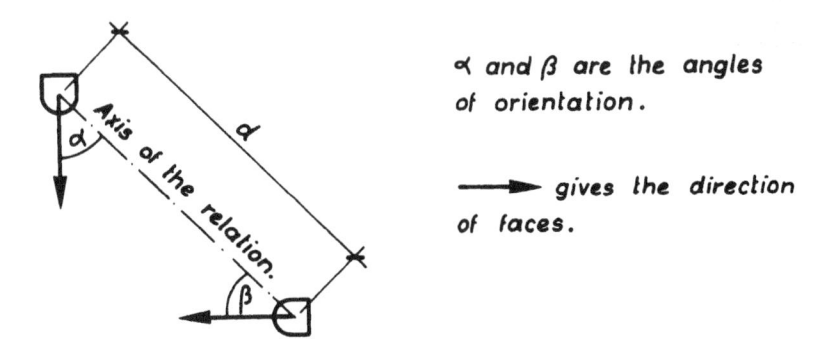

α and β are the angles of orientation.

⟶ gives the direction of faces.

Example: The perpendicular crossing of the two partners' axes with convergent directions is favorable for conversation ("lending an ear").

Figure 2.1. *Horizontal characteristics of a dyad.*

82 Social spacing as a sociological theme of architecture

as 'beeline'. For a given pair, this beeline could be established between two respective points on their bodies, such as the so-called 'Cyclops eye' (Gosztonyi 1976: 805), or the glabellar eye drawn by Hindu women on their foreheads (Buddha, K. Lewin, J. H. Schultz, A. Bodenheimer), or the navel, or any respective point one might choose. This line will, at the same time, give a common axis which determines the station.

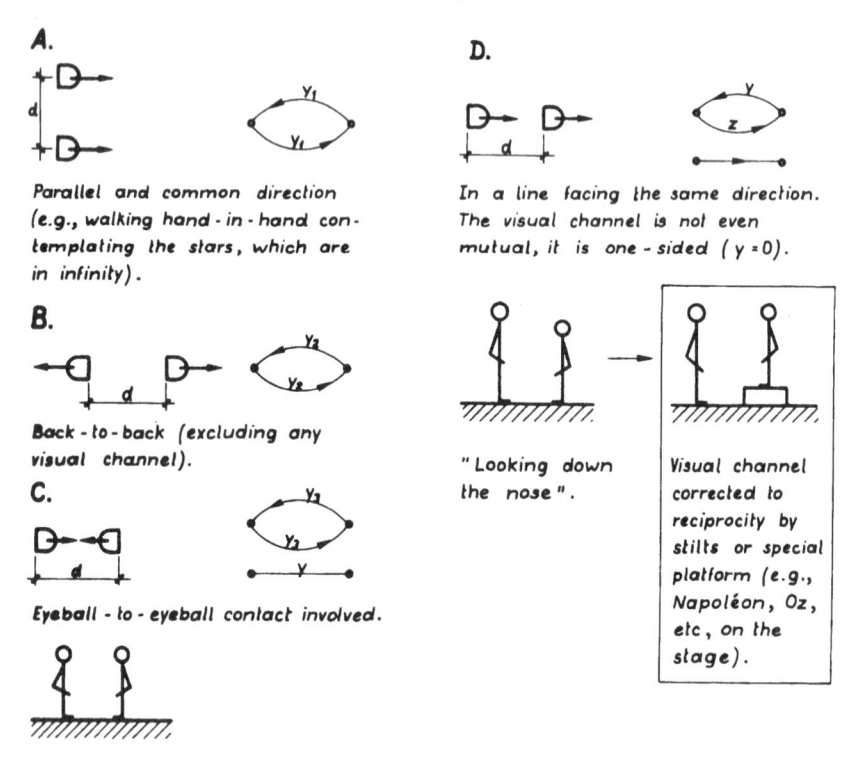

A.

Parallel and common direction (e.g., walking hand-in-hand contemplating the stars, which are in infinity).

B.

Back-to-back (excluding any visual channel).

C.

Eyeball-to-eyeball contact involved.

D.

In a line facing the same direction. The visual channel is not even mutual, it is one-sided ($y = 0$).

"Looking down the nose".

Visual channel corrected to reciprocity by stilts or special platform (e.g., Napoléon, Oz, etc, on the stage).

A, B, and C are reciprocal relations (implying always mutuality) and can be represented by symmetrical arcs or an edge too.

D relation is mutual but not reciprocal represented by 2 adjacent arcs with opposite directions bearing different values (y, z).

Figure 2.2. *Representation of elementary network relation by graph.*

How can one determine the mutual positions when the partners are not in congruent poses (e.g., when one is bowing and the other standing upright)? In a general free-floating situation (e.g., in an aquatic ballet or in an astronautic dyad) the mutual position will be determined by three perpendicular axes and three angles.

We will have, therefore, four classes of data:

(1) the distance in absolute longimetric terms;
(2) the six data of station mentioned above;

(3) all tortional aspects (twisting, turning, etc.); and
(4) data as to whether the receiver is in a static or moving state.

This last point could include considerations as to the change of speed in a stationary or dynamic motion. (Theoretically, when a dyad is in synchronized movement, the network changes, if at all, only in the kinesthesis of the proprioception.)

From the data in classes 2, 3, and 4, we can determine whether the network element is simultaneously mutual or even reciprocal. As the network element inherent in the mutual position is a function of the mode of operation of each expression component (e.g., a voice), and of the mode of operation of each reception component (e.g., hearing), it can allow a (homologous) reciprocal communication 'loop' or a mutual link (simultaneous or with eventual alternating communication), or an unilateral relationship with no possibility for feedback (e.g., where individuals are in a line and facing the same direction). (See Figure 2.2.)

Let us now look at some cases illustrating the data in class 2 mentioned above: it is possible that two partners could be in a reciprocal position but that their statures differ to such an extent that their 'topological' reciprocity cannot be realized in metric terms (see Figure 2.2).

In topological terms, it is a fundamental fact that *no* human sensory receptor field is spherical. Generally, speaking, we can distinguish three primary orientations, all of which allow in a binary situation two choices of direction: forward-backward, up-down, and right-left. We can disregard any differences between right and left sensory acuity because these are generally very minor (see Buytnedyk 1959: 276-277).

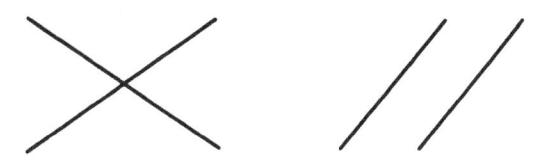

Possibilities in two dimensions.

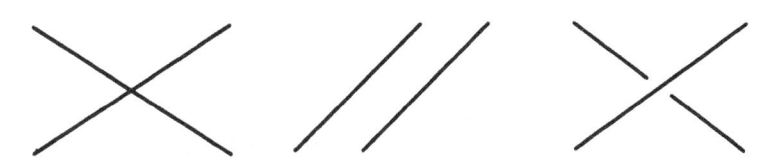

Possibilities in three dimensions.

84   *Social spacing as a sociological theme of architecture*

We can state that the most frequently assumed positions can be defined by crossing, parallel, and skew-line axes (the latter manifesting itself only in three-dimensional systems.)

Let us now look at data in class 3. The human body is not completely rigid but flexible. The carriage can be changed gradually, and, as it changes, so do the reception fields of the sense organs. We know many categorizations of these movements and the resulting 'poses', but these categories have been developed chiefly for the notation of the various postures as corporal expression and not for the consideration of their relevance to the various receiving functions of the body, which constitute our present area of concern. In anatomical terms, we can distinguish three basic possibilities for carriage change:

(a) movements of the trunk, i.e., major 'leaning' and 'turning' (Frey and von Cranach 1971: lateral flexion);
(b) movements of the extremities, e.g., crossing and bending of arms and legs, to which physically minor movements (finger movements, etc.) could be added; and
(c) head movements (Frey and von Cranach 1971: sagittal) such as nodding or turning.

We can observe that, with the exception of the sense of touch, all sense organs are situated in the head; their reception fields (visual, etc.) therefore 'move' with the head. We must also note that among the various movements there is an additive hierarchy in that some movements imply others, while the reverse may not necessarily be true, e.g., a turning of the trunk brings with it the head, whereas a head movement does not necessarily implicate the trunk. (In the case of trunk movement, a compensatory head movement could partially reestablish the previous visual fields, etc.)

Triad and the Microsocial Face-to-Face Communication Network

The triad is the simplest social formation in which a coordinated movement of a dyad gives a 'we' impression in relation to the third party. We will see the importance of this type of movement in a closer analysis of the triad.

A newborn's position relative to the parents' dyad determines a bidimensional relational field. The dyad itself, as we have said, is a linear field. In a network, any number of vertices could be completely localized by fixing their distance (coordinates) from at least four points which are not in a plane.

The face-to-face communication network 85

However, in order to evaluate a network we must know the relative positions of all vertices. Indeed, an individual's position could relate to the position of other individuals in such a way as to utilize channels of different multisensory composition according to the partner involved. A fully exposed network reveals for a given position all of these multilateral relativities. A field with n vertices comprises $\binom{n}{2} = \frac{1}{2}n(n-1)$ relations\(Ankerl 1972a: 56, 279). Only this kind of full exposure allows us to detect positions which are privileged from the viewpoint of perceptual control of the whole face-to-face communication network. Verbal expressions such as 'central figure' or 'elevated position' acquire their concrete and proper sense in the face-to-face communication network.

In situation I of Figure 2.3, the well-surrounded leader, represented by the square, cannot approach any one of his constituencies without increasing the distance between himself and others. The leader in face-to-face communication network II, however, is positioned in such a way as to be able to approach the whole crowd or move off without the dilemma of personal discrimination.

We can also illustrate the analysis of relative network position by comparing a dyad with a triad, where $\overline{ab}_I < \overline{ab}_{II}$ as shown in Figure 1.2.1. Since $\overline{ab}_I < \overline{ab}_{II}$, the communicability between a_{II} and b_{II} is less than that between a_I and b_I insofar as the communicability is 'inversely proportional' to the absolute distances between positions. In an analysis of the entire network, however, we see that while for a the closest point in both situations I and II is always b, the reverse is not true. Because $\overline{ab}_{II} > \overline{bc}_{II}$, the preferential position 'expressed' in relative distance is not reciprocated between a and b. For b, c is closer than a. We can say that in this sense b has a privileged position. We can call upon this insight into the microsocial network later, when it will apply to the analysis of large macrosocial networks where effective analysis of all relationships would otherwise be impossible.

At a party we can observe many illustrations of microsocial networks. By 'dancing' around a partner one can move without increasing or decreasing

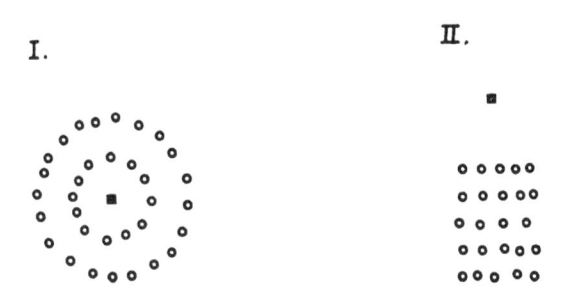

I.   II.

Figure 2.3. *Leader's positions.*

ones distance from the partner. Or, as we mentioned earlier, if a subset of people move in a synchronized way, they create a privileged subnetwork for themselves. Lewin (1969) and Wiener and Mehrabian (1968: 33) speak about 'approach-avoidance' manoeuvres. Of course, the value of a network position is not an exclusive function of distance, nor even of relative distance; one can often compensate for the effects of increased distance by changing one's direction or orientation.

Face-to-Face Communication Network of Large Sets: Macrosocial Network

We must emphasize that in this book we discuss only those aspects of the face-to-face communication network which can be influenced by the enveloping architectural space. In this sense, demograph and even urban sociology — pertinent insofar as the residential structure may give access to macrosocial meetings — will be touched upon only marginally. We treat here only those tools which allow us to deal with the face-to-face communication network of large sets where it would be impossible to analyze all $n(n-1)/2$ relations.

Demography teaches us how to count, at a given moment, the world's population as it is classified in different objective categories (e.g., age, sex, genealogic origin, etc.) and how to represent its distribution by density per square mile or other (more carefully chosen) surface units as reference. It also teaches how to describe the changes taking place within a given population over the course of time, changes due to birth, death, and migration. What can we find in this field that is relevant to the description of the macrosocial face-to-face communication network?

Let us first consider the tools necessary for the description of an instantaneous static state. Even if mutual distance is not the unique variable determining network position, we can nevertheless state that there is a certain maximal distance between individuals beyond which face-to-face communication is impossible; indeed, in terms of face-to-face communication, beyond a certain limit a person may no longer be considered 'present'. This requirement for a certain proximity between nearest neighbors imposes at least an indirect link among *all* participants in the macrosocial network (e.g., hand-in-hand in a closed or endless chain). We can see, therefore, that from the viewpoint of pure sociology the traditional demographic density which relates population to a specified surface area is not directly relevant. As we have stated, the very nature of the social field is relational; vertex is linked to vertex without any reference to surface area. As we have also stated, in an aquatic environment or in a multilevel arrangement, human population may in fact display a three-dimensional network. Additional shortcomings of the demographic density concept have been discussed before (Ankerl

1965: 55: 1974: 576). The application of graph theory to the treatment of topo-metric data will in general be exposed to some extent in the last chapter of the next part which is devoted to the syntax of architectural space systems.

The face-to-face communication network might be better approached via the concept of 'axone density', which does not refer to any surface area at all, but which is calculated as the mean distance among all points in the set. This average beeline distance is a value that is relevant to pure spatial sociology. If we relate it in any way to the volume of the surrounding architectural space (as in the calculation of seating capacity), it becomes (also) an ecosociological value. (The subjective of, if you will, 'human' significance of this objective data — density versus crowding — lies in the communicative possibilities inherent in a network position.)

Density calculated as the mean distance among all vertices can allow a relevant comparison between networks containing similar number of positions, but if their respective numbers are very different, mean distance can no longer yield a good comparison; e.g., even if a crowd should grow in such a manner as to allow its new sections to be no more or less compact than was the original mass (e.g., by adding new edges of equilateral and coinciding triangles), the mean distance between all positions will grow. The indirect character of the 'string' or chain concatenation (the face-to-face communication possibility with a certain polysensory intensity) increases too. We must also acknowledge the practical handicap that it is very difficult to calculate all mutual distances in a large crowd.

We would propose, therefore, that if our density computation is to be relevant, it must take into account the one aspect that is most essential to the maintenance of the face-to-face communication chain; namely, the distance between nearest neighbors. Using this concept, we can construct an index which will not only be easier to calculate but which will, on the theoretical level, allow us to compare any networks without respect to differences in the number of vertices. This density index, which we call umbilical density (Ankerl 1974: 586) is calculated using the mean distance separating one vertex from its nearest neighbor. Additional rules will be necessary for this calculation if we are to avoid ambiguity; among other rules, as in the case of the umbilical cord, one line — or vertex — could be counted for only one individual.

The umbilical density does not, therefore, take into account all possible binary relations in the network, but only those that are 'nearest'. If demographic density concepts such as 'residential presence', 'sleeping density', etc., are insensitive to possible redistributions taking place inside the perimeter of the network's superficial reference, umbilical density is not. For example, whereas global demographic density is not changed by migration on the surface of the earth, umbilical density will reflect any such change in distribution.

In order to more easily handle networks comparing large sets of individuals, it will be convenient to constitute appropriate subsets. If we calculate on a computer the umbilical density by successive integration, we can built-in warning signals which will announce any sudden change occurring in the umbilical density index. Later on we can fix limits, extreme values for the umbilical density, allowing us to form subsets. Each of these can be represented by its center of gravity, giving us a better view of the entire set (control of the crowd).

If the recording device is connected with a computer, all density structuration could be automatically recorded and continuously analyzed. (In this regard, see also Part IV.) To make the recording meaningful for the description of a face-to-face communication network, it is enough to 'calibrate' the distance, orientation, and direction measurements of the positions in accordance with sensory field zones as intervals with upper and lower limits.

There are many advantages to a well-programmed mechanical recording linked to a computer which automatically and continuously analyzes the various regularities occurring among different data. The mechanical recording allows us to observe individuals without influencing their behavior, and, on the level of computer analysis, a well-designed program package — with subroutines — will allow us to confront the face-to-face communication network and its transformations with an actual face-to-face communication structure; here, 'paired-interaction probability' will provide reference for the comparison.

DEMOGRAPHY AS A TOOL OF COMMUNICATION NETWORK DESCRIPTION: AN ENLARGED VIEW

How can we enhance the relevance of demography for objective sociology? Is there a fruitful junction between them? If there is such a junction, the description of the communication network would seem to be an appropriate place to look for it.

From the viewpoint of *pure* sociology, we have dealt with the 'population-effective' present as a set of communication network positions, and with 'migration' as a transformation of these networks. We also said that demography, on the other hand, describes the population — its effective composition and distribution following objective categories — on a global level. It deals with the census of a state, the description of past development, and simulation or projection of the future. The phenomena behind these population statistics and mathematical models of development include (1) the arrival of new subjects by birth (the actual multiplication of a vertex, where mother and child are for a moment at one and the same point); (2) departure by death; and (3) displacement by migration. Considered at all levels of magnitude — micro versus macro, face-to-face versus telecommunication — these states and transformations are, in principle, relevant to the description of the communication network, which serves as a basis for the communication structure, which, in turn, characterizes the social formations. A continuous field of investigation between demograph and sociology would be established (e.g., birth is a demographical fact involving the multiplication of a point, and for sociology, it involves a special communication network element, namely a 'nested' link in the prenatal situation and a distanceless one between mother and the newborn). Unfortunately, however, if we look at the current use of demography by sociology we can see that demography does not provide all of the types of data that it could generate for sociological research.

For example, in studies of social integration related to migration, sociologists need data reflecting the stability and frequency (repeatedness) of communication structures, and on the other hand, the demographic data does not even distinguish migrant and remigrant, etc., so they are sociologically dead data. A similar phenomenon occurs if sociology is to explain why a large crowd, which should assure a dense face-to-face communication network, will in fact often result in only a very minimal face-to-face communication structure. Indeed, sociologists have found (Stokols 1972 summarizes the literature; see also the special issue of *Environment and Behavior*, 2 June 1975, devoted to 'Crowding in Real Environment') that physical density perceived as 'crowding' will often have a negative effect on interhuman communication, especially if the people who are mutually accessible to one another are strangers and their relationships have not been deeply rooted in common personal history (Ankerl 1974: 580). Speaking in objective terms, in order to make predictions about the actualization of a face-to-face communication network into a communication structure, it is necessary to know the longitudinal dimension of the participants' relationships, viz. past face-to-face communication and telecommunication. *Ancienneté* [ancientness] of the common (shared) frequentation of a part of the face-to-face communication network of persons involved is relevant for the network/structure rate prediction.

Indeed by counting — and enumerating — population effectives (according to objective categories) who participate in social communication, over the course of time, demography conveys data basic for the description of social communication networks. Without changing its very nature, this science could increase its sociological relevance in the following way:

(1) The counting could be extended to include identification of the origins of each of the participating individuals. In this respect we could call the study of population samples a kind of genealogical demography which would not

only make a census, a count, but also enumerate the population under consideration.

(2) Another extension complementary to the first would be to generalize demography by adding to its traditional field a microdemography.

(3) As in the case of ethnography, which is 'doubled' by an 'ethnology', here one can also raise the level of interest to an explanatory demology.

Thus, by recording the regularities of human populations, along with tele- and face-to-face communication networks, their transformations, and the generated communication structures, we can reach the whole field of objective (or external) sociology.

The problem of the recording of the face-to-face communication network and structure as dependent variables of the surrounding architectural space will be discussed in the last part of this book. In the same Part IV we will also see how an experimentally induced approach might be used to generate representative longitudinal data as samples.

5

Visible Communication

> — You were lusting, while you were talking.
> — How do you know that?
> — I saw it in your eyes.
> — That was not lust — I protest. The look was caused by my eyeglasses. You see, when you wear bifocals they give off this odd effect that some people could interpret as lust. Ask my optometrist.
>
> Art Buchwald: *The Unlust Life*

If other congeners are in one's perceptual field, there exists a social field. If two or more persons are in a situation where each one can emit signs directly visible to the others, there is a visual presence. The aspects of the situation that determine the transmissible message allow us to apprehend the visual communication network.

The possibility of seeing depends on the visual efficiency and the visible character of the expression (see Argyle 1967). The pattern of use of the network determines the primary structure of communication. In it expressions are transmitted intentionally or unintentionally and received by an observer (this transmission of signs connects efferent and afferent, motor and sensory activities). Our approach leaves the motives of expression out of consideration. Phenomenological interpretations made by essayists (Sartre, etc.) will be outside our scope. Our approach considers the communication network and its use as structure. We will remain at the objective level of analysis, subject to experimentation. This is a physical phenomenal level describing 'expression conversion' into impression through physical transmission. It is at this level that the design of architectural space can influence the communication structure, independently of the importance we attribute to it, and this will be our criterion of pertinence.

VISUAL SENSITIVITY

We can describe visual efficiency either in absolute terms or relative to other channels of polysensory communication, like the auditory channel. Unfortunately, a large number of researchers identify face-to-face or direct communication too closely with oral communication and consider the visual channel purely complementary. (Perhaps ultimately they have a more pronounced interest in the deaf-mute's finger language because it is also an alphabet, although only a manual one.) We can help specify the visual efficiency of our species by considering it in the ethological context.

As we are biaural, we are also binocular, but the visual organs are situated very near to one another — the baseline is about 6 cm. long (Vurpillot 1967: 106) — and on a quasi-plane of the head, on the face. The flexibility of the head and its ability to rotate compensate for the limitation inherent in the directed nature of our sight. Though we cannot fix more than one object simultaneously, we can do so successively. The ears, however, often have difficulty filtering out the wanted word from the babel of voices. We hear everything and we hear nothing. In further contrast to our hearing, we can close our eyes (or one eye, and so make our vision monocular and 'less stereoscopic'). Finally, our eyes are at once the center of sight and of the gaze, a quality we will discuss later.

A given observation position can be described in quantitative terms. We can designate a system of concentric spheres whose center is the midpoint of the baseline, or the cyclopean eye, and each point defined by distance and direction will have visual acuity (in all aspects). Under conditions where the parameters of illumination and transparency are specified, we can determine thresholds of visual acuity in two ways: as a minimum distance of separation between two luminous target points, and as a diameter of a point lighter or darker than its background. These thresholds are the so-called 'minimum separable' and 'minimum visible'. In a similar way, for each point in the visual field, we can specify a differential threshold of chromatic value discrimination, of saturation degree, of brightness or lightness, and of differences in specular or diffusive reflection.

Because of the great depth of the visual field (we can perceive a lighted candle 2.7 km. in front of us) we can only draw conclusions for the entire field if the experimental results are obtained at a wide range of points. Thanks to the more or less symmetrical nature of the visual field, one can establish *'isoptères'* (Piéron 1968: 229) that define points with equal visual thresholds (absolute, differential, crepuscular, photopic, chromatic, etc.). Since the minimum visible can be expressed as an angular magnitude (namely $1''$), in this way its magnitude in centimeters is calculable for each radius of distance.

We do not study visual efficiency for its own sake but rather to determine the visibility of signs. These may be expressed by parts of the body, both clothed and unclothed, and by position changes (by the stable or ephemeral nature of a position, the rapidity or acceleration of the gestures, etc.) in a specific situation (namely illumination, transparency, etc). It suffices to find indicators that allow us to divide an observer's physical environment into intervals. The manner and degree of deformation and schematization of the expressive body in the observer's impression define these intervals. In the following part we will discuss the observer's impression of the optical space as an architectural creation and will reconsider the question of image deformation, but in a different way. We will also treat the more abstract theories of vision, such as those of Luneburg.

The first demarcation in the visual field is the gross maximal limit. As far as the directed nature of the visual field is concerned, the angle of the binocular field is greater than that obtained when the monocular fields of two immobilized eyes are combined. Within this field we can define an angle of central vision, where the image is formed on the fovea centralis of the eyes (see Figure 2.4). We can contrast central vision to peripheral vision, where the image is formed on the macula — the part of the retina outside the fovea — and where the image is less clear. Because the cones and rods — with crepuscular vision — are not distributed equally within the eyes (macula versus fovea), the gross maximal limit of the field changes with color: the blue field is the largest and the green the smallest.

Another characteristic of the maximal field is its 'hole' in the immediate proximity of the body. For anatomical reasons other than those of the eyes themselves and of their positions, the truncated cone form of the field suffers several further deformations. The salience of the nose, the sclera, and the brow ridge have individual and racial variations (e.g., slit eyes) that also vary the visual field.

It is paradoxical that we measure the visual field for the immobilized eye, even though all vision involves some movement (Held in Dubois et al. 1971: 41). Various movements of the eyes, head, and body fill in the holes, the missing parts in our fields. At the same time, these movements express our attention.

Among these expressive movements, the interior movements of the eyeballs and the dilation of the pupil must be considered first, because they reveal receptive stimulation.

Eyeball movement in a given head position defines the field of fixation. We must note that the angle of this field depends on head position. The field of fixation cannot be reconstructed by simply following the head movement; textbook data about the field of fixation imply that the head is in a primary position, i.e., straight forward in relation to the body.

94 *Social spacing as a sociological theme of architecture*

1.

Spatial visual acuity.

―――― = 1'   ―――― = 1"

Minimum separable.   Minimum visible.
(Interspace between contours.)   (Single - fine - line technique.)

2.

Eyes in primary position.

a) Detailed vision in the forea.

b) Vision by macula.

3.

Eyes in secondary position: peripheral region (scanning).

4.

Binocular overlapping.

Horizontal section.   Vertical section.

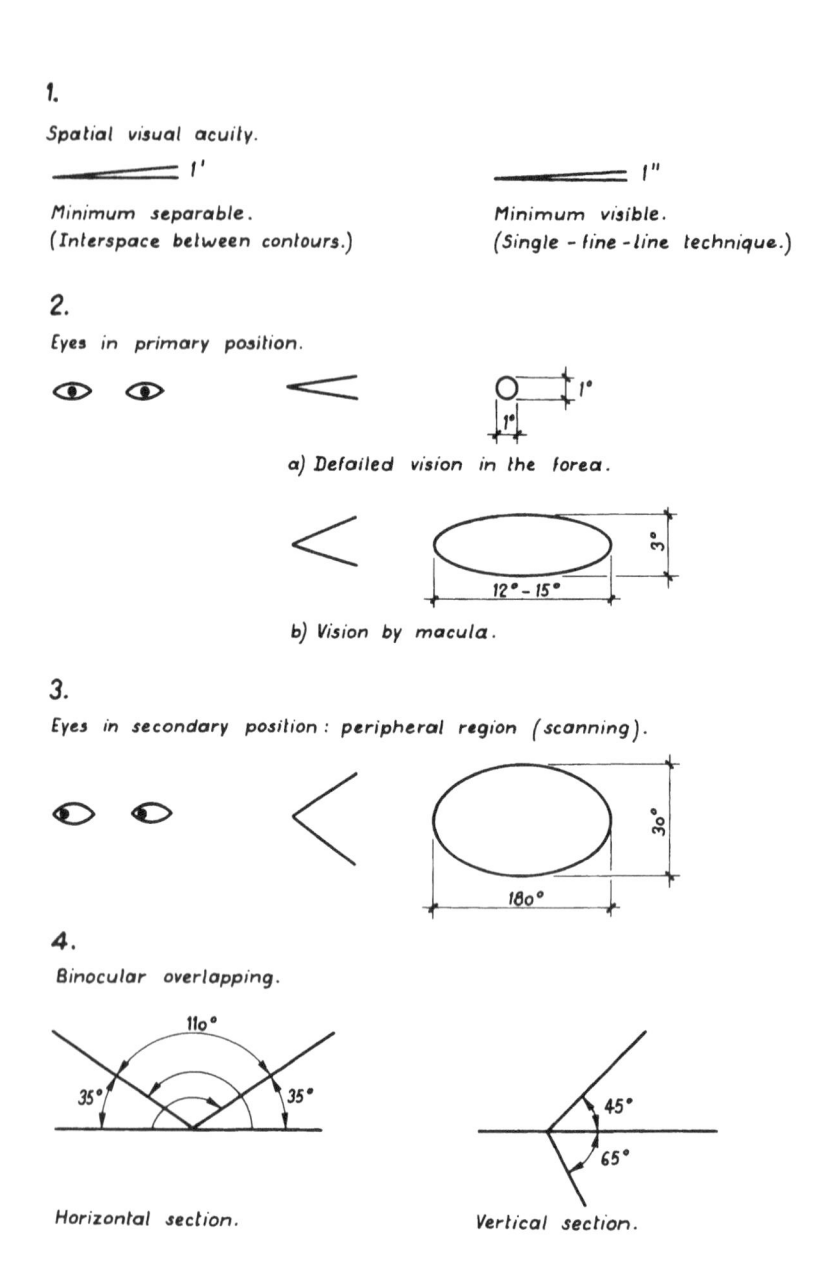

Figure 2.4. *Visual sensitivity. (Schematic representation.)*

We distinguish two main kinds of ocular movements: vergence and version. 'Vergence' is a rotative movement of each eye in an opposite direction. It allows the eyes to move from a near point of fixation to a distance one, i.e., divergence, and vice versa, i.e., convergence. 'Convergence' is two monocular adductions and 'divergence' is two abductions.

In the case of version, the two eyes shift in the same direction.

With the head facing forward, eye movement either vertically or horizontally forms a secondary position; oblique movement forms a tertiary position.

If the neck bends sideward, the eyes make an oblique movement as partial compensation. This rotation is called torsion. Gibson and Pick (1963) say, 'there is an invariant reciprocal relationship between compensatory eye-turning and head-turning.' The head can either tilt or rotate. It is obvious and unfortunate that we still do not have a standardized terminology with precise definitions (Le Grand 1967). Precise experimental descriptions of both the vision and the gaze thus suffer.

Finally, the rotation and flexion of the trunk complete the list of possible movements the observer can make to fill in all the gaps in the visual perception of his surroundings.

Let us now look at the complementary side of seeing, the range of visible expressions, in order to establish the intervals relevant for the visual communication network.

VISIBLE EXPRESSION: INTERVALS OF VISIBILITY

Visible expressions result from various muscular, respiratory, glandular and vascular reactions or efforts.

First of all, pupilary variations, eyeball, periocular, head, and gross body movements can all express attention. By coming closer or receding, our extremities can signify a change in visual attention. Indeed, nearly all movements of our extremities, including those of the fingers, can be a covariance of our visual attention in a quasi-obligatory manner. Facial expressions such as the grimace and smile, especially those of a periocular, perioral, and intraoral (lingual) nature imply very subtle movements. Respiratory reactions imply thoracic movements. Trembling has muscular origins and is visible because of its extensiveness and rapidity.

Among glandular reactions, perspiration changes the lightness and the diffusive nature of the skin's reflectance as well as the roughness of the skin surface. Tears add lenses to the already specular eyeball surface; they act as a 'negative contact lens' blinding the eyes without depriving them of their expressiveness. Goose pimples imply an ephemeral deformation of the skin surface, primarily a change in the specular nature of the skin surface rather than an alteration of the physiognomy. Pilomotor reactions — horripilations and 'creepy-crawly' movements — are other subtle responses hardly visible to the naked eye. Finally, vascular reactions cause changes in the color of the skin — when it is flushed and suffused with color, turning red — or in its lightness — when the skin loses its color, turns pale, and whitens.

These expressions become visible insofar as the movement of the skin surface and/or the changes in its reflectance — specular or diffusive, and the changes in the reflected light's spectral composition — are sufficiently extensive and not too ephemeral. The acuity with which expression can be seen depends upon the observer's position. We can define this position by the distance from the observer's cyclopean eye (Bodenheimer), by an angle horizontal to the observer's median plane, and by an angle vertical to his corneal plane (e.g., a blush is not perceptible in peripheral vision since all colors except blue have a very limited imprint). Thus the visibility of each expression can be predicted by the communicator's relative location in the observer's visual field, a function of his primary, secondary, or tertiary position. However, the impression actually produced — message transmission — depends not only on the communicator's expression but on the receiver's strategy. The 'focused, stabilized and appropriately centered retinal image' itself (Gibson and Pick 1963) depends on the speed, acceleration, and sequence of the gaze and on the rhythmic blinking of the eyelashes (Dubois et al. 1971: 41), which in turn depends on whether the observer engages in an exploratory look — pure 'praxis' (Dubois et al. 1971: 15) — or in a recognition process — 'gnosis' (Hugonnier in Dubois et al. 1971: 356) concerning the subject.

Relying on others' findings (Trager, etc.), Hall concludes that changes in the polysensory composition of the communication network are a function of the partners' mutual positions, and primarily their distance. He suggests four main zones in the face-to-face communication network (Hall 1969: 114; Chapple 1971: 1968; Ankerl 1973). The first zone, labeled the 'intimate' by Hediger of Zurich, goes from 0 to ca. 0.5 m.; the second, or personal, zone goes from ca. 0.5 to 1.2 m.; the third, or social, zone from 1.2 to 3.6 m.; and the fourth, or public, zone begins directly beyond the third zone (beyond 3.6 m.) and is measured straight ahead of the observer. We can note that visibility is a function of distance and also of direction, which plays a greater role in this case than it does in that of touching.

From 0 to 0.2 m. the other's image is considerably enlarged, and it stimulates a very large part of the retina. Certain details and the cross-eyed pull of the eye muscles produce a very unusual vision.

Between 0.2 and 0.5 m. our peripheral vision includes the outline of the head and the shoulders and possibly even the gesticulating hands. This interval allows a clear, enlarged vision (15°) of either the lower or the upper part of the face. Among the various features — lips, teeth, tongue, etc. — the prominent nose is the most enlarged and deformed of all. At a distance of 0.2 m., even in eye-to-eye communication, we can see the other's eye and eye movements in clinical detail: the enlarged iris, the blood vessels in the sclera, etc., but in this microscopic world, the whole eye — as well as the face — appears truly distorted. The expressionistic or the syncopic view of a cubist painter like Picasso could be understood as 'realistic' in terms of certain visual experiences. In this sense certain so-called abstract tendencies could also be seen as a kind of naturalism. Many authors have already noted this phenomenon: the well-known theoretician Giedon (1940 reedited in 1963: 272-273) views cubism as a pictorial art from this zone, which is so close that perspective vanishes. The semiologist Gandelsonas (1972: 82) speaks of 'cubist painting where space is perceived . . . as a dialectic between . . . an observer's ability to make precise readings of frontal planes, and only imprecise reading of peripheral planes.' For Jean Paris (1965) cubism is 'syncope de représentation', 'c'est une pliure de regard'. Finally, the art critic Michael Gibson (1973) writes, 'The battle of cubism can be understood in a number of ways — as an attempt to represent the object simultaneously on a variety of planes, or as E. H. Gombrich suggests, as an attempt to frustrate the viewer who seeks to find an object in the painting, until he is forced to see it as a 2-dimensional surface studded with contradictory clues.'

Between 0.5 and 0.8 m. we perceive the other's eye muscles but even more clearly half of the face. The whole face appears very round; the nose and ears recede. The three-dimensional quality of the skin's texture is also accurately observable: eyelashes, pores, fine hairs, and their changes (pilimotor reactions, sudations, etc.).

Between 0.8 and 1.2 m. we see the other's head. Its size is normal. Allowing our gaze to wander, we can readily perceive facial expressions, as well as the colors of the face and hair, 'sleep' in the eyes, stains on the teeth, spots, and small wrinkles. We can even see dirt on clothing. If the person is sitting, his whole body and gestures already appear in peripheral vision, but his individual fingers cannot be counted.

Between 1.2 and 2.1 m. we can see gestures and the whole body in any position. At 1.2 m. with an angle of 60° we see the upper part — head, shoulders, and the upper trunk — and at 2.1 m. the whole body. In order to establish eye-to-eye contact, as 1.2 m. the gazing eye must shift from one eye to the other, whereas at 2.1 m. part of both eyes is already included in the minimal angle of visual acuity.

Between 2.1 and 3.6 m. we can clearly perceive the other's whole face. At approximately 3.6 m. the feedback from the eye muscles used to hold the eye fixed on a single spot falls off rapidly. On the other hand, both eyes and the mouth (lip movements) are in sharp vision. At a 60° angle a glance can already include a third person, and this interval thus goes beyond exclusively dyadic relationships.

Between 3.6 and 7.5 m. the partner's whole face is in sharp vision. The eyes lose their color and the whole body is seen as flat — e.g., beyond 5.0 m. we can no longer see the thoracic movement involved in sighing. Although the other's face is perceived as less than life-size, the 15° lozenge-shaped area of clear vision can already include the face of more than one person. Hall (1969: 72) brings the following example of the differences between simple exploration and recognition at this distance:

A man with normal vision, sitting in a restaurant 3.6-4.5 m. from a table where other people are sitting, can see the following out of the corner of his eye. He can tell that the table is occupied and possibly *count* the people present, particularly if there is some movement (recognition vs. simple counting.) At an angle of 45 degrees he can tell the color of the woman's hair as well as the color of her clothing, though he cannot *identify* the material. He can tell whenever the woman is looking and talking to her partner but not whether she has a ring on her finger. He can pick up the gross movements of her escort, but he can't see the watch on his wrist. He can tell the sex of a person, his body build, and his age in very general terms but not whether he *knows* him or not.

Persons are seen but not individuals therefore observers can not relate themselves to them.

At a distance beyond 8 m. more and more people, with their whole bodies, enter the sharpest field of vision. While the individual and his expression fade, the 60° peripheral vision can, however, include the gross body movements and displacements of a whole group.

NETWORK POSITION VALUES AND THE VISIBLE COMPONENT OF THE COMMUNICATION STRUCTURE

We have described the visual communication network. The duration of each fixation and its sequence (Lhermitte in Dubois et al. 1971: 317), along with indications about the speed and acceleration in transferring each glance, constitute the visual component of the face-to-face communication structure. Spatial data relevant to the visual exchange, as we have noted, are the angles of the observer's actual field of vision in relation to his primary position and the angles of his gaze within the field, as well as his distance from the 'expressive' part of the observed person's body. Description of the structure should indicate all visible details within both the central and the peripheral parts of the field.

The visible communication structure is realized only when feedback occurs, that is, a gaze is seen by someone. Let us consider the dyad. The positions of the partners could be reciprocal, permitting equal use of the network by each. This situation can be defined by two conditions: (a) the partners must be in the primary position and the plane defined by their base line must be horizontal; and (b) their base line must be symmetrical in relation to a vertical plane. Of course, we must also consider the direction of the two visual fields. (We are disregarding any slight difference in the visual efficiency of the right and left eyes; condition (b) is simply that of central symmetry.) The visual network, like the haptic one, is homologous and allows simultaneous use. In this it differs from the auditory network, for example. For this reason the lapses of the communication exchange — the initiatives, the call, and the responses — must be noted.

Because of its homologous nature, oculo-oculary communication has become the subject of specialized research (Argyle 1967: 'reversible perspective'). The auro-oral circuit cannot be replaced by an auro-aural one.

Finally, distance makes it possible to include simultaneously in peripheral vision more than one person, so the gaze can wander over various parts of several bodies. This ocular communication structure appears in the visual communication network of a group.

There are several difficulties in discussing past research findings in visual communication structure. Some results are contradictory, some not comparable. One investigation will have used unobtrusive methods and rigorous experimental controls; others present results based on research which has not considered all aspects of the communication structure present in the network, as we have enumerated them above. Although many conclusions may appear valid and useful at first glance, we may find that the author, preferring quick, applicable results, has failed to provide a full description and recording of the observed situation. Even journals of experimental psychology often publish contributions of this sort.

Dyadic Relation

Whatever the intention expressed by a movement, no effective communication can flow through the visual network without actual sight of ocular, facial, gestural, or postural expression.

Each kind of expression has its optimal position for the observer. For example, we can see skin structure reactions, like goose bumps, at a distance of half a meter. At one meter we can gain a good impression of three-dimensional facial expression — 'plastic deformation of the face' (Gibson and Pick 1963). We need at least one and a half meters for a view of all gestures, even if the partner is in a sitting position. Postural expressions nearer than three and a half meters cannot be viewed in full, since posture requires empty space to 'deploy' its movements. Thus, the strategy of communication requires either that the receiver concentrate his efforts on expressions for which the given mutual position is optimal or that the partners accommodate their mutual positions to the kind of expression chosen. (In the second case, a displacement transforms the network.) The optimal position makes it possible to gaze without rapid eye shifting.

Oculo-ocular

Hutt and Ounstead (1966: 103) note that gaze fixation is a *sine qua non* of all social interaction. Therefore we must consider the direction of the other's gaze: guessing the direction of a gaze or its fixation point and at the same time the partner's degree of attention as indicated in the pupil opening.

The most significant research in this field has been inspired by J. J. Gibson at Cornell University and by M. Argyle's group at Oxford University. In their exploratory research, Gibson and Pick (1963) asked their subjects to look into each other's eyes in seven different eye positions and from three different head positions. They hypothesize that '... we have good discrimination for the line gaze of another person, at least with respect to whether or not we are being looked at. The ability to read the eyes seems to be as good as the ability to read fine print on an acuity chart, according to our first determination.' From a methodological viewpoint we note that the observation distance was two meters and that ocular expression was not isolated from facial expression; the subjects' faces were uncovered. (To correct this 'negligence' they suggest a replication of the experiment with a realistic model having movable calibrated eyes, with a set of photographs, or with schematic drawings.) Furthermore, the distance of two meters is too close to observe both eyes simultaneously yet too far to see the pupil in full detail. Finally, for the fine print on an acuity chart, they refer to the Snellen test, which is usually applied for a five, rather than a two, meter standardized observation distance.

M. G. Cline (1967: 41-50) states that among the various possible gaze directions, a gaze into our eyes is judged with the greatest certainty. Two German researchers, Krueger and Hueckstedt (1969) replicated this research under modified conditions and concluded that of the seven different parts of the face the eye's fixing is observed with the highest probability of accuracy. At a distance of 0.8 meters we observe a glance with a probable accuracy between 20 and 50 percent — with high individual variations — while at two meters the probability of guessing accurately is not higher than 10 percent, a rate lower than that of a random occurrence (14 percent). We can see how findings obtained without regard to distance or without careful consideration of it are irrelevant for theoretical conclusions and useless for practical application.

J. H. Ellring of the Max Planck Institute (1970) also replicated this research under further modified conditions. He notes that when the distance increases from 0.8 to 2.0 m. (1970: 605), accuracy in determining the attention and the direction of the gaze decreases. But Ellring does not find any privileged prehension for the gazing eye (cf. Cline). Ellring's conclusion must be viewed with reservations because of imperfections in his methods. Indeed, if the nonocular part of the face is not covered, the observer has many cues by which to guess gaze direction from the facial expression (1970: 605).

In summary, to optimalize the information input (Ellring) from the visual point of view, the observer — at a distance of ca. 0.5 m. and in a fixed position — must look at the partner's pupil opening and at the expression of the skin surface, which he can see clearly. At ca. 1.2 m., by shifting from one eye to the other, he can observe both of the partner's eyes and the direction of his gaze. At this range, facial expressions can also be seen clearly. At ca. 3.0 m., the distance used by Argyle (1967: 7) in his experiments, the observer can see both eyes simultaneously, though without their 'intensive details' (pupil, iris, and muscle movements). He can also see gestural expressions. These are the qualitative modifiers of the visual communication network and constitute its significant intervals.

Argyle (1967) studied the arousal effect of visual attention. To isolate purely ocular expression, he covered the partners with masks. R. M. Cross (in Hutt and Hutt 1970) used another device: he drew eyes with different pupil openings and studied the ocular and periocular (brow-movement response, 1970: 142) effects of this isolated expression in the simulated eyes. It seems that the mimicry of predatory animals, such as the butterfly, has guided his approach. The interpretation of results obtained in this way is very tenuous (Gibson and Pick 1963, etc.), namely that the painted gaze will appear to be staring excessively.

Indeed, the gaze — the attention arousal expressed by the pupil opening and the capture of the other's look — can create a feedback loop through the homologous nature of the oculo-ocular relation and thereby accentuate its effects. This is one of the most interesting and essential qualities of the oculo-ocular communication structure. Direction and 'amplitude' (McGuigan and Pavek 1972: 238) in relation to the partners' mutual position are the essential components of this phenomenon. Within the 'ring of the visual battle', that is, at a distance inside 3.5 m., any participant can 'lock' the exchange (informative or emotive) by gaze aversion or by sensory cutoff in order to forestall an over-arousal.

If the distance itself — and so the zone and the visual network value — is a variable in the visual information-collecting strategy, we can regulate the received stimulus quantity by an optimal combination of distance and gazing time. Argyle and Dean (1965) established an approach-avoidance equilibrium (Argyle 1967: 4) which would be regulated at a more abstract level of intimacy; this concept was not formulated, however, in behavioral terms operative in experiments (cf. also Castell 1970: 90). We consider that the concept of equilibrium can also be applied at the level of visual stimulus input without introducing concepts beyond empirical control.

Perhaps, by using Argyle's (1967) method of screening the expression channels (ocular and other) under experimental conditions and in a systematic manner, we can isolate specific effects of the different components of the visual communication structure itself (e.g., reciprocity as synchronous symmetry) and so, in a later stage of research, specify the effects of visual communication on the synchronization of polysensory communication (including oral). By beginning at a more elementary level and developing each stage fully, we can obtain less disputable results.

Taking mutual distance as a parameter and supposing a face-to-face position of perfect homologous reciprocity between two partners as defined before, we can study both the specific effects of ocular, facial, and corporal expression (including gestures) and the combined effects. We can introduce dark glasses, masks, and capes, or we can use a one-way glass. These are artifacts interposed between the partners' bodies. Generally speaking, the first artifact of purely corporal expression appears on the surface of the skin itself, the tattoo. It is followed by clothing, which filters our skin surface expressions, and finally by architectural filters which serve as barriers in the polysensory communication network. For example, a glass wall filters out the acoustical components of the communication stream (Argyle 1967: 7, 12). From the first part, recall that use of artifacts in the laboratory extends the study of face-to-face communication in pure sociology to ecosociology, where physical environment modifies the operation of pure social forces (Drever 1968: 275).

Even if we use completely interchangeable subjects as partners (same sex, age, etc.) and eliminate all inconceivable cases, we must study 15 cases in order to have a systematically built series of experiments. These would include covering or uncovering the eyes, faces, and bodies of both — or of one — of the partners.

Groupal (3 + n)

Group visual communication is produced when more than one person is included at least in the participant's field of peripheral vision and the subject shifts from one to another successively by means of the previously enumerated movements which can influence the fixation line. In the dyadic situation, the partners have only two choices: they can either gaze into each other's eyes or not, or they can shift their fixation line from one body part to another. In groups the shifting is mainly interpersonal. In the dyad, if the subject can also choose his relative position (viz., his position is not sessile), the principal questions were: which details of the other's visible expression (ocular, facial, etc.) will be seen the best? And which polysensory composition of communication is most efficient in a given network position? (For example, nearer than 0.5 m. the tactile component is predominant.) In the group case, distance and position in general determine whether the gaze is concentrated or diffused. While an increase in distance raises the number of simultaneously visible persons, details of sensory input decrease. Beyond 7 m. the public distance begins, and others become 'ants', more and more unrecognizable. The posture and the group's ballet, which changes the network positions themselves, become the most important expression. The number of identifiable participants included within one's fixation line determines whether social formation is micro- or macro-sociological in size.

Micro

In research conducted on various types of groups (informal, working, playing, shopping) in two cities in Oregon, James (1951) found that 71 percent are dyadic, 21 percent triadic, and 6 percent quadruple. Only 2 percent are composed of more than four persons. If a group starts with more than four, the tendency is to subdivide into dyads, triads, and groups of four (1951: 474-477). Stenzor (1950) stated that if round-table configurations dominate communication exchange, response comes from the person whose visual field coincides with the median plane of the last speaker. This statement concerns oral communication, but it is the visual communication network which explains the phenomenon.

We know that communication structures are inserted in the zone system of the communication network. In microformations, the presence of four to five persons, where each sees three to four, forms a circle three meters in diameter; the reception of partners' visible expression, therefore, is not fundamentally different from the dyad. But because of the differences in mutual angular position, the homologous oculo-ocular circuit cannot be maintained simultaneously among the partners. In the dyad a simple relative elevation of one's position determined by the base line produces a privileged communication network position. A group has many relationships, and therefore a relativity of relationships themselves. In terms of graphs,

104   Social spacing as a sociological theme of architecture

round-table arrangements with any number of seats and square-table ones with four seats have interchangeable positions. Other arrangements show some positions to be privileged as a result of better visual control. Figurative expressions like 'superior' and 'central' figures refer to privileged physical positions, but from the angle of the visual communication network, these positions are not privileged in the same way. The Figure 2.5 presents cases (1, 2, and 3) with identical umbilical densities (Ankerl 1974: 586) but different visual communication networks.

Macro (5 + n)

To make our presentation more concise we have discussed problems of visual communication in connection with the number of network participants (dyad, micro, macro), although the directly relevant aspect in determining the visual communication network is the participants' mutual position. Insofar as the face-to-face group involves in its definition a continuous visual network among all participants, either through peripheral vision or through successive glances without any displacement, social formations of different sizes imply different densities or at least new peak densities. For example, a large assembly is impractical without multiple rows, even in a circular arrangement. People on the outmost circle are more than six meters from the central figure, and each can include four or five people, their posture and movement patterns (see case I in Figure 2.3), in his clear vision. If the central figure

1.

Circular network
without central figure.

2.

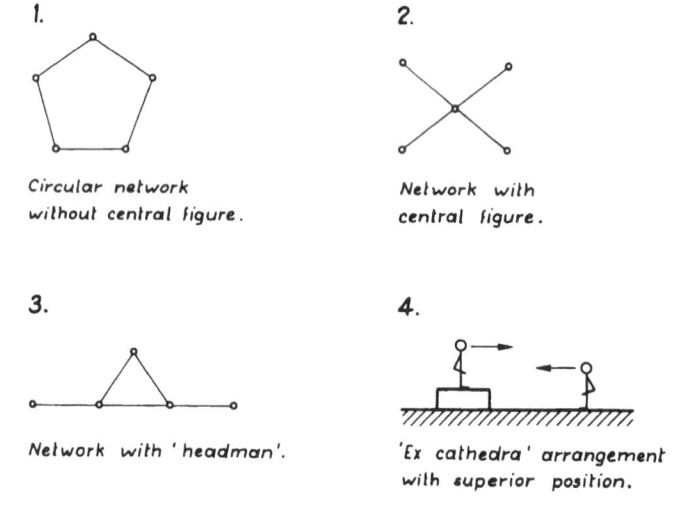

Network with
central figure.

3.

Network with 'headman'.

4.

'Ex cathedra' arrangement
with superior position.

Figure 2.5. *Network and visual control.*

has a sharp vision of four to five people, then the crowd sees him and a dozen people beyond him clearly.

In Figure 2.5.3 the 'leader' has alone simultaneous vision of the others. If he has an elevated position (shown in Figure 2.5.4), his visual control is further facilitated. (Indeed, more visual control is concentrated in the leader when he is in an elevated and in-front position than when he is merely in a central one.)

We have summarized essential aspects of the visual communication network and structure. Optical space by its shape — cross-sections (e.g., podiums) and ground plan (e.g., convex-concave) creating possible visibility gaps — and by its capacity (which relates participants' numbers to density) prefigures the prevailing visual communication network and thus the communication flow itself.

6

Audible Communication

Audition is an extensive, complex sensory modality. Audible communication can be broken down into three phases: production, transmission, and reception of sound. An analysis of reception proceeds from the physical to the perceptual level. Sound emission encompasses several types of noise (handclapping), orally articulated sound (speech), and recitals with prosodic features (used in a restricted sense as sound formed below the glottis). Finally, transmission is affected by reverberation or its absence.

To analyze the auditory communication channel, audibility data are considered in terms of the receiver's spatial position in relation to the communicator. The auditory component of the face-to-face communication network is defined in terms of audibility gradients, which will be limited in this study to sounds produced by human beings. Those aspects of message transmission affected by architectural ambience (by multisensory space in general and acoustical space in particular) that can also be apprehended in external terms (i.e., the substratum of face-to-face communication) will be considered.

In this part, face-to-face communication is examined in the context of pure sociology, where transmission is yet unaffected by the physical surroundings (viz., the architectural envelope). The space is assumed to be anechoic — i.e., a free acoustic field or dead space without reverberation, where sound travels directly from communicator to receiver.

The architectural space within the envelope will be treated later as live acoustical space, where indirect sound affects face-to-face communication; this reverberation also makes the acoustical space with its 'longitudinal depth', etc. (Fitch 1972: 131), perceptible.

Although the whole surface of the human body is marginally sensitive to acoustical vibration, it is the ears — more precisely the auricular canals — which record these vibrations. Humans are binaural, with laterally situated organs. In a static state, the organ positioning permits localization of the sound transmitter. While the efficiency of the auditory field is not uniform in every direction, there is (unlike vision) no direction in which hearing is blocked. The auditory field even extends within the human body, as when we hear our stomachs rumble. Given the permanent alertness of the ears (Simmel 1906: 653), internal noises can form an auditory curtain to isolate people from external stimuli in the social and physical environment. Otherwise, people would respond day and night to every sound of some intensity originating within a defined area. Unlike visible communication, audible communication requires an expenditure of energy by the communicator. People can therefore listen to themselves and establish an oral-aural, autologous 'short circuit', shown in Figure 2.6 (e.g., singing in the shower). In this respect, muteness and deafness are less separable sensory deprivations than the loss of vision and look (expression) (Bodenheimer 1967: 262).

Necessary for visible communication is an external stimulus (viz., source of light) but not a common physical medium. In audible communication air must be shared because a sonor emission is *grosso modo* manipulation of an air column. In visible communication, eye contact establishes nearly simultaneous reciprocity, a homologous circuit; i.e., we *see* the eyes which see us, express emotion, and react to us. This is not the case in audible communication, where one 'lends an ear'. (See Figure 2.1.) Partners can take mutual positions — X on the right-hand side of Z, and Z on the left-hand side of X — most suitable for conversation (Sommer 1974: 62); but if they speak simultaneously, confusion will occur instead of a homologous circuit. Chattering could be viewed as a hopeless attempt to transpose the homologous circuit from visible to audible communication, despite the obvious difference between the two channels.

'Short-circuit' in audible communication.

Acoustical space impression.

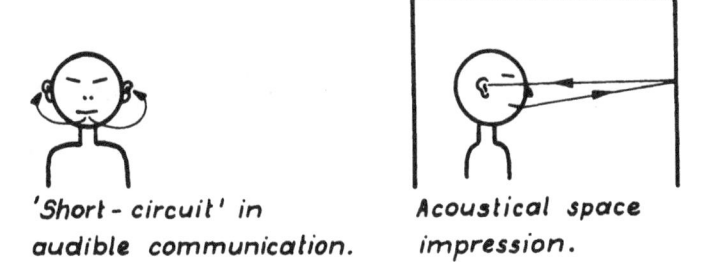

Figure 2.6. *Auditory autolog 'short-circuit'. (Bodenheimer.)*

AUDITORY SENSITIVITY

The audible message, as a sequence of sounds (like all undulatory phenomena), has the two characteristics of frequency and amplitude. These characteristics, together with the determining direction of sound emission, can combine in complex, superimposed arrangements.

(1) The frequency of sound gives the impression of pitch — the horizontal dimension of a graphic representation of sound called wavelength. Ultrasound travels in supersonic waves as high-pitched sound frequencies too high for human hearing. Conversely, infrasound travels in long waves of pitch too low to be heard. Depending on the parameters of individual and situational variables (e.g., training or familiarity with the sound), humans can percieve sound over a dozen octaves, from low-pitched frequencies of 16-20 per second to high-pitched ones of 30,000 per second. If any comparison is possible, the auditory range of human sensitivity is greater than the visual.

(2) The amplitude or volume gives the impression of intensity. It is the ordinate on our graph, indicating energy output in pressure per m^2, measured in decibels. The minimal amplitude constitutes the threshold of audibility, but there is no upper limit, at least in terms of hearing. Instead, there is a point of intensity beyond which sound causes pain, somewhere beyond 130 decibels. Moreover, these points to some extent vary with the pitch; with low- and high-pitched sounds, this threshold is higher. Discotheques which thus far have enjoyed immunity from environmentalists, are known for their projection of these sounds, which often prove injurious to human ears.

Audible human communication does not use the full range of perceptible or agreeable sounds (see Figure 2.7). Considering the fundamentally sequential nature of audible communication, it is sufficient to vary the duration of perceptible sounds with periods of silence or imperceptible sounds to create a structure transmitting a message, even music, without changing either intensity or pitch, e.g., Morse code (Tavolga 1974: 66). The composer Ligeti was correct in saying that music is composed of sound and silence.

A simple sound varied in frequency and amplitude would also be a message-bearing audible communication. Disregarded here are the longitudinal dimension (Fitch 1972: 131) causing deepness by reverberation and superimposition (resulting when the duration of auditory sensation lingers beyond the next sound excitation. Outside the scope of an individual transmitter, sounds of different pitch could be emitted simultaneously by several people (e.g., singing a round), accompanied by instrumental music or handclapping. This could occur in a street mob as pandemonium breaks out; it could be structured by an orchestral score imposing the regularities of meter, rhythm, and tempo. The relative intensity maintained through this complex structuring determines timbre, which allows differentiation of instruments. By this structuring, sound becomes music.

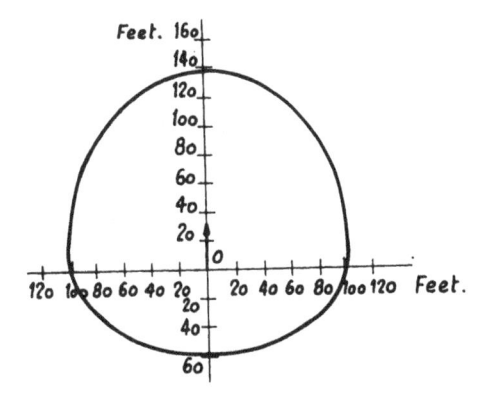

The contour curve shows the limit of distinct audibility of normal speech as a function of distance and direction. The speaker is at 0 and faces in the direction of the arrow. The space is without air motion.

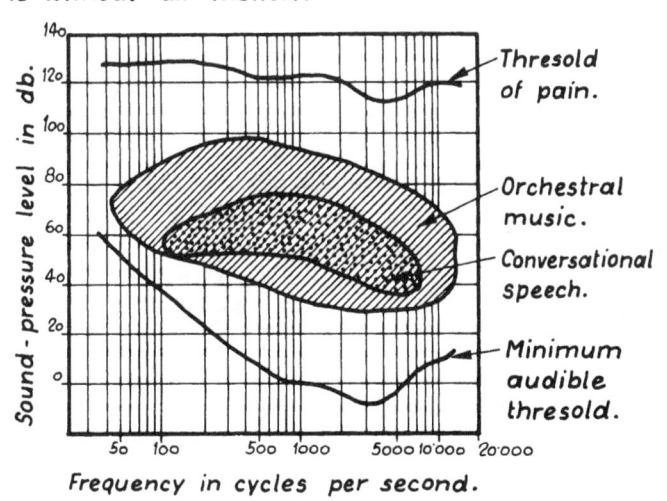

Figure 2.7. *Human sound emission and their audibility.*

AUDIBLE EXPRESSION

Always considering the free acoustical field without reverberation, a first cue in qualifying the audible value of a face-to-face communication network is the capability of localization of the sound transmitter. From this viewpoint,

110 *Social spacing as a sociological theme of architecture*

the auditory field is nearly spherical. Experiments show that sound emission is localized somewhat better in the horizontal direction than in the vertical (Knudsen and Harris 1950: 184). The auditory field deviates from its sphere if the ability to discriminate sound expression is considered. Comprehension increases when the speaker is directly in front of the listener (see Knudsen and Harris 1950: 73 and Figure 2.7). But the interpretation of this phenomenon as proof for the deformation of the spherical auditory field is questionable because of lipreading. The truly auditory component of the face-to-face communication network involves only this ability, which is also present in the dark. The practical complementarity of different sensory modalities again underlines the correctness of the opinion that zones characterizing the face-to-face communication network could be established only on the polysensory level.

Human Sound Emission: the Arbitrary Reduction of the Audibility Problem to the Audibility of Verbal Expression

To qualify relative positions from the viewpoint of the auditory component of the face-to-face communication network, the audibility of human sounds must be compared. At what distance can a human cry be heard? At what distance can a standard voice be recognized? Could all phonetic features be discerned? ('Listening versus hearing': Miller 1956.) What is the optimum distance for reception of specific types of audible expression?

New developments as well as metaphysical remnants generated bias and obstructed research in audible communication. On the one hand, linguistics has recently made prodigious advances; on the other hand, we inherited the scholastic perspective of isolating the human race among the species as an absolutely superior rational animal. Therefore speech becomes the exclusive focus of research in audible communication. First, language had been reduced to the spoken word (neglecting even pictographic representations). Furthermore, linguistic articulation of communication allowed continued application of the introspective approach by interpreting intentional cognitive messages. Nonverbal expressions are often unintended spontaneous outbursts not specific enough for mankind and therefore unimportant (cf. Trager). Thus nonverbal aspects are frequently reduced to the roles of lie detectors (van Koolwijk and Wieken-Mayser 1974: 120), and duration of silence considered only 'negatively as lack of fluency in the speaking' (Mahl 1956: 390; Crystal and Quirk 1964). *A priori* acceptance of these postulates can obstruct research in perspectives important for the field of audible, face-to-face communication.

The generic classification of audible human expression distinguishes oral and nonoral. In oral communication are distinguished vocal sound involving vibration of vocal cords (vowels) and voiceless sound (consonants). According to Trager, vocal sound qualifies the emotional content of oral expression — any paralinguistic features which are neither lexical units nor intonation nor pitch and are not encompassed by linguistics (whispering, breathing, crying, whining, yelling, singing) (Trager 1958: 1-12).

Under the nonoral rubric of audible human communication are, e.g., handclapping and the old Chinese shuffling. All these noises are systematically eliminated from the professional recording of audible communication. This classification followed the source of its origin. All others follow the intention or spontaneity of expression.

The spontaneous could be naso-oral (Trager). A cry is expiratory or inspiratory, sobbing respiratory, laughing expiratory, and sighing or groaning inspiratory. Nonrhinal phenomena include heartbeats and colic wind. All these physiological events could be symptoms of emotional states by virtue of being expressive.

Classification following degree of intention can be more arbitrary than that of the source of expression. Wiener says that the traditional dichotomy between the conscious and unconscious 'is a construct invoked to account for kinds of non-consensual behavior'. A dual-agent model is implied here: 'a consensual response does not occur for particular classes of events (e.g., sex, aggression, adequacy) but some other indicator response does occur which would occur only if the event were, in fact, experienced' (Wiener and Mehrabian 1968: 180). Intention must be viewed not as introspection of an individual mind, but as a communication link in a consensual sense; nevertheless, it could be arbitrary to attribute this intention as being common to communicator and receiver (cf. meaning).

At this point it is only important to know what expression could be intentional, because this fact introduces a variable in the determination of the face-to-face communication network. The communicator can raise or lower his voice, and without transforming his network position, he can make his communication flow (e.g., in a group situation) more or less exclusive by whispering.

The code system of language has a double articulation (Martinet). One is related to a lexicon and another to the syntactic role which specifies how morphemes must be organized in sentences. The most formal application of this role is found not in the original form of expression (oral) but in its transcription (written).

The other level is the phonetic. For a spoken language to exist it must have phonemic universals (Chao 1968: 53; Jacobson about infant language, quoted by Teuber in Dubois et al. 1971: 489). This articulation integrates verbal communication with the oral. Musical aspects also appear in recital of poems (Guiraud 1971: 40, 59; Crystal and Quirk 1964; Wintermantel 1973). Intonation, pitch, and onomatopoeia are considered here, rather than denotative sentence formation, as well as affective, imperative, vocative, and interjectory aspects of communication — whistling, hissing, booing, singing, yodeling (the 'face-to-face long-distance call') (Busnel et al. 1962). On the level of the perceptible significant (de Saussure), all oral expressions become commeasurable, and architectural (especially acoustical) space exerts the greatest influence on audible face-to-face communication. Thus it is considered here only the prosodic level of face-to-face oral communication which considers quantity of sound as function of power (intensity) and number of vibrations (frequency) and complex composition in a given time interval. Included in this category are all metrical phenomena.

NETWORK POSITION VALUES AND THE AUDIBLE COMPONENT OF THE COMMUNICATION STRUCTURE

Because the field of audibility is nearly spherical, distance (the radius) alone varies the position value of an auditory component in a face-to-face communication network. But oral (human) expression is strongly oriented. For this reason (especially if the distance between the interlocutors is relatively limited), if we consider the oral communication in the framework of pure sociology (viz., in dead or 'limitless' space) where only direct sound is received, the angle of the communicator relative to the receiver is a valid position characterizer. The angle beta has importance only if the distance between interlocutors A and B is very short. If angle alpha is not indicated, it is 0 and the communicator himself turns to the addressee. The auditory communication circuit cannot be homologous, even if alpha = 0 = beta. The position of the two interlocutors is symmetrical if alpha equals beta. The mutual position where alpha equals zero and beta equals 90° is optimal for one-sided listening. If the distance is not more than 20-30 cm. (Guiraud 1971: 14-15), the spontaneous sounds of the body (heartbeats, groaning) are predominant (cf. the film *Lipstick*). Within the distance of 20 cm., whispering is nearly inaudible if alpha ≠ 0 and beta = 90° (see Figure 2.1). Even at a distance of 30 cm., whispering has rather the function of muffling involuntary body sounds than of communicating. If the communicator raises his voice, he can easily reach the threshold of feeling.

In oral communication the face-to-face communication network distinguishes two spatial intervals. One, 0.3-1.5 m., for convenience called 'colloquial', ensures good reception and discrimination of phonetic units of a normal voice. In a colloquial situation both conversationalists have a good opportunity to respond by turning the head for a 'speaking situation' (D. Hymes). If third persons are also present and the speaker wishes to exclude one, he can lower his voice and diminish the volume.

Beyond 1.5 m., no possibility of exclusive personal communication can exist any more. The distance of 1.5-4.0 m. is optimal for small-group discussions.

Beyond 3.6 m., the speaker can address the audience publicly, depending on his voice intonation; beyond 6.0 m., public speaking is unavoidable and the style becomes formal by virtue of a more strict observance of grammatical rules. Without technical means like the public address system, verbal communication beyond 30 meters is increasingly replaced by whistles, yodels, and bird calls. These data relevant to the audible component of the face-to-face communication network will be used for the construction of zones of the network on the polysensory level.

7

Osmatic Communication

> Even the most learned man has to let his nose decide for him in matters of love.
>
> Groddeck

> Odors . . . saucy and sometimes tiring in brunettes and black-haired women, sharp and fierce in redheads, it is heavy and pervasive in blondes like 'nose' of some flowery wines: you could almost say that it fits exactly with their manner of using the lips in kissing: firmer and more possessive in brunettes, more personal in blondes.
>
> J. K. Huysmans, *Croquis Parisiens*

Although from the evolutionary viewpoint the olfactory link between living beings and their biosphere is primeval (*animaux osmatiques,* Paul Guillaume) and on the sociological level it is the most universal signal (Sire 1960: 170 ff.) of affection and sexual intercourse, its science, osmics or olfactology, did not develop before about 1910. At that time, Heyninx introduced 'olfactics' by analogy to optics and acoustics, although it is related not to physics but to chemistry.

Identification of odorous substances had originally been made by the human olfactory sense. Zwaardemaker, a contemporary of Heyninx, developed olfactometry, but did not succeed in establishing a standardized odor nomenclature objectively and unequivocally determined by chemical composition, as had been done in colorimetry (cf. odorivectors of Heyninx). This field is now being explored, and development can be expected on a fundamental level. Recent application of new techniques like gas chromatography, mass spectrometry, and the electroantennogram as special neurophysiological techniques contribute to the understanding of the chemoreceptors too (C. Apt). The first authoritative book about the subject, *Animal Communication by Pheromones* (Shorey 1976), appeared only recently and contained over 700 references in the bibliography. This book replaced as a standard work the less satisfactory *Pheromones* (Birch 1974). This state of basic research in the field made it difficult to explore the osmatic component of the face-to-face communication network. Integration of osmatic communication among human beings in the framework of objective sociology required elimination of cultural bias. The tradition of Victorian humanism isolated the human race in a homocentric ivory tower, ignoring what humans have in common with other living beings, especially other animals (optic animal vs. osmatic one). Georg Simmel identifies the common attitude toward this 'inferior organ' for which, due to the element of spontaneity, the human being is not responsible.

OLFACTORY SENSIVITITY

Located on the symmetrical axis of the face are two olfactory organs, a collection of yellowish mucous receptors less than 1.5 square centimeters in area. Their reaction time is relatively long (0.5 second) and the duration of sensation short. The olfactory field is composed of two biconical forms whose apex is the pair of nostrils, extended outside the body and inside the oral cavity. Thus alimentary odors are perceived in the mouth (e.g., wine 'bouquet'). Indeed, olfactory and sapid sensations are allied; both are chemoreceptors. Not by chance has arisen the cliche, *odeur-saveur d'avoine*. The substance to be tasted must be diluted in liquid, the substance to be sniffed must be diluted in gas, and both must arrive at certain mean speeds (cf. osmophoric diffusion and osmatic communication, both discussed apropos of the architectural envelope). Hence the sense of smell is quasi-grafted on the human respiratory ducts.

Osmi-esthesiometry measures odor recognition capacity relative to familiar odors but not by decomposition into basic ones. It establishes also the capacity to differentiate intensities of the same odor as a function of the concentration of odorivector molecules in the gaseous dilution. If human thresholds are compared to those of other animals phylogenetically less developed (e.g., butterflies), it is found that humans are less sensitive; even domesticated animals like dogs and rabbits have more developed rhinocephale. Only if human olfactory sensibility is compared with taste sensibility does the olfactory appear relatively sensitive. Research has found man, under normal conditions, able to differentiate a 5 percent variation in concentration of odorous substances; inability to register fine differences in intensity is

116 *Social spacing as a sociological theme of architecture*

often a result of fluctuation in olfactory stimulus, 'noise at the nose' (Cain 1977: 796-98). Volatility is an important parameter of sensibility. Bees and butterflies can receive messages over distances of more than one kilometer (Ankerl & Pereboom 1974); but for humans, three meters seems the limit. If olfactory reception is not continuous, but intermittent (Sury 1967: 88), odor probably penetrates only momentarily. On the other hand, like audition, the sense is alert day and night. Like the visual field, the olfactory is directed; acceleration of the arrival of odoriferous molecules will raise their concentration, therefore strong inhalation will increase the sensation.

In sum, this section compares human olfaction to other sensory channels and, in an ethological context, to the olfaction of other animals. Reception is rapid because olfaction is directly received by the central nervous system. In some animals (mice), certain odors go through a neurohumoral mechanism; for this reason, the effect is delayed by one or two days (Parkes and Bruce 1961: 1,054). Animals (dogs) sometimes have detailed and specific olfactory souvenirs stored in their long-term memories. This will prove crucial in the discussion of responding pheromonal messages. Wide variation in olfactory sensitivity occurs, depending on the individual and his physiological state. The olfactory sense is probably dependent on endocrine hormone production (Comfort 1971: 412-413). Mitchell and Gregson (1971) describe between-subject variation and lack of within-subject constancy of olfactory intensity scaling. J. LeMagnen (1952) asserts that females have a more sensitive olfactory sense, especially for boar, which derives from musk of urine, exaltolide, and perhaps civetone. This higher female sensitivity perceives not only the chemical message of males (perhaps sexually relevant) but also of other females. In the Biannual Mediterranean Symposia on Olfaction (especially the IVth in 1965 and the Vth in 1967), many hypotheses more or less substantiated by experiments related the dependence of this female sensitivity on menstrual cycle and its duration (cf. Koelega and Koester 1974). The age of sexual maturation (puberty, menopause) and the state of pregnancy (viz., nonmenstruation) show their impact on this sense. Not surprisingly, olfactory communication is that most closely related to sexual intercourse.

KINDS OF ODOR EMISSION RELEVANT TO
OSMATIC COMMUNICATION

Before determining spatial dimensions involved in variation of the osmatic component of the face-to-face communication network, olfactory events encompassed by osmatic communication must be identified.

Many events in the biosphere are accompanied by volatile, odoriferous 'secretions'; in particular, some chemical reactions combine substances from two partners during social intercourse.

Perceptible fragrances may be artificial biosynthetic products from the botanical and zoological worlds. Much research results from the study of flower and insect odor (Kullenberg and Bergström 1975: 59). In a sociology of animals, study of osmatic communication could be considered an investigation of intraspecies relationships (e.g., between dogs) and interspecies relationships (e.g., between cats and dogs). The study of how human beings react to odors of other animal species might be called xeno- or *allo*sociology.

While the subject of this study is osmatic communication among humans, other intraspecies scent communication will be referred to ethologically in constructing sociological hypotheses (homology reasoning and analogical comparison: von Cranach 1977).

While some activities (especially intercourse) are accompanied by processes involving chemical combination (e.g., fecundation), the temptation to group these as 'chemical communication' must be resisted. Osmatic communication must be restricted in scope. Studies in osmatic communication are concerned only with those human chemical processes resulting in emission of odorous substances which characterize the individual (emitter) or signal his mometary internal (biological, emotional) state, and which can be perceived as such by others. The response of others, stimulated by the initial odor emission, reveals the communicative nature of the events. This response can also be a spontaneous odor, can use different sensory channels, and can even be delayed; therefore this is osmatic rather than chemical communication. Sociologists find particularly interesting the odor stimulus which derives not from either partner alone but rather from the mixing of the two (e.g., olfactory perception of intercourse).

Generally speaking, endocrine processes relating internal physiological processes are signalled by exocrine processes (external secretions) producing olfactory stimuli. Because biological processes are continuous, emissions are, too – although they are more pronounced during the active part of the day. These factories of human odor are seldom under our control (e.g., expelling wind). While olfactory receptors are alert 24 hours each day, no odor can be emitted as a 'blocking' curtain (as snoring is in the case of audition) to create an autologous auditory circuit. Osmatic communication is so spontaneous that one is often unaware of it – both during the emission and afterwards. Thus Comfort (1971: 412) calls osmatic communication a 'subliminal language'.

Odor emissions can be classified by source location, chemical processes, or physiological mechanisms (e.g., metabolism, respiration) placing them in the biological context of self- and race preservation (procreation).

Because the face-to-face communication network is related to spatial position and osmatic communication involves physical proximity, the anatomical regions of osmatic communication will be examined first.

Odor emissions come from body openings, of which the most evenly distributed are the pores of the skin. However, not all parts of the skin give odorous emissions of equal intensity. Another factory of human scent is hair. We smell perspiration on the head, in the axilla, in the groin, and similarly on other coated surfaces like the soles of the feet. Insofar as hair seems associated with particular apocrine glands, it redistributes and perhaps recomposes odors. Thus hair color is often associated by the observer with a specific odor. Apocrine sweat and smegma are natural body odors resulting from bacterial activity on the surface of the skin.

Other scent-liberating openings are the mouth, the source of odors from exhalation and the stomach, and the 'strange grouping' of the multipurpose genitalia with their procreative, sexual, and urinary discharge functions, and the anus for the elimination of solid and gaseous wastes. This 'evil' region of heterogeneous functions flustered Victorian prudes and stimulated Freud's imagination (the means of race preservation and end of self-preservation).

On a practical basis, Comfort (1971: 412) distinguishes three categories:

(1) Odor-diffusion tufts.
(2) Breath-axilla complex.
(3) Anal-genital region.

Osmatic messages permit recognition of others as individuals or as members of a social category, or signal a certain emotional state.

A number of hypotheses, validated to some extent, discuss identification of osmatic messages. Once emitted, odor varies in intensity and perceptibility. Some claim that even identical twins have individual odors. Trained police dogs can recognize the odor of an individual through clothing, as can 'trained sensorily deprived individuals'; but this does not mean that the average human has this ability.

Another more ambitious hypothesis postulates that people can recognize various social categories. These hypotheses cannot always be reduced to popular claims, such as the fragrance of blondes. There is experimental evidence that male rhesus monkeys react to the odor of human vaginal secretions containing volatile fatty acids. Identification is related not only to genital secretions. According to some researchers, the originally odorless secretions of male genitals and female pubic and areola regions undergo transformation in the sheltering foreskin where genital secretion alters the musk odor of urine and menstruation. H. H. Shorey quotes an experiment demonstrating that volatile aliphatic acid, a sexual attractant, is higher in young women in the late follicular phase of menstruation than in the luteal phase, where it progressively declines.

Of all states of emotion, the sexual is that most characterized by pheromonal emission. This term is reserved by some authors for genital odors denoting sex and estrous conditions, and by others to include any stimulating odorous substance. As early as 1892, Krafft-Ebing noted that both genitalia and the nose contain erectile tissue which can become rigid after stimulation, thus revealing emotion; he recognized olfaction as a secondary sexual reaction. The sexual index comes from volatile odoriferous substances. Traditionally, musk has been related to sexual arousal; but recently R. P. Michael and E. B. Kerverne reported copulins with sex appeal. Copulins are composed of six fatty acids (acetic, propionic, isobutyric, butyric, isovaleric, isocaproic) whose presence arouses spectacular sexual reactions among male rhesus monkeys. Some copulins are secreted by the human vagina.

Comfort also noted the interesting phenomenon of menstrual synchronization among female roommates; he attempted to explain this through osmatic communication. Parkes, an English researcher, attributes the lowering of menstrual age in our century to the closer contact (and hence osmatic communication) of young girls with men outside their households.

NETWORK POSITION VALUES AND THE OSMATIC COMPONENT OF THE COMMUNICATION STRUCTURE

The human body contains a number of emission sites. On the other hand, olfaction commences at a 'negative distance' from the body, in the oral cavity. To determine network position relevant to osmatic communication, the distance between the source of odor and its receptors as well as all angles enclosed by the common axis of emitter and receiver must be considered.

To smell a clean body, a distance of 0.5 m. or less is necessary. Because this odor is distributed over the whole body, the only significant angles to be considered are those which orient and direct the receiver's olfactory field, not those enclosed by the common axis of the emitter's body. Within this distance, all other olfactory impressions must be included, since the approach of the source cannot weaken olfactory intensity. The composition can change, but intensity is always inversely proportional to distance.

Less than 0.7-0.8 m. from the genital region, the receiver can perceive odor; therefore parallel position cannot assure reception. The naso-anal approach of two dogs (Bodenheimer) illustrates the relative angles needed for osmatic communication using these pheromones. This mutual network position '69' is only possible for humans in a reclining position. Later it will be analyzed in the context of chemoreceptor communication channels (osmatic and sapid).

To contrast to genital odor, exhalation odor of speaking and laughing does not require any specific relative angle, as long as the emitter is no more than one meter from the receiver (Hall 1969: 159-160).

The farthest spatial interval for osmatic human communication is 1-3 m. For example, concentrated foot odors can be perceived at 2.5 m.

Because of the 'staccato' of odor broadcasting and significant individual variation, the spatial zoning imputable to the osmatic channel is less discrete than that of the visual and auditory in the face-to-face communication network.

THEMES FOR FUTURE RESEARCH AND THE AROMATIC DETOUR

The absence of basic research in this field has generally made applied work difficult. Applications to human osmatic communication have been made especially difficult because of the previously mentioned Victorian attitudes and traditions toward natural odors. What gentleman would dare to stand on the street watching the conduct of two dogs? Who seriously believed that the sweat of the working class, as opposed to that of the leisure class, was an honorable odor?

Aversion to the odor of another, especially one of a lower socioeconomic class or ethnic group, may be openly expressed. But who will admit that another's body odor ('B.O.') is appealing? A lady's fragrance is appreciated as long as it is not hers, but that of her perfume. Unlike those in other sensory fields, the manufacturers of perfume will not fabricate what people lack; they never use human substances for scents and reluctantly use animal secretions; instead, they select those most remote from humans – flowers and plants, which preclude the 'perversion' of sexual connotation. Research in human osmatic communication has consequently developed along an indirect, inferential path.

The perfume industry has regarded the entire spectrum of human odor emission from a negative viewpoint of what could be inhibited or obscured (e.g., the research on vaginal odor started with the goal of suppressing odor from vaginal infection; by stating this situation we will not make any esthetic value judgment about the desirability of such human odors, but only describe the general historical context of this research field). The whole washing ritual (and more generally one's entire *toilette*) is more an expurgation of odors than a hygienic necessity. To ensure the permanence of human odorlessness, human odor factories have been removed. Hair and foreskins (as something vestigial and unesthetic) have been cut in the Judaic tradition to keep the human processes from being smelly. On the other side, fragrant perfume was introduced into cosmetics, for which the emitter can take 'responsibility' and which are no longer spontaneous but rather cultural and found even in archaic cultures. But even with these precautions, natural odors could still reach the noses of others, entailing a new strategy – that of reodorizing after deodorizing to neutralize the effectiveness of osmatic communication by interfering with its transmission. To this end research on human odors has been negatively oriented and research on perfumes has been botanically oriented. Before Shorey's book, researchers only occasionally turned their attention to osmatic communication among humans in an ethological perspective. Given the omnipresence of the halo of perfume, pure, not environmental, sociology cannot study natural osmatic communication in a natural setting; therefore comparative ethiological data become even more important.

8

Haptic Communication

Je suis un ours mal léché.

Georges Sarton

All sense organs develop from the skin.

Von Békéssey, 1974

There is not contract without contact.

American Proverb

Haptics involves a conglomeration of somatic sensibilities capable of registering specific permanent and transitory bodily characteristics of another individual. If a message cannot be received in this way, it is intangible and falls outside haptic communication. Concerning the face-to-face communication network, any surface expression not affecting mechano- and thermo-receptors will not be transmitted by haptic channels. For example, a gesture could be merely visible, or else haptic.

HAPTIC SENSITIVITY

Given the complex nature of this sense organ, its definition might be approached by elimination: any message which can be received by an anosmic, deaf, and blind individual must be communicated haptically. Another approach is spatial. No message can be transmitted haptically unless the communicators are at some point closer than 1.2 meters. Haptics suggests the notion of a 'proximoceptor'. Touch, the most personal experience, is also the most exclusive. No given point on our bodies can be touched simultaneously by more than one person. The immediacy of touch constitutes the final proof of being (M. Balint). The apostle Thomas had to touch the stigmata to convince himself of Christ's resurrection. Touching is also the symbol of doubt. The first and absolutely exclusive face-to-face communication occurs between mother and fetus, where the uterus as haptic space is itself the means of haptic communication by its contraction and expansion.

While sapid sensations presuppose penetration of the receiver's body, haptic sensations are primarily received by the body's cutaneous surface (epidermis and dermis), with its three types of nerve endings, and secondarily through joints (including ligaments), muscles (including tendons), and periosteum. All can receive tactile messages (including pressure), thermal messages (heat and cold) on different points, and algesic messages. Distribution of nerve endings on and beneath the skin varies; consequently, spots of haptic sensibility are unequal. Moreover, receptive units of the haptic system each have their own distribution. For example, mammals have some haptic sensitivity in the hair and nails and perceive differences of pressure through tissue deformation; for this reason, the ventral surface is excitable, but not the dorsal one. Therefore, intensity varies, depending on the point where the haptic message is perceived. To limit this discussion, only the most sensitive areas (many in the extremities) will concern us, for they play important roles in haptic communication.

The tactile sensory modality is a proximoceptor and its field the close-range situation; to a limited degree, a somewhat distant relation is also possible. Blowing can be haptically perceived; in a hygrosphere, this 'stretched' haptic sensibility becomes greater. Like a cat's whiskers, the hair reaches out from the skin surface as a feeler. The tactile mode perceives tickling (simple contact), vibration (250-3,000 per second: trembling and palpitation), pressure (compression, quasi-penetration), and prehension. Passive touching requires no movement to receive the haptic impression; active touching involves exploration of the surface with fingers, etc. (slowly: stroking, petting, caressing; rapidly: itching, scratching, massaging).

The mouth and hands (100-200 points of touch per square centimeter) are particularly sensitive regions. With the arms man can actively touch ('tactile scanning', J. J. Gibson) and extend the field of tactile sensibility compared to the state of repose ('brachial space'). Tactile acuity and the spatial, two-point threshold are measured by esthesiometry.

The temperature sense perceives hot and cold by means of separate thermoreceptors. Temperature is not perceived in absolute terms, but only in relation to heat loss (viz., caloric transmission). People feel only the influx and efflux of caloric energy (10-45°C.) with a low sensitivity threshold.

124 Social spacing as a sociological theme of architecture

Direction of caloric flow (endothermic, exothermic) and intensity are perceived, always tending toward temperature equalization of the skin and contacted surface. Physiological zero varies according to individuals and for every state of excitation (W. M. Masters) and every part of the body. Age and sex set parameters. Thyroid secretion influences sensations of hot and cold (hyperthyroidism, hypothyroidism). The metacarpal area of the hands has more thermal sensitivity points than the phalangic, the torso more than the arms. Genital secretionary glands have thermoreceptors without mechano-receptors (viz., tactile receptors). Thermal communication between two bodies touching in a passive situation is not a unique property of convection. Conductivity is also a parameter, which is a function of the color and composition of clothing, subcutaneous fat, and hair. To overall thermo-impression must be added nonconductive, radiant transmission, which permits communication of personal warmth 0.1-0.5 m. away. Also to be taken into account is the rate of evaporation coming from the relative humidity of the sudoriferous spots.

Various haptic impressions of the algesic mode (von Frey) are often reflected in the face: pinching, slapping, digging fingernails into the skin, and other excessive pressures are algesic. Pain is also perceived if skin touches a substance of temperature below 10° C. or above 45° C.

In haptic communication, the communicator and receiver must be in touch; after reception, the latent period between the stimulation and the sensory response is relatively short — as it always is if the process is not chemical, but mechanical or thermal. The effective reaction time is brief. Among different haptic modes, the effect of pressure is most persistent and adaptation slowest. Following is a chart comparing the three cutaneous modes:

Sensitivity	Average number of points in cm^2	Reaction time in seconds
Tactile	17-20	0.1
Thermal	20	
Algesic	170	1.0

PALPABLE EXPRESSION

In acoustic communication it was easy to separate points of emission and reception for analysis. Tactile scanning (active touching) is also an expression, but it is more appropriate to consider haptic communication in the context of dyadic exchange. Namely, though the party who takes the initiative in touching is normally identifiable, the process almost immediately incurs 'feedback'. Later the recording of subconsciously perceived mechanical expression will be discussed.

Warming Up

If someone unintentionally brushes against another (e.g., at a cocktail party), each person's temperature comes within the other's 'heat range', and communicative warmth passes from one to another. Human beings are homeothermal (commonly confused with hematothermal or warm-blooded). Homeotherms maintain a relatively constant internal (buccal, vaginal, rectal) temperature regardless of temperature changes in their environment; they must always have the ability to transmit heat to their milieu. (Designers of Dallas's First International Building (1973) heated 56 stories with electric lighting and the body heat of people inside — an energy conservation strategy superior to those using solar energy in some areas, such as Alaska and Canada.)

If human body parts of different temperatures come within 6-7 cm. of each other, heat is transmitted by radiation. (Some experiments indicate that such transmission can take place at a distance of 40-50 cm.) In touching, where transmission occurs by convection, heat equalization is even more pronounced.

Body temperature differences can be attributed to numerous causes. Bodies undergo diurnal temperature fluctuations; diurnal beings have a higher temperature in the evening than in the morning; nocturnals have a higher temperature in the morning than in the evening. However, this fact is irrelevant for thermal communication between humans, for the night porter remains a diurnal animal, despite his odd hours. Individuals differ in their physiological zero temperature; there are 'cold fish'. With aging, the human body's surface temperature has less upward variation. The cutaneous casing is important for thermal transmission, as are cavities (buccal, vaginal). To be homeotherm, the fat man with a thick subcutaneous layer must have an external temperature lower than the ordinary man. Since female cutaneous tissue insulates better than the male's, her external temperature is lower than his. Body parts do not normally have the same temperature; feet and ears are colder than the mouth and nape of the neck. If two persons of the same temperature make contact with different body parts, then heat is transmitted. Among various thermal transmissions for haptic communication, the most interesting is that occurring when temperature difference is attributable to emotional state. Indeed, difference in surface temperature derives from difference in blood supply to body parts — a physiological phenomenon (e.g., inflammation) or the result of excitement. W. M. Masters discovered that rise in abdominal skin temperature is one of the early indications of sexual excitement.

126 *Social spacing as a sociological theme of architecture*

The nature of heat exchange implies that it can escalate; the warmer being transmits heat first, and this induces the other being to generate its own heat. This communicative mechanism, like olfactory communication, was neglected because subliminal, and therefore beyond the realm of personal responsibility. For 'exclusionist' schools, man as a superior being must not share communication channels with other animals.

Tactually Perceptible Involuntary Body Expression

Even without touching, the 'radiant heat' and breathing (accent, rhythm, tempo) of another can be perceived. Also communicated is the involuntary movement of another's hair (hair-raising, often accompanied by goose bumps).

In passive contact, we perçeive the wetness of mucus, beads of perspiration, or tears. Active touch explores the elbow joint, the popliteal space, skin texture, and the rapidity of its variation (smooth skin or bumps). Qualities of skin can also reveal what part of the body is being touched, approximate age, sex. Among involuntary movements that can be felt are pulse (veins, temples, heart), respiratory rate (thoracic movement), and trembling (shivering, shuddering, quivering).

If light pressure is added to touch, musuclar tension can be felt gradually as it passes from a slack, relaxed state to a tightened and firm one, making from the skin a kind of inexpressive shell.

Intentional Kinetic Expression

Like the discussion of other sensory channels, the level on which these expressive phenomena are considered is what de Saussure calls 'significant' or signifier. Transmittable elementary segments of mechanical expression relevant to the determination of face-to-face communication network position are examined. Categories will be universal in that they depend, on the one hand, on the capacity of the mechano- and thermoreceptors and, on the other hand, on anatomical and physiological capacity used in somatic expression. This line of analytical categorization (cf. F. Deutch) is objective, while objectivity of categorization based on 'universal signification' of gestures and facial expressions is not substantiated by scientific evidence (cf. P. Ekman 1972, 1976). Among 20,000 possible facial expressions, Americans, for example, use only about 30; choice depends heavily on cultural context. For our research strategy, another reference point is Birdwhistell's search for 'kinon', the most elementary movement perceived by *any* sensory channel (though this discussion does not attempt to establish a 'body language'). Only the haptic component of the face-to-face communication network concerns us (and kinesic expression categories only insofar as they 'calibrate' the haptic network channel of the face-to-face communication network to qualify position values exclusively as a function of haptic impressions). For example, ballet can be considered haptic communication until danced not for the limelight but for the participant's haptic pleasure. The purest dance in this sense is the tango, which follows the partners' common eurythmy, even without the dictate of accompanying music.

(1) Passive touching: if active touching is prohibited, body parts of the partners touch each other by chance. The questions which arise are: how does the haptic communication channel vary, following the body part involved? Are the parts involved similar or dissimilar?

If respective parts are similar, contact could be produced on a sensitive spot with greater or fewer points of sensitivity per cm^2., and so the channel would be more or less intensive. If respective positions are symmetrical, the haptic component of the face-to-face communication network is homologous (e.g., encounter back to back). The circuit is not homologous if the relation in the given situation is not perfectly symmetrical (e.g., one partner is much taller; or the confrontation takes place between individuals of the opposite sex, which is a complementary encounter.) Here the fact that left and right sides do not have the same sensitivity will be disregarded (see Scheflen).

If engaged body parts are different, the two have not necessarily the same sensitivity; that person who is involved with the more sensitive part is more engaged in the relationship. If, for example, one's hand is entailed, this prefigures which party has more possibility of switching the relationship from passive-passive to passive-active through manipulation. Indeed, the party engaged with the more mobile body part can more easily switch to active exploration.

(2) Passive impression of active touching: active touching is viewed as expression. Albeit all body parts can theoretically engage in active exploration, the most mobile have a predisposition for that (extremities such as arms and legs and their parts — hands, fingers, feet, and toes). Because of analogous body constitutions, the active and passive roles could be interchanged on short notice; however, the mutual network position would not constitute a homologous circuit since the roles are not symmetrical. Reception of active touching depends on direction (horizontal or vertical pressure) and speed (tickling, grazing, stroking, rubbing) of the movement and sensitivity (determined by body part). In relation to respective umbilical points determining relative stations of participants' outstretched arms and hands, active touch reaches 0.6 m. Beyond this function of reaching another, arms permit clasping another or others (e.g., a whole family) — a protective action, making the haptic relation exclusive.

128   Social spacing as a sociological theme of architecture

(3) Active exploration of active touching: again it is possible to establish homologous circuits in dynamic linkage. The relative position where two individuals are in a face-to-face position with the palms of the hands touching illustrates the best homologous circuit of the haptic component of the face-to-face communication network. It is difficult to find a perfect equivalent of a hand-in-hand (manu-manual) relation in the haptic field. Absence of *al-pari* starting points characterizes embracing and kissing (oro-oral), although reversal of active-passive roles is easy at any moment.

Before discussing the dynamic of mutual arousal, it can be concluded that mutually outstretched arms and outstretched legs of football players constitute absolute limits of the touching component of the face-to-face communication network (ca. 1.2 m.). Keeping someone at arm's length just allows shaking of hands.

NETWORK POSITION VALUES AND THE HAPTIC COMPONENT
OF THE COMMUNICATION STRUCTURE

Structure of Dynamic Exchange; e.g., Sexual Gearing

Because of the proxemic nature of the haptic communication, it is more difficult to establish the value of relative positions for the haptic than for the audible component of the face-to-face communication network. Therefore, the spontaneous and measurable nature of the sexual response (erection, ejaculation) help the researcher to know at which position effective haptic communication can occur. The last stage, fecundation, involves tactile communication with penetration. Although there are different romantic performances (Scheflen) leading to this final phase, yet the stages of the process are in irreversible order. A hand clasp could have sexual connotation before intercourse, but hardly afterwards. Alternative ways may be taken, at least until the point of no return (Brecher and Brecher 1974: 26), as well as speeding up or bypassing some stages (G. Nielsen), and thus shorten the entire duration. This ascending order in the alternative sequences gives a corresponding degree of opening. Every stage determines an equivalent face-to-face communication network position. Sexual exchange is discussed in this section about haptic communication because even if the haptic can carry other messages (not the case with osmatic communication), haptic communication can alone carry the whole sexual train without visible, audible, or even olfactory signals. The research of W. H. Masters showed that the chain of action leading objectively to fecundation and subjectively to sexual resolution (Brecher and Brecher 1974: 33) is a corridor with a physiologically determined length and only the 'doors' (corresponding to particular stages) along this corridor are distributed differently according to various cultural patterns and taboos. The various stages not only are in irreversible order but also correspond to position values of the haptic components in the face-to-face communication network. Sexual exchange is closely related to haptic communication in such a way that not only its real effective form but even the autistic simulation of this exchange (masturbation) is related to it.

G. Nielsen observed American 'rutting' and noted 24 stages. Order is imposed in such a way that its inversion is considered perverse, and the deviating individual as marginal. It normally begins with a hand touch at a distance of more than one meter, after which comes 'hand-to-hand flight', concluding literally in *corps à corps*. The first hand touch is followed by intertwining each other's fingers, then clasping, caressing the back, approaching the breast, an occasional embrace, and then a longer one. The male usually has the more active role. The escalating strategy itself follows stages of haptic components of the face-to-face communication network. The touching series begins with less sensitive, less erogenic zones of the integument (hand, finger, breast, mouth), going from a brief, occasional act to a longer one with more pressure, ending with fusion of complementary body hollows – but still allowing coordinated mobility. At any stage, either party can leave before reaching the point of no return.

In spite of his unreliable method of confessions by subjects of experiments, A. C. Kinsey made the first breakthrough and recognized the necessity of experimental research (1948).

W. H. Masters and V. E. Johnson performed this experimental research in their laboratory in St. Louis. The nature of measured reactions made unobtrusive recordings impossible. The fact to be observed and placement of the instrument on the body tended to deprive the reaction of authenticity by altering quantitative and qualitative results (see Part IV). Nevertheless, this research today represents the best in-depth study of haptic communication in the closest face-to-face communication network zone (sexual intercourse). Direct clinical application of the findings is very debatable. Under observation, reaction became more conscious; the very nature of sexual exchange suggests that it is not usually under strict cognitive control, and deviation from the natural makes it deliberate but less efficient.

In the words of Masters, haptic phenomena are the effectuation of sexual exchanges. He admits the distinction of conventional stages with the reservation that they cannot be strictly delimited.

(1) Excitement by the man is tangibly manifested by erection and lengthening of a relatively small penis (Brecher and Brecher 1974: 19). This phenomenon is accompanied by various muscular and fiber contractions. In women the

130   Social spacing as a sociological theme of architecture

first reaction is moistening of the vagina, which prepares it for penetration. The clitoris is filled with sensitive nerve endings, as are the breasts. In both men and women, voluntary muscles stretch more than involuntary ones, and pulse quickens.

(2) In the plateau stage man reaches the point of no return. His testicles rise, as does the woman's clitoris. Muscular tension can reach a point such that spasmodic movements can occur throughout the entire abdominal region.

(3) Orgasm ensures rhythmic coordination of contractions. At first, intervals are 4/5 second; later the intervals become longer, but the contractions more intense. Even if the apogee of this stage is ejaculation and its accompanying movements, rhythmical contractions occur throughout the body, coordinated by embracing arms. Because of the physiologically precise programming of this exchange and its authentically spontaneous nature, erection cannot be simulated: it is a genuine sexual response. Therefore it is appropriate to look at this phenomenon as a prototype of haptic communication and as a clearly defined social interaction.

(4) Resolution. The return to repose inverts the excitement process. The penis and clitoris return to their original positions; genitalia shrink to their original dimensions somewhat more slowly. Women often perspire on their feet and palms of their hands. If orgasm was not achieved, the return process is slower. Termination of intercourse is marked by a 'refractory period' hindering repetition — shorter for women than for men.

Algesic impression by excessive expression: A particular case

Thermal or mechanical stimuli can by extreme intensity engender pain and so take part in algesic modality of haptic communication. Independent of original intention (Marquis de Sade), sexual relations are spontaneously accompanied by such a stimulus because the addressee's actual state of excitation is not immediately perceived, but only with eventual delay. In turn, the algesic stimulus is often used by adolescents in simulating sexual relations (wrestling, boxing).

The algesic sensation as a negative dimension of haptic communication is seldom discussed (e.g., as a prelude to an affront).

Components of algesic communication are identical with those of thermal and mechanical communication, except that intensity is extremely increased (e.g., threshold of feeling by sound sensation) or the stimulus works with extreme rapidity. Burning instead of warming, digging the nails into the palm instead of scratching, pinching instead of caressing, pushing instead of providing support to prevent a fall — which violate the other's proprioception. In the first interval this happens from 0.0-0.6 m. After that the 'knocking' interval occurs where sensible body parts can be reached by slapping (face), boxing (ears), or kicking (backside). When interrogated, police and gangs are inventive in this respect; their initial posture effectively communicates an algesic threat of torture; e.g., placing the knee between the legs of the sitting victim. These ancient methods do not require instruments of torture.

Genuine algesic communication occurs in battles where both sides retaliate to advances made by the other. Relevant intervals can be read into regulations of various fighting sports (boxing, catch-as-catch can, French or Greco-Roman wrestling).

Group

Multipersonal movement, the 'somatotactical category' unexplored in recent research, will be briefly discussed here (Spiegel and Machotka 1974: 115-116).

Humans are provided with two eyes, ears, and arms. They are thus binocular and biaural, but only the tactile sense allows separate and simultaneous use of arms without difficulty (Y. Hatwell in Dubois et al. 1971: 225-237). For additional contact two legs and the whole body surface are also available. So countless numbers of people can touch each other simultaneously — haptic in a fickle and promiscuous sense! The capacity of simultaneity does not require succession for multilateral contact; thus it is a channel especially suited to group communication.

To categorize haptic group contacts, two basic chemical configurations can be appropriated: the cycle and the chain are shown in Figure 2.8. These touches can be manual in a more or less loose position or brachial involving very close positions. The manual chain sets up a haptic communication flow when a message is sent in a chain reaction by squeezing the next hand in line, or simultaneously in response to a common stimulus. This can also occur in partial form: hand pressing goes not from A to Z, but exclusively between two consecutive points (e.g., from B to C) and perhaps vice-versa as confirmation. We see here the haptic communication flow inherent in a given network.

The difference between the ring and chain network arrangements is the following: in the ring, the circuit is closed and difficult to augment. Every member has a position of equal network value; positions are completely interchangeable, thus no central position exists (Bavelas, C. Flament). Transmission of a message can be confirmed, and even its return speed calculated. In the chain, the network is open-ended. In the case of a specific number of participants there are positions which are marginal for haptic communication, but because of the open-ended character of the chain, they can join one another and so complete the connection of two valences (see Figure 2.8).

132 *Social spacing as a sociological theme of architecture*

Cycle / Ring.

Chain.

A + C + E and B + D.

A + B + C.

Manu - manual series.

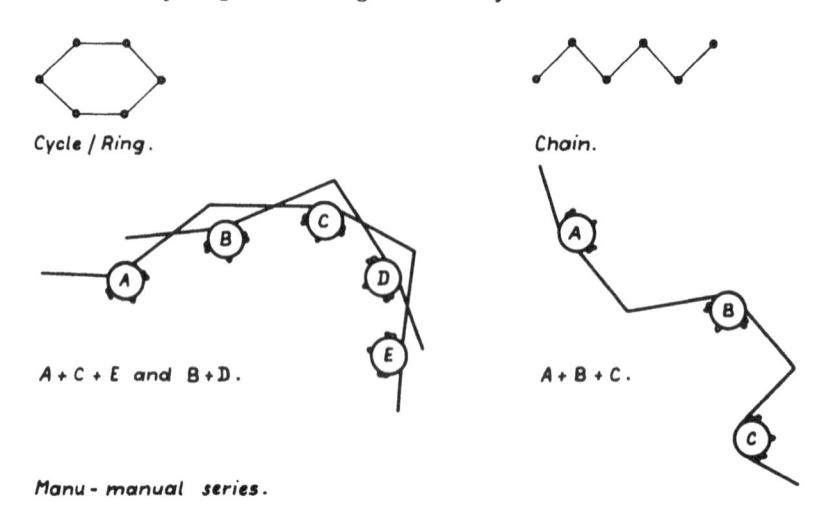

Figure 2.8. *Haptic communication in groups.*

The fact that a manu-manual tie can be realized by looking toward the same side of a line or in all other directions is important on the polysensory level of the face-to-face communication network.

There are countless applications of haptic components of the face-to-face communication network (e.g. games, such as blindman's bluff). Schultz compiled many of these with their rules. The study of these rules intimates the large number of haptic possibilities intrinsic to a face-to-face communication network.

Promiscuity of crowding

The fetish of touching a film star, saint's relic, or cult object brings fans together. This crowding is produced not by lack of space but by the scarcity of some 'preferred' places. It brings innumerable, anonymous persons together to constitute a dense, haptic network. Although crowding brings about the possibility of haptic communication by creating a network, it does not immediately or necessarily generate a communication flow (not even a haptic one) because some can resist haptic exchange; for example, by unilaterally tensing muscles and withdrawing into a shell, becoming 'incommunicado' in a haptic sense. Thus D. Riesman speaks of the 'lonely crowd'.

Indeed, the density of a gathering crowd is its chief characteristic. For example, journalist Herbert Jacob estimates a crowd by multiplying density by area. Density can be calculated in standing, sitting, and reclining positions. If a person has 1.0 sq. m. in a standing position, he can move his arms without necessarily touching someone else (a thinly spread assembly). If one person has approximately 0.5 sq. m. — no more than 0.3 meter between neighbors (according to Stanley E. Jones) — the spontaneous, oscillatory restlessness of individuals make it inevitable that each will touch another.

Maximal density occurs when any displacement becomes almost impossible (e.g., the high point of a pop concert or rush hour in the subway). This situation directly imposes an algesic sensation on any who find themselves with no more space than their bodies require. Usually these situations are temporary, but historical demography shows that in certain slave ships, each person's 'elbowroom' was no more than 0.8 sq. m. — or even 0.1 sq. m. for the night. Today, comparable density exists in the Delaney open-air swimming pool on the Seine in Paris or in the Royal Albert Hall in London, where the audience lies on the floor (an extremely dense arrangement).

Indeed, density is the most essential characteristic of a crowd understood as a network for haptic communication.

9

Sapid Communication

Various types of exchanges occur between man and his physical environment and among men as congeners. Haptic communication goes through the skin, olfactory communication through the respiratory system, and sapid communication through the digestive system, our third assimilative system. Sapid communication as chemical exchange takes place exclusively in the mouth, chiefly on the tongue, and secondarily on the palate, epiglottis, and upper gullet (gustative field) (Kalmus 1958: 104). It is necessary that the saporific substance be dissolved in the buccal cavity and ingested. Man can distinguish four tastes. Without attaching a specific chemical formula to each sensation, they are sour (e.g., citric acid), saline, sweet, and bitter (amaroidal substance). The chemical composition of the latter two especially defies description. The Figure 2.9 shows concentrations of various gustative sensitivity points (taste buds) on the tongue; there is, however, some overlapping. Because of tongue specialization in the sensitivity for various tastes, if the same saporific substance is introduced in a more or less penetrating manner, the taste will be different, as will different concentrations; phosphoric acid tastes sweet when diluted, but sour in high concentration (Kalmus 1958: 106). Because of the chemical nature of the process, the speed of the reaction is slow, but different for each sensation; according to Beaunis, the salty requires 0.25 second, the

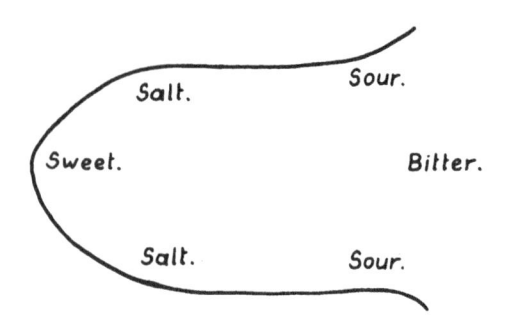

Figure 2.9. *Sapid sensibility of human tongue.*

bitter 2.0 seconds. (This sense also fatigues rapidly, and rapidly recovers.) Thus reactions toward the back of the tongue take more time. The optimal temperature for these sensations is 30–40° C. Salivary secretion, a sign of appetite, facilitates the process. Before joining the other sensation in a polysensory synthesis, the sapid impression first receives the 'support' of the olfactory chemoreceptor, which gives the impression of flavor in the oral cavity (C. M. Apt). (The tongue's skin also provides haptic impressions.) One would expect sapid communication to concern shared sensations of a common meal. But eating at the same table does not necessarily involve sapid communication. In both ancient and contemporary culinary traditions a reminiscence of sapid communication remains. In Africa, the housewife's saliva combines the ingredients of meals; in Swiss fondue, which intimates close relationships, people eat from a common serving dish without tasting each other. The Judeo-Christian tradition of the Lord's Supper (recreated in Communion) represents an alliance sealed by cannibalistic consumption of another's blood.

Different parts of another's body involving mutually specific network positions can be tasted.

An intransitive sapid relationship occurs during the period of lactation.

A kiss is an intensive (cutaneous) haptic message; but because the mouth is an exclusive place for sapid impressions, in linguo-lingual manner, osculation is decisively enhanced by sapid communication.

For visual communication, one specific distance is necessary. The most intimate communication (in the etymological sense) involves 'negative distance' or mutual penetration. This lack of distance is true of sapid communication in kissing and in genito-oral contact, and is also true of haptic communication in genito-genital contact.

10

Polysensory Communication

This study has examined the shaping of the face-to-face communication network in each sensory channel. For a given relative position for each sense can be given a network value as a parameter under standard environmental conditions. But without uniting this field in polysensory reception, zones qualifying the communicative value of each position of a face-to-face communication network cannot be designed.

Intuition suggests that the approach is susceptible of accentuating monotonously and quantitatively the stimuli input of all five senses, as E. Hall's proxemics intimate. However, position values and zones of the face-to-face communication network cannot be established as a unique function of distance. A network position is relative to distance, orientation, direction, and station. On the other hand, the superimposition of different sensory fields shows that information could be redundant, but with approach one sense could become weaker and the other stronger. When someone comes within sight, yet is still far away, his speech is not yet intelligible. When one whispers confidences exclusively in one's ear, he cannot be seen by the listener. Greatest proximity does not clarify auditory and ocular reception of the concerned stimuli. (In a curious manner, the development of telecommunications shows that these two senses are not proximoreceptors.)

Before sharing sensory inputs on a higher cognitive level of the perceptual system, the polysensory reception presents a branching structure with various chemoreceptors, mechanoreceptors, and photoreceptors (cf. J. J. Gibson 1966: 55).

Relative position composed of distance, orientation, direction, and station data determine network value by means of reading acuity value of each sense attached to this relative position. If we use a graident scaling system considering the best possible acuity for each sense as 100 percent or 100 degrees of saturation, one or another sense will be more efficient and predominant in each relative position (see Figure 2.10). If one will communicate by all available sensory channels, he can choose, in the light of this network value, the most efficient polysensory message composition (media mixing). Though Gibson can say that the sensory organs together operate vicariously for information input (J. J. Gibson 1966: 3), McLuhan can also state with reason that the medium itself is the message; affective messages especially are fundamentally affected by polysensory channeling. (Even linguists insist on the spoken origin of language.) Questions of channeling of face-to-face communication are particularly important for our present concern because this is the specific level where architectural enveloping influences the communication processes in particular. Indeed the architecture does not operate more specifically on any other levels of the social communication process.

Speaking in general about the zones of the polysensory face-to-face communication network, we must call to mind that proximity or proxemics does not necessarily involve communication flow (or structure). For example, a crowd does not necessarily involve all types of communication possible in the proximity; it may involve touching, but not speaking. Proximity is not the communication structure, but only part of the network; it only allows its actualization. Approach itself is not an act of communication; it perhaps comes from intention of further communication. This positioning tactic is typically transformation of the face-to-face communication network (cf. E. Porter et al. 1970; Chance 1967).

Finally we underline again that social distance is a soft concept (Cf. G. Simmel, E. S. Bongardus, Ankerl 1972a), if it is unrelated to a position in the face-to-face communication network. It is erroneous to think that protocol prescriptions which vary with culture and society are arbitrary conventions. Distances of three footsteps or positions of physical prominence are privileged locations in terms of face-to-face communication network and give to protocol prescriptions a concrete meaning (cf. Sommer 1969: 62-63) concerning etiquette and intimate positions. The concept of social distance, without this concrete meaning, is only a metaphor. Confusion appears in the text of social psychologist M. Argyle, who states that the normal degree of proximity varies with culture and that every species has its characteristic social distance. There is not any parallel between these two categories; if 'normal' communication distances are changed with face-to-face communication network position, communicability changes (more distant society); but a difference in communication distance between common members of differing species does not necessarily indicate a difference in face-to-face communication network position, since all species do not have an equal 'sensory continuum' (A. J. DeLong). Physiologically, each species has different acuity fields, which is not the case between men of different societies or cultures.

CONSTITUTION OF ZONES FOR THE FACE-TO-FACE COMMUNICATION NETWORK

The five sensory fields are more or less oriented and far-reaching tridimensional fields roughly symmetrical with respect to the central axis (Vurpillot 1967; Wittelson 1976). Certain fields overlap, but that does not mean that their points of optimal acuity coincide. Thus arises the possibility of numerous polysensory 'clutching' of the senses. If we take into account all cases where all or at least one sensory organ operate, we can enumerate theoretically 36 cases.

If all simultaneously operating senses in a relative network position are not necessarily considered at maximally efficient acuity to make possible an order of predominance in the polysensorial profile, 325 possible arrangements (combination with permutation) emerge. Again, it is a question of theoretical cases. For some senses, certain arrangements are impossible (e.g., an exclusive combination between visual and sapid communication where the first predominates). Further, senses operating on a low-level sensory efficiency gradient with low acuity in the third or fourth position of predominance could be interchanged (respectively neglected) without creating a new polysensory profile. For the purposes of this study, it is enough to discuss only crucial cases.

The relative network position to the target is defined by distance, by the six angles determining relative orientation and direction, and by posture (standing, sitting, etc.). Consider a standing posture where vertical angles are 0°. How do polysensory profiles differ with horizontal angles of 0°, 90°, and 180°? (See Figure 2.10.)

Sensory predominance order, established on the basis of the relative operating level (called gradient) of each sense, gives the degree of efficiency of each sensory organ in its own scale. Input value of each sense in terms of information (e.g., recognizing an object) can be compared; yet sensations of different senses cannot be — intersensorily — comeasured, even in the case of two mechanoreceptors (e.g., haptic and auditory). Thus predominance of a sense in a polysensory profile means only that this sense operates— regarding the position of its target — on a higher level of efficiency than does another sense of lower rank.

(1) Now to return to salient cases. E. Hall considers the unique case of *vis-à-vis*, where the horizontal angle alpha = 0°. Disregard possibilities of closing the eyes (which enhances the hearing of song, where lipreading would be irrelevant).

At a distance of 0.0 m. or less (viz., corporal penetration), $d_x \leqslant 0$ meters, in the negative zone $x < 0$ meters (viz., operating in the other's buccal cavity), the sapid modality performs best; the haptic, olfactory, and auditory operate less efficiently. The visual is completely absent in this zone (see Figure 2.10). The predominance order is sapid, haptic, olfactory, auditory:

$$p.c. = (s.h.o.a.)c. \quad v.c. = 0$$

At $0 < $ alpha < 0.5 m., the tactile modality is predominant, closely followed by the olfactory; audition operates, but the lateral position of these

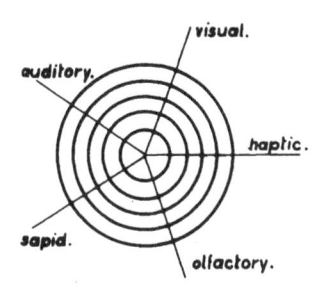

Each radial axis shows a sensory channel. Each concentric circle is a gradient of isoacuity.

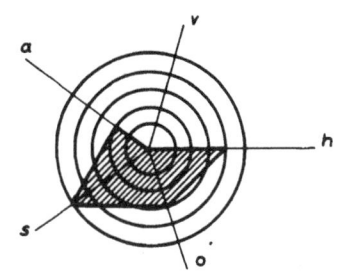

An example: Qualitative assessment of pentagonal profile of polysensory face-to-face communication network position at $d = 0.0m$, $\alpha = 0°$, $\beta = 0°$.

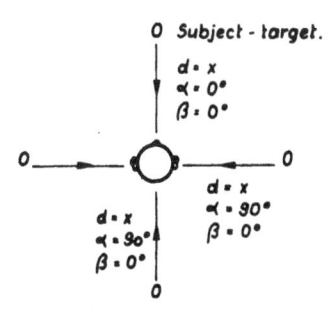

d ... Ray between the target and the observer's 'origin'.
∢ ... Horizontal angle between the observer's vertical symmetry plane and the ray.
β ... Vertical angle between the observer coronale plane and the ray.
(Detailed explanation in the text.)

Figure 2.10. Pentagonal profile of polysensory sensitivity characterizing zones of face-to-face communication network.

140 *Social spacing as a sociological theme of architecture*

senses gives them a handicap (frontal whispering is not heard as well). Vision improves gradually with distance. The ranking order is thus haptic, olfactory, auditory, visual:

$$p.c. = (h.o.a.v.)c.$$

In the zone between $0.5 \leq d \leq 1.2$ m. (especially beyond 0.6 m.), haptic sensibility is lost and vision reaches maximal efficiency for human communication in this ranking (e.g., eye catching). If the feelers of haptic sensibility lose impact, olfactory antennae stretch farther; audition improves. At the upper limit of this zone (ca. 1.2 m.) is the following decreasing order of predominance: visual, auditory, olfactory:

If alpha = 0° is followed farther, the last two senses to be perceived are vision and audition. The latter becomes more predominant until it alone remains. The ranking order is auditory, visual; later, auditory alone:

$$p.c. = (a.v.)c.$$

(2) Along the alpha = 180° axis (ca. $d_x = 0$), the haptic predominates, followed by audition and, to a lesser extent, olfaction. The order is haptic, auditory, olfactory:

$$p.c. = (h.a.o.)c.$$

If d_x is increased, the haptic abruptly loses its efficiency, limiting the capacity to reach back and feel breathing; olfaction scarcely functions; only audition remains. The order is auditory, olfactory; later, only auditory:

$$p.c. = (a.o.)c.$$

The most significant characteristic is absence of vision.

(3) On the lateral axis, where alpha = 90°, in the definition of the polysensory profile it is necessary to specify whether the subject looks straight ahead or whether stationary rotation of head or trunk is allowed, because the senses with a strongly oriented field along this axis are very easily 'out of order'. Indeed, if turns are not allowed, the lateral polysensory pentagon profile is very like that of axis 180°, except that the haptic and olfactory components reach farther.

If rotations are permitted, the most important gain is in vision; but even head turn does not allow transposition of the same efficiency gradient which vision had when the fixation point was straight ahead and the vision is in primary position. By rotation, the very oriented olfactory field also shows an efficiency gain.

Audition increases slightly, especially if the receiver is trying to find the emitter's location, rather than recognize his voice.

After this schematic outline of the polysensory field by its crucial cases, network value of many intermediary positions can be estimated by interpolation insofar as the fields are continuous. A more refined analysis must be based on all new findings of the 'psychology of senses'. This takes into account not only the overlapping of different sensory fields, but also the fact that simultaneous functioning of more than one sense could be enhanced by interaction or inhibited through interference; the difference in rapidity of the proceeding of various senses (mechanoreceptors versus chemoreceptors) affects polysensory synthesis. Other peculiarities of polysensory impression will be discussed in Part III in the context of the polysensory space impression.

FROM POLYSENSORY NETWORK TO POLYSENSORY COMMUNICATION STRUCTURE

If the respective positions of people are known, the network position of each determining the polysensory channel mixture (viz., communication accessibility inherent in position) can be reconstructed. Acuity values must be cross-checked with absolute values of human physiognomy and visible, audible, osmotic, haptic, and sapid dimensions of human expression in order to understand which position assures correct reception.

Because most sensory fields are very oriented, even the simple dyadic network relationship cannot be mapped into a graph by a symmetric arc, but must instead be represented by directed adjacent arcs in such a way that the initial extremity of one arc becomes the terminal extremity of the other (multigraph). The two arcs can have different values which qualify the communication possibilities inherent in respective face-to-face communication network positions. The network value always gives the maximum possible stimuli transmissibility — the polysensory channel capacity without reference to actual usage. In cases A, B, and C in Figure 2.2, the distances are equal but the value of their arcs is not. A and B could be represented with one symmetrical arc or edge, but they could bear different polysensory channel values. In C, the values y and z are also different. Spiegel and Machotka (1974: 129-130) calls these 'mutual position syntropisms', as opposed to synkinetic travel intervals (cf. distinction between proxemic and network transformation). A will be paratrope (⌣ ⌣), B diatrope ([ ]), C protrope ([[), with the technical Greek terms (e.g., apotrope:] [).

142 *Social spacing as a sociological theme of architecture*

The polysensory face-to-face communication structure or flow is the actual usage of the network with a time dimension. Its intensity by definition can only approach but never exceed the network value. Its polysensory composition, volume, and speed result from a selective process. The peculiarity of multisensory channels is that a sole expression can address itself to multiple senses and, at the same time, the response can be given by a sensory channel other than that through which it was received: cross modal reply. These 'mixed immedia' by which communication is transmitted could be written like an orchestral score, so that not only the simultaneity of the polyphonic patterned expression is noted, but the tempo as well. We have already mentioned that speed makes the difference between a grimace and a smile, and speed also determines the receptivity of an expressive event.

Polysensory Bundling of the Face-to-Face Communication

Polysensory communication can be considered from the viewpoint of the face-to-face communication network where coordination of stimuli reception entering through multiple sensory channels is the concern; that is what determines the relative position value in the network. But from the viewpoint of the network, multisensory message emission has intentionally or unintentionally a 'bundling'. The communication network rather than the structure immediately concerns us; however, we will shortly discuss the emission strategy also.

Message content can be informative or discursive, affective and imperative. Informative message content is language-related. For the modern linguist, language is more closely related to speech (Tavolga 1974: 69) than to script. This premise once postulated, vocal-oral expression becomes monopolized by language, and on the other side, all other sensory channels (e.g., visible gestures) subordinated to 'monitoring of vocal utterances' (J. J. Gibson 1966: 75). The behavior of pointing becomes an element of eidetic definition, albeit this behavior is common to primates in general (Tavolga 1974: 68) and proper for commanding. Even if corporal expression could also be received by a haptoreceptor, in this discursive communication it is addressed and received visually. Studies on information transmission (telephone, television) generated 'favoritism for the visible' (G. L. Miller in *Sensation and Measurement* 1974: 131). Yet these two channels could be considered by reference to the extent of their sensory field as far receptors. This type of message is better transmittable beyond 0.5 m. In this zone, the audiovisual becomes dominant and later audition becomes exclusive.

There also exist near receptors: chemoreceptors and haptoreceptors, including thermoreceptors. (Touch, as proximoreceptor, requires contact.)

This distance may occasionally be used for writing linguistic characters in the palm of the blind person's hand, but usually other types of messages are transmitted. If a gesture is made in this zone, it expresses emotion addressed through the haptic, rather than the visual channel. If eye-catching is a means of transmitting emotion and sexual message, to become specific, the sexiferous message needs nearness. Eye-catching as oculo-ocular communication develops in the intermediary zone of 0.6-3.0 m.

Another characteristic of communication in this close zone is that, more and more, spontaneous, unintentional messages prevail (intercourse versus discourse). This subliminal message transmission shared with other animals puts human communication in an ethological perspective. The sexual life of fish is based on tactile and chemical interaction; aliferous and feathered animals (e.g., birds) have a communication system based on the audible (song) and the visible (molting).

Face-to-face communication network zoning can be realized only on the level of polysensory communication. If zones are established, analysis of each network position existing in an etic continuity would be simplified to discrete emic entities. E. Hall suggested four main zones: intimate, personal, social-consultative, and public.

To constitute well-founded zoning criteria, relative positions where significant change occurs abruptly in reception of elementary human messages (with their features appearing on the polysensory screen) must be found. The first consideration for calibration is the size of emitted message particles introduced into the communication channel (e.g., a movement, a physiognomic element of discrete magnitude). On the other hand, zoning implies that reception of these particles could qualitatively change. At or beyond a breaking point of the continuum, specified message particles can no longer be perceived by a specific sensory channel. In this case, message transmission either ceases, or switches priority if the message is polysensorily receivable, or relies on the remaining sensory channel. Zone limits (in terms of relative spatial positions) can be based at switching points showed on the polysensory reception profile where a different sense modality channels communication in an optimal manner.

In light of these criteria, A. J. DeLong's reservations concerning Hall's tactic to reduce the etic continuum into emic discrete units are justified. Indeed, definition of the four enumerated classes originates more from the number of labels available than from results of experimentally founded reasoning about the face-to-face communication network. Before any definitive answer can be given, more systematic experimental research is needed to map the pentagon profile change of polysensory receptivity matched with particles of human expression, thus validating zone limits as relative network positions.

Cross-Modal Communication

Cross-modal communication flow derives from asymmetrical network positions or, in symmetrical networks, from the choice of the respondent (see D in Figure 2.2). The close relationship between message content and choice of channel, even in a dyad tied by a symmetrical network link, causes the correspondent to answer formal speech by a sensual touch or look which better transmits his message. It is also possible to recognize the addressee within a group network by cross-modal communication, even if all network links are symmetrical — speaking to all but one, who is answered through the eyes. Verbal expression can also be responded to with a slap.

H. A. Moss (1974: 190) notes that 'the cry is the earliest . . . signal in the infant's repertoire of responses' and 'milk spontaneously is secreted from the mammary gland in response to the cry stimulus' (1974: 173).

Because relative position determines the face-to-face communication network, to know how given polysensory communication possibilities are used it is convenient to study communication structure in fixed positions (e.g., sitting).

Sommer made empirical studies with different research groups (1969), investigating how relative position affects frequency of verbal communication and how on the other hand communicative intention involved in different social activities (e.g., coaction, cooperation, competition) affects the choice of relative seats, viz., network transformation. Other studies related position to verbal terms (e.g., intimacy; Ball 1973 about 'microspace'). Cross-cultural studies tried to universally define the signification of these words by universal spatial connotation.

Sommer's empirical studies show that competitors choose *vis-à-vis* positions (c, d), conversationalists corner positions (a), coactive readers in a public library more distant positions (e), and cooperants more intimate side-by-side positions (b) (see Figure 2.11).

Specific literature acknowledges Steinzor's studies (Steinzor effect, 1950). In the study, one person takes the initiative to begin talking at a round table. Each has an equal chance to speak next; this phenomenon is inherent in the network position. However, the speaker is *vis-à-vis* along line d (less probably along c, and least probably along a). (See Figure 2.11.) This confirms how much visible communication (gesture, eye contact) affects verbal exchange. The contradiction between this result and Sommer's finding that the corner position (not facing) is the preferred relative position for conversation is only apparent; Steinzor established how the opportunity to speak passes; to Sommer, the preferred position is more efficient for verbal exchange (cf. auro-oral exchange, Duncan 1970).

For these findings, many common-sense explanations can be given. Sommer also discusses olfactory evasion (1969: 37), but we can also mention

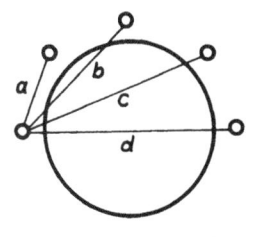

Figure 2.11. *Seating arrangement and communication structure.*

that for side-by-side intimacy the polysensory 'immedia mix' favors the haptic channel. But all of these empiricists' findings are based on intuitions and without theoretical reference, so that the body of knowledge produced cannot become cumulative and systematic.

Indeed, face-to-face communication network must be distinguished clearly from face-to-face communication structure levels of consideration. The movement implying displacement or relative position changes must also be seen as network transformation. The relative positions' network values must be defined by the polysensory pentagon receptivity profiles. Many other diagrams are conceivable as representations. The prime use of these analytic tools allows the perceptual interpretation of mixed immedia, and therefore it is theory-constructing. For example, Hall considers exclusively *vis-à-vis* position and equates network position simply with relative distance ('zones'). Around Sommer's table, six possible graph relations must be distinguished. Five of the six are symmetrical; f is not. Around Steinzor's table are four graph links, all symmetrical. Argyle, in his research about eye-to-eye contact, does not even mention the absolute distance involved.

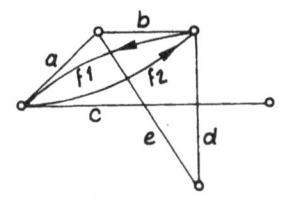

Modification of the face-to-face communication network is where various architectural envelopes can exert the most direct influence on the social communication processes.

III

Communication through Architecture:
What is Architecture? A Sociologist's View

11

Architecture as a Communication Medium: A General Discussion

In the first part of the book we reviewed the precursors of the sociology of architecture, then situated the subject in our conceptualization — architecture among the created objects as the medium of the architect's communication, and its sociological theme. Finally we carved out that topic which in our opinion must have priority in a prolegomenous perspective.

In order to realize this project, in Part II we discussed the face-to-face communication network in detail in order to make it ready in metric terms to become the very specific sociological subject of architectural communication. Indeed, the various sensory spaces created by architectural design find their sociological purpose in the enveloping of a set of virtual face-to-face communication networks.

Now we look into the repertory of the different sensory spaces on the abstract and purely geometrical level, as well as on the physical level where sensory reception of architectural signifiers (de Saussure) are determined. The enclosing space or 'roomraum' is fixed as the basic morphemic element in the architectural communication medium. We will dissect this element to identify its submorphemic ingredients (Chao) to discover what morphological rules apply to its composition, and then to investigate the syntactic rules which organize them (the spaces) into a space system and subsystems.

ARCHITECTURE IS NEITHER MONUMENTAL SCULPTURE NOR A DESIGNED ENVIRONMENT IN GENERAL

Architecture could not be classed with sculpture even if by deserting its proper function the latter were invested with enveloping functions. Architecture does not exist without conveying the impression of a space enveloped by a closed surface. For this reason a history of architecture which begins, like that of E. O. James (1965), with the cave dwelling is less misleading than one which begins with the pyramids, which are in fact monumental sculpture. The first approach to architectural history conforms with a theory of architecture like that of Bruno Zevi (1957). This approach grasps that essential aspect of architecture which specifies that it is a created, enclosed space system.

150 Communication through architecture

Therefore, the characteristics that exist for an individual, and sociologically for twins and multiplets, at the level of natural space formations in the uterus and later in the cave, are also present in the architectural space at the level of created formations. At both levels – created and natural spaces – the separateness of the individual as well as the social intimacy of groups is protected.

Like industrial design the usefulness of architecture presents itself, and so its geometric aspect is an essential feature. The signifier cannot be replaced by any *relais* without dimensional accuracy. Yet in its mode of operation architecture is very different from machines which communicate cybernetically either with a robot or with other machines, and only accidentally with man following strict instructions. The physical virtuality of architecture operates behaviorally as a stimulus (esthetic emotion).

Finally the space or roomraum is the very prime element of our environment. It envelops us, and places us among and relates us to all other objects. For this reason it is a radical error to imagine that architecture finds the fulfillment of its purpose in a kind of large scale envirotecture (e.g., P.Thiel). It is not the comprehensiveness of the task and its scale which determine the classification, but the specificity. In a precise sense we can call architecture only that which commands created spaces allowing full optical, acoustical, haptic (and osmotic) control of the enclosed 'open regions'. Architecture embraces neither designed equipment or furnishings which belong to a separate class, nor purely 'symbolic spaces' such as safety lines (created by lawyers and traffic engineers), nor 'topological spaces' without definite and perceptible geometry.

ARCHITECTURE AND SIGNS

Fundamental aspects of architectural spaces are prefigured in natural spaces like the uterus and caves. Such spaces offer both a protective space against atmospheric space and desired isolation in the social communication field.

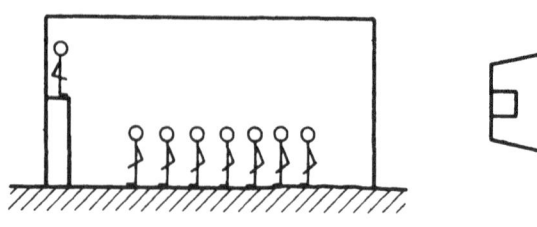

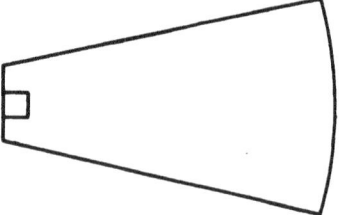

Cross - section.   *Ground plan.*

Promethean space for a preacher.

The space includes virtually a certain set of face-to-face communication networks and through that set it facilitates certain communication structures by enveloping and reflecting them. The architectural envelope's reflection of stimuli perceptible to the senses channels communication (e.g., by excluding voices which are outside, and by adding indirect sounds to direct ones) and also allows the enveloped group through an impression of the space itself to receive an esthetic stimulus.

Natural spaces as well as those designed by the architect share these aspects. The fact that a space is perceived as something designed (communicated by an expedient conscience — Peirce) superimposes on natural spaces a new aspect which draws the designed space into the family of media. In order to select appropriate analytical tools from the existing arsenal for a semiotic treatment of this medium, we must compare it to other media, with which it will have some analogies and differences.

A Closer Scrutiny of the Hypothesis: Space Is the Word of Architecture

Semiotics, the name of a discipline invented very recently by Peirce (Maser 1971: 35), has been rapidly compartmentalized by various schools, (modern, classical, etc.) both in its terms and in its concepts. The consequence has been that very often the application of the term has an obscuring instead of a clarifying effect. In order to forego a general debate or an arbitrary choice about the subject, we begin *in medias res* by posing a hypothesis that space is the architect's word, and by looking at what that implies. Is this statement true, or false, or must it be qualified?

First of all, we have been very imprudent to use the word 'word', which is already outmoded for those initiated into semantics (e.g., Mounin 1974: 222-223); yet we choose it because it is unpretentious and simple to understand, and because of the potential for identifying it with the free morpheme (Bloomfield).

The most significant implication of our hypothetical statement is that architecture can be classed with other structured sign systems (Chao) with a precise repertory. But language is a very specific device of human interactions, and of communication in particular (Tavolga 1974: 51), refined for the transmission of a wide range of articulated messages in abstract terms. Grouping architecture with languages in general would open the way for us to apply the highly developed analytical tools of linguistics. The temptation is great; was it not Cournot (1911) who stated (Ch. II, section 19) that syntax is *'une science abstraite et rationnelle comme . . la géométrie consacrée à l'étude des combinaisons et de l'ordre'*? But of course this grouping, if done without qualification by speaking about 'architectural language', involves bias too. In this case the abstract nature of signs is admitted, and the level

152 Communication through architecture

at which communication is analyzed is relatively isolated from other levels of communication shared by other species. Finally, we 'trail' with us the whole bias inherent in the fact that modern linguistics relates language extremely closely to the spoken form as the original.

It is out of the question to accept as a 'package' (without qualification) the linguistic nature of architecture, but we can state that the role of space in the architectural system is similar to that of the word in language. Pei (1966: 167) says that the free morpheme is a 'minimal unit of speech that is re-current and meaningful' and 'can stand alone'; for Mounin the word is traditionally the *'unité significative empirique'* (1974: 222). In reality the roomraum, namely the architectural space, is the minimal unit with proper signification. Its sociological signification is the set of face-to-face communication networks which is virtually present in the space.

Indeed, from here going 'downward' we can identify the bidimensional surface elements of the space's architectural envelope as infrawords (de la Garza) or submorphologic or prelinguisitc ingredients (Chao), and the formal paradigmatic transformations of a word as the *Grundelement* [basic element] (Klaus 1968: 239) in 'imminent semantics', viz., in morphology, through manipulation of these 'ingredients'. 'Upward' we find syntagmatic chaining occurring in a syntactically autonomous unit which is the sentence. We will see later that, in this respect, the space system is the architect's sentence which is identified by its inner connectedness and its relative detachment from the context of atmospheric space. The space system is that which is the minimal, gramatically complete unit of architectural discourse (cf. March and Steadman 1971: 125, 166). At this level, functional labeling takes place.

After these analogies we will look at what qualifications prevent us from incorporating architecture as a medium of communication completely into the class to which natural language belongs. Eventually we will seek an alternative conceptual structure which can better serve our study than that of linguistics, namely concepts which are used in semiotics.

Differences Between Spoken Language and Architecture as Medium

According to Peirce all communicatory facts involve at least a triadic relation. An object must become a sign, viz., medium or vehicle of a message, and its reference to something signified (Guiraud 1966: 96) (de Saussure), or according to other schools, the referend (referent) must be understood by the receiving subject as signification. This 'minimal semiotic fact' is fundamentally sociological if we consider that the message transmission is an act between analogous minds capable of and intending to communicate (e.g., space designed for a purpose). The language itself as natural 'tongue' is composed of a repertory among whose signs there exist determined relations and a series of implicit rules which order their use. In other words, the semantic field is delimited by the complementary and hierarchical relations existing within the sign stock (repertory).

Morris (1938) perceives three distinct and successive subjects of study in the construction of his theory of semiotics:

(1) syntactics, which studies only the formal relations among signs which bear messages without reference to their signification and their interpreters;
(2) semantics, which studies the relation between sign and signified (referent) (Guiraud 1966: 96-97), i.e., the meaning of signs; and
(3) pragmatics, which takes the interlocutors (users of signs) into account.

Peirce tried to classify all signs in three ways: the sign in its intrinsic system; sign and signified; and sign and its interpreter (hermeneutics). Could it be said that verbal signs as an element of language and space as architectural sign are in all three respects in a common class? Such a parallel must be subjected to close scrutiny, especially the second relation between sign and its referent. In the perspective of modern linguistics all (spoken) languages are chiefly conventional and arbitrary sign systems composed of symbols, which have no natural relation with the signified thing (Mounin 1974: 296). There is no isomorphism at all (Chao 1968: 218-219, 132, 211, 212, 207-208) in the sense that the ground plan of a house is its icon (image) (Mounin 1974: 167). An index (Peirce) or a symptom has a real relation to the signified thing. Even though onomatopoeia has a genuine resemblance to the phenomenon it imitates, this fact is played down more and more by modern linguists as something fancy, even if on the other hand languages seem to be verbal in origin, and the presence of the speaker more and more inevitable in syntactical, logical, and linguistic analyses made in the same circles (Grize, Piaget's discipline in Neuchâtel). The speaker (communicator) is always underfoot, and often in a forced manner. Anyway, in the perspective of a truly general linguistics it seems off-balance to force the spoken origin, especially in the case of languages with pictographic origins (Alleton 1970: 8), and to insist on an acoustically linear thread through all languages (Mounier p. 195; Chao 1968: 68). Nevertheless, for reasons of principle, if languages are essentially characterized by arbitrary signs, the fact that *relais* signs exist must be fundamental; namely secondary or *relais* signs are by definition arbitrary and opposed to any onomatopoetic or imitative possibilities. But even this *relais* is different depending on whether the language is verbal or pictographic in origin. For the verbal, the *relais* is a graphic representation, and for the pictographic it is a pronounced one. For this very reason Indo-Europeans have a better chance of communicatng across different languages by speech, and Japanese and Chinese by writing.

154 *Communication through architecture*

The consideration of language as a spoken form is inherent to modern linguistic approaches and thus linguistics becomes a *science de la parole*. We must take seriously into account the reductive perspective of linguistic imperialism which will be involved if we tacitly accept all its premises by applying this treatment blindly to the plastic arts as Francastel (1960: 285 about *relais* sign) warns us. Indeed if the specific study of pictographic languages could give supplementary insights for the comprehension of the plastic arts — Francastel's specific concern — applying it in architectural semiotics in an increased manner brings other, not less reductive, consequences; namely, accentuation of the prevailing tendency to view architecture as a purely visual art, a tendency which accords only lip service to its polysensory complements. On the other hand, Francastel (1960: 288) also sees a danger in grouping the literary with the plastic arts because the latter for him is a much more synthetic category which does not carry with it the multifunctional versatility of the common language which could be discursive, denotative, and expressive all at once. If this reasoning is valid for plastic art, which is exclusively expressive (cf. abstract painting as pure painting), it is not so for architecture. We discussed this question concerning Prieto's three-way classification of the arts — literary, abstract, and architectural — and we will come back to this question in the next section in some detail concerning the idea that architecture could be the paradigm for all created objects (cf. Hegelianism). Here we state only that architecture is far from being exclusively expressive. If it gives an impression, and so stimulates the beholders, it denotes above all its own purpose — it presents itself.

The 'Echoic' Nature of the Architectural Word: Architecture as Syntactic- or Meta-Medium

If we analyze the special nature of 'architectural words', we see that they cannot be grouped without qualification with the class of signs which for linguistics is the word or the free morpheme. Indeed, words in spoken language are arbitrary, conventional, fortuitous (C.Morris) symbols without any natural or intrinsic links with the represented object. This becomes clearer if the message sender uses the secondary representation of the signifier, the *relais*, which is graphic or written in spoken language and spoken for pictographic language. Any isomorphism (Chao 1968: 212) between sign and object — geometric or other — is excluded.

In the case of space as the word of the architectural medium, the denotated phenomenon itself is completely present in its potentiality, namely the set of all network positions that the space can accommodate in its capacity to hold (e.g., standing, sitting), the web of communication lines which relates these positions directly and which indirectly connects the same positions through the messages reflected on the envelope of the architectural space. Going further, we can say that these various stimuli reflected on the architectural envelope contribute not only to the constitution of all possible face-to-face communication networks, but also allow the people who are included — even though there may be just one individual — to receive a space impression. This impression transmits all essential attributes of the architectural space, namely its volumetric magnitude, its geometrical shape, and the isolating nature of the envelope. This latter hylic aspect of architectural space cannot be neglected insofar as it specifies which perceptible stimuli are reflected and how, or at which point, this reflection is complete. The hylic aspect specifies the sensory isolation of the beholders, isolation which protects against the hazards of the atmospheric space and which ensures sociologically the 'intimacy' of those who are included. Thus because superficial characteristics such as color and sound absorption could influence the impression of the two basic morphemic (geometrical) characteristics of all roomraums, namely their volume and shape, it becomes obvious that the created space as architectural signifier is incomplete without consideration of the space impression and therefore cannot be cataloged without this consideration. The perceptible space is the item of the architectural repertory.

Architects, by using these three ingredients (two geometrical and one hylic) can express and prefigure all sociological and ecological messages, themes which must be and can only be expressed specifically by the architectural medium and not by any other. That is our concern. Architectural morphology and syntaxes find their base in the architectural word which is defined by the above-mentioned characteristics. The architectural word, bearing in and on its intrinsically proper theme, represents nothing but itself — it is presentation. (Curiously, Spiegel reminds us that face-to-face communication also shows a self-presenting nature; cf. E. Goffman.)

Because of the fact that the virtual set of face-to-face communication networks is the proper sociological object of architectural expressions, we can say that the relationship between enveloped face-to-face communication (consisting of a network with its transformation and communication flows) and the architectural space has its analogue in the differentiation of languages according to the semantic level between object language and its metalanguage.

Now we can conclude that the architectural sign shares many aspects of onomatopoeia or echoic words. The signified and signifier have a geometrical isomorphism. The very nature of the architectural sign is to be isomorphic, perhaps also conventional, but not arbitrary (Morris 1946; Chao 1968: 208). By qualifying the architectural sign as echoic word, we do not mean to exhaust its qualification; we will only delimit it in relation to the signs of spoken language. Architectural space as object has real aspects other than its

156 *Communication through architecture*

message bearing (medium) characteristics; and on the other hand, architectural space, like any other object, could also be coded as an arbitrary sign for communication if it seemed convenient. But if the social communication and control process is used in such an arbitrary way (e.g., a big building as a symbol, a pyramid as a power symbol), this is no longer our concern because it is not related to the sociology of architecture, which discusses the specificity of architecture as medium.

One of the fundamental aspects of the architectural medium is its multisensory nature. It has an autonomous and specific relatedness to multiple sense modalities. If we consider the linear nature of spoken communication which has no simultaneity, we can appreciate the fundamental differences. The opposition between spoken language and architectural sign system is not even the same as that between verbal and visual signs. Even if we admit that the same continuity and predictability is not available (Fraiberg 1977) for all autonomous sensory spaces (e.g., optic versus acoustic and haptic space) it is incontestable that space impression is available from other than optical spaces. Our whole conceptualization of architecture is implicitly filled with a one-sided optocentric view which makes it difficult to admit that sensory space other than the optic could be any more than a polysensory complement subsidiary to the visual impression of one and the same space. What we say here is that the architectural envelope can isolate one or another of our sensory communication lines objectively in a completely autonomous manner where various sensory data could not be imputed to a space as a target of convergent polysensory inquiry. The targets are themselves different. (See Figure 3.1.) In this

An analogy in 'multicomposition'.

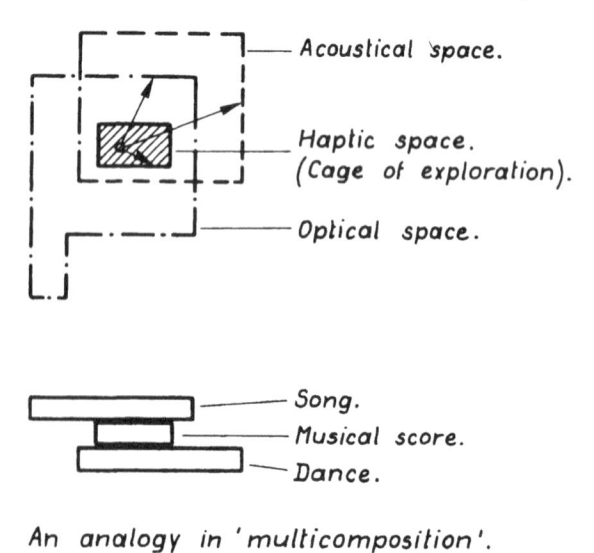

Figure 3.1. *Multisensory space composition without polysensory coextension.*

sense the architectural sign is a multilevel one (H. Reimann), or for Goethe and Schiller a frozen polyphony (Lalo 1951: 25); and there will be not only compound and simple words but complex and complicated ones, as we will discuss later in this part. This will be a fundamental problem of the architectural morphology.

Another basic feature of the architectural space system is the fact that spaces are not made in a row like words in spoken language. If the parallel existence of the different sensory spaces gives a simultaneity, the tridimensional arrangement (not unilinear alignment) of spaces allows the 'reader' of architecture not only to reverse his direction, but also to choose alternative 'readings' with a completely different string order. Depending upon the rule which we prescribe for the reading, we can have a number of different, discrete, and alternative ways. We can conclude that the reading of the architectural space system is multilinear.

Some Implications of the Nature of the Specification of Architectural Expression

There are tendencies to consider architecture in a less down-to-earth and on a so-called more sophisticated or higher level of abstraction and conceptual integration. We must state that most of these tendencies get by on the very specificity of architecture and in reality, by their 'architecturology', invite architects who think too concretely — in their opinion — to venture outside of their range of competence. The new mathematician's aversion for all geometrical quantification and the sociologist's ignorance of problems of spatial behavior promote these tendencies.

Let us see what is at stake. The basic unit of the architectural creation is the roomraum, or so-called 'open region', which defines a set of position points and stimulus propagation lines which could bear face-to-face communication messages. Thus architectural space must not in its nature belong only to the geometrical specifications. The hylic nature of the envelope itself must be specified concerning its isolating quality for sensory stimuli. We know how profound is the difference between a linguistic word and what we have called the architectural word.

First of all, architectural creation cannot stay on a topological level, but must be geometrically concrete or *anschaulich* (Hilbert; Grize 1964). It must have a geometrical shape which is a closed tridimensional envelope. For this reason anyone who claims to see in city planning (urbanism) the generic integration of architecture, its integration on the highest level, misses the point, namely the specificity of architecture. City planning, derived from Renaissance gardening (Bardet 1963: 12-17) is, like the agricultural arrangement, profoundly bidimensional in its origin. That bidimensionalism and urbanistic reduction of architecture go hand in hand, as we can see in many authors like Friedman and Cousin, who think that the chapter on planar graphs in topology is most relevant to architecture. But even where city planning transcends bidimensionality it is often no more than a simple outgrowth from bidimensionality to avoid intersections; it is the concern of traffic engineering. Any tridimensionality which does not create spaces with well-defined, concave volumetric magnitude (Francastel 1960: 292) is not in the scope of architecture. Of course we can speak on the level of more or less dense space systems and distinguish urban and other architectural space systems, but even so we do not change the level of consideration (Ankerl 1974). For the sociology of architecture, circulation or traffic between roomraums is considered as a transformation of the communication network; either a telecommunicative position into a face-to-face network position between individuals by visiting each other; or a face-to-face communication network itself, where a group moves to another room for some reason (e.g., if the original room becomes too small).

Indeed, an architectural roomraum determines a set of face-to-face communication networks of a specific sensory nature and gives the impression of space through a specific sensory channel. For this reason the channel must be not only related to volumetric geometry but to all the hylic characteristics which are relevant to sensory impression. Spaces cannot be simulated as architectural expression if either the 'model' does not have dimensional accuracy or the envelope's reflective nature is not specified accurately (Ankerl 1973). Not only is the impression in the drawing on the desk of a gifted designer (often executed with the considerable draftsmanship promoted in architectural schools) not an architectural expression, but even a model is at best a poor substitute for the architectural expression conveying a very misleading space impression. (A prototype must be a prototype in accurate dimensions.) All these representations of architecture are distorting in their perceptual effect: either they are only unisensory, namely visual, or they are irrelevant from the viewpoint of the thresholds of the actual impression, or both. For the architect conceiving on a level of higher 'sophistication' of topology where there are neither geometric shapes, nor volumetric dimension, nor hylic specification of the space envelopes, there are dead-end streets and professional alienation.

The true sophistication in the architect's conception is the respect for and the deep knowledge and consideration of all possibilities in giving space impression; e.g., detachment of the various sensory spaces from each other, and creation of cross-modal and other 'volumetric sensory illusions'.

Of course the last and worst pitfall inducing professional alienation comes from sociologists who invite the architect to 'architectural commentary' in which the proper spatial effects of the architectural process are replaced by verbal ones in the form of publicity brochures and explanatory comments (*Architecture parlée*). All these secondary representations and metaphors distract us from the medium whose purpose is to express architectural creation. Architecture by extension does not make the process of architectural creation more subtle; rather, it subtilizes its essence.

We see the architect has his own medium and must stay with it even if sociologists and others with more or less reason argue that the architect who adheres to his proper profession has a very limited effect on social processes and change. This argument may persuade someone to change professions, but it is irrelevant for the proper definition of the professional competence of the architect.

*Architecture as a paradigm for the study of human creation –
a short observation*

Many indices point to architecture as an appropriate paradigm for all human creation (cf. Hegel's violinist). Indeed on the phenomenal level space preexists other objects which will be situated in it. (If time is our subjective experience, spatiality is the base for all quantification: Gosztonyi.) It shares with all industrial design the characteristic of usefulness, but it transcends this aspect not only by preexisting (by its primacy), but also through its stimulating and communicative nature. As sign it is unique too, as the linguist Prieto of Geneva, student of Martinet, noted. It is more multisensory than cinematographic art; its reading is multilinear; and we are not likely to find any other sign system which in its morphology and syntax provides a better opportunity for a structural analysis than that composed from spaces. That is the intrinsic virtue of space.

*Some Basic Questions About the Structural Treatment of Architectural
Communication*

We have seen in Part I that endeavors had been made to apply linguistic, semiotic, and communication approaches to architecture. On the other hand, in Part II we have seen how difficult it is and what special care is needed to apply by analogy the conceptual tools developed apropos another field of investigation. It was awkward to apply the concepts of information and communication theory to the field of face-to-face communication because this theory originated in cybernetics (N. Wiener) and in telephone engineering (Shannon and Weaver). We underlined again and again the specificity of the architectural medium, how the architectural morpheme is inseparable

160 *Communication through architecture*

from the signifier itself. We can describe this sign system without referring to specific building materials but we must take into account the hylic aspect of the material (Bénézé 1967: 69, 72, 74) which determines by which modality of his senses the observer is enveloped in an architectural space of given dimensions. The basic geometrical characteristics of the space, namely volumetric magnitude and shape for each unisensory space, and also the manner of its multisensory space composition, must be specified. Such perceptually well-defined space constitutes an item in the repertory of the architectural medium. It must be said that any space which is perceptibly different, allowing various sets of face-to-face communication networks, constitutes a separate item in the (architectural) designer's catalog. How the discrimination of space impression operates becomes a question of great importance when we recognize that, objectively, the differences between linguistic words are discrete, but those between spaces can be continuous or 'infinitesimal'. What is essential to see is that the labeling of architectural spaces such as 'Ballroom Eduard VIII', has nothing to do directly with the repertory of architecture. At its very best the label is a functional one and is superimposed on morphological distinctions by reference to the syntactic use of the architectural words in the space systems (e.g. ballrooms in a hotel). We see here that the structural treatment of the architectural repertory must be based on physical differences, which could be distinguished by the standard observer. Indeed, discrimination thresholds will serve the transformation of the objectively continuous universe of roomraums into a list of discrete catalog items. All other criteria are alien to the structural approach of architectural repertory, and prevent us from producing verifiable categories. At least an implicit knowledge of the architectural repertory and syntactic rules is necessary for a designer to be a competent architect, while an explicite knowledge of them is necessary for scientists and critics who will analyze the particular style of an epoch, of a region, or of an individual designer. Structuralists can study a designer's style through his vocabulary (his word selection, his chosen 'octave'; (Guiraud 1956: 34, 36; Muller 1968: 138), his word frequency (word distribution), and the syntactic patterns which form his particular communication *structure*. (Francastel 1960: 284). Even if he uses ingredients like color, intending to construct illusory geometrical differences for the observer, these must be objective illusions (J. J. Gibson) necessarily inherent in and emanating from some real physical differences projected, for example, from a bidimensional feature in the space shape or volumetric magnitude. By contrast, structural analysis of architectural expression can completely disregard the devious effort of the architect who adds to his 'actual' work (design) something that is not in it by another art, such as skillful essay writing. This is the very reason to look with extreme caution on the architect who speaks and writes more and more and designs less and less (*architectes sans architecture*). 'Architectural semiotics' has also been used and abused for such purpose (cf. Y. Friedman; Francès 1966: 71). Perhaps successes registered in the field of self-commenting by Le Corbusier-Jeanneret — who began his labeling activity by rebaptizing himself from Jeanneret to Le Corbusier — has inspired some contemporary architects who write less well to hire sociologists and semiologists for this kind of incantation where the physical structure of the design is only a vague reference for the 'para-architecture' (*architecture parlée*).

Some authors

The Argentinian semiologist, Mario Gandelsonas, invited to New York, applied (with David Merton's collaboration) concepts of communication theory to demonstrate the particular significance of Peter Eiserman's (1969) and Michael Graves's architectural style. As was the case with Eco's writings, which we discussed in the first part, Gandelsonas does not distinguish architecture from structural engineering. Other authors equated architecture with urban structure — which is often bidimensional and traffic-oriented — and considered streetscapes instead of (enclosed) roomraum systems. In both cases, the lack of specification of architecture keeps — *a priori* — the authors from applying semiology and linguistics to the properly architectural medium as such. For this reason we relegate Gandelsonas's quoted articles to the literature promoting particular architects.

Among the second group of authors who assimilate architecture to urban structures we can mention Max Bense (Stuttgart) and A. Moles (Strasbourg).

Max Bense (Bense and Walther 1973: 16-17) discuss architectural semiotics. Route signals and all other kinds of spatial symbols derived mostly from urban structures, or built environments in general, are discussed under this heading.

In Moles's works, even when he equates architecture with shells, we do not find a consequent application of a space concept, and any spatial demarcation and signals are grouped with architecture. In his work the interest for urban feature prevails too. More recently, he published a book (Moles and Rohmer 1978) about the psychology of space. It is marked by a very strong phenomenologist and culturalist influence which characterizes French circles active in human science. For this reason, it would be difficult to use its categories to denote spaces for experimentation in space discrimination.

Raymond (1968: 174, 1974) and other sociologists of culturalist tradition, not always at ease with geometrical and physical dimensions, had particularly welcomed architects' symbolic activities, such as labeling detached from precise spatial reference. Indeed, this allows sociologists to 'measure' the efficiency of architecture — i.e., considering the 'structure' of architectural communication on the pragmatic level — by simply comparing architectural commentary with the user's labeling — instead of comparing the user's expected behavior with the actual.

Since his doctoral thesis, Hesselgren has worked on the construction of a theory of architecture. On the other hand, he uses linguistic analogies (1967), and he also considers the creation of enclosed spaces and space impressions as the architect's proper task. He has made a systematic effort to study specific aspects of the 'architectural language' and inspire a group of psychologists to study the effective impression of spaces. (We will discuss Gaerling's research later in detail.) Hesselgren also elaborates color maps, but in this field, he departs from the strictly architectural concern (namely the effect of colors on space impression), and studies all kind of color application in the physical — especially urban — (built) environment. Unfortunately, his article (1973: 423-429) criticizing Eco's theses shows a very strong influence of phenomenology. Further, in our opinion, he dissociates too strongly the perception of space from the objective characteristics of its physical features.

Basic Questions in the Morphology of the Architectural Repertory

First of all, for many modern linguistics the use of the term 'morphology' will be surprising in itself. However, we continue to use it as Chao (1968) does, whose linguistic background is a language which has no morphology at all and therefore cannot be considered biased in favor of it.

We defined the architectural morpheme as a perceptible (enclosed) space which has a volumetric magnitude and a geometrical shape, and which is always addressed to a particular sense modality. This means that, on the one hand, the relative location of the different sensory spaces in the multisensory composition is an additional specification to the architectural morpheme, and, on the other hand, it is the observer's impression which establishes the architectural repertory by discriminating spaces with different volume and/or shape.

The primordial problem is that repertories — open-ended or not — should be constituted of discrete items, while (objectively) volume and shape differences are continuous. Even surfaces with qualitative differences, such as broken and unbroken curvatures, angular and rounded corners, could be transformed from one into another by infinitesimal variations. Such is the objective, constructed side, but 'fortunately' the observer's sense organs do not operate in such a way; each one has its threshold (difference limen) below which it can no longer discriminate. Taking these considerations into account to constitute the architectural space repertory, it is enough to standardize the observer and observation conditions and then to find the limit for shape discrimination and the just noticeable difference for volumetric magnitude for various sensory spaces, a task which has never been systematically explored by behavioral science. Of course, although a discrimen (a gray zone) can be permitted, the repertory will still allow the architect to learn the range of discernable spaces among which he has an effective choice. The repertory will be almost open-ended in its superior limit and more restricted anthropologically in its inferior limit, since the space must be accessible for man.

'Discriminability' must be defined. (For example, our decimal or binary numerical systems are clearly established languages composed of an unlimited number of members, each of which can be easily discerned and ordered by its place value: Parry 1967: 86.) In the architectural sign system, discrete units are introduced through the limits of the observer's capability to distinguish between spaces. In reality, repertory items are established by the slightest, or just noticeable, difference in volume and shape which is discernible by the standard observer, and which at the same time is attributable to an actual objective difference between the compared objects themselves, namely spaces. We also exclude all hallucinations or other imaginary differences which are exclusively in the mind of the observer. J. J. Gibson calls them subjective illusions. In short, the impression of difference must come from an objective stimulus difference, which is called 'geographical' or 'near stimulus' (Francès 1966). The experimental construction of the architectural repertory calls for further precision. Indeed, by such variables as recalled experience in our long-term memory, different cultural background, innate sensitivity, or presentation of the spaces in different sequence or under different observation conditions such as illumination, we arrive at different results for the just noticeable difference constructing the repertory. We must introduce standardization, the standardized 'sensor' (cf. Negroponte 1970: 28-29), the 'observer-informator' (Chomsky), the *'architecteur'* (Michael Riffaterre), and also standardized observation conditions. The conditions and human observer which produce the lowest difference threshold (which corresponds to the highest sensitivity) will determine the repertory. We recall Michael Riffaterre's *architecteur* which summarizes all possible reactions of all possible readers of a literary work, by which he identifies any differentiation that can be made on the basis of the work itself, and so he tries to determine the permanent efficiency of this structure.

To establish a space repertory, if not as a closed series but as an open-ended one from which any member could be (re-)constructed, and to establish the relationship existing between discernable morphemes, in terms of the topological transformation which turns one into the other — these are the supreme tasks of architectural morphology. We have here the rules by which to form the morphemes (or here also signifiers), and the differentiators and classifiers which allow us to survey the 'space inventory'; finally beyond the static inventorizing we look for formal variations, the transformations such as inflection and 'gradation', paradigmatic operations generating one form from another.

The complete definition of the architectural space as created roomraum

The roomraum, the morpheme of the architectural medium, is determined by topological, geometrical and hylic criteria.

We will discuss these criteria not for the sake of Prussian acàdemic pedantry, but because the lack of an explicit enumeration of the essential aspects of a well-determined architectural space obstructs part of the horizon where architects can innovate in their expression (Lang 1974: 108).

A roomraum or architectural space is in topological terms an open region (James and James 1968: 306). The definition is based on characteristics of so-called interior points, without yet defining the enveloping boundary surface. Any two points within a bounded region can be joined by a curve that contains no point of the enveloping surface. Defining the space topologically through these curves which join points of the interior illustrates how intimately the set of communication channels of the face-to-face communication network is involved in the definition of space as the free morpheme of architecture. We can say that the set of interior points of the space is topologically equivalent to that of a sphere.

We look now at the topology of the enveloping surface. It must be both a closed and an oriented surface. We can say that normally space envelopes are closed and simple surfaces, surfaces without intersection and boundary curves like Jordan surfaces or those homeomorphic with the surface of a sphere. As we will see in the next chapter, this statement is an oversimplification which must be somewhat qualified because the simple nature of the surface is neither a necessary nor a sufficient criterion. For example, in a space with a floating embedded hole, all its points are equivalent to the sphere's interior points, but its surface is not topologically equivalent to that of the sphere.

The topological definition of the space envelope gives us immediately the two geometrical characteristics of the space: the volumetric magnitude and the shape.

The hylic characteristics must be determined individually for each sensory modality; that is, each sense which can autonomously generate a space impression claims a space with a different shape and volume. Which sensory modality can generate such an autonomous impression will be discussed in this part with all the necessary considerations which must be involved in deciding this question. The sensory modalities (and the hylic characteristics) not only multiply the geometrical requirements, but add brand-new requirements to the definition of architectural space.

If we acknowledge the autonomy of the different sensory spaces, we must not only allow that each can have a different shape or volume but that, even with equal volume and shape, the envelopes are not necessarily coincident, but may be translated or rotated.

When the various sensory spaces do not coincide, then the composition of the architectural space is multisensory or multilevel, and its impression is intricate or complicated (see Figure 3.1). (If the different sensory spaces are coextensive, we call this special case a polysensory space.) The multisensory intricacy of architectural spaces constitutes a compound morpheme if all the different sensory spaces which are simultaneously present are in themselves — or when completed — free forms (i.e., free morphemes).

The intricate multisensory composition of the compound architectural morpheme brings a new element to the definition of the architectural space as experimentally constructed repertory item; there must be a set of coordinates which determine the positions of the different sensory spaces in relation to a reference point and among themselves. This has far-reaching implications:

— On the theoretical level, the experimental construction of a coherent repertory of discernable architectural spaces requires that for an item, all observation data must be collected within a 'perceptually homogenous' space portion as a set of reference points — see hatched zone as common part or 'core' — of this compound morpheme, where for any observation point, all autonomous (and simultaneously perceived) sensory spaces remain (if different in their geometry and location) the same.
— On the practical level, the sociological effect is that someone can share simultaneously different sensory spaces with different persons and so the face-to-face communication network itself becomes very intricate.

Minimal space, or bound form versus free form We have just mentioned that a compound architectural morpheme is composed of sensory spaces which are free forms or morphemes. An unisensory space is a free form if, in respect to this sensory modality, the geometrically defined envelope permits neither entry nor departure of stimuli. To the 'systems theorician' this is a closed system. (We must use the term 'closed system' carefully, because it does not equate with the mathematician's 'closed region'. We should recall that roomraum as free form is an open region.)

166   Communication through architecture

Remaining still on the unisensory level, if leaks are allowed in one direction through the envelope, then the space is a minimal one. It is a bound form or bound morpheme. (In the terms of the systems theorician it is an open system.)

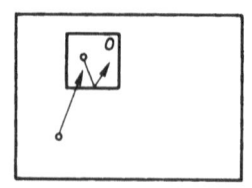

Some input of light without output in the small space (e.g., spy-cell with unobservable observer).

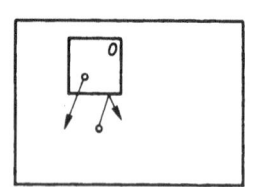

Some output of light without input (e.g., prison cell in an 'open society').

Figure 3.2. *Two possible cases of bound spaces.*

In Figure 3.2 the spy cell and the prison cell in an 'open society' show the two possible cases of bound architectural morphemes. In the first case, someone (the spy, for example) can see out, but cannot be seen from out there; in the second case, the confined person can be seen from outside but cannot see out. There is also no feedback or interactive relation. Of course, leaks in both directions cannot be permitted because that would dissolve — by definition — the conceived space as a morphological entity.

Considering always one and the same sensory modality, if spaces of bound form are associated in such a way that together they now constitute an architectural word which is independent from any other space, as in the free form, we call this combination a 'complex' word. (On the one hand, the compound architectural word is complete because, as a system, it is ultimately closed, as is a free form; on the other hand, it is total, if it is composed of all possible autonomous sensory spaces.) Without losing a coherent concept of the architectural word, we can allow some types of partial incompletenesses, such as a one-way leak concentrated at some spot on the surface (e.g., peephole), or a temporary opening. (For the latter the door is a good example: a door opens, and the conversation is instantaneously interrupted when the 'intimacy-defining' space is momentarily suspended. New persons enter the room, the face-to-face communication network is transformed, and the conversation shifts.)

Finally we must note cases where space shape and volume are only vaguely indicated and the enclosing surface does not assure enveloping in any of the senses just defined. These constructions we do not call architectural spaces or morphemes in a proper sense of the term; they are 'metaphoric spaces' or 'spaces by extension'.

The two geometrical characteristics of the architectural morphemes and a third modifier of the space impression

A space is an architectural morpheme in a proper sense if the recipient, or user-observer, can on the basis of specific sensory input attribute a volumetric magnitude and a shape to the roomraum. However, this space impression (Goldfinger speaks about the sensation of space [1941a] in another sense) depends on not two but three kinds of characteristics. Indeed, each sensory space impression could be modified by superficial characteristics (see Figure 3.3). (We summarize the superficial characteristics under the Basic Texture Elements [BTE] of J. W. Curtis of the University of Washington, even though we define them differently.) For example, the optical space by color or graphics; the acoustical space by the absorption coefficient. Indeed, without changing the actual shape or volume, its impression could be altered by objective means, by design. These superficial characteristics we call *modifiers* (Chao 1968: 68). Of course, the volume impression of a sensory space could also be influenced by a cross-sensory effect, by the simultaneous presence of other noncoextensive sensory spaces. (This effect is not designed in our scheme below.) The shape itself can also influence the impression of the volume. We must remember that all aspects of colors or other superficial characteristics which do not modify the discrimination of volume and shape are, from a purely architectural viewpoint, irrelevant. We look only at the effect which is present on the morphemic level of architecture and not below. Because of the different *modus operandi* of the various senses we can discuss these effects only for each particular sensor space. Observation conditions, too, for the standard observer of the architectural repertory must be defined individually in each sensory field.

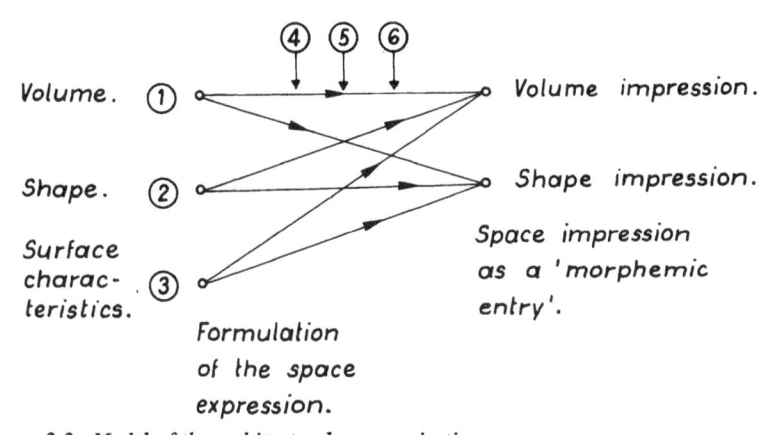

Figure 3.3. *Model of the architectural communication.*

On the other hand, each sensory space as architectural morpheme has only two attributes — volumetric magnitude and shape. In order then to constitute by experimentation the architectural repertory, the subject, or 'standardized observer', will always have the same series of questions.

The preliminary question is, are all autonomous sensory spaces geometrically identical (coextensive), viz., do they have the same volume, shape, and location? This question is necessary in order to know whether or not the observer will report 'additively' (pool) all sorts of sensory impressions about a common polysensory space. (It is possible to create illusions by objectively designed means which seem to make coincident different sensory spaces which are not.)

The experimenter's other questions are the following:

(1) Are the two optical (or haptic) spaces equal in volume, or not?
(2) If not, which of them has a greater volumetric magnitude?
(3) Have the two spaces equal shape?

Applying B. Russell's equivalence theory, which establishes a relation between the property of a class and the belonging to this class, all sensory spaces which for any objective reasons could not be distinguished in either shape or volume are one and the same item for the architectural repertory. By contrast, two sensory spaces having an objectively equal volume and shape, but which are perceived as different for one of these two attributes, are different forms or repertory items. So, a blue room and a red one, with identical shape and volume are different items if and only if either their shapes or their volumes are systematically perceived as different.

Linguistic and geometrical categories

We quoted Cournot on the common roots of linguistic and geometrical categories. Indeed, both show a very disciplined approach, awaking some expectation for an appropriate treatment of the architectural sign system with common reference in geometry and linguistics.

At the very beginning, however, we must warn that many linguistic categories presented as universal (applicable for all languages) were just an unwarranted extrapolation of categories of the Aristotelian logic to cover all sign systems (Mounin 1959: 62). These Aristotelian categories are omnipresent in our sciences. In our particular field of interest, we notice that phonemes have an Aristotelian origin as well (cf. Eco's theory), and that the transformation of similitude is a shape-definer in Aristotle's work (cf. the question of similarity in *Gnomon*).

Architecture as a communication medium 169

After these premilinary remarks, we can approach the problem from both the linguistic and the geometrical aspects of the architectural repertory.

For simplicity we consider now only the polysensory space as free morpheme. Two polysensory architectural spaces are different if the standardized observer can perceive a difference between them either in their volumetric magnitude, or in their shape, or in both. When we consider the difference between two spaces of the same shape, the volumetric difference is generated by the similitude or homothetic transformation. But it is more difficult to specify the exact 'morphism' at which one shape turns into another, viz., the degree of transformational relationships between specific shapes. We know that the sets of points included in each (completely determined polysensory architectural) space are topologically equivalent; that is, each space could be transformed into the other by topological transformation, or that they have a homeomorphism with the set of the sphere's interior points.

A more specific (not generic; cf. Pei 1966: 103) geometrical category is applicable for shapes which have been constructed in a 'regular' way, using bidimensional inframorphemic elements as a generator, and an explicit mode of generation which gives the 'rule'. (The resulting shapes, e.g., cone, cylinder, hyperbolic paraboloid, hyperboloid of one sheet, are ruled surfaces, but not closed ones.) But not all shapes can be generated by an imaginable constructive procedure which goes out from a bidimensional generatrix. On the other hand, the same shape could be produced from a different generatrix *and* by a different rule (though if only one of these two has been changed the resulting shape will be different too). Taking the 'generation' (mode of construction) as a point of departure for constructing generic categories would restrict and atrophy the architectural imagination. (Many authors make believe that engineering requirements, such as calculability and formwork, or econotechnical reasons necessarily limit architectural creation to these shapes.)

In linguistics we distinguish two viewpoints for categorizing morphological units, or morphemes. On the one hand, we distinguish the simple differences between forms (Mounin 1959: 203) as a generic term which 'notices' the differences that prevent one word from replacing another without some change. Among forms there are lexemes which have irreducible semantic differences and so constitute a proper item of the lexicon, and other forms which could be derived from a lexeme by a specific series of paradigmatic transformations — inflections which take a conjugational or declensional form (following grammatical categories or form classes). On the other hand, opposed to this paradigmatic transformation (which can be handled as a morphological difference in the traditional sense of the term, without any direct reference to syntactic function), we find the syntagmatic one,

170 *Communication through architecture*

which is an intermediary stage, oriented toward the syntactic composition, and which categorizes 'words' according to their place in ordered arrangements.

In making these categorizations, we expected them neither to be exhaustive, nor to have the linguists' consensus as a backing. The categories discussed had been chosen not by subscribing to canons of particular schools, but either by their promising heuristic values for our field of application or by their challenging application already undertaken by other researchers in our field of investigation.

In summing up, we can say that the basic difficulty in applying linguistic categories to the architectural medium is that architectural spaces objectively constitute a continuous series — in respect to their volumetric magnitude as well as to their shapes — and on the other hand, linguistics deals with discrete elements. In the case of the architectural medium, it is the observer's limen in discrimination which transforms the continuous series into a series composed of discrete elements which could be ordered in a transitive manner: as a matter of fact, it is easier to constitute an ordered series of volume impressions in a transitive manner (namely, if space A's volume seems greater than that of B, and that of B greater than that of C, this would imply that A also gives a greater volume impression than C). It is more difficult to constitute a transitive series of discriminated shapes as function of the geometrical relationship which relates one shape with another closer to itself than would be a third shape.

Finally, it would be ill-advised to make an analogy between the distinction between lexemes and lexis or forms on the linguistic side, and the distinction between shapes and (absolute) volumetric magnitudes on the geometrical side present in the case of the architectural medium (e.g., seeing in the 'volumetric amplification' a kind of 'gradation').

The direct involvement of the sensory aspect in the architectural repertory as 'anthropometric magnitude' shows us that it is inconceivable to attribute a signification — e.g., a sociological one expressed in terms of the face-to-face communication network — to an architectural space based exclusively on its shape. Thus it is a fundamental — albeit current — error to isolate the semantic difference only on the shape level. In terms of the construction and description of the architectural repertory, it would be erroneous to equate shapes and lexemes. No architectural signification can be given to a roomraum without indication of its volumetric magnitude, too (see Figure 1.2.3).

12

The Geometry of Architectural Morphology: From 'Free Form' to 'Open Region'

> Most of geometry, as opposed to algebra, is built on ratio concept.
>
> Edwin B. Newman, *Measurement*

Just as no one can presume to be a competent Germanist without knowing the morphology and syntax of the German language, so the problems of architectural style cannot be discussed without knowing which are the lexical elements and the morphological and syntactical rules proper to the architecture as a medium. We recall that, among others, Bruno Zevi (1957) defines architecture as a system of spaces. At the end of this part, we will discuss the syntax of the system of multilinearly interlinked spaces, but first we will review the geometrical rules to which all well-formed spaces are submitted. We will do this in a way which does not preclude architectural imagination in the largest sense of the word; that means that we will apprehend the subject beyond the geometrical shapes which are constructed by the conceptual instruments of ancient Greek geometry, which puts nothing more than a ruler and a compass at the designer's disposal.

Our point of departure was the roomraum, the free morpheme of architecture which is the smallest meaningful unit (Pei 1966: 167), and which is independent to the extent that it can constitute on its own a whole sentence, for example an aquarium, or an igloo.

Topologically the space is defined as a three-dimensional open region containing an infinite number of points — that is, we cannot find an interval so small that it doesn't contain a point — but which does not include any points of the boundary surface; and whose boundary surface, or envelope, is such that any two interior points could be joined by a curve that contains no point of the boundary surface.

We see that this definition exactly matches the sociological one, which states that architectural space is a set of face-to-face communication networks. The architectural continuum is defined as a space where the sensorily specified message-bearing stimuli can freely circulate but not leave, and eventually vanish at the boundary surface. The nature of the surface itself is derived from the characteristics of the open region. Indeed it must be a closed surface which does not permit two points to exist which could only be joined by curves of infinite length, since this would exclude, *eo ipso*, face-to-face communication. The Jordan surface, as a genus of surface which is topologically equivalent with the sphere, constitutes a continuum which satisfies these requirements, but we will find that other closed (finite) and orientable surfaces can also qualify (see Figure 3.4).

On the other hand, because of the sensory nature of the architectural space, there must be at least a momentary rigidity (Berge 1966 [1963] :2), that is the space must have a shape and volumetric magnitude related to metric geometry. All these characteristics are determined by the architectural competence (cf. linguistic competence of Chomsky). The determination does not need any outside coordinate as reference, but can be based exclusively on intrinsic or 'local' properties which do not vary in the course of any isometric transformation.

INVENTORY NUMBER IN THE ARCHITECTURAL REPERTORY AND THE INTERNAL GEOMETRY

If prefabricated and stored, each space as an inventory item must be identified by common labels covering completely interchangeable forms. In order to be integrated in a syntagmatic arrangement and later inserted in a syntactic construction, the only transformation which it can undergo is the isomorphic one. In practical terms, it is the operation by which the item is hoisted into place by the crane. This insertion operation will be discussed later in dealing with space systems; for now, we recognize only that it can be either rotation or (simple) translation — rotation fixes the space's orientation and the 'free block' becomes a vector (called *ABC*), while translation preserves the vector's orientation and gives the space its final identity. In neither case does the operation change the internal geometry of repertory items stocked according to their complete equivalence. (We note this here for pure architectural morphology since modifications — such as cutting a door — to a space with internal symmetry, such as a cube, upset the symmetry, and therefore its orientation can no longer be changed without consequence.)

A very particular problem of morphological labeling is represented by spaces which are enantiomorphic or in improper (March and Steadman 1971: 186) or negative (Warusfel 1966: 412; March and Steadman 1971: 48, 114)

The geometry of architectural morphology 173

Space envelopes non homeomorphic with the sphere.

1.

A space enveloped by more than one simple surface.

2.

Dupin's cyclide. A closed but not simple surface.

3a.

E.g., a torus.

3b.

Node of trefoil.

3c.

E.g., double doughnut. Connectivity number : 4.

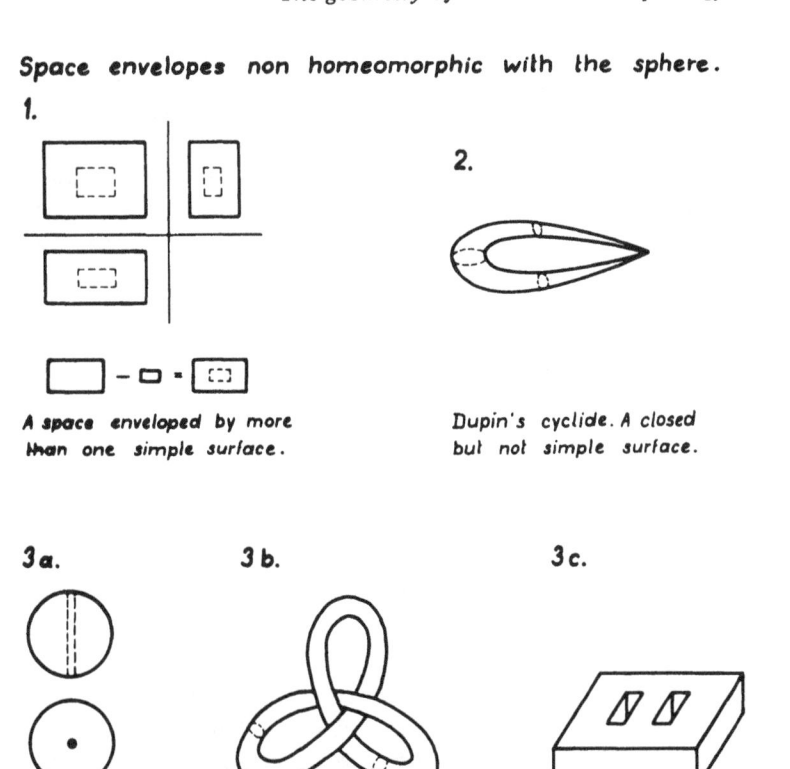

Surfaces inappropriate to envelop an architectural space.

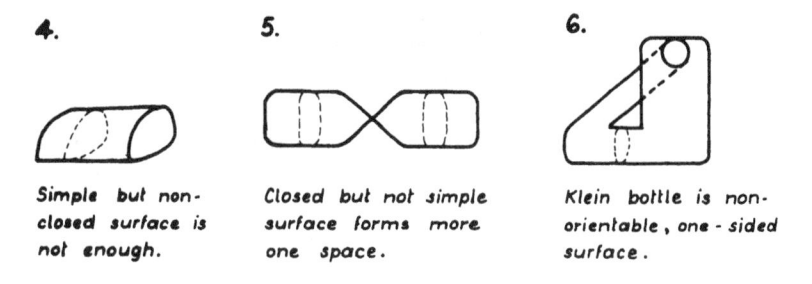

4.

Simple but non-closed surface is not enough.

5.

Closed but not simple surface forms more one space.

6.

Klein bottle is non-orientable, one-sided surface.

Figure 3.4. *Definition of the topological class of space envelope.*

isometry. The most common experience is our shoes. Indeed whether we live in Gulliver's right or left boot makes no difference if we admit the interchangeability of our right and left sides. The shoemaker uses the same quantity of material in every part; but if one part, as inframorphemic element, has been badly cut out, no permutation (cf. Zeitoun 1971: 38) can change a right shoe into a left one. This internal orientation, by which the order of particular points follows a clockwise or counter-clockwise direction, cannot be repaired later. It needs a so-called 'anti-displacement' (Warusfel 1966: 412) or reflection. As a matter of fact, the improper isometric transformation of a bidimensional object needs the third dimension, and for space, a fourth is needed.

In conclusion, in morphological space prefabrication we must catalog under a separate label these 'conjugate dyadics', and we must do this with special care, because the architect is not obliged to produce an equal number of the right and left 'Gulliver shoes'.

TOPOLOGICAL TAXONOMY FOR THE ENVELOPING SURFACES OF SPACE

We have already seen that the architectural word, in order to have a complete meaning, must be an open region as a finite continuum, a roomraum or interior delimited in relation to the *infinite* exterior R^3. We noted that the completely determined architectural morpheme must have hylic characteristics for the specified sensory stimuli related to the envelope's isolating character. Furthermore, all autonomous sensory spaces have in common topological characteristics, as well as geometrical ones of definite shape and volumetric magnitude. Let us first examine the topological characteristics.

It is necessary, but not sufficient, that the surface be closed. A closed surface without boundary curves could consist of one or more roomraums, or even just a pseudospace (e.g., Klein's bottle).

If the surface is closed and simple, then the (enclosed) architectural space is topologically perfect, but these criteria together are not necessary; we can have space without satisfying both of them. (We must think of the closed floating hole in an 'aquarium space'.)

In this sense, an even more 'pragmatic' approach had been made, namely using the sphere's surface as a norm for all roomraums' envelopes, by saying that all space envelopes must be transformable into the sphere's surface by continuous deformation. (Of course, in this context it is not the perfect geometrical convexity of the sphere that makes it the norm, but its topological characteristics: to be a closed, simple Jordan surface.) This is an even softer definition than the previous one. Indeed, some authors think falsely that all homeomorphic surfaces can be changed necessarily into another through continuous deformation — or homotopic mapping, albeit homeomorphism and homotopic mapping are not interchangeable criteria. Homotopic transformation is a sufficient criterion for homeomorphism but it is not a necessary one (e.g., a torus and a node of trefoil are topologically equivalent without having the possibility of being transformed into the other by continuous deformation).

Anyway, even homeomorphism with the sphere surface is not a correct criterion for forming the topological genus of surfaces including all envelopes of a well-formed architectural space. As a point of theory, we must note that a sphere's surface is not even the paradigm for all simple and closed surfaces; there are namely simple and closed surfaces which are not homeomorphic with the sphere, for example Steiner's Roemer surface, which is simple, closed, but nonorientable, i.e., one-sided (Hilbert and Cohn-Vossen 1952: 304). Of course, the latter is also useless for enveloping an architectural space and is mentioned only to show the absence of another interchangeability of criteria.

We are more concerned with the torus and the sphere with floating holes in the middle. Indeed, publicity-oriented contemporary American architects produced giant doughnuts as monoid spaces, which are topologically well-formed, but their enveloping surface, the torus, does not belong to the same topological class as the sphere: both are simple, closed surfaces, but the sphere's connectivity number (n) is one and the torus's is three. The aquarium with the floating hole is also a well-formed architectural space; however, its 'container' (envelope) is not a simple, closed Jordan surface as the sphere is.

We see that all these approaches have not produced the sufficient and necessary criterion for defining the topological genus of all envelopes of well-formed roomraums. Yet, the precision is especially welcome if we are to produce adequate software (Negroponte 1975) to simulate by computer any possible imaginative architectural spaces, which are always topologically well-formed. Therefore an abstract and formalized approach is required. We know that the well-formed roomraum's envelope must be a closed surface at the least. On the other hand, the topological genus of surfaces is defined by the following three numbers: p and q, which together with r can be quantitatively related to each other through the Euler characteristic χ; and also the connectivity number n can be calculated as we will see. If we look for the closed surface as topological genus, the r must be 0 and it is p which defines the different classes of homeomorphic surfaces.

Using the sphere and the Moebius strip as 'paradigmatic tool', we can show the cases of various topological genera. We make dyadic holes on the sphere surface and afterwards close them by strip (which could be a Moebius strip). If the surface is closed and orientable (i.e., has two sides), it is not even necessary to use the Moebius strip for cross-caps.

176 Communication through architecture

The 'No Space': Klein's Pseudospace and Moebius' Pseudodoor

The Klein bottle is a closed surface that is unqualified to constitute a roomraum (see Figure 3.4.6). It is a nonorientable, one-sided surface (Hilbert and Cohn-Vossen 1952: 308, 273). It is a true architectural nightmare in that it is possible to reach any point ('on any side') of the surface without passing through the surface (e.g., a door) or going around an edge. We can cut a Moebius strip from this surface, or construct one by taking a long rectangular strip of paper, giving it a half twist, and pasting its two ends together. The Moebius strips are used as 'doors' to close the sphere's holes in order to define the topological genus of surface.

View of the Architectural Envelope's Topological Genus

A perfect definition contains neither more nor less than it will denote. We state again the topological definition of space: an open region in which any two points can be joined by a curve that contains no points of the enveloping surface; a continuum where we cannot find a distance so small that it doesn't contain a point. These sets of interior points are homeomorphic with those of the sphere, which does not imply that any of its enveloping surface must be topologically equivalent with the surface of the sphere. We mentioned some striking cases as examples.

In order to relate the abstract definition of the topological genus of surface to the formation of architectural words, we tabulate examples of the denoted categories of surfaces. As a general note, we must say that not all conceivable surfaces have already been exhaustively classified, but we proceed here to identify surfaces which are not homeomorphic with any other. We will define the categories in terms of their topological invariants where χ representing the Euler characteristic equals $2-2p-q-r$. In this equation p is the number of handles, q is the number of cross-caps, and r is the number of open holes or boundary curves. p and q characterize the topological genus of surface.

One surface topologically equivalent with that of the sphere is, for example, a polyhedron without a hole in it. This is a simple, closed, orientable surface with a connectivity number $n = 1$, Euler characteristic $\chi = 2$, genus characteristics $p = 0$ and $q = 0$.

The surface of torus or anchor ring (see Figure 3.4.3) is also a simple, closed, orientable surface, but not homeomorphic with that of the sphere. Its topological invariants show the difference: $n = 3$; $\chi = 0$; $p = 1$; and $q = 0$. A variation of this surface is a doughnut with a discretionary number of rings whose connectivity number will be 5, 7, and so on (Hilbert and Cohn-Vossen 1952: 297).

This crescent-shaped surface is known more precisely as Dupin's cyclides (see Figure 3.4.2) (Hilbert and Cohn-Vossen 1952: 219) and is obtained by the inversion from a circular cylinder where the center of inversion does not lie on cylinder (see pp. 193-194 in the original German version of Hilbert and Cohn-Vossen, 1932). The resulting surface is closed and orientable, but not simple (because the vertex is not a simple or ordinary point); however, the surface is completely fit to serve as an envelope of a well-formed architectural word.

We have already mentioned the monoid, where one closed surface, which could be of any topological genus of orientable closed surface, is locked and floating inside another (see Figure 3.4.1). This is also a well-formed architectural word which is enveloped by more than one (simple) closed and orientable surface. The node of trefoil (Warusfel 1969: 107) is also a simple and closed surface which could form a space, but against all appearance it cannot be transformed by continuous deformation into any torus, with which it is yet homeomorphic (see Figure 3.4.3b).

Each of these closed surfaces is usable as a space envelope but has a different Euler characteristic χ and consequently a different connectivity number n, as well as a different p which with q determines the genus of surface. We can conclude that all envelopes for architectural words may not be homeomorphic among themselves because the p could vary.

We remember first of all that the Euler characteristic is the topological invariant which completes other invariants. We see the relationships in the following equations:

$$\chi = 2(1-p) - q - r, \quad \text{or} \quad n = 1 + r + 2p + q$$
$$= 3 - n$$
$$= V - E + F$$

The last equation relates the Euler characteristic to the number of vertices, edges, and faces of the surface of a polyhedron. (Here we do not consider the 'polyhedron' as the simplexes of a simplicial complex; therefore this equation is is not topological but geometrical.)

Of the first two we see that one numerically relates the Euler characteristic to the topological numbers. This also applies to a connected surface: if we add 1 to the largest number of closed cuts which could be made without separating the surface, we obtain n, the so-called connectivity number. We must be careful with this number because some authors do not add 1. The $\chi = 3 - n$ is valid especially for a closed surface; if it is not valid then the surface cannot be a space envelope.

r is the number of the boundary curves of the surface. For example, the cylinder is homeomorphic with a sphere with two holes. Thus r must be zero for all space envelopes.

q represents the number of holes closed by a Moebius strip or cross-caps. If q is not zero, the surface could be closed but not orientable, and so for all architectural envelopes a q must be zero too.

p is the other genus characteristic which with q completes the topological classification of all closed surfaces, hence all with which we are here concerned. p on our 'paradigmatic sphere' is the number of holes closed by handles shaped like a half doughnut.

Knowing that for a surface which could be used as the envelope of an independent architectural word, both r and q, for one or another reason, must be zero, the topological subdivision of the architectural envelopes will be determined by a variation of the connectivity number n since $n = 1 + 0 + 2p + 0$, thus $n = 1 + 2p$.

Denomination	Genus			Connectivity number n	Euler-Poincaré characteristic χ
	r	q	p		
Sphere	0	0	0	1	2
Torus	0	0	1	3	0
Klein bottle	0	2	0	3	0
Moebius strip	1	1	0	2	0
Cylinder	2	0	0	2	0

In this tabulation only the sphere and the torus are useful in the construction of free architectural morphemes.

Now we can ask again why is all this topological delimitation of the envelope necessary, and why do we look for relevant subdivisions? Is that not a pure pedantic luxury, an extravagance for the architect of human habitat?

We observed that the well-defined 'topological status' of the envelope is necessary for any creative architectural form simulation by computer. The subdivisions stimulate the architectural imagination on the topological level before it moves to the geometrical level. Of course, for emphasizing the geometrically 'noncommittal' nature of topological homeomorphism, mathematicians like to design 'patatoides' (Warusfel). We have tried here to relate it to some geometrical possibilities. Indeed, pocket spaces are often used for exposition halls, the sterile cage, or in other cases where the different autonomous sensory spaces are incongruent in their complicated multisensory composition. How interlocked syntagms are facilitated by variations of the topological genus will be shown when we discuss space systems.

Finally, we must repeat that if in economic terms one of the highest expenditures is for low income urban housing, also called 'basic housing' (B. J. Frieden), its design is not necessarily the unique or even the most exacting task for which architectural competence is called.

THE GEOMETRY OF CONCAVE SHAPES

In order to accomplish our task we must go back to the etymological sense of geometry. Indeed, if we give a description of space ripe for an enumeration in a repertory without binding the architect's imagination and desire to communicate by secondary and technical considerations, we should pay more attention to the analytical tool used by the geographer to describe a formation which results from the earth's natural history than to the tools 'handed out' to create architectural shapes. These latter tools, instead of being used to describe freely created space, have become a sort of norm for the creation itself, a prefiguration by which the imagination is channeled. In many cases, especially in our civilization, the geometrician's preference for easily describable shape, the architect's dependence on the ruler and compasses in his drawing, the engineer's preference for calculable structure, and the industry's for convenient formwork construction have become the supreme determinant and true shackles of architectural communication, of what space can and cannot be created. Technical and scientific progress appears in a reversed perspective; instead of enlarging or realizing possibilities which are at least equal in quality and variety, this progress restricts the potential — in our particular case the optimization of shape for architectural communication effects — for the sake of false economies. The mass-produced substitutes do not replace the genuine shape in its true complete character. Let us look at this question in order to substantiate our claim that the traditional catalog of accepted geometrical shapes restrains the architect's repertory in an undue manner.

We can observe that contemporary architectural shapes which we like to call 'highly imaginative' are for the most part generated in one of three ways: revolution, translation, and eventually the helicoidal mode. The curves used for generating the surface are for the most part derived from a conic surface. By this 'generation' we can obtain only five surfaces, all quadric (also called second-degree) and second class. Among them is the hyperbolic paraboloid, which combines excellent characteristics; it can be generated by revolution and translation and so is very easy to construct — namely the framework — and it has a shape with interesting sections and perspectives (cf. Giedion 1971: 23; Van Lier 1959: 316, 318 about Candela). But as with all limited catalogs it could become redundant in all its syntagmatic combinations and volumetric magnitudes. We also mention here the common right prism which is used almost exclusively in 'housing boxes'. The quadric surface represents a very restricted repertory. We also notice that the quadric surfaces are continuously concave if they are closed, but among them only the ellipsoid, an affine variant of the sphere, is a totally closed surface, while the hyperbolic paraboloid is not an envelope but only a 'roof'.

Let us turn our attention now to the geographer's geometry, where we find analytical tools for describing the accidental shapes of nature. There are inspiring approaches in Haggett and Chorley (1970: 70), partly reproduced from Bunge (1966: 72), as well as in the works of the Laboratory for Computer Graphics and Spatial Analysis at Harvard University, directed by B. J. L. Berry, which also tries to serve geographers.

Finally, in order to free the architect's creative imagination, we must eliminate obstacles of a terminological nature. Even if the geographer's landscape is full of potholes, his conceptualization parallels that of mathematics applied to the physics of solids. Both look at the object from outside. The geographer is not here chiefly to describe natural caves, and so, both the geographer and the physicist, spheres, whether global or smaller, are viewed as perfectly convex bodies and not perfectly concave. Indeed if the globe and other spheres of the physical world are compact and impenetrable, then by contrast the envelope of architectural space is seen first and foremost from the interior of the roomraum. If, for example, a surface is wavy, which part is called convex and which one concave depends exclusively on whether we look downward or upward at it. These are not terms of internal geometry referring to intrinsic characteristics of the surface. If we call the sphere perfectly concave and adjust the whole terminology of the architectural geometry to that, we have underlined that its primary sociological and ecological purpose is 'caving'. With this inversion of the applied terminology we eliminate the implicit effect of the conventional terminology which suggests appreciating architecture more by its facade than by its spaces.

Definition of the Architectural Shape

The definition of the architectural shape will be a very elementary thing, but again it is not useless to be very explicit in our effort to clear up any confused ideas. We find in the field of architecture 'form' or 'urban form' (Rapoport 1977) as a generic term and a nomenclature given to particular shapes. Indeed the Aristotelian-sounding 'form' used by gestaltists has no suitable unequivocal meaning for its use in scientific research. Therefore we have no intention of using this concept. Anyone with an interest in the soft science of architecture can find a relatively inspired survey of this nebulous concept in *Droit à la Ville*, written by the Marxist philosopher Henri Lefebvre.

A second source of confusion is the inconsistent usage of geometrical terminology. If we ask someone to mention geometrical shapes, the answers may be sphere, ellipsis, prism, triangle, equilateral triangle, isosceles triangle, right-angle triangle, square, quadrangle. Among these terms only the sphere, equilateral triangle, and square denote a class that could be called 'a shape'. The full set of terms denotes geometrical classes of different degrees of abstraction. Indeed, there is full reason to reserve the word 'shape' for a class of objects, objects which have in common that each individual member of the class could be transformed into another by homothetic transformation. In more familiar terms we can say that they are similar and the homothetic transformation − or 'transformation of similitude' − is a kind which preserves the ratio and the angle invariant. This is a particular case of affine transformation, namely the equiaffine.

A shape as a class is a class of neither equality nor identity, but a class of equivalence. We can symbolize it either by ($\stackrel{e}{=}$) or by the symbol of similitude ($\sim$). Having a common shape involves neither an identity transformation nor an isometric one.

An architectural repertory item involves an isometry, i.e., from the viewpoint of their internal geometry, thus no differences between objects can be discerned. All individual pieces of each member of the repertory are intrinsically equal, having a common shape and volume. Now to fix the identity of each one, we must consider their external geometry, namely we must locate it, giving it coordinate values, orientation, and direction. More than one space cannot have a common location since the identity class denotes by its definition only one object.

For example, the sphere, which is − as we will see − a paradigmatic enveloping shape second to none, is determined by a parameter, the radius. In order to belong to the shape class denoted by 'sphere', the location of individual spheres is irrelevant. Concerning the location, a set of concentric spheres constitutes a one-parameter family of surface, the radius being the arbitrary parameter, while the set of all spheres is a four-parameter family.

If the definition of the shape is now clearly remembered, we can add that the representation of a geometric object by matrix is unequivocal, but it is far from being transparent. In reality, in this representation the reference to external coordinates could be involved, and so it is often difficult to find an equal shape in the different aliases of representation. They could easily be misread in two ways: thinking that two geometrical objects have the same shape which do not, and vice versa, or reading as different shapes those which are the same. For this reason, to identify a shape we must always compare it to the canonical, or normal, form of matrix.

What Kind of Geometry Commands the Renewal of the Architectural Repertory?

We noted earlier the fact that cultural, historical, and scientific imperatives imposed some discipline on the architecture of our civilization, a discipline which today seems outdated. In reality, architectural expressions of our civilization have been limited to very 'usual' or 'regular' shapes, terms which are frequently used but badly defined. (We must except from this the 'gaudi'sk' architecture, where walls are rarely straight or angles right, where the surface is rarely not undulating, and what Pevsner [1977: 113] calls 'fiercely extravagant repertoire', 'fantastical savagery', 'an entirely free . . . asymmetrical . . . indescribable . . . unprecedented architecture'.) Our architectural catalog is composed largely of so-called geometrical shapes opposed to nature, restricted for all practical purposes to the rectangular polyhedron, the right prism, a framed environment (H. E. Ross 1974: 59) and shapes generated from conic sections which appear as a praline of free fantasy. If we compare these to the architectural repertory of the Far East, we become aware that it is not the earth's gravitational pull which makes regular, rectangular architecture necessary. The introduction of static calculation, where calculability is a requirement, and the abandonment of the master builder's empirical approach to construction according to drawn representation have brought exact copies, precise standards, even stereotypes. Robert Wehrli's doctoral thesis (University of Utah) reveals how even peculiarities of bidimensional drawing — right-handed versus left-handed design — can influence architectural expressions, in addition to the previously noted servitude to the compass and rule. Today many authors tend to make Euclid a scapegoat, the one who is responsible for the impoverishment of our geometry.

If the building trade with its framework requirements seems to restrain the repertory of the architectural medium, then we must consider the new, very economical materials at our disposal (often coupled, it is true, with high quality requirements at the building site) which allow practically any kind of shape. Think of the various plastics and synthetic materials such as polyester, plexiglass, polyurethane treated with radioactive isotopes. Even concrete construction has developed from ferroconcrete, first seen as an artificial stone, which has become a material which can be constructed into a thin self-supported membrane like an eggshell, to a stressed-skin structure made from surprisingly thin timber, or quality concrete without ribs or steel reinforcements. They are all-tension structures following the whole tent tradition in architecture (e.g., German Pavilion at Expo '67 in Montreal) and the inflated domes. We will discuss the geometry of these structures regarding their merits for architectural expression. What is important here is that, on the one hand, the shape becomes free; ribs are no longer necessary, spans can be unbelievably large, uninterrupted by support from the ground, and even rise need not necessarily become higher with the larger spans. So shape as well as volume and floors can have greater variety. On the other hand, the statics calculation of these structures is appealing for a 'new geometry'. In other words these new materials could be fully used if geometry keep pace with them. If we are to counter the narrowing effect of mass production by the building trade with the richer possibilities opened by computer application, which exhaustively explores the combinations of a limited number of inframorphemic ingredients, we need the geometrical tools which can describe all kinds of shapes.

We also need this new geometry to develop the morphology of a larger, more complete architectural repertory. The construction of this repertory at a new frontier must take its departure from the characterization of individual points of closed orientable surfaces. Irregular shapes whose 'generation process' is not immediately obvious can also be approached point by point. We must apply differential geometry in order to treat 'potatoid' shapes, this geometry of any closed orientable surface. Afterward, if we have apprehended any different class of points which could be found on the surface, we can question the characteristics of the complete set of points and so describe the whole surface by its invariants.

Differential characteristics of any point of a closed surface

The architectural envelope has been identified topologically as a closed, orientable surface delimiting one continuous open region. From a geometrical viewpoint this surface must be of finite degree, viz., a straight line can intersect it a finite number of times (e.g., the envelope which is continuously concave is quadric). In opposition to a transcendental surface, these surfaces are also called algebraic in the literature.

Differential geometry always characterizes the intrinsic properties (u, v) of each point of the surface. To characterize one point on the surface we can make an infinite number of intersections with plane surfaces of different orientations, and so cut out an infinite number of curves. If we characterize the surface point by certain intersections, our choice should be motivated so that it does not become arbitrary.

At first we consider the point's tangent plane, if it has one. After that, we choose all surfaces (this number is still infinite) which include the normal line, a line perpendicular to the tangent plane at this point. These are the normal planes since the normal line is included in all of them. For each plane we can find the circle of curvature of the curve, which is the circle having at this point the same tangent as the curve on its concave side. Thus R is the radius of this osculating circle; its reciprocal is the curvature of the curve ($1/R = K$).

The first general division of surfaces in respect to their points depends on whether or not there is a K value in any direction at this point. If not, the surface at this point is not differentiable. We can also say that the Dupin indicatrix cannot be formed.

184 Communication through architecture

– If at a point of the continuous surface there is no direction where the K has a value, this point is a vertex or corner. The implication of this characteristic for the immediate neighborhood of this point is not necessarily that the vertex is situated at the end of (or on) an edge. If it is at the end of an edge, even this does not imply that all or any of the faces deliminted by the edge in the point's neighborhood must be plane, although one face could be a plane. But if all faces are plane, there must be at least three converging edges at the vertex, and the surface forms a polyhedron.

– If only one of the surfaces K at this point has a value, the point is on an edge without being on its 'end point' or vertex. If $K = 0$ at this point, the edge is a straight line. If the edge is a straight line because the point's only calculable K is 0, then the neighboring faces could be either plane or curved. But if the faces are all planes, the edge must be a straight line.

– If K at a point equals 0 in all directions, the point is either on a plane face or on a point of inflection implying that the surface is not continuously concave, but concave-convex.

Now if the surface is continuously differentiable, we can have planelike parts, floors for example, without having either an edge or a vertex.

We can sum up the thought in the following manner: edges, vertices, and planar faces are mutually less involved than the 'architect's intuition' tells him; the freedom of combination is greater than spontaneously supposed. The systematic approach enlarges the repertory of available spaces. It follows that the characterization of a single point of a surface, with or without a vertex, by no means characterizes the whole surface; e.g., vertices and exclusively straight edges do not imply that the shape is a polyhedron, nor does the existence of a set of planar points necessarily involve edges or vertices and vice versa.

The systematic approach requires that the existence of nondifferentiable normal curves – the rupture in the differentiability – constitutes a criterion for a first large division of closed orientable surfaces. Indeed, information theory tells us that without precluding the geometrical 'name' of the whole surfaces, we can discriminate certain architectural morphemes from the others without taking any other consideration into account than difference on one single striking point and thus eliminating the possibility that two surfaces have the same shape.

Now looking at the points which have a K value in all directions, how do we make quantitative differences? We could calculate theoretically the integral value of all Ks: $\int_{(2\pi)} K d\phi$. But we know that there are two directions for which K has an extreme value in absolute terms, maximal and minimal, and also that these two directions are always perpendicular to each other.

The geometry of architectural morphology   185

These are the principal directions, and the radii are ρ_1, ρ_2. From that we can calculate either the total normal curvature or Gaussian curvature $K = 1/\rho_1\rho_2$ or the mean normal curvature K_m (or $2H = 1/\rho_1 + 1/\rho_2$). Both characterize the differentiable point of the surface now as a whole. ($1/\rho_1$ and $1/\rho_2$ are the principal curvatures.) We can also formulate these magnitudes in functions of the fundamental coefficients of the first (E, F, G) and second (D, D', D'') orders of the surface.

These curvature values (K, K_m) geometrically characterize a point in its infinitely near neighborhood. But these magnitudes do not measure the shape as such at this single point. It does not present the homothetic invariants in isolation, but includes all intrinsic isometric invariants. So, for example, all spheres with various radii do not have equal K; only the K and K_m of corresponding points on the two surfaces have a constant numeric relation. This constancy could not appear in the case of a point, and so must be discussed in the context of the characterization of the whole surface shape.

If we consider not the magnitude of ρ_1, ρ_2 but their numeric and algebraic relations we discover a first subdivision of the differentiable points of a surface. Indeed the principal normal curvatures could be numerically equal or not, having the same or opposite signs, or they could be zero. These regulations appear in K's variations.

Surface points:

1. Elliptic point.
2. Parabolic point.
3. Hyperbolic point.

Dupinian surfaces:

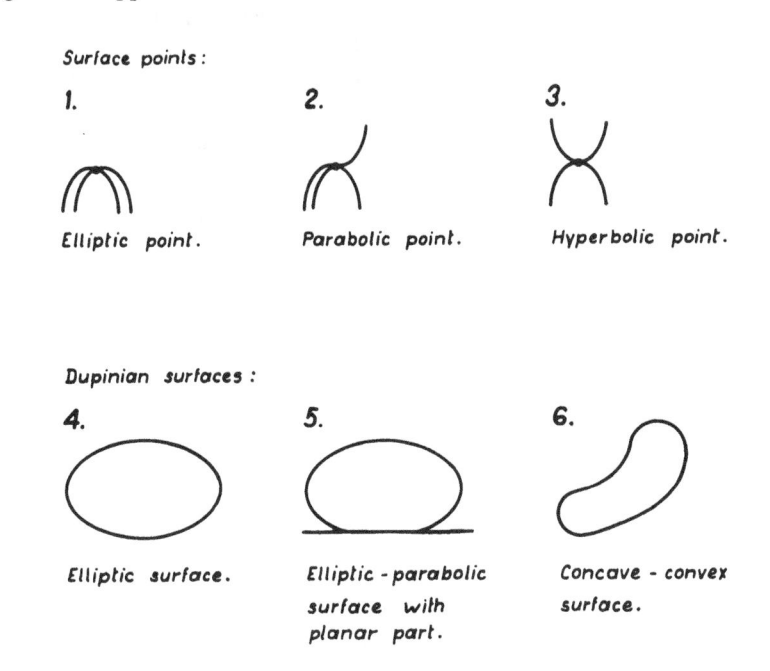

4. Elliptic surface.
5. Elliptic - parabolic surface with planar part.
6. Concave - convex surface.

Figure 3.5. *Dupinian surfaces.*

If $K > 0$, the osculating circle is on the same side of the surface, and the radii have the same algebraic sign, then these points are called elliptic points (see Figure 3.5.1). All the sphere's points are a particular case of elliptic points, since not only is $K > 0$ but $\rho_1 = \rho_2 = R$. When we discuss the sphere's geometrical excellences among closed surfaces, we will see that its main section gives its own osculating circle.

If $K = 0$, the point is called parabolic (see Figure 3.5.2). It is developable because at least one of the ρ must be infinite. If both ρ_1 and ρ_2 are infinite, the point lies in a plane.

If $K < 0$, the surface point is a hyperbolic one, implying that the center of the osculating circle is on the opposite side of the surface (see Figure 3.5.3).

Now we must distil the properly homothetic characteristics of the point. We will do that in the context of the characterization of the whole set of points of the considered surface. We will see that for a closed orientable surface delimiting a continuum there are some relations among its own points that are necessary in order to assess the whole surface shape. The preceding classification only assures that the point is in one of the three classes from the viewpoint of concavity. As a matter of fact this classification groups points which are related in a family through affine, but not equiaffine, transformation.

If we consider the problem of properly defining the characteristics of one point (in its infinitely near neighborhood) which are exclusively relevant to the surface shape, we must look for 'similitude characteristics' of the point which preserve the constancy of angles and distance ratios. Considering the use of the fundamental coefficients, it is the first fundamental quadratic form of surface which determines angles and distances ($ds^2 = E\,du^2 + 2\,F\,du\,dv + G\,dv^2$) and therefore $\cos\theta = F/\sqrt{EG}$. So points are similar if $F^2/(EG)$ is constant. This is useful to say, at least for clarification of the definition.

Considering the whole surface: Engineer Dupin's indicatrix

1. *Dupinian closed surface* We consider now the three 'concavity classes' — elliptic, parabolic, and hyperbolic — and how this tool can characterize whole continuously differentiable closed surfaces. Could each type of point alone constitute such a surface or must certain of them be combined with other types of points? Within such surface classes could the numeric value of the Ks be used for further subdivision? If this value varies from point to point on one surface, are some interrelationships of the distribution pattern inevitable? How could surface families be created with specified degrees of relationship?

Two principles of classification emerge:

(1) All points of a particular closed surface have a positive K ($K_{xyz} > 0$), or are zero or negative. We could call them K_+, K_0, K_- surfaces. In this case

a whole surface could be characterized by one of the three types of points. (We must guard against the confusing terminology often prevailing in mathematics dictionaries (James & James 1968: 90, 122, 293, 341, 355), which applies the same adjectives — elliptic, hyperbolic, parabolic — not only for classifying surfaces, but also for constituting subdivisions within them (e.g., 'pseudospherical surface of elliptic type'). It is much clearer to say that points K_+ and K_- could alternate on a surface when speaking about a heterogeneous or mixed surface.

(2) The other classifying principle could be more strict, requiring that the surface at all its points have an equal K.

In general, a surface whose total curvature K has the same positive value at all its points is called spherical, and those having the same negative value pseudospherical; but in the case of a continuously differentiable closed surface only the sphere can have an equal K value at all its points, namely a positive one.

We can classify the continuously differentiable closed surfaces in three main categories:

(1) A surface cannot be closed and continuously differentiable without having elliptic points. Elliptic points are the only type of points which could alone constitute an architectural envelope, namely a homogeneous surface (see Figure 3.5.4). This surface is totally concave and has no geometrical affinity with concave-convex surface. The 'regular' elliptic surface, i.e., where K is invariant at every point, is the sphere.

(2) A parabolic surface, if it is Dupinian at all its points, i.e., differentiable $(\partial y/\partial x)$ and closed, must contain some elliptic points. Surface categories 1 and 2 are totally concave ($K_{xyz} \geq 0$) while the elliptic-parabolic (category 2) surfaces in addition have a planar part (quadric surface or surface of second degree.) (See Figure 3.5.5.)

(3) The surface having hyperbolic points cannot be closed without having elliptic points too. These surfaces are concave-convex and the presence of hyperbolic and elliptic points implies that between the two there must be a parabolic line — or inflection points — making the transition between the two (see Figure 3.5.6). This is the most mixed surface type among the closed continuously differentiable surfaces.

1.1. *Elliptic surfaces* All points of the elliptic surface have a positive total normal curvature value. Any elliptic surface can be obtained by affine transformation from the sphere which has a constant curvature.

1.1.1. *Sphere, the closed surface par excellence* It is not for nothing that we speak about the atmo*sphere* or the hygrosphere (J. J. Gibson 1966: 9). To define an open region in topology, all points must be homeomorphic with those included in the sphere. This was our topological definition of the architectural word. Concerning the closed orientable surface itself, we always also ask the question: are its points homeomorphic with those of the sphere?

Geometrically the sphere is perfectly regular, and it is unique in that it defines the regular surface itself in a certain way. Hilbert enumerates 11 geometrical virtues of the sphere. In point 10, he affirms not only that the total curvature K of a spherical surface has the same value at all its points, but that individually all its ρ_1, ρ_2 and its R in general are the same. Point 8 says that K_m of the sphere has a minimal value among K_m of all totally concave surfaces. We can add that the sphere is the only closed surface which could be entirely approached by a polyhedron with equal numbers of edges and of solid angles, a quality which shows that the sphere's excellence transcends that of all the other continuously differentiable closed surfaces, and relates all closed simple (or Jordan) surfaces among them as their paradigm.

The seventh virtue of Hilbert's enumeration is that the sphere is the only closed surface which has a minimal V^2/S^3. V is the volumetric magnitude of the enclosed space and S that of the enveloping surface. We call this the index of isoconcavity. Closed surfaces of many shapes can have the same isoconcavity index, but no other can have $1/36\pi = 0.0088$, which is that of the sphere. The sphere contains the maximum of volume with the minimum of surface. We will see that this index is particularly relevant for the impression of acoustic space.

Even though it is difficult to square the surface of a sphere, or to cube its content, it is the sphere which helps us to osculate points of the closed surface. It is also the sphere which helps us to characterize a whole closed surface by the radius of the smallest circumscribed sphere, as well as by those of the largest inscribed sphere, spheres the relative locations of whose centers are themselves used for characterization (cf. centroid), especially if the surface is topologically homeomorphic with that of the sphere. The constructions which exploit parts of the sphere are numerous.

1.1.2. *Ellipsoid* Ellipsoids are closed surfaces all of whose sections are affine with the circle. If the normal section in respect to one of its three axes of symmetry is a circle, revolution is its mode of generation. Depending upon which of the two axes, the longitudinal or the shorter one, of the ellipsis is the axis of revolution, the resulting shape is called a prolate or oblate ellipsoid. All ellipsoids generated by revolution are called spheroids. For example, the filtering ensemble in Hibbing, Minnesota, by J. C. Taylor is an oblate ellipsoid.

1.1.3. *Ovaloid* Ovaloids are closed surfaces which are always concave and are composed from a semiellipsoid and a semisphere. A naturally occurring example is the egg. The ellipsoid part could also be replaced by a hyperboloid of revolution of two sheets, or a paraboloid of revolution as a particular case of the elliptic paraboloid, because these surfaces are elliptic too. Like the golden section, the shell of the golden egg is a preferred subject for mystification by the architect's alchemy.

1.2. *The partly parabolic surface* We attach particular interest to the fact that a completely concave architectural envelope has parabolic points, since this assures, on the one hand, that the surface part having this set of points is developable, and, on the other hand, a more practical consideration, that there is a planar surface part (which is useful as floor) of space in the gravitational field. We have seen that a set of parabolic points on a closed surface must be combined with elliptic points, or all points will not be differentiable. Among the surfaces with parabolic sets of points we find the cylindrical and conic surfaces, and also the developable helicoids.

Among the cylinders, a parabolic surface whose generator curve and mode of generation we can recognize, we can distinguish numerous types: the cylinder of revolution and the sinusoidal cylinder.

Among the cones, the cone of revolution is the more frequently used in architectural practice.

1.3. *The partly hyperbolic surface* All points of a continuously differentiable closed surface can never be hyperbolic. Even the name is misleading since surfaces grouped under the name hyperboloid are not surfaces all of whose points will be hyperbolic. We also noted that the hyperboloid of two sheets is composed of elliptic points. Among the quadric surfaces are the ruled paraboloid, which has a rectilinear generator but whose points are hyperbolic, and the hyperbolic paraboloid.

1.3.1. *Hyperbolic paraboloid* For modern constructors the hyperbolic paraboloid appears to be a surface which offers the most possible advantages. Indeed it is a surface which is ruled as the cylinder *and* simultaneously generated by translation. And yet the fact of its being a ruled surface facilitates not only the statics calculation, but the concrete's formwork and its removal. This surface could also be better simulated by small, very small, rectilinear elements. This is no negligible advantage because it is very often difficult to create and remove the formwork of a thin, self-supporting membrane (eggshell principle).

First and foremost, the application of the hyperbolic paraboloid in modern architecture bears the imprint of the Spanish concrete engineer Felix Candela. Faber (1963) discusses Candela's works in detail, as well as the influence of the engineering architect Eduardo Torroja on him. We can mention some examples.

Candela conceived — in collaboration with the architect Jorges Gonzales Reyna — the Cosmic Ray Laboratory of the University of Mexico in 1952. This is a one-inch-thick (thin shell) four-legged shed whose roof is composed from two hyperbolic paraboloids with a surface of translation. One of his warehouses (Vallejo, D. F. Mexico) looks like umbrellas of hyperbolic paraboloids defined by a network of left-handed quadrilaterals. During the same period (1956) the Iglesia San Antonio de Las Huertas (St. Anthony of the Orchards Church, Calzada Mexico, Tacuba, D. F.) was erected under the imprint of the same architects, namely Enrique de la Mora and Fernando Lopez Carmona. The Restautant Los Manatiales at Xachimilco, D. F. Mexico, constructed in 1959, was created by Candela with the architect J. A. Ordonez. The shape derives from a bitangential penetration of four hyperbolic paraboloids generated by translation. The very spectacular Iglesia de San José (St. Joseph the Laborer Church at Monterrey, Nuevo Leon) was designed by architects de la Mora and Carmona (1959). It is composed of two hyperbolic paraboloids by two left-handed quadrilaterals symmetrical with respect to a vertical plane. The next year Candela erected the Chapel of San Vicente de Paul at Coyoacan, D. F. Mexico. In this case there are three hyperbolic paraboloids defined by one left-handed quadrilateral which are rotated around a vertical axis. In the same year (1960) he created, with A. T. de la Pina as architect, an open roof which could be seen on both sides, showing that it is a thin membrane. It is geometrically a bitangential penetration of two hyperbolic paraboloids with a common vertical axis. This is a sales office building at Guadalajara, Jalisco.

Other architects also became active in hyperbolic paraboloid construction. The technician of Le Chaux-de-Fonds, Jeanneret–Le Corbusier designed the Philips Pavilion at the Brussels World's Fair in 1958. It is composed of multiple hyperbolic paraboloids which have one or more generators (C. Siegel). The information pavilion at the same World's Fair was created by the engineer R. Sarger and the architectural office of L. J. Baucher. It is also a hyperbolic paraboloid defined by a left-handed quadrilateral on a square plane. We see how these so-called very original constructions became fashionable and often a pure combination of two variations (Ankerl 1958).

1.3.2. *Ruled hyperboloid* The ruled hyperboloid is the other quadric surface whose points are hyperbolic. The new cathedral of Algiers is a ruled hyperboloid of revolution conceived by R. Sarger. Herbé and Le Couteur were the architects. Its axis is vertical, which gives a blast-furnace impression to the building.

The geometry of architectural morphology 191

1.3.3. *Other identified, partly hyperbolic surfaces* Cylindroids and conoids could have hyperbolic points since both are ruled surfaces. The first type has as directrices two curves and one straight line, while the second has the inverse number of directrices.

Favini conceived a service station near Milan whose shape combines a sinusoidal conoid with a parabolic surface which is a sinusoidal cylinder.

The porch roof of the UNESCO Palace in Paris (1953-1956), created by the architect Marcel Breuer and engineers P. L. Nervi and B. Zehrfuss, is also a cylindroid whose directrix is a parabola.

Among the other surfaces not homeomorphic with that of the sphere is that of the torus, the one most used for the annular vault. It is sometimes penetrated by a conoid (bitangential penetration torus-conoid). Along the line of penetration the surface loses its differentiability.

The reservoir at Rabat, Morocco, is a truncated cone with a base covered by a depressed cupola and surrounded by a depressed torus.

The hangar of the airport at Marignane, France, designed by engineer N. Esquillan and architect A. Perret, is covered by narrow vaults in equatorial zones of anchor rings.

1.3.4 *Surfaces with zero mean curvature* If the mean normal curvature K_m is zero, then ρ_1 and ρ_2 must have opposite signs and K (total curvature) must have a negative value, or at least cannot be positive; and so if the surface is not planar, it must be hyperbolic under the stated requirement. (In terms of the fundamental coefficients of second order of the surface, $ED'' - 2FD' + GD = 0$)

Even if this requirement is not sufficient, a surface with $K_m = 0$ is called a minimal surface. James and James (1968: 236) specify that a 'minimal surface does not necessarily minimalize the area spanned by a given contour; but if a smooth surface S minimizes the area, then S is a minimal surface.' It is also the minimal surface of a surface which is not closed but has a boundary curve. According to Plateau if we blow a soap bubble which has a closed boundary curve without double points, the resulting surface is always the minimal one.

The catenoid, according to Meusnier, is the only minimal surface of revolution. It is generated by the rotation of a catenary about its axis. (The

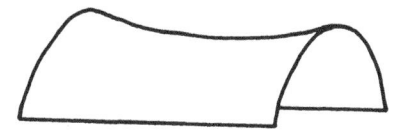

192 *Communication through architecture*

catenary is the plane curve in which a uniform flexible cable hangs when suspended from two points.) We find this kind of shape in a cable-suspended tentlike construction such as the German Pavilion at Expo 1967 in Montreal, Ile St. Hélène.

Earlier we discussed the developable helicoid among the parabolic surfaces. Yet the right helicoid — right in respect to the directrix plane — is the one and only real ruled minimal surface.

2. *Non-Dupinian closed surfaces* We call a surface non-Dupinian if a normal curvature cannot be calculated at all points and in all directions, so that the Dupin indicatrix cannot be calculated for all points of the surface. Surfaces are not closed and Dupinian if they are hyperbolic or developable. Only elliptic surfaces satisfy these two requirements; the others must be either elliptic-developable ($K_{xyz} > 0$) or hyperbolic-elliptic-parabolic (which has some $K = 0$, some $K > 0$, and some $K < 0$ points). Otherwise some points must be non-Dupinian.

Concerning the non-Dupinian points which are on edges and vertices, we have seen how they do or do not involve each other as well as the developable planar surfaces. Through all these mutual freedoms and constraints we can establish classes of closed surfaces which are all situated between the two extremes, namely the Dupinian surfaces which are differentiable at all points and those non-Dupinian surfaces which have only nondifferentiable and developable points, viz., where the Dupin indicatrix vanishes. They are called polyhedrons. Their great advantage is that their surface is always squarable and their volumetric magnitude cubable; moreover their differentiable surface parts are planar, which is appropriate for a floor as well as for syntagmatic composition of spaces, since flat surfaces are endocompatible, that is, can be mutually and jointlessly adjacent. In order not to restrain the architectural repertory without valid reason, we must repeat that these advantages are always present in the case of polyhedrons but are not exclusive to them. Further, these advantages are not a *sine qua non* for a well-formed architectural word, as our classical tradition would make us believe.

A more subtle question arises in this respect in the formation of the architectural repertory. We note that, from a purely formal viewpoint, the existence of one single point on a surface which is differentiable and its absence on another surface is a sufficient discriminating cue for saying that the two cannot have the same shape. But, on the other hand, in an infinitesimal process we can multiply the faces of a polyhedron in such a way that it approaches any curved surface. We say that this surface is reticulated. The history of architecture shows that this is not necessarily a purely modern trait; we find innumerable subdivisions of roofs and vaults also in other epochs (quadripartite, sexpartite, and fan vaults, stellar vaults, liernes, and so on). The circle is the unique surface which can be approached infinitely well by a regular polygon, but other surfaces with curved boundaries could be by other polygons.

The general consequence of this fact is that two surfaces, one continuously differentiable and the other non-Dupinian (albeit geometrically nonisometric), are not necessarily as easily distinguished on the perceptual level as being nonisometric as we could expect. Indeed, eventually two surfaces, both continuously differentiable, can be better distinguished than can a Dupinian from a non-Dupinian. Because architectural communication is accomplished by the impression of the created spaces, the architectural repertory cannot be constructed only on the basis of purely geometrical — or topological — differences; the final judge must be the most sensitive human observer perceiving the difference in a standardized observation situation. Of course, only just noticeable differences which are based on actual objective difference enter the repertory construction. In order to constitute two different repertory items, two criteria must be satisfied: the items must (a) have an objective difference which is (b) also perceptible. So classes and subclasses of the architectural repertory do not coincide directly with the geometrical or topological ones.

In contemporary times, the ease of calculating surfaces composed from flat or near-flat faces has made this kind of shape fashionable, especially those composed from very small triangles. These could be calculated, namely as nonreticulated massive structures. We will discuss these structures after a treatment of the polyhedron.

2.1. *Polyhedron* A closed surface which is exclusively bounded by plane polygons is a polyhedron. Most spaces that we call 'rooms' belongs to this geometrical class. If we fix neither the shape of the faces nor their number, nor the number of the sides of the enveloping polygons, this class has an infinite number of possible shapes. From a topological viewpoint any genus of orientable closed surface, whether or not it is homeomorphic with the sphere's surface, could have the shape of a polyhedron. On the other hand the genus of the surface fixes its Euler characteristic and that imposes a definite numeric relation between the number of edges, vertices, and faces: $V - E + F = 2 - 2p - q - r$. This formula makes a distinction between a polyhedron with and without holes but shows us that continuously concave and concave-convex surfaces are topologically equivalent.

2.1.1. *Regular polyhedron* We have already seen that the concept of regularity, if it has any well-defined sense, is related to the repetition of the chosen elements which generate a symmetry in the modern sense of the term, and which is no longer understood as something exclusively bilateral. In our specific case, let us state that the polygon's regularity which is implied in the polyhedron exists insofar as faces and vertices are equivalent (Hilbert and Cohn-Vossen 1952: 89) and in that they participate in the perfect regularity of its circumscribed circle. We can make an infinite number of polygons which are regular, and so their vertices are all situated on the circumscribed circle and all their faces touch the inscribed circle. If we try to make an analogy with three-dimensional shapes, expecting to have an infinite number of regular polyhedrons with an analogous relation to the circumscribed and inscribed spheres, we will see that this analogy is unfounded. As a matter of fact there are only five of them. This finite number can be deduced from topological requirements (Hilbert and Cohn-Vossen 1952: 471, 490-495). Indeed Plato, among other authors, has enumerated them, and Pythagoras has proven their limited number.

All regular polyhedrons have an equal number of edges meeting in each vertex. However, we can distinguish two families among these five polyhedrons. In the first we find the tetrahedron, the octahedron, and the icosahedron. Their faces are all triangles. The second family has a common characteristic that three edges meet in each vertex. They are the cube or hexahedron, the dodecahedron, and the tetrahedron. We see immediately that the tetrahedron is privileged because it participates in both regularities, which infers in terms of graph theory that it is its own dual. We will remember this privilege of the tetrahedron when we look for a polyhedron which is most appropriate to approach the various Dupinian surfaces.

The first family, namely the triangular polyhedrons (tetrahedron, octahedron, icosahedron), have the characteristics that they are not deformable and so are also statically determined systems. They are geometrically rigid shapes. Indeed the geometrical composition of a shape by hatching is rigid if it is done by adding triangles to a basic triangle. (The bidimensional simplex is shown in Figure 3.34.) $E = 3(V - 2)$ where E is the number of edges and V is the number of vertices.

We now turn to the question of approaching the Dupinian surfaces by a regular polyhedron, a sort of inverse process from that used when we approach the closed surfaces by the osculating spheres. The following statements must be made:

– There is not an infinite number of regular polyhedrons at our disposal, as was the case with the circle which could be approached infinitely well simply by increasing the number of sides of the regular polygons.

– The sphere has the privilege that it too could be approached infinitely well by some polyhedric surfaces which have an equal number of edges and equal angles. Angle here means the solid angle, viz., the interior and not the polyhedral angle. The number of such polyhedrons is 18: 5 regular polyhedrons and 13 semiregular ones, also called Archimedian polyhedrons. These 18 polyhedrons are those which could be inscribed in the sphere.

Finally we see that the triangular polyhedrons are not deformable, and among them the tetrahedron is the only one which can constitute on its own a covering surface. The octahedron and the icosahedron must be sectioned, which means that in the process of approaching the sphere they lose their geometrical rigidity; for example, a half-octahedron or a pyramid.

3. *Assimilation of the curved or Dupinian surface to the polyhedron* Having revealed that, on the one hand, the sphere among the closed surfaces has unique geometrical qualities and, on the other hand, the tetrahedron among the regular polyhedrons as an approach to the sphere has its own, the temptation is great for architects who look for a miraculous, unique, and ideal solution to develop hermetic ideas from this shape as a starting point.

We first address the question from a practical viewpoint. If we approach the sphere by a tetrahedron, we must bear in mind that the bar of the formwork cannot be longer than 2 to 3 m., so we can never approach a sphere whose diameter is larger than 3.80-5.60 m. Both ancient and modern (geodesic) domes easily have diameters which vary between 16 and 30 meters. Fuller's polyhedral geodesic domes, constructed in Baton Rouge (1958) and at the American Pavillion at Expo '67 in Montreal (destroyed by fire May 21, 1976), have diameters over 100 meters.

From a more fundamental viewpoint it is not at all interesting to look for a 'canonic' ideal shape. Architectural communication must express many different sociological and economic concerns. It is time for architects to renounce the search for the perfect natural or ideal shape. There are *many* optimal shapes corresponding to different requirements for architectural expression. And so different Dupinian shapes could be approached by various polyhedrons.

The following considerations must be kept in the forefront:

– The polyhedron composed from equilateral triangles has geometric virtues which we have evoked. These virtues could also be present if these triangles are inscribed on other than planar surfaces, e.g., we choose three points on a sphere's surface in such a way that the shortest mutual distances inscribed on this surface should be equal. The lines of these distances will be the three sides of the geodesic triangle.
– We stated that only the triangular polyhedrons are composed from equilateral triangles. The evident advantage of approaching continuously differentiable Dupinian surfaces by a polyhedron is that a continuous surface becomes divided and is composed from a discrete and finite number of inframorphemic elements, namely the surface facets. On the other hand, if these elements have the capacity to become infinitesimally smaller and smaller, some requirements for a 'perfect approach' become less important. If the planar triangles become small enough – we must think about the while 'tangential procedure' – the differences between planar and geodesic vanish,

and the overall shape itself becomes semispheric, semipolyhedral, quasi-polyhedral. The result of this sufficient 'miniaturization' is that, on the one hand, the geodesic could be approximated in statics calculation as planar elements, a calculation which anyway is always just an approach of the effective force, and, on the other hand, the perceptible differences vanish too. In this sufficient 'miniaturization' of the elements it is less important to preserve the regularity − that is, the equilateral sides − of the triangles than to preserve the trilateral character of the polygonal facets, that is, to ensure that they remain triangles.

− If we approach the circumscribed sphere from a different series of regular and semiregular polyhedrons, constructing also quasi-regular ones with mixed semipolyhedral and semicurved surfaces, we can choose among four kinds of modification processes − bisection, division, maclage, and pyramiding − of the polyhedron's nontriangular facets.

Bucky, our alchemist, dr h.c. and dr. h.c. . . . . (29 times) It would be hard to find another amateur architect who, like LeCorbusier, could better typify the search to justify some particular invented item of the architectural catalog as something natural and universally, uniquely superior than Richard Buckminster Fuller. He first constructed a 'Dymaxion House', which was a huge hexagonal structure hung by cables from a central mast that poked through the roof. But his true reputation is related to the geodesic domes with very large spans constructed after the Second World War. Truthfully, these constructions have an inherent convincing beauty, but it is false to think or say, as he and his Design Science Institute (founded in 1972) would pretend and teach, that these constructions are based on a deeper understanding of the 'eternal laws of the total Universe', on the application of 'omni-interaccommodative generalized principles' (Fuller 1972), and that the advantages of these architectural catalog items transcend all other items in every respect.

What is the matter? The large domes are geometrically cuboctahedrons, which are semiregular polyhedrons composed from two regular polyhedron types, cube and tetrahedron. They have the unique property of having edges all of which have the same length as the radius of the circumscribed sphere. In addition, the network's points are centers of equal tangent spheres which are disposed in the space in the most compact manner. On the one hand, these geometrical qualities offer possibilities for the statics calculation, and, on the other, the possibility of this compact arrangement, this endocompatibility of complete adjacency as syntagmatic solutions, opens ways in the construction of space systems.

But we must note that before him, Schweder's dome and Zeiss-Dywidag lierne, both self-supporting structures, demonstrated already very analogous solutions.

Bucky did not discover this shape by a new statics calculation technique, but by the most traditional approach, the trial and error method (Kenner 1973; Alexander 1964: 76-78). The cuboctahedron was only subsequently related to his 'energetic-synergetic geometry'. In order to make his doctrine more unified he tried to rename his dymaxion (Kenner, professor of English literature at the Santa Barbara campus of the University of California, in his 1973 book about Bucky describes its original baptism) as a body with vectorial equilibrium.

Another very popular way to attribute a universal significance to a particular architectural expression is to relate it to natural shapes. Reference to the radiolar design of the cuboctahedron in nature had already been made in the last century by Ernest Haeckel (*Kunstformen der Natur*) according to Weyl (1967); and a picture taken by electron microscope by William Bragg in 1924 (just three years before Bucky's suicide attempt in Lake Michigan) confirmed the cuboctahedral structure of the atom. But this kind of natural 'occurrence' is totally irrelevant to justify a chosen architectural solution or to judge its appropriateness. Buckminster's geodesic shape and 'omni-directional equilibrium of force' has crystallographic perfection, an advantage in nuclear biology where the gravitational field is not asymmetrical, but it offers no economic or other advantages on our globe where unidirectional gravity dictates structural shapes.

Bucky's architectural spaces are pleasant, as many other architectural spaces are, and pleasantness is a sufficient justification in itself without other unnecessary pretensions that is often forgotten.

General measures for specifically architectural shapes

Topologically speaking, the surface forming architectural spaces belongs to the closed, orientable surfaces whose interior points are all homeomorphic with those of the sphere. It is necessary to enumerate in an exhaustive manner all admissible surfaces which could potentially form an item of the architectural repertory. We must try to develop a device which apprehends items of this infinite group from the geometrical viewpoint without imposing any arbitrary limits on them.

It must be made clear that the topological and geometrical characteristics to which the discernibility of these items is related could be and will be different for the various sensory spaces. For example, a reticulated polyhedron approaching a Dupinian surface in an optical space is, beyond a certain limit, indistinguishable from the Dupinian surface itself, while the same minor geometrical difference can be perceived in a haptic space.

In order to classify the architectural envelopes we noted topological differences: surfaces homeomorphic with the sphere and those with other

198 *Communication through architecture*

genus characteristics. These constitute lexical items of the architectural repertory. We also noted differences of solid geometry for morphological classification: Dupinian and non-Dupinian surfaces, and so on. Among the shape indicatrixes we must pay particular attention to those which are exclusively related to closed surfaces. Curvature and other characteristics can be calculated on other kinds of surfaces but the volume-to-surface ratio, in appropriate form, is a proper characteristic of a closed, orientable surface. Even if it does not identify a shape in its individual property there is interest in exploring various forms of these ratios in relation to particular sensory spaces, especially to the acoustical one.

Various global shape indicatrixes of geographers

We have already noticed that the geographer's geometrical interest can inspire us and enlarge our horizon because he is obliged to apprehend 'irregular', accidental shapes and so to devise tools useful also for the designer of an architecture of free ('ungeometrical') shapes.

But a geographer's task, if it is not to consider the shape of the whole globe, is rather to describe, not closed surfaces, but surfaces with boundary curves.

For this reason their shape indicatrixes often establish relation between the area (A) and the boundary curve or perimeter (p or L). Perhaps they note the distance between the farthest points (l = major axis) or the position of certain specific (characteristic) points, like the centroid. We will list some of these, even if most of them cannot be directly applied in our field because they are related to surfaces with boundary curves. We find them in Haggett and Chorley (1970):

(1) Horton calculated in 1932 the A/l^2, called a 'form ratio', which was revived by Hagett (1965).
(2) Miller introduced in 1953 the 'circulatory ratio' $4\pi A/p^2$ in order to classify and compare surface shapes.
(3) Schumm used in 1956 the area (A) and major axis (l) in the 'elongation ratio $[\sqrt{A/\pi}]/l$.
(4) Stoddart used in 1965 the "ellipticity ratio' $4A/\pi l^2 \sqrt{1-\epsilon^2}$ where ϵ gives the relation between the major and minor axes of the ellipse.
(5) Boyce and Clark formulated in 1964 the 'radial-line ratio' $\Sigma_i(t_i - 1/n)$ where t_i are the normalized radial axes from centroid vertices and n represents the number of vertices.
(6) Blair and Bliss developed in 1967 the 'compactness ratio' which closely matches the description of the continuously differentiable (or Dupinian) closed surfaces. The precision of the formula is conveyed by its differential nature: $A/\sqrt{2\pi \int_A t^2 dA}$ where t is the radial axis from centroid to small dA.

According to Haggett and Chorley (1970: 70-72), this ratio is also useful for the description of fragmented and punctured surfaces.

It is interesting to observe that all these ratios give the value 1 for the circle. In all shape indicatrixes the circle as measure is implicit. The shape used by Bunge is an exception in that he uses equilateral polygons.

What can we learn from how the geographer measures shapes? Certainly the magnitude of the surface area can be a characteristic for the closed surface too. But because of the fact that geographers do not characterize closed surfaces, the volume could not appear in their indicatrixes; yet volumetric magnitude is a fundamental characteristic of the (enclosed) architectural space.

For the closed orientable surface the radii and the location of the centers of the largest inscribed (radius represented by $\dot{r}$) and smallest circumscribed (radius is $\bar{r}$) spheres are used in the characterization (cf. eccentricity of the ellipsoid). But magnitude in absolute terms cannot characterize a shape in a neat manner; the numerical relation between $\dot{r}$ and $\bar{r}$ and the relative locations of the two spheres' centers will be relevant for the shape (Polya and Szegoe 1951: 2, 278).

Centroid If we set fire to a solid sphere over its complete surface at the same moment, and if the sphere is physically homogeneous, the burning front will be successively smaller and smaller concentric sphere surfaces and the last burning point will be the center. The search for these consecutive burning surfaces is the search for the internal boundary of a circular neighborhood. Of course the method could be applied to any compact homogeneous body closed by an orientable surface. Whether this continuously shrinking surface remains a continually closed surface or becomes, according to the original shape of the closed surface, more than one closed surface before the whole body vanishes, the last burning points are very interesting characteristics, especially of irregular shapes. The fire always spreads along the normal line of the surface, which can change its shape at every moment. So, for example, if the fire, before completely vanishing at one or more points at the same time, was to form during the burning process more than one closed surface, the original surface would necessarily have been convex-concave; however, this implication is not strict because — conversely — there could be not only continuously concave but also certain convex-concave surfaces which do not break up into more than one closed surface during the burning process.

Isoconcavity indicatrix (i): *a proper characteristic of the closed orientable surface*

The dimensionless numeric relation between the superficial area of a closed surface and the enclosed volumetric magnitude characterizes the shape in

200 Communication through architecture

some way, although one numeric value does not specify one shape exclusively. The unique case of the sphere is the exception, where shape and i are converse criteria.

The indicatrix $V^2/S^3 = i$ we call the isoconcavity indicatrix. A shape always has a determined i but an i can be realized by different shapes. An i fixes a class of isoconcave equivalent shapes. Each numeric class of i fixes a degree of *arrondissement* — rounding in the etymological sense of the term. Applying 'symmetrization' to transform a shape, the next shape cannot have a lower i than the original one.

After this definition, and before we study symmetrization as a transformation process, let us see what the significance of this indicatrix is in applied terms.

In order to characterize an acoustical space it is very important to calculate the Sabine formula, which gives the reverberation time and which is instrumental in producing the impression of acoustical space. We will see in the section about acoustical space that this formula could be calculated and formed in a unique function of i and V without other specification of the space's shape: the shape is there fully represented by i. $T = f(V, i)$; or $T = c \cdot \sqrt[3]{iV}$.

Further, any increase of the i represents a shape which is more economical, in the sense that with less surface we have more enclosed cubage. In more technical terms we can say that among the isepiphane envelopes, those having a greater i use less material for the same volumetric magnitude and lose less heat per time unit as well.

The fact that acoustical optimalization of a common space usually requires lower i values than haptic optimalization does not change the significance of the i as characterizing the orientable closed surface, which is the architectural space.

Symmetrization Concerning the numeric value of the i, we can state that for any i we can find at least one shape, *if* the value is less than 0.0088, or, more precisely, less than $1/36\pi$. The i has a maximal value which in fact determines *a* shape, namely the sphere. There is no other shape which satisfies this i value, and there are no other i values which determine one single shape in an unequivocal manner. This is the unexcelled quality of the sphere.

Let us imagine a physical model. We have a closed surface constructed from a material which is completely flexible but inelastic. It is surface-preserving. If we begin to inflate it, at every moment the i increases. During this expansion process the material could pass through very different alternative shapes which become more and more similar to the sphere. The elliptic-hyperbolic shape finally becomes elliptic; the polyhedron also approaches the sphere despite its developable nature. The end product of this series of transformations is its approximation to the closed surface with minimal mean curvature (K_m), to the completely concave and perfectly symmetrical surface, the sphere. The operation of transformation which increases the *i* of a shape is 'symmetrization'.

Jacob Steiner introduced this transformation on the bidimensional level in the last century. The problem that this process solved was to find the maximal area which could be included by a closed line of determined length. He discovered the method of construction without proving its general validity. In analytical terms, this is the isometric problem, and the isometric inequality must be solved in the framework of the calculus of variations.

H. A. Schwarz applied the solution of the isoperimetric problem to the isepiphanic by applying it to the closed surface and its enclosed volume.

We find extensive literature on this question, beginning with Schwarz's own writings. Polya and Szegoe (1951: 3) state that according to Pappus's book Zenodorus had already discussed this problem. They introduced the concept of volume-radius ($\bar{V}$) and surface-radius ($\bar{S}$) these being the radii of the sphere which has a volume and an area respectively equal to those of the considered space. Using $\bar{V}$ and $\bar{S}$ we can express the isoconcavity indicatrix $I = V^2/S^3 = (1/36\pi) \cdot (\bar{V}/\bar{S})$. If the considered space is a sphere then $\bar{V}/\bar{S} = 1$.

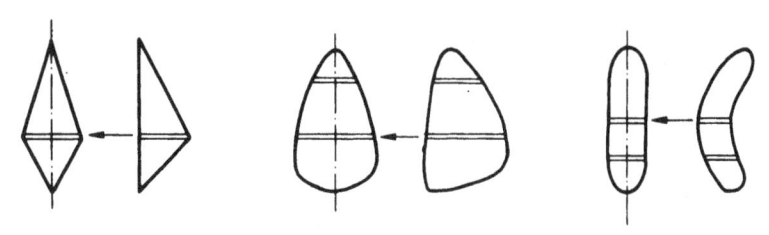

Figure 3.6. *Symmetrization.*

How can we present Steiner's symmetrization transformation to non-mathematicians? And what is the procedure for carrying it out? Draw a simple closed curve in a plane. Choose any straight line as an axis, then cut out infinitely small sections from the surface, sections which are perpendicular to the axis, and displace them to the axis in such a way that the axis becomes the axis of symmetry for all sections. Next, choose an axis of another orientation and repeat the operation. If it is sufficiently repeated, all shapes become more and more round and eventually become circles (see Figure 3.6).

Schwarz's three-dimensional symmetrization, with which we are concerned, is accomplished in an analogous way; however, the symmetrization must proceed tridimensionally by adding f'' and f''' to f', corresponding to the three axes. The process inevitably produces a sphere after enough repetitions. During the whole procedure of symmetrization, the space preserves its volume-radius ($\bar{V}$).

Isoconcave mapping: the problem of the isoconcave shape simulation in an architectural laboratory

The symmetrization of Schwarz is a transformation which approaches the maximum of V/S by successive transformations of the shape in such a way that V remains invariant.

We try now to relate the symmetrization transformation — and the isepiphane problem in general — to our specific problem, namely the isoconcavity indicatrix. This indicatrix is, on the one hand, applicable to the space determined by a closed orientable surface, and, on the other hand, the i can have particular significance for establishing the architect's space repertory, especially insofar as it gives an auditory impression. Therefore we now examine the possibility of 'equiconcave mapping', viz., how the architect can generate any number of shapes all of which have the same i in common. We will see how physical modeling, computer simulation, and mathematics can contribute to its solution. This approach promises to identify for the architect the most desirable shape among the limitless number of different shapes, but with the same concavity (indicatrix) preserved.

Let us begin with the physical model, which will acquaint both sociologists and architects with the method more easily. In light of the fact that the experimental proof of the isepiphane problem itself had been easily realized (Hilbert and Cohn-Vossen 1952: 224, 226-227) by the bubble's behavior, it is not unusual to approach the generation of isoconcave shapes by experimenting on physical models. As a matter of fact, the generation of a discretionary number of isoconcave shapes is mathematically an underdetermined problem in that there are an unlimited number of solutions.

The task is that the architect will generate as many isoconcave shapes as he needs to find the shape that is convenient in other respects for his design. A shape i and all of its deformations preserve invariant the height between a flat floor and a flat roof, so the shapes will vary only in the horizontal cross section. To realize this physical model it is enough to find a container like a right cylinder or prism with a short-sided polygonal base. We fill this container with sand or a similar substance and begin in whatever manner the designer wishes to deform it horizontally, taking care that the sand at the 'roof' remains flat and at the same level. The architect can vary the cross section at his discretion until he finds the shape which he prefers among the shapes which are all isoconcave.

Let us now consider simulation by computer. The computer approaches the problem in an experimental way, so we can have great expectations for its application to this problem. K. C. Knowlton and L. Harmon distinguish from a logical viewpoint four types of computational tasks in the field of computational graphics:

(1) Data to picture (output of calculation as a graphic data display).
(2) Abstract to picture (graphic simulation, picture generation).
(3) Picture to abstract (picture analysis, pattern recognition).
(4) Picture to picture (visual design, digital design processing).

We are concerned here chiefly with the second kind of application, namely generating isoconcave space shapes. Among other laboratories, the Laboratory for Computer Graphics (SYMAP) at Harvard has tried to represent tridimensional arbitrary surfaces especially for geographers. This research has shown that either the surfaces must be made up of flat components (facets), or a very large number of contour surfaces must be stored, or the surface's mathematical expression must be found. Even if mathematical formulas could be generated which determine not one surface but a set of an undetermined number of surfaces, the available computer algorithms and the digital equipment have to be developed especially to aid in the geographer's task. Indeed, it is a basic heuristic problem that computer programs of the generation of any desired number of solutions in a mathematically undetermined system, viz., which shows an infinite number of solutions, has not yet been developed. We will discuss this question in more detail in the section dealing with the syntax of the architectural opus. Isoconcave spaces represent a problem of this type. In addition, the number of solutions is not only infinite but the variations of V and S are not discrete but continuous. We can state that the digital computer, which operates on discrete data by performing arithmetic and logical processes on digital data, is more fully developed than the analog computer, which processes data in the form of continuously variable physical quantities. The family of isoconcave closed surfaces is describable by differential equations, so that the application of the analog computer could open new perspectives for simulation of isoconcave surfaces.

The simulation of space by computer can help the client to choose the most pleasant shape within an isoconcave equivalence class, but this creates even more general problems. Indeed, models must be (a) photographed from the interior (the concave side), (b) in a manner which renders the impression of three-dimensional space, (c) in their natural size; and they must render, finally (d), the multisensory space impression. We are far from satisfying all these requirements by any modeling.

The mathematical measurement of the area (S) and of the volumetric magnitude (V), which are involved in the isoconcavity, implies that for the area we can find a square of the same magnitude, and for the volume a cube of the same volume. The method of exhaustion of Eudoxus, which promises to find the area and the volumetric capacity of a given closed surface, is the best for our task. This method proceeds by exhausting any desired error margin. For example, $\overline{r} < \overline{V} < \dot{r}$.

Isoconcave spaces and other families of architectural repertory items

In order for two spaces to be different items among the architectural words, two basic criteria must be satisfied: (1) they must have objective topological or at least (solid) geometrical differences, and (2) these differences must be able to be perceived by the beholder. This second point implies that, on the one hand, the differentiation of the item among architectural words is sensory dependent and can vary from one to another type of sensory space; and, on the other hand, because the just noticeable difference, or difference threshold, has a discrete value, the otherwise continuous volume or shape difference between spaces becomes discrete; so the catalog of architectural words will also be composed of discrete units.

Because this differentiation is a function of the particular sense we consider — before discussing all autonomous sensory spaces individually — we can look here only for 'critical points' of topological, geometrical, or metrical differences which could be sensorially captured. This allows us to construct a hypothesis for experimental testing. Concerning the differences in volumetric magnitude we can expect that if $V_1 > V_2 > V_3$ objectively, and the beholder can distinguish the difference between V_1 and V_2, and between V_2 and V_3, he will also be able to distinguish the difference between V_1 and V_3, viz., there is a transitive relation in the series. In contrast, if we consider our shape discrimination capacity, we cannot expect that shapes — in formal terms — with more significant topological or geometrical differences can necessarily be better distinguished (e.g., a discriminability between two ellipses with very different ϵs does not necessarily involve a better discriminability between the circle and an ellipsis). The closeness of topological and geometrical relationship defined by the type of transformation (e.g., affinity) which relates one to other (i.e., allows one to be mapped onto the other) is not *directly* relevant to the discriminability of shapes.

We will recall now some topological and geometrical classes of spaces and relate them among themselves in order to keep them in mind for the experimental construction of the architectural lexicon and repertory, a construction that we will discuss, one sensory modality at a time, in the next chapters. Of course, it will be particularly interesting to relate the topological and geometrical categorization to i, the isoconcavity indicatrix, because this is a characteristic proper to space.

(1) Topological genera and i. We know that the sphere's i shows an absolute limit, and the maximal i is about 0.0088. That means that *all* closed surfaces whose interior points are homeomorphic with those of the sphere — and so can constitute an architectural word — but which are in another topological genus than the surface of the sphere can never reach maximal i. So, for

example, the torus has an $n = 3$, and the sphere has an $n = 1$. We cannot say in the genus $n = 3$ it is the torus which will show the maximum of i in this topological category. If a sphere is stuck through with a needle, this transforms the sphere into the genus $n = 3$, and it can have a higher i than any torus can (see Figure 3.4.3a). For each shape in a genus we can find the one which has a maximal i. Among the tori, for example, the one for which the r of its generator circle and the R of the rotation are equal has a maximal i.

(2) Among the continuously differentiable closed surfaces, the ellipsoid of revolution allows a relatively easy specification of its shape differences. As a matter of fact, the ϵ as numeric eccentricity characterizes the ellipsoid shape. It varies between 1 for the sphere and 0 for the paraboloid; $0 < \epsilon < 1$. In a series of experiments we can see for each autonomous sensory space at what $\Delta\epsilon/\epsilon$ level a just noticeable difference appears. Theorizing that for certain sensory spaces, e.g., acoustical, the i change will be the directly relevant aspect, it could be interesting to see how ϵ and i values are related. Actually there is a *negative* correlation between ϵ and i.

For other continuously differentiable surfaces, if all points of the surface have a constant K_m, the diminution of its value implies in principle an increase in the i value, by invariant volume.

(3) Concerning the correlation between i and different characteristics of the non-Dupinian closed surfaces – among them the polyhedrons – it is difficult to make general statements. The maximal i of the sphere could be approached equally well by either a Dupinian surface – by increasing the ellipsoid's ϵ – or by polyhedrons. We remember that in two dimensions, the S/L^2, where S is an area enclosed by a closed curve and L the length or perimeter of the closed curve, the maximum which characterizes the circle could be approached at discretion by a regular polygon for which we increase the number of its edges or vertices. This is an infinitesimal process and so the approach could be 'infinitely good'. We start with the equilateral triangle, which has $S/L^2 = 0.0482$; then for the square, if calculated as the next step, we have 0.0625, and so on, until we reach the circle, for which $S/L^2 = 1/4\pi \approx 0.079$.

Concerning the investigation of space shapes, we can state that if we order the five regular polyhedrons according to the number of faces (k), that which has a higher k also has a higher i.

	k	i
Tetrahedron	4	0.0026
Hexahedron (cube)	6	0.0046
Octahedron	8	0.00535
Dodecahedron	12	0.0067
Icosahedron	20	0.00725

Tetrahedron (T). 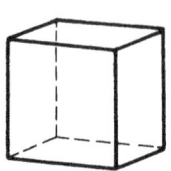   Hexahedron (C). 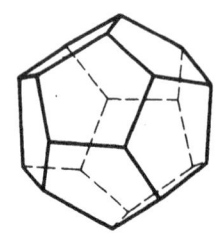   Dodecahedron (D).

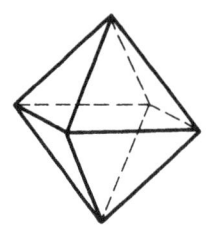

Octahedron (O). 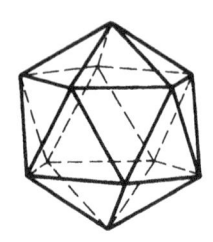   Icosahedron (I).

In principle we can assume that among the polyhedrons with the same number of faces, the regular polyhedron has the higher i value.

Finally, concerning the regular polyhedrons, we can note that all five have a $V/S = \dot{r}/3$, where $\dot{r}$ as we already know is the radius of the largest inscribed sphere in the closed surface. On the other hand, we have already mentioned that $V/S = \sqrt[3]{i \cdot V}$, and is a relevant magnitude for the acoustical space discrimination. We can conclude that all space discrimination which depends entirely on V/S differences will show these differences among regular polyhedrons exclusively on the basis of $\dot{r}$ differences, regardless of whether the regular polyhedron is a tetrahedron, cube, octahedron, dodecahedron, or icosahedron.

13

Acoustical Space

WHY BEGIN THE DESCRIPTION OF THE ARCHITECTURAL MEDIUM WITH ACOUSTICAL SPACE? SOME CONCEPTUAL CONSIDERATIONS

Perhaps it is surprising for many who have learned that architecture is a visual art to begin the description of architecture with acoustical space. Even for those who see architecture in a somewhat broader perspective and take into consideration the polysensory impression of architecture, the discussion begins with (and is largely exhausted in) optical space, it is followed by some consideration of the auditory component of the space impression, and it then vanishes in some elementary remark about the contribution of other senses. The one-sided visiocentric bias has its effect not only on the researcher's paradigms but on the architectural praxis itself. Fitch (1972) notes that modern theater design, for example, is oriented more to the visual than to the acoustic. But he reminds us that the ear has a habitat, and that the 'acoustical engineer errs when he accepts the task of trying to convert the architect's visual cliché into aurally satisfactory experience.' This statement could be illustrated by the acoustics of the Oliver Theater, the largest of the three theaters in Britain's new National Theater complex opened in 1977. Orchestra Hall in Minneapolis, opened in 1974, constitutes a happy exception. Although some minor echo and overloading problems are noticeable on the side of the hall, sound comes off the stage with unprecedented volume so that even a pianissimo can be heard everywhere. This results from the fact that from the very beginning the architects Hardy Holzman Pfeiffer, of New York City, and Hammel, Green and Abrahamson, of St. Paul, conceived this hall in close consultation with the acoustician Dr. Cyril M. Harris. Even the 'visual architects' admitted that the acoustical space required a backdrop for the orchestra that looks like a stage set for Romper Room.

In the part about face-to-face communication, we began with visual communication in order to focus the reader's attention on the fact that this communication as a whole could not be exhausted in purely verbal communication, especially if, along with discursive content, affective and imperative content are equally involved. In this chapter the attention must be somewhat redirected from the optical space to the acoustical one.

Even though it is not generally acknowledged, we tend to suppose that the metric precision of our visual impression over the auditory one also assures an automatic predominance of the impression of optical space over that of acoustical space. As a matter of fact, the visual cue permits a better localization of the direction of our interlocutor, the estimation of his distance, and, overall, a better perception of the spatial relations, but it is always the objects and their relation *in* the space which are in question, not the space impression as such. Still, this latter impression precedes the previous ones and appeals to a different psychological mechanism. For the space impression, auditory sensory input, compared to the visual, has some genuine virtues. The auditory impression is more direct, while the space impression coming from it is more synthetic. As Gaerling (1969-1970: 250-268) observes, the visual space impression can be composed analytically; relative volume can be estimated by multiplying the estimated edges, and so on. The acoustical sense gives a direct impression of the space to be enveloped by a closed surface, even before its shape and volume are estimated, by casting one's ear around. G. Révész (1950: 27-28) noticed that acoustical space has the specificity to give an immediate global impression; in acoustical space, the primary sensory material can be more easily apprehended.

The auditory sense gives an immediate impression of space as a reverberating continuum. We will see that the reverberation time — and the mean free path — as objective characteristics of room acoustics provide us with an impression which is independent both of the position of the source of sound (according to Sabine's second law) and of the position — location and orientation — of the beholder (sonic waves easily avoid small obstacles by diffraction; J. J. Gibson 1966: 81) So the impression of acoustical space is not pieced together but comes more in one piece, is less contingent upon the observer's location, and is more invariant.

The observer's capacity to distinguish — beyond a certain threshold or limen — spaces with geometrical differences solely on an acoustical basis is one of the two necessary conditions so that we can speak about acoustical space as an autonomous sensory space, i.e., creating a space impression without being simply one of the sensory components contributing to the impression of a polysensory space. The second condition is that the envelope of the acoustical space be able to be physically detached from those of the other autonomous sensory spaces, namely the optical and haptic ones. Indeed we can easily conceive a space envelope which reflects only acoustical waves and not optical ones (e.g., a glass wall). In turn we need to consider modern construction materials to admit that acoustical envelopes can also be conceived of separately from tactual ones; and yet we can objectively construct an acoustical space from sound curtains which are not solid in the sense of resistance to mechanical pressure of the haptic kind. An acoustical space is physically constituted if a closed surface — as a reverberating envelope — determines an open region with rigid geometry. Because of the possibility of an autonomous acoustical space, it is inappropriate to speculate, like the philosopher P. F. Strawson and the architect R. Abraham, that if all impressions other than the auditory one are suppressed, we have created 'no-space', a concept used by Strawson as a device to represent concretely solipsism.

PHYSICAL CONDITIONS OF THE PERCEPTIBLE ACOUSTICAL SPACE

Physically, a sensory space capable of giving a space impression is formed when a surface encloses a continuum in which the waves which could effectively stimulate the sense organ in question circulate without notable refraction. In order for the stimulation process to induce a space impression, the beholder must feel himself, or his concerned sensory organ, enclosed in such a way that he can try to attribute a volumetric magnitude and a shape to the 'object' which gives the impression. In this respect it is unimportant whether the estimated volume is more or less accurate.

We look now at the process by which sensory data which are necessary for the acoustical space impression are produced. There must be an observer, human or mechanical, in the space; a source of sound, and a filling of the milieu which allows the propagation of sound vibration. The envelope created by the architect is in fact specified by changes in the acoustical resistance of the material which makes the enclosing surface. Because of differences between the viscosities of the filling and the envelope, the condition of propagation of the sound waves changes and the resistance causes reflection. These reflections provide the necessary sensory data for the space impression. As the attention of the observer is directed to the acoustical space — the object of his curiosity (J. J. Gibson 1966: 23, 28-33), he is not primarily interested in the direction and other attributes of the sound as it comes from the primary sound generator since the acoustical space impression is revealed more by the reflected sound. (The number in the figure denotes that the sound comes from a primary (1), secondary (2), or tertiary (3) source of sound.) Thus walls, ceiling, and floor become secondary and, by multiple reflections, even tertiary sources of sound. The span of time between receiving the original (direct) sound and receiving the reflected one, the variations of its attributes — like the 'onomatopoeia of a sound or canon' — allow us to have an acoustical space impression. Theoretically this process of reflecting would go on for an infinite period of time if the envelope did not 'decimate' the sound by *absorption* at each occasion of reflection (Dungen 1934.)

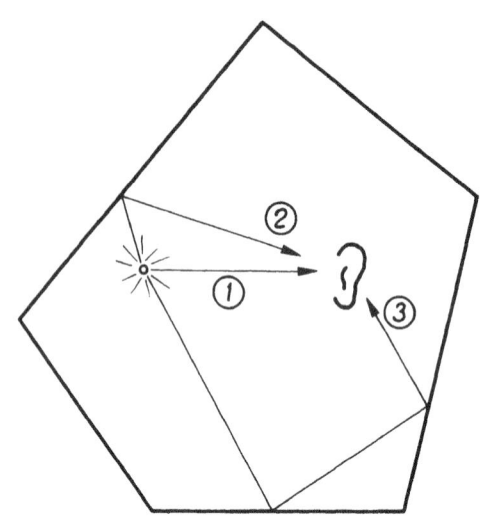

In sum we can say that the acoustical space impression is produced by the space envelope which becomes an indirect source of sound. An anechoic room, where we hear only direct sounds and all others are absorbed by the envelope, does not create any space impression. In this circumstance the acoustical space vanishes, becomes infinite, and cannot claim any space attributes, namely volume and shape. The space is dead. For this reason this construction could simulate the situation which was discussed in the previous part, where audible communication occurs in the context of pure spatial sociology without any interference from the surrounding physical space, viz., in a free acoustical field. The perceptible acoustical space is a live space 'perpetuated' by reflection. As long as the ratio between the reflected and the direct sounds is high enough, the acoustician says that there is liveness in the room. So we can expect that the characteristics related to the reverberation (time lag and resonance) will be relevant to architectural communication in general and to the acoustical space impression in particular.

Acoustical space shares the universal attributes of all architectural spaces, namely having a volumetric magnitude and a shape determined by the enveloping closed surface. How does the architect convey these two attributes as a message in the acoustical space? How does he produce a chosen acoustical space impression?

For creating space impression, which has volume and shape, the architect could use three acoustical elements, although the end impression might also depend on one of three circumstantial parameters which are not determined by the creation of the architectural envelope (see Figure 3.3). For the acoustical space envelope the architect determines the volume (1), the shape (2), and the absorption coefficient (3), all of which are permanent features of the acoustical space. We see on the model that volume and shape are the only attributes which are communicated as general space characteristics, and the absorption coefficient is a subsidiary or peripheral inframorphemic component which could catalyze a room's acoustic illusion by inducing the observer to take absorption differences for volume or shape differences.

What must we know about the three circumstantial parameters? They are the sound generator (6), the medium of propagation (4), and the receptor (5), which bring us into psychoacoustics. Let us discuss each one individually.

It is a peculiarity of the process of acoustical space impression that the observer himself can generate sound (6) without using an artificial source of sound (like a flashlight in the case of the optical space impression). So we can program and monitor our voice for an optimal echolocation. In general, then, the primary source of sound could also be the observer himself (see Figure 2.6), another person in the space, an animal, or a natural or artificial source located either in an interior point of the space or on the space envelope. J. J. Gibson distinguishes natural, animal, vocal, musical, and technological sounds. If we look for an optimal design in the experimental study of the acoustical space impression, we must consider that frequency, intensity, and sequence — continual, intermittent, or abrupt sound emission — affect its precision. There are many experimental studies on the perception of emitted sound, but none on the acoustic space impression. Based on researches into the auditory localization of objects, we can advance the hypothesis that it is especially the frequency of the sound which influences the precision of the acoustical space impression.

Concerning the receptor (5), if we study the threshold of the discriminability of various acoustical spaces for construction of the architectural repertory, we must standardize the ear's auditory capacity as well as the condition of reception. The audibility normalization must be so precise that a mechanical recording could replace the observer and simulate the sensory data input which at any time could be interpreted, i.e., perceived by a standard human observer. The standardization could proceed by statistical means, eliminating interpersonal ('social') and intrapersonal variations. Of course the mechanical recording implies that the observer cannot dynamically modulate his voice in response to each voice reception (Lehman 1969: 3, 1961: 9; J. J. Gibson 1966: 77, 16). The introduction of the mechanical recorder implies also a static observation point, or a robot with very sophisticated programming. In the case of acoustical space impression, because of Sabine's second law, the displacement of the observer and of the sound generator does not promise an important improvement in the precision of space discrimination.

The filling (4) or the medium of propagation has an absolute and a relative viscosity in order for an acoustical space impression to be possible.

212 Communication through architecture

An absolute level of viscosity is necessary to transmit the sound – there is no sound propagation at all in a vacuum – and a relative one in order that the relative homogeneous internal propagation of the sound may transform into reflection by which the architectural envelope manifests its presence. The clearest sign of the acoustical envelope's existence is that the filling and acoustical curtain are not composed of the same state of matter – liquid, gaseous, or solid – either because they are from different matter or because there is a critical difference between their temperatures.

In connection with absolute and relative viscosity of the matter as a condition of the acoustical space impression, we can speak about a paradox of propagation and a dialectical relation between envelope and space. As a matter of fact the minimal viscosity is a qualitative condition necessary for the sound propagation, but quantitatively, friction attenuates the sound power (similarly, we cannot advance without friction). We will see that the air absorption, the quantitative moderating effect on sound propagation of which is expressed by the attenuation coefficient m, depends on temperature and relative humidity.

Reviewing the whole propagation process, the ideal geometrical acoustics calls for the straight-line propagation of the sound; but physical acoustics takes into account the heterogeneity of the medium with its varying acoustical

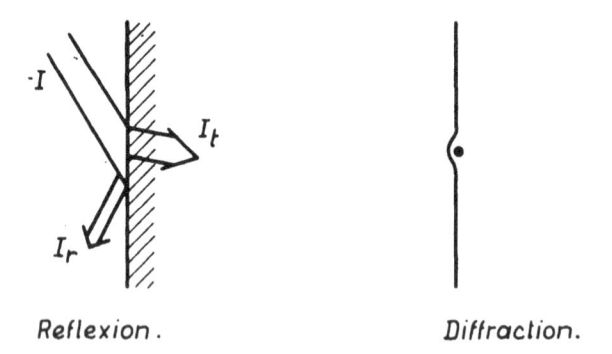

Reflexion.   Diffraction.

Figure 3.7. *Sound behavior at obstacle.*

resistance. Any difference in acoustical resistance is a small one, the sound avoids it, is diffracted, or scatters (see Figure 3.7). Refraction is a change of direction imputable to the speed variation (Sondhaus). If a resistive material is encountered on a large front – namely the architectural envelope – some sound waves turn back and reflection occurs. If there is a large difference between the medium's viscosity and that of the envelope, for example a concrete wall around an air-filled space, very little sound is transmitted and nearly all is reflected. As a matter of fact according to the law of the conservation of energy, the I (intensity of the incident sound) $= I_r$ (reflected) $+ I_t$ (transmitted).

We consider room acoustics, the acoustical space impression, so for us the $R = I_R/I$ is particularly interesting. Of course, all sound phenomena are fundamentally temporal, and the formula's variables must be understood by time units. If there is a sound emission in space for a certain duration and neither the internal absorption nor the transmission I_t is high, the density of the sound energy increases continuously.

THE REVERBERATION TIME AS THE MOST IMPORTANT VARIABLE OF THE ACOUSTICAL SPACE IMPRESSION

The main link between acoustical space and its impression is assured by the reverberation time (T_R). It is a variable which depends exclusively on the objective characteristics of the constructed acoustical space, characteristics grouped under points 1 to 3; it is independent of the circumstantial parameters grouped under 4 to 6; i.e., the T_R is a variable which is calculable from data in 1 to 3, and it is perceptible by the observer. The architect who learns by experimental science how the beholder maps the reverberation time into spatial data — also making use of other subsidiary data such as the transmission-frequency characteristics of the resonance — can communicate more efficiently through the acoustical space.

If a continuous sound emission occurs in an enclosure that we call acoustical space, the vibration increases for a period of time; then the density of the sound energy reaches a stationary state when the energy loss and the supply compensate each other. If the emission stops, the vibration continues for a period of time with always-decreasing intensity. We can arbitrarily choose a limit to the decrease in intensity of the initial pressure, and we can measure the span of time necessary to reach this decrease. This time varies in different acoustical spaces and makes possible their comparison. We call reverberation time (T_R) the time which is required for a specific sound to die away to one-thousandth of its initial pressure, which corresponds to a drop in the sound-pressure level of 60 decibels. For this very reason the reverberation time is alternatively symbolized by T_R and T_{60}. If for example the stationary sound intensity is I, the T_R is measured when the intensity becomes $I.10^{-6}$.

How can we calculate this T_R as a function of the objective characteristics of the acoustical space? We can anticipate that the sound energy loss comes from absorption.

Each time that the sound waves encounter the envelope, some of them are not reflected but absorbed. Quantitatively the degree of absorption depends on the envelope's 'acoustical impedance', which is itself in close relation with this material's viscosity:

To a lesser degree, the internal friction occurring in the space itself encountered on the sound's path speeds up the attenuation of the sound's intensity.

The number of reflections depends upon the space's geometry and can be formulated in a function of the mean free path (m.f.p.) (Knudsen and Harris 1950), also called d. The m.f.p. is a direct function not of the space's shape but of the numeric relation between the volumetric magnitude (V) and the envelope's surface magnitude (S), namely m.f.p. or $d = 4V/S$. The T_R will be a function of d and of the absorption coefficient α. $T_R = f(d, \alpha) = f(S, V, \alpha)$. The α calculated by W. C. Sabine is $\alpha = 1 - R^2$ where $R = I_R/I$; so in the metric system Sabine's $T_R = 0{,}04\alpha^{-1} \cdot d$.

Sabine's second law makes the important statement that the T_R in a given space is independent of the sound source location as well as of the observer's position. For this reason, Fitch (1972: 138) insists that T_R is a unique number characterizing the acoustical space, the 'vessel as a whole'. However, without becoming too technical, it is necessary to mention that in order to be valid, some conditions must be fulfilled. The initial I must be in a stationary state of sound distribution, and the sound emission must be diffuse. (This condition is used in the deduction.) The mean free path d characterizes in a statistical sense all paths when the shape is such that the difference between the longest and the shortest paths is not over a certain limit. This is realized if the shape is regular enough, which means here that it is relatively close to being a sphere.

We remember from the preceding chapter that the isoconcavity indicatrix $i = f(V, S) = V^2/S^3$ characterizes the shape as it approaches the sphere and the sphere has the exclusive privilege of having $i = 1/36\pi = 0{.}0088$, which is also its extreme (maximum) value. So we can say that the d is representative if i is high enough.

The Significance of Reverberation Time for Architectural Communication

We see that T_R is a function of d, and α. ($T_R = f[d, \alpha]$) But i as well as d derive from a relation between V and S, and not directly from the shape of the space, so perhaps d and consequently T_R could be expressed as functions of i, the isoconcavity indicatrix. On the other hand, if the impression of the space depends chiefly on T_R, the isoconcavity indicatrix could be considered as a specific shape characteristic of the *acoustical* space. For this reason we are very interested in pursuing the necessary mathematical transformations of the T_R formula in order to make more explicit for the architectural designer which manipulation of the shape and volume of the space becomes efficient for the observer of the acoustical space. If $d = 4V/S$ and $i = V^2/S^3$, then

$d = 4\sqrt[3]{Vi}$ and $T_R = f(V, i, \bar{\alpha}) = 0.161\bar{\alpha}^{-1} \cdot \sqrt[3]{iV}$. So if the designer fixes the V he can change the shape without changing the impression of the acoustical space. It is sufficient htat he does not change i. Any other shape change has no effect on the acoustical space impression at all. If he has a canvas tent (S), he can see in $T_R = 0.161\bar{\alpha}^{-1} \cdot \sqrt{iS}$ how the shape change affects the space impression by modifying i through V. This clear distinction of the main effects of shape and volume changes on the acoustical space impression is especially useful for the composition of polysensory spaces; this knowledge allows the architect to manipulate the common space envelope according to the optimal requirements of other spaces — optic and haptic — in such a way that this does not affect the acoustical space impression at all. This manipulation of absolute magnitudes (V, S) and ratios (i) along a constant T_R could be made experimentally on a physical model. We know by deduction that certain shape changes never affect the i. We also recall that all regular polyhedrons which have an $\dot{r}$ as radius of the inscribed sphere in common have an identical V/S. That means that it is sufficient to keep the $\dot{r}$ unchanged and the architect can choose any $n + x$ sided polyhedron without affecting the acoustical space impression. Other shape families could be identified which preserve a constant V/S and so T_R.

Manipulation of the Acoustical Space Impression by Absorption

Systematic errors — or, improperly speaking, illusions — in the space impression can be intentionally generated by the architect if he has a refined insight into the effects of sound absorption. Because the acoustical space impression is a total one and chiefly created by the T_R, the architect can expect that in the case where AS is perceived without the help of other sensory data, changes in $\bar{\alpha}$ will impress the beholder as being a change in the geometry of the given space.

What do we learn from recent research in room acoustics about sound absorption? It distinguishes two kinds:

(1) Absorption which occurs on the occasion of each sound reflection from the space envelope. This is represented by the average absorption coefficient $\bar{\alpha}$.
(2) The medium in the space which causes internal impedance, expressed by the attenuation coefficient m.

The absorption coefficient α depends on the porosity of the material (cf. acoustical impedance), or on the relative fixity of the enveloping surface, because the sound spreads by mechanical vibration. Indeed, not only does the surface, whether it be an air curtain or a liquid or a porous material, influence the α, but the flexural vibrations themselves use up a certain amount of the incident sound energy by converting it into heat. The Sabine formula for T_R can be applied only if $\bar{\alpha}$ is relatively small compared to unity. This occurs less and less frequently, because the frequent acoustical faults of modern spaces, which are composed only for the eye, are very often corrected after the fact by application of highly absorbent acoustical panels. In this case it is necessary to introduce in the T_R the value of the effectively reflected fraction (I_r) of the sound (I). If $\bar{\alpha} = 1 - R^2$ where $R = I_r/I$, we must use $1 - \bar{\alpha}$ or more simply R^2. So $T_R = 0.161V/[S(-2.3 \log_{10} R^2)]$ or $T_R = 0.161V/S(1 - \bar{\alpha})$.

How can the architect use the magnitude of absorption to modify the space impression?

We know that if the absorption becomes $\bar{\alpha} = 1$ (unity), viz., $I = I_t$, the acoustical space is a dead space which can simulate a free acoustical field and gives the impression of 'open space'. It is a kind of 'negative hallucination'. We can hypothesize that, if the $\bar{\alpha}$ increases, the acoustical space gives the impression of larger and larger rooms, so that the increase of α would be projected by the beholder in a systematic error in the volumetric magnitude. By $\alpha \approx 1$, the acoustical space impression disappears.

The $\bar{\alpha}$ shows the *average* absorption coefficient resulting from $\bar{\alpha} = (\alpha_1 S_1 + \alpha_2 S_2 + \ldots + \alpha_n S_n)/\Sigma S_n = a/S$ (Knudsen and Harris 1950: 150). The acoustical space as architectural expression could thus be manipulated by the dispersion of α_1, α_2 and by that of S_1, S_2. But if the chosen α_1, α_2 has a high variance, the T_R cannot be calculated by the Eyring formula, and the more detailed Fitzroy integral formula – also called the Millington formula in the French technical literature – must be applied: $T_R = 0.161V/[-\Sigma S_i \log_{10}(1 - \alpha_i)]$ (Purkis 1966: 98-99). Even this estimation is valid only if the individual S_is are not too small; that is, if the enveloping surface is not broken up into too-small pieces. The T_R is in principle not affected by the placement of individual panels S_1 and so on. These considerations show the architect's freedom to manipulate the acoustical space impression; without having his hand tied in the composition of polysensory spaces, which must also satisfy requirements other than acoustical.

The internal attenuation coefficient m could be introduced into the Eyring formula as follows: $T_R = 0.161V/[-2.31S \log_{10}(1 - \bar{\alpha}) + 4mV]$. It is the air humidity and the room temperature which mainly determine the m. As the temperature rises, m increases, but as humidity increases, m decreases (at 10-20 percent humidity, m has a maximal value). On the other hand, its effect is affected by the volume. From this situation we can conclude that for osmotic space, air conditioning affects the acoustical space, but for its intended impression the m is not an important variable in the hand of the architect. It is a parameter which must be taken into account, especially in major spaces with important volume.

In general terms we can state that empirical data show that m has the greatest effect on the sound propagation when it has a frequency higher than 1,000 or even 2,000, and the architect must not forget that the human voice has a frequency between 1,000 and 4,000 cycles per second, as mentioned in the previous part.

RESONANCE AS ANOTHER VARIABLE OF THE ACOUSTICAL SPACE IMPRESSION

So far we have discussed only the T_R as a clue to the observer's space impression. But a reconstruction of the acoustical space by the observer could be aided by other supplementary variables, meaning that in certain cases the difference between two spaces having the same T_R could be detected by acoustical means.

In reality each room does not react in the same way for sounds emitted at different frequencies. Each room has a code, and if someone can find and tune this frequency, like 'open Sesame' it will reveal its 'secrets' and define more completely its characteristics. A room can have one or more specific frequencies, or 'transmission frequency characteristics'. The periodic impulse at this frequency amplifies the acoustic pressure, and these sound waves will oscillate with a sensibly higher amplitude. Of course, the phenomenon as such allows us to distinguish acoustically different spaces. But the discrimination can go further because from previous polysensory space experience, the beholder can associate a specific resonance with a specific geometry of the acoustical space, perhaps constituting quantitatively ordered series according to the space's volume.

The acoustical space has in this respect two characteristics: a normal or resonant frequency (f_c), and a specific number of modes of vibration (N), a region where there is a relatively uniform transmission-frequency characteristic.

If we find the f_c of the room, we can calculate $N = 4V(f_c/c)^3$, which gives for mode per cycle $dN/df = 12Vf_c^2/c^3$. This formula is valid beyond an inferior limit of frequency, namely, $> 4c/\sqrt[3]{V}$, c is the velocity of sound.

What is instructive here for architectural communication through the acoustical space?

From $N = f(V, f_c, c)$ we see that N is a function of V but it is not influenced by S or by the i. If by previous experience the beholder has learned that at the normal frequency f_c each room reveals its volume without interference from the room's S or i, his impression becomes more specific and can discriminate smaller differences between various existing acoustical spaces. So far in general there are very few research findings about acoustical space perception, which could be at least indirectly relevant for the acoustical

218 Communication through architecture

space impression, and we must refer again to Black's research discussed in Part II.

In sum we can say that each room has a normal frequency f_c which reveals to the beholder new differences concerning the geometry of the space, and if the beholder finds the f_c and can further distinguish the variations in the N, he can perhaps order various acoustical spaces according to their volumetric magnitudes. This is particularly likely if the amplification is not attenuated by an increasing amount of absorptive material, which deprives the room of its timbre and smooths out the transmission-frequency characteristic.

ACOUSTICALLY HETEROGENEOUS SPACES AND THE IMPRESSION OF THEIR SHAPE

First we discussed the T_R which characterizes and distinguishes the acoustical spaces in a very general manner; namely $T_R = f(V/S, \alpha) = f(V, i, \alpha) = f(S, i, \alpha)$. It does not, however, give a specification for the impression of the space shape. The indication conveyed by i does not point specifically at *a* shape anyway.

By means of the resonance, the impression of f_c and $N = f(V, f_c, c)$ conveys to the observer supplementary global space characteristics. Both characterize the acoustical space as a whole, and both are susceptible to giving more clues to the volumetric difference than to specifying the shape.

Even these characteristics are not equally perceptible in any one location in *all* spaces. In certain spaces the acoustical pressure is not diffused throughout the whole space in a uniform manner. Heterogeneous properties of the acoustical space are the most related to the space's shape, and so could reveal it. Of course, this impression of the shape of the acoustical space is not accessible to an observer who must stay at a single observation point. He must have several listening posts. The comparison of these impressions is evidently facilitated if these posts are related by a kinetic or even dynamic exploration.

Loudness Difference and Shape Impression

Concerning the shape, we know already that if the space's envelope is a continuously differentiable surface, it is inevitable that at least one part of the surface be concave, that the center of the principal osculating circles $(ds/d\theta)$ be situated inside the space, and, in addition, that at least some surface points have a positive total curvature (K). If the surface is continuously differentiable, and not all points are elliptical ones, some must have an

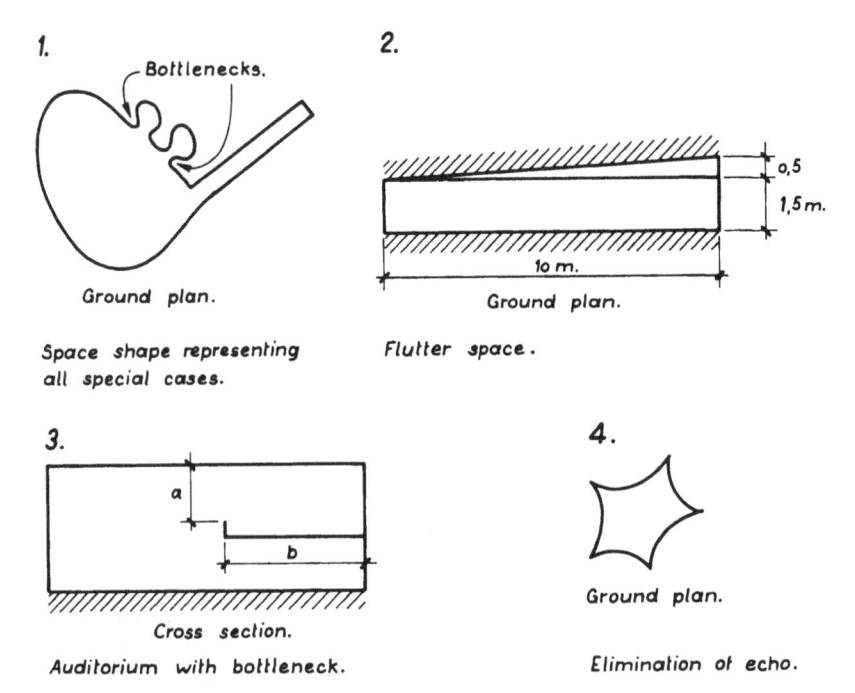

Figure 3.8. *Special cases of acoustical space shapes.*

osculating circle with its center in infinity. (A flat surface spot has both a total curvature and a mean curvature of zero.)

Sound foci

If the sections of the enveloping surface are ellipses, we find two foci which have the property that lines drawn from them to any point on the surface make equal angles with the tangent (and the normal line). It follows that if the surface's α is low, for example a polished metal surface, somebody approaching the focal point hears a monotone sound louder and louder with ever-greater intensity. This phenomenon is even more accentuated if the sound emission is concentrated in the opposite focal point. In a space filled with a mass of humanity, the interlocutors situated in the two foci can entertain a privileged dyadic communication above the others' heads. This effect of the indirect sound could be exploited in a motion picture if the director were to walk with the sound camera back and forth around the foci. This ellipsis effect is not limited to the space with near-ellipsoid shape; even the cylindrical drum with an elliptical floor shows it because our ears are more sensitive to 'horizontal than vertical sound events'.

If the space's *i* approaches its maximum by becoming a sphere, or at least a cylinder with a circular base, there is only one focus. A speaker finding himself at this focal point hears his own voice much louder than others around him do. The overestimation of his own voice invites him to lower his voice more and more until it is barely audible. The self deescalation occurs very often in the open-air classical theaters because they are circular and neglect the acoustical component of polysensory space compared to the optical one.

Fortunately in the history of architecture we seldom find completely regular circular polysensory spaces; but in order to detect a specific spherical or concave surface part by this focal effect, it is enough that this surface part have the necessary extension and be in a relatively voluminous space.

Dead spots

The other side of the phenomenon could be revealing too. Indeed, according to the principle of the conservation of energy, if the acoustic pressure is very high in the focal point, elsewhere it must be low or even very low, viz., under the average. We can detect in an extreme case of loudness deficit a kind of counterpoint or dead spot where we can hear only direct sound.

Echo

Sound foci and dead spots show up even if the sound emission is a monotone, but most sound — verbal and musical — originated by men has such a structure that its accumulation in the form of direct and indirect sounds can generate 'antistructures' which destroy its perception. We can distinguish two sounds if we receive them in not less than a 0.006-second interval. According to this fact, if the beholder hears a sound repeated, blurred or masked, he can guess that the indirect sound covered a distance 1.5 m. longer than did the direct one. When the indirect repeated sound is distinctly received, the echo shows that the difference of distance is even more than 2.0 m. (cf. the gallery of Albert Hall in London). If this echo is perceived in a focal point, the beholder can guess that the distance between the focal points $SS' \geq 2.00$ m., or if the beholder hears his own echo in a spherical shape with a unique focus, he can conclude that the radius is at least 2.00 m. Spaces with convex surface parts suppress all these shape cues, but the architect must pay for that with edges and noncontinuously differentiable surfaces (see Figure 3.8.4 and Voder room of A.T.T. in the U.S.A. Knudsen and Harris 1950: 184).

Flutter space

Now we imagine two cylinders with a common axis whose radii have a difference less than 1.5 m. ($r_1 - r_2 \leq 1.5$ m.). See Figure 3.8.2.) When we increase the radii to infinity, always observing the condition of inequality, the result is a straight corridor of infinite length.

In fact, if the beholder observes a multiple echo, he can be certain that he is in a 'flutter space', that is, in an extremely long corridor which is narrower than 1.5 m. and whose walls are parallel with a maximal tolerance of 1/20, smooth, and not very absorbing. We must note that such precision in the acoustical space impression is possible only if the surfaces are not too absorbent.

COMPLEX ACOUSTICAL WORDS OF ARCHITECTURE

Until now we have considered the impression of the acoustical space as a morpheme which has a minimal autonomy; namely, if sound leaves the space it does not return, or, if it comes in, it does not leave. There are acoustical spaces which are intermediary cases, in the sense that sound originated in one space goes out and with modification and delay comes back; but this back-and-forth still does not imply a free circulation. Each component of this complex acoustical space preserves its own T_R as the main objective acoustical characteristic. Reality always challenges our conceptualizations involved in our understanding. Churches have naves, transepts, choirs, sanctuaries, chapels, and organ chambers; theaters and auditoriums have foyers, anterooms, and balconies. Secondary spaces often have a volume and concavity very different from that of the main auditorium. The connection between them causes a bottleneck, with the consequence that each will have its own different T_R, assuring its respective autonomy.

We have seen how the variation in the 'cartographic' distribution of the loudness of sound can give cues to the space's shape. Now we are confronted with a much more fundamental problem, namely how the identity of an acoustical space as a unit of expression can be 'shaken' when the ubiquitous T_R splinters, and sounds from various parts of the complex word of the acoustical space remain in mutual interference and reverberate into each other.

Let us examine the processes. Sound is initiated in the major space section and spreads into the smaller recesses restrained by a bottleneck. In the recesses the T_R is longer than in the large part of the complex acoustical space, and so in the smaller space, for example a gallery where $b/a \geq 2$, sound reverberates longer, exactly by $\Delta T = T_{R2} - T_{R1}$. (See Figure 3.8.3.)

So the smaller room begins to 'accumulate sound reverberations' and then feed them back into the major space. Now even before the end of the sound event, sound returning from the recess can be observed in that part of the major space which is near the bottleneck (cf. the Oliver Theater, London, near the front of the balcony). The observation of this feedback, especially because it comes precisely from a recess, where the sound did not originate, allows the beholder to know that the acoustical space is a specific complex word composed from more than one morpheme.

ACOUSTICAL SPACE IMPRESSION AND THE EXISTING VARIETIES OF POLYSENSORY SPACES

Considering architectural spaces either from the viewpoint of the prevailing doctrine of architectural design or from that of the history of architecture, we find that the acoustical space impression is a subject that has been and still is systematically neglected. Completely ignored until it backfired, consideration of the acoustical space came as a late corrective. This snub was the fruit of a visiocentric reductionalism which taught that from whatever position the beholder could see well he consequently could also hear well. This doctrine had a classical tradition which shaped the famous Greek theaters — the $\theta\acute{\epsilon}\bar{\alpha}\tau\rho\omicron\nu$; but even the appearance of the modern physical and mathematical theory of room acoustics at the beginning of this century did not bring an automatic improvement of the praxis. A very 'classical' example is the Lincoln Center for the Performing Arts in Manhatten, where the whole plaza, including its relation with neighboring Fordham University, constitutes — in visual terms — an exemplary complex. But despite considerable expenditures for acoustical studies, it was necessary to reconstruct the Philharmonic Hall three times.

Another basic shortcoming in the field of room acoustics is manifested by the fact that there is practically no study which is directed not at the auditory usefulness of a space, but directly toward the impression of acoustical space as such; that is, studies which teach us how the communication from architectural expression to the user passes through the acoustical space.

Considering the history of architecture on a truly empirical basis, we can see that neglected periods treated as secondary can be important in certain respects other than optical. We have in mind here the rococo, an outgrowth of baroque architecture. Both baroque theaters and the sequences of rooms in the rococo residence provide an extremely rich experience from the viewpoint of the acoustical space. This could be confirmed by the experience of blind people. In rococo suites, the vestibule is followed first by a marble hall with an acoustical quality all its own, then by the majordomo's [butler's] quarters — a room with a stone floor. Then come various rooms with more nuances in tonality: the large dining room where music *de table* was played; the salon with damask walls for chamber music; a smaller room reserved for the fine sound of the harpsichord or spinet; and finally for those who preferred the murmur of the ladies' intimate confidences to the gentlemen's *fumoir* [smoking room], the boudoir with its special acoustics.

We cannot and will not consider systematically all varieties of the acoustical space for each different type of room according to its 'auditory functions' across different civilizations, nor even in the history of our own architecture. But because of the relatively neglected state of acoustical space as compared to optical space, we will try to discuss some significant developments in the field of the former in relation to its (acoustically relevant) objective characteristics.

By reviewing such cultic spaces as churches, we find great variations in the T_R, both in different historical periods and within a particular period. Almost accompanying the transformation of a religious movement, the sound events in the cultic space changed too: at different times preaching, collective prayer, even individual witnessing from the public or small discussion groups. General confession shifts to individual confession, or chant to organ music, or orchestral and other instrumental music become predominant or even exclusive. In our time the ecumenical trend makes the architect's task even more difficult (e.g., the small interfaith chapel of 'baroque design' at M.I.T. in Cambridge, Massachusetts, where 'post-Bach' and 'romantic' music cannot be played). To cite some examples from the past to illustrate the qualitative difference in the T_R among spaces serving similar religious purposes, both the Roman basilicas and the Gothic cathedrals in the Middle Ages had a T_R = 6-8 seconds. Modern churches have one of 0.9-2.0 seconds. The Reformation, particularly Lutheranism, accented preaching, and the walls no longer remained bare stone but were decorated with wood and furnished with family loges like the bourgeois opera houses. Accessories increased the absorption coefficient. This trend was so strong that even the Counter-Reformation could not deter it but had to fight the Reformation by preaching. The emphasis was not on music any more, but the debate turned to verbal rhetoric. Baroque church spaces are rich in decorative folding surfaces, causing the V/S ratio to decrease — the V itself decreases too in absolute value — to which the increase of sound absorption must be added. So the trend here is toward a lower T_R. Contemporary 'auditoriums' (e.g., interfaith) could not become multipurpose without paying for it with a very high sound absorption and so with a low T_R.

Speaking in general, modern multipurpose auditoriums, where an assortment of concerts and theater productions are performed, make optimization possible only at the lowest level of requirements, viz., avoiding faults without looking for the best acoustical effects.

As a matter of fact, the functional optimization of the space's T_R must be considered from the viewpoint of sound event frequency. Speeches, chamber music, and philharmonic orchestras of our time have very different frequency spans. Because the design of the optical spaces predominates in the composition of polysensory space, the optimization calculus determines first the V and the S. With these two values the architect of the acoustical space has the α almost exclusively at his disposal. Today a space's T_R is designed as a function of the expected sound frequency and of the volume; $T_R = f(f_c, V)$. For spaces where speeches are delivered, the designer chooses $T_R = 0.7$ second if the $V = 10,000$ cubic feet, and 1.08 seconds if $V = 1,000,000$ cubic feet. For a motion-picture theater, where both speech and music are heard, the $T_R = 1.0 \sim 1.4$ seconds; in school auditoriums $T_R = 1.0 \sim 1.5$ seconds; and in music conservatory auditoriums where chamber music is often performed the $T_R = 0.9 \sim 1.4$ seconds.

Considering the range of acoustical spaces in the architectural repertory insofar as variations of T_R distinguish the different items, among modern spaces the beholder has $T_{R1}:T_{R2} = 1.3$ as a maximal range. But if we include spaces of other epochs (in our history), the range of discrimination becomes much larger — 1:10. We mentioned that the architect can expect the observer to discriminate between various acoustical spaces (ΔAS) which are discernible not solely on the basis of their ΔT_R but also through differences in resonance (f_c, N), and to perceive the heterogeneity of an acoustical space by its region where echoing, for example, could reveal shape differences (e.g., octagonal synagogues with high domed ceilings often echo).

We have already noted the lack of important research in the field of the acoustical space impression as such. Some rudimentary steps have been made for studying the orientation of those born sightless or accidentally blinded. But this is a very different research problem. Otherwise, experimental science has approached the acoustical space, when at all, as a simple component of the impression of the polysensory space. Truly the problem must be seen in a much broader perspective, and acoustical space impression must be systematically studied even if the architectural space is complicated by the noncoincidence of the acoustical, optical, and tactical envelopes. Blindfolding and darkness are the appropriate devices for these experimental studies of the acoustical space items of the architect's repertory.

In the programming of these studies we must resist the temptation offered from the contemporary sound equipment industry, which studies the acoustical space only for the optimal location of loudspeakers or stereo telecommunication equipment. This presents a double jeopardy. These studies, if they are to be well founded and relevant to the theory of architecture, must be preceded by a systematic study of impression of acoustical space without the complication of such artificial equipment.

14

Optical Space

PHYSICAL CONDITIONS OF THE CONSTITUTION OF OPTICAL SPACE

We turn now to optical space and the conditions which make it an autonomous element in the architect's repertory. The task requires us to answer three questions:

– What are the minimal criteria for an optical space to become an architectural morpheme? (This is the condition of definition.)
– What problems are inherent in bringing about the impression of optical space? (This is the condition of experimentation.)
– Last, to avoid redundance, what are the specific conceptual differences between optical and acoustical space?

Optical space, like all completely constituted space, is a minimal meaningful unit of the architectural medium when a beholder can perceive a space to which he can attribute volume — more precisely, volumetric magnitude — and a (concave) geometric shape. The accuracy of the perception is not important here, only the fundamental condition that the space can be discriminated from another space on the basis of volume and shape. This is the essential requirement for the experiential existence of optical space as a concrete item in the architect's repertory.

Many researchers, in fact, while trying to determine the objective effect (Hebb 1972: 49) of the architectural envelope on the communicative behavior of the enclosed groups, leave implicit the question of which spaces can be distinguished by the subjects. Without asking that, they proceed to study the communicative behavior and even the evaluation the beholder makes of a certain denotatively unspecified space (see Küller 1974; Acking and Küller 1973). At first glance this phenomenological social psychology seems very productive. But closer consideration reveals that without the arduous experimentation necessary to determine the beholder's discrimination capability, no affective or other effects can be correctly attributed to any optical space. To this extent such research lacks sure foundations.

It is environmental optics which tells us how the 'structure of data' pertinent to the formation of the optical space impression takes shape (Baird 1970: 288; J. J. Gibson 1966; Purdy 1958).

In a very schematic way, we can say that under relatively homogeneous conditions of the propagation of photonic waves within a closed, optically isolating surface, a structure of emitted and reemitted rays occurs. This 'space-filling network of rays' is a potential source of stimulation for a definite receptor at any point in the space. The luminous flux appears as a 'luminous efficiency' in the eyes. Even if we take into account other psychologists' criticisms of this theory, it is reasonable for our purposes to take J. J. Gibson's systematic theory at least as a basis for discussion. Whenever necessary, we will indicate our reservations concerning his theory and its inherent limits. In Gibson's perspective (1966: 188, 190-210) there are eight stages necessary to constitute a perceptual synthesis of a space:

(1) radiation from a luminous source,
(2) scatter-reflection of light from the surface,
(3) the set of all convergence points in a medium (cf. Leblanc et al. 1958: 251),
(4) the ambient light at a stationary convergence point,
(5) the effective array at a stationary convergence point (the photo),
(6) the same at a moving convergence point (the film),
(7) figural motion within the ambient array,
(8) kinetic optical occlusion and edge formation.

This classification is not free of doctrinal opinions. Indeed, Gibson himself tells us that the information about optical space cannot be analytically apprehended, on either systematic or practical levels, by isolating sensory impression as raw data apart from the (informational) treatment of these data by the beholder (Gibson 1970; Johansson 1970), because, in his opinion, the reception of an impression is in itself a selective process which includes feedback between reception and treatment of information. On the other hand, he holds that visual impression is closely related to the muscular work of the eyes itself (e.g., measuring magnitude by contraction) and, in more general terms, closely related to proprioception. (This is exploration — or, in Pavlovian terms, investigation — where the impression is considered as feedback.)

In the perspective of systems theory and other schools of thought, it is fashionable today to posit the inseparability of phenomena (Gibson 1966: 46); but this is to forget that experimental verifiability depends upon an analytical approach. Indeed, Baird (1970) suggests, not without reason, that many of Gibson's statements cannot be experimentally verified or refuted. In particular he calls the statement that a moving person is a more natural observer than a stationary one pure speculation. We continue to distinguish static observation in the experimental design for the study of optical space discrimination. In order to determine the threshold of discrimination capability by static observer we distinguish data which can be recorded by photomechanical means, thus excluding feedback between sensory input and information processing, which will later be interpreted by the beholder. We speak of space impression in the case where discrimination is based on actual sensory data differences and data from long-term memory are neutralized. On the other hand, we regard as being in a 'black box' all aspects of the process of data transformation which belong to physiological psychology because they are irrelevant to our present subject. This 'black box' — the observer's mind — receives the data of observation from a fixed position and reveals the differences perceived among optical spaces — presented in rapid succession (cf. short-term memory) — by replies to paired-comparison or forced-choice questions put by the experimenter.

The results of such research would enable the architect on the one hand to know which are the truly discrete items in his repertory, and on the other to see how redundance or scarcity of cues to the distinction of spaces allow him to create spatial illusions by generating systematic errors.

What are the operational conditions (Déribéré 1964: 60) for objective definition of optical space? There are four architectural variables and three parameters:

(1) There must first be a luminous source which emits transversal waves. Its characteristics are its luminous flux and its relative location in the space. (Its location could even coincide with part of the architectural envelope, but that remains a parameter of the space impression, not an architectural variable.)

(2) The space-filling medium must be transparent and distinctive from the envelope. Thiel (1961: 56) reminds us that a fog curtain could be the wall of an optical space. A relatively homogeneous and transparent medium assures 'regular transmission' (Leblanc et al. 1958: 225). The rectilinear regularity of the wave propagation is indispensable for the reconstruction of the source by the receiver. In the case of optical space we can be even more precise and require only the absence of a nontransparent medium, since neither an atmosphere nor a hydrosphere is strictly necessary in it. It could be a pure vacuum (Alexander 1964: 169, n. 17).

(3) The spectator must have at his disposal an optical receptor with a standardized minimal sensitivity (Déribéré 1959: 42, 48; Leblanc et al. 1958: 209). As we have mentioned, at this stage of consideration the function of the receptor must be detached from any subjective factors, and so possibly simulated by robot eyes. The possible use of the recording of impressions by robot has not yet been explored in a sufficiently differentiated manner. As a

matter of fact, with appropriate equipment we could go beyond the mechanical recording of photometric values in terms of energy and record values of luminous photometry which give the brightness of different rays arriving at the same observation point.

(4) The reflecting closed surface is the architectural variable. The optical space is perceived because the enveloping surface causes a change in the direction, quantity, and composition of the received luminous rays. In short, the surface becomes a nonprimary (secondary, $n + 1$) luminous source. This process is a *sine qua non* for the impression of optical space. It is, in fact, the regularity of reflection which allows the spectator to have an impression of the enveloping optical space. (Paradoxically, a mirror surface assures such extreme regularity of reflection that this kind of optical space becomes imperceptible.)

The optical space is filled with rays of light coming from various sources: primary or direct, called D or B rays (depending on whether the experimenter refers to albedo or to white light; Déribéré 1959: 54, 116; Geldard 1953: 16-17; Dourgnon and Krossaw 1949: 1-9); R rays, reflected once from a secondary source, e.g., the architectural envelope; and M ray light, which results from multiple reflections. The relations among light rays at different stages of propagation — R/B, M_{n+1}/M_n — their 'redirection', new quantitative and qualitative composition, all provide the cues necessary for the impression of optical space. The number of these reflections is objectively proper to the specific closed surface which constitutes an optical space. R. C. Oldfield describes this concisely.

The impression of being located in a specific optical space, which arises from this series of reflections, may be complete or relative. This is to say that optical space, like other sensory spaces, may be a free morpheme or a bound one. The optical space is a free morpheme if no optical stimulus emitted within it leaves for an adjacent space, and vice versa. This does not rule out the wall's absorption of some amount of light at each reflection, not does it exclude the possibility that the wall itself be a partial primary light source, thus enabled to reemit perceptible (reflected) light. Such a part of the surface is a luminary one and so a quasi envelope of the perceived optical space. The optical space as free form thus assures complete intimacy for those inside it and complete protection from external light stimulus.

On the other hand, light can either enter or leave a space without necessarily destroying the impression that one is in a specific optical space. A space which satisfies just this minimal criterion of sensory space constitution is a bound morpheme (Welsh). The minimal criterion, as we learned before (Beuchel 1969; Forrester 1969: 17; Y. Friedman 1971: 29, 35; Klaus 1968: 636), is that light stimuli can go, out from the space or come into it, but never both; in short, if there is feedback between spaces they are not discrete optical spaces, autonomous units in the architectural space system.

We may consider other cases in which the optical space is something less than a completely free form. (A special case is the door opening, which unites spaces temporarily.)

An extreme case of vanishing of the envelope occurs if the material is completely absorptive, reflecting no light at all. The optical space would be complete in the sense of being totally isolated; but people within it could not perceive its dimensions. In fact it suffices to have either a completely absorbing envelope or a completely luminary one to render the optical space imperceptible. Some architects, such as Abraham and Schapiro in 1969, have created 'vanishing' spaces of this kind. It is pretentious, however, to call them hyperspaces; they are in reality hypo- or quasi spaces. We will discuss illusory constructions in more detail later.

The Specificity of Optical Space in Relation to Acoustical Space

There are analogies and differences between the sources of optical space impressions and acoustical space impressions. We restrict our comparison to the differences, and study them through the four aspects involved in the space impression.

(1) In the case of both vibratory events and wave emissions, space impression occurs within limits; that is, we do not perceive ultrasounds or infrasounds, ultraviolet or infrared waves. The first difference between the photon's transversal waves and the sound's longitudinal ones is that the first are propagated rigorously in a straight line and cast shadows, while the latter are more easily deflected. (The diffraction of light waves constitutes an exception insignificant for our purpose; see Gibson 1966: 213; Leblanc et al. 1958: 214.)

Light waves travel through space at a speed of 300,000 km./sec., which does not vary significantly in different media. In fact, we have already pointed out that a medium is not necessary at all for their propagation. Sound waves, on the other hand, do need a medium, and one of a certain density (e.g., air), for their propagation, which goes on at the speed of 0.34 km/sec. In practical terms this means that an optical space darkens almost instantaneously, while an acoustical space retains aftersounds.

(2) Concerning the source of emission, there is a significant difference. Without some mechanical aid the human observer cannot originate the wave emission necessary to explore an optical space. In an acoustical space, the emitter and observer could be the same.

(3) The process of reverberation against the envelope is roughly analogous in both cases, but photonic waves undergo different selectivity on the wall, as we shall see.

(4) The most significant difference appears in the act of observation. Unlike audition, our vision is not circular but highly oriented. We do not have panoramic sight. This difference has basic and far-reaching implications. The highly oriented nature of our visual field brings it about that in face-to-face communication, eye-to-eye communication can become predominant. For the same reason, i.e., orientation, in static position our visual register does not yield uniform and direct information about the whole space as such. The impression of acoustical space is virtually independent of the observer's position within it. The T_R provides an immediate and overall impression of the acoustical space to a completely immobile observer. J. M. Fitch is right to insist that the architect must learn the exact limits of our vision in order to understand optical space impression as well as the visual component of polysensory space impression.

The implication of this fact for the experimental construction of the repertory of optical spaces will be clear if we consider the role of specular areas for static exploration of the optical space, and also if we compare space impressions obtained in static and those obtained in dynamic exploration.

Optical Properties of the Architectural Envelope

We have seen that the impression of optical space originates in the reflecting properties of the enveloping surface; but our impression of the shape and volume of the space undergoes modifications due to other aspects of the surface than its geometry, aspects which are no less inherent in the architectural design of space.

In order for the architect to be master of all the means by which he can create spatial illusions and so change the character of optical space, he must study those aspects of reflection which are pertinent to changes in the optical space impression.

Aspects of reflected light: differences in reflecting surfaces

Reflected light is always a function of the incident light ray. The surface can diminish, transform, or even – if we consider the phenomenon within a limited span of time – increase the incident light. The surface's reflecting qualities cannot be defined in absolute photometric terms; instead, the surface as secondary light source is described in terms of reflectance, the coefficient of reflection.

In reflected light we find three basic factors and one accessory one:

(1) the relative quantity of incident light reflected,
(2) selectivity, the ratio of light reflected measured by wavelength,
(3) the directional distribution, in relation to the angle of incidence,
(4) sometimes, temporal retardation (phosphorescence).

We have here an energy aspect expressed as relative intensity, a spectral factor expressed in a set of curves, and finally a geometric one (Boynton 1964: 6).

1. *Reflectance* For the beholder inside an optical space, it makes no perceptible difference if the nonreflected light is absorbed by, or passes through, the enveloping surface. The science of lighting measures reflected light (F_ρ), according to the principle of the conservation of energy, as a residual magnitude, viz., $F = F_\rho + F_\tau + F_\alpha$. The reflectance ($\rho$), is calculated as $\rho = 1 - (\alpha + \tau) = H/E = F/F_\rho$. As a matter of fact, the luminous flow is the most 'solid' of the basic concepts in lighting science. Luminous flow (F), erg/sec measured in lumens (lm), is photonic energy which produces a luminous sensation evaluated by relative luminous efficiency (Déribéré 1959: 5; Leblanc et al. 1958). When we relate this energy to a surface unit of reception, we speak of luminance (E) measured in lux (lx); if we relate it to a surface unit of emission, it becomes luminous emittance (H). Reflectance is a reemission and as such can be apprehended as $H/E = \rho$. In the case of reflection — or secondary light source — we speak of lightness (or grayness) of the surface, in the case of primary source the luminous intensity is called brightness.

2. *Diffusion of the reflection* The reemission from a point on the reflecting surface may vary with the observer's position. When we consider light reemission from a given direction we speak of luminance, $L = H/\omega$ (or E/ω). The total F_ρ results from the integration of the H/ω values around a hemisphere of the surface whose center is the designated point of reemission.

Before considering the spatial distribution of the luminous (re)flow, we must fix its parameters. Distribution will depend on the angle of incidence. If the designated surface point does not have symmetrical properties, the reflectance will be a function not only of the vertical angles of incidence and reflection, but of the two horizontal angles as well. Thus the table describing the reflection will show four modalities. Moreover, since each value in this table is a function of the wavelength of the incident light as parameter, to each value respectively there must be added the spectral composition as specification (Gillod 1957: $RE = f[\lambda]$).

The large number of 'parametric' dependencies of the values opens a wide range for the architect's play with optic materials. We can grasp the extent of this range by examining its extreme limits.

2.1. *Regularity of reflection* If the immediate environment of the designated point is flat, the line perpendicular to this surface bisects the angle of incidence and reflection of a beam of light. Even if some part of the incident light leaves the space, passing through the envelope (and so $E \neq H$ and $\rho \neq 1$), as long as all reflections proceed along the same beam of rays we speak of regular or direct reflection (Déribéré 1959: 8-9, 54). All deviations from this case result from unevenness in the surface of the microenvironment of the designated point. (Other diffusion phenomena are produced fundamentally by the retransmission of light which has already crossed the enveloping surface.) Regular reflection is the property of what we call a specular surface, e.g., polished metal or silvered glass.

The invention of the mirror gave man a tool to know himself and his surroundings better than he could from the natural mirror of water surface (J. J. Gibson 1966: 215). But a plethora of specular surfaces, e.g., a hall of mirrors, removes any reference to distance and creates what the Swiss author and architect Max Frisch calls a Desert of Mirrors. This visual inexistence of specular surfaces can afford a city planner a useful device for integrating modern space systems into historical surroundings. In fact, if the new construction has mirror facades it shows no other identity than what it reflects of the surroundings. A good example is the John Hancock building in Boston with the adjacent Trinity Church.

2.2. *Perfect diffusion* This is the opposite extreme from regular reflection. The term describes unvarying uniform distribution of luminance in all directions of the hemisphere. The so-called Lambert Law (or Cosine Law of Light Emission) characterizes the totally mat surface, like milk glass, blotting paper, or woven materials (Leblanc et al. 1958: 225, 339). In practice, materials with perfect diffusion are very rare (e.g., Ripolin's wall, Leblanc et al. 1958: 225; Déribéré 1959: 53, 87; 1964: 11; Geldard 1953: 16-17). If in addition to perfect diffusion there is 100 percent reflectance, viz., the wall is opaque ($\rho = 1$, $E = H$), a perfect filter.

In general, intermediate cases, namely variation of luminance as a function of diffraction, can be measured in Taylor's apparatus by the Ulbricht (or integrating) sphere. The variation is calculated by $l = L/E$. If the diffusion is perfect, l/π is constant. To make the 'imperfection' in diffusion directly comparable, viz., independent of the variation of reflectance, it is better to constitute the following indicator: $L(F_T)/H(F_T) = l$. If the surface is a perfect filter ($E = H$), the two preceding indicators give the same result.

3. *Spectral composition* From the point of view of color a beam of light may have, on the one hand, a distinct wavelength (hue) and, on the other, several wavelengths in various proportions. If a single wavelength is present we have monochromatic light. In contrast, if the beam contains a variety of wavelengths nearly uniformly distributed along the spectrum of visible rays, the light is white. So we can say that the architectural surface as a secondary light source is selective and produces a quantitatively differentiated reflection by its pigmentation.

In conformity with its pigmentary properties, the surface does not return all rays but only those of certain wavelengths, and that according to a fixed coefficient. The ρ of the color red, viz., light with the shortest wavelength, is the lowest, which means that its 'return' is the least. Green's return is greater, and blue's even more. Finally, total white light has the highest ρ. (In fact, the sum of the coefficients of all colors gives the coefficient of white.) If the reflectance is zero, the surface is black.

Thus the spectral composition of light informs us of the relative presence of various rays with different wavelengths.

4. *Deferred and transformed reflection* Reflection is usually considered an instantaneous effect of incident light, especially because of the great speed of light propagation. This is, on the one hand, a phenomenon of spatial redirection of light and, on the other, one of eventual absorption of the various wave components. But to be more precise, the reflecting material does not manipulate incident light only in mechanical ways by the microscopic irregularities of its surface; deeper within itself the material may manipulate received light on a chemical or nuclear level. Because of the deferred nature of these 'responses' the surface can appear to us as luminous on its own. In reality the phenomena are more complex. Like an accumulator, the material may send back the light after a delay. Furthermore, this delay could be used by the 'receiving surface' to act as a transformer and to reflect light composed of wavelengths other than those of the incident light. Perhaps the most spectacular transformation is made by photochromatic glass and other surfaces which transform invisible ultraviolet light into visible waves.

Opalescence, fluorescence, and phosphorescence count among the qualities of extraordinary architectural surfaces. The first describes the 'blurring' of a reflection into shimmering, iridescent light; the second, reemission as longer waves than those of the received light; and the third, fluorescence with the addition of delay. Today's large variety of artificial materials provides an unimaginable range of effects for the designer to influence the impression of optical space. He can create focal points to give special impressions from 'privileged' observation points, for example, by redistributing diverse spectral compositions in a variety of ways.

Since 1898 the American Society for Testing and Materials has established voluntary standards for test methods to classify and give specifications to various materials. Generally it gives preference to tests under conditions of ultimate use. In order to promote the use of the psychology of perception by architects as an auxiliary science of their art, it would be desirable that all materials bear specifications related to perception, e.g., purity of color related to degree of saturation. In particular, the ASTM could extend its activities systematically in the direction of space impression, perhaps using the type of experiments proposed in this book to relate optical characteristics of materials to their effects on space impressions. Some work of this kind has already been done and reported in 'Sensory Evaluation of Materials and Products', Part 46 of the 1976 *Annual Book of ASTM Standards*.

Of course, such developments will go to waste as long as architects prefer 'intuitive insights' to scientifically based 'perception data' about materials. Schools of architecture should emphasize applied psychophysics as an auxiliary science to design in the same way that applied physics is to structural engineering.

The Five (plus One) Peripheral Variables of Optical Space

The various surface qualities which can affect optical space impression are peripheral variables of optic architecture. We call them peripheral because they act 'on the fringes' of the space impression, acting upon the two basic variables, viz., volumetric magnitude and geometric shape. They are 'superficial' in the root sense of the term.

We count six classes of variables and apprehend them first on the physical level. Based on this first level, we can go further to the psychophysical one, where intervals are measured in terms of difference thresholds (just noticeable differences).

(A) Spectrometric attributes, with two aspects:
(1) The specific quality of a monochromatic material; in physics the specifying wavelength (λ_s), in psychophysics the hue (λ/n).
(2) The purity, or in psychophysical terms, saturation (chroma) of the color.
(B) Attributes of intensity, with two modalities of appearance:
(3) Reflectance (ρ); in psychophysics, lightness or grayness.
(4) Luminous emittance; in psychophysics, the brightness or luminous efficiency of a luminary surface.

(C) Diffusion:
(5) Spatial distribution of luminance.
(6) Distribution of properties 1-5 on the enveloping surface, first seen as developed or rolled out, then in connection with curvature in the surface.

Spectrometric surface characteristics: scientific analysis vs. subjective dogmatism

One of our primary goals is to contribute to the construction of a science of architectural communication, which will in turn help to work out a sociological theory of architecture.

Scientific theory of architecture has long been claimed as its own by one or another dogmatic school with an exclusively visual and subjective orientation. We need mention only the abstract, esoteric, and confused notation of colors promulgated by Edouard Jeanneret, 'Le Corbusier'. This arbitrary chromatology served as doctrine during the renaissance of polychromatic architecture around 1900-1930 (Déribéré 1959: 25; Fitch 1972: 215).

In this effort we encounter obstacles similar to those in many other nascent sciences; there exist already dogmas and terminologies whose arbitrary and unscientific character presents endless pitfalls and blind alleys. Before we can proceed to conduct exact empirical research we must sweep away such 'alchemical' constructs, which lack any precise foundation in physics.

Harmony of colors, the chromatologist's dream

One such subjective scheme gives the title to H. Pfeiffer's book, *L'harmonie des couleurs* (1966). By referring to Klee and the Bauhaus, Pfeiffer (1966: 24) defines the harmony of colors as the chromatic union of affinities among colors and their combinations. Many other such systems have been constructed, all natural, all universally valid – and all different. What they have in common is a foundation in the confusion of science and art, psychophysics and esthetics (Thompson d'Arcy, H. van Lier, Borissavlievitch).

Psychosociologists recognize the fundamental conventionality of all esthetics with wide variations among cultures (Francès 1968). Under such conditions it is clear that the search for a natural harmony can have no scientific basis. Gerard (1958) emphasizes how purely intuitive the views of the colorists are.

Color nomenclature, ethnoscience, and 'emics' But how do colors receive their names, or go unnamed? Do universal psychophysical laws of vision impose the names, or are they just arbitrary and fortuitous?

The study of diverse societies reveals that both the specific colors and the number of colors which show on the mental map are subject to wide variation. Authorities also disagree: Newton posited seven colors in the solar spectrum, believing in the number's magic properties, while others suggest four fundamental ones (e.g., Pfeiffer 1966: 5, 9; Bouma 1971: 235; and Geldard's critical review). Vasarhely proposes six (1970: 141); the basic ones, red, blue and green, plus mauve, yellow, and gray (although the last is achromatic and should not be considered as a color). We note that Klee built his painting on red, blue, and yellow (see his painting Bildarchitektur: Rot, Gelb, Blau, 1923, in the Art Museum of Berne).

In comparative ethnology (ethnoscience), two approaches have been taken to the study of color perception. One has been to determine the taxonomy of colors used and understood by a given people. The other, 'cross-cultural' study, goes beyond simple ethnographic description and juxtaposes different taxonomies in an attempt to compare the mental maps of many or all human societies. The first studies are said to proceed on the emics level, the second on the etics level. Berlin made an emic analysis (1970) of the color nomenclature in 100 different societies and found that the number of 'named' colors varies from 2 to 11, and that all societies which recognize the same number of colors always name the same colors. That is, if a people name five colors, for example, the names are always the equivalents of white, black, red, green, and yellow. If they name only two, they are always the 'achromatic colors', the extremes of the lightness scale, black and white. Still, we must consider these generalized findings with some caution.

From physics to psychophysics of colors

In view of the above, we can see the necessity of beginning our examination of color in purely physical terms, i.e., we start with the length of the transversal waves and proceed methodically to the point at which the brain perceives color, i.e., evaluates optic sensation. In physics we describe colors by three variables: specifying quality, i.e., the wavelength; purity, i.e., relative uniformity in wave length of the rays of light; and luminance, i.e., 'light' or 'dark' shades. The first two are closely related in terms of chromaticity, but the third must always be indicated as a parameter in color specification. Note that specifying quality and purity are functions of the length of the wave(s) while luminance (intensity) is a function of wave amplitude.

To designate specifying quality we turn to the spectromagnetic spectrum, whose full range lies between 10^{-14} and 10^8 meters of wavelength (Geldard 1953: 16; Boynton 1964: 17; Chapanis et al. 1949: 57). Within this range the visible spectrum lies between ultraviolet (4 · 10^{-4}) and infrared (7 · 10^{-4}). As far as the spectral composition is homogeneous, viz., composed of a single specifying wavelength, we speak of a monochrome. In this case the purity factor is equal to unity. If other colors are present, the specifying wave length (λ_s) becomes (simply) dominant (λ_d). To the extent that the wavelengths which complete the spectrum to whiteness, viz., the complementary ones (λ_c), are present, the light becomes achromatic and the purity factor is zero. Thus a color is as much pure as the λ_c are absent.

The three chromatic coordinates From the physical point of view, any specifying wave length can be constructed from the three chromatic coordinates which we call basic colors. Although some colorists have reservations about this concept, we think it useful on both spectrometric and colorimetric grounds to hold to a trichromatic system based on red (R; 700 mμ), green (G; 505.5 mμ), and blue (B; 478.5 mμ) (Baird; Geldard 1953; 57-58). If we mix all three at equal levels of purity and brightness we achieve the achromatic 'color' (Boynton 1964: 17: unique match). On the subjective side, the result is the color white. The chromatophanometer of Piéron determines these levels.

We must recall that colorists and phenomenological psychologists sometimes use systems of other than three colors. Pféiffer (1966: 10-11) uses four 'fundamental' colors and even considers systems based on 5, 9, or 11 colors which he thinks have 'natural affinities'. Hesselgren maintains that color impression cannot be attributed to the synthesis of tristimuli.

To bring order to the existing confusion in color theory, we state some epistemological rules. First, although spectrometric differences can be translated into colorimetric intervals, the reverse cannot be done (Déribéré 1959: 51-52). The procedures followed by the makers of coloring materials to achieve the desired color are of little relevance to the experimental study of perceptual color syntheses. The process can be either additive or subtractive without affecting the result and its perception. Finally, as we learn more about the physiology of color perception we find in the field of physical spectrometry solid grounds for experimental studies in colorimetry. For example, a Harvard team in 1967 won a Nobel prize for showing that the three basic colors reach the 'mind' by three distinct channels.

For these reasons the experimental psychologist can use the trichromate-tristimuli system of Piéron as a heuristic device. Psychological arguments can be adduced for the three-color system. These colors have maximal saturation

238 *Communication through architecture*

compared to all others (although not equal among themselves), as well as the lowest difference thresholds.

Saturation The three physical variables in vision are measured by purely optical means completely independent of any physiological sensitivity. If we fix a 'light of reference', the size of the observed area and the distance of observation, we can make measurements concerning the optical characteristics of the surface from a standard 'observer of reference'. The measurements of this sensor will be less precise than those of physical optics, but they will relate more directly to our study, especially if the standardization approximates the conditions prevailing in the case of architectural space impression. Indeed, such conditions are essential if valid conclusions are to be drawn from the observation. We can note that the optical space envelope is generally seen from a distance of 2 to 50 m.

In general the mensuration of psychophysiological variables — namely lightness, hue, and saturation — can be improved by using robot-eyes as a standard observer, such as Hardy's spectrophotometer, which measures luminous efficiency.

The reason we discuss the problems of transition from physics to psychophysics under the heading of saturation is that it is the least precise of the three mentioned data (Holmberg 1964, 1965). The basic problem is to determine sensory intervals (Déribéré 1964: 117). Saturation degrees cannot be matched directly with the physical purity; the relation between the two is about as loose as that between taste and chemical composition. What we measure is simply the number of discriminations that can be made between the absolute threshold or limen and the maximal purity (Piéron 1968: 387). This gradation is expressed by the suffix '-ish', as 'greenish' (Pfeiffer 1966: 10-11; Piéron 1968: 74). We normally distinguish 23 intervals of saturation (Geldard 1953: 42), 65 of brightness (Pfeiffer 1966: 34), if we observe from far enough away (Piéron 1968: 322), and around 20 hues — for Ostwald 21, for the German DIN norms 24 (Déribéré 1964: 114-118).

We will see later how the perception of hues may vary according to the context of presentation. When two color fields are well separated, the 'just noticeable difference' is much lower than if the difference in color alone serves to separate contiguous fields.

The three variables we speak of are different vectors (Grasmann in Krantz et al. 1974), but not completely separable one from the other; there is some obligatory correlation among them. Thus, not all the points on the frustrum of a (truncated) pyramid, which we use for a graphic representation of colors, will be occupied. In the German DIN system and other analogous ones we can show how an equal saturation of color can be kept, even if we change the degree of brightness, and vice versa, for any given color. Still, according to the obligatory correlation between vectors, there remain the following restrictions:

— The maximal saturation of a color can only be achieved at a determined degree of brightness; but this degree varies according to color (correlation among modifiers; tints; Geldard 1953: 54).
— The shade of gray, i.e., the degree of maximal saturation, also varies according to color. When the color reaches maximal saturation at a higher degree, the required brightness factor is lower (Déribéré 1964: 117).
— Each of the three basic colors reaches its saturation point a different degree, but all do so at a higher point than any other color. Geldard (1953: 42) and other authors correctly point to the much lower maximal saturation of yellow. (It had namely been suggested to consider the yellow as a fourth fundamental color with the three basic ones.)
— Finally, we can state a correlation between saturation and the direction of reflected light, in the sense that regular reflection from specular surfaces has the effect of desaturating the color of light (E. Barthès 1957; Déribéré 1959: 87-88).

A model for the chromatic variables on the envelope

The frustrum of a pyramid (Lambert) can represent all possible combinations among hue (H), saturation (S), and brightness (B). Thus every section cut through the pyramid gives a page of the color atlas, which leaves certain areas blank for combinations which cannot be made.

The figure 3.9 shows the horizontal section as a triangle. The vertical axis, W, represents the achromatic aspect; it shows brightness, i.e., the shade.

Z' is complementary color of Z.

W... Origin of the vertical axis.

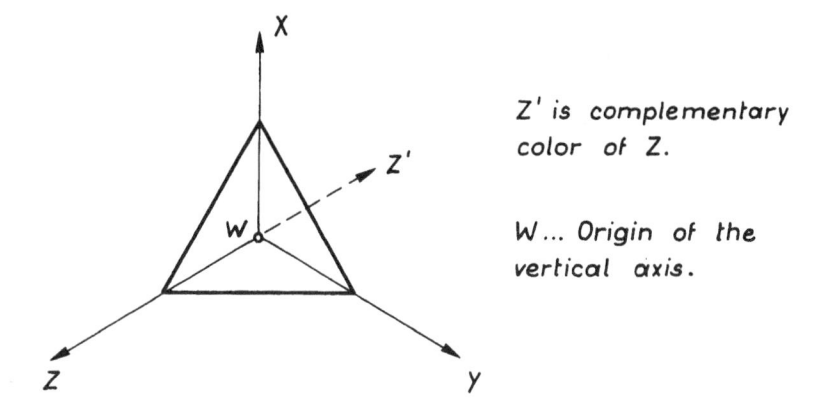

Figure 3.9. *The base of the 'trichromatic pyramid'.*

240 *Communication through architecture*

The *XYZ* system can be converted into the RGB one (Red-Green-Blue). Horizontally, from the origo represented by the axis *W*, the polar angle, i.e., the direction of the vector, shows the hue. The length of any given radius shows the color's saturation. Because the three basic colors have the highest degrees of maximal saturation, their bisectors meet at an angle of 60°; but because those degrees are not equal, the pyramid's sections are not equilateral triangles.

For optical space, thus, chromatic variables are peripheral. They originate from the color of the light and the pigmentation of the envelope. Their colorimetric properties are defined by the diffusion of reflection along the spectrum.

Intensity characteristics: surface lightness and luminous quasi surface The standard enveloping surface is a reflecting one. The lightness of the surface is (or ought to be) determined by the reflectance of the material chosen by the architect, and may vary from white to black. If the surface becomes completely black the optical space vanishes.

Even before the architect determines what variations of reflectance he wishes the enclosing surface to have, he must decide if some areas of it will be primary light sources. (See Figure 3.10.) Such areas then become (luminary or) quasi surfaces of the optical space, having brightness but no lightness. Thus the first decision about intensity attribution is between reflection and luminosity, (*r*) and (*d*). Concerning *d* spots we speak of quasi surface, i.e., not closing in but opening out. Moreover, the fact that luminous surfaces cannot bear shadows has an important consequence for the impression of optical space (J. J. Gibson 1966: 194, 212-213).

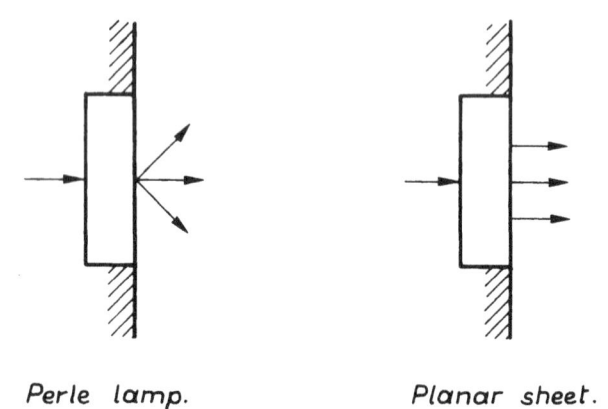

Perle lamp.   Planar sheet.

Figure 3.10. *Luminous surfaces.*

The architect can choose to treat some areas as intermediate between r and d, or even use one and the same area as both reflecting and luminous. If an area's luminance is relatively low and its reflected flux relatively high, it appears at one time to be reflecting and at another to be luminous. A commonly observable case is the window, which is luminous during the day and reflecting at night. (Fitch 1972: 120-121).

Fluorescence also presents a 'hybrid' case in that it reflects light selectively and emits its own light as well.

The sky as quasi surface: a special case We have described luminous areas on the surface of the envelope of an optical space as quasi surfaces. These areas tend to make the impression of the space indeterminate, especially if they are large, and invite the observer to complete his impression from his own imagination. Perhaps the most interesting case is atmospheric space, the ultimate context for all architectural texts or space systems. The observer always attributes specific geometrical characteristics to the sky even in cloudless weather. In one geographic location or another, the sky seems, e.g., 'higher' or 'lower'.

We also attribute colors to the sky, azure in general and red at sunset. We see the sky as blue because of the polarization of sunlight. The phenomenon called Rayleigh Scattering occurs when the size of the scattering particles in the atmosphere is small in relation to the wavelength of the light. Blue, of course, has a relatively short wavelength.

We should note also that the atmosphere is composed of many layers of varying density and temperature, which can function as a series of lenses to produce vertical distortions like the fata morgana — truly imaginary cities.

Specular attributes of a surface We have established two main classes of variables in optical space: geometrical ones, shape and volume; and peripheral ones, which affect the observer's impression of the space but do not affect the space itself. We now discuss the second class in more detail.

Our first distinction is between bright (b) and mat (m) reflection. This difference in reflection may arise from a cause other than the properly superficial characteristics of the surface, in the sense that a rough surface is, in principle, a geometrical phenomenon (Leblanc et al. 1958: 339; Fitch). But we continue to class brightness and matness characteristics among the peripheral variables because the same mat or specular reflection which may vary according to the light's direction or spectral composition may be caused by the surface's molecular structure, by prismatic effects, opaline glass, fabric, or blotting like wallpaper covering, and so on.

Again, we have said that architectural geometry is related to 'minimal monumentality'; cavities inaccessible to human beings are geometrical spaces but not architectural ones. For this reason we apply here the criterion of scale. If we have the impression of only one light ray which returns after multiple reflections in the cavity, this minicavity is assimilated to the superficial characteristics and treated as another peripheral variable. But if the

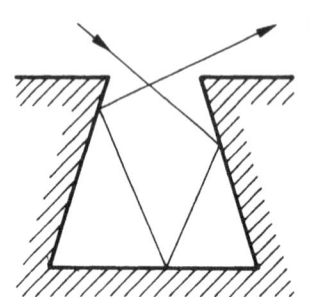

Only one light ray output.

reflected light waves produce an impression of the geometry of the cavity, e.g., by shadow, we treat it as a properly geometrical variable of architectural space.

J. J. Gibson has established an entire hierarchy of surface qualities (1966: 12, 191, 212, 208) such as layout, facet as micromirror, fine and coarse grain, and finally, plastic texture. Within this scale the architect can create pictorial and graphic structures on the surface by manipulating its microstructure, varying brightness and matness characteristics only.

With regard to matness, it can have, in the extreme case, only one modality, which we have called perfect diffusion. But in opposition to brightness it can have multiple modalities. As we have said, the diffusion of a mat surface can be uneven according to direction; and there is a continuous series of matness variations which could be reduced to a manageable number by establishing difference thresholds on the psychological level. A further possibility of enlarging the number of matness modalities lies in the variation of the light's spectral composition. Thus the architect has ample means for designing graphic or pictorial structures on the surface. The variation of the direction of diffusion is an important device in the formation of optical space because it can produce dynamic (e.g., focal) effects. In fact, there is a very wide range open to subtle play with the diffusion factor. Because there is a continuous passage from microtextures (which influence diffusion) to larger ones, the architect can alternate between smaller and larger scales. While this may make the study and anticipation of the effect more difficult, the effect itself will be no less interesting.

Another subtle device would be to place the light source at such a point that, depending on the observer's position, a pigmented surface would actually appear to change its configuration of colored areas.

Architectural orthography and orthopictography of surface arts

Architectural orthography operates on three levels:

(1) The surface has light-isolating properties, even before it becomes part of the envelope. The developed surface already has the two spectrometric characteristics, reflectance or — if the surface part is luminary — luminous emittance and specular attributes.
(2) The distribution of the above properties can produce one or more graphic or pictorial surface structures.
(3) Finally the surface is erected to form the optical space envelope in the gravitational field and each surface point with the enumerated optical specifications finds its relative location on it.

These are not meant to be temporally successive steps but logically discriminable aspects of the process. It behooves the architect to keep all three in mind during the design process so as to use all available means to create ingenious optical space, independent of other sensory spaces. The complicated task of composing multisensory space is a logically subsequent step.

1. *The homogeneous surface* In order to distinguish the task of designing the superficial character of the surface (e.g., wallpaper or tapestry) we speak of the designer here as 'architecturist'. This means simply that the architect can at this stage create the pattern himself or choose among already fabricated materials designed by other professionals.

As TV transmission techniques do, we divide the surface into grids of small squares whose size will be determined by the 'minimum separable' (Geldard 1953: 83; Attneave 1954: 188). To each of these units the architect can assign different characteristics. Should he decide the surface will be homogeneous, he simply chooses once for all points. But since the character even of a homogeneous surface affects the impression of optical space, the choice must also be made by the architect. Only a completely random distribution of surface characteristics renders unnecessary the choice of peripheral variables. How many attributes must be chosen for a homogeneous surface?

(1) The specifying quality of the surface, perceived as the 'report' (exact reproduction) of a color under standard white light. This quality has a

constant modality situated among the three coordinates of the basic colors. For simplicity, we can say that there are ten minimum discernible hue intervals, including achromy.

(2) The purity of the color, perceived as saturation. Whatever the number of hue intervals accepted, we can generally distinguish about 20 degrees for saturation.

(3) Whether the surface is to be luminous or reflecting. This binary choice also determines whether the following step is to be taken in terms of brightness or lightness.

(4) If the surface is luminous, we measure its brightness; if reflecting, we determine its lightness under a standard illumination. In both cases we distinguish about 60 intervals between white and black.

(5) The unevenness of diffusion according to direction. Between specular reflection and perfect diffusion we distinguish eight intervals. (For this purpose we assume symmetry of reflection, ignoring the possible variation of spectral composition by direction.)

A rapid calculation of the combinations possible among the five types of attributes shows us that the architecturist has in fact $10 \times 20 \times 2 \times 60 \times 8 = 192,000$ possibilities at his disposal, and that only for a homogeneous surface!

2. *Astructurality: total heterogeneity of the surface* The superficial characteristics become peripheral variables of the optical space and affect the impression of its dimensions. Even if uniformly distributed, they can enlarge or contract the space impression.

If the architect wishes to construct a pure case in which only the geometrical attributes will affect the impression of the optical space, it is not enough to make the enveloping surface homogeneous. In order to neutralize the effects of surface characteristics he must distribute them in such a way that every minimal unit has an equal chance to receive any attribute ($p = 0.50$), i.e., the distribution must be random (Zusne 1970: 277; Berlyne 1966: 9-22). This statement takes on scientific validity as soon as we specify a technique which allows us to make such a distribution (Bachelard).

We do so in three steps:

(1) the surface is divided into minimum separables, based on the absolute threshold of the standard obseving eyes (Attneave 1954: 188; Aubrée 1968: 2),

(2) we assign as an autonomous stimulus to each unit one attribute of each class of surface characteristics (we already know the number of modalities for each), and

(3) finally, we apply the contingency table of stochastic calculus to make the distribution.

2.a. *The size of the minimum visible* The theoretical definition of minimum separability requires that each unit be able to exert a stimulus during 100 msec. independently of adjacent units. But the required unit size changes with each of the five classes of characteristics. Thus, to be safe, the architecturist must effect the distribution for the smallest units. In colorimetry, for example, the standard is to consider a field of $2° = 2.22'$ surrounded by a white field of $40°$ (Déribéré 1964: 101). Using this angle and the fact that 5 m. is an average observation distance, we can calculate the size of the minimum visible.

2.b. *The calculus of nonredundancy and complete heterogeneity* Total heterogeneity occurs when the observer sees neither regular nor surprising change. How can we apply the principle of random distribution in our specific case? Following Attneave's instructions, W. H. Price and E. F. Chiburis converted Snedecoren's decimal contingency table into a binary system. Thus Attneave's field has a random distribution of characteristics with binary modalities, e.g., each unit has an equal chance to become white or black.

The systems of the envelope's optical characteristics are relatively independent from one another. Except for the third class, all have more than two modalities. On the other hand, all the rest have more than two modalities, and so Attneave's binary system cannot be directly applied. In order to find a random distribution of the modalities of all characteristics, the procedure is the following: we convert the values of a contingency table into various numerical systems according to the number of modalities in each class of characteristics. Next, we superimpose the independent numerical series. Thus we can assign determined combinations of attributes from each class to each unit. By random distribution with the 192,000 possible combinations of surface attributes we have calculated, not even in a space of considerable size will there be an area of repetition.

3. *Graphic and pictorial features* We turn now to surface attributes as means for graphic or pictorial structures. They serve the impression of optical space by articulating the enveloping surface. In the words of Vasarhely (1970: 123), 'polychromatic architecture emerges from monumental frescoes.'

Independently of the architecturists' intentions, artistic features stand out substantially through absence of complete homogeneity or complete heterogeneity, and through the presence of various regularities and surprises in the patterns. The definition of regularity is not without problems. The mathematician Zeitun attempts a definition through combinatorics: regularity consists of repetition in a population of enough size so that we can judge that the repetition is not random. A Touring machine can generate a series of regularities *ad infinitum* if it is composed of a finite number of operations (von Bertalanffy 1968: 22). In information theory, the information itself is defined as nonconformity with a prediction, and the prediction itself is possible as a function of expected regularity (Kraehenbuehl and Coons 1959: 510-522).

Our task now is to discuss the surface arts as far as they are relevant to the architect's task, namely to modify the impression of optical space. We do not discuss the arts in a general way, but only in their properly architectural function. Thus, for example, we ignore the purist school, which maintains that painting must be strictly bidimensional without any three-dimensional connotation. We also avoid the 'imperialistic' tendency of some architectural schools which completely subordinate other plastic arts, e.g., by reducing painting to tapestry (Le Corbusier, cf. Vasarhely 1970: 123, 126). In short, we analyze the plastic arts only in the context of their architectural, 'space-modifying' effects.

Vasarhely is certainly one of the most conscious exponents of architecturally relevant painting. While baroque architects used ceiling frescos to emphasize verticality – and Gothic builders did so by properly geometric means – Vasarhely's monumental mural paintings are applied on the facade of polychrome architecture (Vasarhely 1970: 102, 123). This seems to be the most methodical exploration of pictorial structuration of the surface (see also his *Yellow Manifesto* of 1955). This structuration depends neither on the figurative content nor on fortuitous distribution of pigments. He sets out to produce specific ambiguous space effects he calls kinetic, giving a flat surface the appearance of being curved without specifying the direction, or sense, in which the curving takes place, e.g., enlarging or confining the space.

Vasarhely also tries a more universal approach to the original in painting. In fact, he does not use original and copy but constructs his pictorial creations from two sources: a prototype, which is not itself a painting, and an original algorithm which allows the construction of multiples with serial permutations (1970: 102). This technique opens an easy way to integrate his pictorial structuration into our repertory of the architectural media. We anticipate that this repertory will integrate all architecturally relevant aspects of surface arts: hue, saturation, lightness, and diffusion, as well as all types of pictorial and graphic structures.

To be more concrete, we can speak of the scenographic effect through the architecturist's correct use of his orthography and orthopictography, by which he can bring about the mental transformation of perspective.

3.a. *Graphics* We return to the division of the surface into the smallest separable area. We use this definition both to identify the main types of structural surface and to describe the structures in permutational and combinatorial terms (Vasarhely 1970: 13). We consider each of these spots a punctual dimension which cannot be subdivided in any sense (Thiel 1969: 54). In physical terms, we perceive a spot as a point if we see a rupture in the continuity of the surface attribute and the punctiform element itself seems a minimum visible (cf. Anti-Impressionist Pointillism of Seurat). In more practical terms, any type of figure is called punctiform which has a clearly inferior dimension in comparison with its neighboring environment *and* whose shape has relatively equal distance from its center in all directions, i.e., its boundary seems to be roughly circular. The structures have such names as stippled, spotted, dotted, mottled, and speckled (cf. Tachism). Of course, structures using punctiform elements cannot be developed without having, as Zeitoun stated, a sufficient number of them on the surface.

We speak of linear structure if the zero degree of freedom of the point is relaxed to have one degree of freedom. We can see in the line an innumerable series of our elementary spots (dominos) so arranged that none is isolated nor has a neighbor in all directions. In a line, each element has two neighboring points, or at least one (Klaus 1968: 570) which assures continuity ($\Delta d \to 0$), but there is no continuity in any other direction of rupture.

Any one-dimensional structure can be rectilinear or curvilinear. The first cannot be inscribed on any other than a flat surface (i.e., one whose radius of curvature has infinite length). The curvilinear line can 'stay' on a flat plane or 'follow' surfaces with various curvatures, e.g., volute, helix, spiral.

In practical terms, the line may be more or less large. In fact, the linear nature of our script has an effect on the way we draw a line, whether we use crayon, pencil, pen, ink, or brush. We are well aware of the close relationship between Chinese painting and their pictographic, nonlinear writing system.

To sum up, we can say that if the freedom of continuity of the elements is no higher than degree one, we have a graphic structure (J. J. Gibson 1966: 229). For the realization of such a structure, it is not necessary that all points, isolated or on a line, have homogeneous optical attributes. It is enough that any one attribute contrast at each border to the neighboring background. If this difference is constantly preserved the structure appears. An abrupt change of difference ($\Delta d; y'; y''$) in the value of an optical attribute reveals the structure's presence and allows the distinction within it between punctual and linear. If an attribute shows gradual change on a line or in both dimensions of the surface, it designates an element of the punctual structure where it reaches its extreme value.

3.b. *Pictorial structures* If the various parts of a surface differ in at least one optical attribute at least gradually, with no difference in the degree of freedom of any of the component parts, i.e., all parts have bidimensional freedom, we speak of painting, having gone beyond graphism. In his chapter on 'painting and architecture', Vasarhely (1970: 124) tries to dematerialize the art of painting. He shows how the same work of 'form-color' could be imprinted on stained glass, mosaic, tapestry, painting, fresco, or mural. We do not touch here on the point that painting may or may not be defined as form-color 'fixing'; in his different, perhaps more general point of view, the architecturist will use any means to impart optical structure to the surface. We cannot speak of equality among various 'imprints' of the same form-color pattern because they will certainly differ in one or another of the five possible optical characteristics.

In the history of our architecture we find paintings on the ceilings of churches, like Michelangelo's in the Sistine Chapel, which have the architectural effects of seeming to expand or contract the optical space impression. In addition to direct effects achieved by abrupt (see Anquetin's paintings called Cloisonism by E. Dujardin in 1888 and the Post-Impressionists in general such as van Gogh) or gradual changes in optical attributes, the fresco exerts an architectural effect also through its representational content.

Since the birth of abstract art, the latter effect no longer comes into play; the pictorial surface is completely divorced from subject matter (e.g., the abstract expressionist Jackson Pollack created painting by spattering on huge canvases placed on the floor). Moreover, as we noted, they are more often murals than paintings on a ceiling and are even seen on external facades. We know the special importance of the wall, compared to the roof, for the sociological denotation of architecture. (Facade paintings are for us less important here because we are less concerned with the streetscape of the atmospheric space where it exerts its influence.) What we find especially relevant in modern art is that the artist — the cubist in particular — is constantly aware of the spatial effect of his work. This effect becomes more calculable in contemporary mural paintings than was the case in representational frescoes, and they are more easily integrated into architectural media.

To sum up, the effect of abstract painting on the impression of optical space can be more systematically explored by using the division of the surface into minimum visible (areas), and so better articulated (submorphemic) components of the optical space. The effect can also fit the requirements of serial industrial production without becoming monotonous, thanks to the application of combinatorics in the programming algorithm.

Before we discuss the application of combinatorics for a systematic use of peripheral variables, let us note that the architect should keep in mind two objectives in their deployment:

(1) precise modification of the optical space impression,
(2) ambiguous modification of the optical space impression.

Indeed, surface attributes can even generate contradictory effects. We need not think that architecture must always provide maximal legibility – as in telecommunication, or in the choice of the direction and orientation of the roads (K. Lynch). Fortunately, architects are asked to design systems other than clear subway corridors. These other, perhaps major, spaces, at a level beyond mere functionality, can give ambiguous space effects for pure joy (R. Venturi).

This structure shown in Figure 3.14.2 does not allow ambiguity, since the observer does not see the spots as being behind the line. When we determine the location of the spots we also put a limit on the line's location.

On the other hand, Vasarhely's kineticism produces surface structures which imply two complementary modifications of the optical space. In fact, we attribute a nearly imperceptible movement to the surface part through which the convex impression will be transformed into a concave one, and vice versa. Both 'final impressions' show identical curvature; only the orientation changes. (The true geometrical plane of the surface part functions as an axis plane of symmetry for the complementary surface impressions.)

The implication of these two complementary and inverse deformations is that the observer sees two optical spaces with equal magnitude of enveloping surface but different volume. It implies the change of the concavity index ($i = V^2/S^3$), which is an important complex characteristic of acoustical space.

The static illusion of reversed perspective has been known to psychology for more than a century. In the case of Necker's cube and Schroeder's staircase (1858) the reversal occurs so rapidly (Cesarec 1963) that these phenomena are used to study the oscillation of an observer's attention. The gestaltists studied figure inversion also, as background versus form. In these cases, the change in qualitative relation was studied without assuming a precise quantitative relation between the two possible spatial solutions of the picture, i.e., depth. Because the illusory rotation was not necessarily isometric, namely $I \neq a*a^{-1} \neq a^{-1} * a \neq I$, it is more appropriate to speak of figures with ambiguous impression than of inversion.

Computation of the architecturist's combinatorial cases

Before turning to the experiments necessary to learn the quantitative effects of each surface characteristic, and in order to be complete in our strategy, we must count the possible combinations.

First, as has been said, when all surface areas have the same attributes of all optical characteristics, the number of intervals in each characteristic produces 192,000 permutations. This is the total of all possible absolute effects of optical characteristics on a homogeneous surface.

Another step in the study of surface effect is to vary the attributes of one or more optical characteristics from one spot to another on the surface. In a systematic approach, we can start to calculate the variation by considering the left and the right, the upper and the lower, in relation to the central. We can show the calculation and the scale which is thus at the architect's disposal. With the surface divided into 24 parts, and the architect varying only one characteristic, which has only two modalities, e.g., being luminary or reflecting spots, he can choose among $2^{24} \cdot 24! \approx 10^{31}$. This 'relative' effect adds to the first step, which deals with absolute effect.

If the surface is large enough to comprise several elementary spots, attribute variation can produce distributive effects independent — more or less — of what the surface characteristics are used for. The attributes involved, with their absolute and relative effects, become only instrumental for delimitation.

We can think of the problem of map coloring, called also the four-color problem. According to Headwood, if there is no overlapping it is enough to use four colors, or four other attribute variations, to distinguish all the countries on any plane map (this conjecture was finally proven in 1977). On the surface of an anchor ring, delimitation of all possible configurations needs seven attributes. In the design of such structures the surface attributes are wholly interchangeable without affecting the structure itself.

By distinguishing the geometrical aspects of surfaces we can differentiate various arts of surface structures. We contrasted the graphic mode, the art of punctual and (recti- and curvi-)linear dimensions, and the pictorial one. In the choice of modes, the size and shape of the developed surface are the determining criteria. It is not very important which class of optical characteristics is used for delimiting boundaries. (See Figure 3.11.) A complexification occurs if overlapping structures are superimposed or if the geometrical structure consists of *gradual* variation in attributes. In the first case, the different structures can enter into composition, one or the other can prevail 'visually', in short a hierarchical order can be established among them. In both cases, a correlation between geometrical structure and optical characteristics occurs. From the geometrical viewpoint, the gradual structure is a continuous one, as opposed to the previous ones, which were discrete. Such structures cannot be created if the optical characteristics used do not have a certain minimal number of modalities. On the other hand, the gradual modality change can bring out nongradual structures; namely at its extreme values it can be used to draw lines — in a graphic sense or as a boundary for pictorial effect — or to

Optical space 251

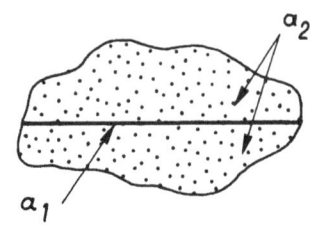

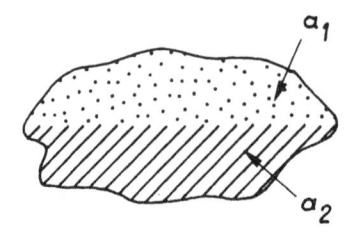

Graphic structure.   Pictorial structure.

(1, 2, n are the modalities of "a" optical characteristics.)

Figure 3.11. *Graphic and picturial structures.*

make points. In addition, the hierarchical order in the superimposed structures depends on the characteristics used. Hebb's experiments (1972: 48-49, fig. 7) show that not only for humans, but for all primates which have a sense of chromatic discrimination, this last takes precedence over all other optical characteristics. If one structure is delimited by a characteristic which has a large number of modalities, the designer can resort to strong attribute differences — i.e., big leaps in intervals — to compensate for the primacy of chromatic delimitation. (We recall that the number of intervals varies between 2 and 60 according to the characteristic.) Further, the architecturist's work becomes even more complicated if he uses more than one characteristic for imposing emphasis on one of the overlapping structures. Finally, we must note that the priority in perception of geometrical structures depends on shape itself, e.g., squares and circles are more quickly distinguished than composite figures.

The mathematical handling of the simultaneous manipulation of multiple characteristics is easier if we choose those which have the same number of modalities. In that case we can use block design in experiment (see Part IV for more detail). Vasarhely's system, for example, comprises 30 shapes and 30 colors (1970: 129).

We began this section with the enumeration of the three main aspects of the architecturist's orthography. The main types of peripheral variables were the surface's optical characteristics, geometrical structures (or, in more general terms, distributive effects), and relative position in the erected state. We treated the first two in more detail, taking into account possible interaction among them. We now look at the effect of the erection of the envelope upon its optical space.

The surface becomes closed and located in the gravitational field. Some surface areas may become curvatures and, eventually, new neighborhoods. The various surface structures of the envelope add their effect to the impression of the space's true geometry. In this context the architect has the opportunity to turn the architecturist's simulated space into perceived architectural space.

The erection of the envelope has its own combinatorics. For the most common cases mathematicians already have appropriate treatments, the customary prismatic spaces. Polya studies the case of a free-floating cube, — viz., with no consideration of its direction and orientation within the gravitational field — having two possible attributes. He shows that ten permutational schemes are possible in this case. If there are three modalities, the number of permutational possibilities is reduced to three. Of course, the mathematics of spaces with freer shape, i.e., composed not only of plane faces, for the design of an experiment series is more difficult to manage. The trial and error approach will hold a larger place in the study of the architecturist's contribution to the optical space repertory. (Of course, there are many aspects of greater or smaller interest for study, such as lines of inflection.)

In the next pages we assess past and future experiments which may contribute specifically and quantitatively to the construction of the architectural space repertory through optical space impression.

Perspective is particularly interesting in the understanding of surface structure's space effect. Indeed, perspectivity operates through transformation and preservation of cross ratio and unchanged neighborhood (March and Martin 1972: 25). In this respect it is worth noting that J. J. Gibson (1950) concentrated his efforts on gradients. We will look at his experiments on the space effects of grades of density gradients. We will see that regular change of density gradient, in either the graded manner of graphic structures or the smoother progression of painting, namely the systematic difference of spot distribution bases on perfectly regular spacing of elements (Gibson 1950: 84, fig. 33) has the maximal chance to simulate space shape and so influence optical space impression.

THE VISUAL IMPRESSION: CALIBRATION OF THE REPERTORY OF OPTICAL ARCHITECTURE BY EXPERIMENTAL CATALOGUING

An optical space stands as an individual word-form (or graph) in the architectural repertory if it cannot be brought into congruence with any other item by isometric transformation, viz., by simple translation or what is called proper rotation. In addition, word-forms which have equal angles, ratios, cross ratios, and neighborhoods and differ only in volumetric magnitude are similar and can be subsumed under *one* name as *a* shape. These distinctions are valid for all sensory spaces and for polysensory composition as well.

Easy as it is to label architecture a language (Preziosi), there has not yet been a serious effort to construct an architectural repertory at least of the most common part of it, optical space. Some arguments can be made against such an enterprise:

— Sensory spaces commonly have two attributes, volume and shape. The latter allows several word-forms, related by homothetic transformation.
— The surface characteristics which typically distinguish the spaces of various sensory modalities do not contribute to the specification of the repertory items, only to their qualitative distinctions.
— The repertory items differ on a continuous (R) scale, not a discrete (N) one, and so cannot be drawn up in a list.

Nevertheless, architecture is a medium of communication, and it is not enough for the architect to make designs only for his own pleasure. The designed space does not become part of the medium without being discernible to the addressee, the beholder. For communication to occur, the two mental mappings of space, the designer's and the beholder's, must at least partly coincide. Indeed the projective transformation of the optical space which the latter undertakes constitutes a necessary part of the communication process. For this very reason the surface characteristics of a space become involved in the construction of the space repertory in a quantitative manner by modifying the impression of the space.

Finally, the existence of difference thresholds allows the beholder to 'transform' continuous phenomena into discrete ones, which can, in fact, be listed. The designer can anticipate this transformation and use the distinctions as part of his medium. This is what we are calling calibration.

For these reasons it is worthwhile to undertake the construction of the repertory of architectural space as part of the description of the medium, and to deal with the repertory of optical space on its own.

Which questions pertain to the task? What indications of methodological and substantive concern can we find in the research in fields adjacent or analogous to ours for choosing the most promising hypotheses for experiments in the architectural medium?

Taking optical space as the most studied of architectural spaces (Clouten 1970), we try to deepen our knowledge of the experimental design devised to construct the repertory of the architectural medium on it (as a paradigm). In these experiments there will be features valid for the investigation of all types of sensory space and some especially chosen hypotheses inherently restricted to a particular sensory modality.

In all the sensory investigations the question series will evidently be the same, as will the approach of submitting the different spaces to a standard observer (see Holmberg et al. 1967: 1, on group data). Another common feature will be the experimenter's lack of interest in the method that the observer follows to discriminate spaces; this remains his secret (Black Box method). We only use theses about the mental process behind the subject's response as cues for organizing the question series economically. Responses of 'yes' or 'no' will be requested to a series of questions, organized in order of increasing complication, concerning the comparative volumetric magnitude of spaces and the discriminability of their shapes. The goal of the questions will be to designate intervals according to the smallest difference, below which the subjective probability of discrimination approaches zero. Such a repertory will allow the architect to address the most sophisticated beholder and remove the danger of refining beyond the point of perceptibility.

To avoid 'noise' and pitfalls in the experimental series we hold to the 'paired-comparison' method. This ensures that the subject can always give a binary, i.e., yes-no, response and eliminates the need for external standards and previous references (see the simultaneous presentation done by Hochberg and Hochberg 1952 and by Holmberg et al. 1967 on model). We avoid less classic methods which are not related to the difference threshold concept, although that concept is not without problems. The advantages of our method are numerous. Principally, it avoids important cognitive biases. If we ask the subject of our experiment to compare two optical spaces presented in a quasi-simultaneous way, long-term memory, with its related problems, will not be directly mobilized. The requirement of preexisting standards unduly intellectualizes the discrimination process, and makes it impossible to get and use data from a variety of social classes and civilizations. Other proposed methods go even farther from the target problem and are even more fraught with epistemological peril. Even in the case of forced choice (Sweets), if the beholder must compare two labels (e.g., names of two shapes), the problem of language usage arises, and we know that '*Verbal* report of experience is a critical part of the study of perception' (Haber 1970: v).

Of course the yes-no answer to our questions is also a verbal one, but it is on a clearly unsophisticated, even primitive, level. We ask for comparison of a simple aspect — 'Does this have greater volume than that?' — of the space, which is a prime frame of reference for other impressions in the space. The impression occurs, and the response is made, on an immediate, all-encompassing, and preperceptive level, before any cognitive bias can interfere.

A clearer source of bias would be the temptation to the experimenter to add phenomenological questions about, e.g., 'spaciousness' — implicitly about claustrophobia — or even about 'gestaltgoodness'.

The minimal result of the well-established series of questions is an ordered series of optical space impressions. Cohen and Nagel (1944) rightly say, 'Isolated facts do not constitute science and . . . the object of science is to find order among facts. 'The difference threshold concept holds the promise of a numerical, viz., quantified, series, which is the ambition of all scientific research.

The Question Series

The experimenter's questions aim to determine discernable volumetric differences between, and shapes common to, two spaces; both exclusively as functions of objective variation.

For comparison of volume, the simplest case takes two optical spaces with equal shape and surface characteristics. The experimenter begins to inflate a shape-preserving space envelope, i.e., he exerts a homothetic transformation ($y' = k \cdot y$) on it, until the point at which the answer to the question about equality in volume becomes 'no'. He goes to the next question, 'Is A larger than B?' If the response is correct, this assures that the original discrimination in volume was not random. The result can be put into the catalogue with the threshold value. Next to be ascertained is how the threshold difference varies as a function of shape and as a function of absolute magnitude of volume, even if the result is expressed as a percentage. Further, does regularity of difference, if in fact it seems to be present, show on a linear scale of percentage, or on a logarithmic or asymptotic one (Gilinsky 1951)?

After the series of volume differences has been catalogued for each of the shapes considered, a more complex task begins, namely to identify equal and different volumes in optical spaces of different shapes. We can expect these intershape comparisons to give higher thresholds than the previous same-shape series. We may even be able to form a hypothesis about calculating the new threshold on the basis of the two previous ones (e.g., a Cartesian product of the two previous results: $1_1 * 1_2 = 1_{12}$).

We turn now to shape discrimination. These responses cannot be catalogued in simple numerical terms, as was the case with volume differences, even though these judgments involve quantitative comparisons as well as topological ones. The observer's task here is to recognize similitude, i.e., homothetic transformation. To prevent confusion between isometric and homothetic transformation, and to distinguish shape-preservation from volume-preservation, the series must begin with equal shapes with varying volumes. The next stage conducts shape comparison on the basis of standardized volume. The cataloguing becomes systematic if discernible shape differences can be related to some kind of geometrical constants.

Optical surface characteristics do not constitute a separate question series. Their effects, if any, precipitate a systematic deviation in the judgment of volume or shape; but they are not themselves subjects of question series.

Indications from Knowledge About the Visual Field

Any impression of optical space, and its perceptive mapping, which is based on data input via the retina (Hebb 1949; March and Steadman 1971: 26) comes through a geometrical transformation made on the screen of the visual field. But this field is not homogeneous; if the visual receptor is located at the center of a spherical optical space, even though all the surface points are topologically equal, that will not be the beholder's impression of them. When we fix our gaze, the impression of any point will vary as a function of three values of polar or spherical coordinates, viz., one radius and two angles, whose origo is the observer's position. In fact the polar coordinates are a more appropriate reference for describing the visual field, as well as the optical space, than the Cartesian coordinates. The visual field is highly oriented in the horizontal plane and even more in the vertical. It also has absolute limits not only in distance but also in angles. Thus, from a fixed position, the whole enveloping surface cannot be seen. As we noted before ('Visible Communication' in Part II Figure 2.4.4) the binocular nature of vision 'stratifies' our horizontal field by overlapping images.

The diversification of the various points in the field is nearly total; the exception is the field's symmetry in respect to the median plane, the vertical plane which is our head's axis of symmetry. We do not attribute the same axis role to the frontal plane.

In approximate terms, we can say that one of the absolute limits of our vision is a vertical plane including the base line which connects the centers of the pupils. In front we see roughly a half ellipse with a horizontal major axis and two semiminor axes, the longer for the lower part and the shorter for the upper (J. J. Gibson 1950: 100, fig. 47).

We can divide the envelope into minimal, just detectable spots. The size of these minimum visibles can be calculated as a function of the radius (r) measured from the observer's eye: $r \tan \alpha$. Indeed, minimum visible requires an angle of $1''$, while minimum separable requires $1'$ (Sweets 1973: 991; Geldard 1953: 83; Boynton 1964: 15).

To locate the spot for binocular vision we need angles. The angular opening necessary to detect a spot changes as a function of the three angles which locate the point in the field. When the observer estimates the size of spots located under different angles, the errors vary.

In order to determine the differences in vertical, as compared to horizontal, error, a simple test is to ask for estimation of two sticks, one in vertical, the other in horizontal position, whose retinal images, i.e., apparent projective size, are equal. The length of the vertical stick will be overestimated compared to that of the horizontal, and quantitatively the resulting difference will approach the inverse proportion of the major and minor axes in the ellipse of the visual field a/b (Vurpillot 1967: 134). This difference seems to explain the well-known horizontal-vertical illusion (Kuennapas 1957, 1959).

Another variation in estimation results from the relative horizontal position. Horizontal sticks placed in the zone of fixation are overestimated in comparison with others located more on the periphery (Vurpillot 1956; 1967: 118-119). Osgood (1953: 250) emphasizes that the point of momentaneous fixation serves as reference for the whole orientation of the visual field.

Binocular disparity allows the observer to go beyond estimation of the apparent projective length, the result of estimating the angle's opening (arc tan r/d), and make an estimate of the 'radius' or distance and thus of the objective apparent length of the thing beheld. (See Figure 3.12.) Baird (1970: 61) thinks that the whole of spatial perception — volume and surface estimations, etc. — can be reconstructed from errors inherent in estimating the relation of distance and size (G. Simondon; see also Gaerling's research); for this purpose it is enough to choose an appropriate exponent for the relation. The hypothesis seems attractive for constructing a theory, but we will see later that, for several reasons, Baird's 'axiomatic reduction' is debatable.

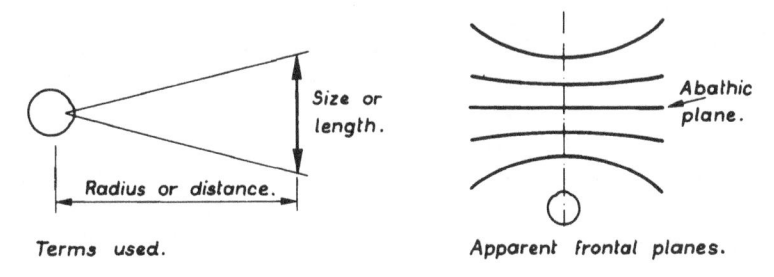

Figure 3.12. *Distance estimation.*

It would indeed be of interest to find some constancy in the estimation of the distance-size relation, both for the general characterization of the visual field's various points and for formulating hypotheses about the estimation of volumetric magnitude. The thesis concerning this constancy holds that, in the complex calculation involved in the perception of objective apparent magnitude, the observer takes into account the projective apparent magnitude; therefore if he overestimates the distance he will necessarily underestimate the size (Kilpatrick and Ittelson 1953; J. J. Gibson 1966). This would mean that the cone of distance-size suffers cumulative error. But experiments show that if the estimate of size is not helped by cues from the observer's familiarity with the object (Hochberg and Hochberg 1952), the overestimation of distance does not necessarily imply underestimation of the size; even the contrary can occur. Gruber (1954) calls this the size-distance paradox.

258 *Communication through architecture*

Further, distance estimation of points in the visual field shows certain regularities. First we can state that errors in distance estimation remain under 1 percent (Jenkin and Hyman 1959), and relatively long distances — beyond 40 m. — especially outdoors, are usually underestimated (Gibson and Bergman 1954). We will discuss the conditions and validity of these findings later. Distance estimation of variously located vertical sticks allows us to map the apparent frontal planes, viz., distance variations in the median plane. In fact the apparent frontal planes take curvatures along a cylinder with a vertical generator (Ogle 1950; Le Grand 1956) The plane as it approaches the observer appears more and more concave; as it recedes it becomes flatter, until it finally turns convex. Between the distances where the apparent frontal planes appear concave and convex, there is a privileged distance at which the plane appears in its true flat shape; this distance is called 'abathic'. It varies among individual people from 0.4 to 1.85 m. and averages 1 m. This distance characterizes the individual's visual field; it is therefore important to test it among our experimental subjects and take it into account before homologizing their results.

A device for ensuring that the observer perceives the 'true value' of at least one length is to display an ellipse with the major axis vertical. The estimate of the length of that axis is normally accurate, and experimenters regularly use the device as a control for a subject's other responses. By contrast, the designer who aims at 'controlled illusion' (Birren 1961a, 1961b: 42) must be certain to withhold anything like this device and to eliminate multiple optical clues which may let the observer correct his distortions. In addition, an optical space which does not allow full use of the parallax capacity of binocular vision encourages errors in distance impression (Fried 1964). Obviously, if the architect wishes to maximize the legibility of the optical space he must do exactly the opposite. In either case he will have an experimentally constructed repertory from which to make a conscious, reasoned choice rather than an intuitive leap.

The curvature of the visual field

Besides Baird, only Luneburg, to our knowledge, has attempted a mathematical description of the visual field. Luneburg cites experimental evidence for the claim that the whole visual field of a stationary observer can be described by Bolyai's hyperbolic geometry, characterized by a total normal or Gaussian curvature $K < 0$. Granted this, the visual field has two parameters: K, the negative total curvature (with individual variations), and σ, the individual characteristic of the binocular sensitivity for depth perception. These constants can be determined by specific experiments (Zajackowska 1958: 66-78) and indicate as well the individual's abathic distance: $x_o = f(K, \sigma)$. As a function of these two constants, the various surface spots undergo a geodesic deformation according to their positions in real space. Later we will see that the description of the visual field by hyperbolic geometry gives interesting inferences, such as this: there will be no similar triangles, because if two of their angles are equal the two triangles must already be isometric.

From the visual field to experiments in optical space impression

We have discussed objective surface characteristics relevant to the optical space impression and then also data on our visual field in relation to this impression. A survey of available special literature allows us to make the following general statements:

— Among all the fields of space perception, that of visual perception has received the most research;
— The literature uses the term 'space perception' in a more general sense than we do, viz., to mean perception of any object present in the space. We restrict the investigation about space perception to investigation of the open region included in the space envelope;
— Experimental results in the literature often seem contradictory; but closer inspection shows instead that they are only noncomparable; namely, experimental conditions and methodological principles vary and produce results of uneven reliability. We find this opinion also in the work of Vurpillot and of Haber; the latter surveyed some 4,000 publications.
— Given this state of the literature, we must be doubly cautious in using it for our specific goals.

Problems of standardization in the experiments To have compatible results from experiments in optical space impression, we must know precisely:

— the observer's position, observation time, and degree of immobilization;
— the volume, shape, and surface characteristics of the optical space;
— the 'algorithmic order' of presentation of the spaces for paired comparison and that of the binary questions asked about them.

If we use a mechanical observer to register the visual data, we need to simulate human binocular vision adequately by the correct choice of lens, fixation, film sensitivity, etc.

For an observer to see the whole envelope of an optical space his vision must be panoramic. This is precisely what distinguishes true space impression, with panoramic perspective, from pictorial space (J. J. Gibson 1966: 198).

Being, as we noted, highly oriented, the visual field could be 'panoramized' either by allowing the observer to turn his head (O. W. Smith: 388-389) or to use a mirror, or by making part of the enveloping surface specular. The use of a small scale model of the space is ineffectual because the interpretation of the results of its observation presents nearly insoluble problems (L. Holmberg).

If the observer turns his head around completely, he can locate 150 million different points (Piéron 1967: 123, 135). Head turning, obviously, approximates the ordinary conditions of space perception, but it brings in the problem of isolating the purely visual information. Indeed, eye contraction already gives other sensory input than visual, but in the case of head movement the proprioceptive input is no longer a negligible source of information. On the other hand, not even head turning permits complete exploration of optical space if, for example, there are corners or recesses. Before using or matching any experimental results, freedom left to the observer must be carefully considered.

The use of specular areas can give a good simulation of the normal conditions of space observation, since mirrors do not necessarily 'impoverish' the space's image. This can, however, accentuate 'incongruities' which direct vision would hardly detect. This is the reason why painters often work from a mirror.

In this respect, the observer's *position* is also a parameter. A convenient solution to the panorama problem would be to station the subject with his back to the wall. But the choice of a standard position requires taking other considerations into account.

As we know, minimum visible is a function of angle opening, and so the size of the smallest detectable spot depends on the observer's distance from it. The capacity for color discrimination also varies with distance, and that too must be standardized, e.g., at 1 m. (Birren 1961b: 83), which is at the same time the average abathic distance (where the normal error of estimate of the plane's flatness is near zero).

In 'space perception' experiments researchers have used 'architectural laboratories' with quite different volumes (cf. R. C. Hulsebius's volume effect). Even in indoor experiments, our particular interest, the space studied varied widely. L. Holmberg operated in a 'full-scale laboratory' of 62.5 m.^{3}, with 2.5 m. the constant height and the floor surface 25 m.^{2} (i.e., 5 × 5 m.). In his interdisciplinary research project — psychology and architecture — Gaerling (1969-1970) used simulated spaces, namely photos. C. Jeanpierre conducted his experiments in the CSTB laboratory in France in a space of 7 × 3 × 2.12 m. O. W. Smith (1958) worked in a hall with a floor of 108 × 2.75 m. Jenkin and Hyman (1959) had their subject observe a wall from a distance of 9 m. Of course Gibson and Bergman's outdoor experiments (1954) involved even greater dimensions, a grass surface between 47 and 350 m. long.

For all the above reasons, we find ourselves in a real quandary. If we place the observer with his back to a wall, his observation distance varies from one part of the envelope to another (see Figure 3.16.1). Nor, indeed, can we find a single standard distance satisfactory for the valid use of research results about all characteristics which contribute to the optical space impression; a distance which seems preferable in one respect has adverse effects in others. We are forced to compromise. In order to achieve a cumulative use of various results, all reports should be accompanied by a careful description of the conditions of observation and their scientific purpose. Crosschecks will permit results from other research contexts and goals to be adapted to our present concern.

Pitfalls of the 'schoolmaster's space perception' We have noted that researchers in the field of so-called space perception study all kinds of extensions which are within space and, for heuristic reasons, observe very simple elements, e.g., lengths. Our problem now is to find ways of using those results for a different purpose, the study of the impression of the optical space itself. We must avoid from the start the mistake of thinking that the optical space impression is necessarily a synthesis of certain perceived components which any observer would make. This we call the 'schoolmaster's pitfall'. It would negate every epistemological advantage of our method of eliciting simple binary responses to carefully planned paired-comparison questions. By the possible use of 'invented eyes' or 'robot eyes' to fix the data entry level, and then by restricting our study to the responses alone, we leave the whole process of data evaluation by the subject in a 'black box' and deal only with the results. This allows individual variation in the process among subjects with different backgrounds, including the possibility of a direct 'grasp' of the optical space.

The schoolmaster has many 'apparently promising' temptations to reject this approach, although it involves very few unproven premises. There is the lure of the most 'economic' method, the one which would possibly give the least error in the estimation process. Some researchers look for optimal information processing for the same purpose and even try to 'describe' it by computer simulation. Such research may be useful for many purposes, but it does not guarantee that the simulated process is the one which an observer will effectively use. We cannot assume an obligatory process for transforming the impression data into units of information (J. J. Gibson 1966: 28; cf. the tv 'scanning process').

The schoolmaster's problem is that he wants to be 'correct' and thinks it is enough to follow the formula he taught us in school: volume is the product of length X height X width, or of floor surface X height. Period. Indeed, Swedish researchers Gaerling, Kuennapas, and Thegtsoonian show us that we have abundant experimental data about errors in length estimates of lines, vertical and horizontal, at varying distances from the observer, as well as data about the distance estimates themselves, which we can use to construct hypotheses about standard errors of volume estimates. We determine the exponents and coefficients to be used on the subjects' errors on one-dimensional (length) and two-dimensional (surface) extensions and calculate the error we expect in volume estimate as follows: $V = c \cdot [(B^m \cdot D^n)^p \cdot H^l]^q$ where B^m, D^n, and H^l are the length estimates in various positions relative to the observer, and q the proper subject of the research into volume estimation itself, as p was for floor-surface estimates.

Still, not everybody in every culture had a schoolmaster. Nor do we all follow the schoolmaster's methods all our lives. The attempt to reconstruct the processing of information that takes place inside the 'black box' inevitably involves the use of unproven premises. We can spare ourselves tedious labor and unverifiable results by resolving at the outset to leave the black box closed.

APPLICATION OF PAST FINDINGS TO THE USE OF PERIPHERAL VARIABLES FOR SPACE IMPRESSION: ELEMENTS FOR HYPOTHESES

We saw that the calibration of the repertory of optical architectural units depends on the way experimental findings answer two types of questions. First, where is the threshold above which the observer can recognize differences in volume or shape between two nonisometric optical spaces? The complementary questions check the results of the first: what spaces, with objectively different shape or volume, appear, nevertheless, systematically either homothetic or volume-preserving?

The systematic error of estimate in a serial paired comparison of the shape and volumes of optical spaces depends objectively on the following aspects of the spaces:

– the six (5 + 1) optical characteristics of the enveloping surface,
– the absolute magnitude of the volume,
– the geometrical properties of the shape and, in nonhomothetic ('heterothetic') comparison, the relative 'geometrical relationship' – e.g., affine transformation – between the shapes in terms of topological transformation.

The practical purpose of this research is to let the designer communicate more effectively by rightly anticipating effects in quantitative terms and so avoiding details too fine to be perceived. The use of the repertory of optical spaces – established by a systematic series of experiments – will permit the architect to give his spaces the optimal formal and functional legibility, e.g., better orientation in circulation (K. Lynch), or, where he wishes, to use systematic error of volume estimation to create illusion, either in order to solve economically conflicting design requirements, as baroque architects did, or simply for the sake of playfulness (Déribéré 1959: 126-127 about *trompe l'oeil* architecture; Birren 1961b: 42).

Space Effects Created by Hue (Hue as Opteme)

Colors exert a direct emotional effect on the beholder. Children as yet unable to distinguish shapes, group objects by color, and the role of color in categorization remains predominant throughout life. Here, however, we are concerned only with the specifically architectural effect of color, the ways in which it can seem to enlarge, contract, or otherwise modify an optical space. To anticipate such effects we seek a 'calculus of ambience'. Our architectural heritage teaches us how color was used in the past. Byzantine mosaics, even though faded by time, are instructive. Austere periods, like the years following the Reformation, refused systematically the use of colors in architecture.

As a first step toward learning the effects of colors F. Birren (1961b: 47) lists them in order according to their effects of seeming to situate a surface spot nearer to or farther from the observer. His list is the following: (yellow), white, red, green, violet (blue), and black. The list begins with the yellow as the most 'approaching' and ends with the violet. This means that the colors in their approaching effect follow the order of chroma brightness: the yellow color, which reaches its maximal saturation at a lower degree of brightness than those of the three basic colors, brings the surface nearest to the observer. (See also the section on saturation.) The order of the three basic colors on this list is important; it shows that the basic color with the lowest wavelength — and lowest maximal degree of saturation — red, has the strongest approaching effect. Indeed, the whole list follows the order not only of chroma brightness but also of wavelength.

Quantitative data show that the shift from approaching to receding effect occurs between red and green where popular language makes the distinction between warm and cool colors. We will discuss later the question of including white and black in this list.

We may note that physiological psychologists have explained the space effect of colors by charting the retinal color field (Geldard 1953: 67; Fitch 1972: 91, fig. 23). The field's extension follows the order: gray $>$ blue $>$ (yellow) $>$ red $>$ green. Not only the extension of the various retinal color fields is different; their elliptic shapes vary too. For the colors' 'deepening' effect, the criteria are the relative positions of the centers of gravity of the

264 *Communication through architecture*

various retinal color fields. On this subject Ivo Kohler and my colleague at M.I.T., Richard Held, have conducted experiments. The Figure 3.13.2 shows the results. This chart shows not only the order of the deepening effect, it also shows that in the farther region the blue component becomes predominant. This can also be seen from an aerial perspective (Vurpillot 1967: 124).

The limits of the visual field of the right eye for each of the basic colors. (Test object is a small, homogeneous patch of light of moderate intensity. Perimeter and campimeter are used.)

Centers of gravity of the retinal color fields. (Schematic representation.)

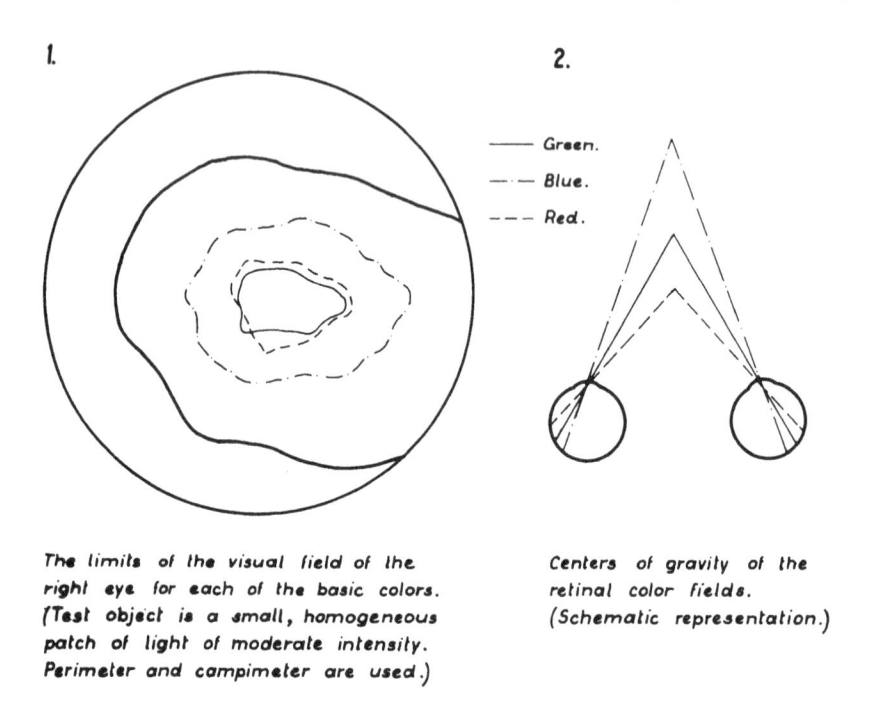

Figure 3.13. *The retinal color field.*

Experiments in the colored spherical phone booth

We seek the most productive hypotheses to learn the effect of surface colors on the optical space impression. Although we normally measure volumes in cubic terms, we must remember that the 'paradigmatic' or, for some authors, archetypical shape of a closed surface, necessary for space enveloping, is the sphere. Having only one datum of magnitude, the radius, the sphere offers a particularly good beginning for experiment.

To determine the effect of colors on optical space impression, we may construct one series of spherical 'phone booths' with monochrome interiors and others with differently distributed, even iridescent, coloration. As for the (interior) volume, it is tempting to choose a radius of one meter because, on the one hand, it is the average abathic distance and, on the other, the effect of color decreases with distance. But an appropriate choice also involves other considerations, chiefly the coronale plane of the head.

In the monochromatic series, we make the hypothesis that the volume of the blue sphere compared with that of the red will be consistently overestimated, and that the estimates of the green will fall between the two. This

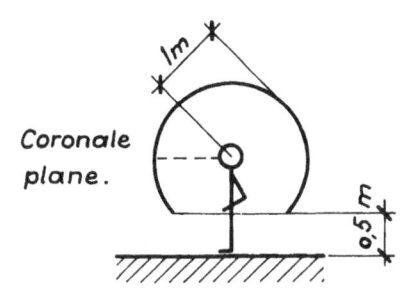

effect, like all surface effects on the optical space impression, will be more pronounced in the absence of cues revealing that the spheres under comparison are in fact isometric. We can predict that the magnitude (in percent) of the systematic errors will diminish with the increase of the radius.

We now consider seeming shape modification due to surface color. Because of the well-known horizontal-vertical illusion, i.e., the general overestimation of vertical length, we may risk an initial conjecture: spheres without color variation will be seen as prolate ellipsoids of revolution. Of course, this must be verified before all else, by a series of paired comparisons which evoke binary responses to precisely focused questions. The results of these experiments may be systematically evaluated according to the affine transformations which relate ellipsoids among themselves and to the special case of the sphere. (Note, by way of example, that if the observer sees a difference between the sphere's horizontal axes according to parallel or perpendicular situation in relation to the observer's base line, this implies that he did not perceive the sphere's vertical axis of revolution.) The experimenter must rigorously avoid introducing verbal labels like 'sphere' or 'ellipsoid' into the questions asked, or he spoils the results from the very outset; namely if the subject takes a 'sphere' for a 'sphere', this is a precise recognition of a shape defined always by a transformation of similitude. Saying about two spaces that they are both 'ellipsoids' is verbally a very similar statement; but in its content it is vague and not necessarily related to a homothetic transformation, essential for shape identification.

Shape modification can be expected if the experimenter applies iridescent colors in various orders along the vertical axis of the sphere. Results could again possibly fit in a scheme of affine transformation which relates sphere and various ellipsoids of revolution.

266 *Communication through architecture*

After these affine transformations produced by the subject's mental mapping of the colored sphere, we can leave the field of distributing colors according to symmetries inherent in the ellipsoid of revolution, and generate spheres which are so colored that the optical space impressions will be of various ovaloids.

We see now the general design of experiments for integrating these optemes, namely hues, into the catalogue of effects upon the impression of optical space.

Space Effects Created by Lightness

We have already referred to the hypothesis that white surfaces appear closer and black ones farther away than their true distances. Research of long standing further maintains that light surfaces also appear to be larger than dark ones (cf. the size-distance paradox). A more nuanced view now replaces this: if black seems to be farther away than white, the various shades of gray seem even farther; yet, at the same time, the size of a gray spot will undergo more significant diminution than will the size of a black one. The spot with average lightness seems most in the background, the darker gray more so than the lighter.

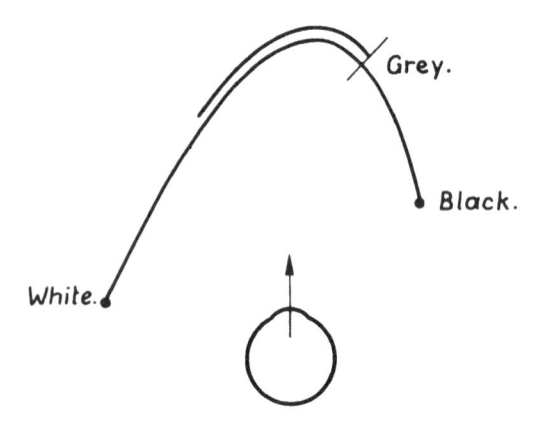

Effects of shadow

If a surface part does not receive light directly from a primary source, it is in shadow. If the light in a space is diffuse, e.g., in a cloud of smoke, or if the space is completely concave, there is no possibility of shadow. Obviously, the illuminated side of a protrusion is always nearer the light source than the shadowed side (Vurpillot 1967: 124); thus shadow is a useful means to distinguish optical spaces which are completely concave from those which are convex-concave. The class convex-concave can be subdivided accordingly as shaded and illuminated parts are separated 'smoothly' by a line of points on the curved surface — differentiable in all directions — where the light is tangent, or by an edge. Finally, the border of the shadow, straight or curved, also reveals the geometrical character of the separation line itself.

Effects of chroma brightness

When the architect uses color, he must keep in mind that the effectiveness of color depends in part on the intensity of the light, and this varies with hues. In fact, if the luminous directional reflectance does not reach 20 percent ($\rho < 0.2$), colors become achromatic and their effect vanishes.

The multiplicity of reflection also affects the color's effectiveness adversely (Déribéré 1959: 114).

The diminution of light intensity, whether due to the weakness of the primary source, as in a movie theater, or to low reflectance, or to the distance between source and observer, affects the color impression in a differentiated manner. We recall that in the case of blue we can distinguish light intensity gradients of 1/205-1/288, while in the case of red we can distinguish gradients only of 1/16-1/70. With the diminution of luminance (L), blue-violet, and later gray-violet, become predominant, even where the 'warm' colors, red and yellow, prevailed before (Luckiesh; Birren 1961b: 44-45, 81, 95; Ferre-Rand). Since blue-violet and dark gray both have an enlarging effect, we may advance the hypothesis that the darkening of a space makes it larger.

Space Effects Created by Saturation

Valentine (1962) thinks that, as a dark surface part recedes in relation to a light one, the part of a monochrome surface with a higher degree of saturation also recedes in relation to one with a lower. Since he carried out his experiments on a floor, Valentine attributes this effect to the principle of gravitation.

We have already noted that saturation presents delicate problems of measurement, and very special prudence is required in calculating its effects. The saturation scales of the three basic colors are different, their maximal saturation points are different, and so different lightness values are involved. When we compare the saturation effects of different colors we cannot use maximal saturation because the difference in lightness could 'spoil' the results. Where direct interpretation is impossible, factor analysis may eventually give acceptable results. Birren (1961b: 77, table XIII) reports on a comparison made between two colors. The experimenter added to them white and black in turn and found that in the first case, yellow excepted, the surface appeared to advance, and in the second to recede. But this method does not make clear whether the effect is attributable to the change in lightness or to the change in the degree of saturation.

For this reason, the safe course is to compare the effects of saturation in parallel by different color and tint series in a zone of relatively low saturation where the same degrees of lightness can be freely combined with various saturation degrees of any colors.

The process of properly imputing effects to surface characteristics, indicating quantitative predominances and discontinuities, is a tiresome one and ill meets the pressures on the practicing architect. It is also full of pitfalls. There is, indeed, a very extensive literature available to the architect, full of cookbook recipes, but generally unsupported by controlled experiments.

Space Effects Created by Diffusion Differences

Specular areas enlarge a surface. In terms of the interaction of surface characteristics, colors diminish in degree of saturation when reflected by a mirror. In the optical space, colors transmitted by a luminous surface tend to prevail over those on reflecting parts (aperture color versus object color). Finally, if the entire enveloping surface is specular, the optical space becomes imperceptible (cf. Charlie Chaplin's mirror maze). E. Barthès has developed an experimental calculation to separate systematic space errors due to specular surfaces from those due to color.

Space Effects Created by Luminous Surface Parts

The distribution of the luminous surface spots and areas (luminaries) influences the impression of the optical space. We know, for example, the 'planetarium effect', by which small points of light distributed over a very dark surface seem to enlarge the space dramatically.

Some authors report that black apertures, like windows at night, make the optical space seem larger. But we can interpret this kind of effect otherwise and perhaps more accurately. In spaces where the light intensity is low and its constancy is independent of the day-night rhythm, and where the observation position is fixed (we have just described a movie theater), color loses its effect, the shape and volume of the space become ambiguous and

Optical space 269

freely exposed to the imagination. The effect is not so much an impression of expansion (memory is not allowed to come into play here) but increased uncertainty. We can test this hypothesis by the fact that, in these circumstances, errors of estimate increase, but randomly; there are reports of contraction as well as enlargement (Rodieck 1977: 1,195).

Space Effects Created by Optical Surface Structures

Should the enveloping surface of an optical space be homogeneous and have equal illumination (E) at every point, it will therefore also have equal luminance (L) at every point. But this does not mean that at any point in *any* optical space the observer perceives equal lightness and equal chromatic composition at every point of observation. It is precisely this difference, since it depends on the observer's distance from the envelope's various points, that permits him to form his impression of its shape and volume. Moreover, since the impression is in fact an interpretation, the designer can modify it. He can impart an optical structure to the envelope which creates the impression of an optical space whose geometry is different from the true shape and volume of the space. Thus a two-dimensional feature like textural change can generate a three-dimensional impression. Pictorial and other surface structures serve the architect in this way as generators of systematic space error.

Gradients; the calculation of the tridimensional effect of surface structure

Let us take a close look at the regularities ruling the above-mentioned phenomenon.

Even a monochrome surface with equal luminance, if it is not parallel with the observer's frontal plane, will reflect color and light unequally at the level of retinal reception. The farther parts of the surface will give the retina less lightness and more violet light than the closer ones. Experience makes clear that observers tend to project the differences in gradients of lightness and hues, usually in specified depths. Since the depth impressions caused by these data are general and quantitative, attributing to each point on the observed surface a certain direction of inclination, the architect can reverse the process by imprinting a similar structure of gradients on the surface and so 'replace' the first one. J. J. Gibson speaks of the gradients of the surface's pictorial structure or texture.

The same effect can also be generated by graphic structures. If there are regularly distributed parallel installations on the surface, such as pipes, or if the graphist has set out lines or bars in equidistant arrangements ($a_i = a_2$) (see

Fig. 3.14.1), the retinal image of the lines and intervals, i.e., the projective apparent image, will result $a'_1 \neq a'_2$. The observer transforms the regular differences into the projective apparent image of the surface (J. J. Gibson 1966: 28). Thus the architecturist's contribution is to change the space impression by designing the projected structure on a surface whose position is predetermined by the architect according to other requirements.

Experience shows that reconstruction of the gradient system is a highly sophisticated process, which allows the observer to see other than planar surface shapes. In general, the gradients at a point express the variation of a magnitude, which varies with the space's different points, in the direction of the maximum (Piéron 1968: 186). In Gibson's theory of spatial impression, the gradient is the key notion; it allows us to recognize 'change and disparity of pattern' (J. J. Gibson 1950: 261-263). The observer can even sense curvatures (e.g. sphere, also edges) if the surface bears regularly distributed structures or textures which, in accord with the complexity of the curvature and its changes, are sufficiently dense. In fact, in this image the regularly distributed structure will be transformed into regularity of a higher order, exponential or logarithmic, showing no longer the y but y', y'' as characteristic.

Which particular aspects of the optical space's envelope have the 'architectural merit' to be simulated by a gradient structure? Which surface characteristics are the right tools? Before answering, we must discuss the limits of the use of gradients for generating systematic space errors.

Gibson and Bergman (1954) resourcefully constructed a pseudotunnel to show that the monocular observer follows the logic of the designed gradient structure and draws the expected conclusion about the tunnel's depth; but his measurement of the inclination of the gradients is very imprecise.

Thus we can term the structure a cue for spatial perception, but little more; its efficiency is dependent on the observer's familiarity with the milieu, e.g., familiarity with the geometrical nature of the urban environment. That is what makes it possible to assign spatial position to the enveloping surface on the basis of gradient structures; they will not conform with expected regularities.

Furthermore, although not our concern at this point, variables of binocular disparity are powerful sources of control of depth impression, because by giving a third angle of reference they sustain our space perception during daylight. Gruber and Whitehouse designed experiments in the conflict of information from gradient structure and binocular disparity.

Denis-Prinzhorn (1960: 202) found that the possibility of creating systematic errors in distance estimates increases in the following order: binocular vision with texture, monocular vision with texture, binocular vision without texture, monocular vision without texture. This series indicates that texture is more important for distance estimation than binocular disparity.

Finally, a pictorial gradation of the surface by turning the 'warm' colors toward the violet range does not permit the observer to locate the surface's points continuously by distance estimation. This structure invites the observer rather to attribute a direction to the surface than to gain a more precise impression of its inclination.

Optical space shape simulation by surface structure

To induce the observer to 'see' an enveloping surface with the desired characteristics of distance and curvature, the architecturist must imprint the graphic or pictorial structure on a surface sufficiently distant from the observer for the effect to succeed. Moreover, the structure must simulate, as a cross-section, an equidistant distribution on the projected surface (see Figure 3.14.1). Of course, the design must include features in sufficient number and density for the observer to 'see' regular equidistant distribution on the surface as apparent objective distribution (Vurpillot 1967: 134).

The designer can also simulate surfaces other than flat ones, even those with complicated curvature. The best procedure for this is to use at least two design features which simulate equidistant distribution along the two principal directions. Note that, according to Gaito (1959) and Zusne (1970), it is more common for the observer to mistake a curved surface for a flat one than the reverse.

The architecturist can also use these tools to simulate convex-concave surfaces, without edges. For this the most delicate task is to simulate the line of inflection where the observer has to evaluate not only y and y' but y'' too (J. J. Gibson 1950: 62). This calls for continuous design features such as increasing, decreasing, accelerating, and slowing the distribution of luminance.

To simulate an edge it is enough to draw a line on the surface and arrange the appropriate gradation of luminance on the two sides of it. Gibson suggests that the most effective simulation is to draw lines on the surface which simulate the normal lines of the two half-fields (see Figure 3.14.3). In this way the feature simulates the inclination of the half-fields and also implies the edge. It should now be clear how other shapes, e.g., corners of cubic or conic spaces, can be simulated by the use of surface features.

By contrast, the Figure 3.14.4 shows design features fail to produce a clear image of the enveloping surfaces. They imply lack of continuity or closing. The optical space impression becomes ambiguous; there seems to be only a partial possibility of estimating volume and recognizing shape.

1.

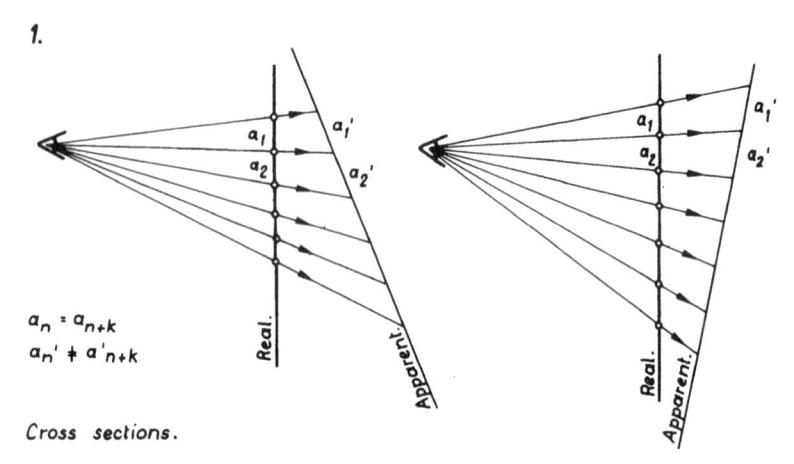

$a_n = a_{n+k}$
$a_n' \neq a'_{n+k}$

Cross sections.

Apparent 'displacement' of a surface as a function of line distribution according to the apparent image of equidistant real distribution.

2.

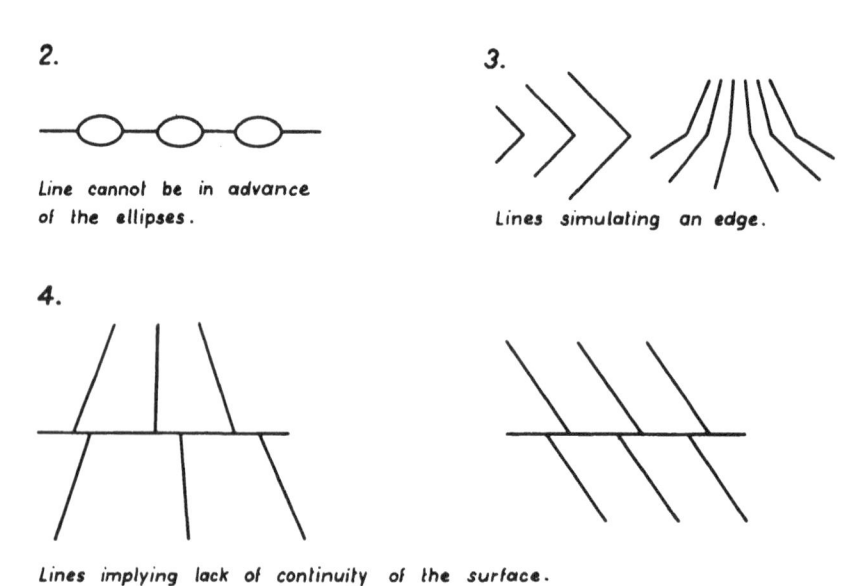

Line cannot be in advance of the ellipses.

3.

Lines simulating an edge.

4.

Lines implying lack of continuity of the surface.

Figure 3.14. *Space effects of graphic surface structures.*

Emphasis on Features Through Choice of Means

In general we can say that the architect has a task similar to that of a theatrical set designer in that each uses surface features to create optical space impressions. When he is using more than one technique to imprint a desired feature, the architect must know which will predominate. There may be situations when certain visible surface textures are clearly imposed by conditions other than optical, and if the architect wishes to have other optical space impressions, he must add some predominant visible surface structure. Here the task is to eclipse one effect with another.

When the architect chooses among the five types of surface characteristics in order to imprint a feature most effectively, he will recall that, in general, features expressed by difference of hue are more striking than those expressed by difference of luminance. General experiments with both humans and other primates with color vision, and others made in the more specific context of psychology applied to the architectural environment all confirm the principle.

Among the hues, red and orange eclipse features in other colors. More systematically, we can say that the distinctiveness, or legibility, of colored graphic features shows the following decreasing order of preference:

— yellow on black;
— green on white;
— red on white;
— blue on white;
— white on blue;
— black on white;
— white on black.

We know from experiments on both normal subjects and tritanopes (those who have the rare congenital condition of blue and yellow blindness) that the distinctiveness of the border between two colors is weakest when blue is involved. F. Birren says (1961b: 51 and fig. 53), 'When, however the contrasting colors are arranged in fine lines or dots and when the eye is forced to blend or confuse them, contrast is lost and the hues will cancel each other ...'

When features are expressed by difference in luminance, the luminance of the larger surface area affects the appearance of the smaller. Thus a gray graphic structure on a black background seems clearer than one on a white one.

We have already seen that the correct use of colors can make part of a surface seem to be near to the observer. For example, we can make it yellow and distribute the other colors so that the part we wish to appear to recede is in the blue wavelength range. A less crude effect would result from starting with a bright blue and modulating to a dark blue or gray, and similarly by going from yellow to white.

These effects are best achieved when color gradation and graphic structure suggest the same optical space illusion. This is not always possible; we have noticed before that the architect must sometimes deal with a surface feature he is forced to install, such as some kind of required equipment or an unavoidable result of some material used. If such a feature is generally familiar it is useless to try to mask it, although the attempt is often made. A more sophisticated strategy for achieving the desired impression of the optical space is to apply other structures to the surface, independent of the undesired one, and give them predominance by using the kind of optical means we are discussing, such as color.

In a 'hopeless case' the last resort is to create ambiguities in the space. We need only think of Van Doesburg's 'Composition' to see how shadows can be simulated by the gradation of corners (J. J. Gibson 1950: 96, fig. 44/2).

If the junctions of the surface cannot be seen as closed, the observer may perceive the same surface either as fluted or as circinate. A simple framing can diminish the lightness of a surface by seven grades (Birren 1961b: 49).

Although it is our wish to apply human science to the medium of architecture, we must not forget that the invention of spatially effective features is not a scientific task. We simply present the full range of expression inherent in the medium, quantitatively by combinatorics, in the hope of enlarging the conceptual horizon. On the other hand, if the architect should invent new effects, the scientist can come to his assistance by evaluating, quantitatively if possible, their likelihood of success.

The chance of success for any effect is greater when the observer is unfamiliar with the space. But, given the observer's familiarity with a space or a surface, we can displace the cue, making it a false reference and so a tool for creating yet more illusions. Clearly, this calculation operates on a higher level of perceptual organization, and its success is very dependent on particular sociological variables (Vernon 1952).

The chance of success for creating systematic space errors is greater as (a) the illumination of the space is weaker, (b) the observer is in sessile position, and (c) the observation distance is greater — conditions which are often satisfied in major architectural spaces.

INTERACTION OF THE MAIN VARIABLES IN OPTICAL SPACE IMPRESSION AND PAST RESEARCH

The fundamental characteristics of all architectural space are volume and shape, and we have already seen how peripheral surface attributes can influence the impression of each. We now consider how the shape of the space can affect the estimate of its volume and how volume acts as a parameter for the discrimination of shape (Zusne 1970: 274).

(1) The ability to perceive the equality or difference of the shape of two spaces can be affected by
— their relative volumetric difference, as well as
— their volumetric magnitude in absolute terms.

Shape discrimination *per se* depends on the geometrical relationship between the compared spaces. We hypothesize that the task of discrimination is easier as the geometrical transformation which relates the shapes is more complex.

(2) For estimates of volumetric magnitude, the 'just noticeable difference' in a paired comparison will depend on:
— the kind of shape which each space has, even if it is the same for each, and
— the kind of difference between the shapes in a cross-shape comparison.

The just noticeable volume difference will be a function of the absolute magnitude of the volume, either in a linear (percent) relation, or an asymptotic, or other, e.g., absolute limit of vision.

1. *Shape Impression of Optical Space as a Function of Change in Real Shape and Volume*

We now wish to know which previous studies in form perception relate directly to our present concern, the establishment of an open-ended repertory of created optical spaces.

Zusne (1970) reviewed some 2,000 studies in preparing a synthesis of research done on so-called form perception. He grouped them in five areas (1970: 274-275): (1) shape, (2) length of a line, (3) degree of curvature, (4) direction, and (5) number of sides or inflections in contour. The scope of Zusne's study diverges from ours in two respects:
— he treats form perceptions chiefly in two dimensions, and
— he defines 'form' in a much less operational way than we do.

His 'form' is the phenomenologist's *gestalt* or configuration, and for most purposes is inoperant in the context of experimental science.

We use the term 'shape', and by it we denote only those geometrical structures which are related by similitude in the strict sense of the term, homothetic transformation. A shape of architectural space means an equivalence defined by the identity of the following relations:

$$y' = y \sqrt[3]{V}; \; x' = x \sqrt[3]{V}; \; \alpha' = \alpha.$$

Among more recent contributions to the study of the perception of spatial features we find valuable articles on the application of information theory to the field by Shepard (1963) and Attneave (1950), but their focus is not specifically in the direction of optical space perception.

Goldmeier's book (1972) — one of the most recent on the market — seems relevant at first; but it turns out to be no more than an English translation of the 1936 German with a small added chapter about information theory. It shows all the influence of the gestaltists of the 1930s, as did the disciples of the Bauhaus (Giedon). In any event he treats only bidimensional shapes.

Consequently, it seems best to stay on the solid ground of the clear definition of space in terms of shape and volume, to which we can assign a program of experiments, an 'algorithm' which will generate a repertory of architectural spaces. Repertory items, differing in shape, will be defined as follows: two spaces of effectively different shapes constitute different items if, when presented to the standard observer in standardized conditions with standardized volumetric magnitude, they can be distinguished by that observer. Thus the possibility of a yes-or-no response to a question about a paired comparison is the criterion for the distinction of an item.

Isometry and the optical space impression as a function of the observer's position

When an observer considers two isometric spaces, he may have difficulty in realizing that they are in fact equal in shape and equal in volume, that difficulty incidentally arising from different observation conditions, namely position. We must deal with this possibility here because it is more important in the case of optical space than in that of acoustical space.

We recall from our study of the visual field that length estimate depends on the 'horizontal-vertical illusion' and that the field's curvature affects the comparison of distance and length. Rock (in Goldmeier 1972: 10-11; cf. p. 91) also noted that parallels, horizontal lines, and the vertical symmetry axis are lines whose direction is clearly seen. A 'deviation' or 'violation' of a vertical symmetry axis which, like the observer, has a left and a right side, is much more obvious than a deviation from a symmetry axis with any other direction.

The observer's standardized position in relation to the space must be defined in two ways: in terms of the space's internal geometry and in terms of vector in the gravitational field, i.e., in standing or reclining position (see Figure 3.16.2).

The first problem is easily solved, since repertory items, the spaces, always have morphological specifications. The impression variation caused by standing or reclining position presents a more complicated problem for spaces not in a condition of weightlessness, e.g., in spacecrafts. In fact, positioning in the gravitational field is an objective characteristic of the space, externally imposed, which goes beyond the simple relation of space and observer. For this reason, we discuss at the end of this part ways of specifying standard observation necessary for the architectural repertory.

We have been discussing the effects of geometrical rotation and translation for cataloguing architectural spaces, which are isometric transformations, cases of similitude with $k = 1$. Here we will note a peculiar case, for the sake of completeness, and deal with it later. This is the 'flip-over' or improper rotation of the same space, by which the space changes in neither volume nor proportion, but goes from 'right-handed' to 'left-handed' by passing through the fourth dimension.

Shape equality and volume variation

Our next task is to determine the possibility of recognizing a shape equality even when the k of the affine transformation of homothetic type is not unity. The volume varies, and we also speak of conformity mapping.

According to Hebb (Goldmeier 1972: 6), 'Forms transposed in size and position are easily recognized in terms of common parts of figures, such as lines and angles.' This refers, of course, to bidimensional figures. An affine transformation of homothetic type leaves the edges qualitatively unchanged — parallel lines remain parallel, straight remain straight — and the angles quantitatively so as well.

What do we know about errors in angle estimates?

According to H. P. Bardan, and especially to M. B. Pratt, we can expect the systematic error of estimate to be higher as the angle deviates from the familiar right angle of the Cartesian coordinates, or its fractions. We also know that systematic errors of estimate come in alternate zones, now an overestimate, now an underestimate. Errors show at a minimum around 90°, 45°, and their multiples. At the subdivision of the right angle by three, i.e., around 30° and 60°, we also see errors at the minimum. The regularity goes through all 360°, e.g., 270° is perceived through its complement, 90°.

278 *Communication through architecture*

Overestimates show at a maximum around 50° and underestimates around 120°. The alternation is shown in the following figure:

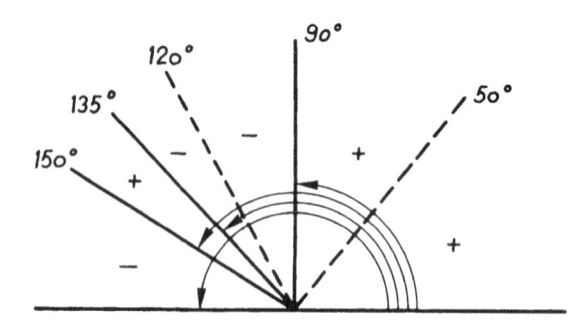

Of course, these experimental data are culture-dependent and related directly to our 'cornered' urban civilization. Nevertheless, they do suggest hypotheses about the recognition of the identities of optical spaces if they are conformable polyhedrons, some of which will be easier to identify than others. Further, findings about angle estimates will help us form hypotheses about shape identity recognition of optical spaces with broken edges.

Certain systematic errors of angle estimate can be used as starting points to generate false shape identities. M. Weiner constructed an optical space with a trapezoidal floor so shaped that the observers saw the space as rectangular with systematic error. The deformation was so constant that the observer was ready to misperceive the shape and angles of other objects in the space in order to preserve the rectangular space impression and the coherence of the system of seen objects. This perception process conforms with our general hypothesis that the roomraum, the space, is the prime reference for our perceived physical environment. In the next few pages we will look at the other side of shape impression errors, the case where the observer sees two spaces with different shapes as being the same.

Shape impression differences and the degree of geometrical relationship

In the field of discrimination of volume differences, it is much easier to organize experiments and survey results than in the field of shapes. We saw in the chapter on the geometry of architectural morphology that the description and classification of all possible shapes of enclosed surface as a topological category of homeomorphism is a very difficult task. It is even more complex to explore the observer's ability to discriminate among them.

We cannot make the assumption that the possibility of discrimination follows the same order of priorities for all sensory spaces. A program of experimentation must be designed to catalogue discriminable shapes in each type of sensory space, taking account of the findings of 'space perception' investigation in the relevant sensory modality. An obvious handicap is that existing experimental data are limited to bidimensional shapes and, too often, only to so-called regular ones.

In order to define the discriminable optical shapes on a comprehensive basis, we need an algorithm to assure that the shapes have been presented to the experimentees in the most economical manner from the heuristic viewpoint.

We seek to learn which striking features of shapes serve the observer as differentiating cues that two spaces do not have the same shape. These features could be described in terms of the geometrical transformation which connects them; but this definition of detected differences will not necessarily follow the order of the degree of geometrical relationship stated in terms of this transformation (affine, not affine, etc.). This is only a first indication.

An interesting approach has been taken by Coulon and Kayser (1969: 103), who established an algorithm for the automatic recognition of polyhedron patterns. Their method could be extended to the recognition of other patterns. This algorithm may help us develop the most appropriate series of shape presentations to the subjects, but we must not forget that 'human pattern recognition' (Goldmeier 1972: 1) does not necessarily follow the most economic course, like automata proceeding according to software designed by specialists.

J. P. Smith's doctoral dissertation (1964) also gives interesting ideas for programming the experiments for an optical space repertory. He does not study the common catalogue of so-called regular shapes, but instead searches systematically for gross features (e.g., number of turns) of randomly generated shapes.

Which gross features of a closed surface give cues for discriminating between optical spaces with different shapes?

Even if we take a cubic measure of the volume enclosed by a surface, the common characteristics of all closed and simple surfaces is that they can be transformed into a sphere by Schwarz and Steiner's symmetrization. Thus we begin the series of shapes to be compared by the subject with the sphere and one of its affine transformations of one-dimensional strains — elongation or compression ($x' = r$; $y' = k \cdot r$) — which gives an ellipsoid. We know the sphere is characterized by the fact that all its points have positive and constant total curvature. Abandoning the ellipsoid's symmetry axes but keeping the positive total curvature, which is no longer constant, we come to the more relaxed continuously concave shapes which we call, perhaps a little too freely, ovaloids (elliptic surfaces). Within the family of ovaloids we next test for discriminability between ovaloids with and without a surface part which has zero total curvature, i.e., is flat, yet not showing edges (elliptic-parabolic surfaces). Still in the family of closed surfaces whose points can be derived in all directions, viz., they have neither vertex nor edge, the total curvature of some points is negative (partly hyperbolic surfaces). These surfaces, e.g., Cassini types, have a closed line of inflection points, which is important for optical space impressions in that shadows appear.

The next step in the series of experiments is to compare optical spaces which have points whose total curvature cannot be calculated, i.e., surfaces with salient points. These can be observed and counted.

A further step away from the sphere is the appearance of edges, which may be recti- or curvilinear. Both are compatible with any surface, whether having finite or zero total curvature (flat). If not all points of the surface have zero total curvature, the edge can even be a closed and continuously differentiable (not polygonal) line, viz., it has no salient point. Every part of an edge which is a closed line or is limited by two salient points is called a segment line. Like salient points, segments can also be counted, and give an important cue for space discrimination.

The possibility of having various types of geometrical points on a closed surface enlarges the number of mixed shapes for optical spaces. This class of shapes goes beyond the repertory of shapes which are classified by their geometrical affinity. 'Mixed' thus means in this context those shapes which are, as it were, biform on a kind of line between two pure types, the sphere and the cube. As examples Figure 3.15 give some details from the history of architecture.

Polyhedral shapes have only points with zero total curvatures, viz., flat surfaces, or points with no curvature at all, like rectilinear polygonal edges and salient points. In modern Occidental architecture these are the most common shapes, including even the geodesic designs of Buckminster Fuller (e.g., U.S. Pavilion at Expo '67). In fact, the latter provide prime examples of the difference between purely geometrically defined spaces and perceived optical spaces. By sufficient reduction of the size of individual flat surfaces, the designer not only achieves in a polyhedron the mathematical approximation of a curved surface, but also eliminates the visual difference entirely. We discussed this in very precise terms earlier in this chapter.

To sum up, there are three classes of striking features which aid in space discrimination:

(1) Qualitative: the observer of the spaces under comparison identifies, by yes-or-no answers, the presence on both envelopes of inflectional lines (allowing shadows), lines, line segments (recti- or curvilinear), and salient points, external or internal (convex or concave).

(2a) Quantitative: these geometrical features can be counted as discrete elements on both surfaces.

Ancient tent,
Grec and
Hellenistic.

Tunnel vault,
round dome,
Romanesque
or Norman.

Pointed arch,
Gothic.

Bulbiform cupola,
Oriental, Orthodox (Kiev).

Modern tent
(e.g., W. German
pavillon at Expo '67).

Figure 3.15. *Roofs*.

(2b) Volumetric: discrimination may be made by comparison of continuous magnitudes (e.g., value of curvature).

The discrimination by criteria 2a is clearly more difficult and less reliable than the first, especially in terms of the immediacy of the comparative space impression and the time allowed the observer. The 2b criterion is the least reliable. Comparison of continuous magnitude is notoriously more subject to error than comparison of discrete numbers; and for correct discrimination of shapes in this context, the observer must also discriminate between relative and absolute differences. (Differences are relative when the proportions are preserved, so the spaces have equal shapes and differ only in volume.)

This order of priorities for the reliability of shape identification is valid for the distinction of different shapes as well as for the recognition of shape equality in different optical spaces which have different volumes.

How do these criteria apply to various classes of shapes?

Among polyhedrons (see the chapter about geometry), we call those shapes regular which have isometric faces of regular polygons and congruent polyhedral angles. There are only five of these, the 'Platonic' polyhedrons. Among these five classes the number of faces may vary from 4 to 20; but every regular polyhedron's faces have a characteristic number of edges, and its vertices a characteristic number of adjacent edges, and these numbers are always less than five. Further, humans have the innate ability to form immediate impressions of phenomena whose elements do not exceed five in number.

We can therefore make the reasonable hypothesis that in a comparison of two optical spaces which have different volumes, recognition of shape equality is realized with less error between regular polyhedral spaces than between irregular polyhedrons. In fact, to recognize regular polyhedrons the observer need not measure ratios (see above, on class 2b of gross features), but only count edges.

For the same reason the shape equality of two regular hexahedral (cubic) optical spaces is recognized with less error than that of other rectangular hexahedral prisms, although mathematical terminology is confusing here, calling *all* right prisms with regular polygons as bases also 'regular prisms' (James & James 1968: 284).

In the case of ellipsoids, the experimenter may proceed from the hypothesis that, because of the horizontal-vertical illusion, the observer will find it more difficult to perceive shape equality and even isometry in two optical spaces if the major axis of one is horizontal and the other vertical, even though these axes, and the minor axes, are all equal.

Irregular polyhedrons of different shapes are more easily distinguished than are shapes without edges and corners, since the former contain countable features, thus permitting the application of criteria as in class 2a. The distinction of shape differences among continuously differentiable optical space envelopes gives more error, unless it can be based on the criteria of class 1, e.g., one shape is convex-concave and so has a line of inflection, while the other is wholly concave. In this case, the criterion of class 2a applies very seldom (e.g., convex-concave shapes with different numbers of inflection lines and maximum points). For this reason, angles play an important role in shape equality recognition because they preserve their absolute values in homothetic transformation. But, according to Gaito (1959), angles subtended by straight lines are better estimated than those subtended by curved ones.

The same rule applies to mixed shapes, those which combine curved surfaces, flat faces, and edges. In these cases the positive recognition of shape equality is rarely possible due to the necessity of applying the criterion of class 2b, which makes error the most probable. In order to predict the probability of distinctions among complex shapes of this kind, we must try to define shape complexity and even, if we can, try to quantify the degree of complexity in given cases.

Information theoreticians define complexity as lack of redundant information (D. E. Berlyne), i.e., irregularity. Heckhausen seeks a phenomenologist's definition (1964: 168-173), while Day's definition (1965) is guided by physical difference. Seiler and Zusne (1967: 884-886), defining complexity according to information theory, relate the observer's tendency toward simplification directly to the degree of complexity and the observation time allowed. Indeed, if this time is shorter, the observer further underestimates the shape's complexity. We may also note here that, according to Hitchcock et al. (1962), error in the estimation of surface area increases with complexity of shape.

Because we hope to extend the repertory of optical spaces beyond the received catalogue of 'the few standard geometric forms', we are very much concerned to integrate complex shapes into it. It is inevitable that any listing, open-ended or not, will have a gray area where distinctions are less clear than we wish; but it must be a principle of the construction of the architectural repertory that the discriminability among the items show a generally transitive order. The user of the repertory must be able to say that if 1 and 2, on the one hand, and 2 and 3, on the other, can be discriminated, 1 and 3 must be even more clearly distinguishable. Otherwise the ordinal indications will be useless.

Without oversimplifying the findings of Zusne and W. Crossman (1955 in Piéron 1968: 89), we hold that accuracy of discrimination in 'gray areas' can be increased by lengthening the standard observation time (by Δt) and by complementing the static optical space impression with dynamic exploration.

2. *Volume Impression as a Function of Shape Variation*

We have discussed the recognition of equal shapes of optical spaces and the discrimination of differences of shape. In these paired comparisons, the volume was a parameter. We now examine the recognition of equal volume in optical spaces with different shapes and the discrimination of differences in volumetric magnitude between optical spaces with equal shape. In these comparisons, shape is a parameter. As we have stated, the difference threshold or the just noticeable difference in volume can be formulated in two ways for each experimental series; first, in absolute terms (ΔV): second, in relative terms, as a function of the absolute volume — $\Delta V = f(V)$ — by establishing some mathematical regularity.

The results of these investigations will provide the degrees of comparison which allow us to enumerate optical spaces as repertory items which have noticeably different volumes.

We look first to past findings for heuristic aid in designing an appropriate experimental series. For example, in the field of bidimensional research, we note that Mansvelt (1928) long ago stated that when the area included in a circle or square increases, the systematic error of estimate increases in the direction of overestimate. Anastasi (1936: 201-225) proved that this same tendency is even independent of the shape. But these findings are valid only for plane figures.

284   *Communication through architecture*

Volume estimates of rectangular parallelepipeds

Our everyday architecture is ordinarily comfortable with only one space shape, the rectangular parallelepiped. It is conveniently described by cubic measurement and fits compactly into a system which uses other rectangular prisms. It is thus not surprising that research into space volume estimates has also been limited mostly to spaces of this kind; and so we must mainly examine the findings on this subject.

Research carried out in various laboratories in Sweden merit our particular attention because it gives the psychologist's answer to the architect's questions. Gaerling (1969-1970: 250-251; 130), in G. Goude's Stockholm laboratory, studied volume estimates of optical space in the perspective of Hesselgren's (1967: ch. 39-40) theory of architecture. He gives us the occasion to submit the classic 'schoolmaster's space perception' to a close critical analysis.

As we said, his assumption is that volume estimate can be 'heuristically' deduced from estimated distance and vertical and horizontal length. The remaining problem is to find exponents which allow us to show how one- and two-dimensional errors affect three-dimensional ones quantitatively, i.e., errors in estimates of the volumetric magnitude of optical space. Real volume $V = (B \cdot D)H$, where B = base or length, D = depth or distance, and H = height or vertical length. In order to find the apparent volume, the impression of volumetric magnitude $V_i = [(B^m \cdot D^n)^p \cdot H^l]^q$. The specific research target is to determine the value of q, but prior research must determine the B, D, and H estimates by establishing m, n, and l. The formula follows the schoolbookish assumption that volume will be estimated through basic area estimate, also called 'ground-space'. Basic area thus has its own exponent p which will be multiplied by H^l. In mathematical terms, the volume estimate seen by Gaerling is a nonassociative multiplication because a definite mental processing of information is assumed, viz., $B_i = B^m$, $D_i = D^n$, and $A_i = (B_i \cdot D_i)^p$; finally $V_i = (A_i \cdot H_i)^q$. Moreover, in this estimation process the position of the various dimensions of the space with respect to the observer are fundamentally differentiated. The volume estimate is assumed to be a process of synthesis which follows a set order, and one in which one- and two-dimensional estimates are not just cues but fully quantified factors.

Length estimate ($B_i = B * m = B^m$): a survey of the literature on length estimate shows there is no consensus on the absolute value of m or about the very operation which relates m to B in order to produce B_i. We would write in a postulational algebraic system: $B_i = B * m$.

Certain authors hold that magnitude and direction of estimate error depend on absolute magnitude, not in a linear (percent) manner, but in another, undetermined so far; and, on the other hand, error also depends upon distance, which Gaerling includes in p.

The partial consensus we find concerning B estimates is that the error varies from 3 percent to 10 percent of the length; but there is no further consensus about regularity of estimates. Thus we have no valid heuristic reason to accept the schoolmaster's volume estimation scheme; it would mean accepting another unproven assumption without founding our research any more firmly.

Height estimate ($H_i = H * l = H^l$): we have already seen that H_i as a function of B_i, i.e., vertical to horizontal, is normally overestimated. According to Kuennapas (1957, 1959), this overestimate follows the inverse ratio between the horizontal and vertical axes of our visual field. M. C. Williams places the degree of overestimate at about 7 percent. There appears then, to be a consensus that, given $B_i = B * m$ and $H_i = H * l$, $l > m$.

Distance estimate ($D_i = D * n = D^n$): the literature suggests two kinds of general consensus. One holds that the error with increased absolute distance grows steadily in the direction of overestimation. The other holds that errors in distance estimate within architectural spaces do not go beyond narrow quantitative limits. Two additional parameters apply to distance estimates: when two equal distances are compared, the one set on a solid ground is much overestimated in relation to another seen on an air line. This relative overestimate can go as high as 18 percent (M. C. Williams). On the other hand, binocularity increases the precision of these estimates (Fried 1964).

We should recall some important experimental findings. J. J. Gibson (1950: 183) found that errors generally increase with distance, yet estimate is most precise at the abathic distance, ca. 0.4-1.85 m. Jeanpierre (1968: 11) performed his experiments in a room measuring 7 X 3 X 2.12 m. He varied the distance to be estimated from 1.5 to 4.9 m. and within this range found that errors and systematic overestimates increase as a function of distance. Le Grand (1956) found the average error in distance estimate at 6 m. to be 0.5 percent, while Jenkin and Hyman (1959) found it less than 1 percent at 9 m. Given the narrow range of error at these distances, and the persistence of overestimation, we can assign to n a value greater than unity (1). But Gaerling follows the hypothesis of Gilinsky (1951) and Kuennapas (1960: 187-92; Kuennapas 1968: 523-529); he accepts for $D_i = f(D)$ an asymptotic function $D_i = A \cdot D/(A + D)$, according to which the distance estimate would be an underestimate, $D_i \leq D; A \gg$.

Basic area estimate $[A_i = (B^m \cdot D^n) * p = (B^m \cdot D^n)^p]$: we recall that $m \neq n$ because B_i's systematic error is greater than D_i's. In fact, distance and length are not distinguished in this formula according to the intrinsic characteristics of the 'floor-space', viz., width vs. length, but in relation to the observer's position. In the formula, the shape of the floor plays a varying role, accordingly as observation is made from the 'end of the corridor' (case B) or from the middle (case A). (See Figure 3.16.3.) According to the supposed m and n values, the estimate of the corridor from the end will be better than the one from its middle. Further, according to the formula, p must be a constant simply for correcting the 'error of multiplication' between the two factors, and should be independent of any shape characteristics. In our earlier discussion of the visual field we examined the size-distance relationship on the objective apparent level of the estimated target. We also looked at the controversy concerning the paradox of the compensation for a distance overestimate by a size underestimate (see Gruber). In these terms the area estimate would depend more on its shape than on the observer's position. With respect to this question, Gaerling also follows Gilinsky's formula, which makes any overestimate mathematically impossible (Vurpillot 1967: 133).

Volume estimate $[V_i = (A_i \cdot H^l) * q = (A_i \cdot H^l)^q]$: obviously, in the transition from B_i to A_i there is an analogy to that from A_i to V_i, but there is also a notable difference. Volume, in fact, presents a unique situation. B has surface area as a frame of reference (surface effect) and the floor A the space itself (volume effect), but volume itself has no superior dimension as frame of reference; it is the ultimate reference for any phenomena within the space.

To sum up, we see that the Swedish school tried to clarify volume estimate by determining the exponents m, n, p, l, and q. In agreement with other researchers, the consensus is that $l \leqslant m > p > q$ (Taghtsoonian 1965: 392-402, sets $m = 1$; Gaerling and Künnapas set $m = 0.8$). The series can also be completed as follows: $1 \geqslant l > n > m > p > q$.

We must have reservations about the use of the schoolmaster's method of volume estimate as a general framework for all experiments. It excludes *a priori* the observer's spontaneous response and demands instead derived responses of theoretically calculated magnitudes. Gaerling himself (1969-1970: 268; 128) acknowledges the discrepancy between the predicted and actual results of the observer's estimates.

Yet research in volume estimate remains vitally important to the construction of an optical space repertory with thresholds calibrated quantitatively to give degrees of differences: despite the lack of consensus in past research findings, even from the first rudimentary repertory, architects can see, with a probability near to one, that two spaces with a volume difference over 20 percent are never wrongly ordered according to their volume.

Effect of shape on volume comparison: experiments on rectangular parallelepipeds In establishing context we recall that the threshold of noticeable volumetric difference depends on the shape of the space under comparison, even when the shapes are equal. The researcher can also look into a complementary problem, namely the observer's capability to identify volume equality in two optical spaces with different shapes specifically chosen for the purpose. Errors can be measured in probability of right responses as well as in random or systematic distribution of errors in both directions.

L. Holmberg headed an interdisciplinary team for the Department of Psychology and of Theoretical and Applied Aesthetics at the Institute of Technology of Lund (Sweden), which investigated the effect of the shape of optical space upon volume estimate. Their first, concern was methodological in relation to psychology in general. They sought to learn the extent to which volume estimate is affected by presentation of a space in small-scale model as compared with presentation of the space in natural size.

They used a rectangular parallelepiped with a volume of 62.5 m.^{3}. The height, 2.5 m., and thus the floor area, were constant; the proportion of floor length and width varied from 1:1 through 1:1.5, 1:2, 1:2.5, 1:3, to 1:3.5.

We have already seen that the isometry of a corridor presented to the observer in different positions is not recognized (see Figure 3.16.3). $V_A = V_{Bi}$ but on the level of volume impression $V_{Ai} < V_{Bi}$. The volume of the corridor seen from the end will be overestimated in comparison with that of the same corridor seen from the middle. Holmberg's results do not provide a good control for this finding, or others, because he maintained extremely relaxed observation conditions — for example, his subjects could return repeatedly to the compared rooms. His results show that as the shape of the parallelepiped goes farther from the square floor area the optical space overestimate increases. The order of overestimate is as follows; $A < B1 < B2 < C$. (See Figure 3.16.4.)

On a small-scale model he found that, with a floor space ratio $L/l = 1:3.5$, volume overestimate reaches 1.5 of the true volume. Like all errors in space estimates, this decreases with dynamic exploration.

Interpreting the results reported by Menchikoff (1975: 49), we can say that if Holmberg had also varied the space's height he would have come to the generalization that the elongation ratio as a general shape characteristic determines the volume overestimate — as it increases, so does the overestimate. With rectangular parallelepiped shapes closer to cubic the overestimate approaches the minimum. Figure 3.16.5 shows Menchikoff's table that plots the results of the subjects' comparative estimates between a room 1 meter wide, 1.5 m. deep, and 2 m. high, and rooms of other dimensions. The results came from the formula $R = aS^n$, where S represents the effective ratio between the standard 'gauge' and the compared counterparts (length, area, volume), R shows the estimate of the relation, and n is a constant. We can see that the error in the height estimate is always an overestimate, while the surface and volume are first underestimated and later overestimated. The fact that the overestimate of volume begins to occur earlier than that of the basic area indicates that it is the overestimate of the vertical dimension which brings on the former.

288 Communication through architecture

1.

Ground plan.

Standardization of observation point.

2.

Cross sections.

Ellipsoidal space and gravitational field.

3.

Observation of a corridor.

4.

The order of overestimate.

5.

Errors in volume, basic area, and height estimates.

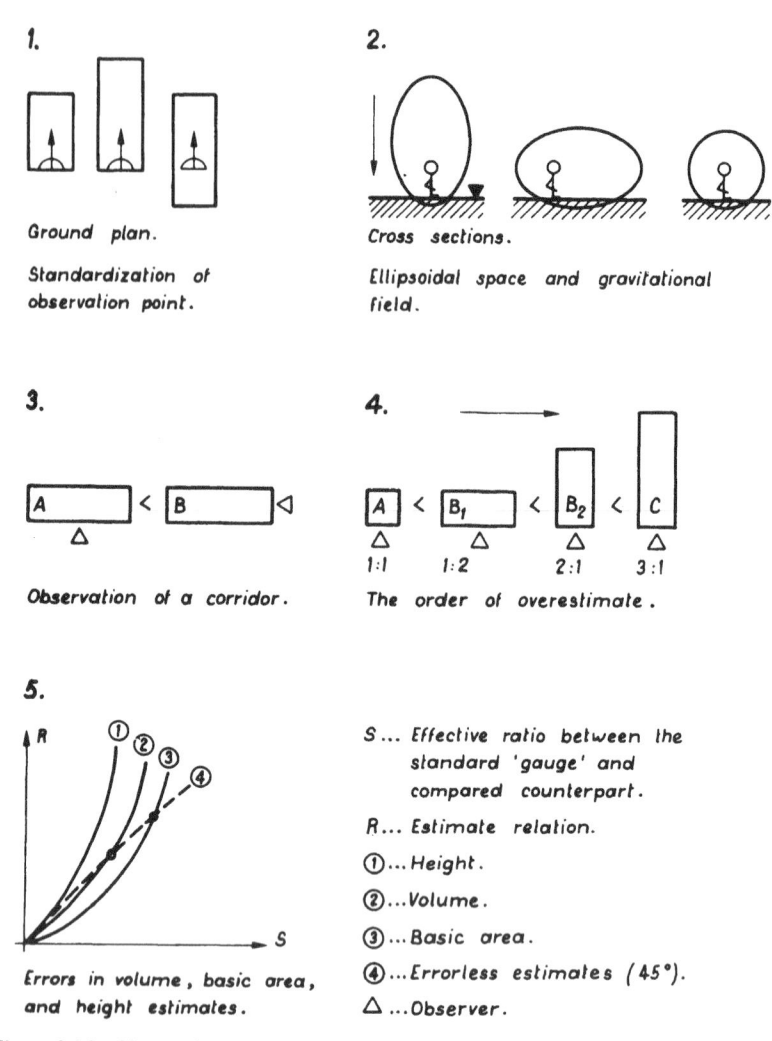

S ... Effective ratio between the standard 'gauge' and compared counterpart.
R ... Estimate relation.
① ... Height.
② ... Volume.
③ ... Basic area.
④ ... Errorless estimates (45°).
△ ... Observer.

Figure 3.16. *Observation point and errors in volume estimate.*

Degrees of noticeable volumetric difference in relation to the gross shape characteristics of optical spaces

In the series of experiments designed to construct the repertory of the architectural medium, the subjects are not asked to give volume estimates, but only to identify noticeable differences in paired comparisons. (Therefore the results, i.e., range and constancy of error, coming from studies about volume estimates, for example, formulated in m.^{3} or other scales, are only material

Optical space 289

for hypotheses. This is especially true, when we are using findings from bidimensional surface estimates.) As we now approach the conclusion of our treatment of optical space, we attempt to treat noticeable volumetric difference in a more general perspective, one which includes all kinds of space shapes.

As we saw in the discussion of geometric morphology, shapes in general can be characterized by Schumm's elongation ratio, by Blair and Bliss's compactness ratio, and by Miller's circulatory ratio (Haggett and Chorley 1970: 70).

The striking feature of all these formulae is the presence of pi, an indication that the sphere is the measure of space shapes. We ordinarily measure volume in cubic terms, but volume can always be treated, both mathematically and perceptually, in terms of circumscribed and inscribed spheres. In

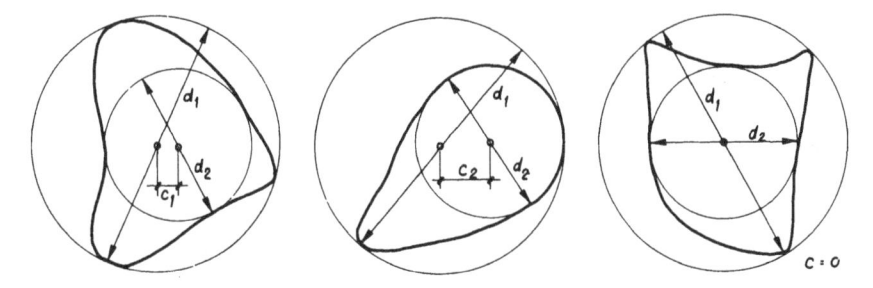

Cross sections of three spaces with various "c" values.

this context, errors can be related chiefly to three shape variables:

– difference between the length of diameter of the circumscribed and inscribed spheres;
– complexity of the shape as expressed by the 'behavior' of the enveloping surface between the two spheres;
– the distance between the center points of the two spheres.

The approximation of the volume in terms of two spheres depends on the impression of the two diameters. In the case of rectangular parallelepipeds, the shorter diameter coincides with the length of an edge, the longer with the diagonal, which is not on either surface. Moreover, as we have seen, length seen against a solid ground is overestimated compared to length seen on an air line. Thus when the observer apprehends the volume of a shape in terms of a circumscribed sphere whose diameter is on an air line, the experimenter can expect a compensation between over- and underestimation effects. Geometrically, in these volume comparisons the sphere represents the simplest case, since it is the most compact shape, has the maximal concavity index, V^2/S^3, and serves as the measure of all others. Of course, estimating a sphere in terms of cubic measure is not at all simple; but our concern is with comparison and not with measurement. We can thus prepare a series of spaces with relatively low degrees of noticeable volumetric difference.

The literature on magnitude estimates often relates the range and constancy of errors in relation to a shape's complexity and compactness. We will see shortly how this is done on both bidimensional and volumetric levels.

Complexity and compactness on dimensional levels lower than the volumetric

An understanding of the influence of shape complexity and compactness on magnitude estimates of lower dimensions, e.g., length or surface area, aids the formation of hypotheses for experiments in the sociology of architecture in two ways: even before comparing volumetric magnitudes the observer receives cues from the enveloping surface, and perhaps is helped through bidimensional analogies. Experiments have long shown that the estimate of the longest linear measure and of the perimeter often give cues for the surface estimate.

The surface of an optical space may show edges of widely diverse shape and curvature as cues for volume estimate. Della Valle and others (1956) found that if an edge is a complex broken line or a curved one, the error in estimate is positively related to the line's deviation from the rectilinear. The difference between the length of a broken line or a curved one and the length of its chord — resp. base of the angle — determines the error. Gaito (1959) found that most aspects of broken lines are more accurately judged than those of curved lines. Earlier studies (Takagi 1926) showed that 'the amount of overestimation of arcs increases with increased curvature.'

Pfeiffer (1966), and Warren and Pinneau (1955) established the order of overestimation of areas in intershape comparisons as shown in Figure 3.17.1. Menchikoff (1975: 50) interpreting the findings of Lauer and Pearson, as well as of Franken, shows another order (see Figure 3.17.2).

A survey of the last 50 years' research shows little consensus on magnitude and direction of systematic errors. The only general agreement seems to be that in intershape comparison the area of a triangle, especially an isosceles, is overestimated in comparison to that of a circle or square.

Peter and Smith (US) find that the longest linear dimension is overestimated (Menchikoff), and so the elongation ratio becomes a source of overestimation. However, as already mentioned in the context of shape discrimination, J. P. Smith (1964) generates 30 two-dimensional shapes at random and finds that 'figures which are the most "compact", or the least "stretched out", are perceived as relatively large in area.' Note that he uses the term 'compact' in quotes; the magnitude of error in estimate relates, according to Smith, to the perimeter, the number of turns, the ratio of width to height, the length, breadth, external area, and angle of tilt. Poffenberger

Optical space 291

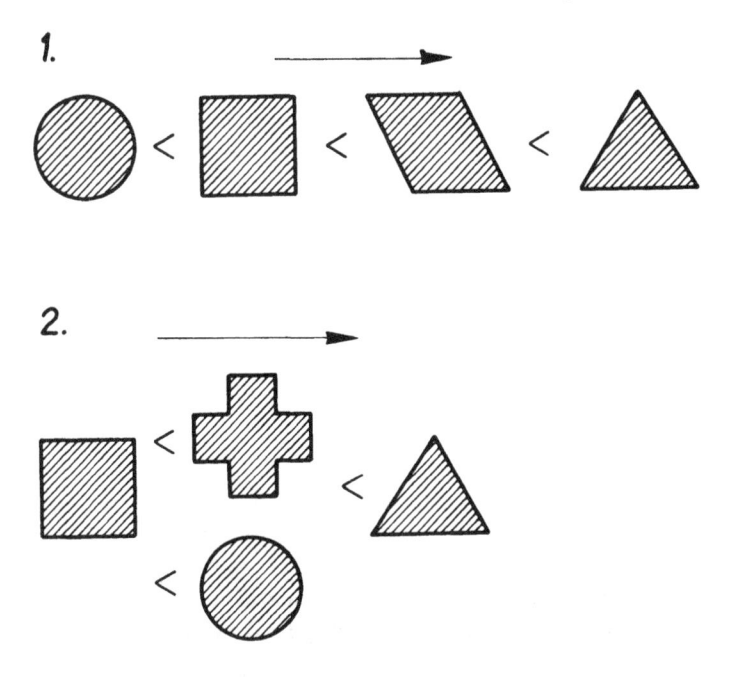

Figure 3.17. *Order of area overestimation according to different authors. (Schematic representation.)*

finds that areas with irregular outline, compared to regular ones, are overestimated.

We see that compactness and complexity figure in the prediction of both constancy and range of error. The basic problem lies in the low formalization of the concept of compactness and complexity which is used by various authors.

Concerning magnitude of error, we can add E. Wagner's finding that the area of circles and triangles is estimated with more error than that of squares and rectangles in general. This can hardly be related to difference in complexity; it is due rather to the fact that areas are measured in rectangular units.

Prospects for further research in volume comparison

The first and persistent temptation is to transpose results of bidimensional researches directly into volumetric ones. For one thing, there is little consensus even on the bidimensional level about the magnitude and direction of errors in area estimates. For another, most of the analogies for such a transposition stand on shaky ground, although Goldmeier says (1972: 120), 'In perception there seems to be a tendency to structuring . . . [information inputs] . . . in terms of the minimum possible number of dimensions.'

For example, if we try to make a hypothesis about volume comparison between the sphere and the cube through findings about area estimates of circles and squares, we immediately face the problem that squares are proper parts of the surface of a cube, but a sphere has no circular lines, only imagined cross-sections. As we noted, and as J. P. Smith reminds us by underscoring the concept of 'external area', lines on a surface are overestimated in comparison with those on air lines. The change in context, like the volume effect, can distort estimates by nearly 20 percent (R. C. Hulsebius: 18 percent).

There are other conflicts between findings about bidimensional and volumetric estimates. Lauer states that prisms with higher elongation ratios are more likely to be overestimated than those which are more nearly cubic. R. G. Pearsan finds in 1964 that volumes of optical space are overestimated as they have fewer axes of symmetry and are less compact (Menchikoff 1975: 50). This contradicts J. P. Smith's findings and prevents direct transposition of bidimensional findings into volumetric terms.

Problems also occur when architects apply the results of investigations of the impressions of various three-dimensional objects to space (impression). Merchandiser, for example, has studied volume estimates for purposes of packaging (Franken), but the results cannot be used directly for experiments in noticeable volumetric difference of optical spaces. The packaging research looked at estimates of convex shapes of relatively small dimensions, while our concern is concave enclosed volume on an architectural scale.

To sum up, the 'algorithm' of experimental design to construct systematically a repertory of optical spaces must respect the following principles:

— On the conceptual level, before the researcher tries to relate findings about volume estimate to total shape characteristics like compactness, complexity, and the like, he must define them in formal and mathematically operational terms.

— A distinction must be made between the effect of shape characteristics on the size of noticeable volume differences and the effect of the dispersion of errors, respectively, on the reliability of the experimental data. It may be that shape complexity has greater effect on the dispersion than on the threshold of discriminability.

— Results of investigations in other fields must be used only with the most extreme care. Findings about two-dimensional estimates or estimates of convex volumes are not directly relevant to the determination of noticeable volumetric differences in optical spaces. It is also necessary to recall that discrimination between optical spaces on the basis of volumetric magnitude does not in itself involve cubic measure, however subjects may use the latter.

15

Haptic Space

In our discussion of haptic communication in Part II, we noted that, of all sensory modalities, the haptic system as a whole is the most versatile in terms of the sheer variety of stimuli, mechanical and thermal, which it explores. As for haptic space itself, there has been relatively little study of the way we form impressions of it; far less than in optical and acoustical space. While environmental optics and environmental acoustics are now well-established fields of research, environmental haptics is still in its infancy. First, therefore, we attempt to clarify the concept of haptic space in terms of an autonomous space impression quite on a par with impressions of acoustical and optical space. We then turn to an evaluation of past research on haptic impressions and look for directions which future investigations might fruitfully take.

With J. J. Gibson (1966: 50) we adopt the terminology established by Géza Révész, the founder of the School of Psychology of Amsterdam. He includes in haptics all sensations which result from simple contact, pressure, pain, and surrounding temperature which deviates from physiological zero. By stating that haptic space is conceivable we imply that there are architectural spaces which can be fully explored by the haptic system alone. In experimental terms, we make the hypothesis that a subject, either blind and deaf or normal but placed in a soundless, odorless, and lightless surround, will have an impression of being enclosed in a space with normal objective characteristics, viz., shape and volume. Gibson (1966: 303) defines the conditions of sensory deprivation necessary for haptic space experiment as 'complete darkness and utter silence' where the adjacent surfaces, enveloping what would normally be a polysensory space, can only be apprehended by haptic means.

Like acoustical space, haptic space is perceived through mechanoreceptors, but the impression differs in two important ways: first, the impression of haptic space requires direct physical contact with the enveloping surface, contact between the convex tegument of the body and the concave envelope of the space; and second, haptic space is perceived by the whole body.

The complete haptic space may be defined in linguistic terms as a free form without further completion. It is a closed system: no palpable signals may enter or leave it. As examples we may cite a spacecraft, a compression chamber, or simply a closed room. This does not mean that the other sensory spaces associated with the haptic space must be coextensive with it; the window of a spacecraft does not make the haptic space within the craft any more or less closed.

On the other hand, the *minimal* criterion for haptic space to be an architectural morpheme, even if it is a bound form, is the same as for other unisensory spaces: palpable exchange cannot take place between haptic spaces on a mutual basis, i.e., a palpable message may leave or enter a space but not both. Again, a temporary aperture, e.g., a door, or even a potential elasticity in the enveloping surface need not be considered an infringement of the discrete shape and volume-preserving nature of the haptic space.

In thus conceiving the haptic space we have felt it important to free its description from the tendency to 'opticalize' it, given the highly visualistic bias of our language. As Révész (1950: 34) and Whorf, among others, have noted, metaphoric transposition of the terminology of optical space has a long tradition (Aristotle), even though the genesis of all human space impressions is to be found primarily in the haptic exploration of uterine space by the embryo.

For a more detailed look at haptic space and its unique sensory definition — *all* autonomous space impressions attribute shape and volume to a space, but each sensory modality is unique in the way it does so — we direct the reader to the work of Révész and his pioneering Amsterdam School. Yet we should register the following reservations about that work: Révész has been strongly influenced by the philosopher Husserl and has accordingly put himself in the phenomenological tradition of psychology, which makes it difficult to use his paradigms in conducting controlled experimental research. Moreover, he has been excessively involved in criticism of the essentially visualistic orientation of gestaltist psychology (Scholtz 1957: 299 ff). This brought him, at least provisionally, to this definitional equation: haptic = nonoptic (Révész 1950: 26). A more precise equation would be haptic = nonoptic + nonacoustic. It is also important to note that haptic is the only noncephalic sense system.

PHYSICS OF HAPTIC SPACE

We analyze the impression of haptic space in three stages:
— the physical characteristics of the envelope (Révész 1950: 48, 'objective space'),

— the palpable signals whose propagation is merely impeded by the envelope, and
— the evaluation of palpability as a mechanical stimulus in terms of the efficiency of the haptic system (J. J. Gibson 1966: 40).

Mechanical Stimuli

Mechanics is the science which describes those physical encounters which produce impressions through touch, always leaving aside the special case of acoustical vibrations. There are three types of mechanical stimuli.

(1) Temperature. The motion of the molecules within an aggregate attribute to it a certain degree of temperature. The normal human being can perceive a deviation of 0.15°C in the temperature of his environment from the so-called physiological zero, 32°C on average. This sensibility is measured by thermoaesthesiometry. Over time, a change of 0.5°C per hour is noticeable (McIntyre and Griffiths, in Canter and Lee 1974: 17-18).

(2) State. In any aggregate, the distance between molecules can vary from 1 to 1,000 units of the mean distance. Attraction and repulsion set the molecules in motion and the resulting collisions are more or less violent and frequent according to the momentum and initial mean distances of the molecules. If the molecules' arrangement is so dense that they can only oscillate, the aggregate preserves both its shape and its volume and we call it solid. The extreme case of solidity is the rigid body, defined as one in which the distance between any point and the center of gravity as origin does not change to a perceptible degree over time. If the cohesion holds only the volume constant, we call the aggregate liquid; in modern physical terminology, this is plasmatic matter as opposed to condensed, or solid. This means that volume constancy is preserved during any geometrical transformation, as we saw, e.g., in Schwarz's series of transformations, or 'symmetrization'. Finally, the minimal cohesion in the 'aggregate' called gas allows the molecules to take on the whole shape and volume of the space, but at a relatively lower density, or cohesion level, than that of the envelope.

The passage from one physical state to another occurs on a quasi-continuous scale. The temperature of an aggregate may change, and thus the amount of molecular agitation in it, causing progressive modification of the physical state of the aggregate. In this sense the three states of matter exist only in a relative manner; there are varying degrees of, say, solidity, elasticity, viscosity, and so on. Nevertheless, the body's elastic tegument informs us directly about the various degrees of consistency of matter by deformation of tissue. Haptometry (Fraisse) tries to measure stimuli objectively. When the observer's mechanoreceptors in the skin are pressed against a substance, the degree of resistance, i.e., of compression or deformation, reveals its relative viscosity or solidity. Thus we can attribute to any substance certain qualities of consistency: whether or not it is compressible or deformable, and whether either process is gradual or reversible. There are some striking instances of combinations of these qualities (cf. liquid crystals).

If a substance preserves its geometry completely under pressure – in mathematical terms $\overline{c} \cdot \overline{d}(g \vee \overline{g}) \cdot (r \vee \overline{r})$ – it is rigid. If it undergoes abrupt and irreversible deformation (changing continuity but not volume), it is frangible. If the deformation is gradual and irreversible $-\overline{c} \cdot (d \cdot g \cdot r)$ – the material is plastic; if the deformation is gradual and reversible, it is elastic.

Liquid matter cannot be deformed because, by definition, it preserves only its volume. Viscous materials have relatively low fluidity.

(3) Size. Solids which preserve their shape can be counted, and can collide in an elastic or inelastic way. The absolute threshold of our haptic sensitivity does not allow the impression of clashes between molecules. The aggregate of molecules must have a minimal mass to be perceptible by the tegument of the body. The minimal size is not the same on all parts of the body; on some parts we have 200 points of haptic sensitivity per cm.^{2}, on others only 5 (Chauchard 1965: 65). The minimum threshold is 2 mm.; that is, on no part of the body does the cutaneous spatial sense distinguish two points of contact any closer together than 2 mm. The sensitivity of points of contact is measured by the esthesiometer.

Haptic Envelope

Discontinuity in the consistency of two materials is what constitutes the surface of a haptic space envelope; the denser material determines the shape of the other by containing it.

In order for a haptic space as such to be complete the envelope cannot be completely heat absorbing at all points; at least some part of it must reflect heat. We are able to distinguish air temperature and the mean radiant temperature of the enclosure in a 'climatic chamber'; but we cannot distinguish between the impression of radiant and of convective heating.

Finally, the envelope of the complete haptic space, as free form in the architectural repertory, must be strong enough to repel a projectile, protecting the enclosed space and maintaining its own stability. This characteristic may also allow the observer inside the space, under certain conditions, to form an indirect impression of it, necessarily vague, by rebounding objects like rubber balls.

What are the architect's main practical use of haptic space?

Because of the extremely heterogeneous composition of the haptic sense-system — Piaget calls it 'tactile-kinesthetic', and others 'somesthetic and kinesthetic' — most haptic spaces turn out in practice to be only partial, in one or another sense. First, only a part of the whole envelope may be perceptible to all components of the haptic system. Second, and much more important, the degree of mechanical isolation provided by the envelope is very relative. We should consider the haptic space envelope in three sets of terms: (1) the thermal quality of the material; (2) its 'ballistic' or protective properties; (3) its compactness, which hinders molecular penetration by internal friction. We will discuss the last aspect more carefully in the next chapter, on hermetic space; even if the envelope's porosity is perceptible to the haptic system, molecular compactness is important mainly for the osmotic and sapid components of polysensory space.

(1) Concerning the envelope's thermal quality, heat loss is inversely proportional to the V/S ratio. That ratio is largest in the sphere, another feature of that shape's unique position (March and Martin 1972). We can also express the V/S ratio as a function of the isoconcavity index, $V/S = \sqrt{i \cdot S}$.

(2) The resistance of the architectural envelope to the transmission of messages by contact, pressure, pain, or projectile is described by the mechanics of solids. It is an application of the mechanics of molecules (cf. internal friction versus friction) to macrophysical contacts. When an object collides with the surface of a larger object, either of the following two results can occur:

(a) It may rebound or ricochet, following the law of elasticity (aa) or inelasticity (ab). By this means we perceive the wall's solidity.
(b) It may pierce the surface.

In either of these cases the envelope may suffer permanent or temporary deformation. An elastic surface takes an impression (aa) which is reversible, conforming to the shape of the touching tegument both in and out (J. J. Gibson 1966: 123-128). A hard and fragile surface may undergo permanent deformation (ab).

If the object pierces the surface (b), it may pass on and leave a hole or, if the surface material is plastic, it may hold the projectile and conform to its shape.

(3) The haptic space may be filled with a liquid or a gas, even in a hyperbaric state (>1 ATA), e.g., compression chamber. There are also wet chambers with specifically high humidity. If the filling matter is gaseous, part of the envelope could be liquid (e.g., water surface). In this case, a colliding object will either rebound or be absorbed. As stated above, it suffices for the establishment of a perceptible haptic space only that the enveloping material have greater cohesion than the filling matter.

Modern tents and other ephemeral spaces

In many nomadic cultures, we see in the development and refinement of 'tents' a conception of architectural space which seems to approach the separation of haptic from other sensory spaces and a subtle differentiation of its various characteristics. The book by Bidault and Giraud (1946) is an excellent source of examples. The technical aspects of constructing tents have been the subject of considerable innovation in modern times. On the model of Theodore Olivier's apparatus, first constructed in 1930 and now in the Conservatoire des Arts et Métiers in Paris, the principles of tent construction have been applied to concrete. These various concrete structures, e.g., shells and prestressed units, enlarge dramatically the range of shapes and dimensions where tent-construction principles can apply, but they deprive the haptic qualities of the spaces of most of the subtlety which traditional tents had. For new impulses in the field of *flexible* strcutures we must look to suspended tents, like the German Pavilion at Expo '67 and to the so-called air house, or inflated bubble.

The air house goes back to an English invention in 1917, which compressed 30 mm WG above atmosphere (0.003 atmg. = 0.003 kg/cm.^{2}) between two sheets of canvas. Today we use synthetic fabrics 0.8–1.2 mm. in thickness to inflate spaces of desired shape and volume. The airhouse at the Hanover Fair in Germany was more that 50,000 m.^{3}, dimensions never seen before in canvas. In the modern air house, the haptic space itself has hyperbaric pressure of 0.003 atmg., which is imperceptible to humans; but access to the interior space must always be through revolving doors or double-door airlocks. The air house as haptic space resists the most common external shocks.

Which aspects of these modern tents bear upon our concern with the sociology of architecture?

Both types of modern tent construction, suspended and inflated, give great freedom of choice of the shape and volume of a haptic space. The technique of inflation permits a geometry based on complicated criteria, which can originate from other aspects of the polysensory space such as the acoustical (e.g., a concert hall, which requires a specific V^2/S^3, i.e., volume^2/cloth surface^3). The fabric of the air house preserves some of the flexibility and versatility of the traditional tent.

In addition to the envelope's elasticity, the tent affords another valuable opportunity for constructing a complicated multisensory space, the use of translucent or transparent material. The history of the construction of the Cathedral of Palma de Mallorca, with the poor illumination of its main nave, tells us much about the importance of this problem.

An important sociological aspect of the air house, in addition to the multiplicity of its uses, is the rapidity of its construction. It is easy to inflate and transform, equally easy and cheap to deflate by intention or destroy by accident. The cost of this architectural material is far lower than that of any other, but its service life is brief, ca. 12-15 years. Many theoreticians of architecture (cf. the 'vast spatial envelopes' of Schulze-Fielitz 1971: 22-35; Y. Friedman) see an advantage in the instantaneous and ephemeral nature of this construction. But, as we made clear in the first part, architecture is more than a 'covering for groups'.

Architecture, in fact, aims to construct an artificial envelope which, fully developed, protects man and society against the hazards of atmospheric space. It succeeds to the fullest only when the envelope is shaped in required dimensions and is subject to human control.

A service life of 12-15 years, a period of less than a generation, certainly allows rapid change in social institutions; such a short duration may even encourage it. If the urban landscape becomes dominated by short-lived structures, their rapid deterioration may give impetus to the moral amortization of the social institutions they contain.

A further problem with inflated structures is that they do not permit multilevel space systems, a specific feature of urban architecture.

In short, we think that these structures enrich the repertory of available spaces and allow us to diversify the urban landscape. But even in our neonomadic society, it is naive to see them as a substitute, rather than a supplement, for solid constructions of (ferro-)concrete or other traditional constructions.

A related problem has to do with the filling medium of the space. In principle, the haptic space impression does not depend upon a medium, as does the acoustic; the haptic space could even be a vacuum. The observer needs oxygen for respiration, but not for exploration of the space; artificial breathing equipment would suffice.

On the other hand, in the case of both the air house and a hydrospheric (viz., liquid filling) space where aquatic ballet can be performed, the stability of the space's shape may depend on the cohesion, e.g., viscosity or pressure, of the filling.

These and related problems are increasingly important today as more and more work is done in deep-submarine or outer-space conditions. We can actually contemplate complete and solely haptic spaces, where sight and hearing are not available, without any filling medium, with a hyperbaric medium (7 to 10 ATA), or a liquid one at varying pressures. There is already a good deal of research about behavior in such spaces, but it is generally more concerned with the effects of varying conditions of respiration on perception and performance than with the effects of various filling media on the haptic space impression itself with standard breathing conditions.

HAPTIC SPACE IMPRESSION

Haptics includes more information than the tactilism named by Franck (1957), which used only the tactile function as its source. Haptics deals with space exploration in the following terms:

— the geometry, i.e., volume and shape, of a haptic space,
— the manner and degree of isolation of the envelope against caloric, ballistic, and vibratory transmission,
— the permanence of the geometry realized by the rigidity of the envelope.

For the design of haptic space experiments, the impression occurs when the subject can gather information about the space only through the haptic system. In practice, it is not necessary to block the taste-smell system; at least temporary blindness and deafness suffice. To gather data from a variety of settings we can list four basic experimental cases:

— sensorily normal subjects in dark and soundless space,
— sensorily normal subjects, eyes blindfolded and ears stopped,
— congenitally blind and deaf subjects,
— subjects blind and deaf as a result of accident.

Von Senden made the most complete compilation of observations with blind subjects, but his data, which come from nonexperimental settings, are frequently unreliable. Still, taken together with Révész's approach, and contributions from the blind, such as Henri (1962), they provide indications for further, more controlled researches.

Von Senden (1960: 21) poses the problem in the following terms: 'Do the tactual impressions of the blind provide them with what can properly be described as an awareness of space in the same sense as the visual one?'

The debate about the 'hierarchy' of sensory handicaps is also implicit in Révész's work. It is not our intention to compare haptic and visual handicaps, nor do we share St. Augustine's interest in 'superior' and 'inferior' senses (see J. Cohen 1969). Rather we hold to Locke's principle that a space concept must be formulated in sensorily indifferent terms. In fact, each sensory modality has its own 'information-gathering process', and Révész states that, unlike the other senses, the haptic system often obtains information by reconstruction.

For comparison of various optic and haptic multisensory compositions, data obtained from a congenitally blind person who has just become sighted can be compared with data from an accidentally blinded subject who has just recovered sight. The results are (experimentally) valid as long as the experimenter does not try to draw far-reaching metaphysical conclusions. If, for example, the haptic space impression is studied *in statu nascenti*, the results must not be interpreted as a justification for a nativistic philosophy. Birth should instead be considered as a passage from uterine space into atmospheric, troglodytic, or architectural space accompanied by progressive development of awareness.

Another problem we encounter is the visual bias of our language, which Whorf pointed out. Questions about space, especially polysensory space, tend to be phrased in ways that ask for a visual description of it. Such questions are incomprehensible to the congenitally blind (Henri 1962: 32, 37 n.1, 49). For this reason questions about haptic space discrimination must stay on a level unaffected by linguistic bias. Thus, to avoid bias, we ask only which space in a paired comparison has greater volume. In the same way we note the discrimination of shapes in terms of geometrical relationships alone. We never ask the subject to choose names of shapes from a catalog.

Experiments in haptic space impressions must also take into account the fact that the haptic system is a proximoceptor. This problem is especially acute in this section where we consider stationary space impression. But even a prison cell as architectural morpheme must allow the inmate to stretch his limbes without reaching the haptic envelope in all directions.

The roots of this problem go very deep; are tactile and kinesthetic sensations, in fact, separable at all? Does their experimental separation have any heuristic value?

Except for kinesthesia, all haptic sensibilities involve epidermal contact (Kenshalo 1968). We should, however, recall our observation that the various components, thermal, vibratory, and algesic, of the sensation obtained by skin contact, as well as kinesthesia itself, are defined in an imprecise way. How can we isolate 'contact impression' from kinesthetic? For experimental purposes we can define the stationary impression by imposing certain observation conditions. We prohibit the subject from moving himself and instead transport him on a wheelchair which never accelerates more than 2 cm/sec^2. In this case the observer receives no information from locomotion per se. Even though he moves about, i.e., is moved about, his impressions are always those of a stationary observer.

This case has both analytical and practical importance (Révész 1950: 147–148). The haptic space impression clearly requires some motion; but so too does the optical space impression, involving as it does some input from the muscles of the eye (Held; Michotte 1946; J. J. Gibson 1966: locomotional theory). We thus have a relative isolation of the stationary haptic space impression.

We can round out our investigation of the stationary impression of haptic space by considering stimuli which we can class as 'haptotropic'; the observer seeks and finds cues from the haptic space, without actually touching its envelope, in the way that an experienced swimmer knows deep from shallow without touching bottom (Chauchard 1965: 78). Even if we cannot distinguish between radiant and convective heat, radiant temperature can be a clue to the nearness of the haptic envelope. The sensation of air movement, even a simple draught, can be a cue to the volume of the space or to some peculiarity, such as a recess or opening. In this respect, note the thermal mapping made by Clouten (1970: 125) of the Court House of Montgomery County, Dayton, Ohio, and think of the blind man's use of his (white) cane. Of course, such 'haptotropic' impressions work on a less direct level than touching; the subject needs previous space experience to allow him to draw inferences about the haptic space from his sensations.

In sum, the two main types of impression, stationary and dynamic, can be distinguished in haptic spaces, as also in the case of optical and acoustic ones, but with more difficulty. The stationary haptic impression includes inputs in experimental conditions where passive contact and active touch (J. J. Gibson 1966: 133; Révész calls the latter 'moving touch') are permitted, as well as locomotion, but only that which involves negligible kinesthetic, or proprioceptive, sensory input.

We will examine the dynamic exploration of haptic space, together with that of other sensory spaces, after our discussion of the polysensory space impression. The dynamic exploration of *any* sensory space involves the co-ordination of kinesthetic, motor, and afferent events (Teuben in Dubois et al. 1971: 488).

Proximospace

We can classify haptic spaces according to the movements necessary to gain an impression of them. There are spaces whose exploration requires locomotion, and others where bending or turning is enough, i.e., the envelope is within arm's reach (Ross: 1974: 57). There are even those minimal spaces where the envelope is in constant touch with our tegument, such as telephone booths, bathing cabanas, or elevator cages. We seldom notice the constriction, because we are in these spaces only for brief periods – but the exceptions to that normal rule are striking.

Claustrophobia and its manifestations represent the psychological reaction to restricted space. An extreme case of an inescapably long sojourn in a restricted space is very much before us today in the form of spacecraft. Both extremes – cosmic space and the confines of a spaceship – have induced researchers to learn more about the haptic space impression and the relevant physiological limits. The haptic envelope differs from clothing in that it sets clear limits to the motions of the person within it. In terms of physiological criteria, we seek to learn how long, and in how small a space, a person can function before the 'straightjacket effect' becomes a direct threat to health. For the sociology of architecture, however, we are primarily concerned to discover which characteristics of the geometry and surface (e.g., softness) of haptic spaces influence their ordering by their perceived (volumetric) 'spaciousness'. Is it the objective volume? Is it related to a particular shape feature? Is it related, e.g., to the diameter of the largest inscribed sphere as a sort of bottleneck? Or to the maximal straight line, the diameter of the smallest circumscribed sphere? Little research has been conducted in this area, despite its obvious importance.

To understand the discrimination of haptic space in close contact ('near space': Révész 1950: 38-40), we must first determine the least shape difference which can be perceived by touch. Continuous exploration by the fingers allows the discovery of microfeatures on the space envelope and the discrimination of uncommon free geometrical shapes. Static cutaneous pressure permits recognition of shapes, e.g., of the faces of polyhedrons (cf. stereoesthesiometry of Toulouse and Vaschide). Experiment also identify cues to the impression of curvature and solidity the haptic envelope.

Below a certain threshold, the observer cannot distinguish individual features, 'shape of room' (Révész 1950: 38-40). The difference between two spaces cannot be expressed in geometrical terms, only in terms of texture. Various components of the haptic impression, like touch-pain, add to the sensory inputs and reveal the surface texture as coarse, granular, prickly, and so on. A mural, simply as painting, would not be part of the haptic space impression; but a heavy layer of paint could be explored, like a sculpture or bas-relief. Some painters, like Pollock, Tapiès, Soulages, and, especially, the Italo-Argentinian Lucio Fontana (d. 1969) pay careful attention to the haptic effect of their works.

Through pressure exerted by various parts of the body's tegument we explore the cohesion, or relative hardness, of the haptic envelope (J. J. Gibson 1966: 123-128). The feet feel the floor's carpet, the back the wall, and the fingers the ceiling (Fitch 1972: 176). It is important to note which part of the body is involved because different skin areas have different sensitivities. S. Weinstein claims (in Kenshalo 1968) greater sensitivity to pressure for the *left* palm and fingers, but other studies show no lateral difference (Carmon et al. 1969). Sensitivity to differences in temperature is a function of the way the physiological zero varies from one part of the tegument to another. This, for example, explains why it is inadvisable to heat a space through the floor; the soles of the feet are especially sensitive.

Past Findings and Prospective Research in Haptic Space Impression

Previous research by psychologists and physiologists has generally concentrated on only one component of the haptic system, and so gives little information about the impression that results from the cumulative effect of the various haptic inputs.

Much research, inspired by humanitarian concern, has been conducted by groups involved with the blind, but the usefulness of it for our purposes is limited. The studies usually include all nonvisual modalities, not the haptic in isolation. Further, because they aim directly at practical application, they have little theoretical significance. Work of this kind has been done at the Non-Visual Perceptual System Laboratory of the University of Louisville and the Institute of Rehabilitation, Industrial Home for the Blind in Jamaica, N.Y. The findings have been published in *New Outlook for the Blind* (e.g., Milton and Clark 1968: 265-269; Foulke 1969).

Von Senden's study also deals with the haptic space impression in the nonvisual context, viz., both haptic and auditory, especially in the case of the blind person who has become sighted by an operation.

The recent studies by Worchel (1960: 27) also look into the haptic impression in the context of blindness. He finds that even the congenitally blind have no handicap in tactual recognition of form. He confirms our previous observation that the subject's real difficulty in conveying his impression of haptic space is mainly due not to his blindness but to the visual imagery of the language he is asked to use.

Révész focused solely on the haptic impression. Despite his excessive polemic against gestalt psychology and his preference for phenomenology, and the possible effect of this on his approach, his heuristic principles are worth examining with a view toward further research, under better experimental conditions. We can summarize them in the following way (Scholtz 1957 299-333; Révész 1950, 1953):

— The stereoplastic principle: haptic prehension grasps an object in totality, and estimates volume without examining detail. This principle applies to a compact convex object, perceived from its exterior.
— Successivity: haptic exploration proceeds from point to point, while optical exploration normally proceeds by skipping about. In the case of listening, successivity is even stricter. The haptic explorer can at least choose his own rate of speed, and even reverse the process.
— The kinetic principle: motor activity is more pronounced in haptic exploration than in other types; but the muscular involvement does not necessarily imply the predominance of kinesthetic input. We will discuss dynaminc exploration later on. Here we only point out that the subject cannot know whether or when he accomplishes a full 360° turn; unless he makes it in a near space, as long as it is not cylindrical, it affords at least one point of reference.
— The metric principle: by the use of terms like 'foot' and 'arm's length', the language itself illustrates this, despite its preference, as we noted, for

visual metaphors. Of course, the blind man lacks an 'eye for detail', but the thumb has the last word on symmetry, congruency, and the like.

The remainder of Révész' principles are either too vague or else too specifically related to his controversy with the gestaltists.

Let us now summarize the heuristics applicable to further experiments on the impression of haptic space.

In the everyday concept of space, the haptic component is always implicitly present. It was our first, prenatal experience of space, and it is also the final confirmation of the protective function of architectural space. So too the fact of solidity, confirmed by haptic exploration, must be clearly implied in multilevel space systems. Although the static impression even of optical space has limits, in this case the haptic field is especially restricted. On the other hand, the shape and volume of proximospaces too close for a visual impression compared quite accurately by direct haptic exploration (Henri 1962: 37). In fact, that is the best way of exploring the 'minimal living space'. (For rapid exploration, the space's circumscribed sphere should have a radius not greater than arm's length.) Haptic exploration permits the observer to discover microshapes in the envelope, and, by finding discontinuities or changes in its curvature (y'), directly to distinguish nonisometric spaces (von Senden 1960: 47, 53-54). The incompleteness of the haptic space, viz., the discontinuity of y, is also well 'grasped' according to the principle of successivity.

The 'explorability' of the envelope is not the same in all its parts; the biggest handicap is normally the height of the ceiling. (Spacecraft constitute a different case; Schulze-Fielitz 1971: 19.) Since most spaces are located in a field of gravity, simple walking explores the floor's slope quite accurately (Aubree 1968: 4/3.25; Jampolsky). Blind and deaf people develop keen sensitivity to information gained from walking.

Jose R. Bernardino, an architect at Columbia University and City College, describes (1970) some intuitive applications of this observation to the construction of a home for the blind. Primarily, the architect should avoid any abrupt changes in the floor, like steps, whenever possible. He should strive for a construction in which the change of floor level is well signaled.

In the multisensory context, Bernardino suggested that, since a blind person lacks about 87 percent of normal environmental information, the architect make the space more stimulating (cf. Goffman 1963) by enriching the textural and thermic variety of the envelope and characterizing the differences between spaces in this way. The enrichment can also be acoustical and olfactory.

The thermic aspect of haptic space is interesting. One of the most obvious signs of passage from one space to another is the change in temperature. Barnes (1963: 870-877) observed that the higher the temperature of a space, e.g., a sauna, the more the distance between people tends to be underestimated, and vice versa (cf. public vs. private and intimate space, and relation to dress).

Finally, the experimenter can study the ways a subject explores a haptic space envelope farther than arm's length away from him at every point. We have mentioned tossing rubber balls; but the only relatively efficient 'tele explorer' of haptic space is the blind man's cane (Foulke 1969).

16

'Osmotic' and Hermetic Space

IS THERE ANY SUCH THING? SOME CONCEPTUAL CONSIDERATIONS

The objective condition for complete autonomy of any sensory space as free morpheme is that no communication can pass through its envelope in either direction in the relevant modality. The minimal criterion for the existence of a sensory space is that communication can go only one way, in or out; this is a bound form. We are concerned here with 'leaks' in face-to-face communication; other transmissions, e.g., a phone call, belong by definition to *tele*communication. Some sensory communication, e.g., osmatic, cannot be spatially extended even by telecommunication.

A second condition involves the observer. A space takes part in architectural communication only if the message can be received through the relevant sensory system in such a way as to let the observer guess the shape and volume of this space. The objective condition for its realization is that the envelope reflect the substance or waves which stimulate the receiving organ efficiently enough to register.

How do these requirements apply to our taste-smell (flavor) system, which relies primarily upon chemoreceptors?

We know from experience that volatile substances, carried by atmospheric or hydrospheric media and received through metabolic or respiratory exchange, transmit essential messages for living beings. It is easy to imagine a hermetic envelope which excludes any osmotic passage — not only in the case of a sealed container or a space vehicle (Fitch 1972: 108). The true problem is to conceive of an osmotic space without a haptic envelope.

Osmotic space requires exclusion of osmosis through the envelope. Hermetic space is a completion of haptic space by osmotic isolation, creating a closed biosphere. The haptic 'explorer' can gain a good impression of the relative consistency of the envelope; he can distinguish perforated walls, even to fine degrees. But haptic exploration cannot detect characteristics which make the envelope semipermeable, where molecules of a certain maximal size, or solutions of a certain concentration, can traverse it either by endosmosis or exosmosis. This kind of space is not distinguished by the mechano- and thermoreceptors of the haptic system, but by the chemoreceptors which respond to osmatic stimuli. Hermetic space is thus the completion of haptic space.

'RESPIRED AND INGESTED SPACE'

There are few odorless spaces, and when we breathe we bring odoriferous substances into our oral and nasal cavities (J. J. Gibson 1966: 144; Geldard 1953: 289; Bodenheimer 1967: 274). In aquatic spaces we encounter soluble substances which are saporific and may or may not be palatable. The distribution and concentration of these sources of stimulus vary. By contrast, a hermetically enclosed space tends, through constant emission of odoriferous substances, to increase the concentration of these molecules and to distribute them more evenly within itself. The envelope also absorbs odoriferous substances and reemits them at varying rates, giving the impression of the osmatically isolating nature of the envelope. Thus a boudoir is easily distinguished from a *fumoir* [smoking room].

It is clear that odors, even those reemitted by the envelope, cannot by themselves provide a direct impression of space shape or volume. The case is like that in which a swimmer perceives that he is in a large body of water because he can taste salt. In all such cases, the observer may gain some sort of impression of shape and volume, but it will always be based on inference rather than resulting from input of the chemoreceptors. From the given odorivector (Piéron), the observer infers the geometry of the actual space through its function (e.g., a smoking room) on the basis of his knowledge, gained from prior experience, of the dimensions of spaces with similar purpose. So, on the one hand, the odorivector gives the observer cues about polysensory space, that is if all the mechanical envelopes, viz., acoustic and haptic, coincide and so constitute, with the osmotic, a hermetic space; and he interprets the cues by 'associative concatenation'. On the other hand, the 'hermetic sealedness' of the space cannot be conveyed without some inputs from senses other than the taste-smell system.

AIR CONDITIONING

As distinguished from taste, olfactory impressions, received through respiration, result from the pressure, gaseous composition, and nongaseous aerosols of the ambient atmosphere (Fitch 1972: 62). These characteristics, as well as temperature and humidity, are affected by air conditioning, although that fact is almost never considered in designing the system. Similarly, a liquid filling medium is determined by pressure, composition of the solution, aeration, and temperature.

With regard to pressure, Adolfson (1974) and H. E. Ross (1974) conducted experiments in both gaseous and liquid media. All spaces with hyperbaric ambient air were considered together, while a dry compression chamber was used to simulate 'wet' space; for a diver at 60 m. under water the experimenter counted 7 ATA, at 90 m. 10 ATA, and so on. The experiments showed that at 4 ATA the subject's reasoning and immediate memory are affected (Adolfson 1974: 64-65). 10 ATA seems to be another threshold; beyond it, psychomotor functions — hand, foot, and manual dexterity — deteriorate seriously. The perceptual and psychosensory functions are affected only beyond 13 ATA; the subject becomes 'drunk'. After a second exposure, however, habituation diminishes these effects significantly. There are also experiments concerning behavior in hypobaric (<1 ATA), ethereal space (Chouchard 1965: 53-54; J. Cohen 1969: 43). Here the effect proper to subnormal pressure is often difficult to distinguish because the hypobaric medium is associated with rarification of components, including oxygen molecule (O_2).

Sensations received by the chemoreceptors bear closely upon the metabolism in relation to respiration and ingestion. For this reason, in the context of self-preservation, human sensitivity to negatively valued chemicals, like the asphyxiating, narcotic, or toxic molecules, has the lowest threshold. On the other hand, humans have high sensitivity to scents and appetizing molecules. Adolfson's experiments show that the effects of hyperbaric atmospheres diminish when the air is composed of O and He in the ratio of 20 : 80, as compared with a composition of O and N in the same proportion. Nitrogen has no taste or odor but is more narcotic and heavier than helium.

How do the nature, concentration, and homogeneity of saporific and odoriferous particles influence the impression of a hermetic space?

Bodenheimer (1967: 274) states the hypothesis, not yet experimentally verified, that the volume of an 'ethereal' space, where heavy odoriferous molecules are less concentrated, will be overestimated in comparison with that of a highly perfumed one. In fact, claustrophobia is related to the sensation of a lack of oxygen, imminent suffocation, or gassing. Experimentation should be able to determine the effects of various odoriferous substances, in various concentrations, on volume estimates. Because these substances are perceived as volatile, their concentration in a space, remaining constant over time, conveys the impression that the space is hermetic. In fact, the homogeneity of the odor in the space depends on both the constancy of its emission and the hermetic character of the envelope.

Formerly, the habitable space, like an igloo, was multifunctional, and odors mixed because various vital functions were performed in the same place. Nowadays air conditioning, on the one hand, promises us osmotic separation within one and the same haptic space, but, on the other hand — in reality — a badly connected system can produce mutual olfactory pollution in spaces which are far more removed from one another in distance as well as in function.

Researchers have tried to find neutral odors, using Peruvian balsam, carbonic acid, etc., to produce a 'zero point' in odor. But Henning and other specialists consider this 'camouflage' of existing odors, not the true production of odorless space (Geldard 1953: 290).

The technology of air conditioning has shown us ways to separate the envelope of osmotic space from that of haptic space. We know that rain washes odors from the air (J. J. Gibson 1966: 18); air conditioning does so by passing the air through a 'fine water spray' (Fitch 1972: 77). We can separate osmotic spaces, even horizontally, with fountains. A mechanical means is to filter out large airborne particles by creating a 'screen' of air. The highly sophisticated use of electric charges to form an osmotic screen allows even clearer separation of osmotic and haptic envelopes. Thus we have a haptic barrier and an osmotic filter which latter is not mechanical at all.

SUMMING UP

We can say in conclusion that the mechano- and chemoreceptors which report odors and savors can contribute to the impression of space. We can also imagine an envelope which acts exclusively to separate osmatic messages. But in most cases the osmotic envelope, which prevents mechanical penetration, coincides with the haptic one, causing the haptic space to become also hermetic. In fact, even when the osmotic envelope is objectively distinct from spaces otherwise defined, the observer is almost never in a situation to receive an impression of 'osmotic space' apart from that of other mechanical — haptic and acoustic — spaces. In short, osmatic stimuli are not enough to attribute shape and volume to any roomraum, at least not for a sessile observer. In theory, the observer can, by walking or swimming, find limits where the concentration and distribution of osmatic particles change noticeably and abruptly.

The normal contribution of osmatic phenomena to space impression occurs in the context of polysensory space by indirect means. Odorivectors are inherent in some spaces which, by their constant use for specific functions, are infused with characteristic odors, e.g., boudoir, kitchen, etc. Thus the observer attributes expected shape and volume to the space through its function. As we will see in the discussion of the polysensory space impression, odorivectors are more important in confirming the space impression established by other sensory inputs than in constructing a space impression on their own.

17

Multiplicity of Sensory Spaces and the Multisensory Composition

PHYSICAL COMPOSITION OF MULTISENSORY SPACES

The Architectural Morpheme and Multisensoriality

Let us pursue our analogy between architecture and spoken language. Both can convey strictly functional messages, as in scientific discurse or spaces for industrial purpose (e.g., engine room, kitchen). Both can bear poetical meanings as in literature and in spaces which create esthetic responses (e.g., a well-designed music room). This is why we reject 'clear readability' (K. Lynch) as a kind of supreme criterion for 'good gestalt' in architecture. That is valid for traffic engineering, say, or any kind of industrial spaces, just as it is for expository prose; but 'complexity and contradiction' (Venturi 1966) also have a place in the creation of architectural spaces. Just as the social activities housed within the architectural space are divided between cooperation and competition in an ambiguous way, so too does the space itself meet contradictory requirements and leave some of its aspects open to the imagination of various users.

These general observations apply directly to the present chapter because the multisensory composition of architectural morphemes unavoidably creates ambiguity. The architect can use the separability of the various unisensory envelopes to meet the requirements of the individual space, optical, acoustical, haptic, or hermetic, even if each must have a different shape and volume. But when we question the observer about 'the' space, sense modality unspecified, we often get a variety of responses. One observer may identify the space with the haptic space, another with the optical, and so on. This is not necessarily a cause for worry, except, of course, in experimentation; it may very well represent the architect's choice of 'scherzo' or compromise.

The fact of ambiguity in architecture itself, however, must not suggest that we can be anything but rigorously precise in the scientific metalanguage used for its description. Especially here, where the composition of architectural morphemes on a multisensory level is like the use in language of compound words. The social sciences have experienced too much confusion already from using the ordinary language of observed populations to attempt scientific descriptions of various human activities. We need to develop the sociological theory of architecture not in the terms which the population uses to describe its reactions, but in a metalanguage corresponding to scientifically founded concepts. Only this kind of knowledge can help the architect execute his design more efficiently.

Multisensory intricacy, properly understood and employed, can be regarded as the true completion of architectural morphology. Yet the very intricacy of it demands the most careful study in order to preserve the consistency of the architectural repertory under construction in this work.

The first problem is to specify the observer's position as part of the definition of our compound word. If the observation is static, the experimenter should always specify the sensory modality of the space whose shape or volume the subject is to indicate in response to the paired comparison. In reality the subject may attribute at the same time different volume and shape to the optical space, the acoustical space, and so on. This simultaneity constitutes the very essence of the multisensory intricacy.

The second problem in keeping the repertory free of ambiguity arises when the observation is dynamic. Our next chapter will treat this detail. For now, we only remark that within all sensory spaces simultaneously observed from a fixed point there is a zone shared by all. If the subject leaves the shared portion, on the one hand, the multisensory observation conditions for perceiving the unisensory space, whose envelope he did not cross, nevertheless change; on the other hand, by means of change in multisensory composition, at least one of the unisensory spaces to be observed will be different.

Multisensory Composition of Space

We know it is possible for an observer to attribute volume and shape to a space which encloses him only in respect to one sensory modality. We can define the hylic or physical conditions created by the architect, as well as the sensory ones proper to the space impression. We conceive of acoustical, optical, and haptic spaces as autonomous and, at least theoretically, osmatic spaces as well. All are explored, by definition, through a single sensory system.

But what about seeing a glass partition, for example, and thus exploring a haptic space by visual means? A misconception. If it can be seen at all the partition is to that extent not transparent. The optical space is not a free form but a bound one; the glass partition is the separator between two bound morphemes, which perhaps constitute a complex word.

A subject proper to this chapter is the exploration of unisensory spaces in the context of interference by other sensory spaces under normal conditions, i.e., all senses are functioning and all classes of input available.

When we introduce the simultaneous presence of a variety of sensory space we open up a new field of investigation, that which deals with the impression of the relative location of the various spaces. This requires us to derive an entirely new kind of question which we can build into our series of paired-comparison experiments.

Within this framework a special case will appear, the coincidence of two or more spaces whose sensory modalities differ but which are geometrically identical. This case is important both in theory and in practice, and so we reserve for it the term polysensory. This will distinguish it from the various multisensory spaces, compound morphemes made up of autonomous spaces. The experimental importance of this special case is that all the senses have a single, common envelope as target. In this context, the different sensory data can be pooled and act simply as optical, acoustical, haptic, and osmatic components in the exploration of a space without restrictive sensory specification. The practical importance is that this process is what the common user thinks of, rightly or wrongly, as experience of 'normal' architectural space.

How must this new series of questions be deployed in the experiment series concerning unisensory space impression alone?

To avoid ambiguity, as well as disorganization of the observer's information processing if the entire series of questions is to be put in a single sequence, the series must begin by asking if the envelopes of the various unisensory spaces coincide or not. Thus we determine whether or not the observer has an impression of polysensory space, meaning impression of same geometry and same location of all sensory spaces.

This part of the question series will also reveal the effectiveness of the architectural design. The architect, for example, may have attempted to generate systematic intersensory space errors which would 'transpose' one or another sensory space envelope and create illusory coincidence of the envelopes.

If the observer perceives both spaces in the paired comparison as polysensory, the experimenter proceeds to ask the same question he does in the case of each unisensory space:

— Which of the two has greater volume?
— Do the two have the same shape?

The polysensory impression will result from an input process $PS_i \leftarrow (AOH)S_{a, v, h, o}$ and thus the discrimination threshold may be lower than in the case of individual unisensory impressions (ΔV). It is also possible that the space will not seem coextensive. The impression that the compared spaces are not polysensor may be based on one or more of the following conditions: one or all of the three sensory spaces may, or may seem to differ in shape or volume or both, i.e., lack geometrical congruence, or one or all may be displaced in relation to the others by translation or rotation. Finally, the coincidence may be partial, as in the previous example of the glass partition which separates two bound morphemes. This investigation must be carefully programmed on the combinatorial as well as the sequential level, especially because the question must be kept simple, generally understandable, and answerable by yes or no without complex mental operations.

New aspects of these questions concern the tasks of localization and of geometrical comparison of spaces with different sensory modalities. Both require skill in intersensory comparison. In the older literature we find this subject listed under 'heterogeneous matching' (Harper in *Sensation and Measurement* 1974: 91). More recently it has been named 'cross-modality matching' and abbreviated CMM (Dawson in *Sensation and Measurement* 1974: 49).

Investigations of the case where $(AO)S \neq HS$, $(AH)S \neq OS$, and $(HO)S \neq AS$ reveal the predominance of one or another sense by determining thresholds of discrimination.

Finally, in the case of spaces which are not polysensory, we may investigate how, and to what extent, the simple presence of one sensory space may interfere with the discrimination thresholds of another modality. For example, we set two different optical spaces (OS_1 and OS_2) for paired comparison, which have parameters of variously located and dimensioned acoustical and haptic spaces. We have already discussed the influence of other parameters on these thresholds.

In all these experiments, we must always keep in mind the principle that only those data are relevant to the repertory of the architectural medium which are perceptible to a standard observer and caused by some objective physical difference between the compared spaces.

We now see architecture as multimedial in the sense that one and the same component of architectural communication can both aid and hinder its reception. When the observer can find parallels among the signs of the various sensory modalities, he 'reads' them better. Thus at a poetry reading, if he has a written text, he can immediately correct a mishearing. This is the basis on which we stated the hypothesis above; discrimination thresholds are usually lower in polysensory than in unisensory spaces.

On the other hand, when the receiver is unable, for whatever reason, to detect concordance among the simultaneous sensory signs, comprehension of any one kind of sign suffers from the presence of the other. For this reason we state the following hypothesis: when the observer judges the various sensory spaces to be noncoextensive, the discrimination threshold of all the spaces will be higher than when each was presented in the exclusively unisensory context.

Further, when there is objective noncoincidence among the sensory spaces, the very definition of the compound morpheme causes problems. The various spaces must be parceled out in smaller units where the observer perceives one and the same space in all sensory modalities (see Figure 3.20). By listing all the parcels of one sensory space where all impressions remain homogeneous, we see that the compound architectural morpheme can exist in a theoretically unlimited triple weaving; it must therefore be apprehended on the level of higher composition, the syntagmatic. For reasons of economy we discuss this aspect of multisensory space composition in the last section of this part, which deals with space systems and subsystems.

Combinatorial Topology in Multisensory Composition

For unisensory spaces, we have used topological geometrical definitions, describing shape and volume, and hylic ones, specifying sense modality and degree of isolation (bound or free forms). Multisensory spaces require in addition a topological and geometrical definition of the relative location of the component unisensory spaces. A further complication results from the necessity that all the observation data be homogeneous and able to be pooled. This means that the number of possible static observation points is limited to those within the subregion of the multisensory space which the same three unisensory components occupy in common. These subregions serve as reference and qualify repertory items. We now count the possible topological combinations exhaustively, to avoid unwitting omission, before we eliminate those which cannot be realized. In Figure 3.18.1 we use the logical trefoil for illustration.

If we consider all possible subregions with different combinations of the three components, including the one where all are absent, we reach the total of eight as shown in (3) in Figure 3.18.

Because 111 is the observer's position, it must be present in all compound architectural morphemes. On the other hand, 000 can take part in none. Thus, to calculate the number of all possible variations, we combine six of the eight subregions and find $2^6 = 64$ topologically different cases.

In addition to this purely topological enumeration, we must note immediately that some direct metric constraints apply in terms of relative volumetric magnitude as the bottom two examples in Figure 3.18 show.

316 *Communication through architecture*

1.

Bidimensional représentation of the general case of non-coextension.

2.

Optical space. Haptic space. Acoustical space.

A case of tridimensional possibility.

Impossible case: more than one optical space.

3.

AS	OS	HS
1	0	0
1	1	0
1	0	0
0	1	1
0	0	1
0	1	0
0	0	0

111 is the shared parcel to which space impression in a repertory item is referred.

$$\begin{array}{c} AS \\ OS \\ HS \end{array} \quad \begin{array}{c} 011 \\ 111 \\ 100 \end{array}$$

An example of the application of the notation.

$$\begin{array}{c} AS \\ OS \\ HS \end{array} \quad \begin{array}{c} 100 \\ 101 \\ 111 \\ 011 \\ 010 \end{array}$$

Metric constraint: $(V_{OS} + V_{AS}) > V_{HS}$

This topological arrangement implies that the volume of haptic space must be smaller than the sum of the volume of the acoustical and optical spaces.

$$\begin{array}{c} AS \\ OS \\ HS \end{array} \quad \begin{array}{c} 100 \\ 101 \\ 111 \\ 110 \end{array}$$

Metric constraint: $V_{OS} < V_{AS} > V_{HS}$

The volume of the acoustical is larger than that of the optical or the haptic space.

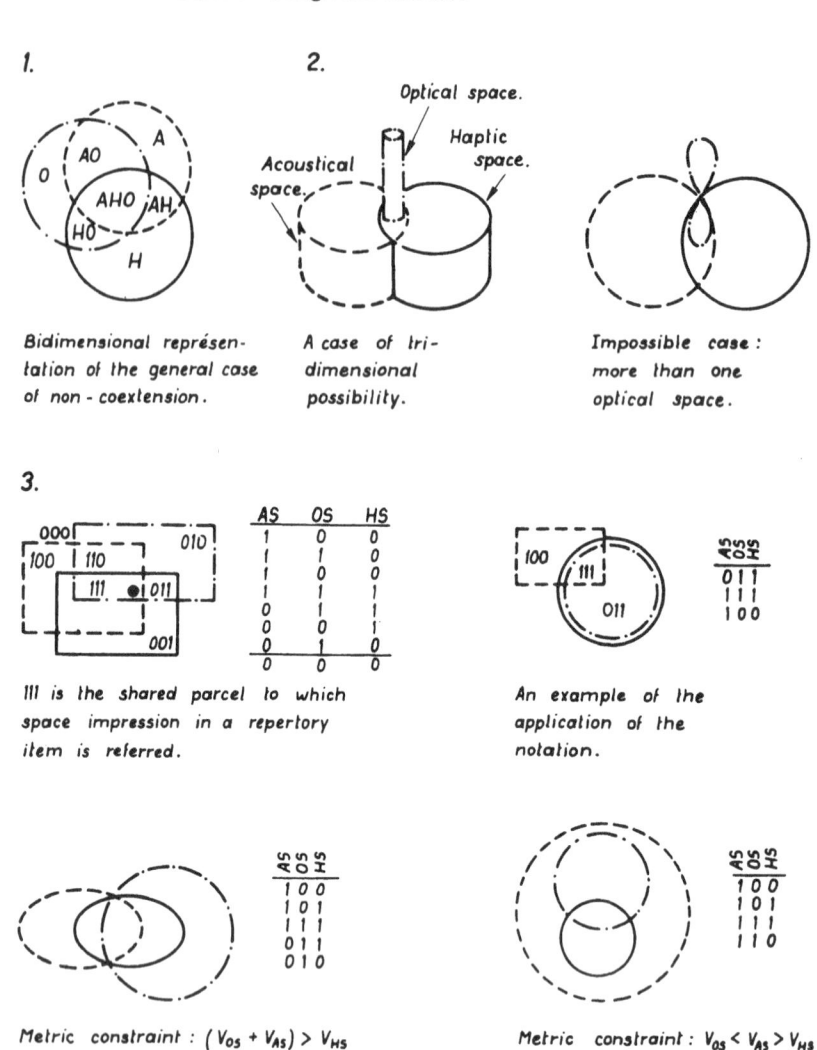

Figure 3.18. *Notation of multisensory composition of a space and of the metric constraint implied.*

Geometrical Transformation in Relation to Multisensory Composition

With a view toward geometrical transformation of an architectural space, what, and how many, are the characteristics which the experimenter can vary?

The geometrical definition of every sensory space comprises location, specified by two coordinates, u and v, and an angle, α; volumetric magnitude, a single datum; and shape, for which the number of data involved is variable.

On the basis of these data the experimenter can distinguish the following types of cases:

(1) In geometrical terms the simplest case is the complete coincidence of all three sensory spaces. This results in a polysensory space, produced by identical transformation ($\equiv$), a 'conformity' or matching. Data about the shape and volume of any one space suffice to define the whole configuration.

(2) The isometry of the three spaces may be preserved, without a common location. In this case the spaces are equal, or congruent; volume and shape data are in common, but not location data. Isometric transformation relocates one or all of the spaces in two principal ways:

(a) translation (T); $u \neq 0$, or $v \neq 0$, or both, and $\alpha = 0$;
(b) rotation; $\alpha \neq 0$.

(3) *Either* the shape *or* the volume of one or all of the component spaces remains invariant during the transformation. The three are equal in only one respect, and so are equivalent ($\underline{e}$). Here again there are two main types:

(a) homothetic transformation, or transformation of similitude: volume can change (if $k \neq 0$) but not shape. If $v = u = \alpha = 0$ we have the special case of concentricity or 'nesting'. (See Figure 3.19.1.)
(b) 'Schwartz transformation' (symmetrization); volume remains unchanged during shape transformation.

We can even conceive of other parameters, like the isoconcavity indicatrix V^2/S^3 as invariant or 'transitive quality'.

Polysensory Space

A fully polysensory space involves three coextensive sensory spaces. There can also occur partially polysensory spaces where only two sensory spaces are perceptible and coextensive. They may result from two types of conditions: input is unavailable in one sensory modality, either because of lack of stimuli from the space (e.g., darkness) or because of sensory deprivation on the part of the observer (e.g., tactual agnosia, Révész 1950: 11, 97). We can conjecture that the discrimination is lower in these cases than in the case when a third noncoextensive sensory space is present and interferes.

We now proceed to fully polysensory spaces, those all three of whose sensory envelopes coincide. As we indicated, the subject must first be questioned about the location of each unisensory space, his impression of their geometrical identity being necessary for the impression of a polysensory space.

Once that impression has been verified, we can try to learn how the pooling of various sensory data functions as a 'molar' perceptual system (J. J. Gibson 1966: 51); $(AOH)S_i = PS_i = (PS_i)_{a, v, h}$.

SPACE IMPRESSION AND PAST FINDINGS

Spatial Illusions: Polysensory vs. Nonpolysensory Space Composition

In polysensory space the architect can create two types of illusion in terms of localization: either he can make an objectively coextensive envelope seem disjoined, or he can make an objectively disjoined envelope appear coextensive (e.g., first case: $PS \leftarrow (AH)S_i + OS_i$; second case: $(AH)S + OS \leftarrow PS_i$).

In the first case, we have already seen how the architect can cause part of an enveloping surface to appear to move forward or back by the right selection of surface characteristics (J. J. Gibson 1966: 310). This disjunction may involve only one envelope or it may imply the accompaniment of a related space (J. J. Gibson 1966: 294).

For the illusory coincidence of an envelope, the procedure is similar but must be executed with greater precision ($OS_i = AS_i$ versus $OS_i \lesseqgtr AS_i$). In the first case the impression transforms identity into inequality; in the second, inequality into identity. We make the hypothesis that if the various sensory spaces are in 'concentric location' (e.g., nesting), $u = 0$, $v = 0$, $\alpha = 0$, the chance of effecting the second type of illusion is better. The creation of any kind of illusion is easier when the observer remains static (Handel and Buffardi 1968: 1,026).

Sensory Means: Optemes, Acoustemes, and Haptemes

We now consider the ways in which the architect can use the surface characteristics we call optemes, acoustemes, and haptemes as submorphic elements. Which arrangement of which elements effects the desired space error in the polysensory context?

Multisensory composition 319

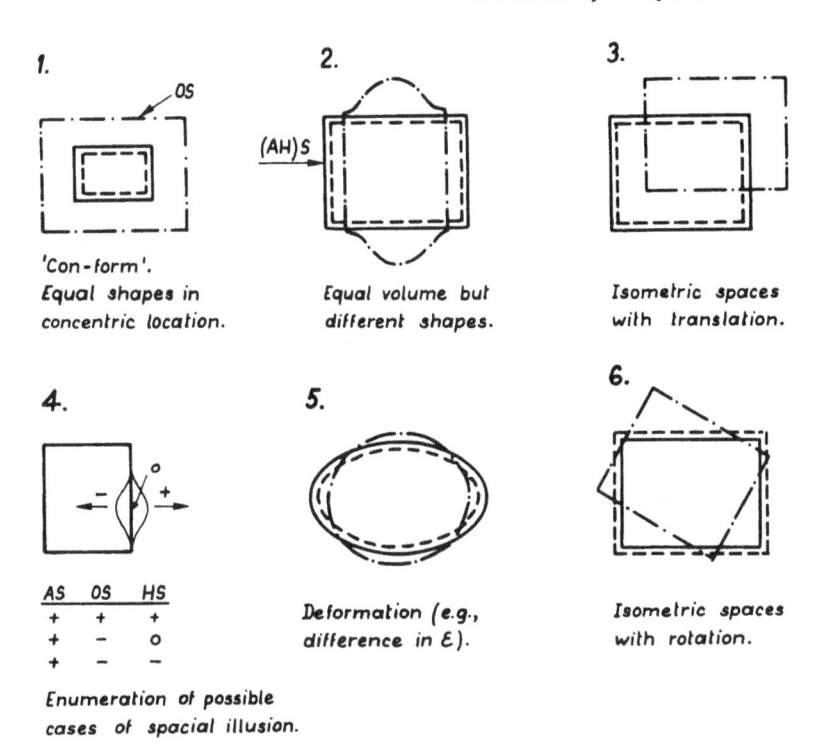

1. 'Con-form'. Equal shapes in concentric location.

2. Equal volume but different shapes.

3. Isometric spaces with translation.

4. Enumeration of possible cases of spacial illusion.

AS	OS	HS
+	+	+
+	−	0
+	−	−

5. Deformation (e.g., difference in E).

6. Isometric spaces with rotation.

Figure 3.19. *Cases of illusion of multisensory space identity.*

To create either of the illusions of location mentioned above, the architect must 'push' the impression of one or two of the envelopes toward (−) or away from (+) the observer (see 4 in Figure 3.19). The effect is obviously heightened when one moves one way, one the other. There are 24 possible arrangements of the relative positions of the three envelopes (+, −, and 0). We can eliminate the cases +++, —, and 000 because these affect only the shape and volume impression of the polysensory space, not its identity (viz., in these cases the envelopes all move together in the same direction).

Of course, this sort of combinatorial enumeration is 'mechanical' to the extent that it includes cases which are of no practical use. Yet we hold to the approach because it is exhaustive and may draw attention to cases hitherto overlooked. We must avoid, however, inferring from this enumeration the false notion that the various unisensory illusions function on the polysensory level in a simple additive way. If two senses convey the same illusion to the observer, we can expect this multisensory rhyming to give a false confirmation of one by the other. There is no guarantee that the effect will be cumulative by addition; even sudden disappearance of the effect can take place. These effects must be measured experimentally in the proper multisensory context.

320 Communication through architecture

Concerning optemes, acoustemes, and haptemes, each operates through any or all of the three types of surface characteristics: (1) the structure, or texture, of the surface, (2) the manner of reflection, (3) the intensity of reflection. The last determines whether the space is a free or a bound form.

These three types exist in all three sense modalities, giving ($3^3=$) 27 possible combinations which, multiplied by the number of possible 'envelope-moving' combinations, come to 648 cases of illusion, each different from the other either in the effect intended or in the means used to achieve it. Further, we recall that each of the three types of surface characteristic has a large number of modalities within it, different for each class of sensory envelope, and so counted individually for each space. We can now see that the architect has, at least in theory, no less a wealth of combinations available within his media than does the composer or writer.

It is possible to conceive of some synthetic materials whose characteristics might even combine different illusory stimuli, e.g., between acoustic and haptic 'softness' of echo and touch. This is difficult, however, because the scale of 'minimum separables' differs among senses.

Finally, the architect can enhance the illusion of the envelope's receding or advancing by varying its intensity of reflection, i.e., by making it a bound instead of a free morpheme. A bound sensory space loses some of its autonomy and depends on other spaces for support; it can thus more easily be 'moved' or made to seem coincident with another sensory space.

Past findings: A critical review We now look for any equvalencies or internal relationships which may exist between specific optemes, acoustemes, and haptemes. If they exist, the architect could use them to produce illusions in multisensory space impression which go beyond the simple addition of unisensory effects, a kind of heightened synthesis ($v*a*h$ where * is not + but, e.g., ×; visual = v, auditory = a, haptic = h.)

We know that certain colors 'push back' an optical surface, as do certain reverberation qualities in the acoustical space. Is there a relation between the length of the respective light and sound waves involved in resonance?

In fact, why not avail ourselves of the insights granted to certain chosen ones, like the German Eidetikers, who perceive deep relations between impressions in different sense departments? This approach holds the promise that, beyond the contingency of individual senses, we will find pure forms (cf. Handel), as the gestaltists hoped. Perhaps we may discover that common sense dear to scholasticism: For our immediate concern, the architectural media, we see the prospect of composition which is not merely optical, not even polysensorial, but supersensorial.

We find discussions of equivalency between color and touch in Descartes. Goethe, in his *Farbenlehre*, posits a relation between colors and music. Wellek observes colored hearing, or synopsia, and colored olfaction too. McDonald Crichtley (1975) discusses synalgia, a constant association of certain sense impressions, e.g., color, with sensations of pain. All kinds of practitioners rush to any indication of intermodal associations, seeing them as objective relations between sources of stimuli, saying their perception is inevitable, and applying them as valid scientific findings. Pfeiffer (1966: 10-11) goes back to the 'temperature of the colors', warm and cool. Villey (1914: ch. 4) sees hope for the blind in dermoptic sensibility. Thiel (1969: 56) applies the theory to architecture. We are grateful to Mrs. de Vienne, of the famous Reading Research Institute of Maine, for her assurance, 'It is certainly a scientific explanation of the relation between sonor vibration and color waves.'

Recent research allows us to explain the phenomena of intersensory associations. Their origin is not in some deep relation between stimuli per se, but in previous experience, where certain polysensory experiences produce constant associations, as of red blood with the pain of a laceration. The phenomena are also of the eidetic type, when the individual projects vivid interior imagery onto the exterior world. The latter are particularly common among children, and the occurrence of these associations early in life, when they are not rationally analyzed, reinforces their strength. Even embryos have concomitant sensory experiences.

Even the universality of certain associations is amenable to this explanation. The red of blood, for instance, is associated with warmth. This kind of association becomes 'codified' in the language and is as conventional as the language itself. Of course, polysensory association may act as inspiration for some artsists; Rimbaud, for one, associates vowel sounds with particular colors. But no treatment of such associations as objective phenomena has the least scientific foundation.

By contrast, research into the functioning of intermodal sensation shows that some sense departments are closer than others in their mode of operation, and so their effects are more easily conjoined.

We have seen that discrimination thresholds vary with the sense involved as well as with the task. The observer proceeds in one way comparing a shape with another one known to him (gnosis); in another way when describing a 'strange' one (proxis). In general, shape recognition is an operation of the 'logon', volume estimate one of the 'metron' (MacKay 1950); but both belong to the field we can properly call space perception. Research into the areas of orientation, locomotion, and localization has explored other capabilities in subjects. But when we try to use past findings about volume impression for our present inquiry we encounter the recurring problem that most of the research was done on convex objects rather than concave ones, which are our concern.

The problem of analogy and transposition of results becomes even more complicated in the context of multisensory space; a complex interaction occurs among the senses and poses new challenges in addition to those of unisensory spaces. The architect can use this fact in two ways. By exploiting the difficulty of localizing the various unisensory spaces which are simultaneously present, he can confuse the subject and gain freedom to create illusory effects. On the other hand, he can simplify the multisensory composition into a polysensory space and provide the subject with a more precise impression, since the joint effort of the senses now results in lower discrimination thresholds.

We have already discussed the investigations of J. J. Gibson in our chapters on visible communication and on optical space. Gibson also looks for a method of information processing common to all the sensory modalities and tries to detach the individual systems from the sensory inputs peculiar to them. He argues that one type of energy which stimulates specific receptors can be replaced by another (1966: 53). This free substitution seems attractive and relevant in a discussion of polysensory spaces, but the theory is open to objection on several grounds. Primarily, the possibility of substituting one type of energy for another as a source of information is extremely difficult to substantiate by evidence, since no perceptual system can be completely detached from all stimuli (1966: 46). For this very reason the energy inputs from the sensory receptors remain the objective points of reference in the process of space impression. In fact, instead of 'desensorizing' the perceptual systems, Gibson's theory tends to generalize a particular theory of the visual system, viz., 'visual kinesthesis' (1966: 200) to apply to all other sense departments. Johansson (1970: 67-74) sees clearly that in Gibson's theory proprioception, as 'purposive action' (J. J. Gibson 1966: 33-34), especially when it is realized by locomotion, fills the role of integrator of the perceptual systems. Gibson himself concedes that his theory of the perceptual systems 'goes hand in hand with a theory of proprioception'.

Gibson is not, in fact, an expert in acoustics (1966: 293) or haptics, and so his theory is one-sidedly visual. Indeed, the thrust of it leads him to eliminate the stationary impression as a stage of optical space exploration, the fifth stage (1966: 194).

Other contributors are inspired by problems raised by the gestaltists and try to treat them with the most sophisticated experimental design and setups. They distinguish clearly between experiments concerning the systems of spatial orientation and of space analysis, and they admit the integration of stimuli on more than one level.

Localization has to do with the subject's situating himself in a space so as to make active movements within it or even manipulate it. These activities involve an orienting system, an 'egocentric' space where distance and direction can be measured in absolute terms.

Recognition and discrimination of shapes are different tasks of perception, and use the shape 'analyzing system'. Held and Hein show that the angles and proportions which characterize a shape can be recognized by the subject as well as striking points like 'corners' (Held 1968: 347) or 'contour breaks' (Held and Hein 1967: 302) *without* involving the perception of 'direction, distance, and other magnitudes' (Held 1968: 318).

To contrast localization and shape recognition, we find in the literature distinctions between quantitative and structural (MacKay) and between vectorial representation and topological mapping (March). Experimental procedure needs clear operational definitions and must avoid using terms as synonyms without definition, such as 'Gestalt', 'form', 'configuration', 'structure', and 'pattern'. This makes the findings vague and liable to 'epistemological deterioration'.

Most of us seem predisposed toward accepting dichotomic, bipolar systems (right, left) based on simple linear ordering. But the polarity between the task of orienting, involving metron, and that of shape recognition, involving logon, does not cover all perceptual tasks. Thus the estimate of volumetric magnitude, for example, requires measuring, without becoming a task of localization.

Nevertheless, the distinction bewteen the tasks of orientation and shape recognition lets us draw some useful conclusions. Held (1970: 318) states that 'locus specific information' is chiefly necessary for the control of our movements. In consequence, the absence of 'feedback from motor output' (Held and Hein 1967: 302), 'self-produced locomotion', 'motor-sensory feedback loop' (Held and Hein 1967: 100), and the 'lack of response-produced visual feedback' (Held 1968: 341) affect the orienting system almost exclusively. The control case is the 'movement-deprived animal' (Held 1970: 322) which loses practically nothing of its capacity for 'figure recognition' (cf. J. J. Gibson's theory).

We can make the following observations:

– Research on spatial orientation systems has no relevance to the subject of this chapter.
– Since shape recognition is not affected primarily by 'motor-sensory feedback', research on shape discrimination by a static observer constitutes a valid stage in the inquiry.
– In the polysensory context, the proprioceptive component is not very useful for visual shape recognition. In the strictly defined area of shape recognition, all the senses operate in a relatively autonomous way (Handel and Buffardi 1968) and intersensorial feedback, like other corrective interventions, has little learning effect.

We reemphasize the limits of these remarks: they bear upon shape recognition only, and have little to do with the comparison of volume. The subject's capacity to perceive the coincidence of the various sensory envelopes — i.e., their relative location — belongs to the metric field which, again, is not usually the case with shape recognition.

There are two drawbacks to the use of the findings of Held's team and other researchers for learning about multisensory space impression related to gestaltist influence:

For all practical purposes the research was done solely on visual shape recognition, not multisensory (Révész 1950: 149-150).

In the space recognition research, investigators use confusing terminology and often ill-defined concepts. After looking through the 40 works which Zusne (1970) presents, after surveying 2500; Haber's 80 (1970), after checking 4,000; and the bibliography of Sleight and Duvoisin (1952), which includes over 2,000 titles, we can state that no definition of 'form perception' is so drawn as to be clearly delimited from the metric estimation task. In this entire literature, the term 'shape' as distinct from 'form' conveys no precise geometrical concept. Barthley (1958), a gestaltist, calls the target of observation 'form' and its perception, 'shape'. But for Alluisi (1960: 195-203) 'shape' is the stimulus, 'form' the response. Held also uses 'form' in the unspecified manner of the gestaltists.

In constructing the repertory of the architectural medium we use only experimentally operational concepts. Thus shape is defined in the geometrical sense by homothetic transformation. We also wish to enlarge the repertory to its full potential, yet maintain it on the primary, sensory level, not the secondary, symbolic one (Francès in Piaget 1967: 188-189; see also Hebb's identity). For this reason we speak of 'impression' (not perception) obtained through paired comparisons without the necessity of previous knowledge, and we discuss it as shape discrimination, not form recognition.

Wapner and Wapner (1957) achieved the development of an axiomatized theory of the sensoritonic field. Held uses it here and there, but does not cite it. Certain of its six postulates are relevant to our concern with multisensory space impression.

These authors regard space perception as a result of the integration of all sensory stimuli, acoustical, haptic, and optical, received at a given instance, whether external or internal in origin.

They maintain that an equivalent impression can be created by different combinations of subjective states and objective stimuli. The criterion for equivalence lies not in specific causes, but uniquely in the fact that all combinations, at the given moment, are equal on the sensoritonic level. Thus in this respect it is of no interest whether the stimuli are transmitted by extroceptive (e.g., visual), proprioceptive, or introceptive (e.g., visceral) modalities (postulate III). The architect, of course, is mainly interested in those impressions which can be created by the manipulation of objective space attributes and which produce more or less invariable states in the organism (cf. postulate II). What is important here is that the same state can be produced by different objective spaces through illusion, and by different combinations of sensory spaces through varying the multisensory intricacy of the unisensory spaces. Equivalence has to do with the total impression, and postulate V lists three kinds, one of which is intersensory substitution (Scagnelli, 'intersensory equivalence'). Under postulate VI they deal with vicariant transmission (cf. J. J. Gibson 1966: 3). Postulates III and V refer to the effects of stimuli which are merely present at the moment of observation without being its target. In our context, these stimuli are the noncoextensive sensory spaces which, by their simple presence – in multisensory awareness – can disturb the shape discrimination and volume comparison of two spaces of the same unisensory type and also raise their thresholds.

Illusions of coextensive identity

We have noted that the architect, by the use of surface characteristics, can alter the apparent relative location of coextensive (uni)sensory spaces. The reverse of this occurs when two or more spaces do not coincide, but the fact is concealed from the observer.

For the design of a series of experiments on this effect we distinguish three basic cases, which can also be combined:

(1) The real objective volume difference bewteen the spaces disappears.
(2) The real objective shape difference disappears (see 2 in Figure 3.19).
(3) The pure case of apparent dislocation of polysensory space occurs when isometric sensory spaces are translated or one space undergoes a rotation in relation to the others (see 3 and 6 in Figure 3.19).

Experiments will tell us the cause of the impression of noncoincidence by determining how the subject resolves conflicting impression. For example, in the first case, the response to the question about volume attributed to the 'new', apparently polysensory, space will show whether the smaller space seemed larger to the observer, or the reverse.

Some indications from past findings It is difficult to find any research directly relevant to our present concern. Most investigations in the field of resolution of sensory conflict and illusory coincidençe have been devoted to problems of orientation and localization, not to space impression (Piaget; Aubrée 1968: 5); the results, therefore, have very limited relevance to our concern especially the problems encountered in cases (1) and (2).

Jackson (1953: 52-65) studied conflict in localization of visual and auditory sources and found that the subject follows the visual input more than the auditory. Further, in the presence of conflicting visual signals, auditory localization suffers in both precision and speed.

Rock and his associates carried out experiments prompted by Berkeley's statement, 'Touch educates vision.' (Rock and Harris 1967: 96). They wanted to prove that, for localization and orientation, the precision of vision (1967: 97-99) 'captures' (J. C. Hay) and standardizes the haptic impression, thus producing a 'unified or unitary impression' (Rock and Victor 1964). To their credit, they developed a highly sophisticated methodology. For example, they considered the possibility of unconscious tactual input (1967: 103), and they elicited responses in drawing, rather than language, becuase it 'involves both vision and touch' (1967: 97) and eliminates the 'Whorf effect', the visual bias of language. These precautions could not, of course, eliminate the bias resulting from the fact that all the subjects came from a lettered and clothed culture (Montagu 1971: 114; K. Stewart 1975; 105). The results of Walther's manual skill tests show that Brazilian subjects with lower IQ performed better through touch than European ones with higher IQ. We must consider this seriously, as well as Révész's doctrine of 'optified haptics' (1950: 103-104), before concluding that the physiological capacity of vision singles it out to be the 'clearinghouse' for all sensory inputs.

Scagnelli (1969) presents a better-balanced view of the problems of intersensory perception, if only because he has no polemic purpose. He finds that normal subjects tend to receive more information through vision. If 'unfamiliar geometrical designs are encoded via visual' they are better recalled than if they are encoded via haptic. Yet he makes the necessary reservations; the difference is only significant if subjects have higher education and if the recognition task is mediated by verbal. These parameters clearly qualify the award of hegemony to visual, as related to (cultural) socialization and not to physiological base.

It is important to note that Scagnelli's experiment was, like Rock's, bisensory, not trisensory. But it differed from Rock's in that the subject's task was to *recognize* geometrical design.

At the present stage of the growth of our knowledge, it would be an arbitrary and paralyzing restriction to accept the visual as the normative standard. Even Vurpillot, who tries to make optical representation of polysensory space the only possible one, adds the qualification 'far-space'. The implication is clear; in near-space the haptic predominates. And the haptic system increases the effectiveness of dynamic exploration.

Polysensory Meshing

Once the subject supposes the coextension of the various sensory spaces, whether it is real or apparent, he begins to pool the sensory inputs, using one class to check another to improve volume estimate and shape discrimination. On the other hand, in noncoextensive multisensory space, when the subject tries to define each component, unisensory space, the target-irrelevant data from the other spaces interfere and reduce his perceptive efficiency. A third way of exploring the multisensory field involves intersensory or cross-modal comparison. Here the subject compares volume or shape of simultaneously present spaces of different sense modalities which are not perceived as coextensive.

Handel and Buffardi (1968) studied pattern recognition in various uni- and bisensory presentation series. Although they worked in temporal, not spatial patterns, their results are worth our attention. To compare relative 'ease of (pattern) identification' (1968: 1,026), they presented patterns in all possible bisensory combinations, as well as the three 'main' unisensory modes. Using as stimuli light (v), tone (a), and vibration (t), they presented the cases a, t, and v, and the bisensory cases at, av, and tv.

They find, among other things, that when the subject is to recognize one series of patterns by variation of location and another by variation of sense modality, the probability of success is greater in the second case. This agrees with the observation on temporal pattern recognition made by P. Fraisse, that signals are integrated in priority by the sensory modalities.

Comparing the three modalities we find that neither the individual efficiency nor the possible combinations are interchangeable. As for the relative efficiency of the individual senses in the temporal pattern recognition; the acoustical does best and next the tactual, with the visual last. Among the bisensory combinations, the visuo-tactual improves efficiency most markedly. In fact, it is the only combination in which the two senses together produce recognition faster than either would alone. Remember, however, that the context of these findings is temporal; they cannot be applied directly to the recognition, still less to the discrimination, of the shapes of various sensory spaces simultaneously presented. Still, these results suggest some physiological relationship in the reception processes of the various organs, which may possible also be effective in space discrimination. In fact, both the acoustic and haptic systems respond to vibratory events (Handel and Buffardi (1968: 1028) refer to von Békéssy); the difference is only in the amplitude of the waves (Chauchard 1965: 37-39). This may explain the fact that audible and palpable signals are more often confused than is the visible with either of them. Moreover, temporal patterns presented alternatively in both the acoustical and haptic modes are less well recognized than those presented in each individually.

Can we make any further heuristic use of these results?

In experiments about multisensory space impressions, the subject's very first task is to determine the relative location of the component unisensory spaces. This is a task of localization, but we cannot directly apply to it findings about the localization of primary sources of stimuli, e.g., light or sound, because the space envelope is not a primary source. It is localized by its function as a reflecting surface, i.e., as a secondary source of stimuli. If the subject reports that the component spaces are not coextensive, we proceed, through the series of questions outlined, to have him locate them and distinguish their volume and shape through paired comparison. If, however, the subject reports a polysensory space, in which all the sensory envelopes coincide, we are able to study, again through paired comparison, the process of information pooling. That is what interests us now.

J. J. Gibson looked at the perceptual system (1966: 14-16, 50, 53) in the following aspects: mode of attention, receptive units, anatomy and activity of the organs, and, on the other side, the stimuli available and the external information obtained.

We noted that hearing and touch respond to similar vibratory events and that the data obtained are not redundant, due to the specialization of the relevant organs for vibrations with different amplitudes. Vision, on the other hand, like touch, operates by successive fixations (Révész 1950: 130; cf. Vurpillot 1967: 102) and thus achieves precision. Audition gives an immediate total impression of the space which is also more independent of the observer's location. For this reason the auditory space impression is even further removed from the spatial orientation than is the visual or tactual. Von Hornbostel (1966: 55) sums up the comparison: 'Touch and vision are overlapping senses and with redundant input of information. Taste-smell are superordinate perceptual systems.' Thus in the cooperation of the senses, a process not additive but 'kaleidoscopic' (Gibson), we have perceptual systems and subsystems. For our concern we can say that 'optemes' and 'haptemes' complement each other in space impressions; for example, in a polysensory space where a line of inflection also separates areas different in both color and texture.

There are two parameters involved in the polysensory impression: (1) observation time, a parameter of the stimulation process itself; and (2) the absolute dimension of the observed space.

(1) The temporal parameter has two aspects, duration and speed, the latter itself having two phases, external propagation and internal processing of stimuli.

When external propagation is slow in comparison with the dimensions of the space and the location of two sense organs, as in stereoacoustic reception, speed gives cues to space impression through the time differential. Adding now the duration necessary for the sensory input processing, we make the hypothesis that various polysensory space impressions can be 'prejudged' differently according to which of the sense departments produces the space impression first.

We are all acquainted with the delayed reception of thunder after we see a flash of lightning as an example of the difference in the speed of propagation between a mechanical and a photonic event. Most architectural spaces are not large enough for this effect to impinge on the space impression; but the timers at an indoor track meet still watch for the flash of the starter's pistol, and not just out of habit.

In internal processing, stimuli from the chemoreceptors go slowest. Because of the simultaneity of auditory reception, if the duration of the observation is short, the acoustical component predominates. When the duration is longer, thanks to the effort of the visual process, it increases the precision of the space impression. Even more time is necessary for the complete visual input because this field is more oriented than the auditory field. By a similar step-by-step process palpatation brings new and greater detail to the mental mapping of the polysensory space. The auditory system can make little or no use of additional time for enriching the space impression.

(2) Finally, architectural space, being by definition an envelope for human beings and groups, varies only within certain absolute spatial dimensions, where the efficiency of the sense organs also varies. In near space the haptic impression dominates, in the middle range the visual; beyond a certain range, polysensory space can only be perceived by auditory means. In all these cases, of course, we are speaking only about the static impression, where neither time nor movement is allowed without limit. In fact, practical limitation is the very essence of our space concept and of architecture in particular.

OUTLOOK FOR FUTURE EXPERIMENTS: QUESTIONS AND HYPOTHESES

In comparison with unisensory space experiments, the polysensory area is a much larger field for experimentation, specifically in the following ways:

— the impression of unisensory spaces in paired comparison (AS_i, OS_i, HS_i) is now replaced by polysensory comparisons ($PS_{i[a, v, h]}$) or by partially polysensory ones ($[OA]S_i$, $[AH]S_i$, $[OH]S_i$);
— the relative localization of noncoextensive unisensory spaces;
— the paired comparison of spaces of the same sense modality in the interfering presence of other sensory spaces;
— the intersensory comparison of volume and shape impressions of spaces simultaneously present but not coextensive.

A point should be made about the practical possibility of effecting the separation of the various sensory spaces. At the present stage of the development of construction materials, not all separations are possible. More precisely, not all can be effected in both directions, one nesting the other. On the other hand, some remarkable developments have occurred which meet extremely difficult requirements, such as the isolation of an autonomous osmotic space by electric filtering alone. More usually, however, the separation is imperfect, as in the case of a glass barrier which can be detected by its reflections, and the desired free form of the unisensory space devolves into a bound one.

1. Polysensory Space Identity: Illusions of Coextension

As we know, illusions of coextension can go two ways; either noncoinciding envelopes are perceived as coinciding, or the reverse. A special case of such illusions is the bound form of sensory space which is perceived on one side as a free one, e.g., one-way glass taken for a fully isolating optical envelope. It may occur in various cases of multisensory intricacy, e.g., $(OA)S$ vs. HS.

Illusions of coextension can have the following causes:

— the impression of an isometric transformation, i.e., translation or rotation (see 3 and 6 in Figure 3.19);
— homothetic transformation (see 1 in Figure 3.19); or
— 'deformation' as topological transformation (see 5 in Figure 3.19).

To effect these illusions the architect can use the surface characteristics of the sensory envelopes, those submorphemic features we call optemes, acoustemes, and haptemes. He deals not only with the manner and quantity of the envelope's reflection, but also with its relative 'permeability', which distinguishes the bound form from the free one.

Normally the architect causes 'affirmative' illusions through a specific sensory envelope. He can use another envelope for 'support', false confirmation of the illusion, or design the other envelopes so that they at least 'tolerate' the unisensory illusion.

Optemes are particularly useful for creating illusory deformations, as we saw in Vasarhely's painting. By applying homogeneous optemes such as mirroring, the architect can stretch or shrink the space. The optical effect can be so strong that, instead of contributing to the impression of increase in the polysensory space as a whole, it causes the polysensory space to seem to dissolve into its component unisensory spaces, which cease to give the impression of coextension.

Acoustemes have little effect on shape impression. If used for illusion, they affect rather the impression of volume, e.g., an absorbing envelope seems to stretch the polysensory space. Thus it does not seem promising to explore the effects of acoustemes per se, separate from other sensory effects. Acoustemes can indeed be supportive, especially in combination with haptemes, e.g., to create an illusion of coincidence.

Haptemes have the unique function of providing final confirmation, solid proof, of a space impression. For this reason, they are unlikely to succeed as principal causes of a space illusion; they can, however, serve as 'false witnesses'. Moreover, some kinds of hapteme can 'soften' the starkness of solid presence; elastic or furry surfaces (cf. exposition of soft sculptures in Zürich, November, 1979) are less likely to serve as solid references, and therefore they allow illusory effects in other sense departments. Materials warm or cold to the touch can positively enhance the impression of expanded or contracted space, respectively.

The development of sophisticated construction materials, to the point where they allow the perfect separation of any space from any other in any combination, would facilitate the task of the architect as a creator of illusions. He could fully exploit cases where the normal observer would make strong assumptions about the coextension of certain spaces, separating them in fact while confident that they will be perceived as being together. Of course, subjects learn to anticipate the new effects; the 'illusionist' always designs for a 'naive' observer.

Given the materials available today, the most promising direction for the creation of illusions of coextension seems to be the combination of free sensory morphemes with bound ones. Use of one-way glass is shown in the following figure:

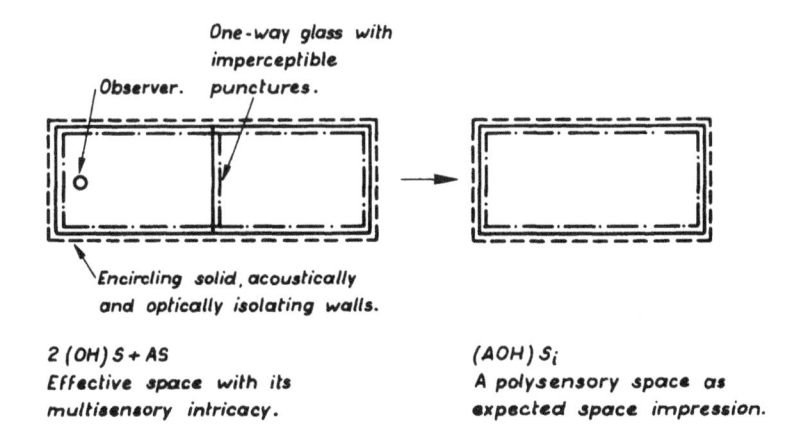

One-way glass with imperceptible punctures.
Observer.

Encircling solid, acoustically and optically isolating walls.

$2(OH)S + AS$
Effective space with its multisensory intricacy.

$(AOH)S_i$
A polysensory space as expected space impression.

2. Discriminability of Two Polysensory Spaces

After the paired comparisons of unisensory spaces, viz., AS_1 vs. AS_2, OS_1 vs. OS_2, and HS_1 vs. HS_2, we now encounter four new cases of conjunction: one is complete, the polysensory space: $(AOH)S = PS$, PS_1 vs. PS_2; three are partial: $(AO)S_1$ vs. $(AO)S_2$, $(AH)S_1$ vs. $(AH)S_2$, and $(OH)S_1$ vs. $(OH)S_2$.

It is our general hypothesis that discrimination thresholds are never higher in polysensory conjunctions than in unisensory impressions, and are

332 *Communication through architecture*

most often lower. For the impression of volume, the threshold will be quantitatively lower; for shape, those with closer relationship defined in terms of geometrical transformation become discernible, e.g., ellipsoids with smaller ϵ difference. A quantitative restriction of this hypothesis is that the lowering of thresholds cannot be understood as additive; according to 'sensoristasis' the lowering of the threshold will be less than expected from the addition of different sensory data.

In the case of a fully polysensory space the application of the hypothesis is unrestricted. In all cases of partial coextension we assume that the third sense is unavailable, as in darkness, and so cannot interfere with the partial impression.

Research in adjacent fields suggests the following hypothesis: the discrimination threshold of (OH)S is never higher, and usually lower, than that of either OS or HS alone.

The combination of acoustical space with other sensory spaces improves the difference threshold of the volume impression. This is especially important when the observation time is short. The acoustical space impression depends mainly on reverberation time, which is a function of the ratio between volume and surface. For this reason the auditory component of the space impression improves discrimination in the special case where the difference consists in texture. This microshape difference strongly affects the superficial extent of the polysensory space's envelope and exerts its influence on the space impression through the isoconcavity indicatrix V^2/S^3, while the visual component of the space impression does not take it into account.

3. Interference of Other Non-Coextensive Sensory Spaces with the Comparison of Two Isosensory Spaces

We turn to the case of a space simultaneously present with the observed, or target, space but not coextensive. The effect of such a space is parasitic; if it does anything to the thresholds of discrimination for the target spaces, it raises them. We hypothesize, in fact, that the presence of the parasitic space is more disturbing as it varies less from the target space. All findings must be based on paired comparisons.

(1) Interference by acoustical space:

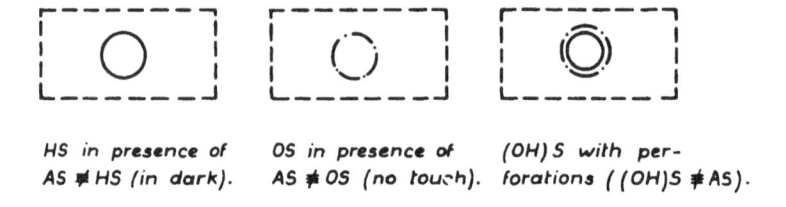

HS in presence of   OS in presence of   (OH)S with per-
AS ≠ HS (in dark).   AS ≠ OS (no touch).   forations ((OH)S ≠ AS).

Acoustical interference raises the threshold of volume discrimination for the impression of *OS*, *HS*, and *(OH)S*. It does not affect the shape discrimination of the object spaces.

(2) Interference by optical space: a parasitic optical space destroys the already doubtful possibility of shape discrimination in acoustical space. It also interferes with the haptic space (*HS*) impression, and so with the impression of *(AH)S*, in terms of both shape and volume.

(3) Interference by haptic space: a parasitic haptic space may affect the acoustical space impression, and very likely will interfere with the optial space impression in the same way as did the parasitic optical space with the target haptic space.

Interesting hypotheses can be developed as a function of the subject's cultural origin. The parameter would be the literacy or illiteracy of the society.

Unisensory interference occurs in nine cases, as below; to complete the table of possible cases we add the three in which bisensory spaces interfere:

OS → *HS*	*AS* → *OS*	*HS* → *AS*	*(AO)S* → *HS*
→ *AS*	→ *HS*	→ *OS*	*(AH)S* → *OS*
→ *(AH)S*	→ *(OH)S*	→ *(AO)S*	*(OH)S* → *AS*

It has not been our purpose to discuss systematically all the possible cases and hypotheses, but simply to give some indications of directions for research.

4. *Intersensory Space Comparison*

There are architectural morphemes in which the various sensory spaces are not coextensive. The experimenter must ask two series of questions about them to determine, (1) how the subject locates the component spaces, and (2) how he discriminates shape and volume among them, i.e., the thresholds.

Questions about the relative positions of the component spaces involve characteristics which are not intrinsic to the spaces themselves. The problem is one of intersensory localization, in which the observer's efficiency depends strongly upon his position.

If the acoustical space undergoes isometric transformation only, it is more difficult to perceive the location difference than in the case of the other sensory spaces. If the noncoextension comes not only from isometric but also from other homothetic transformations, the volume difference is a good cue to indicate the noncoextensive nature of a multisensory space, because volume, as we noted before, is the space characteristic best perceived by the acoustical system.

For volume and shape comparison of the component spaces in a compound morpheme, the simultaneity of their presence makes the task easier than in the case of successive presentation of same-sense spaces for paired comparison because memory is less involved. Yet this advantage is slight compensation for the additional difficulties inherent in the intersensory comparison. Thresholds are sure to be higher, and the problem of localization makes volume and shape discrimination far more complex. The field is an extremely complicated one, and so will be the last to be explored.

18

Space Impression Through Dynamic Exploration

'Time is imaginary space.'

Whorf

THE MORPHOLOGICAL CONCEPT AND THE DYNAMIC EXPLORATION OF SPACE

We first discussed the sensory space perceived individually, as a free form. Next we dealt with the compound architectural morpheme, carrying over from the first series the condition that the observer be stationary. We now remove that condition, and find two main areas of investigation before us: the dynamic aspect of the exploration and the kinetic.

By 'dynamic' we mean that the subject not only uses passively obtained data to explore a space, but also actively seeks material by motor activity (efferent versus afferent). This kind of input is not part of the impression in static or even noninert (Piéron 1968: 6) states, i.e., through stationary movement (without acceleration, negative or positive), or transport. Of course, sensory input from motor activity does not come from displacement exclusively; some muscular activity is involved in any afferent process, e.g., the eye muscles involved in the space impression discussed before. Some authors emphasize this excessively, even where sensory input from the muscles is negligible. For our discussion, dynamic exploration means that motion is not merely a performance, but a source of information. A further aspect of the dynamic exploration is that the observer is in control of his own movements, start, orientation, direction, speed, and stop; therefore he can devise an overall dynamic strategy, adjusting the sequence of sensory input through feedbacks. We will see that this dynamic strategy — with appreciable rate of acceleration, positive or negative — is possible without the observer's own motor activity.

For space exploration, displacement as such presents an awkward problem. In a multisensory composition whose spaces are not coextensive, kinetic

336 Communication through architecture

exploration can be defined unambiguously only if the experimenter confines the subject's movements to the area common to all the spaces, which we have called the shared parcel. This assures that the spatial envelope remains homogeneous for all sense departments during the whole exploration (see Figure 3.20).

Architectural text.

Its acoustical spaces (AS).

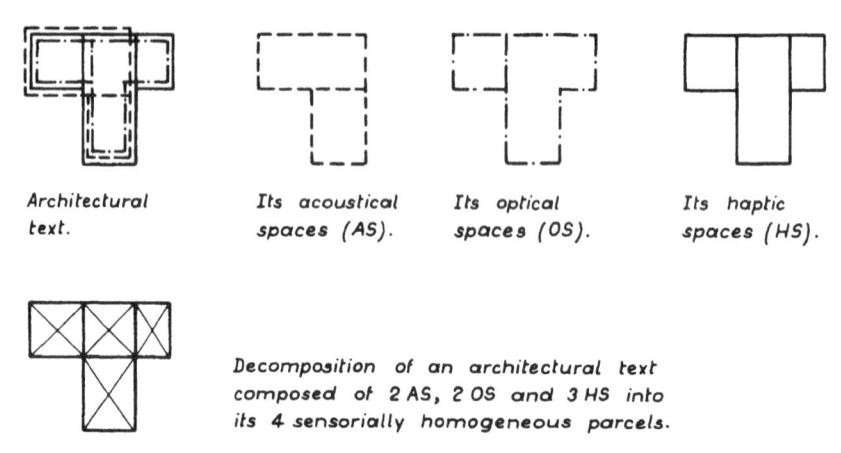

Its optical spaces (OS).

Its haptic spaces (HS).

Decomposition of an architectural text composed of 2 AS, 2 OS and 3 HS into its 4 sensorially homogeneous parcels.

Figure 3.20. *Sensorily homogeneous space parcels.*

Kinetic exploration involves the choice of multiple points of observation, the possibility of rotation of other movement, e.g., of the limbs, which does not change the observation point, and movements which are, in mathematical terms, translations. Thus, kinetic exploration implies a set of observation points and organization in terms of sequence and speed.

Clearly, kinetic exploration is most closely related to haptic space impression. The haptic space experience, even sessile, depends more on movement than the experience of optical and acoustical space. Moreover, the haptic envelope will obviously confine within itself the kinetic exploration of other sensory spaces, but this has practical effect only if it is inside the other spaces. This haptic limitation to the exploration of any sensory space is even stronger if we consider the human explorer as an earth-bound biped (Robinson 1973), whose movement is restricted to a bidimensional platform.

We thus distinguish two stages of exploration, the rotational and the translational or mobile. We can visualize the distinction by associating the rotational stage with embryonic movements in uterine space and the translational stages with infantile movement after the release from the umbilical cord. Like the comparison between still and motion pictures, these stages are not only heuristic devices but represent effective stages in the genetic reconstruction of space impressions (Piaget), where successive steps are increasingly rich in sensory data.

Dynamic Reading of Architectural Space

Dynamic exploration, like others, by definition proceeds from interior points of the sensory space. But because the various observation points are not equivalent for obtaining a space impression, the sequence of these points is important. The observer has his choice among possibly innumerable routes; but no matter what his choice, his first impression is always determined by the entry point.

A monadal space (No access without destruction; e.g. a strong room) Paradigmatic valence $d(x) = 0$.

Spaces with paradigmatic valence $- d(x)-1 -$ differing only in door position.

Spaces equivalent in morphology and paradigmatic valence: $d(x) = 2$.

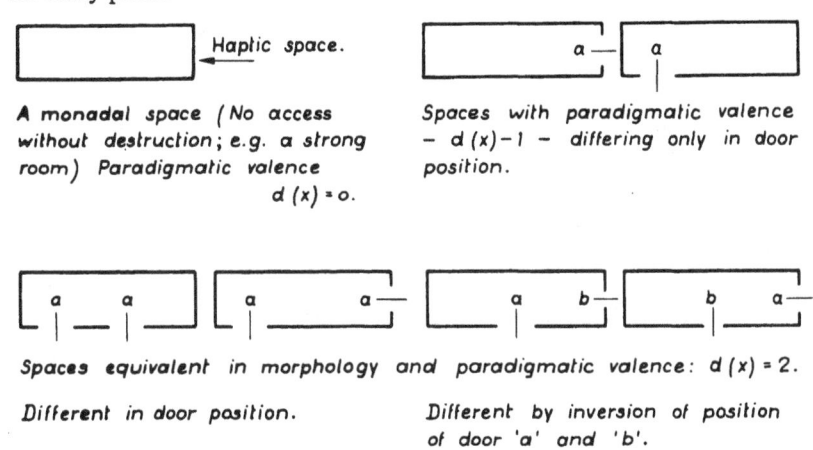

Different in door position.

Different by inversion of position of door 'a' and 'b'.

Figure 3.21. *Morphological equivalence and paradigmatic valence of space.*

Apart from artificial situations, entry points are the doors which connect spaces either to one another, thus creating space systems, or to atmospheric space. They are provisory openings, not definitive joiners of specific spaces. They are designed already in the roomraum as a prefabricated unit, but transcend its strict morphology as defined by shape, volume, and envelope characteristics. Since the space with its doors can be integrated into a variety of systems, the door specification relates the morpheme to the syntactic construction through the intermediary, syntagmatic level. We distinguish two types of door characteristics, one expressed as discrete value, the other as continuous:

– the number of doors, which gives the paradigmatic valence of the space (see Figure 3.25), and
– the emplacement and size of the doors (see Figure 3.21).

'Space, time, and architecture'

We take the title for this section from the famous book by the Zurich engineer Giedion (1963). Since its original publication in 1940 the book has been translated into many languages and has been widely influential. Gropius, in his preface to it, says the work equals that of Toynbee in prophetic value. Others, like Hajnoczi, regard it as a reinterpretation of our traditional concept of architectural space. In the introduction we find the promise of an 'objective analysis' of the 'secret synthesis in our civilization'.

Yet a survey of the literature indicates that Giedon's thesis, that the solid forms of architecture are received in sequence through subjective experience, is not a new idea at all. In fact, we consider the importance attributed to the work greatly exaggerated — even in the light of all three volumes of *Eternel Present,* of which the quoted is one volume. The methodology is prescientific and, with respect to empirical operationality, the concepts are no more useful than those of the French philosopher E. A. Chartier, called Alain.

Like most attempts at synthesis, the work begins with an arbitrary historical survey of the architectural art. It starts with the monumental external effects of the pyramids, and sees the creation of enclosed spaces as a subsequent stage. After the transitional period of the XIXth century (Paul Frankl), architecture reaches its zenith with the synthesis of external and internal (cf. von Lier). As a faithful disciple of Wölfflin and Gropius, Giedon thinks that Dadaism and Futurism have essentially and comprehensively defined architectural space.

In this doctrine of the inseparability of time and space we see an unwarranted extension of Einsteinian concepts. In practical terms, architecture becomes dynamic through the automobile; it leaves behind the classic catalogue of regular shapes and becomes streamlined. As an engineer, Giedon sees the hyperbolic paraboloid as the new ideal shape, both streamlined and geometrically describable.

Looking at architecture as we do from the viewpoint of the science of social behavior, we prefer the theory of architecture of B. Zevi, who considers (interior) space the essence of the art, and the history of it by E. O. James (1965), who begins not with the pyramids but with paleolithic caverns. We are convinced that architecture can only be specified by its dual purpose, to create a durable shelter from the elements and to provide the necessary 'intimacy' for polysensory communication.

The aims of framing and stability in no way preclude the existence of mobile spaces or deny that space exploration takes place in a dynamic sequence over time. But, as often happens, the scientific approach to the description of physical phenomena is unattractive to authors with prophetic intent. It is a slow and complicated process, with no place for quick conclusions. Its reward, however, is reliable and lasting information. There is, of course, a place for prophecy in this and all fields, as well as for scientific approach; but the distinction must always be kept clear.

Actualization of the Space Impression

Meyer-Eppler (1969) and Klaus (1968: 570) classified sign systems according to the type and number of spatiotemporal dimensions involved. Only the manual alphabet used by deaf-mutes includes all four dimensions; architecture has three.

But time does somehow have its place in architecture; it seems worthwhile to examine this more carefully. In the first place, the space impression is not based on a single instantaneous exposure; the observer reconstructs a completely adjacent order on the basis of successive impressions. In more technical terms, we say that the observer identifies geometrical configuration through its aliases, which are present in successive impressions. Let us be clear; time is not involved in architectural communication in the same way that space is, even in the case of dynamic exploration, where the successivity of sensory input is explicitly admitted. True, all space impressions are constituted this way, but only insofar as all sense impressions occur over time.

A photograph, even if it is panoramic or produced by a laser beam, presents an image of an optical space made from an instantaneous exposure. The observer can examine it repeatedly. A recorded sequence of echoes actualizes the acoustical space to the subject in a more rigorously imposed way. The static impression of haptic space, defined by simultaneity, is more difficult to determine because of the observer's deep involvement in this class of impressions.

The space impression depends on the processing of data, over time, which are inherent in the space; but the observer in this case has far more freedom in regulating the process than any other, e.g., a concert audience. Let us consider the process of dynamic space exploration, which we take to be the most complete and complex one, including all the previously discussed stages, as well as the temporal aspect of the impression at its maximum.

We say the process is complete because the observer not only can use all his capacities in the exploration, but also has full control over the sequence in which and rate of speed at which he does so. By 'capacities' we mean not only afferent data of the senses available in stationary observation, but self-produced movement as well, which brings input from kinesthesia, sensation of direction, and speed change by vestibular proprioception.

We distinguish two principal stages of the gathering of space impressions, stationary and dynamic. The most restricted case on the stationary level is the static, where the subject is in 'positional rack' (J. Cohen 1969: 59), rotation being prohibited and afferent input received in the passive state. To allow haptic exploration of a large space, the experimenter permits, during the first stage, not only rotation but also horizontal and vertical transport, as long as the movement remains rectilinear and the velocity constant and governed by someone other than the subject. This is the stationary stage, where no — or only negligible — reafferent input comes either from motor activity (kinesthesia) or from vestibular proprioception of speed change through the programming of the process by feedback.

Beside the information coming from the self-produced movement, there is a further possible benefit from dynamic programming, the *en route* use of feedback by which the subject himself optimizes the exploration process and selects his own changes of speed and direction.

There is a connection between our present topic and the stationary space impression discussed in the previous chapters. We refer to the eight stages in Gibson's proprioceptive theory of exploration of the visual surround. At the first level, optical space exploration can be simulated by a photographic image of a space based on instantaneous exposure. Not even at Gibson's fourth stage is the subject allowed to turn his head. At the fifth stage comes the zenith of the stationary exploration. Visual kinesthesis, with the ambient array at a moving convergence, occurs at stage 6 (J. J. Gibson 1966: 200).

But Gibson's theory, like Giedon's pictorial reading of the architecture, concerns only visual exploration; motor and proprioceptive input only complete visual perception, and haptic or polysensory space is generally ignored.

What are the specificities of dynamic exploration of space?

Still in the context of the stationary impression, we were able to consider its multisensory character, even though the displacement restriction proper to this stage prevented some of the sensory departments from contributing, especially the kinesthetic proprioceptor.

— At the first stage beyond the static impression, we add a multiplicity of observation points. Displacement per se is not yet more than a negative aspect, i.e., slow movement from point to point allows more to be forgotten.
— Further, the subject can choose his own path, thus determining the sequence of his impressions. The direction of the path is usually reversible and the subject may choose alternatives ($P_1 P_{2a} P_3$ or $P_1 P_{2b} P_3$). These are all objective data which can be managed by combinatorics. In the complete graph we can include directed graphs to indicate 'paths' and 'lines'. We show on the edges the time spent traveling in either direction and on the vertices the time spent standing at each point. In order to carry out this kind of enumeration we must transform the continuous nature of the possible orientations into discrete numbers.
— The observer can regulate all the temporal dimensions of his exploration, not only the time at various points but also the speed and acceleration of his displacements. It is important to note that the subject can alter the speed or change the direction of his motion, in either case making a contribution of his

own energy to the process. In this way displacement represents not simply time lost between observation points but a positive source of data for the space impression. The command of his speed changes permits a strategy of dynamic exploration, and the personal (muscular) effort adds to the impression of the contributions of kinesthesia and of the vestibular orienting system (e.g., slope of the floor). The observer's control of his accelerator shows that the reading of an architectural space is closer to reading a literary text than to listening to a piece of music.

We see that experiments about space impression cannot be carried out properly and compared with previous ones if, in respect to the subject's freedom of movement, the researcher does not have a clear response to the following questions:

(1) Does the experimentee remain in a fixed position or can he also move along a straight line with constant speed? (Static and mobile versions of stationary movement.)
(2) Can he also accelerate, decelerate, or change the direction of his motion? (Dynamic movement.)
(3) Does he move by the force of his own motor activity? (Dynamic movement without kinesthetic input.)
(4) If he is transported, does he himself control the characteristics – direction, velocity, acceleration – of motion? (Dynamic exploration strategy without kinesthetic input.)

THE TEMPORAL ALIASES OF A SPACE

At the opening of this Part, we noted that an architectural space can be defined as an open region, and equally well defined as a set of face-to-face communication networks, which is its sociological theme. We now seek to define it as a set of alternative paths for its exploration.

The architect has little power to affect the time dimension of the reading of a space by imposing a predetermined sequence on it, still less to affect the speed of the reading (scansion). (He can do so in a very limited way by slopes and other characteristics related to the fact that by our displacement we are in relation to the haptic space.) Given, then, the freedom of the space impression from temporal limitations, we look for conditions which allow an analytical enumeration of the possible paths for exploring the space. Our goal is to determine through a series of experiments which paths permit the most effective exploration.

The first condition is that any exploration, at least on the morphological level where we are now concerned, deals with the local geometry of the space, which can be perceived only from some interior point. We thus exclude an infinite number of exterior points.

A second limitation is that the explorer must stay within the haptic space, usually on a bidimensional floor.

A third condition is the paradigmatic valence of the space; not all parts of the walls have doors, so not all parts can serve as starting points.

Despite these limitations, the bidimensional floor of the space still contains an infinite number of possible paths. Even though the floor has a closed curve as boundary, by virtue of the continuity of the surface it contains an infinite number of lines, which are unidimensional.

We were able to reduce the infinite number of possible spaces to a discrete number of repertory items on the practical basis of the limit to the human capacity for discriminating sensory phenomena; we determined thresholds. In the same way we now seek a practical consideration which will let us count the possible paths of exploration as aliases inherent in a space (March and Steadman 1971: 182). Without this we cannot complete the experimental series necessary to the construction of the architectural repertory.

We solve the problem by noting that man moves by walking. Despite variable length of stride, the step-by-step motion resolves the continuous line into discrete elements. We need only think of the flagstones in a garden path, which actually impose a predetermined length of stride upon the walker. (Stairs are also constructed of steps. Their dimensioning, which follows the well-known formula $2h + l = 63$ cm, implies a standardized footstep.) Bechtel (1967) saw in his study a device for unobtrusive experiments. He registered the movements of people on a floor made of tiles of a suitable size which were connected to a recording apparatus. By division of the floor into tiles of suitable size, we can not only record the effective paths of exploration, but also devise a method to enumerate all the possible paths which can occur in dynamic experiment.

For the standard size of the tiles of our experimental floor we choose squares with a 60 cm. diagonal, the centroid representing the position of each. We establish rules for 'moves' as if in a chess game (see 1 in Figure 3.22). The subject, like the King in chess, may move from any starting point to any adjacent or diagonal square. Thus from any interior point he has eight choices, a very high number for our purpose. For easier experimental design and data interpretation, the researcher would prefer two-choice situations. At this stage, however, we are still committed to exhaustive enumeration; beyond the restrictions already set, we add no new ones, e.g., the installation of temporary barriers. We have, in effect, reduced the floor of the haptic space to a set of edges and vertices, and imposed rules of circulation (e.g., exclusion of jumping). We now have the framework for enumerating the possible paths of exploration by the use of situs analysis or graph theory. However, we see immediately in this context that without some further traffic rules, the number of paths will be infinite, since the subject can retrace a step as often as he wishes. In fact, the directed graph of his movement could be infinite on a floor of only two squares.

In establishing further rules we must keep in mind the goal of our research, the enumeration of paths which permit original space impressions. The purpose of exhaustiveness is to prevent the inadvertent omission of a potentially promising route. Thus, further restrictions must be founded either on objective characteristics of the physical space or on those of the perceptive process, e.g., negligible difference. Let us illustrate the task by the simple case of a floor composed of three squares. If the subject may begin his path at any of the three, we find that there are six directed graphs of simple paths, three by simple permutation and three more by enantiomorphic transformation, viz., reflection: $P_{1,2,3} \neq P_{2,3,1} \neq P_{3,1,2} \neq P_{1,3,2} \neq P_{2,1,3} \neq P_{3,2,1}$ (see Figure 3.27). (The last three are converse graphs obtained by reversing the direction.)

An objective limit inherent in the physical space to the number of possible paths comes from what we have called the paradigmatic valence of the space: the emplacement of doors prefigures the first and last impression in the exploration. For example, if there is only one door, the path must necessarily be a circuit whose two extremes, the initial and terminal points, coincide. In any case, those points will always fall at one door or another; in the context of our investigation, other possibilities can be dismissed as artificial and pointless.

Original Exploration Paths

How can we describe, in terms of the theory of graphs, those paths which promise original syntheses of space impression through dynamic exploration? The possible peculiarities of any given space prevent a full answer at this stage. We can only discuss how to predict an original impression as a function of the path chosen. For preventing repetition we note also that, from a strictly mathematical point of view, the analytical description of these paths will be analogous to that of the syntax of architectural space systems, the subject of the next chapter. Still, the subject's path in the space normally remains on a bidimensional surface, the floor, and is thus a particular case of the 'reading' of a space system. For this reason the application of graph theory will be discussed in the next chapter in general terms. (As a point of method, we should mention in advance that some authors mistakenly assume that all phenomena which occur on a flat surface can be described by a so-called planar graph. This is not the case, since graph theory does not admit the intersection of lines on a surface at points other than vertices.)

344 Communication through architecture

The first step in dealing with paths by graphs is to divide the space into squares whose centroids represent each as point or vertex (see 2 in Figure 3.22). We have established the basic rule of circulation that the subject moves only from vertex to vertex, like the king in chess. This network is not yet a path which is oriented and described by directed graphs: no directions are indicated on the edges. Using the terminology of Claude Berge, we say that an 'edge with an arrow' is an arc, which indicates direction of motion. Thus there is no possibility of mapping the edges on a chess board as arcs of a possible path onto a planar graph, even though the board itself is flat.

1.

Possibilities for paths
(A step = max. 60 cm).

2.

The physical reality of the floor is replaced by the network of a non-directed graph showing possibilities for path. (1 edge = 1 step).

3.   4.

$d = 1$ $d = 2$

Possibilities for paths and paradigmatic valence.

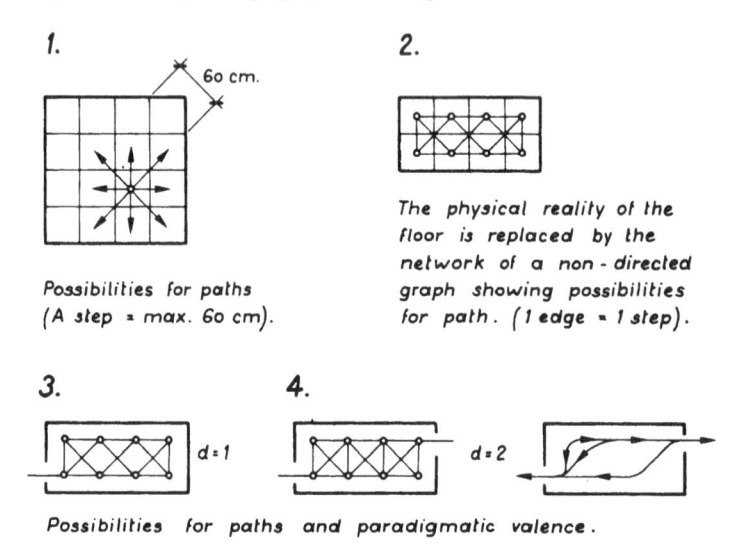

Figure 3.22. *The division of the floor in discrete elements for enumeration of possible paths.*

Our task now is to select paths, 'routes' (in Ore's terminology) which promise original space impressions.

We avoid redundancy in terms of the graph by seeing to it that the subjects (1) do not meet more than once on the same square or (2) do not travel more than once through the same arc. For Berge, an arc is a 'directed edge'; thus to pass from b to a is not a repetition of the passage from a to b. We know from everyday experience that to walk a street in both directions gives two different impressions of it. The first requirement gives a so-called elementary path (E), the second a simple one (S). It is easy enough to satisfy both at once, but hard to reconcile the search for original impressions with the goal of exhaustiveness, viz., including all edges and squares. Euler and Hamilton each tried to find the best combinations between originality and completeness, viz., formation of the most precise space impression with the least investment of time and effort. Euler dealt with the famous Köningsberg bridge problem — the tourist to visit all parts of the city but use no bridge more than once — and Hamilton with a comparable one, a traveler who does not touch any square more than once (Warusfel 1969: 182, 185; Ore 1963: 18). Here we illustrate the problem of the number of cases involved in the application of this or that rule of circulation.

We take a small floor, comprising only six squares. Now we consider the number of possible paths conforming to the rules under two conditions: first, the space has one door, the paradigmatic valence one; second, two doors, valence two.

We enumerate all the simple circuits (total and partial graphs and subgraphs) whose start and end is the (same) doorsill. The number of arces in each circuit (i.e., its length) varies from zero to six. Static observation, a simple 'look-in', is represented by a so-called nul graph (Ore 1963: 131), and the full circuit by the total graph of six arcs. Proceeding empirically we count 47 semi, or symmetric, or nondirected graphs, all the cases where the circuits are composed of different edges. In these 47 different configurations the explorer may choose 213 simple circuits, all beginning at the same door but involving different routes (viz., paths). (See 3 in Figure 3.22.)

We now consider the same space with two doors. We count all the simple partial graphs which start at one door and finish at the other, with no duplication. The observer can follow 176 different paths, maintaining the required originality. In none of these cases, one door or two, is the graph an elementary one: the observer may return to a previously visited square if he arrives from a different angle (see 4 in Figure 3.22).

In summation, the originality of sensory input during dynamic space exploration depends less on the elementary nature than on the simple nature of the path or circuit. Returns to a point from different angles bring new perspectives. For this reason, alternatives of exploration can be described only by directed graphs which can relate two points instead of an edge, with two arcs distinguished by opposite arrows. Note that a converse graph gives a different impression from one which has been reversed. Finally, it is not only the direction of the individual steps but their succession which affects the dynamic space impression, and we have taken this into account in our examples.

NEW TYPES OF IMPRESSION IN DYNAMIC EXPLORATION

We have mentioned the fundamental aspects of time and movement involved in dynamic exploration. Let us now look more closely at vestibular proprioception and the orienting system which contribute to the space impression by input from dynamic transport.

We observed that dynamic exploration allows a multiplication of observation points and choice of the sequence, of the tempo, and the direction of the movement (orthokinesis vs. klinokinesis, Fraenkel and Gunn 1961). Within the same exploration schedule two aspects allow dynamic exploration to transcend the stationary.

Walking or cycling, as opposed to passive transportation in a wheelchair, illustrates the first aspect; the activity itself provides its own sensory input, adding to the space impression by kinesthesia. (This is comparable to the geokinesia of certain animals.)

By comparing the driver of a private car and the rider on public transportation we see the second new aspect of dynamic exploration. The driver controls the steering wheel and the accelerator, while the rider can resort, at best, to an emergency brake. The driving is thus a model of movement which includes feedback, or retroaction, and its use in further decisions (von Békéssy in *Sensation and Measurement* 1974: 9).

The subject obtains impressions about aspects of his self-propelled movement through tactilo-kinesthesia, and about direction and speed — during transport — through vestibular proprioception (cf. just-appreciable rate of acceleration or deceleration). There is a very close relation between tactilo-kinesthesia, the synoptic system of muscles and joints, and the vestibular organ, the nonacoustical portion of the inner ear. They can function without visual or auditory reference and complement one another in proprioception (cf. 'proprioreceptor') giving particularly rich input to the haptic impression. Even though the relation among these sensations is one of the closest, it has been very scantly explored. We know that nearly all sensory input involves movement, which in turn gives further, unintended, input. Authors have preferred to discuss the often-conflicting relation between visual sensation and proprioception (e.g., 'muscular reporting' in the process of focusing), or the relation between hand and eye coordination, than the internal relation between kinesthesia and vestibular proprioception. Yet proprioception is more fundamentally involved in orientation during displacement than in the functioning of the visual and auditory systems, where its input is secondary. For this reason it is far more important in dynamic space exploration than in the stationary level because of the new factor of self-produced movement. (In the process of locomotion the subject can even count his steps, turns, and half-turns as a source of information.) Let us look now at what relevant studies there are.

Von Holst (1954: 89-94) distinguishes among the (afferent) sensory inputs a reafferent (Klaus 1968: 506; cf. exafferent) one which comes from the skin or elsewhere and reports about the organ's own activity. Mittelstead developed a theory of functional control of eye and other movement by reafference as a feedback. In fact, as we indicated, the experiments carried out on sensory-motor coordination — which work like lock and key (Teuber in Dubois et al. 1971: 488) — were mostly related to sight. Held and his collaborators and students (Efstathiou, Bauer, Steinbach) at MIT studied especially oculo-motor coordination and the coordination of eye and hand (Steinbach 1969: 366, 375). Without denying the value of these studies, which grow naturally from the visual research field, we recall that for our purpose we need more data on the field of tactilo-kinesthesia proper related to the haptic and orienting systems before we take up problems of polysensory coordination (e.g., data about arm-leg coordination, etc).

We learn from Held's group that only self-produced, voluntary movement has adaptive and learning effect on the accomplishment of the orienting task (Steinbach 1969: 113, 366). To the extent that the orienting system affects the space impression through dynamic exploration, this conclusion is relevant to our concern. But its validity depends on the role of sight in orientation, and so it cannot be applied immediately to dynamic exploration of all sensory spaces, e.g., the haptic. We should recall that if we consider sight in the polysensory space impression and in the polysensory orientation its role is different.

Programming of Dynamic Space Exploration by the Experimenter and by the Subject

The observer, as we have noted, can and will optimize upon attributes of his chosen path of exploration. This strategy varies according to the purpose of the movement. In a corridor — viz., place of transit — for example, the best use of the space is likely to be mere speed. But in a once-in-a-lifetime place, Rome, Jerusalem, the Forbidden City, or Mecca, for example, the opposite is likely; he will take the necessary time to fix the impressions upon his memory. For us, the task is not to learn what the observer's own purpose may be, but to determine what discrimination thresholds relate to a given aspect of an exploration path, and how to find the best. (So we consider the observer's decision-making process only in an indirect way, namely by formulating hypotheses about its influence on his discrimination threshold.) For correct imputation, the experimental design will proceed by successive relaxation of the strictness of the observation conditions imposed upon the static observer. The experimenter will observe the differences in thresholds. In this series of imputation by factors, the effect of the subject's freedom on the exploration strategy will appear as unexplained improvement of the discrimination threshold, a residual factor. The general hypothesis is that every new relaxation in the observation conditions will probably bring on a change for the better in the discrimination thresholds, but we must be careful.

These improvements are not additive, and there are illusions of movement as well as sensory illusions due to movements which occur even when only the path is imposed upon the subject, not the speed.

What aspects of the exploration task can the experimenter relax for the subject?

We recall the possible stages of relaxation in terms of 'lineup of the subjects' for experiments.

The first was the static, involving no displacement.

Close to this is the stationary, which involves only rectilinear transport with fixed velocity, as in a wheelchair. Here the experimenter can add 'angles' and 'cinematic' observation, i.e., an infinite number of continuous observation points.

When the subject is exposed to change of speed or direction, the vestibular organ, which registered in the static state only the position (i.e., gravitational field), now reveals the dynamic aspects of the movement.

If the experimenter turns over control of the vehicle to the subject, the programming of the exploration itself becomes dynamic; there are feedbacks and en route adjustments.

The fullest vestibular and tactilo-kinesthetic input results from self-produced displacement. There is a direct relation between effort and acceleration, and the efferent (motor) activity brings its own afferent input through kinesthesia.

For every stage of relaxation of the static observation conditions the experimenter can note the improvement in space discrimination, and thus show how the architect's space repertories differ accordingly as the observer is static or freely moving. The use of many intermediate relaxation stages can yield more detailed insights, e.g., free circulation within limiting barriers. The experimental design is basically the same for the investigation of every stage of relaxation. The subject has to distinguish shape and volume in paired composition, and the experimenter notes how each aspect of relaxation improves the just-noticeable difference, with the ultimate goal of finding the conditions of exploration which produce the lowest thresholds.

A group of East German psychologists, headed by Hecht (1972) and inspired by the logician Georg Klaus, elaborated a model of dynamic exploration patterned on the functioning of conditioned reflexes. According to this model, the subject first has an afferent synthesis. In order to confirm or reject the expectation based on the first synthesis, he undertakes motor activities to obtain a corrected synthesis by reafference. This gives a temporal structure for the exploration activity, interrupted at times for decision making. As regards time, the process is both continuous, with periodicities and periods of latency, and segmented by leaps which are discrete units. This structure suggested to Klaus a simulation of the process by 'cooperation' between an analog and a digital computer.

The final goal of our experiment in space impression through dynamic exploration is to discover the lowest threshold of discrimination, as far as it is a function of the optimal path and temporal sequence, by admitting self-produced and self-programmed movements.

Dynamic Exploration of the Various Sensory Spaces

1. *Acoustic and dynamic*

Of all the sensory space impressions, the acoustic is the least improved by dynamic exploration. (By 'dynamic' here we mean actual motion through the space, not mere feedback due to the subject's own choice in sound emission; this latter can take place even in the static stage.) The fact is that acoustical space is perceived virtually instantaneously, and the observation position is seldom important. At the motile stage the subject may better locate a sound source other than himself, but not the shape and volume of the space. Even if the space has a peculiar, e.g., labyrinthine, shape, or dead spots for sound, and so requires more than one observation point, a full acoustical impression can still be obtained at the stationary stage. Finally, if the sound used for the impression has 'scanning', it can hinder the optimal exploration of the space by preoccupying the hearer and dictating the rhythm and tempo of his pace. This effect may show also in polysensory space exploration.

2. *Haptic and dynamic*

In contrast to the acoustic space impression, the least affected by dynamic exploration, we now examine haptic space impression, the most closely affected by it. Exploration through movement involves vestibular and kinesthetic sensations closely related to the skin sense, somesthesia. Corzier noted the geokinesis of some animals, which are stimulated to increase pace by slope inclinations. If also observed in the case of humans, the pace of exploration could be a cue to the situation of the floor in the gravitational field. These vestibular and kinesthetic sensations are absent in a zero-gravity space. The haptic explorer has no sense of up and down, and cannot even count his steps (von Senden 1960: 37). But he can explore the entire envelope, including the ceiling, which is not normally the case, due to gravity. In fact, in zero gravity, the blind circuit of nearspace, ca. 1.5 m. diameter, explorable in the static condition, now has no limits at all.

The dynamic exploration of haptic space goes according to a completely different strategy from that of optical space, where the observer can estimate distances along sight lines in the air. Haptic exploration of space, in zero gravity or not, is circular, following the envelope closely (see Figure 3.23). Thus the closed nature of the envelope is the first noted fact. Because haptic exploration relies strongly on the hands, which let us find right and left, clockwise and counterclockwise, systematic progress is relatively easy (cf. Usnadze and Natadze of Tbilisi in *Perception de l'espace* 1959: 295). The difficulty comes in knowing when the circuit has been completed, especially when the surface is homogeneous or has repetitive features, such as more than one door. The sense of the concavity of the envelope is the only cue to knowing whether the observer leaves the space through an opening. Sometimes the temperature difference of the wall may also disclose the fact of passage from one space into another.

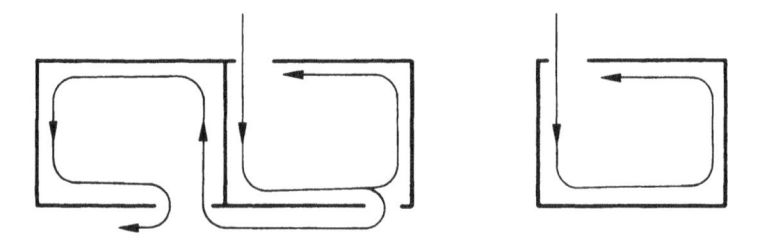

Figure 3.23. *The blind by dynamic exploration of the haptic space usually follow the wall.*

Apart from the exploration of the floor shape compared to the wall, dynamic movement, in the sense of acceleration, gives no new cues for the space impression. Moreover, the fact that the observer can choose his own speed lets us expect better discrimination than in the stationary situation, with a constant speed imposed by the experimenter.

3. *Optic and dynamic*

Some optical spaces are so shaped that they cannot be explored without translational transport; but this can be effected at the stationary stage. The 'temporal sampling of ambient array', this 'successive sampling' made by the beholder of simultaneously existing space features, can be recorded by a camera attached to the subject. This will simulate approximately the process of gathering the data, as far as it is affected by head movement, but not by eye movement.

Past experiments suggest hypotheses about the effect of kinetic exploration. Piaget and Morf (1954) found that lengths fixed visually at a later moment or for a longer time are overestimated. From this we can draw conclusions about the effects of reversal of the path and of its tempo for the impression of specific optical spaces. For example, a complicated shape detail will occupy a self-propelled observer longer than other parts.

Steinbach's work suggests that insofar as the orienting system affects space discrimination, as is the case in dynamic exploration, passive transport does not improve results (1969: 366). That happens only when the displacement is self-commanded and the subject has an 'intact sensory-motor feedback loop, complete with motor outflow and subsequent visual input' (1969: 375, point 1). More research is necessary in order to attribute, in a precise and quantitative manner, the improvement of the optical space impression to specific aspects of dynamic exploration such as speed change or self-produced movement.

Many outstanding examples in the history of architecture call our attention to the fact that the effectiveness of planned illusions of optical space depends upon the specific path which the observer follows. We see this especially in Baroque architecture, e.g., the Galleria of the Palazzo di Spada in Rome, and many examples in the Vatican.

Finally, M. Weiner's experiment with trapezoidal space in 1956 shows how effective space illusions can be nullified by contradicting haptic input (Menchikoff 1975: 50). In a room with a trapezoidal ground plan, the subject perceives it as rectangular and so distorts all other impressions accordingly (cf. A. Ames's effect). Movement and somesthetic input correct the illusion. We have already discussed Held's work concerning the subject's localization capacity in the case of conflict bewteen optical input and various proprioceptive inputs.

4. Polysensory and dynamic

We seek now an overall view of the whole exploration process. We can say that the best path is the one which gives the lowest discrimination thresholds. If this can be attained by more than one path, the most rapid one and the one least demanding of effort should be considered the overall best. On the other hand, when the experimenter, in the course of comparing alternative paths, reaches the point where increment in advantage, in terms of effort, rapidity, or precision of the impression, becomes negligible, further study is otiose. Let us see which considerations are important to polysensory exploration.

Each sense has its preferred path of exploration with its own tempo, its own 'strategy of move and wait' (Held et al. 1966: 887), despite von Békéssy's

352 Communication through architecture

assertion of the analogy of the senses. Thus in polysensory exploration, aspects of the chosen pathways may be results of 'dispute' among sense departments. It would be prejudicial to future research to accept a general, Aristotelean, proposal that the most rational path is dictated by the visual system. Thus the belief of many architects that seats which provide a good view also provide good hearing has often damaged the usefulness of multifunctional auditoria. We cannot expect to find such kinds of harmony to identify a path which is best for all senses equally.

With respect to tempo, the auditory component of the exploration of polysensory space registers very quickly (the exceptions have been described) and requires only one observation point. The visual component does not benefit from rapid locomotion. The beholder's rate of translational motion must be low; and the transport serves principally, to link observation points where rotational motion is critical for visual input, and that needs time. The haptic explorer goes along the wall more rapidly and benefits from kinetic exploration more than he would from various static positions.

As for length and direction of paths, the visual beholder needs less length than the haptic explorer, who works with feelers. The spectator can see distant points at the same time, and needs walk only to link strategic central locations. He saves effort, while the haptic explorer must circumambulate.

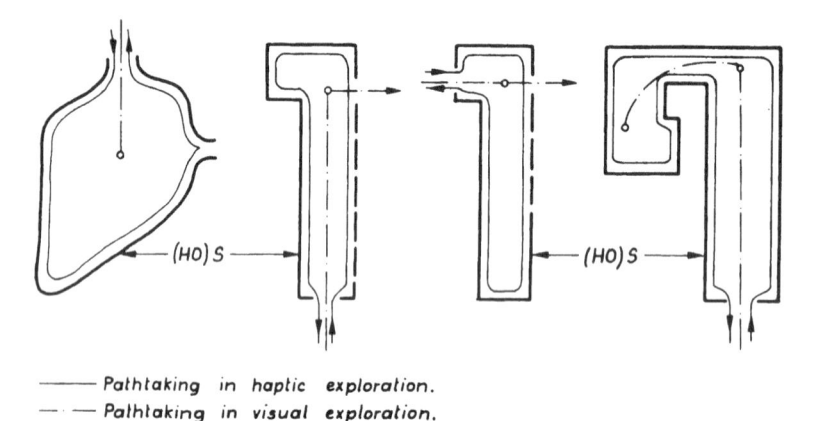

———— Pathtaking in haptic exploration.
— · — Pathtaking in visual exploration.

Complete dynamic exploration of a (HO)S.

Given these differences in the predilections of the various sensory organs, we can recognize with relative ease which system dictates which rhythm or path of polysensory exploration. In total darkness, for example, haptic exploration is the only kind available, in ordinary circumstances.

Finally, we can say that exafference, especially that which comes during displacement, presents its input through the haptic system. The feedback loop, which governs speed, orientation and direction, also functions as intermediary among the various senses, selecting the preferred path of one over that of another.

Space Illusion in Dynamic Exploration

Dynamic exploration presents new opportunities not only for more precise space impressions but also for illusions caused by kinesthetic and vestibular sensations.

There is a first possibility on the kinetic level under stationary conditions; the observer can be moved at a speed too great for the sensory input process, thus diminishing the acuity of perception. If the transport remains rectilinear at a constant speed, his motion and that of the entire surround is interchangeable for interpretation, and so change of relative position can be falsely attributed.

An even more disturbing phenomenon is that acceleration can be falsely gauged by proprioception, and self-produced motion can go unnoticed or be erroneously registered. In dynamic exploration, the illusory effect can be direct, and indirect in self-produced motion. Since the feedback loop also depends on ex-afferent input, erroneous data about motor, i.e., efferent, activity draws the subject into imperfect programming (cf. cervo loop).

Laboratory investigations by H. A. Witkin also show this kind of illusion in circular movement, the so-called 'haunted swing'. Subjects confined to a fixed chair within a rotating space perceived themselves as tilted and the room as upright when the reverse was true. This illusion was successfully exploited at the Midwinter Fair in San Francisco. According to J. Cohen (1969: 60) the psychologist R. W. Wood reports it in the following terms:

The device was worked in the following way: The swing proper was practically at rest, merely being joggled a trifle, while the room itself was put in motion, the furniture being fastened down to the floor, so that it could be turned completely over. The curious and interesting feature however was that even though the action was fully understood, as was my case, it was impossible to quench the sensations of 'goneness within' with each apparent rush of the swing.

The vestibular component of proprioception can also create illusions, not only in a dark and soundless room but also in a polysensory space where the visual input cannot act as a corrective when vestibular sensation is intense because of extreme forces. O. H. Mowrer motorcycled at high speed within a circular velodrome, a cylinder 30 feet in diameter. Centrifugal force permitted a riding position horizontal to the ground. Vestibular sensations were powerful, and he perceived himself upright over a flat ribbon with a rotating 'wheel of observers' at his side.

Abraham's illusion

The architect Abraham and the acoustical engineer Schapiro (1969) created a 'space' equipped with a feedback apparatus so programmed that sensory inputs conveyed to the subject negated the benefit of each new step in dynamic exploration and reinforced the space illusion. Through this objective device, dynamic exploration became a Sisyphean labor; in this 'haunted' space, whenever the subject tried to touch the apparent envelope, it disappeared.

It was, in fact, more a stage than a space, an optical and acoustical pseudospace where the envelope coincided with the source of luminous and sonorous stimuli, and was thus imperceptible. In it the subject had, not a space illusion, but an outer-space one, the impression of roomraum reduced to nothing. The haptic space was absent. There are other examples of no-space impression, where shape and volume cannot be attributed to the surround, in an absolutely dark and soundless night. The label given this space by its creators, 'hyperspace', is misleading; their whole creation is rather a 'zero zone', a pseudo- or hypospace.

This is not meant to imply that autoregulative and autoadaptive space engineering is not a suitable complement to permanent architecture.

19

Syntax of Space Systems and Subsystems

> '... distributional analysis is an elementary method, and involves merely the statement of relative occurrence of elements, in this case morphemes.... To establish the method for its own sake, or for possible application to non-linguistic material, no prior knowledge should be used except the boundaries of elements.'
>
> Z. Harris

FROM MORPHOLOGY TO SYNTAX: MORPHEMES, ULTIMATE AND IMMEDIATE CONSTITUENTS, AND THEIR CONSTRUCTION

Having discussed in detail the various cases and different layers of architectural words and their formation, it would be useful to recall some concepts developed in the beginning of this part, by applying them to the construction of architectural sentences.

After his development inside the uterine space and subsequent birth, man continually experiences changes in the space around him. The sociological theme of these spaces has been defined by the sets of face-to-face communication networks, which are inherently possible in a specific space. Space change is produced by displacement or transfer. The system which makes this possible can be thought of as a transformer or converter, either of one face-to-face communication network into another, or of a telecommunication network into a face-to-face one. The former takes place when an existing group moves from one room to another; the latter, when somebody stops using the telephone to converse and physically goes to see the person to whom he was speaking.

On closer inspection, we can see that the transfer from one space to another implies a temporary suspension of the autonomy, at least, of the haptic spaces between which the transfer takes place. It is a temporary adjunction (Whitehead and Eldars 1964: 102-103; Bense 1971: 11: 'spatial and temporal character of adjunction'). Because the displacement is a continuous phenomenon — going through spaces and from space to space — the accessibility of one space to another could be either direct connectivity or indirect connectivity. Direct connectivity usually involves the two spaces being physically adjacent.

While discussing the architectural medium in this part, we have tried to relate its different elements and relationships to the concepts of semiotics and general linguistics, in order to make it possible to apply some of the paradigms and conclusions of those disciplines. In discussing the architectural repertory, we have considered spaces in terms of their internal properties, such as their geometrical properties (March and Steadman 1971: 36, 183) and the reflecting quality of their enveloping surfaces. In the framework of morphology, we distinguished among repertory items those which cannot be transformed one into another by paradigmatic transformation as separate items of the architectural lexicon. Examples of such items are enveloping surfaces, such as a sphere and a torus with one ring, that belong to different topological genera and therefore cannot be mapped onto each other either by continuous deformation or by any geometrical transformation.

In discussing the dynamic exploration of the architectural morpheme (or space), we have introduced the concept of paradigmatic valence, which implies the question of direct accessibility to the space. (In terms of graph theory, this valence is described by incident arcs or by two demi-degrees of a vertex for possible distinction between exits and entrances [Berge 1966 (1963): 7, 86].)

In order for morphemes to be combined into syntagmatic arrangement, they must have a matching valence, just as two spacecraft must have openings of equal size if they are to be linked; but in order for the morphemes that form a syntagm to become an idiom — to be joined without a gap in a compact arrangement — they must also be geometrically compatible, namely adjacent. A syntagm is, in other words, an ordered positioning of neighboring morphemes with matching doors. (We have already shown in an earlier section that the bound morpheme demonstrates an interface which is ready for syntagmatic relation on the sensory level.) The architectural morpheme — or space — acquires its complete identity from its syntactical positioning (see Figure 3.28). This position affects the reading of morphemes, or impression of them through sentence stress. (Because of the importance of the syntactical position of the morpheme, during experiments the subject's spatial orientation will heavily influence pattern recognition in his impression of a space.) Coming from this broader integration of morphemes, it is seen as an element of decomposition, namely the ultimate constituent (Klaus

1969: 239). In this process of sentence decomposition the hierarchically higher component (than the ultimate constituent) is the immediate constituent. This level of substitutable part of a sentence has a very particular significance for the architectural utterance. We have already mentioned direct and indirect access between one space and another. There is indirect access between two architectural morphemes when they belong to the same sentence, yet are not directly connected. An architectural space system, as a sentence, can be read linearly in more than one way. The different paths that can be taken to get from the same initial space to the same terminal space in the space system can be called components. These multiple — alternative — ways of reading the space system constitute the immediate level of the parsing of an architectural sentence. As the space system itself, these paths or components can be described objectively just as the structuralistic approach describes archaeological finds. These paths, as possible partial graphs of the graph of the architectural sentence, are an integral part of an architectural opus. We do not discuss here either what could be considered a complete perusal of an architectural space system, or what could be only a scanning of it. (We will later apply Eulerian and Hamiltonian criteria to construct graphs that pass through all locales in an architectural space system at least once without necessarily going in both directions through all of the doors in each locale.)

How do we determine what constitutes an architectural sentence in a space system that forms a continuous web of interconnected spaces? The proper level in this web where the architectural space system can be called a sentence is defined by complete purposefulness uttered by it. Architectural words bear complete meaning; an architectural sentence utters purposefulness. Indeed, at this level, the space system becomes designated by its purpose. On the other hand, the participating space becomes a locale with an assigned function.

A further and final determination of the architectural work with all its constituents is realized by its situation in respect to atmospheric space, which provides the context for all architectural texts. This geographic location also gives unique identity to all created spaces.

It must be emphasized that the architectural opus cannot be equated with the so-called building. Indeed, the delimitation of an architectural text is defined by the fact that all its locales are connected among themselves without 'going out' in the contextual space. Therefore gates and windows determine a proper architectural opus without respect to how loosely or tightly it is wrapped by its facades.

We see that all this analysis of the architectural opus does not involve the designer's intention (Harris 1952: 3-9), but by using the same symbolism a designer can use this structuralistic description in his creation.

What makes all this consideration complicated, apart from the multiplicity of readings of an architectural space system, is that the architectural text is properly characterized by at least three sensorily autonomous textual webs.

INFRASTRUCTURES, SYNTAGMATIC ARRANGEMENT, AND SYNTACTICAL CONSTRUCTION: BASIC QUESTIONS

Considered properly in isolation, an architectural morpheme can be embedded in the lithosphere without having an interface. However, if the architect constructs a space system with bound forms, with membranelike interface walls in a compact system without solid residuals, or gaps, the adjacent spaces become geometrically codetermined by each other, in the pattern. These remainders, coming from construction of a system without respect to geometrical compatibility, can exist between directly accessible spaces as well as between inaccessible, back-to-back spaces — nonpunctured walls (March) or partitions between two architectural sentences of nonconnected texts — in a manner which may or may not be perceptible to the beholder who walks within the space system. These questions of syntagmatic arrangements are not all proper to the construction of the architectural sentences as such. Indeed, as in the case of the 'exploration labyrinth' (the Villa Pisani labyrinth in Santarcangelli 1967: 258) constructed for rats by the researcher at ETH, only the conceiver can have knowledge of certain gaps as well as certain hidden neighborhoods. What must be clearly said and understood here is that the existence of gaps or adjacencies, as far as they are for the beholders imperceptible, do not constitute an integral part of the architectural text. For this very reason, heterogeneous architectural texts packed in structures called buildings — like words arranged above and below each other on a page — are not properly units of an architectural medium unless their facades make envelopes for the atmospheric space. It is here where architectural infrastructure (cf. Zeitoun 1971: 38; Friedman 1975: 12) must be distinguished from structural engineering.

In the case of interfaces, especially when complex words are composed from bound forms, the syntagmatic connection requires a geometrical complementarity of the participating units beyond their topological neighborhood. If morphologically (geometrically) incompatible morphemes are brought into direct accessibility in the construction, the architect has the following choices:

— he may fill the gap;
— he may leave it inaccessible;

Syntax of space systems and subsystems 359

— or he may put a purely relational space as a floating element between the spaces, which will not have any lexical meaning but express only a syntactical relationship, an empty or function word.

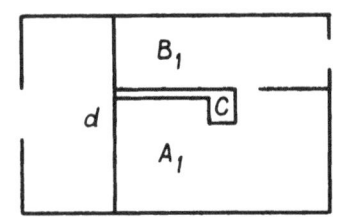

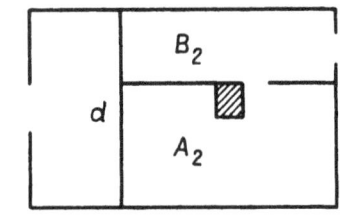

If the geometrical difference between A_1 and A_2 is imperceptible, the inaccessible C makes no difference between the two space systems as architectural texts; neither does interface d, if there is no direct accessibility, and therefore the adjacency remains latent, imperceptible.

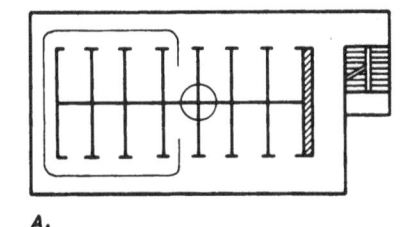

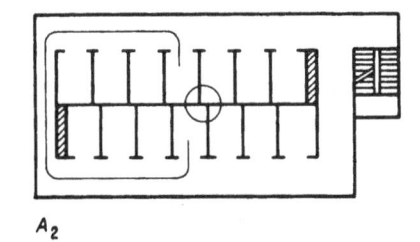

If the difference in adjacency between A_1 and A_2 is not perceptible to the beholder (e.g., by difference in 'functional', — Fitch, — ecological, or walking distance), the syntactical orders of these two architectural communications are equal.

On the other hand, all effective adjacencies which are neither used for allowing direct access nor perceived by the beholder as neighborhood, viz., having latent accessibility, are architecturally irrelevent and do not take part in the network of architectural communication.

Of course, for the sake of composition, the designer can construct adjacencies without punctures, a so-called no-road map, an antimap (March and Steadman 1971: 268) as antigraph to the graph of the actual 'readable' structure of the architectural communication (assured by the piercing of the walls by doors or by bound relations in complex words. See 1 in Figure 3.24.) It might be useful for the conceiver to know that modifications of the existing structure could be done inexpensively but which do not contribute to the description of the actual architectural text. Indeed, the antigraph itself can be understood in yet a different way; it can show all direct accessibilities latent by adjacency, but in this case it is not a complementary graph ($\bar{G}$) to the

360   *Communication through architecture*

1.

[Ground plan showing rooms A, B, C, D]

Edges express symmetrical arcs, resp symmetrical accesses.

Ground plan.

A — B — C — D

Syntactical graph of architectural communication.

2.

The complete graph.

3.

C — A — D — B

The complementary graph of the architectural text. ($\bar{G} \triangleq 2.-1.$)

4.

The graph of all adjacencies. (Texttopological connex; 'infrastructural' or syntagmatic graph.)

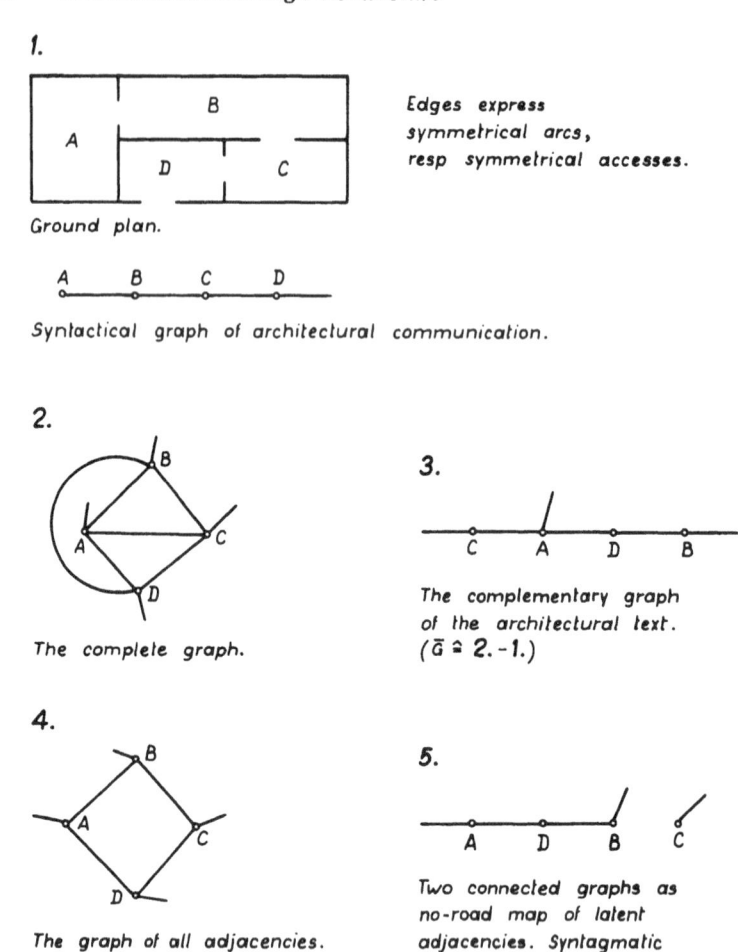

5.

A — D — B   C

Two connected graphs as no-road map of latent adjacencies. Syntagmatic potentialities. ($5. \triangleq 4.-1.$)

Figure 3.24. *Graph of an architectural text and other graphs used in analyses.*

graph describing the system of the effectively connected spaces because the complete graph includes relations between all spaces, even if they are not adjacent. The complementary graph (see 3 in Figure 3.24) of the complete graph has an importance for the architect-designer because, as we will see later, by introducing empty or relational words (e.g., transition rooms, corridors) the architect can create direct accessibilities for his 'reader' without having a spontaneous adjacency on hand which is inherent at the syntagmatic level.

Syntax of space systems and subsystems 361

On the other hand, it is also possible to have more than one puncture in an interface separating the same two rooms and therefore the graph relating the two vertices will have more than one arc.

Frequentation: Access to Spaces

Let us turn our attention to the 'reading' of the space system by frequentation. It is the actualization of the architectural communication.

A first observation concerns the act of passing from one space to another. Conceived as an ambulatory process, it is most immediately related to the haptic space. In order to make the passage, it is necessary to suspend, at least temporarily, the separation of two haptic spaces by the opening of the door.

Because this haptic root runs throughout the space system, the blind person's impression of the space system is particularly instructive. We have already noted von Senden's observation (1960: 41). If the doors (sliding door or hatch) are already open when a blind person goes through, he considers the two rooms as one (see Figure 3.23). Further, von Senden noted, recalling the Cheselden case, the born-blind subject realizes that he is *in* a room — he hears that it is part of a house though he cannot conceive that the so-called house is bigger than the individual rooms. (The Wild Boy of Aeyron, who came out of the wood and into history just in time for a brand-new century, the 19th, reportedly said, 'A room is larger than a house since if I turn myself I see always a room but not a house.') At first glance we would draw the simple conclusion that his experience of a space system differs even more in a negative way from that of the polysensory explorers than was the case with the impression of individual polysensory space; but on the other hand we note a particular point in the case of the blind's reading of the space system, namely, it is 'unspoiled' by a preconceived concept of the space system which is mediated through the house for the sighted person. Indeed, the blind truly experience space sequences without considering purely topotextual adjacencies present only by virtue of the packing of the space system in a building, a packing which is irrelevant for the architectural space system as a 'piece of reading'.

So the door must be a *temporary* opening.

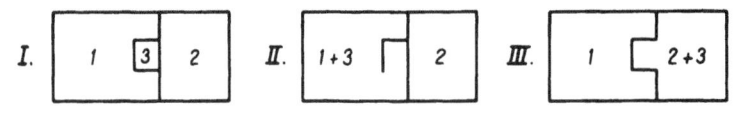

I. | 1 [3] 2 | II. | 1+3 ⌐ 2 | III. | 1 ⌐ 2+3 |

Stages of access.

This can be strictly realized by a lockage where a 'dummy space' is used.

All temporary openings between two haptic spaces are described by an arc of a graph, which, along with an arrow, can also bear a value (see Figure 3.25). The temporary opening must relate two haptic spaces, otherwise it is a pseudodoor (*porte à Charlot*) (see 7 in Figure 3.25). It could be a two-way or only a one-way door (revolving door with barrier, turnstile shown in 3 in Figure 3.25). It could also be adjacent in the sense that more than one door relates two spaces. (Multiple graph is shown in Figure 3.30.) The opening, even if it allows circulation in both directions, does not necessarily mean symmetry in a quantative sense (e.g., a trapdoor at the end of an attic staircase for the garret). In this case we assign different numerical values to the two opposite arcs. A directed graph with numerical values assigned to its arcs is called a network (March and Steadman 1971: 268). The completely symmetrical opening is the revolving door without barrier. (It also functions as a lockage.)

Secondly and finally the space system as path network consists in the set of all possible directed graphs which can be inscribed in the accessibility graph. Indeed the graph of accessibility, which gives connectivity, shows the space system with all its alternative readings. As we will see, in order to enumerate the possible readings we must limit the iteration of the itineraries.

Architectural communication is realized by frequentation of the space system. Among the set of possible paths, some will be used more frequently, others not at all. The actual frequentation, perhaps mapped in graphs, objectively records the communicatory events occurring between architect and beholder.

Geometrical Implications of Adjacency

We have stated already that architecturally relevant adjacency involves the possibility of puncture to allow a beholder to pass through. For this reason, if the adjacency occurs at the meeting of vertices, this secondary adjacency is architecturally irrelevant (see 1 in Figure 3.26). In order to have an architecturally relevant adjacency ensuring accessibility without gap, the two spaces or enveloping surfaces must have a relatively extended contact area which can become an interface by sharing a common curvature — or more exactly, an equal absolute value of the curvature (K), but with opposite signs, namely $-K_1 = K_2$, where 1 and 2 represent the two adjacent spaces.

What is the geometrical implication for the two participating spaces, if they can be 'stacked' without imposing on them any paradigmatic transformations but those involved in syntactical positioning (March and Steadman 1971: 173), namely the two isometric transformations, rotation and translation?

Syntax of space systems and subsystems 363

1. Swinging door.

Revolving door.

2. Door opens in one direction.

3. Revolving door (turnstile) with barrier.

Strictly symmetric arcs (qualitatively and quantitatively), expressed also by an edge.

Qualitatively symmetric but quantitatively asymmetric.

One-way, directed arc. (Antisymmetric graph.)

4.
$d^+(x) = 3$
$d^-(x) = 3$
$d^+(x) = d^-(x)$

Albeit all doors are not symmetric.

5.
$d^+(x) = 4$
$d^-(x) = 4$

6. Trap.
$d^+(x) = 1$
$d^-(x) = 0$

7. Pseudoaccess ('porte à Charlot', loop).
$d(x,x) = 1 \neq 0$

Paradigmatic valences.

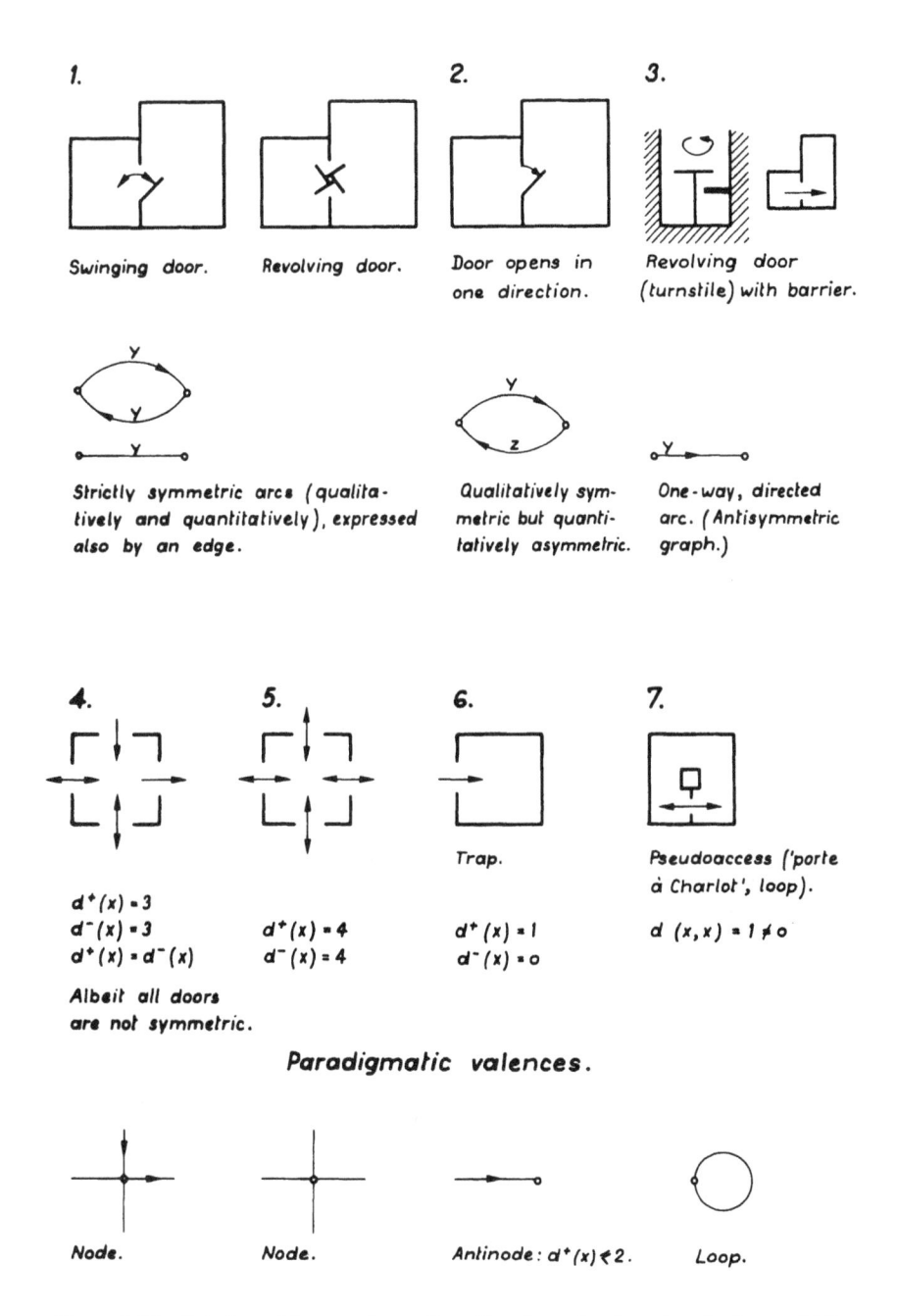

Node.

Node.

Antinode: $d^+(x) \leqslant 2$.

Loop.

Figure 3.25. *Notation of doors and paradigmatic valence for the network of accessibility.*

364   *Communication through architecture*

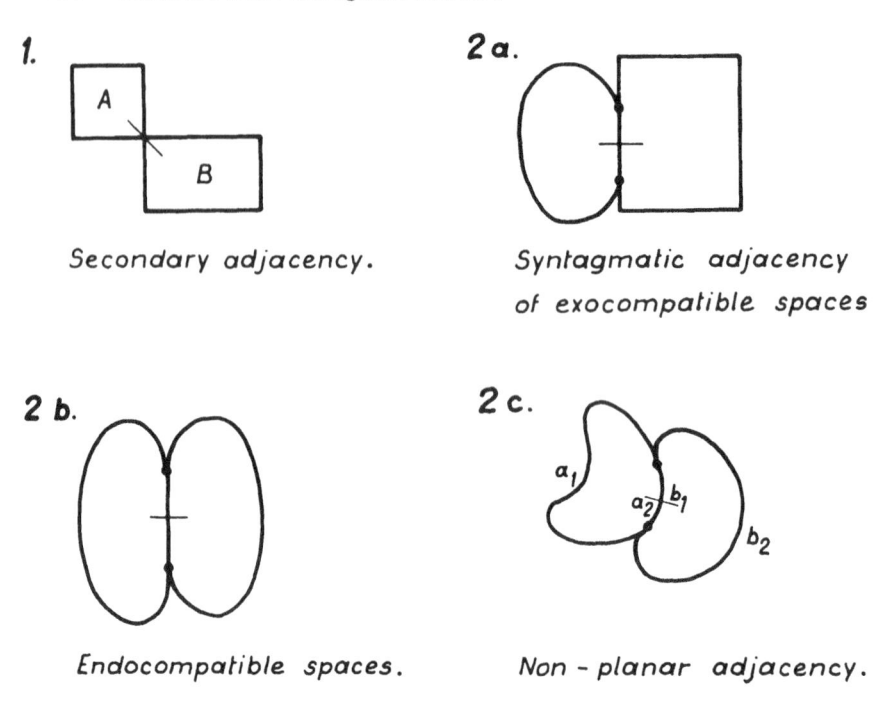

1.

A
B

Secondary adjacency.

2a.

Syntagmatic adjacency
of exocompatible spaces

2b.

Endocompatible spaces.

2c.

a_1, a_2, b_1, b_2

Non - planar adjacency.

Cross sections.

Figure 3.26. *Adjacencies and syntagmatic arrangement.*

We can find two groups of shapes which can be adjacent to another isometric space. We call them endocompatible (see 2b in Figure 3.26). It is evident immediately that if each space envelope has a plane surface part, the adjacency of the two spaces is facilitated. In this case the adjacency is described by $K_1 = 0 = K_2$. The importance of the plane surface is further underlined by the fact that adjacency can be understood also between rooms in superposition, i.e., on different floors. However, a flat surface part is not absolutely required for adjacency. (There are curved doors too shown in 2c in Figure 3.26.) But in this case, two continuously differentiable envelopes, viz., without edge or vertex, cannot be compatible if they are completely concave. They are only endocompatible if they are convex-concave. And even in this case the adjacency does not occur at corresponding points of the two (endocompatible) envelopes. If we consider compatibility between two envelopes of different but continuously differentiable shapes, at least one must be concave-convex (exocompatibility shown in Figure 3.26).

Adjacency clearly implies geometrical requirements. Now how can this be realized for various architectural lexicon items, envelopes which are

Syntax of space systems and subsystems 365

classed under a different topological genus? Does there exist a topological genus which excludes, *eo ipso*, endocompatibility? This does not seem to be the case. But the participation in an adjacency of space envelopes with different topological genus *enriches* the types of contact areas involved. To the simple stacking by juxtaposition we can add nesting and even interlocking. Anchorring spaces can adjoin each other by possibly multiple intertwining. They can have a geometry which makes them endocompatible.

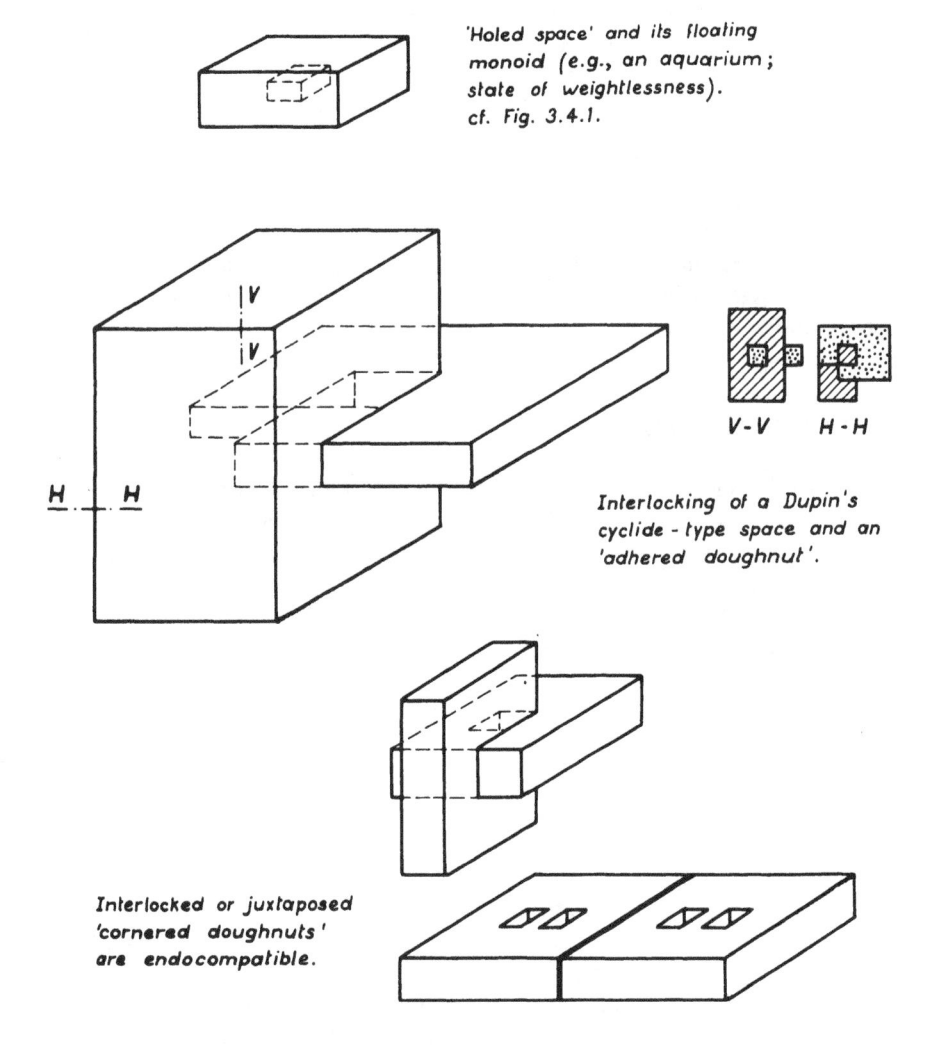

'Holed space' and its floating monoid (e.g., an aquarium; state of weightlessness). cf. Fig. 3.4.1.

Interlocking of a Dupin's cyclide-type space and an 'adhered doughnut'.

Interlocked or juxtaposed 'cornered doughnuts' are endocompatible.

Some syntagmatic arrangements in axiomatic representation.

Spaces with more than one closed surface as envelope can, of course, create adjacency through nesting, which by definition makes an interface, viz., contact area, from the whole envelope of the embedded space (monoid, Berge). This is an adjacency between nonisometric envelopes, an exocompatibility.

To the particular types of adjacency proper to this topological class, we add the simple juxtaposition among endocompatible isometric anchor rings and those of various lexical items viz., topological class as well as an anchor ring with space whose envelope belongs to the sphere's lexical item ($p = 0$). For example, a prism-shaped space can be imbedded in an anchor ring ($p = 2$), placed in its middle like a cigar.

Finally, two spaces can have more than one contact area. This is very important for the insertion of the two-space syntagm in the architectural text but for the internal relation, namely mutual accessibility of the two spaces, this fact is of negligible importance. Indeed, with a single contact area, the two spaces can be directly connected by two doors of equal size, or of different sizes and importance (i.e., a main entrance and a secondary door that is not necessarily a back door). Both cases are represented by a multiple graph shown in Figure 3.30.

Syntagmatic vs. Paradigmatic Operations

The morphemic characteristics of a space are defined intrinsically by the internal or local geometry without involving any external reference (March and Steadman 1971: 36, 183-187); this definition of a repertory item was a stage in the determination of the architectural space system.

The paradigmatic transformations relate spaces with different shapes or volumes yet without any external reference which would locate them. The paradigmatic operations which establish relationship between shapes are numerous. They tell us how to find another repertory item which preserves unchanged certain characteristics of a shape but which, in other respects, is accommodated to specific syntagmatic arrangement. The paradigmatic transformation of a space which leaves the shape unchanged but varies its volumetric magnitude is a homothetic one. If the space is expressed by a matrix of cubelets, the transformation of similitude means a scalar multiplication.

In order to make the description of the items of the architectural repertory (or word stock) fit for use, it is not enough to ensure that one designation does not represent more than one item (viz., to be unequivocal), but the same item must not appear under two different names (van Hout 1969: 16). The double name of one item is the problem of alias, and the unequivocal definition, which does not permit one item defined by internal or local

Syntax of space systems and subsystems   367

geometry to cover noninterchangeable spaces, is the problem of enantiomorphic spaces.

Alias

Even in a space with only one door, the subject has the option to walk around it in a clockwise or counterclockwise direction (see Figure 3.27). In either case, we do not represent the same space by the same matrix. The two matrices truly reflect the differences experienced by 'left-handed' and 'right-handed' people in their space impressions; however, here we are concerned with the objective description of the space as a repertory item, and in this respect it is one and the same space. It is a postmultiplication of permutation (*P*) which allows us to eliminate the alias which differs only by the order of enumeration of the relative coordinate values of the corners of a space which is one and the same.

Aliases.   Permutations.

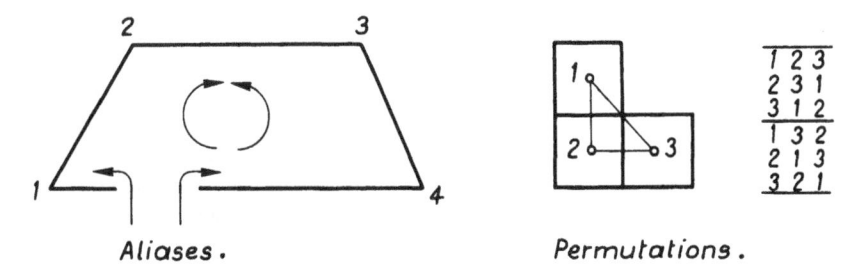

Figure 3.27. *Aliases of pathtaking on the floor.*

In general, by always using an ordered equation and by choosing an appropriate coordinate system we can realize that the item is not only defined without ambiguity, but its matrix also clearly shows its shape and volumetric parameters. It is called the canonical or normal form. It is in our interest to choose as origin the unique point (u, v) which does not change its place during syntagmatic transpositions that occur before hoisting the room into its definite syntactic place by crane.

Enantiomorphism

Enantiomorphic shapes, as in the case of left- and right-handed gloves or shoes, pose another problem. An objective difference exists between them although the local geometry does not show it. Internal properties — neighborhoods, ratios, angles, and distances — are the same in both shoes. Still, if the prefabricated room is not a mongolian yurt which can be turned inside out, items with a negative or improper isometry (Warusfel 1966: 41) must be specified before delivery. (The difference could be as trivial as a right-hand or a left-hand door.) They do not belong to the same class of substitution.

It is the transformation which specifies the relationship between different spaces. Enantiomorphic spaces are related among themselves by reflection (R). It must be carefully distinguished from the syntagmatic operation of rotation (S) since both are isometric and preserve equivalences $ABC \stackrel{e}{=} DEF$, implying $|ABC| = |DEF|$ because $\{|A|, |B|, |C|\} = \{|D|, |E|, |F|\}$. Twin spaces which are enantiomorphic spaces are related to each other by improper or opposite symmetric transformation. As a matter of fact, *all* transformation can be defined by a matrix and its determinant. *All* differences and similarities between rotation and reflection as transformation are revealed together by these two data.

Transposition as a syntagmatic operation

After excluding any ambiguity among morphologically predefined elements attributable to alias or to enantiomorphism (Negroponte 1970: 20-21), we next submit them to a syntagmatic operation, placing them adjacent to each other and connecting them in a syntactical arrangement by doors. These blocks of adjacent spaces become the immediate constituents in the analysis of a syntactical system such as the sentence.

We know already that a room obtains its complete identity by its syntactical position in a specific architectural text. Let us now discuss the operations which the unequivocally identified repertory item must undergo to obtain its identity.

(1) The first operation is a syntagmatic one which fixes the space orientation. In the warehouse repository the prefabricated space can be stacked without respect to its orientation. But as soon as it is definitely affixed to another space, its orientation becomes significant. The so-called free block becomes a vector expressed by symbols: an A becomes A, ABC = DEF becomes $ABC = DEF$, where the elements are ordered $(|A|, |B|, |C|) = (|D|, |E|, |F|)$. Spaces which are isometric are equivalent; those which, in addition, have the same orientation are equal. This does not yet fix the definitive place of each item in a particular syntactic unit, only its position (e.g., which is the floor and which is the ceiling).

Rotation (S) is the isometric operation that fixes the space orientation. Rotation is characterized by revolution which leaves unchanged the place of one single point, namely the origin of the revolution. This unique point (coordinates u, v), which does not change its place during subsequent rotations, is an important point of reference. (For example, a cube whose faces have different colors can have 3.4 = 12 different orientations in relation to a surface.)

Of the three axes present in all spaces, the vertical one has a particular significance on our earth. We have a particular term for one kind of vertical rotation, namely the half-turn (H) which is also called 'improper translation'. By this operation the second part of a duplex house can be reconstructed from the first if they are to be isometric. The half-turn is simply a case of rotation where two angles have a zero degree opening and the third, 180°. Therefore H is represented in all respects by the matrix of S.

(2) Alibi. After the space has obtained its definitive orientation as vector, the translation (T) specifies its place for the syntactical construction. This operation can be understood in terms of transportation by an elevator or by railroad, which does not turn the objects. After all other transformations, transport provides the space with its identity (I), viz., the space morpheme obtains its definitive address, it becomes a locale, and is architecturally completely determined (see Figure 3.28). Even though $ABC = DEF$, but $ABC \not\equiv DEF$ because $(A, B, C) \not\equiv (D, E, F)$, March and Steadman (1971: 185) call the transformation which carries the space to a new address an alibi. First the morpheme became a vector by a syntagmatic operation such as rotation, and now, by translation, it has become a positioned vector which not only has a defined internal geometry and a determined orientation, but also a location.

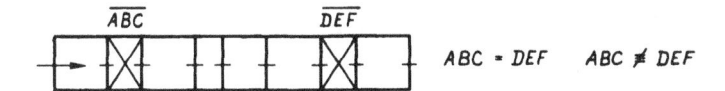

Figure 3.28. *Equal morphemes and their identity in the syntactical arrangement.*

Of course breaking down the various transformations into various stages — paradigmatic, syntagmatic, and syntactical positioning — is not a necessary procedure as such for all construction. Perhaps it is more clearly called for in the case of prefabricated rooms and blocks than in other cases.

We can sum up all these operations by the following formula:

$$Q = m \cdot R^i \cdot S \cdot Q' \cdot P,$$

where:

m = scalar premultiplicator which refers to a paradigmatic operation changing the volume of a space;

R^i = reflection matrix for improper isometric transformation which does not belong to the syntagmatic operation in architecture;
S = rotation determining the orientation and direction of the space making a vector from the free floating morpheme;
$Q' = T$ = translation which makes a positioned vector from the space;
P = a permutation matrix as postmultiplicator which shows the various aliases of an objectively single space (it also holds for expressing the alternative ways the space can be explored − clockwise or lefthanded);
Q = the full identity of the space.

In a more traditional way translation and rotation can be summed up by the following set of equations:

$$x' = (x - f) \cos \alpha - (y - g) \sin \alpha$$
$$y' = (x - f) \sin \alpha + (y - g) \cos \alpha$$

The same equations may also be expressed as matrices with addition of the nonisometric, therefore paradigmatic, transformation as a scalar premultiplicator:

$$\begin{bmatrix} x' \\ y' \end{bmatrix} \leftrightarrow \begin{bmatrix} m & 0 \\ 0 & m \end{bmatrix} \cdot \begin{bmatrix} \cos\theta & \sin\theta \\ -\sin\theta & \cos\theta \end{bmatrix} \cdot \begin{bmatrix} x_1 & x_2 \\ y_1 & y_2 \end{bmatrix} + \begin{bmatrix} f \\ g \end{bmatrix}$$

For simplicity's sake this formula is for bidimensional features; in the case of space the matrix is 3 × 3 instead of 2 × 2.

Some questions of enumeration of cases of syntagmatic arrangement under prismatic restriction as form class Because an overwhelming proportion of the architectural spaces of our time has the shape of a quadrangular prism (or rectangular parallelepiped), and also because the cubelet is a convenient element used for decomposition, a certain number of mathematical studies have been carried out to enumerate the possible cases of adjacency between two shapes with 'prismatic restriction' (e.g., combining two phone booths), and also to enumerate all the cases of adjacency that a cube can have with other cubes. (Indeed, one cube can have in a three-dimensional arrangement 14 adjacent cubes at once.)

From these works we can draw the following conclusions:

(1) The number of possible syntagmatic arrangements between two rectangular prisms of different shapes which is at the architect's disposal is joyfully

high. We enumerated 1,764 cases of different three-dimensional syntagmatic arrangements between two oriented and positioned rectangular prisms.

(2) A critical analysis of a published enumeration made by the self-named Important Members of the Cambridge Trinity College Mathematical Society reveals mistakes (see March and Steadman's enumeration, 1971: 118-120 and 272-274, reprinted in uncorrected form by the MIT Press in 1974). Indeed, it is a fact that by using computer analysis for enumeration, it is relatively easy to develop programs which eliminate all repetition (that is, they make the enumeration disjunctive), but which make it much more difficult to guarantee an exhaustive enumeration.

We have intentionally not discussed here this enumeration of the rectangular prism's possible syntagmatic arrangements, since it could be inconsistent with our objective to enlarge the architectural repertory to pay particular attention to an arrangement between the conventional shapes. Therefore we will discuss the question of possible arrangements in a broader context which goes *beyond* the Procuste bed of the prismatic restriction.

MATHEMATICAL DESCRIPTION OF ARCHITECTURAL SPACE SYSTEM IN GENERAL

In order to make the description of a phenomenon clear and its manipulation easy and precise, there is a well-known advantage in using mathematical language. This is an acceptable general statement but its application does not go automatically without qualification. Indeed, Alexander (1964: 61-62) clearly exposes the criterion for a heuristically useful application of mathematical notations. In order to be adequate, the applied symbolism must cover the whole scope of the problem in a uniform manner and therefore allow manipulation of at least all nonnegligible variables. Other applications are either illusory or based on naive assumptions often metaphorical in nature.

As a matter of fact, when we apply mathematics there are pitfalls for readers who are unfamiliar with the internal problems of mathematics itself, and who, in addition, have a mystified view of it. The way is open to abuses. The possibility of this mystification comes from the relatively difficult and therefore esoteric character of the field. In order not to depart too far from the proper concern of this book, and at the same time to lighten the weight of the mystical power of mathematics, we posit here some facts.

The claim that modern mathematics creates a manageable and efficient language which is completely abstract must be understood more as a program than a reality. In this context we also see that the devastating critique exercised against Euclidian geometry is much more irrelevant for the geometry of architectural spaces than some authors applying topology in our field like to imagine.

Considering the present state of the mathematical art, we find developed systems but not a systematic development. Solutions are often worked out following the author's fantasy for solving technical or hobby problems which are fragmentary, isolated, and anecdotal. To demonstrate this it is enough to check the peculiar headings in mathematical dictionaries under which we can find solutions to otherwise significant problems.

It must be said explicitly that mathematics as a whole is *not* an axiomatized system except for certain well-isolated enclaves. The stock of available knowledge is in very different epistemological states, which allows an unexpectedly large part for proof by authority. Indeed, under-the burden of the authority of reputed mathematicians, some conjectures had been used as sure findings (e.g., Euler's conjecture had been accepted for two hundred years until 1960, when Bose, Parker, and Shrikhande proved that it was not only undemonstrable, but even false).

Finally the language itself, if it is artificial, unfortunately does not guarantee the development of a context-free, uniform symbolism which is exempt from all sources of equivocation. (An equivocation can come either from double meaning of a term, or from synonyms.) If the natural languages show the contingency of their historical development, in mathematical symbolism we find a Babel artificially created by men of science. (Indeed, even one and the same author uses different symbolism in different ages of his creation without deep motives.)

This development does not make scientific communication easier. Among others for even deeper reasons, we must say that for the epistemological hardening of the findings of the social sciences, as well as those of the so-called 'architecturology' (Boudon, Friedman), the development of a disciplined and strict conceptualization which allows experimental control — namely, which uses objective concepts and unequivocal terms — is more important than the exclusive use of mathematical language.

Critical Analysis of a 'Scientific Architecture' and the so-called Topart

Jean Cousin and Yona Friedman are two French architects — the first coming from the French colonies, the second from Hungary and Israel. Without working together they illustrate very well a broader tendency present in contemporary architectural thought. Yona Friedman anticipates that through the application of the theory of graph a 'scientific architecture' can be developed. Jean Cousin hopes to create a new style, the Topart which consists of an architecture created on graphs. (Of course, to add mathematical precision and to show that this debate does not affect the pertinence of the graph theory as a special field of mathematics, we must note that the graph can always be associated with the incidence matrix.)

The success of these enterprises depends on the response to a question: are all the most important aspects of architecture represented in a graph network?

In a short presentation we can say that graphs are composed from a discrete number of elements and bilateral relations between them, which can be directed or symmetrical. The vertices can be completely interchangeable or bear labels; in the latter case a numerical value can be assigned to edges or arcs, thus we call the graph a 'network'. What we must see clearly is that the theory of graph comes from analysis situs, viz., belongs to topology, and it facilitates the manipulation of the set of the participating discrete number of elements and their links, but not qualities which are denoted in the labels. They are there only to say that the elements are *not* interchangeable, and not to say why, in which aspects, and so on.

On the other hand, architecture, insofar as its essential specificity consists in created space systems, communicates space impressions, which are geometrical and sensory in their nature, and continuous in their numerical characteristics. In the representation used by the mentioned authors these truly essential aspects of any architectural system are relegated to the labels of vertices which cannot be manipulated. All topological representation which leaves the geometrical properties in parentheses leaves there the essence of architecture itself. For this reason geometry in its most primitive form, the geometry of banal spaces, is the true domain of the manipulation of our art. The French mathematician Warusfel (1969: 11) is completely correct when he says that abstract Riemann space belongs to the theory of relativity and not to our everyday life, where space has human dimensions (meso versus macro or micro) and is shaped by the architect.

We come to the conclusion that the architectural designer on all levels of manipulation — unisensory space, multisensory composition, syntagmatic arrangement and syntax — is chiefly concerned with geometry in its banal metric form. The perceived space involves shapes which require rigidity, an aspect present in geometry but absent in topology (Alain 1963: 177, 189; Berge 1978: 2). Further, because of the sensory nature of the space impression, not only shape but volumetric magnitude is involved at the first moment of architectural creation. Therefore tridimensional metric geometry cannot be banned as outmoded from the architect's studio. Indeed, it is involved on all levels of the architectural creation: on those of space creation; on those of the physical adjacency of these spaces in order to arrange them in a compact space system through syntagmatic arrangements as immediate constituents of a syntactical construction; and finally, even in metric distance which is involved in the design of the indirect accessibility of spaces in an architectural text.

All this rehabilitation of geometry for the architect does not mean to refuse to use topology in architectural creation, but it would be amatuerish to think that in our time topology replaces geometry, and to command architects to abandon geometrical conception. We said at the beginning of Part III that determination of the space envelope's topological genus helps to distinguish between architectural lexicon and repertory.

On the other hand, coming back to the use of topology for architecture made by Friedman and Cousin, besides some mathematical errors they overestimate the importance of the network representation in the architectural design. Indeed, these graphs simply show the accessibility system or syntactical links of spaces. Therefore *this aspect* of the architectural text can be manipulated on the graph, but not architecture as such. We see at once that anyone who designs using this tool exclusively reduces architecture to urbansim (Whebelle 1969), more exactly to traffic engineering. Their designs expose how the use of a preferred mathematical tool impoverishes the creation itself. Indeed, the preoccupation with planar graphs is related to this traffic engineering which seeks the third dimension only for circulation without intersection and where the whole fundamental nature of space created by a closed tridimensional surface has been forgotten. (It must be said, incidentally, that it is a false hope to reconstruct the three-dimensional system in a planar graph by applying bijective correspondence.)

The Topart, and Firedman's 'scientific architecture', do not open new avenues for architectural creation. They are reductive doctrines which, instead of broadening the architect's horizon, reduce his whole scope to the problem of the traffic engineer who seeks the shortest, smoothest and most continuous path with the minimum of interruptions. Their proponents are prisoners and not masters of the means they use.

Multisensory Intricacy of the Space System and its Representation

In the previous section we made a critical analysis of the representation of the architectural space system by graphs and concluded that only syntactical links can be apprehended successfully by that means. In order to apply graphs even on this level it is necessary that we first solve problems emerging from the multisensory intricacy of architectural words. Indeed, not only on the unisensory level do bound morphemes require a closing-up into a complex word which has a free form, but acoustic space, optical space, and haptic space can be compounded in such a manner that their simultaneous envelopes are not geometrically identical. We have seen already on the morphological level that determination of the space impression (considered in an experiment) in an unequivocal manner necessitates that, on the one hand, the question specifies which sensory space's volume or shape must be discriminated by the subject, and, on the other hand, in order to assure that the subject has a homogeneous space impression and speaks always about the same acoustical, optical, and haptic space, he must not leave a common parcel which is shared by the same optical, acoustical, and haptic space. In general terms, this multisensory intricacy of architectural morphemes can include seven parcels which show different space experiences because their multisensory space composition is objectively different (see 3 in Figure 3.18).

Of course, this is an isolated multisensory space composition for purposes of morphological consideration. In reality, the problem is even more complicated because the multisensory morphemes of the architectural medium are embedded in syntagmatic arrangements of various extents. How can we master this complicacy by using graphs to represent the syntactical construction of the space system in all sensory spaces at once?

We now give a solution to the problem under the assumption that if we consider a large-enough space system, we will ultimately arrive at a closed surface which contains at the same time the set of all sensory spaces included in a common envelope.

We use the method on three cases which employ all rules and allow universal application to any trisensorily composed space arrangements. In Figure 3.29 the first column presents the topological situation. The second shows the polygraphs which reproduce all adjacency relations between all parcels indicating which sensory space is involved. The A and O graphs deal individually with each unisensory space arrangement without respect to the multisensory space composition. The polygraph is an analytical tool which shows all relations but on which we cannot count how many unisensory spaces are involved. This second data is revealed on the A(coustical), O(ptical), and H(aptic) graphs. From the polygraph we can easily and perfectly reconstruct the graph showing the adjacency arrangement of any unisensory space system. The rule is that we consider only relations which were given in the polygraph by the line representing the sense modality under consideration. On the other hand, all vertices which would become isolated on a 'unisensory graph' must be integrated with that point to which they were related on the polygraph by another link representing *another* sense. This operation is necessary so that the unisensory graph has not only the right number of vertices but that the possible labels of vertices are exact (e.g., addition of the parcels' volumetric magnitude to show the volume of the unisensory space). Of course the 'unisensory A, O, and H graphs' and the polygraphs are not converse; namely, from the polygraph we can reconstruct

376 Communication through architecture

1.   Polygraph.   A-graph.   O-graph.

$n_P = 7$
$n_{AS} = 3$
$n_{OS} = 5$

2.

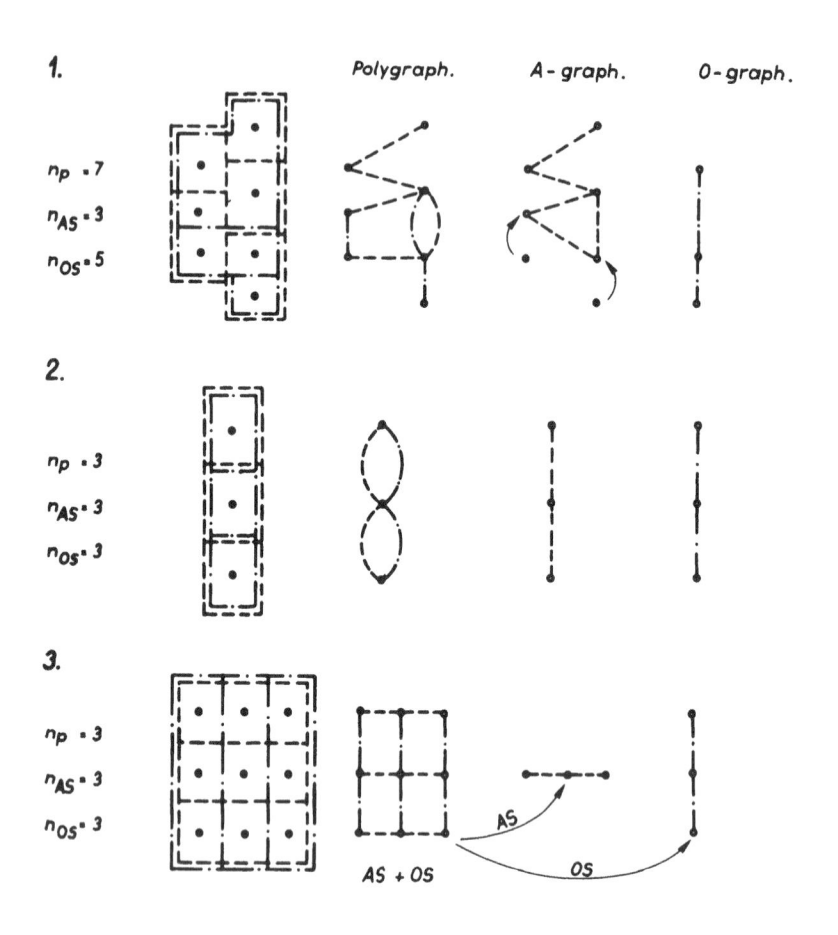

$n_P = 3$
$n_{AS} = 3$
$n_{OS} = 3$

3.

$n_P = 3$
$n_{AS} = 3$
$n_{OS} = 3$

AS + OS   AS   OS

n_P : Number of participating homogeneous space parcels.

n_{AS} : Number of acoustical spaces (-----).

n_{OS} : Number of optical spaces (—·—·—).

Figure 3.29. *Notation of a bisensory compound spaces and their unisensory space components by graph.*

any 'unisensory graphs', but we cannot decompose the A, O, and H graphs into the polygraph showing all homogeneous parcels and their relation to the compound space composition.

ARCHITECTURAL TEXT, ITS GRAPH AND SYNTAX

By the critical analysis of the application of graphs for the description and design of architecture, we tried to fix properly the limit of the significance of this representation. In the next section we gave techniques for the integration of the multisensory aspect of the architectural space system into the representation by graphs. We can discuss now substantial aspects of the representation of the syntax of the architectural text by graphs.

The syntactical order of the architectural space system consists in a system of direct and indirect accessibility of the spaces provided by the connectivity of the system. The syntactical order prefigures a set of potential readings of the architectural text, while the ultimate and immediate constituents of the sentence construction — as far as they are prefabricated in the morphology — prefigure their own possible participation. Indeed, the paradigmatic valence realized by puncturing the space envelope for access (e.g., doors) determines the two demidegrees, namely inward and outward, of the locale. As immediate constituent the graph of adjacent spaces shows the potential for direct accessibility. This graph of physical infrastructure does not assure access but makes it possible without introducing grammatical artifacts, architecturally 'desemanticized' (Guiraud 1967: 41) empty words, or expletives such as corridors. They are architecturally amorphous locales (function words) and have grammatical rather than lexical meaning. Therefore the graph of adjacencies is fundamentally a nondirected one. Arcs in the syntactical graphs can also appear without arrows, but they represent, in fact, symmetrical arcs. Vertices of the adjacency graphs are not linked by arcs but by edges.

To present the whole picture of the analysis of the space system with all its layers, we see the sentence as an autonomous unit at the center of the syntax. It is from this point downward that morphemes and syntagms are chosen as constituents to be entered in a syntactical composition as elements of major form classes, namely parts of speech, and upward that an architectural opus is spun. The sentence is an autonomous component of the graph which gives purpose to all spaces as locales, and on the level of a graph it shows links (isthmuses: Berge 1966 [1963]: 190) which, if deleted, disconnect the system into two components (e.g., closing the door of an apartment). On the other side, the architectural opus is defined by the fact that the space system is connected without passing through the atmospheric space as context. In common language we would say 'without leaving the house', but this is misleading because the architectural opus as such is not the building — since a building can include more or less than one architectural text — but the connected space system. Of course, as a sentence can be a one-word sentence, or an opus a one-sentence work, nothing prevents the architect from making a one-living-room apartment, or a big tent for communal living, or from constructing apartments, duplexes, or individual villas.

To truly present in a nutshell the whole context in which the graph of syntactical composition as a point of junction of the architectural text must be considered, the implication of the constructed architectural text for its beholders remains to be established. Indeed, the architect can provide many degrees of freedom in which the beholder can read the opus and gather from it the architect's message. In terms of graphs, all cases are situated between two extremes. At one extreme, we have the case where all spaces are antinodes (Berge 1966 [1963]: 123) having only one entry and one exit. The order of reception is determined like a speech for the audience (cf. Alexander 1966: 6). At the other extreme, we find the complete graph where from any space there is direct access to any other and the beholder is completely free. The latter can be realized by adding the necessary number of corridors, stairways, and elevators to the adjacencies given in the syntagmatic arrangement.

In general the plurality of reading order is inherent in the architectural space system as a three-dimensional system. The mapping of the actual frequentation reveals the beholder's strategy.

Network of Accessibility and Paradigmatic Valence

Festinger's well-known study on the MIT campus (Festinger et al. 1950) and Calhoun's study of rats (1966: 46) drew a relation between (residential) distance and frequency of association. It is clear that for sociological purposes the mutual accessibility of spaces is the relevant factor. Let us review now all aspects which are relevant in the determination of the mutual accessibility of spaces in a space system.

We can distinguish direct and indirect accessibility. In the first case the subject can go from one space into another without passing through other spaces which are meaningful architectural units. Direct accessibility requires either an adjacency of the spaces or function spaces. The whole substance of function space consists in its paradigmatic valence, namely how many doors it can manage on its surface.

Adjacency itself has no relevance to the syntax of architectural constructions without the paradigmatic valence of the spaces involved — namely its doors or other openings which allow actual access. While the adjacency is represented by edges of nondirected graphs, the graph of accessibility is fundamentally a directed network composed of arcs which can bear numerical value characterizing the accessibility.

Two spaces can be directly connected in both directions by more than one arc indicating, for example, main entrance and side door. It is a multigraph.

The indirect accessibility must also be understood in a directed manner; one's connection to another does not imply the converse.

Accessibility has always two meanings: a topological one and a metric one. The graph shows the topological connectivity. Metric accessibility is measured in terms of the physical distance that the subject must travel to arrive at the destination space. This can be displayed by the number attached to the network's arc. The adjacency of two rooms as such is irrelevant in determining their topological connectivity and metric distance in the syntactical construction of architecture. For the possible sociological effect of the accessibility of spaces, it is the metric distance which counts. More precisely, it is the time and effort involved in the access which gives an architectural syntactical construction its immediate sociological significance.

Let us illustrate the question in terms of graphs. Each locale has a paradigmatic valance which determines its readiness to be directly connected by adjacency to another locale. The paradigmatic valence shows the number of possibilities of coming and going in the space. If all openings are not at least qualitatively symmetrical, i.e., the subject can go in and out, the paradigmatic valence is composed from two demidegrees — one inward $d^+(x)$ and another outward $d^-(x)$. In short, the paradigmatic valence of a space is represented by $(d^+[x] + d^-[x]) \cdot 1/2$ and by the ratio $d^+(x)/d^-(x)$, which is equal to unity if all doors are symmetrical. The converse is not necessarily true (see 4 in Figure 3.25).

If the space has only $d^+(x) \leqslant 2$ it is called an antinode in respect to its paradigmatic valence for the graph. All other spaces are nodes. If a space has only one door, it is pendant and its path is blind. (See Figure 3.30.) In this case the architect did not leave any choice to the beholder for how he might gain access to the room.

If an access, for example a door, is qualitatively symmetric — $d(x, y) = = d(y, x)$ — that is, if we can go in and out by the same door, but at the same time the accessibility in terms of effort or time is not equivalent, then it is quantitatively antisymmetrical $(x, y) \in U \Rightarrow (y, x) \notin U$, which is signaled by the different numbers indicated on the opposite arcs. The case of antisymmetry is not of only theoretical interest for the architectural space system. There are many instances where at the same access line the facility of passing is not the same, as, for example, doors which open in only one direction, or steps, or other cases of 'elevational symmetry', though some authors (P.E.

380 *Communication through architecture*

Multigraphs.

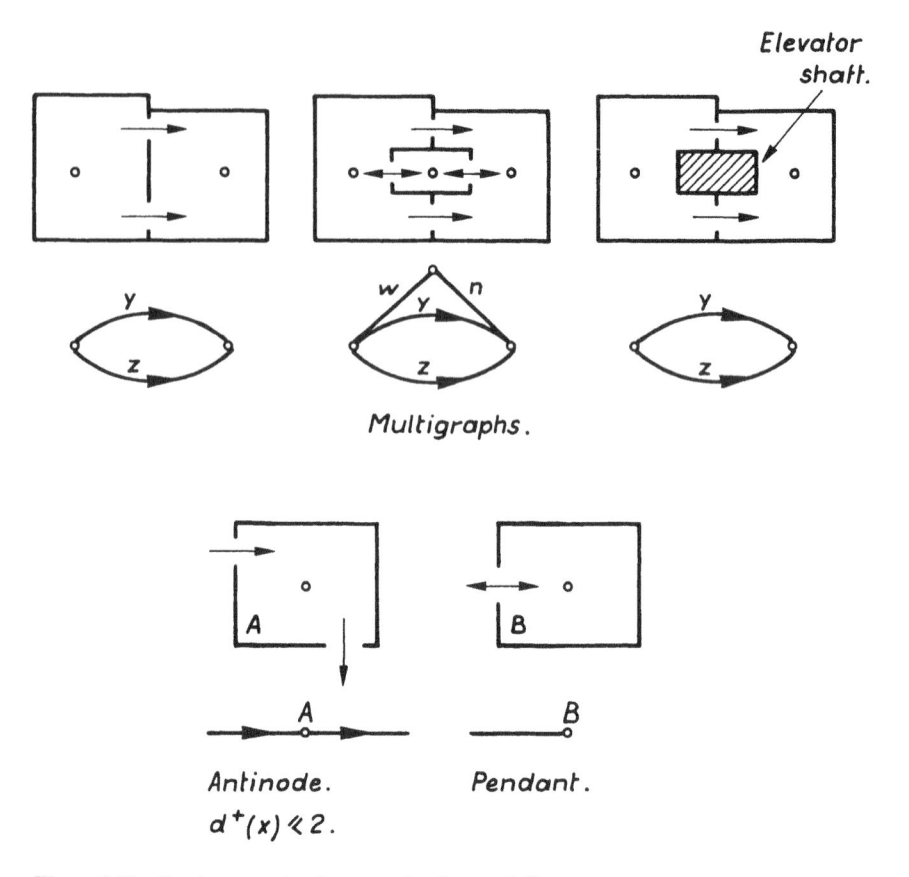

Antinode.
$d^+(x) \ll 2$.

Pendant.

Figure 3.30. *Further notation in network of accessibility.*

Tabor) have measured that the loss of time due to antisymmetry between different floors is qualitatively less important than the naive observer would expect.

We will see later that the paradigmatic valence of a space having only symmetrical *adjacent* arcs can be visualized by the dual representation of the graph of the space system where edge becomes side (see Figure 3.34).

Generally speaking, we can say that the graph of the syntactical construction of architecture is composed from arcs, from edges (showing symmetrical arcs), and from multigraphs which represent multiple-door relations between two spaces. We must hasten to say that the participating locale's paradigmatic valence prefigures greatly the architectural opus, leaving the beholder a determinate amount of freedom for alternative exploration. We call a network of the architectural text homogeneous, or regular, if all locales have an equal paradigmatic valence.

It would be wrong to think that the architect is obliged to construct the same space system even if he changes neither the number of spaces nor the number of doors involved — namely their paradigmatic valence. Indeed, these two data do not necessarily identify all the isomorphic graphs as a class of substitution (see Figure 3.32). We will see that the order of connection can vary within the use of the same words. What is important to note is that the syntactical order of the architectural opus consists in the set of possible alternative paths of the explorer.

Function words; transit spaces

We have learned that the syntactical requirements of an architectural sentence can contradict geometrical and other topological desiderata.

(1) The architect wishes to establish a direct accessibility between two spaces which by their geometry cannot be adjacent: syntagmatic incompatibility. (2) The architect wishes to realize a space system in a one-level composition which conflicts with requirements for a set of indispensible direct accesses among locales. We will see that a space system composed of more than four units cannot assure direct access among all locales by a (complete) planar graph. If we impose more than $3(n-2)$ relations (Euler) to a planar graph, the lines must cross at other points than a vertex. (We will discuss the question of planar graphs later; however, we warned that it is misleading when some authors suggest a necessary isomorphism between a planar graph and a one-level syntactical arrangement for an architectural space system.)

As we can see, the origin may be different, but the remedy is the same for solving the problem of direct accessibility between spaces without adjacency. The grammarian, whether architect or writer, introduces in the text a conceptual and morphological artifact, namely the empty word. It is a word, but it has no meaning. It is desemanticized (Chao 1968: 100, 80; Chomsky 1972: 114-115; Guiraud 1968: 41) from any theme, but it is also 'phonetically' empty, understood as a residual or added space whose geometry is not determined by intrinsic requirements. It is a pure product of its syntactical function. It attempts the impossible task of giving direct access to nonadjacent meaningful units. The numerous puncturations of its envelope by doors, etc., reveal its substance, which consists in its paradigmatic valence assuring access. Esthetically we evaluate its geometry with great indulgence, since a corridor is not here to stimulate peripatetic discussions but for traffic. We even accept straight corridors 300 m. long, such as we find in the newly constructed (1978) headquarters of the Johns-Manville Company near Denver, Colorado, where the Architects Collaborative of Cambridge, Mass., and the

Space Design Group introduced this absurd tunnel as artifice by stretching out Le Corbusier's LaTourette (1955). Indeed, corridors do not mobilize the form recognition faculty of the beholder but rather his orientation capacity; and at this point we are very exacting with relational spaces. Relational spaces can be esthetically indifferent but must allow easy orientation without crossing incompatible circulation lines. We are entertained by burlesque scenes in films where busy waitresses with trays full of plates run into elegant clients; where the physician collides with his patients; or where actors get mixed up with theater-goers in the confusion of badly organized circulation lines behind the scenes.

The meaningful words as lexical items are an open-ended list in a family which is always enlarging by thematic inflection or otherwise. Function words constitute a closed group. They are disciplined by syntactical control. In respect to architecture we can group them (1) by their paradigmatic valence (number of openings), and (2) by their orientation in the gravitational field. Corridors, vestibules, and other spaces are designated for horizontal circulation; vertical elevators, stairways, ramps, and escalators are designated for nonhorizontal circulation.

As a conceptual artifact, a basic characteristic of the empty word is that it does not figure among the meaningful lexical units. Indeed, if we begin to include one its role is immediately dissolved by this simple fact: namely, the two rooms to which it gives access will no longer be in direct access because of the corridor which is interposed between them. It must be a nul element which does not increase the number of vertices in the graph. This 'nullification' or process of ignoring insignificant spaces is an artifice of accountancy.

It is the very logic of the nul element (Cousin 1970: 115) that to omit it, or to diminish its occurrence or its role in a large and strongly connected architectural opus, can be considered a sign of the elegance of the syntactical construction.

Sense and Non-Sense: the Twisted Architectural Network

Before going into the more technical discussion of the architectural syntax and its application in architectural texts, we will try to eliminate some misunderstandings which are deeply rooted in the common perception of architecture. We discussed in Part I, and in the first chapter of this part, that the public is acquainted with many an architectural opus without having had the opportunity to open these opuses, to penetrate them. (Architectural opuses are also often shown to the public exclusively via a hasty photograph of their exterior.) As we said in Part I, the relation between the (natural) atmospheric space and the architectural space system is an important issue of the composition; generally speaking this puts a text in its context but does not alone give it a proper reading.

Men learn to read nature. It is chiefly composed of such convex impenetrable shapes as mountains and only marginally of caves and other concavities, which are often discovered by chance. Those who see architecture in terms of *buildings* apply this schematic type of reading to architecture. But what is pertinent and revealing for nature does not apply to architecture, which is a space system. The packing of space systems reveals the architectural opus marginally, and in a misleading manner. Indeed, this *convex* shape expresses often indistinctly the number of spaces included — especially in our time when spaces are often smaller than in previous periods — even less the syntactic composition (i.e., the space system with its proper utterance). At best, the superficial reader circumambulates and is invited by the architect — who relies on deceptive effects to encourage this — to pass through the so-called main facade and then 'absorb' the whole building in a two-dimensional reduction. The most curious of the explorers tries to guess the architectural space system by the order and number of windows and doors. Arab architecture, which deliberately turns its back to the streetscape, makes it especially hard for those pursuing this awkward and uninitiated approach.

As a matter of fact this reading — speaking in mathematical terms — is an involution of inverse type which twists the sense of architecture. It is an appropriate way to read nature as lithosphere, but applied to architecture, it is a preposterous 'denatured' reading of it which maps it mentally into nature. During this pyramid-type reading, countless aspects of architecture remain ignored or confused, namely impenetrable gaps are confused with space and simple space adjacency with an actually connected space system, and the multisensory intricacy of the architectural space system is ignored.

It is the specific task of the architect to create man-controlled (that is, free from natural hazards) *concave* space systems. As we said in Part I and elsewhere (Ankerl 1974: 578ff), urbanism, at least in its common form, which simply invites the architect to complete a landscape — often already ruined by ill-advised traffic engineering — by a streetscape, cannot be considered architecture's apotheosis. Even if the geometric scale of urbanism is larger, it uses only a marginal and derivative aspect of architecture. (Of course, urbanism devoted to a completely controlled arctic or underground city establishes a truly new relation between architectural space systems and the whole surround, and therefore between architect and urbanist.)

Perhaps some readers are surprised to see that in considering the architectural space system we involve its reading in such a predominant manner. For them we must recall that the syntactical order of an architectural text

384 Communication through architecture

has been defined — represented in terms of graphs or of matrices — by the set of possible reading paths inherent in it.

Atmospheric Space as Context: U *Graph*

If an observer from outer space could perceive pervasively the 'architectural milieu', he would behold first of all a set of adjacent concavities, spaces planted in the earth's crust in the immediate environment where the atmosphere encounters the lithosphere. Around the earth's spherical surface,

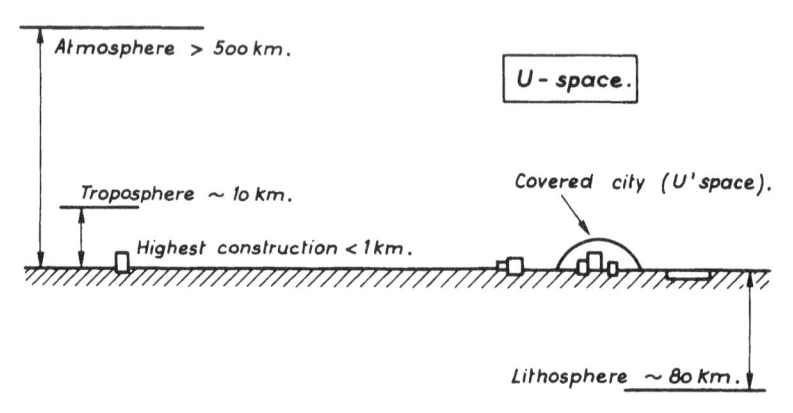

architectural space systems are relatively closely earthbound with some parts penetrating and some sticking out perpendicular to the earth. Our illustration is disproportionate even if we consider the world's tallest skyscraper, namely the Sears Tower in Chicago, which is nearly half a kilometer high (444 m.) and has 110 floors. Its penetration of the lithosphere is even more modest. However, the figure illustrates that all architectural texts as connected space systems can be adjacent either to another architectural text — with which it is not directly connected — or to natural spaces such as caves, to the compact lithosphere, or finally to atmospheric space.

As we have just recalled, architectural texts — meaning 'readable' pieces of communication — are enjoyed by frequentation which implies access through connectivity of the locales; therefore among the adjacent environments only natural cavities and atmospheric space can be considered as context to the text. The extension of natural caves by architectural ones is of interest for theoretical reasons as well as for sociological ones because they reveal a fundamental sociological phenomenon, namely the cryptic one (e.g., catacombs) (see Georg Simmel about secrecy). But atmospheric space is a central issue in the description of the total architectural space system not only for quantitative reasons, in that there are more doors which open to the atmospheric space than doors which lead to caves. Atmospheric space also has the unique property of being the universal context (U) of all architectural texts. Indeed, it is a universal space of reference for all architectural opuses which are defined by contrasting them to the U. Thus, an architectural text is *an* opus insofar as its composing spaces are directly or indirectly intercommunicating without having to go 'out' into natural space which is not controlled by men against the hazards and rigors of the atmosphere. It is this definition of the architectural opus which is intrinsically architecturological, and which replaces the 'building', long considered as the architectural work. In the next section we will discuss the proper architectural meaning of buildings contrasted to urban contextual space.

The U as contextual space is omnipresent, and all architectural opuses bound by gravity to mother earth communicate with her just as we did at our origin through the umbilical cord. Indeed, the U must not be confused with so-called outer space. U is atmospheric space. Space systems created elsewhere in spacecraft or on the moon do not have a natural space as context through which the inhabitant can communicate between architectural opuses without encasing his whole body in an artificial envelope resembling architecture (cf. spacesuit, vehicles, mobile architecture in the proper sense of the term). Further, even when accustomed to more precise spaces such as the uterine, cave, or architectural ones, the beholder can attribute the space characteristics, namely volume and shape, to the firmament (Vurpillot 1967: vi-133). After this discussion of architecture's U key, we can try to reply to the question: which representation in the graph of space systems would be appropriate for it?

We can either give to this vertex a special label or simply locate the U vertex at infinity as the so-called vanishing (ideal) point is. Thus all the graphs of all architectural opuses become open ones. Because the criterion for an architectural opus was only the internal connectivity, it is possible that one opus has more than one gate leading to U space, and therefore its graph has more than one edge of infinite length, which results in more than one infinite face. We will see its significance during the discussion of dual graphs.

Urban space as contextual U' *space*

We have repeated in this book many times that city planning cannot be understood as the integration of architectural space creation at the highest level of synthesis. We noted that our city planning has a bidimensional origin such as we find in agriculture or in landscape architecture, and in its recent development, in many respects, it is only traffic engineering which has been added, or at best streetscape architecture. This is not truly a creation of controlled spaces, which is the architect's specific task, but a completion of the natural landscape (Schulze-Fielitz 1971: 10, 42). His *Grossklimathalle* [giant climate-controlled dome] as a kind of macroenvironmental envelope is what we could call urban space (1971: 22). Under an arctic climate or on a planet without atmosphere, it can serve as contextual or reference space for other architectural spaces which are envelopes of mesoscale. It simulates functions of the atmospheric space (U) on a high level of control as it is proper to the architectural spaces. As a 'wet nurse' it includes the architectural texts and as context relates them indirectly as the atmospheric space did. U' is truly global space in the architectural sense of the term and its creation enlarges the range of possible solutions.

The Architectural Text and its Subdivisions: The Sentence as the Largest Grammatical Unit

We have established that the architectural opus as text is defined not by physical adjacency, not by how the spaces are packed in so-called buildings, but by the network of accessibility among a set of morphologically labelled spaces. In this very sense, opuses and their subdivisions will be distinguished by the system of vertical and horizontal openings such as gates, doors, or continuous elevators.

In the breakdown of the architectural space system into its successive layers of construction — and we mean here construction in the purely architectural sense of the term — two main levels emerge: *opus* and *sentence*. As we have already said, an architectural space system constitutes an opus to the extent that the beholder can go from one space into any other without crossing the doorstep leading to U space. It must be understood clearly (see D in Figure 3.31) that for a windowless multistoried space system where all levels are equal and are related among themselves by an elevator, it makes no difference from the strict viewpoint of its *internal* order (Z. S. Harris 1952: 9 and n.9) how deep it is planted in the lithosphere and how high it thrusts into the atmosphere. As a matter of fact, studies show that people who frequent the Place Ville-Marie in Montreal judge the underground character of a windowless space not from its actual situation (it is built on sloping ground and has interpenetrating levels), but from its entry points — one on the street level, and the other through an underground tunnel from the Hotel Queen Elizabeth.

The fundamental element of architectural discourse is the architectural sentence. If we compare the strict order commanded by syntax in the internal construction of a sentence with that relating (successive) sentences among themselves in an opus (as total discourse), we see the fundamental nature of the sentence as an organizer of language.

Syntax of space systems and subsystems 387

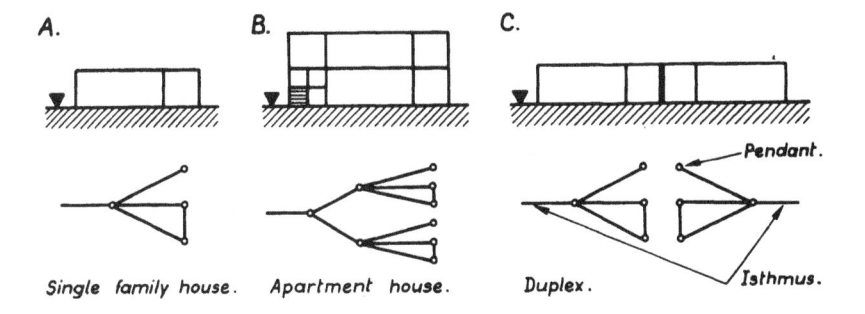

Single family house. Apartment house. Duplex. Isthmus.

Dwellings with the same internal arrangement inserted in one – A and B – or two (C) architectural opuses.

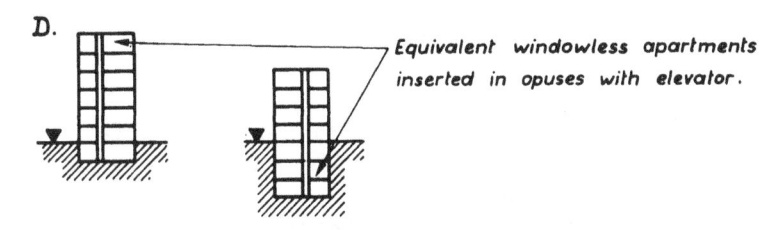

Equivalent windowless apartments inserted in opuses with elevator.

Figure 3.31. *Architectural text and its subdivision.*

When a space as a recurrent and meaningful unit enters into a syntactical composition, it loses its multipurpose nature and acquires a specific value through the major form class in which it is used as part of a sentence. The architectural sentence has a label which assigns a purpose. Prefabricated spaces also have a label under which they are stocked, but this is a morphological one indicating shape, volume, and surface characteristics and paradigmatic valence. In the labeling of the sentence it is not only new topological characteristics which are added – namely the syntactical arrangement into which the spaces are entered – but a denomination referring to the purpose. This new significance affects also the free forms or spaces inserted in the sentence by adding to each of them a denomination revealing its purpose in the sentence (e.g., 'an apartment' is a sentence denomination, while 'a living room' is a space denomination). In a well-formed architectural sentence, it is not the given name itself or only the furnishings and fixtures which provide space with this functional specification, but its architectural identity within the sentence.

The question now is to distinguish nonequivalent sentences on the same objective level as we did with the architectural morphemes. We must avoid the pitfall of the tyranny of words that we have spared ourselves and our readers through this entire book until this point. We will adopt the approach of the structural archaeologist who describes the space systems of civilization about which no written document, and therefore no labels, remain or can be deciphered. This is a tool not only for description but for proper architectural design; that is, a well-written architectural program must indicate the requirements in objective spatial terms. The sentence is here apprehended as the largest grammatical unit.

In order to distinguish between two space systems, e.g., an apartment from a theater, we have two objective tools; looking for the relation among the minimal units of utterance — or predication — which is the sentence in its internal arrangement, as well as discovering its relation to other sentences as part of an opus.

In the Indo-European languages the period serves as a mechanical distinction for a sentence, while the internal arrangement shows whether it is well formed or not. We will see that the differences noted between the strict discipline commanding the word order within a sentence and the looser one commanding the sentence order is even more pronounced in architecture (Ankerl 1972a: 280-281).

One architectural sentence is distinguished from another in the opus in general by an isthmus (Berge 1966 [1963]: 184, 190). Strictly speaking, an isthmus is an edge — i.e., a door — which, if closed, divides a connected space system into two components which are subgraphs of the whole connected system (see Figure 3.31). How can we apply this concept to our specific question? Space systems which can be closed, or cut off from the world, by a single door are rather rare; already the fire regulations of wood-constructed US settlements do not allow this even if the normal functioning of the architectural sentence does not itself require it. An architectural sentence by its nonlinear order need not be terminated by 'a period'. There could be several doorsills where the system can be locked, which because they are in plurality are not isthmuses in the strict sense of the graph. The sophistication and the multiplicity of the internal connectivity of the network in comparison with its possible relative isolation from other parts of the opus make its external determination.

The internal order is the basic criterion. Any grammarian can subsequently put in the forgotten period in a text composed of well-formed sentences, insofar as the sentence internal order determines its place completely. It is its property to be significant without immediate context. The internal order will be described by a sophisticated network linking vertices with individual morphological labels which make them noninterchangeable. The number of the included spaces, their morphological labels, and their relatively imperative or incidental position, which comes from the major form class (e.g., predicate) that 'hired' it, as well as the pattern of the syntactical network, determine the sentence. The morphological character of the central spaces and their relation in the syntactical network give the major types of sentences. Within a class we can distinguish subclasses where the central spaces may vary in certain respects or where, through their number and relations, they allow us to distinguish various styles and creations of various significances (e.g., extended simple sentence, complex sentence).

This abstract grammatical description of architectural space composition reveals how narrow-minded it is to concentrate architectural attention on the two poles of current interest, namely housing and city planning. Indeed, the structural description of architectural space systems shows that there are major areas of creation, and we do not refer to taller and taller corporate headquarters where a large number of relatively small rooms are stacked, but to libraries, theatres and other 'cultic spaces' where the specific task of the architect emerges fully.

Of course, some will object that a purely structural description will make it impossible to distinguish between hotel and hospital; however, if we consider the function of certain space systems in the depth of their full lifetime (March and Martin 1972: 332-333) even this structural description reveals how close were the purposes of a *Hôtel de Dieu* and a *Hôtel de Bellerive*, both 'hospices' at the moment of their construction.

READING ARCHITECTURE: FROM NETWORK TO FACTORS

We already have mentioned that the syntactical network of the architectural space system can be a multigraph, providing more than one direct link between two rooms, either a completely directed one or a partially directed one having symmetric arcs allowing two-way communication. The reading of architecture proceeds by the choice of a path in this network. P. K. Cadwell says: 'We move from one space to another by making maps, mapping one space into another.' According to the characteristics of the network, some passages can be imposed, some excluded, and others are facultative. If the network is not composed exclusively from antinodes, as is the case in an exposition hall with strictly one-way traffic, usually the beholder can make an infinite number of trips. It is this aspect that makes the reading of architecture so different from the reading of literature. Both are realized in a string but the literary text has only one string or factor (Berge 1966 [1963]: 111), all its words are simple points of articulation — $d^+(x) = d^-(x) = 1$ — or antinodes. It cannot be reversed either by symmetric arc or by multigraph; it has neither circuit nor more than one factor. It bears its instruction for reading in an intrinsic manner.

Even if not all reading strings are possible in a particular architectural text, the number remains infinite until we specify a reading instruction. We can specify more than one instruction, and on the other hand, most individual instruction can be realized by more than one reading. The enumeration of the possible itineraries realized under a specific reading instruction reveals clearly the architectural message inherent in the network. It reveals also not only the text but its insertion in the (contextual) U space: where in the text is the point of origin? Is there more than one starting point, or must the initial and the terminal arc be incident to the same vestibule as vertex?

Various Possible Reading Instructions

How a system of spaces must be read depends on the concern of the beholder, as well as the space system's purpose. Is it a church or a factory? Is the beholder a tourist or a regular visitor? Or a fugitive? The optimization of each purpose has a corresponding instruction for reading: (short, abbreviated, extended read, etc.). Let us discuss some of the most frequent instructions.

(1) Perusal, scanning: the realization of this objective is relatively clear for the literary text, despite the 'discovery' of speed reading. We must read every word, even if the speed or rhythm is not specified. If we apply the same instruction in precise terms to the reading of architecture, we see immediately that it is not specific enough for this complicated system. But on the other side, even if we allow limitless 'mileage', certain specific instructions cannot be carried out in some networks.

An exhaustive reading can be specified as a visit to all locales. Even if we fix the vestibule as the point where the path or circuit can begin and end, and all locales are not antinodes with only one entrance and one exit, this instruction can be realized by an infinite set of paths which include an infinite number of repetitions for the forgetful visitor.

Another rule must be added, namely that the path must be the most concise possible, including the minimum number of iterations, viz., of redundant impressions. If we can choose a route without passing more than once through any locale, viz., by an elementary path, the factor which means an itinerary in terms of graphs, is in this case Hamiltonian (Berge 1966 [1963]: 7, 107, 111). If there is only one vestibule, we speak about a Hamiltonian circuit — a factor of one circuit — where only the vestibule is visited twice.

Usually Hamiltonian paths are partial graphs of the network, not using all doors, but some networks do not possess Hamiltonian paths, or circuits, and to realize the exploration of all rooms implies repetition; therefore the factor of exploration becomes a graph that is longer than the network. We mean here topological length which is measured by the number of arcs (doorsills).

Written from left to right, or vice versa, from top to bottom, or vice versa, all linguistic texts must be read in only one way, passing from one determined unit to another in a determined manner. This applies also to the reading of the Chinese text (Chao 1968: 13). With the architectural system this is not the case. Not only can we become acquainted with the locales in various successive orders, giving them different grammatical stress, but it is also possible to enter a room by different doors and so approach it from more than one angle if it has a high inward demidegree as paradigmatic valence. This implies that even if identical twins with identical thoughts visit the same room, each will have a different mental map of it, if each sees it first from a different angle or doorstep. Therefore to be sure that the objective conditions of a perusal are truly granted it is not enough to prescribe a passage through all locales, but it is not without interest to ask: from which side did you approach it? A scrupulous reader, e.g., a professor of history of architecture, will try to pass not only once through all rooms but also through all its doors, viz., integrating in its factor all possible arcs. By this means all objective conditions of an original experience are exhausted. Of course, the professor will spare his energy and try to make the least number of repetitions. By chance, there are networks where this task can be realized — namely passing by all doors in both directions without crossing an intervening door more than two times. This path is called a simple one (Berge 1966 [1963]: 7). (A simple path does not necessarily run through all doors.)

Euler volunteered as an amateur tourist guide of Königsberg and proved that it is impossible to cross all seven bridges over the river Pregel around the Kneiphof island without crossing at least one bridge more than once. Following this, some authors call a circuit which uses every arc once and once only a 'Euler line' (Berge 1966 [1963]: 167). It must be noted that the Eulerian criterion is more exacting than the Hamiltonian — namely that no one can cross all thresholds if he does not enter all rooms at least once — and therefore the Eulerian circuit is topologically always longer than the Hamiltonian. But this does not imply that an Euler graph must necessarily have a Hamiltonian circuit. We will see later that their relation is more complex. Finally, we must say that the Eulerian circuit is not directly relevant for our present concern. It is formulated for a graph where all arcs are symmetrical (viz., edges) and the satisfaction of the Eulerian requirements does not guarantee that the visitor pass all thresholds in both directions, which would be the relevant requirement from the viewpoint of perception. The Eulerian circuit only assures the beholder that at the end he has closed all doors — if that was what he wished to do. The Eulerian circuit is not a factor but a semifactor (Berge 1966 [1963]: 187). Euler does nothing more than to 'convert' a symmetrical graph into a directed one, both of which have the same length and include the same vertices. (In other words, he adds arrows indicating only economical use of doorsteps.)

(2) Skimming transit: the previous instructions to visit all locales or even to enter them by all possible doors with the least possible iteration was an

unambiguous one. However, because many networks possess neither a Hamiltonian path, nor a circuit, nor a simple path running through all doors once, its realization can be very time-consuming. Even the objective itself presupposes that upon his arrival at the gate the visitor does not have any information which would make one locale more interesting or valuable than another.

Opposite this exhaustive (and exhausting) interest, the visitor can consider the whole space system as an obstacle. A labyrinth is an example of this kind of senseless wandering. The Minotaurian visitor looks for the shortest way out; in terms of a graph, the shortest path, called directed distance $d(x, y)$ (Berge 1966 [1963]: 119). If the visitor is compelled to see some locales at any price, the reading instruction can also be expressed as the directed distance among these spaces. Art Buchwald describes this kind of strategy for a digest visit in his 'Twenty Years Later' (1974):

One of the main reasons I came back to Paris was to celebrate the 20th anniversary of the breaking of the six-minute Louvre. It was exactly 20 years ago to the day that a young American student named Peter Stone amazed the world by going through the Louvre Museum in 5 minutes and 19 seconds. As everyone knows there are only three things worth seeing in the Louvre Museum — they are the Venus of Milo, the Winged Victory and the Mona Lisa — the rest of the stuff is junk. For years tourists have been trying to get through the Louvre as fast as possible, see those three things, and then go out shopping again. . . . Peter said: "I did some exhibition running at the Prado in Spain and the Tata Gallery in London. The Russians invited me to run through the Hermitage in Leningrad. It was the first time the Soviets had ever asked an American to race through one of their museums.

The discussion itself of these frequentation strategies serves not only the visitor but the architect whose art is to create the syntactical arrangement which makes it easy for the visitor not to miss major spaces (e.g., by putting 'isthmus-doors' in them) and to find rest rooms only if needed. The architect ought to anticipate the paths and circuits which are possible in the network.

The formulation of the reading instruction becomes more difficult if the beholder must find the best solution where the cost of iteration is compared to a loss by omission. The graph shows the topological distance, namely how many doors must be opened before reaching all specified spaces. However, door opening is only one of the possible costs; time and effort are even more proportional to the metric distance of the three-dimensional banal space, taking also into account its situation on the gravitational field (e.g., slope). Of course, any of these variables relevant to the calculus of economy of the visit can be introduced in the graph as a numerical value of the network's arcs, but it cannot be manipulated by an operation made on the graph. Prihar (1956) exposes a technique which makes any of these aspects of the itinerary topologically manipulable. In order to schematize complicated and extensive graphs, some authors 'close up' the graph by suppressing all points which are antinodes. The presence or absence of these points does not affect many of the graph's important characteristics. Prihar uses this fact in the opposite way. He introduces between vertices as many antinodes as dummy points as is necessary to show the relative physical characteristics labeled on the original arc in relation to the others. In this case the counting of the arcs shows the physical characteristics which are truly relevant in the visitor's strategy; that

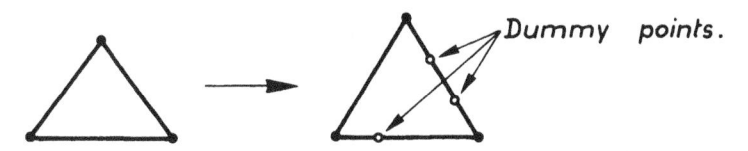

Expanding the graph by dummy vertices.

is, the number of dummy nodes that can express the physical length between the center of gravity of the two linked rooms, an 'ergonomic' value necessary for passing from one space into the other, or even the time needed (ecological distance).

1. *Perusal*

Hamiltonian and Eulerian sequences We have seen that the Hamiltonian path or — if the space network has only one gate linking it to the U space — circuit, would assure a unique visit to all locales of the space system; on the other hand, a scrupulously designed exploration in the sense of perception would involve not only a visit to every locale but an entering by all possible doors. We know that Euler proposes chains and cycles which do not consider that passage through a door in opposite directions involves two different experiences. Despite this fact, we discuss also the Eulerian solutions for two reasons: conveniently, we find well-established theorems concerning the solution of Euler's problem; and secondly, we can apply his solution to our problem by inversing his itinerary and thus counting it twice.

We will respond to the following questions:

— How in a given network does the existence of a Hamiltonian or Eulerian itinerary imply the existence of the other?
— How do structural characteristics of the network and the location of entrance and exit doors determine the existence of Hamilton's and Euler's itinerary?
— How might the visitor find them?

We know that on the one hand, all elementary paths are simple ones and, on the other hand, all Hamiltonian paths are elementary and all Euler lines are simple ones, but from that we cannot draw a conclusion about any implication between Hamiltonian (*H*) and Eulerian (*E*) lines. It would be an interesting thought to draw conclusions about *H* from *E*'s existence in a given network because Euler's theorem allows us to find *E* easily. In a given network all four of the possible cases can occur. Euler's theorem says that the beholder can traverse all doors exactly once, if there are zero or two locales which have an odd number of doors. This theorem applies to multigraphs where there is more than one door between two locales, and exposes at once the necessary and sufficient conditions to construct the Euler line. (For the sufficient condition cf. Fleury's algorithm for tracing the Eulerian cycle.)

The first striking observation that an architect can make is that the possibility of an Eulerian reading of the space system does not depend directly upon some kind of complicated syntactical criterion but exclusively on the paradigmatic valence of the rooms, and the Eulerian conclusion does not depend on an absolute number of some paradigmatic types of rooms, but only from their even or odd number. (Here is where the syntactical criterion is hidden: Berge 1966 [1963] : 165ff.) Indeed, if there are two locales with an odd number of doors, this must be the locale of the entrance and that of the exit, where the architectural space system is connected to the *U* space. If there are no locales with an uneven number of doors, the network has instead of a chain an Eulerian circuit. It is impossible to have an Euler graph — which means one where we can find an Euler line (Ore 1963: 24) — with only one locale with an uneven number of doors (*tertium non datur*).

It is a much more arduous task to determine whether a network has a Hamiltonian reading or not, how many there are, how to find them (in terms of an algorithm), and where the space system must be connected to the *U* space to have at least one Hamiltonian.

C. A. B. Smith demonstrated that if a network is homogeneous by having only locales with 3 doors, it is always possible to find Hamiltonian circuits of even number.

(In the next section we will discover the preeminent importance of the locale's paradigmatic valence for the visitor's orientation capability in a space system. Gordon Brest's empirical researches (Canter 1970: 122-129) show that neither the length of the path nor the geometrical intricacy of the corridors are what determine the probability of losing one's way in an extended space system, but the possibility of alternative paths, and yet this latter is a direct function of the spaces' paradigmatic valences.)

The Hamiltonian reading depends entirely on the locale's paradigmatic valence. It means not only that the circuits can be inversed but that the reading can start at any point, i.e., the architect is free to choose the street door, or '*U* gate'. All locales are topologically equivalent in the network. (As a closed circuit it can be used in the construction of a prison or cloister.) If the space system with this homogeneous syntactical network has 20 spaces (e.g., a dodecahedric arrangement) all with different morphological labels — namely, they differ either in shape or in volume or in superficial characteristics — we can enumerate 400 varieties of original Hamiltonian circuits ($20^2 = 400$).

Furthermore, Redei's theorem shows that any complete graph (i.e., all vertices are symmetrically linked) has a Hamiltonian path. It must be noted again that all complete graphs are homogeneous, otherwise called regular, in that all locales have an equal paradigmatic valence. Because this kind of homogeneous space system has no proper syntactical order, these theorems have only very limited architectural significance.

Until J. D. C. Little elaborated in 1963 a complex algorithm of branch and bound which solves the problem in its generality, the search for a Hamiltonian path had been made by simple enumeration, which is a very laborious, often impractical procedure (A. Kaufmann 1968: 377s, Warusfel 1969: 184).

Perusal with minimal rereading There are a large number of networks where we cannot find Eulerian or Hamiltonian reading lines, and the observer must choose a complete reading with some rereading, or an incomplete reading; in short, redundancy or negligence. We can also infer from Euler's theorem that, if the space system has more than two locales with an uneven number of doors, in order to go through all doors at least once, the visitor must q times repeat the traversing of a doorsill — $2q$ being the number of locales included in the system.

In more general terms, in order to find either H or E or exhaustive reading lines with minimal redundancy, in this undertaking it is useful to find two particular configurations in the graph; namely a tree, and a cycle which is elementary and simple. In terms of the compartment theory of Riscigno and Serge the first is also called 'mammillary structure' and the second 'catenary structure' (von Bertalanffy 1968: 21).

(1) A tree is defined as a finite connected graph with no cycle and possessing at least two vertices, which implies among other things that every pair of locales is connected by one and only one chain. In order to visit *all* locales in the network with the lowest number of repeated visits, the guide must always direct the public, where there is a choice between more than one door, to the door which does *not* lead by the shortest way to the exit (Berge 1966 [1963]: 152ff). All other decisions do not affect the economy of the exploration. It is possible that there is more than one solution of equal length, e.g., in the graph of seven locales we can enumerate six solutions in which the frequenter must pass through doors ten times. Of course, they are solutions of equal topological length, but that does not mean an equivalence in the observer's experience, namely the sequences do not have the same order.

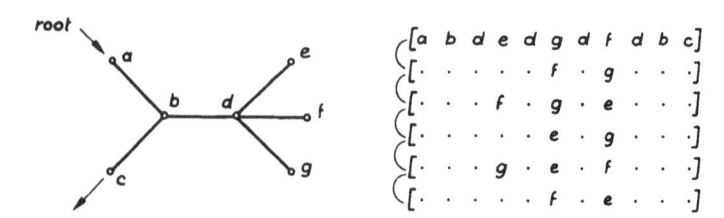

396 *Communication through architecture*

```
       root
          ↘                    ⎛[a  b  d  e  d  g  d  f  d  b  c]
           •a        •e        ⎜[·  ·  ·  ·  ·  f  ·  g  ·  ·  ·]
              ╲   ╱            ⎜[·  ·  ·  f  ·  g  ·  e  ·  ·  ·]
               b  d            ⎨[·  ·  ·  ·  ·  ·  e  ·  g  ·  ·]
              ╱   ╲ •f         ⎜[·  ·  ·  g  ·  e  ·  f  ·  ·  ·]
          •c        •g         ⎝[·  ·  ·  ·  ·  f  ·  e  ·  ·  ·]
```

(2) If the network is an elementary and simple cycle the reader must follow the same rule as he did in a tree. (We recall that a simple and elementary cycle is a finite chain which begins and ends at the same locale, and we can return to the starting point without passing through the same door or locale more than once, with the exception of the starting locale.) Of course, the most economical visit to such a network is possible if the visitor can start and end the visit by the same vestibule. In technical terms, that means that a biconnected graph must be transformed into a strongly connected directed graph. There are two solutions (Berge 1966 [1963] : 198). If the entrance and exit are in different locales the visitor realizes the most economical, least redundant exploration by following the same instruction which guided him in the 'tree', e.g., the shortest exhaustive exploration in the figure is (*abcdefe*).

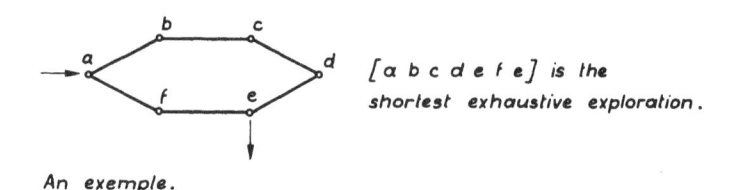

```
          b      c
       ╱─────────╲
     a             d    [a b c d e f e]  is the
       ╲─────────╱      shortest exhaustive exploration.
          f      e
                 ↓

     An exemple.
```

At first glance, someone might guess that because all more intricate networks are composed 'graphically' of trees and cycles, the same rule could produce the most economical exploration of any network. This is not true. Only the very laborious procedure of trellis promises to find the solution with complete certainty (e.g., Young's solution; cf. Little's algorithm).

2. *Skimming*

Speed-reading techniques (Evelyn Wood) were not invented for literary masterworks, but because of the drab and bureaucratic texts we must read in our daily life. It is not otherwise with architectural texts. For this reason it is an appropriate and practical task to find ways to read which are not exhaustive but which skim the text by passing through the nonnegligible passages.

We can consider two cases:

(1) The frequenter will visit some locales if the cost in detours is not too high. (The detour is determined in relation to the shortest way to pass through. We recall the labyrinth.)
(2) The frequenter follows the architect's ideas and visits some locales which have a central situation in the syntactical composition of the space system.

In mathematical terms, both cases can be reduced to the problem of finding the shortest path with the fewest door openings between two locales. The difference between the two cases lies only in the way that the unavoidable locales are chosen.

Let us consider the second case, because there are two problems: one for the architect, who chooses the central locale and arranges it in the syntactical construction; and the other, the problem of the reader's instruction. We can characterize the syntax of the architectural text by some aspects related to its 'readability'. The path we take crossing the fewest possible thresholds we call the distance between two locales. The architect can calculate in the design process the distance from any locale to another; in a symmetrical graph where all doors can be opened in both directions: $d(x, y) = d(y, x)$. In respect to one locale we will have some with direct access [$d(x, y) = 1$ as minimal distance] and others which are at the farthest point from it [max $d(x, y)$]. The sum of the distances of all other locales we call 'associated numbers' (Berge 1966 [1963]: 119). A locale or locales which have the least associated numbers are centers and those which have the highest are called peripheral locales. There may be more than one center or none at all. The number of door-crossings which are necessary to reach the farthest locale from the center is the network's radius, and the longest distance among all the shortest paths leading from any locale to any other is considered the network's diameter. In short, the radius is the longest of (directed) distances from the central locale and the diameter is, altogether, the longest possible (directed) distance in the whole network.

The necessary detour for visiting chosen locales in a space system depends heavily on the average distances prevailing in it. In a network with two-way doors it is $\Sigma d(x, y)/m$, where m = number of locales.

We can say that to read only the kernel sentence of a complex sentence means for the architectural medium to reach and leave the central room passing from the entrance to the exit by opening the least possible number of doors — namely, using the path that we call topologically the (directed) distance (refer to the earlier discussion of topological and banal geometric distance; see also Chomsky 1965; 1972: 44; Apter 1970: 134).

There are various techniques for finding the (directed) distance between two locales. H. W. Kuhn suggests a physical model. Reconstructing the graph by a net where the strings have equal length, if we stretch out the net by holding the two points between which we will determine the distance, by noting the points which are on the stretched line, we can enumerate the locales through which this shortest way goes. (For this method the graph must be a symmetric one, also called a semigraph.) If on this model the lengths of the edges are proportional with the physical distance or time required for passing and so on (cf. ecological distance), it solves the problem of the shortest way in a manner other than assuring the least number of door openings. In this respect, we must recall Prihar's algorithm. Other methods give only the lowest number of necessary door openings, but do not enumerate them. Again, others are comprehensive by indicating at the same time the distance (in terms of door openings) between any chosen rooms. They are more or less time consuming, which is an important aspect if the size of the networks makes the method virtually unmanageable. L. R. Ford's graph traversing technique produces the list of all distances between any points. By attaching appropriate number values to the edges, we indicate the physical length, or the time and effort needed, etc., and thus we can choose the easiest way among the topologically shortest paths if there is more than one solution. This technique can easily be programmed for the computer. There are also *matrix methods*, like the *'cascade algorithm'* (J. D. Murchland). This is an iterative procedure (Berge 1966 [1963] : 67). Haggett and Chorley also outline a large number of applied methods.

Finally, as mentioned already, there are the paths 'inscribed' in a network, or in other words, the possible readings of an architectural space system which reveal its syntactical construction. In order to discover if two graphs are only aliases of one and the same isomorphic graph, we can test them by prescribing the same instruction, e.g., always turn to the next door on the right-hand side. If the traveler arrives at the initial locale in both graphs by the same number of steps, they are isomorphic, viz., it is one graph with two different representations (aliases).

Finding the visitor's way out All appropriate readings can be considered for two types of people: the connoisseur or initiated person and the naive visitor or 'tourist'.

In the first group is the architect himself, who knows the syntactical properties of his system and who, if he wishes to find the exit or any other locale, knows before starting that there are shorter or longer ways.

The naive tourist, in order to find his way out, is satisfied with less-demanding methods. He will simply have reading methods which exclude the possibility of returning to the same locale before reaching the exit.

Returning to a locale shows him in a clear way that he is looking for his way by a wrong method.

In psychological terms, the architect's orientation task is recognition (Simon 1969: 39) and the visitor's is exploration. We address this latter task and suggest ways that architectural communication can make it easier for the visitor.

A fugitive from prison, or a naive visitor lost in a labyrinth or catacomb, could use some advice from the topologists for finding the shortest way out, without any local knowledge: if the space system can be represented by a planar graph, respect the following rule: in any locale, always take the door at your extreme right. This rule allows the individual to reach the end of any confusing and intricate network without ever having to cross one door more than twice.

Tarry (1895: 187) gave more general advice: never cross any one door twice in the same direction, and in any room go again through the door by which you first arrived only if no other choice is available. Of course, this last rule involves some memory work or marking unless the door may be locked after crossing it.

The marking can be conveyed by the architect through his medium. Where a jurist or administrator would apply arrows, the architect can use shape as an indicator. While still preserving the shape of a certain cross-section of the space, which he consider *a* circuit in the maze, he can continuously enlarge it. And that is only one of many properly architectural means.

How Can We Study Frequentation and its Effect on the Reading Experience by Experiments?

In order to construct the architectural repertory we studied first the impression of the various sensory spaces and their multisensory intricacy in a stationary position. Here the subject made paired comparisons between spaces by using his immediate memory. This exercise involved his capacity to compare volumetric magnitudes and to explore and recognize shapes.

Relaxing the sessile observation conditions into motile ones was a next step. By allowing the subject to choose a dynamic exploration strategy, to walk around, to begin the exploration where he wished, and to finish where it seemed to him appropriate, we introduced basically the following novelties: the choice of the sequence of the detailed impression obtained, depending on which door he entered, and both the use of a feedback loop in programming the exploration and the input of the motor activity itself for the space impression. Therefore, not only the psychological literature about pattern recognition and exploration became relevant to the scope of the problem, but research about orientation in the space (Held 1968).

400 *Communication through architecture*

Now in this chapter, where the architectural word is not considered in its morphological aspects but as part of a major class form which allows it to enter into syntactical compositions, what new branch of psychology becomes relevant in order to learn more about the space impression and the means of architectural communication?

Indeed, each space achieves its identity in the space system by its connection, which is prefigured by its paradigmatic valence. As many entrances as a space has anticipates the number of aliases and sequences that are possible in the space impression building. It is the syntactical construction which determines the immediate previous space experience in relation to each door. The variety of space experiences depends on the syntagmatic adjacency of other spaces. (Of course, this adherence and so experience interference can be amplified by the interfaces used in bound forms and by intricate multisensory composition.) However, the truly new syntactical effect on the space impression comes from the (grammatical or) sentence stress. Indeed, a space impression of a locale which finds its definite identity in an architectural text depends not only on the possible immediately preceding space experiences — determined by the number of doors and by the adjacent locales — but on all the reading sequences which are inherent in the syntactical construction. The syntactical construction allows a set of possible sequential orders. On the other hand, in many of these sequences the beholder sets up a different mental map in his mind. If spaces *A* and *B* are separated by a more-or-less long path or by a sequence of spaces which are more or less filled with new

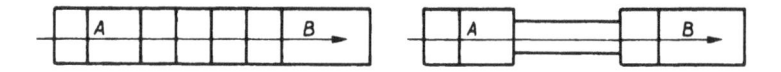

space impressions (see figure, by interesting spaces or an empty corridor), then they are not compared and mapped one into the other by the same mental process. Anyway, the effect of the sentence stress on the space impression cannot be understood without considering mnemonic aspects going beyond the span of apprehension of the beholder's immediate memory (Piéron 1968: 261).

If the beholder's orienting system gives an increased input in the space impression considered from the angle of sentence stress, it is even more involved when we turn to a field of experimental investigation which is completely different from what we have considered in previous chapters concerning morphology; namely, in order to choose his reading sequence, the beholder searches for an impression of the syntactical order itself of the sentences, where the alternative reading paths are inscribed. For this latter investigation, interest turns to an impression of the relational words, if any — e.g., corridors, stairways — words which remain outside of architectural semantics because they are by definition desemanticized. At its worst, this is the exploration of the impression in a labyrinth. Going astray means having a false impression about the syntactical composition of the space system.

(1) Orientation. The actual impression of spaces included in a system depends on the reading path which can be objectively described by its two aspects: the sequential order and the time used. In respect to these, the reader can choose the duration of his visit and the door by which he leaves a room. We consider first the exit.

For epistemological reasons, in all previously mentioned experiments we left out of consideration the subject's intention, which we used only in the 'antechamber' of scientific theory, where hypotheses are constructed, and we continue to follow this principle to assure that conclusions are not less reliable than those of other experimental sciences. (In turn we consider it as manifested in the relative speed.) Indeed, independent of his intention, the visitor has as many choices — neither more nor less — than the paradigmatic valence of the space, the number of exits — in technical terms, the outward demidegree of the locale. The objective parameters of the choice are the number, size and location of the exit doors in respect to the space's possible axes of symmetry and in respect to the subject's actual entrance. In this respect the (diametrically) opposite doors, if any, or the doors to the extreme right and extreme left have particular significance.

In order to analyze the effects of each parameter present in natural situations, the experimenter first reduces the number of parameters present. As we have seen in the previous section, the two-choice situation offers heuristic advantages (see also G. Winkel's researches: Held 1968: 339; G. E.

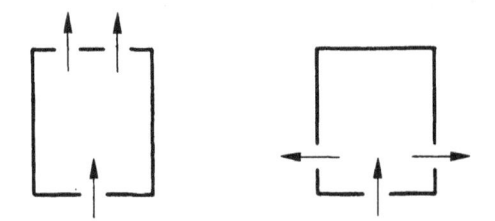

Schneider's two-choice apparatus; also Hamilton's method for the less redundant, exhaustive round trip of the world (Berge 1966 [1963]: 107) on a homogeneous graph where at every point there is a two-choice situation except at the entrance). We know that any choice — even multiple — is composed implicitly or (for the 'enlightened' subject) explicitly from binary choices situated on different levels of a 'tree'. Because of the bilateral organization of human behavior affecting our orientation system (cf. lateralization), the topological requirement for a two-choice situation — $d(x)^- = 2$ for the vertex's outward demidegree — must be completed by a properly geometrical one, i.e., that the two exit doors be situated symmetrically to the axis of the entrance door. This setup allows one to study properly effects of lateralization upon the orientation. (We can mention here that a space which is an antinode $d(x)^- = d(x)^+ = 1$ is the best experimental setup to study the subject's interest in a particular room by the relative time spent in it since there he cannot spend time choosing doors appropriate to his traversing strategy.)

There is a problem of lateralization. In viscera the neural control systems often depart grossly from bilateral symmetry and only in vertebrates and other Bilateria are the sensory central motor loops that control behavior bilaterally organized. As we mentioned before, the hemispheric differences in cognitive processing — and the following systematic asymmetry — even if it is minimal and indirect, and uncertainly related to minor anatomical (brain) differences of trivial functional significance, is more far-reaching in its consequences involving the grouping of major mental activities of two groups. According to theory, the right-handedness or left-handedness of the subject would influence how information processing would be lateralized, on the one hand analytical–linguistic, sequential auditory data (e.g., verbal), and on the other hand, spatial holistic — even nonsequential auditory — data (e.g., identifying sound sources) (Nottebohm in Harnad about songbirds, D. W. Shucard, Paul Saltz in J. Herron's volume, Sackeim, Wittelson etc.). Our proper concern in this section is neither the 'perceptual asymmetry' nor lateralization in sessile situations but the systematic asymmetry in the neuromotor activities which affects spatial orientation in its motile form (choice in turning).

The special literature — physiological and psychological — about lateralization in the human brain and nervous system, and the closely related issue of hemisphere interaction, has grown rapidly in the last years. Despite this fact, not a single major issue has been definitely resolved. For this reason we cannot go further than to mention the relevance of the problem and to indicate possible further solutions for our present concern. Our question is how species-specific and individual human handedness produce a rightward turning bias.

(2) Time vector in the mental mapping of space impressions. In the morphology for constructing the architectural repertory the subject compares, in sessile and later in dynamic exploration conditions, the volume and shape of two spaces in immediately successive presentations. Regarding the temporal aspects of the experiment, the duration of the observation and the possible reversion of the presentation (*AB* versus *BA*) were the unique parameters. For a similar comparison of two locales in a given architectural space system there are time parameters related to the events occurring 'between two'. Indeed, along with the time used for sensory inputs from the compared

spaces, there is a storage time which depends on the distance between the two locales. In the syntactical construction it is also possible that the linkage is directed in such a way that reversion is or is not possible. Further, the comparison could be multiple, mapping not only the geometry of one locale into that of another but into more than one (e.g., a visitor or employee chooses among rooms). In this case the result — the response of the subject to questions about relative volumetric magnitude or 'affinity of shapes' — depends upon sequences determined by the syntactical order prevailing in the given space system. The sequence parameter can become a long list of potential sequences enumerated by permutation.

For the actual experience of locales in a space system and of the system itself, the sequential order used and the absolute and relative time spent in each locale are the revealing data. The relative speed at which the beholder crosses each room reveals its meaningfulness for him (P. K. Cadwell) or his familiarity with it (Simon 1969: 38-39). These two reasons for slowing down can be clearly identified if, in the first case, the space supposed to be a meaningful lexical item is an antinode — as mentioned above — or if, in the second, it is a locale functioning as a relational word in the system.

It is the research about memory that is relevant to our present concern. In order to construct, in a heuristically rewarding manner, an appropriate series of experiments about impressions of spaces localized in a specified architectural text, it is necessary to hypothesize about parameters of memory, but there is no consensus about this subject among psychologists. Some authors have tried to approach the subject from the viewpoint of artificial intelligence, analyzing the process for computer simulation (dubbed EPAM). The crucial concepts are what is *an* item and what are the time limits. We will consider the questions within the scope of our problem, namely discriminating the shapes and volumes of spaces in various locations in a space system which requires storage of differentiating cues.

The process involves three main steps:

— an uninterrupted period of sensory input,
— rapid-access storage, and
— large-scale long-term memory (LTM).

The first step has already been a part of comparative experiments discussed in a previous chapter. The basic question here is the number of items or chunks which can be retained error-free within a given span of time. According to the author, this ranges from two to ten — some authors opt for the magic number seven (see the literature in Ankerl 1972a: 56, 298 n.35). The vague nature of the concept 'chunk', which is a conceptual reduction of heteroclite elements to be stored, does not allow us to come to a conclusion.

The semipermanent access storage as parameter is also, in quantitative terms, a very 'soft' concept. While its existence is not contested, its delimitation in time is not established. It is a storage span of apprehension which does not yet involve mnemonic fixation. Of course, its dimensions are number of items (item span) and time span. It is clearly an intermediary stage between information reception and storage by LTM (cf. learning; W. S. Maki). Some speak about immediate memory (Piéron 1968: 261), others identify it with the short-term memory (STM) (Simon 1969: 33), and its span of time is reckoned between 1-4 seconds to one hour.

For us the question of time span for the STM is critical, because the exploration of a space system varies exactly within this time span. Is it necessary for the comparative exploration of spaces in an extended architectural text to transfer impressions to LTM, which involves according to some estimates five seconds per item, and not necessary in a shorter one? Certain authors pretend that items which reached the LTM will never be forgotten, although they may become irretrievable for a time. But as we know from our everyday experience memories can surge again at any time in a spontaneous manner (Buschke 1974).

A last question concerning relevance of memory research for our problem is how the comparison of two spaces is affected not only by the time necessary to reach one from the other in the system, but also by how significant spaces intervening in the path between the two interfere in the comparison by distraction. For example, major spaces make the path longer in time because their size distracts the beholder and slows him down.

We believe we have now situated the new parameters proper to the impression of spaces as they are located in the system and as they must be explored in experiments.

Past applied studies

There are applied studies more or less close to the subject of space impressions in architectural texts. A first topic of research concerns orientation in space systems, that is, how not to get lost in the maze of corridors, stairways, and elevators. (In the vast over- and underground corridor network of MIT there are free phonebooths from which the lost visitor can call for information.) We recall Philip Tábor's work (Cambridge, UK) about circulation in a hospital that depended on the syntactical aspect of the space system. David Canter published (UK) a volume of papers presented at a conference on environmental psychology (1969). Gordon Best (1970: 122) determines the principal parameters of the space system which are relevant to losing one's way. But as we see, these studies concentrated on circulation, if you will, on the impression of relational architectural words such as corridors.

Another more substantial contribution could be expected from research about mental mapping which would study the process of integration of successively experienced environments over time. David Stea's approach (1973) as a psychologist seemed to be truly relevant to our subject, namely mental mapping of architectural spaces, by working with the architect Raymond Studer (Providence, R.I., 1965). However, Stea's subsequent cooperation with a geographer increased only the scale of the study but did not make an essential contribution to the understanding of architectural space impression. In his volume (1973) we do find numerous contributions to mental geography (J. F. Wohlwill) and an even more comprehensive approach concerning the mental map of the whole globe (Thomas Saarinen). These subjects in themselves are pertinent for study but we also see some dangers in this tendency. It is a kind of fascination with scale that we have already observed in city planning, where fully controlled genuine architectural spaces are neglected. Of course, there are technical facilities to obtain a bird's eye view of atmospheric space (e.g., by helicopters). However, there are considerable heuristic arguments for beginning the research of mental mapping in closed architectural space systems, which are in mesoscale, and which allow manipulation and experimentation. This kind of research would lie in the field of our present study. We will discuss methods of these researches in Part IV.

RECOGNIZABLE OBJECTIVE PATTERN IN ARCHITECTURAL TEXTS: THE USE OF DESCRIPTIVE TOOLS

Structural Archeology and the Historiography of Architectural Styles

It is not the system of this book which dictates to us the subject of this section, but for reasons of opportunity, namely that we have arrived at a point where we dispose of the description of the architectural space system on all levels (and this can give a significant input for the development of the historiography of architecture). On the other hand, this use of description also gives us a momentum which indicates which aspects of the text's syntactical description of the system by graphs are particularly relevant or interesting and are therefore to be developed.

We suggest that architecture is an art which may be particularly well described by a rigorous taxonomy based completely on objective (external) aspects, namely lexical, morphological, paradigmatic, syntagmatic, and syntactical ones. In order to apprehend architecture as a medium, we add the dimension of the perceptibility of spaces by the beholder. This taxonomy would allow a 'structural' classification of the space system according not only to its functional aspects but also according to the regional, epochal, and personal *style* which finds objective expression in it.

Considering this issue at this stage allows us also to consider exhaustively not only each level of elaboration of a style, levels with their own properties, but also the necessary or chosen interplay of those levels — syntactical graph versus geometrical morphology — as further style characteristics. We will discuss how topological features determine choice on the morphological level, namely solid geometry, and how far the inverse configuration expressed in dual graphs truly reflects geometrical implications; e.g., planar graph and regular prism (Cousin 1970: 88; Berge 1966 [1963]: 214). Within the possible freedom and beyond the random occurrence, the consistent option for some combination — e.g., selection within the major form classes (Chao 1968: 69-70, 65) and involved omission (as a characteristic of the architectural expression) — the chosen relations and orders (Alexander 1964: 6) reveal by their coherence the existence of a style.

This archaeological approach to architecture tries to apprehend the subject by intentionally disregarding, and consequently leaving in parentheses, aspects of architecture largely debated in our history of architecture, and often the subject of passionate ideological controversies.

— Archaeological structuralism must find the essential characteristics and boundaries of styles, epochs, and regions of architectural history *without* considering functional denominations of establishments but as they are revealed by their objective aspects. Thus description remains independent of labelling and concentrates on the architectural space system. The immediate advantage of this approach is that this 'archaeology' of architecture will handle with equal ease the architecture of various periods and regions. We know that the continental Chinese architecture and that of the island of Japan did not imply a definite place for heavy furniture, and even the architecture of our civilization did not prefigure a definite place for furniture until the 18th century.

— The archaeology of architecture tries to apprehend the structural characteristics of architectural styles in an *intrinsic* manner instead of interpreting them within the framework of a cultural history. This holds true where its interrelation with the fine arts is considered, as far as surface arts are used and can influence space impressions (especially thresholds and errors in volume estimates and shape discrimination).

— In the same line of incontestable distinction of styles promised by these objective methods, the experienced space system, namely the message transmitted by the meaning attributed to architecture will not become a tool of descriptive characterization. Architecture will not be considered as one of the possible symbol-bearing vehicles or as a channel through which a culture alternatively transmits one and the same connotated (symbolic) message. We consider the architecture in its particularity for that which cannot be conveyed by any other means, namely what the space system denotes. The 'architectural channel' as message transmitter is considered in its perceptible nature, and, on the other hand, the communication flow that the architect actually conveyed by his created space system will be apprehended by the aspects of its effective frequentation such as chosen pathways, speed and stays, and so on. (The beholder's preference is manifested by his behavior, by the 'beaten path'.)

The archaeological structuralistic characterization of the architectural style, epochs, and regions will not exclude other approaches to a study of the subject. This approach only pretends an exclusivity as an indispensable first step for serious future interpretation and before any ideological discourse can be pursued with some credibility, as, in a trial, the unimpeachable fact-findings preceed pleadings.

Levels of Objective Apprehension of the Architectural Styles

The inventory of an epoch's architecture reveals characteristics which are obligatory in a set of space systems and again other characteristics which show variations and are facultative revealing personal style. The first set of characteristics is used occasionally if not systematically by social morphology (P. H. Chombart de Lauwe, A. Cuvilier) to describe the large one-room tents – architectural word sentences – where Amerindian families live; other architectural sentences help to describe large Chinese families, and so on. These uses of objective description of architectural space systems in sociology show how precise instruments can serve multiple purposes by skillful sampling extracted from the whole range of aspects of the architectural medium. Let us now present the exhaustive enumeration of all levels where this medium can be apprehended by its external aspects. We will be succinct because it is largely a recapitulation indicating the compulsory directions where syntactical description must be further developed.

– The morphological elements, architectural words chosen for the syntactical construction of determined space systems, are characterized partly by topology and partly by solid geometry of the spaces, as well as by the hylic characteristics of the enveloping spaces – as submorphemic ingredient – as far as they influence the sensory impression of the space. We consider free morphemes, as well as bound forms which must be closed up in complex words, and the intricacy of the multisensory composition of the architectural (compound) words.

– The paradigmatic valence expressed by the possibility of temporary openings giving accessibility are topological characteristics as well as geometrical ones – especially in multigraphs – as far as they are main entrances, back doors, side doors, and other doors.
– We refer to the syntagmatic level where we are concerned with adjacency of spaces, which implies possibilities of syntactical linkage. The difference between interfaces used for linkage and those which are not used for intercommunication – no-road-maps, or antimaps (Ore 1963: 129; March), versus roadmaps – is itself a significant grammatical characteristic of the space system. As the map of nonrealized potential linkages provides supplementary grammatical characteristics of the space system, the relational words – corridors, stairways – that are introduced linkage requirements are characteristics too.
– The proper syntactical characteristics are the number of rooms – as elements of major form classes – with specifications that participate in a given space system, and the network of actual connectivity which prefigures the potential paths of reading, namely the components which are inherent to this graph. This internal structure of the text will be discussed further in terms of graphs. The connection to atmospheric space gives the architectural opus contextual delimitation.
– Finally, the actual use of alternative readings, the graph of actual frequentation which indicates not only the frequency of use of doors but the duration of stays in the rooms, the relative speed and acceleration, completes the external or structural characterization of the use of the architectural medium by a society, viz., through its particular actors: frequenters as well as individual architects as creators.

Grammatical characteristics of architectural texts

An architectural text (as delimited by the contextual U space) has been defined as a space system where from every locale we can reach any other, directly or indirectly, without going outside the system into the atmospheric space. Therefore an architectural text is represented by a connected graph. (In contrast, to be *an* architectural text it is not necessary that a locale which is directly accessible from the U space be a simple articulation point or an articulation point at all; a space system can have more than one 'vestibule'. The internal connectivity is the necessary and sufficient criterion.) In terms of graphs the syntactical structure of a space system is determined by the number of participating locales n, by the number of intervening doors (their directed or symmetric nature) m, and their distribution. We will look for the descriptive tools which characterize a syntactical structure in an equivalent or

Syntax of space systems and subsystems 409

converse manner; any diagram that represents one and the same graph must allow that their isomorphic nature be recognized, and no two diagrams which do not represent the same graph could be taken for ones having a relation of equivalence.

Of course, the requirement for an architectural text to be connected immediately imposes some relations between n, m, and their distribution.

A first grammatical classification of the space system comes from its topological extension determined by the set of participating rooms (the *manyness* of the locales). Theoretically this series is an infinite one, as is the set of positive integers. (We disregard the question of bound spaces which can be considered, for example, two and a half rooms, and in this case it is the set of positive rational numbers.)

Within one class of manyness, *all* syntactical constructions are situated between two extremes: the complete graph, where all rooms have intervening doors, and the graph where all rooms are antinodes. The latter case is derived from the requirement that isolated rooms are not admitted, namely, the set

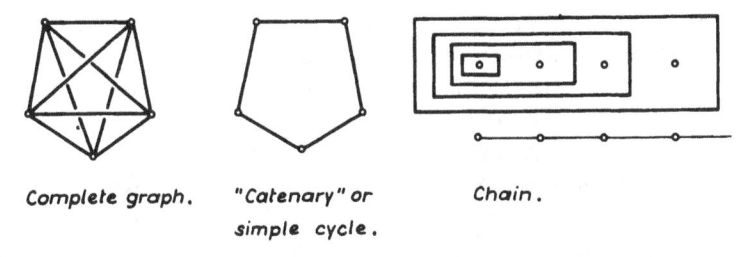

Complete graph.   "Catenary" or simple cycle.   Chain.

of spaces participates in a text as far as it is in a connected graph. This inferior limit for m shows the case where the architect imposed one reading sequence — with the possibility of reversion — a simple and elementary path. (The locales would be simple articulations if the minimal connected graph were not a cycle but a chain.) So, to be a text the following numerical relation must be respected: $(n - 1) \leq m \leq n(n - 1)/2$.

Both extremes — the simple cycle and the complete graph — are homogeneous (or regular) graphs where every locale has the same number of doors (the 'catenary' structure always has two doors and the locales are antinodes).

Between these two cases of 'maximal' and 'minimal' door 'saturations' there are numerous heterogeneous cases where not every locale has the same number of doors, i.e., they are not homogeneous graphs. We see then that the architectural text of n locales can have $n(n - 1)/2 - (n - 1)$ different degree of homogeneity; however, this number bears only a very limited interest because this does not enumerate all the possible different (homogeneous) graphs with n number of locales. Indeed, graphs which are equally homogeneous and have the same number of locales are not necessarily isomorphic and it is the

410 Communication through architecture

isomorphic graph which properly identifies a syntactical class in its equivalence. We use an example of two nonisomorphic graphs shown in 1 in Figure 3.32. Albeit both are composed of one pendant locale which has $d(x) = 1$ as paradigmatic valence, three locales with $d(x) = 2$, and one with $d(x) = 3$, but their syntactical order varies. We can see the different possible lines of readings immediately. A's minimal complete reading line is 1, 2, 3, 2, 2, 3, 2, 1 and B's is 1, 3, 2, 2, 2, 3, 1. Even the lengths of the two readings are not the same.

The incidence matrix (Berge 1966 [1963]: 141ff) helps us to identify the truly isomorphic graph among the possible aliases. (See 2 in Figure 3.32.) Different uses of the incidence matrix will be discussed later. A very simple rule for recognizing aliases — representation of the same thing in two different forms — is, in the case of square matrices, that if columns and rows can be interchanged, the two matrices are identical (Warusfel 1969: 269).

Let us suppose that the syntactical structure of an architectural text had been unequivocally apprehended. In order to characterize the structure we can use the parameters which we evoked in the section where we discussed the various readings of architecture. They are, as we recall, associated number, average distance, central and peripheral locales, radius, and diameters. Of course, other quantifiable parameters can be developed. These parameters allow us to find general statements about the syntactical structure of the text by formulating theorems as a function of these parameters.

One of the theorems (Berge 1966 [1963]: 197-198) states that if an architectural text (as connected graph) where all doors are intercommunicating (viz., symmetrical arcs) does not have a cycle, all its central locales must have just two doors. Indeed, it is the predicate in the sentence which is central, obligatory, and independent.

1.

2.

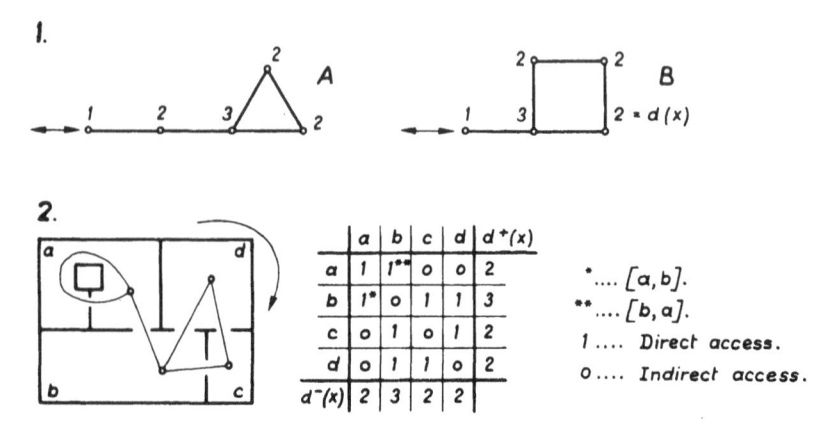

Figure 3.32. *Isomorphism of a graph and its incidence matrix.*

Another theorem states that under the same conditions – symmetrical doors and connectivity – peripheral locales (as defined) can never have more than one door.

Use of Certain Stylistic Requirements by the Architect

In order to demonstrate that architecture is a communicative event, we tried to relate the text's characteristics to the reading inherently possible in it. Further, we tried to see the usefulness of the objective structural characteristics of the architectural opuses for apprehending not only their functional but their stylistic, epochal, and regional variations.

Now we will consider these various topological characteristics and the manner in which they overlap other, geometrical levels in order to show the designer which syntactical means are at his disposal and which syntactical decisions have implications on other levels of the space construction. We will again disregard the message expressing intent of the architect. In turn, we will give a critical review of some deeply rooted doctrines in the architectural heritage, which are presented often as essential principles of the craft.

This alchemy looks for ideal forms – often expressed in perfect proportions – and its source is sought in nature, which must have harmonic qualities – especially those of the human body (e.g. Le Modulor of Le Corbusier, 1951) – and also in mathematical speculation. Curiously, these archaic tendencies are not disturbed by technical progress and are applied even on the modules used in prefabrication.

In this search for perfection the following beliefs emerged:

– the existence of a divine proportion expressed in its mathematical excellence but without any functional relativity;
– the architectural beauty of some regularities which, in fact, are present only on the two-dimensional surface of the designer's table (we will see the lack of differentiation between regularity in pavement and regularity in crystallography);
– and human proportions, projected out of all proportion on a building, that would somehow 'humanize' architecture.

Our effort will focus on how topological and geometrical (syntactical versus morphological) design options are mutually implicated. How can chosen composition rules be applied to an open-ended space system, and on the opposite side of the extension, how can those same rules be respected in order to complete an architectural text within limited intervals? (We will make explicit, as the occasion arises in the text, the implied universal beliefs concerning the supposed advantages, if they occur, for each stylistic option.)

Planar restriction

Fortunately the human being has the privilege of being motile and 'rootless', although he does not move with the same ease vertically as he does horizontally. Therefore it is of interest to give specific consideration to the one-level space system. In order to realize it, the designer must follow syntactical as well as morphological restrictions which are formulated for the architectural medium by topological and geometrical requirements.

A graph is said to be planar if it can be represented on a plane in such a way that the vertices are all distinct points, the edges are simple curves, and no two edges meet one another except at their terminals. If a system has only four locales, a planar arrangement is topologically always possible. Systems with a higher number of locales can be put in a one-level arrangement only if there is a restriction on the number of doors assuring intercommunication among rooms. If transit locales — relational words which would not be counted among the graph's vertices — are not considered, the number of doors (m) as a function of the number of locales (n) involved in the connected system must be limited to $m \leqslant f(n)$: the numeric relation is stated in the Euler theorem $m \leqslant 3(n - 2)$. This reflects the fact that the face of a triangle is the two-dimensional simplex (see also Figure 3.34). That is, the planar system which is most saturated by doors must show a diagram made from triangles. However, it is wrong to attribute, as some authors do (e.g., J. Cousin), much significance to this theorem. It states a necessary but not a sufficient criterion for a planar graph: it also does not state that all planar graphs having the same Euler characteristic are necessarily isomorphic. It is Kuratowski (1930: 271) who formulated the two tests whose applications on a graph establish *positively* its planar character. Kuratowski's theorem says that the necessary and sufficient condition for a graph to be planar is that it should possess no partial subgraphs of either type 1 or type 2. (Negative results from these two tests assure that the graph is a planar one.) To be planar a graph must not have (see Figure 3.33):

(1) a complete pentagonal graph within it as subgraph (K_5);
(2) a (hexagonal) bipartite graph ($K_{3,3}$) (also called three houses with three wells).

From this elegant representation in diagram we can say that a graph is planar if and only if it does not contain within it any graph which can contract to a pentagonal graph or hexagonal graph. (Contraction here means suppression of all 'symmetrical antinodes' — rooms with just two two-way doors; Ore 1963: 95–96, 30.)

The Euler theorem is also not a sufficient criterion for asserting categorically that a graph is planar, but it gives many very useful quantitative indications about relations existing within the planar graph. We will discuss its

Syntax of space systems and subsystems 413

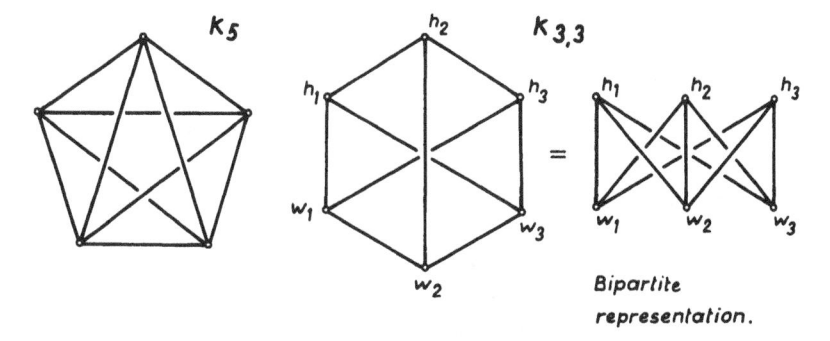

Figure 3.33. *Kuratowski's pentagonal and hexagonal graphs.*

application in three respects: graphs with infinite faces, dual graphs, and the calculation of the number of function spaces necessary for giving direct access to all pairs of locales in a unilevel arrangement. The mathematical presentation will be somewhat short since we have already discussed the relation of the Euler characteristics to other topological characteristics in the chapter on the geometry of architectural morphology earlier in Part III.

Considering the polyhedrons, we had the Euler theorem $\chi = f + n - m$, where the value of the Euler characteristic χ — defined by the surface topological genus — is $\chi = 2$ and f is the number of faces, n = number of vertices, m = number of edges. Now for the planar graphs, f is a face whose sides constitute a simple and elementary circuit in the graph — or 'minimal circuit' (Ore 1963: 129) — and whose number can be calculated by the cyclomatic number (Berge 1966 [1963]: 27; or circuit rank, Ore 1963: 129) $\gamma(G) = = m - n + 1$ where m is the number of edges or doors and n is the number of vertices or rooms).

We know that all architectural texts are connected to the U space as context. This link or edge is an opening to a vertex which is in infinity. Euler's theorem always counts among the faces of the graph the infinite face which has as boundary the graph's maximal circuit — in plain language we would say the graph's contour. Therefore 1 must be added to $m - n$ in order to have the $\gamma(G)$. In this logic, if the architectural text is related by two doors to the contextual U space, the graph will have two infinite faces. (A graph composed of one edge relating exclusively to the vertex in infinity has two faces, both infinite, so it has one edge and one vertex being in infinity. See Figure 3.34.) As dual graph we would say it is the representation of the Iron Curtain continued by the Bamboo Curtain or Great Wall of China around the earth. In the case of a planar graph the Euler characteristic χ is 2 because the plane is a sphere with a radius of infinite length. (To be complete we recall that χ can be numerically related to h, $\chi = 3 - h$. If h is a positive integer, not larger than the graph's connection number, the graph is h-connected; and if not larger

414 *Communication through architecture*

than the graph's cohesion number, it is h-coherent. If $h = 2$, the graph is biconnected and bicoherent; but for a planar graph — our present concern — $h = 1$.) From this we have the triangular weaving of the planar graph which excludes any links that cannot be realized in one-level space arrangements. $3 - 1 = 2 = \chi = f + n - m$, the triangle weaving gives $m = 3(n - 2)$ since $f = 2(n - 2)$.

We introduce now the concept of dual graph G^* of the polygonal graph G. It can be constructed only in the case of the planar graph. Its utility is to make — as we will see later — *anschaulich* some implications of syntactical design decisions for the geometry of the spaces constituting the architectural text. Dual graph (G^*) is constructed by the following method: within each face, including the infinite face, put a vertex v^* and link them by edges e^* each of which always crosses its dual, the edge e. The faces f^* result from the construction. The principle of duality says that the theorems applicable to a graph become applicable to its dual if we replace in them each element by the dual element and each operation by a dual operation (James and James 1968: 121). We see that the dual graph G^* of the architectural text's graph is a closed one 'circumscribing' the space system's contour (see Figure 3.34).

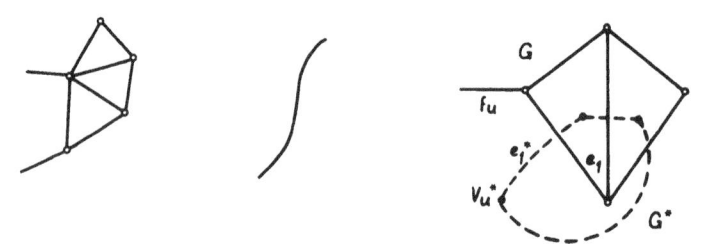

Open graph with   Graph with a virtual   Graph G and its dual
bidimensional simplexes vertix at infinity.   graph G* (a closed graph).
as finite faces.

Figure 3.34. *Open planar graphs and the dual graph G^*.*

Indeed, the architectural text by its links to the U space is represented by a graph having an infinite face (or faces) too, but its dual graph will not have an infinite face as no architectural space has infinite 'ground space'.

Finally we consider the grammatical implication if the designer insists on requirements contradictory in themselves, or wishes, for example, to have more doors between a larger number of rooms than a one-level space system can support. The number of unrealizable intervening doors (or direct accesses) can be calculated if we subtract from the number of edges in a complete graph the number resulting from the trangular weaving expressed in Euler's theorem:

$$\bar{m} = n(n - 1)/2 - 3(n - 2) = n^2 + 7n - 12.$$

Syntax of space systems and subsystems 415

We see the lacking doors increase by the number of rooms in quadratic order: $f(n^2, n)$. To realize direct accesses between rooms over the 'critical' number coming from Euler's theorem [$3(n - 2)$], the architect has two solutions: remaining on one level he must add more and more corridors as functional words — especially to avoid heterogeneous crossings (diners with cooks, etc.); or he must break out into the third dimension. We will see in the next section that there is no compelling reason to stay on one level, especially in urban architectural space systems (Schulze; March and Martin 1972: 35; Ankerl 1974: 579) where multilevel construction is necessary for more fundamental reasons than direct access among spaces. But if the architect insists on numerous direct accesses on a single floor, he must face an excessive increase in the number of corridors. If we accept Hill's conjecture, the number of intercommunications that the corridors (which as we know are desemanticized locales whose number is not counted among n) must channel increases biquadratically as a function of n: $f(n^4, n^3, n)$.

The multistory space system as repetition of the ground floor: critical considerations

We see at first glance the advantage of a multilevel arrangement from the viewpoint of the direct mutual accessibility of rooms as well as from the viewpoint of minimal effort of access in terms of physical distance and time, especially if there are elevators. Tabor's researches (1971) show that among locales of equal frequentation, circulation with minimal effort is assured in a multilevel arrangement whose global shape can be approached by circumscribed and inscribed spheres whose radii differ the least. (It is the space system arranged in the most compact package.) We showed also that a cubiform room can be brought into adjacency with 14 other cubical spaces even if all remain isometric.

Yet even if the necessity of a multilevel arrangement in urban architecture is recognized reluctantly, its construction is exposed in the name of law and order to regulations of questionable utility. Often an absolute limit on the number of levels is imposed for dubious esthetic criteria (e.g., streetscape is supposed to be better) or for narrow-minded economic reasons (e.g., saving the installation of an elevator). Another product of bureaucratic esthetics is a requirement suggesting plane facades with 'elevational symmetry'. Further, the structural engineer presents his requirements for spatial arrangements to accommodate his calculations. The overall result is that, as the unimaginative architectural space was an outgrowth of the floor which is already called the 'ground space', the same simplification occurs in the construction of space systems by bringing all levels vertically in line over the first or ground floor.

416 *Communication through architecture*

This reduction of the R^3 to R^2 comes from the agrarian origin of urbanism, seeing the crops planted in a two-dimensional arrangement and growing in the third one (Schulze-Fielitz 1971: 9–10). Topologically also the handling becomes easy, the problems of three-dimensional graphs are reduced to those of the planar by matching the single-level arrangements in a one-to-one correspondence. Of course, man is not a bat; he is an erect biped animal (*erectus*) with a clear sense of verticality, but this argument is only valid for the verticality of the walls of a room and does not command the vertical syntagmatic order of the three-dimensionally composed space system. A space system with repetition of a planar arrangement on all levels is a pseudo-tridimensional syntactical order.

(1) A space system where the different levels are related among themselves *only* by a through-going transit column, can be reduced to a ground plan represented by a planar graph (see 1 in Figure 3.35). At the same time,

1.
Elevator shaft

All stories are independent.

2.
$h_n \gtrless h_{n+1}$

Possible direct access between corresponding rooms of successive stories.

3.

Coplanar locals on all stories but no longer one-to-one correspondance.

4.

Tridimensional arrangement without story - system.

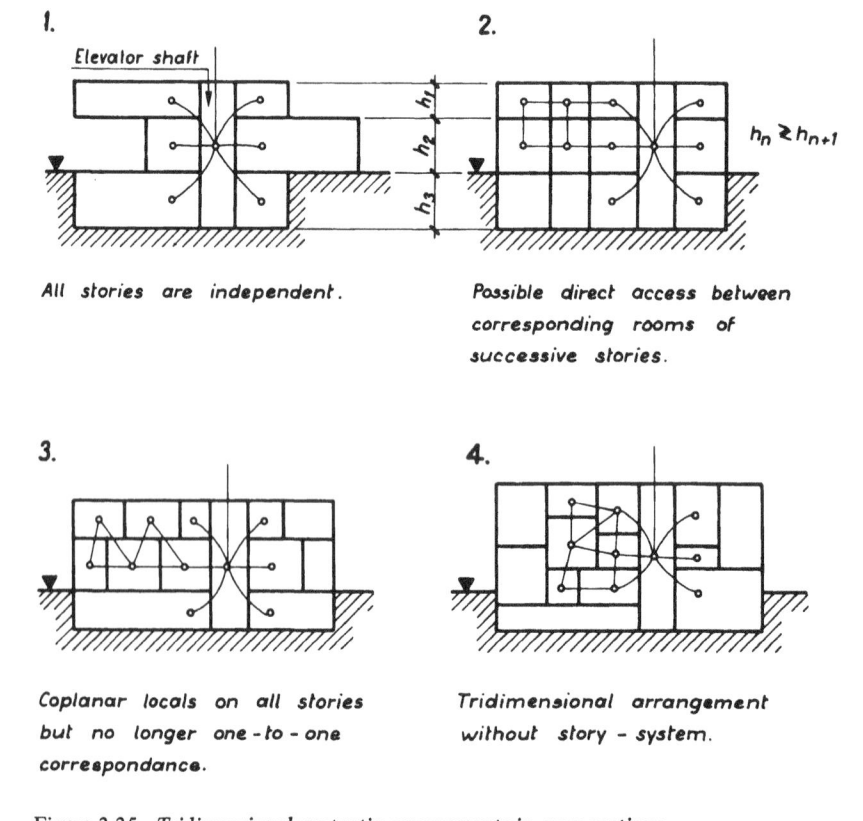

Figure 3.35. *Tridimensional syntactic arrangements in cross sections.*

especially if the vertical gullet includes an elevator shaft, all floors gain an increased independence, namely the nth and the $(n + k)$th levels become interchangeable from the viewpoint of circulation (Ankerl 1973). The gullet, if there is only one, allows rotation at pleasure at the various levels. (However, the elevator car must have doors at more than one side. The changing directions at each level add — the numbers of those levels painted on the appropriate doors of the car — a variety to the otherwise monotonous repetitions at all levels.) This system can be applied underground or underwater, as well as in a system growing out into the atmospheric space where the variety of vistas is added. Levels can even be motile in a heliotropic way, following the sun's attraction.

(2) We can also leave the architectural sentences in a one-to-one correspondence in the vertical syntactical arrangements but insert multilevel sentences by using internal stairways (see 2 in Figure 3.35). According to studies carried out in Le Corbusier's residential building in Marseille and its copy in Berlin, internal stairways give the impression of having one's own house. (The stair hall connotes the so-called family mansion.) The syntagmatic or adjacency graph is a bijective (Warusfel 1969: 84-86) or bipartite one. Even in this case theorems valid for planar graphs no longer apply.

(3) A further relaxation and so enrichment of possible syntactical arrangements in comparison to those restricted to the planar graph consists in space systems which preserve only horizontal flush surfaces; locales remain coplanar but because locales on all levels are no longer in a one-to-one correspondence, the syntagmatic arrangements allow increased accessibility — syntactical links — among locales on various levels (see 3 in Figure 3.35). The relation between levels is no longer bijective, which involved a one-to-one correspondence of locales between levels (and implied both surjection and injection), but only surjective.

(4) A last step toward the free play of the syntactical imagination and relief from planar restriction occurs when the inserted spaces are not necessarily coplanar. (Compare this with the previous case 3 where the superimposed locales on different levels could have different ground plans but their height on a coplanar level is covariant.) In this case if we preserve a syntagmatically compact space system where all space envelopes are interfaces — namely they are not impenetrable gaps in the system — the heights of all locales (e.g., galleries) can differ (see 4 in Figure 3.35). If gaps are admitted, the freedom is even greater and only the near-horizontality of the floors is required as a condition for walking. This syntactical arrangement breaks with the story system itself, which is composed of a discrete number of levels expressed in positive integers. Mezzanines, split-levels, intermediate floors, and entresols appear.

We can conclude that theorems of planar graphs have only a very limited usefulness for urban architecture, and tendencies which try to force multi-level arrangements into extended planar systems by a one-to-one correspondence at each story are reductionist and at the same time limit the scope of architecture, especially in certain types of space systems, namely those for administrative or domestic purposes.

Regularities and rhythms in composition of architectural space systems

Regularity, and the research of symmetry in particular, is a favorite subject of architectural treatises. We have considered regularities on the level of geometrical morphology of the architectural spaces. We can also conceive of regularities in syntagmatic composition allowing compact adjacencies among spaces, and finally on the level of syntactical topology it appears as a (regular or) homogeneous graph composed of spaces with equal paradigmatic valence.

However, a close look tells us that the terms 'regularity' and 'symmetry' are mostly used in a very equivocal manner, and not only by architects.

Created or discovered, the characteristic of regularity from the viewpoint of information theory is that within a sufficiently large series of elements — even if the number is infinite — a repetition occurs which makes it easier to encode the set of information in a less-large number of chunks or items.

Bilateral or axial symmetry is a special case of regularity. (Because it suggests a clear hierarchical order — namely it assigns central and peripheral locations to points without ambiguity — it has been used to express authority.)

Historically we find regular or Platonic and semiregular or Archimedean polyhedrons in the vocabulary of Greek artists and philosophers (Critchlow 1969) and also a preference for such shapes and spatial arrangements. All these tendencies can be understood under the research heading of a kind of 'philosopher's stone' for a construction which, by discovering a unique numerical or geometrical relation which bears a critical ratio, would make the opus incontestably perfect, e.g., the golden section; the miraculous shape of the cubelet evoked by the Old Testament as *Unterbrachtstein* (Critchlow); then Thompson d'Arcy's rediscovery in nature of the spiral of Archimedes; and, very close to the sociology of architecture, Calhoun's doctrine (1966: 52-57) about the incomparable perfection of the hexagonal domestic arrangements of the cells in a beehive. As we stated at the beginning of Part III, the pernicious nature of these hermetic researches consists in reaching for *one* unique magic formula ensuring the most perfect solution appropriate for all cases and in all respects. Unfortunately, these tendencies have been revived in our modern time in order to promote the construction of modular systems by assembling the space system from prefabricated spaces. (We must note here for the record that prefabrication does not call for monotonous space systems. At any rate, it would be difficult to increase the monotony already present in some English and German row houses.)

Contemporary definitions of the 'regular' and 'symmetrical' After this presentation of the general and specific context of the problem we can bring the clarity necessary for understanding these concepts in order to apply them on various levels of the architectural composition with their imbrications, namely geometrical, syntagmatic, and syntactic.

Concerning this question we can observe in present-day mathematics a tendency to apprehend the concept of regularity and symmetry on a more abstract level and, on the other hand, an increased interest in irregularity where linear programming relates to the extreme of a function.

In mathematical treatises and dictionaries we find the term 'regular' to be synonymous with 'homogeneous' (Berge 1966 [1963]: regular or homogeneous graphs). On the other hand, it appears that a 'regular' point is also a 'simple' or 'ordinary' one (James and James 1968: 275, 307). 'Regular' in its pure form implies uniformity, repetition in its precise sense in information theory, redundancy (Attneave 1954: 186) implying predictability as a cognitive virtue. Approached from its antonyms it is opposed to irregular as well as to singular (James and James 1968: 334-335). It must be noted that neither of these distributions can be classified as random. (See our discussion about random distribution on the surface of optical space.)

Further, we find use of the term 'regular' in a gradually attenuated sense — 'semiregular'. Also Polya and Szegoe (1951: 151) speak about 'sufficiently regular function' and Warusfel (1966: 131) about a 'regular part'. In this gray zone appears the term 'rhythm', related to dynamics, largely used in biology, but also in architecture where — as we will see — the multilayer character of the composition facilitates its application.

In mathematical terms, regularity is inseparably related to symmetry. Indeed, positively defined in the sense of contemporary mathematics they are converse, one implying the other.

The 'symmetry operation' verifies automorphism where the latter is a characteristic of regularity (Hilbert and Cohn-Vossen 1952: 56-57). On the other hand, symmetry is not equated with axial or bilaterial symmetry any more (Weyl 1967; Yale 1968) which distinguished a major axis of total reflection and a minor axis of partial reflection (March and Steadman 1971: 35). Today it is applied to cyclic phenomena. Cyclosymmetry involves variables remaining unchanged under every interchange of two of the variables. The symmetry group includes also rotation and inversion (March and Steadman 1971: 40) and it is not difficult to generalize the bidimensional concept to include crystallographic symmetry (from polygon to polyhedron, $R^2 \rightarrow R^3$).

The minimal number of elements necessary for symmetry is two sets of points and another point, line or plane as axis. As an operation it is evolution mapping by which we can construct symmetrical configurations. Applied two times in succession it transforms the given geometrical figure into itself. Even this abstract definition which transcends bilateral symmetry — by adding plane and center as possible axes to the customary axis line, and rotational and elevation symmetry in R^3 — remains in the framework of geometry.

Now regularity is related to symmetry as a multilateral repetition of the operation, e.g., an 'n-fold symmetry'.

In order to apply the concept in the syntactical composition, we must go beyond the definition inherent in solid geometry. In graph theory we have isomorphism, regularity — including symmetry — defined as an automorphism. (We have used these concepts already: a graph where all vertices had the same degree, resp. for us the same paradigmatic valence, was a regular graph; a directed graph where all 'doors' are two-way doors way composed of symmetrical edges.)

Applications in the composition of the architectural space system It appears immediately that total regularity, namely homogeneity, is a completely predictable system perhaps desirable for some communicative purpose, but because of its evident monotony is architecturally not very expressive. In order to create significant structures, the variety must play on the invariance. This permutation gives structures which can be considered elements of style.

Because of the multilayer nature of composition of the architectural space structure, this nonmonotonous regularity can be achieved by various means; for example, creating regularity on one or more, but not all, levels, and leaving irregularity or singularity to others. Of course, we cannot rely on a completely blind combinational procedure because of the imbrications existing among these various levels. We can also create the desired rhythm by considering only one level where we create semiregularity, various regularities (dephasing), or zones of regularity within a singular or random general context.

a. *One-level regular arrangements* We enumerate now all one-level space systems composed of right prisms with equal polygons as bases which can constitute an infinitely extending space system. The strict regularity consists here in the possibility of always having the same ground plan as 'pavement'. The whole task is interesting only if it constitutes a compact system (Warusfel 1966: 409) where all walls are interfaces adjoining two spaces to their full extent. For this reason the syntagmatic (or adjacency) graph shows the network. But it would be erroneous to think of a converse relation existing between the space system composed of equal prisms in compact arrangement and its dual graph. Indeed, the *same* dual graph could represent architectural texts composed of various spaces with other shapes. Cousin attributes an undue importance to the representation of a graph by diagram.

It must also be recalled that the syntagmatic graph is an adjacency graph which does *not* oblige the architect to open all vertical faces with an intervening door and thus to equate the syntagmatic graph with the syntactical one. If the doors are distributed sparingly, the space system can have morphological and syntagmatic regularity — that is, a composition of prismatic spaces without gap — without necessarily having syntactical regularity too.

Because the system is conceived as one of infinite extension, at any moment of its development the syntagmatic graph has infinite faces or, in other words, is an open graph (Cousin).

We find three n-sided polygons which are endocompatible and can be used for constructing a compact space system which has only isometric regular right prisms. They are $n = (3, 4, 6)$. They can be recognized by the fact that their syntagmatic graphs are homogeneous or regular (see Figure 3.36 and Ore 1963: 102). If we relax the restriction and are already satisfied if the right prisms are only isometric but no longer regular, we can enumerate eight other shapes which constitute what we call an endocompatible space system, namely a compact one-level space system which is composed of one item of the architectural repertory. The prisms composing these eight cases are in four classes, $n = (3, 4, 5, 6)$. Since the regularity in these eight cases does not consist in the individual room's geometrical morphology, the regularity is exclusively syntagmatic — grammatical and not lexical. The choice of the composing words is regular but not the words themselves. It is again the syntactical network realized by opening a door on all edges of the syntagmatic graph — providing the reading possibilities — which reveals the properly grammatical specificity of an architectural text.

It is shown in Figure 3.36 that there are space systems composed of right prisms with isometric triangular floors, but those which are composed of regular right prisms have only one type of minimal circuit (3_1). Another has two types: $(^1 3_2)$ one right-hand minimal circuit goes through different isometric locales four times, counting the initial–terminal as one, finally returning to the initial locale; the other left-hand minimal reading circuit leads back to the initial room by passing through eight adjacent isometric locales (including the first). Another syntagmatic arrangement of rooms with equal triangular floors may have two other readings by minimal circuits which pass through 3 or through 12 locales before closing the circuit, depending on whether the reader is left or right 'biased' $(^2 3_2)$. Finally there is a fourth arrangement for rooms with equal triangular floors which offers three possible readings by a minimal circuit, where a circuit passes through 4, 6, or 12 isometric locales (3_3). Here the circuit is not only a function of the left or right bias of the reader but also of the door which it crosses first.

422 *Communication through architecture*

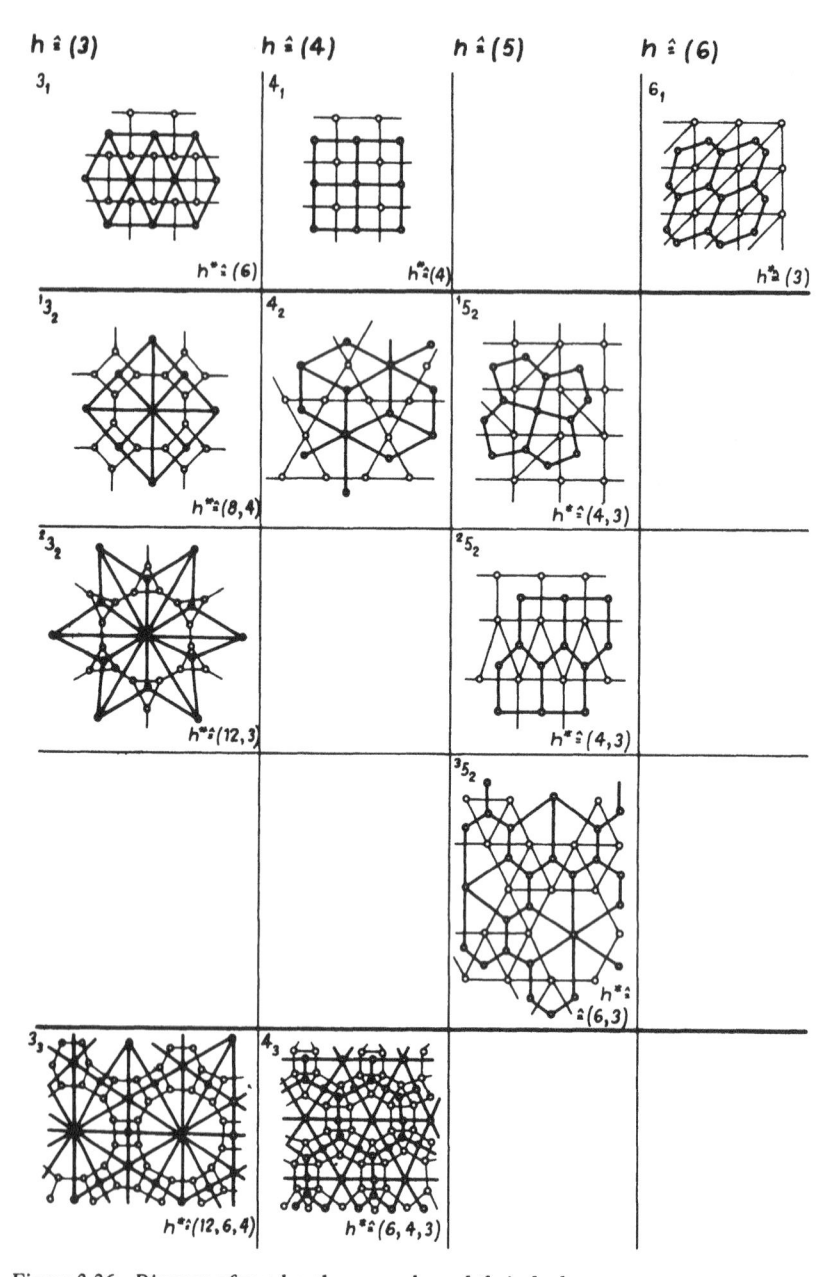

Figure 3.36. *Diagram of regular planar graphs and their duals.*

These differentiations of space experiences as a function of the space's internal regularity and as a function of the syntactical regularity, as well as the implication existing between the shape and the syntactical arrangement (if, of course, the architect wishes to realize the syntactical arrangement in an elegant manner by a compact syntagmatic composition) are very interesting not only for stylistic reasons, but for making clear in theory the existence of different levels of consideration and their interrelatedness.

The architect must realize before any application that the isometric shapes of solid geometry and isomorphic topological graphs are not converse concepts and are not equivalent; only isometry implies isomorphism.

We will see that in some cases the adjacency graph can be represented by a diagram, itself visualizing an infinite network of regular pavements. It is misleading, however, to speak of inversive configuration (Cousin 1970: 88) since (a) the syntagmatic or adjacency graph of all 'planar' systems composed of the same elements (e.g., right prism with triangular floor) cannot be represented by a diagram composed of the same polygons; and (b) the diagram is only a possible representation of a graph but must not be equated with it. Some amateur mathematicians with a background in architecture made this mistake. For example, in Cousin's book (1970), we find the correct number of one-level space arrangements composed from isometric right prisms, namely 11; but it is probably taken from other sources in a confused manner, because afterward in the enumeration we discover the regular right prism $n = 3$ twice presented in different diagrams and by contrast the case $n = 6$ of regular right prisms is omitted (Cousin 1970: 75-76, figs. 90 and 91). Yona Friedman enumerates four classes of open planar graphs which have minimal circuits of equal length, $n = (3, 4, 5, 6)$, but he neglects to say that there are 11 graphs of this type among which *not one* is isomorphic with any other, and under these circumstances we do not see what he means by speaking about four 'general models' (Friedman 1975: 85-86).

If architects wish to know more about this subject they should read the books of Fejes Toth or Steinhaus (1969) instead of those just discussed.

In summation, we can enumerate only three regular right prisms which constitute an endocompatible one-level space system without gap. Using Schaeffli's notation system (p, n) where p = edges adjacent to a vertex – or in terms of a graph the degree (h) – and n = number of sides of a polygon of ground plan – or in terms of a graph the length of the minimal circuit – they are shown in the figure on page 424.

On the other hand, these floor shapes allow some combination where, by subdivision, the architect can weave compact space systems composed of no more than two shapes or by the same shape but of different volumes. We can

1.   2.   3.

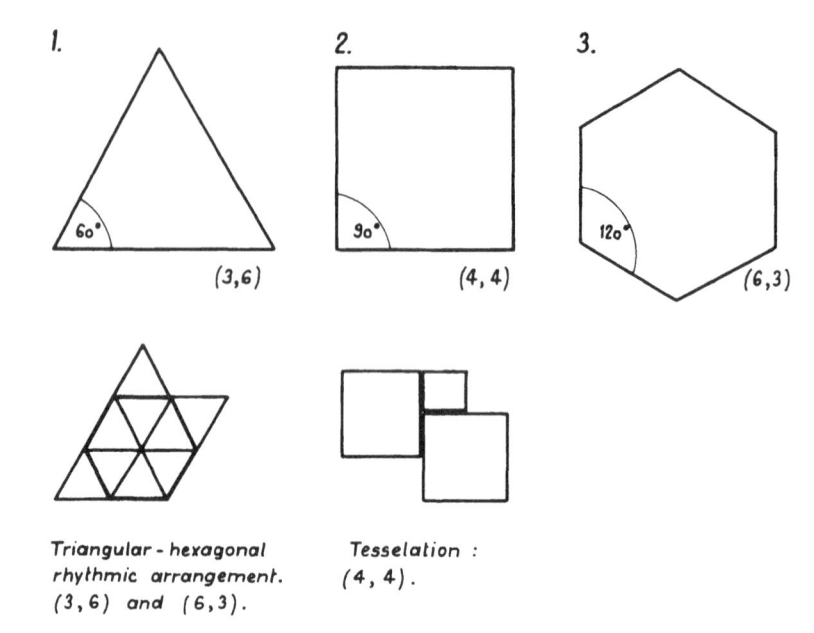

(3,6)   (4,4)   (6,3)

Triangular-hexagonal rhythmic arrangement. (3,6) and (6,3).

Tesselation: (4,4).

call these texts partially regular and the result is a rhythmic arrangement. There are two systems:

(1) The (3, 6) and (6, 3) can be combined to give various triangular-hexagonal rhythmic arrangements with the possibility of inserting the right prism (which is a parallelepiped) having a rhombus or regular deltoid as floor surface.

(2) The regular space system composed of quadratic floor surfaces allows in its tesselation only spaces with quadratic floor surfaces, therefore a rhythm can be introduced merely by varying the size of the checkers, i.e., by subdividing them.

We see that the hexagonal space system in a beehive is not a unique paradigm for the habitat system. Attaching the quality of absolute excellence to the numbers 6 and 12 in the composition of space systems as Calhoun does (1966: 52-57) is no more than an expression of personal preference. In reality there are three regular shapes and among them the triangle, as the simplex of dimension 2, has more unique qualities than the hexagonal system – as we noted at the beginning of Chap. 19. But even so, Wright's cult of the equilateral triangle smells of a hermetic doctrine again.

The 11 different topological compositions of the one-level space system constituted from isometric spaces allow generation of semiregular (Gheorghiu and Dragomir 1978: 229) texts which can be extended endlessly without having to use more than three items of the architectural repertory. It is sufficient to constitute the dual of the diagrams representing the 11 cases of

Syntax of space systems and subsystems 425

isometric space composition. Indeed, in Figure 3.36 the 11 original diagrams show a syntagmatic graph of the semiregular space systems. We see from this figure that there are cases composed of two shapes. The polygon can have (n) 4 and 8 sides, 3 and 12, 3 and 4, or 3 and 6, of which the last two can be constructed in two different syntagmatic arrangements. Three different architectural repertory items may be combined to form two semiregular space systems: in one the polygons have (n) 12, 6, and 4 sides; and in the other 6, 4, and 3.

Finally we recall that even after the choice of a particular syntagmatic arrangement the architect still has the possibility to bring further rhythm into his text by the syntactical decision to open certain interface doors but to leave others blind.

Do not forget that other forms than the regular polyhedron can constitute a regular system (i.e., homogeneous syntagmatic graph), for example Kevin's polyhedron, which we will discuss shortly.

b. *Nonplanar (regular) syntagmatic arrangements and crystallographic regularity (restriction)* We recall that all bidimensional constituents in themselves are submorphemic for the architectural text. Even the three single-story space systems constructed exclusively from the so-called regular right prisms are not composed of regular shapes in the proper sense of the term. Quadratic tesselation makes an exception because by appropriate choice of length all spaces can become cubic (regular hexahedrons). We look now at the tridimensional regularity of the syntagmatic arrangement. However, we must remember that the geometry of spaces becomes an architectural word only through its created impression; and that the syntagmatic arrangement becomes part of the architectural sentence through the syntactical (accessibility) network which determines the text's reading. Therefore, at least in those sensory spaces where the beholder is more sensible for horizontal symmetry than for vertical, the absence of regularity is less important in the vertical dimensions than in the horizontal. We think here of the optical word of the architectural text.

We discussed regular polyhedrons in the chapter about geometrical morphology. The cube or hexahedron is the only right prism among the regular polyhedrons. The five regular polyhedrons have isometric (i.e., congruent) regular polygons as faces as well as congruent polyhedral angles. The semiregular polyhedrons which embody some of the preceding criteria group two kinds of spaces: (a) faces are regular polygons and solid angles are congruent; (b) faces are isometric (i.e., congruent) and solid angles are regular. Archimedes enumerates 13. (The figure shows a semiregular prism and antiprism according to his denomination. See p. 426.)

In order to study their syntagmatic graph in a tridimensional compact arrangement, we cannot make the same use of the dual graph as we do in the

426 *Communication through architecture*

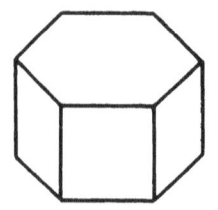

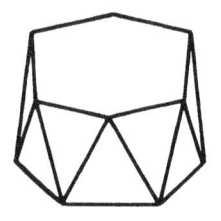

case of planar arrangements. In a three-dimensional arrangement the dual graph can be conceived only if the diagram of the original graph is developable on a spherical surface (that is, the planar surface itself can be understood as a spherical surface with a radius of infinite length). Because of this restriction the dual graph is no longer a tool to make explicit mutual implications occurring on the various levels of architectural composition (morphological, syntagmatic, and syntactical).

Which regular and semiregular spaces can compose a compact space system?

(1) Only the cube among the regular spaces is syntagmatically endocompatible, viz., can constitute a compact space system on its own. Its syntagmatic graph is also regular (i.e., homogeneous). Further this completely regular system — regular by its morphemes and by its syntagmatic composition — allows the degree of the syntagmatic graph to vary between 6 and 14 without losing its regularity. As we have seen in Figure 3.36, the change of degree means that different numbers of rooms can become intercommunicating if the architect decides to link them syntactically by doors. The architect can also change the (physical) metric relation between the linked spaces without modifying the degree of the homogeneous syntagmatic graph or renouncing its homogeneity. Metric freedom exists in the first case in Figure 3.37.1 but not in the second case; namely, distance *a* can be changed without affecting the homogeneity of the syntagmatic graph of the space system, i.e., this 'metric freedom' does not apply for a syntagmatic graph of any degree. (See also 3_1 and 4_1 in Figure 3.36.) If the architect allows other cubes than isometric ones in the system, new syntagmatic arrangements become possible.

While in the architectural morphology the sphere had some unparalleled 'virtues', in the syntagmatic context the cube has some.

(2) The tetrahedron and the octahedron cannot constitute individually a compact space system on their own. They can do it together, but they do not form a completely regular space system because the vertices of the syntagmatic graph will bear more than one morphological label, namely tetrahedron and octahedron.

The dodecahedron and the icosahedron are incapable of constituting a compact space system of any kind, not even if we arrange them with semiregular spaces.

Syntax of space systems and subsystems 427

1.

2.

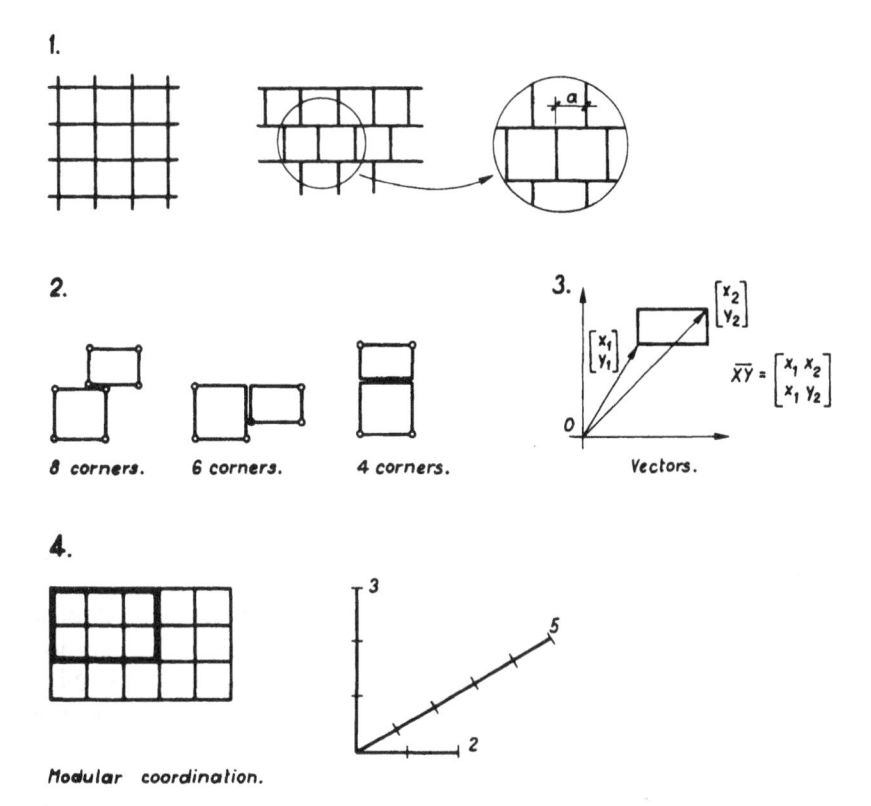

8 corners.   6 corners.   4 corners.

3.

Vectors.

$$\overline{xy} = \begin{bmatrix} x_1 x_2 \\ x_1 y_2 \end{bmatrix}$$

4.

Modular coordination.

Figure 3.37. *Aligning rectangular parallelepipeds.*

(3) The frustrum of the cube (*A VI*) or (3, 8, 8), also called Kevin's polyhedron, with $6F_8 + 8F_3 = 32$ faces as semiregular polyhedron, can constitute a compact space system on its own, i.e., the syntagmatic graph's vertices will have only one label. Having a homogeneous degree of 32, this space system is also regular on the syntagmatic level but not on the level of the architectural morphemes. We can call it an Archimedean rhythm.

(4) If we relax now the requirement for morphological regularity, that is, if we admit semiregular spaces in the space system, we see that it is again the cube which can be combined in a compact system with semiregular spaces, namely the cuboctahedron, which has 14 faces with the formula $6F_4 + 8F_3 = 14$. It is the $A\overline{II}$ case in Archimedean enumeration and has the code (3, 4, 3, 4) in Emmerich's notation system. This $C + A\overline{II}$ system as syntagmatic graph has on its vertices labels of regular shapes (*C*) as well as semiregular ones ($A\overline{II}$); the facts that there is more than one label, and that the syntagmatic graph has 6 *and* 14 as degrees, further relaxes regularity on the syntagmatic level.

In summing up we can say that among the 5 regular and 13 semiregular polyhedrons — we see again how the so-called 'round number' has no significance beyond the decimal system — we can enumerate only four cases where either a regular or at least a semiregular polyhedron can constitute a compact space system in a network which can be infinitely extended. The cube is regular at all levels of consideration — as morpheme, and in the syntagmatic composition having always the same degree. Two other regular polyhedrons can compose a compact space system which has only regular morphemes but whose syntagmatic graph is semiregular, having degrees of 6 and 14. The space system of Kevin's polyhedrons is composed of semiregular morphemes but the syntagmatic graph is regular, having a degree of 32. The composition constructed of cubes and cuboctahedrons 'infringes' on the regularity on the level of the participating morphemes, namely one space type is only semiregular; furthermore, having a degree of either 6 *or* 14, it is also only semiregular on the level of the syntagmatic graph. The privilege of all these systems, regular, semiregular or semisemiregular — if we consider all levels together — is that from a very limited number of composing morphemes we can construct a *limitless* compact space system. Three of the five regular polyhedrons (Warusfel 1966: 307; Schulze-Fielitz 1971: 10) and 11 of the 13 semiregular ones cannot participate in any of these kinds of systems. Notice that the regular polyhedrons composing these systems must have either triangular, quadratic, or hexagonal faces — not pentagonal — and these polygons also constitute the so-called regular right prisms which were capable of making a compact one-level space system.

This enumeration of regular and semiregular three-dimensional space systems puts at the architect's disposal compact space arrangements where, by choosing syntactical links (by breaking openings in the wall for doors), he can impose various rhythms chosen on a stylistic basis. He may freely choose the constituting space's morphology and construct space systems with gaps or add relational words, so the architectural opus consisting in word choice and links transcends the adjacency constraints extolled in the compact packing in 'buildings'.

Critical review of the application of some rules of composition from the beholder's viewpoint In any creation the communicator must, on the one hand, master context restrictions, and, on the other hand, meet internal requirements which can be practically expressed in the contractor's program in factual terms. This program can also state stylistic rules which must be respected. The querying of traditional rules of composition which architects, like other craftsmen, receive from generation to generation is a particular task of our book. In fact, traditionally the question asked is *how* to implement the rules, but in our time we question their *foundations*, their rationales

(M. Borissavlievitch). Does the application of a certain rule to the architectural space system provide unmatchable perfection? And even more pressing — is the intended effect 'communicated', namely, is it perceptible at all?

In our skeptical time we challenge disrespectfully the pertinence of time-honored rules. These formulas are related mostly to symmetry, or repetition of a complex kind, or in terms of the traditions 'analogon' (Bouveresse) where the constituents in relation to themselves and to the opus as a whole manifest a harmony (Ravaisson) which makes the opus indisputably complete, resp. perfect. This perfection can be tested — as we showed to some extent in the preceding sections — first by asking if the solution is intrinsically unique in topological and geometrical terms, or if it is in fact only one case among others that has been discovered, in which case its perfection would not be absolute but only relative; second, on the practical level, we ask questions about the perceptibility of the effect as well as the universal relevance of a 'perfect' solution when specific contexts are not considered.

The task of completion itself can be conceived in different senses. The architectural opus can be inserted in a limited context, for example between bulkheads (see 1 in the figure), and a harmonious completion becomes a task of appropriate subdivision which itself can be conceived as a finite or an almost-infinite operation. The irony of war-devasted Europe was that the

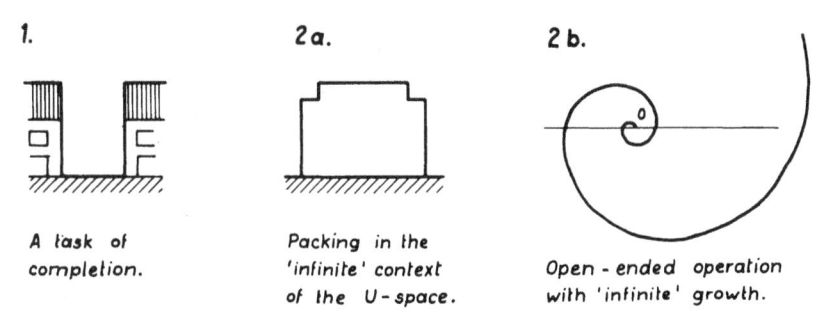

1.

A task of completion.

2a.

Packing in the 'infinite' context of the U-space.

2b.

Open - ended operation with 'infinite' growth.

subdivision of space became an inglorious infinite operation. On the other hand, we have the 'infinite' context where the completion of an opus can be conceived as a packing giving to the space system a compact inverse shape in the (contextual) U space (see 2a in the figure); or a complete composition can be perceived as an open-ended operation with 'infinite' growth (see 2b in the figure). This last case conforms more with the modern evolutionary and progressive *weltanschaung* than the previous one. In this case the formula of 'magic proportions' must be applicable in perpetuity, e.g., by a Turing machine. It will be a recursive formula, a growth in terms of recurring topological variables, e.g., modules (Warusfel 1966: 344). (As an architectural task, we can consider Le Corbusier's museum of infinite growth: Schulze-Fielitz 1971: 38. Indeed, a museum must be infinite.)

430 *Communication through architecture*

Even if the formulas transmitted through the generations showed absolute topological or geometrical perfection, it is still pertinent to question if this perfection is perceptible elsewhere than on the designer's drawing table. Is it truly transmissible to even the most sensitive beholder, e.g., another architect, the *'archilecteur'* of architecture (Michael Riffaterre)? This 'esthetic from down' (Bouveresse) has already been launched by Fechner and produced pertinent modern research results (R. Francès). The esthetic effects become explicit and verifiable. An immediate advantage of this inquiry is that if there is, for example, more than one 'perfect proportion' the architect can choose the one which is perceptible, a *sine qua non* condition for any communication of esthetic emotion.

By applying the enumerated criteria, we could discuss the application of harmonic division and progression in relation to various architectural tasks. Grosso modo, the architect can encounter three situations:

(1) In one case the requirements and his freedom to maneuver — his variables for determining the spaces' morphology and syntactical linkages — are balanced and can be solved like a system of equations where numbers of equations and of unknown quantities are equal.

(2) In another situation the degree of freedom is high and the number of solutions is infinite. This gives place to imagination, yet an indeterminate system is very difficult to handle; namely, it is partially determined and it is difficult to make explicit aspects of restrictions. It is difficult to do by mathematical means (e.g., the Diophantine equations do it for a restricted problem). Because of this lack of a heuristically workable approach to solving indeterminate systems, it is — of course — hard to elaborate computer software (algorithms) for producing a desired number of numerical solutions. (We have seen that the isoconcavity requirement for the acoustical space is this kind of situation.)

(3) Finally there are the more common cases where there are more requirements and restrictions than alternatives. The architect must compare heterogeneous requirements and find an appropriate compromise. For this very reason it would be grotesque to overdetermine the program by so-called esthetic requirements which in the end are neither uniquely perfect nor perceptible, and therefore become remnants of uncontrolled speculations.

In concrete terms we will discuss these questions in four particular contexts.

— How can rectangular parallelepiped spaces be packed in a syntagmatically compact system in such a way that the space system in its inverse form, that is, its facades in the atmospheric space, read as a rectangular parallelepiped?
— How can the conformity of 'internal' and 'external' requirements be realized under the more restricted condition that all spaces in the system as

well as its extrusion into the atmospheric space be a regular rectangular parallelepiped (or regular hexahedron), which is the cube?
— What is the architectural efficiency of the proportions by (sub)divisions (regular dissection; harmonic division)?
— What regular progressions perpetuate a chosen modular system?

a. *Alignment* Alignment means here that spaces are stacked in such a way that in the common external contour the lowest possible number of edges appear. The simplest case which can demonstrate the mathematical instrument is two right parallelepiped spaces of equal height which allow a planar treatment (see 1 in Figure 3.37). The problem can emerge in the design process in association with other requirements (Whitehead and Eldars 1964). The design function of an alignment can be economical, namely looking for an enveloping surface which is the smallest for a determined set of spaces and which will minimize heat loss or realize more adjacencies of locales. But very often the purpose is for the atmospheric space, namely to create a convex image of the space system as a rectangular parallelepiped. Even if that is so we must advise the architect that the esthetic contribution from architectural space systems through bidimensional facades on the streetscape as part of the *U* space is far from self-evident (e.g., row houses). Further, it can be said beforehand that research which tries to generate esthetic emotion from the beholder by imposing the shape of the concave space on the space system's packing itself is pointless. These effects remain in the realm of the designers and draftsmen because the beholder cannot efficiently compare the shapes of spaces read in their concavity with the shape of the so-called building which he reads in its inverse (convex) extrusion in the atmosphere. But this question has been already debated in other sections.

Depending upon the relative difference between the shapes of two constituting rectangular parallelepipeds, the composition can produce between four and eight corners (see 2 in Figure 3.37). In order to find the minimal number, we must consider the spaces in terms of vectors. In the case of a one-level space system composed of rectangular parallelepipeds of equal height, each space is determined by two vectors which make a matrix

$$\overline{XY} = \begin{bmatrix} x_1 & x_2 \\ y_1 & y_2 \end{bmatrix}$$

where x and y can have numerical values or can even represent equations (see 3 in Figure 3.37). The comparison of the two shapes by a zero–one matrix allows us to say whether or not the two spaces can be packed in another rectangular parallelepiped. All the optimal packing processes can be monitored by the constituting spaces' matrices. This applies also to the problem of arrangements discussed in the following sections.

b. *Cubelets and the so-called perfect rectangle* Is it possible to construct a one-level space system composed exclusively from cubic spaces in such a compact syntagmatic arrangement that they occupy only and fully a rectangular ground plan? This way of posing the problem makes the so-called 'squared rectangle' or 'perfect rectangle' (a problem which intrigued many mathematicians until Morton solved it in 1925) relevant to our concern. It is typically a bidimensional problem of tesselation; transposed in terms of the composition of space systems, it involves a one-level system with equal shapes and various volumes as well as with varying height which, considering the relatively narrow variations in human tallness, involves a minimal height and therefore (because of the cubic shape of all spaces) a minimal extension of the building site itself. On the other hand, because of the various heights of the locales the same system can be repeated on more than one level only at the price of gaps between superposed spaces. That the cube is a privileged shape is incontestable. The cubelet is not chosen by chance as the measure of volumetric capacity (cubage). It is the square's privilege to construct a compact system of the same elements. In dimension two there are three regular shapes — triangle, square, and hexagon — which can form a compact pavement but in dimension three the cube is the only one among the regular polyhedrons which produces again in all new compact arrangements a cube as packing. This endocompatibility of cubes gave considerable momentum for mathematical research. However, before discussing the solutions to this problem we underline the limited merit of the whole problem; namely the packing for any architectural text's quality.

Strictly speaking, the mathematician's problem was: what is the smallest number of squares which can be packed in a rectangular polygon which is not a square? It is proven that under 9 as critical number there is no solution; at 9 there are two; and over 9 there are numerous solutions (Berge 1966 [1963]: Appendix 3). Morton found this critical number by an experimental approach (trial and error). The general solution comes from R. Sprague, the self-styled 'Important Member of the Cambridge Trinity College Mathematical Society' (March and Steadman 1971: 272-274), who discovered it in his leisure time during the Second World War (1937-1940), and who completely ignored the results of Morton's work. By his description of the discovery, another 'Important Member' of the same society, W. T. Tutte, tries to create a saga (see Gardner 1963: ch. 17) with the typical self-righteous vanity of the so-called *Grandes Ecoles*.

In fact, a more general approach to the problem can be obtained by applying Kirchhoff's first law. (We applied his second law earlier in connection with the incidence matrix characterizing the locale's paradigmatic valence.) Of course, the Kirchhoff laws themselves result from the application of mathematics to problems of electricity and in terms of mathematics itself, we find the solution under the rubric Green's function of the second kind solving 'boundary value problems'.

But let us now look at the two critical solutions and describe their characteristics in terms of syntagmatic graphs, which concern us here.

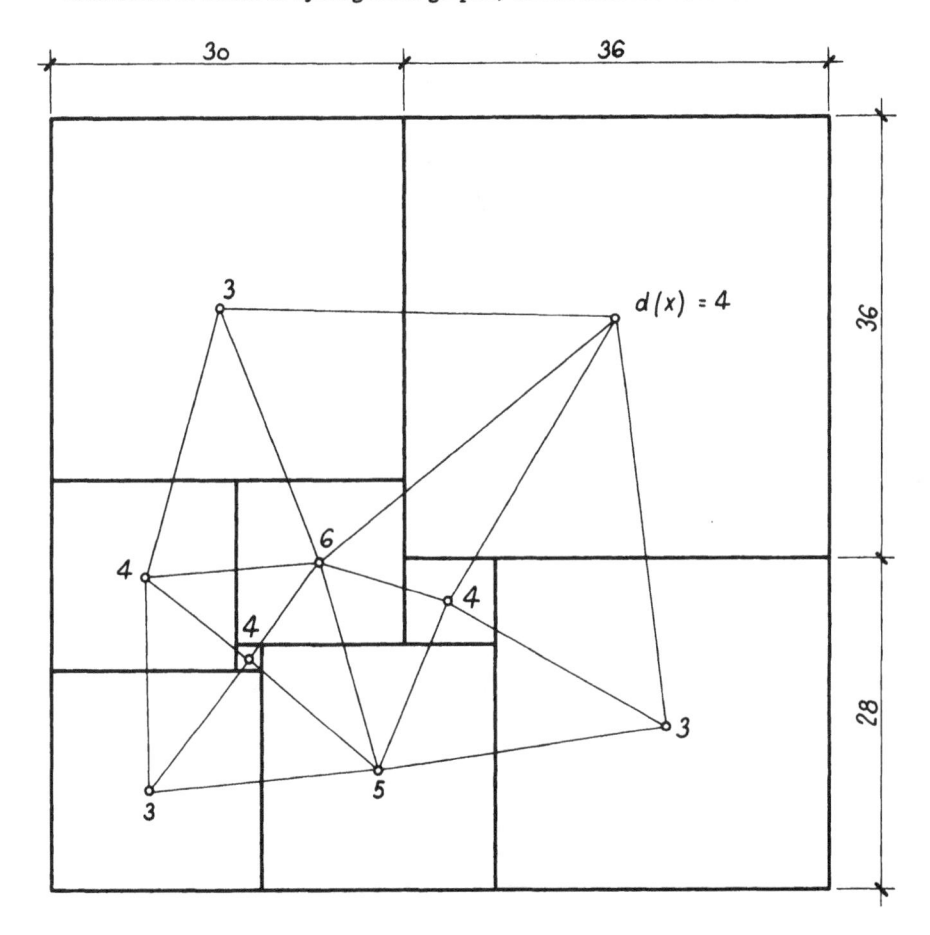

Morton's squared rectangle with syntagmatic graph and paradigmatic valence of rooms.

We can see that the two solutions have, from the viewpoint of their syntagmatic graph, individual characteristics in common. Both have an index of equal centrality, as well as radii and diameters of equal length. Both also have two peripheral locales with equal indices. In contrast, the first space system has only one central locale while the second has two, one near to the center of gravity and the other whose geometrical location is more 'eccentric'. This fact shows again how characteristics related to geometrical morphology

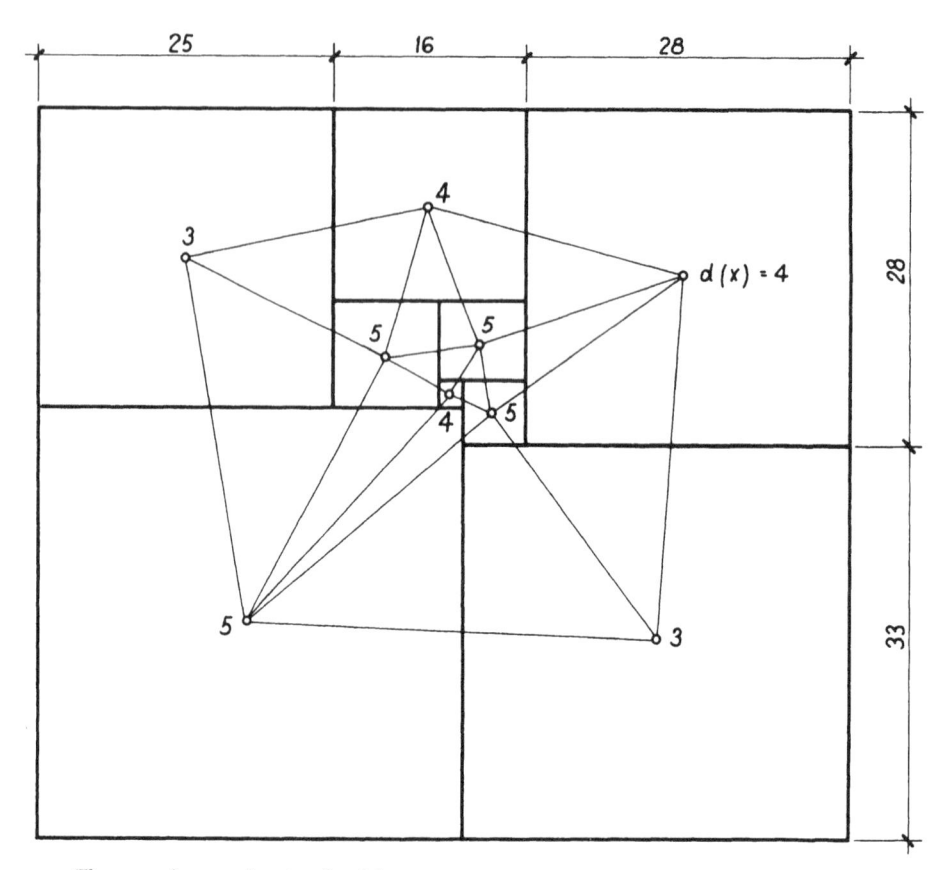

The second squared rectangle of 9 squares.

and those related to syntagmatic — and also to syntactical — arrangements are autonomous layers of composition. (For that matter, we expected this difference between the two systems, since the first has a locale whose paradigmatic valence is six, and the second has only two locales with a valence of five.)

c. *Golden section and modules for infinite growth* In the tradition, praise for the golden section is unmatched. From Vitruvius — *De Architectura* in ten books — to the Red and Blue series of Le Corbusier, recognition of it goes through Fra Luca di Borgo, Kepler ('one of the treasures of geometry'), Ziesing, as well as Paul Valéry, who exclaimed '*quel poème que l'analyse de ϕ*', and the list goes on (March and Steadman 1971: 236; Bouveresse 1976: 58-59). The dissident voices are very rare (Alexander 1959). Indeed, in this exaltation there is no limit; the golden section's value is unique, universal, and without flaw. It is invested on the speculative level with an exclusive quality in number theory in Euclidean geometry; animate and inanimate nature and all creation are imbued with it. We can read it in the human body in relation to the navel. It transcends all the branches of the major arts, which reproduce it for its supposed power to arouse an incomparable esthetic (emotional) response. In the light of this general context we will examine the merit of the golden proportion for the creation of architectural space systems.

The golden section is a harmonic division, meaning that the entity is divided externally and internally in the same ratio without being symmetrical. The division also relates parts among themselves as well as to the whole. Using a line, we can formulate this proportion — $a : b = b : (a + b)$ — or if we take a as unity in ├──a──┼────b────┤ then $1 : b = b : (1 + b)$, which gives the equation $b^2 - b - 1 = 0$ and $b = (1 + \sqrt{5})/2$, namely $\phi = 1.61803398875$, which is an irrational number algebraically incommensurable. While it can not be reconstructed by addition, neither is it a transcendental number as e and π are, and therefore it can still be represented geometrically by means of Euclidean geometry, namely by ruler and compass. The first quality of this section is the existence of a geometric average: $\phi = \sqrt{a(a - b)}$. It is the middle term in the geometric progression which allows continuous proportion. We will see in connection with the Fibonacci sequence that if we begin a sequence with unity and we put ϕ in the second place we can construct from these two a recurring sequence which is either geometric (viz., multiplicative), additive, or subtractive.

1, ϕ, ϕ^2, ϕ^3 where $\phi + 1 = \phi^2$, $2\phi + 1 = \phi^3$, and so on.
1, ϕ, $\phi + 1$, $2\phi + 1$.

The consequence on a bidimensional level is that we can subdivide a rectangle into a sequence of nesting rectangles where all have the proportion $1 : \phi$ *ad infinitum* (see 1 in Figure 3.38, and Scholfield 1958: 138).

Two questions arise:

(1) Is this truly a unique quality of the golden section or does the architect have other choices even while preserving these qualities?
(2) Do these particular qualities have special merit in the composition of architectural space systems for the created esthetic atmosphere? Are they appreciable?

— Ad 1. According to Scholfield and Choisy, the Renaissance designer used another regulating line (Le Corbusier — *tracé régulateur*), namely $1 : \sqrt{2}$ and $1 : 2\sqrt{2}$. This ratio is also an irrational number, therefore indivisible by cubelets of measurement, but it makes it possible to subdivide or fold a sheet of paper in format A_1, A_2 without leaving any remainder (see 2 in Figure

1. 'Whirling squares' (J. Hambidge) pattern generated by nesting golden rectangles.

2. Folding in format A_1, A_2, etc.

3. Bidimensional harmonic arrangement of boxes within boxes.

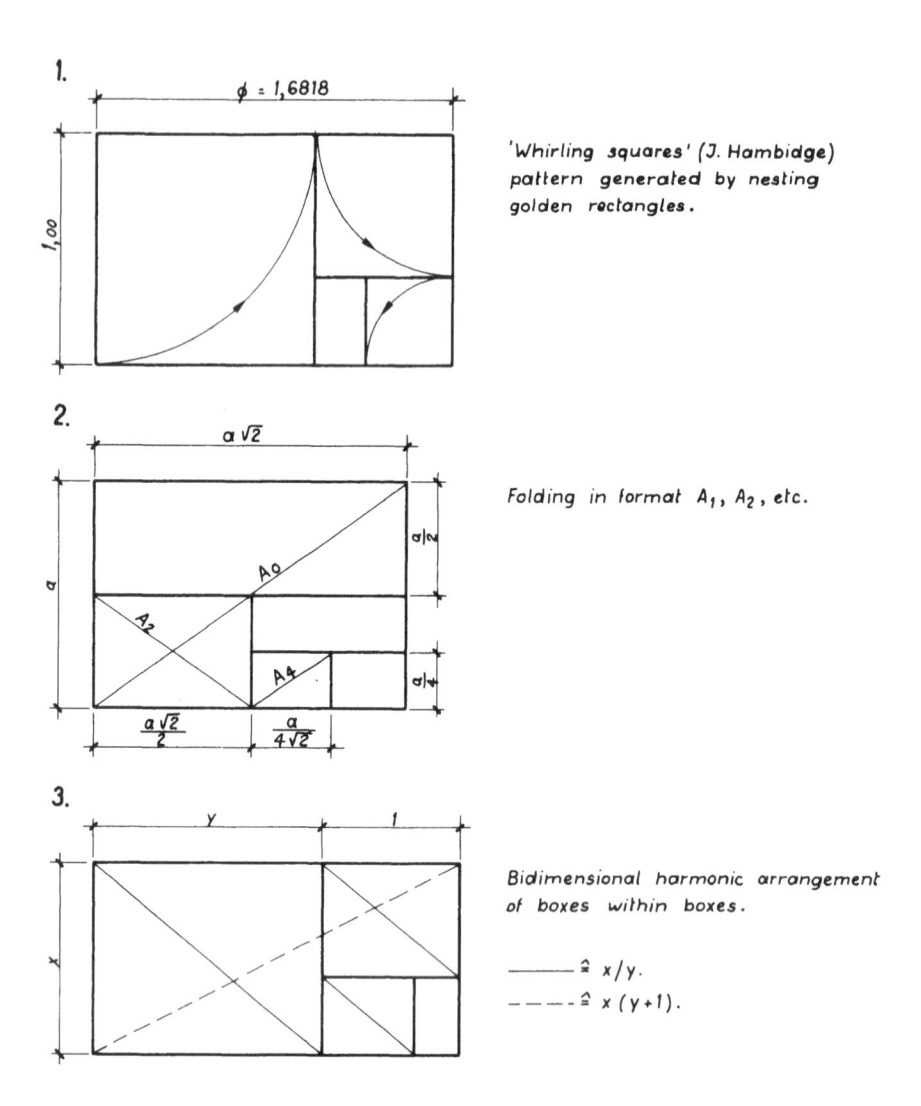

———— $\hat{=}$ x/y.
-------- $\hat{=}$ $x(y+1)$.

Figure 3.38. *Bidimensional harmonic arrangement.*

3.38). If A_0 is equal to unity (1 m^2) then $1 = a \cdot a/\sqrt{2} = a^2/\sqrt{2}$. It is also a harmonic proportion and there are more than two. We recall that the $\sqrt{2}$ comes from the Socratic research for finding the side of a square which has double the area of the original square.

As a matter of fact, we can find many proportions which are harmonic and can be folded and nested just like $1/\sqrt{2}$; namely $1/\sqrt{3}$ or $1/\sqrt{5}$. There are also rational numbers like $1 : \sqrt{4} = 1/2$ or $1/x = x/3$.

With regard to the successive nesting property of a sequence of proportions — the harmonic arrangement of boxes within boxes (cf. in syntactic analysis, N. Chomsky; Chao 1968: 70; Simon 1969: 48) — the golden section is only one of numerous possibilities. In general terms, any number fits which satisfies the equation $1/x = x/(y + 1)$, viz., $0 = x^2 - y - 1$. In geometrical terms, the last remaining rectangle has the proportion $x/(y + 1)$ and the next one, obtained after subdivision, x/y (see 3 in Figure 3.38).

— Ad 2. The merit of perpetuating the golden section in the arrangement of ground plans can be argued for more than one reason. In the last century Fechner proved that subjects can distinguish the golden section from others. Alexander (1959: 425-426) adds that the error remains within a margin of 3 to 4 percent. However, in 1955 Lawlor qualifies this statement by finding that socialization is an intervening variable and the golden section is only appreciable for a subject coming from the 'Atlantic civilization'. If so, the esthetic value and even the perceptibility of the golden section is not rooted in the nature of things (Ankerl 1971a).

Its application in the composition of an architectural space system calls for still other reservations. The golden section is applied to bidimensional phenomena which from an architectural viewpoint are submorphemic. Further, all proportions which are not within a space but transcend it are, *eo ipso*, imperceptible. (We except now the bound word and the multisensory compound word, where more than one space can be perceptible at the same time by way of different senses, and we disregard them because all claims made so far in the literature for the quality of the golden section are only optical phenomena.) How could a person other than the designer himself perceive the proportion which is inherent in two spaces if they are not simultaneously considered? These objections are completely valid for all harmonic divisions. They are diversions for the drawer's eyes, as well as for the armchair architectural historian who analyses ground plans or ruins more than historic space systems that are still extant.

Charles Gwathmey, one of the well-known contemporary US architects, intervened at the last AIA congress (Dallas, May 1978) during a panel about architecture to say that 'abstract, ideal spaces' must be created. Looking for a perfect space and space system is a metaphysical undertaking which seems to have no end. Even the research on squared rectangles is more relevant than that which applies the golden section to create emotion by truly architectural means.

Modulars (and Leonardo Fibonacci of Pisa) We come now to the last point which must be considered for the application of regularity in the construction of space systems, namely a modular system which allows limitless growth.

Wittkower (1960) notices that, until the Renaissance, designers took most interest in harmonic division, and the idea of infinite progress only emerged at this time. In the organic world, the 'infinite' growth of the vegetable kingdom is the paradigm. Thompson d'Arcy asked how a tree could grow without visible limit, remaining always itself by realizing the program of its seed. For Goethe the logistic or growth curve is the symbol of the limitless harmonious development of life.

The modern construction industry introduced prefabrication where a limited number of repertory items are used in architectural communication. Our question is: how can we construct space systems — permitting extension at our discretion — with a limited number of repertory items without becoming monotonous? (Chao 1968: 66, 70) In other words, how can the restriction of repertory items be compensated by a variety of syntagmatic and so syntactical arrangements?

With reference to number theory, we can find geometrical prime factors in spaces with various volumes and shapes. They are prime factors in the sense that they help us to find the greatest common factor as well as the least common multiple for a space. 'Combinatography' can have two tasks: to look for all variations which are possible by using a limited number of items; or to go out from desired sentences to look for the largest syntagmatic blocks which can be used in all these sentences as immediate constituents.

The European Productivity Agency, among others, suggested in 1950 a system of modular coordination and standardization (Ehrenkrantz 1956) by the following formula (see also 4 in Figure 3.37):

$E = \{x | x = 2^i 3^j 5^k, i, j \in Z_+, k \in [0, 1]\}$, where
2, 3 and 5 are prime numbers;
i and j = any positive integer (including zero);
and k = binary value.

This system is tridimensional, also proper to architecture. (It can coordinate submorphemic elements as well as morphemes in syntagmatic and syntactical arrangements.) The proposed numbers are rational ones which belong neither to arithmetic nor to a geometrical sequence, but they constitute a Fibonacci sequence. Fibonacci, a very productive mathematician in the Middle Ages, contrived a sequence where from two numbers a third one is constructed, and each succeeding number is the sum of the two immediately preceding.

This sequence allows various general applications. The designer can choose the first two numbers in a manner which seems to him to be the most appropriate to his actual task. He can even begin it with 2 equal numbers like 1, 1, which gives 1, 1, 2, 3, 5, 8. ...

The sequence allows regularity in *both* directions: in the direction of expansion as well as in that of division. James and James note (1968: 145): the ratio of one Fibonacci number gives the sequence 1/1, 2/1, 3/2, 5/3 which has the limit $(\sqrt{5} + 1)/2$. The members of the sequence which begins with 1 and 1 are easy to calculate; members of many other sequences cannot be so easily calculated. Any member of the 1, 1 Fibonacci sequence can be calculated by the formula

$$u_n = \{[1 + 5)/2]^{n+1} - [(1 - \sqrt{5})/2]^{n+1}\}/\sqrt{5}$$

We remember $(1 + \sqrt{5})/2$ is the golden section ϕ and the formula can be stated in the following manner as well: $u_n = \{\phi^{n+1} - (1 - \phi)^{n+1}\}/\sqrt{5}$.

We can also place the ϕ as second number in the sequence, which gives 1, ϕ, 1 + ϕ, 1 + 2ϕ, 2 + 3ϕ. This sequence has a geometrical progression as we have mentioned before, namely $1 + \phi = \phi^2$ and $1 + 2\phi = \phi^3$ and so on. We see that the golden section appears in this perspective as a particular case among the large number of possibilities inherent in the Fibonacci sequences for modular coordination.

IV

Studying Space Effects on Face-to-Face
Communication by Experimentation:
Experimental Sociology Begins with the
Sociology of Architecture

20

Systematic Observation and Inferences: Epistemological Foundation

> 'Physics is the paragon of exact science.'
>
> Bertalanffy

We are now in a position to discuss which approaches and experimental methods can be used to reveal the etiological relationships existing between created space systems and the face-to-face communication process which takes place within them. Indeed, the logic of our topic demands that, within the interrelated process of social communication, we single out for study those effects upon direct or face-to-face communication which a created space system specifically generates.

After a Prolegomenon, in Part II we treated face-to-face communication analytically, and in Part III we studied the architectural media as means of communication. In simplified terms, therefore, we can say that Part IV attempts to determine the effects of phenomena presented in Part III (the X variable) upon the phenomena viewed in Part II (the Y variable).

Before going further we would like to explain why a field which appears at first glance to be part of applied ecological sociology seems to us to represent a more general paradigmatic vanguard for the development of experimental sociology. We must make it clear why the sociology of architecture involves the use of more reliable objective concepts than *verstehende* sociology, which bases its findings on introspective sources as well as objective ones. In short, we must justify the title of this chapter: why experimental sociology should begin with the sociology of architecture. This question has already been dealt with in general terms in Part I; here we will elucidate its consequences for our present inquiry.

The creation and measurement of space dimensions can be made in an unequivocal manner, especially on the mesolevel where architecture is situated. Furthermore, the space itself is the reference frame for estimating and locating all real objects and subjects within it; it is the prime factor of the physical environment, the point of departure.

Moreover, architectural space, with its closed envelope and finite volume, allows us to apprehend the concept of space in its most precise form, as roomraum. By using architectural space, we can obtain a variable for the sociology of architecture, as well as for sociology in general, which fulfills the requirements of exactitude necessary for experimental research.

This part will clarify how the very nature of architecture enables us to create situations which lend themselves remarkably well to experimental investigation. Not only are such situations in the privileged position of being able to simulate the real world better than laboratory experiments usually do; they can also be controlled just as effectively, giving results fully as reliable. We will see that sociology, conceived on the empirical level of the communication process, can in fact be more genuinely scientific than psychology, because of the fundamentally external character of social behavior.

However, the experimental sociology of architecture as part of the study of man in his environment is still in the 'preparadigmatic' stage (Rapoport 1977: 14). This can be exclusively attributed neither to the fact that it is a new area of study nor to its being a remote field in applied sociology. Rather, the situation is due to inappropriate research strategy which attempts to evaluate communication without first dealing adequately with perception and properly describing the network and structure of communication.

This part is divided into four chapters. The first deals with the importance of experimentation to the etiological inferences in science in general, and in sociology in particular. The second chapter discusses experimentation specifically in the sociology of architecture. The third chapter examines in detail the necessary elements of models in the experimental sociology of architecture. And the fourth chapter shows that a longitudinal experimental design is heuristically the most promising direction for research, in order to make results epistemologically commensurable – as results must be if they are to be scientifically cumulative.

EXPERIMENTATION AND ETIOLOGICAL INFERENCE

The paradigm of science is physics. This is true not in a metaphorical but in a historical sense. All other efforts of intellectual curiosity and investigation, which do not follow this paradigm – comprehension, intellection – must be considered erudition. But this does not imply some hierarchical order in determining the epistemological validity or attractiveness of two approaches.

The formulation of a proposition already shows, *prima facie,* its scientific character. A proposition is stated in explicitly defined abstract terms which do not allow more than one interpretation. (Not allowing more than one level of interpretation precludes any 'deeper understanding' dependent on one's degree of initiation.) Furthermore, such propositions must become an integral part of a science representing a systematically organized body of knowledge, in which every element has its well-defined status. A sentence is either a postulate, a deduction, or a statement which may be checked directly by experimentation. It is the presence of these latter sentences, which are relevant to sensory experience as well as to application in the real world, which makes an exact science empirical.

Indeed, the systematic organization of a comprehensive field of knowledge, the exactness of the proposition, the explicitness of concepts, the presence of rules for the definition and the postulation of axioms, the exclusion of contradiction, and the tendency to completeness (and axiomatization); all of these are preconditions for an experimental science, but all of these can be shared as well by other exact sciences. This is a point to stress; because many authors attach an excessive importance to the use of sophisticated mathematical processes — mathematicalism — in order to upgrade the scientific character of sociological studies, particularly those in environmental sociology. In fact, however, the most sophisticated mathematical or statistical treatments of data cannot bring improvement to the science, if the concepts used are not formulated in terms which permit abstract theory and empirical data to be related to one another by the process of experimental verification.

The sociology of science underlines the ritual and conventional aspect of the scientific praxis. Still, we must recognize that the full-blown procedural ritual common to the exact and experimental sciences has a productive function and produces tangible advantages. A simple empiricism, whereby one accumulated and stockpiled various statements, would be a waste of time, and the results of dubious validity. However, the integration of knowledge into a science as a comprehensive, organized whole permits the accumulation process to proceed heuristically in a most rewarding way. In addition, it improves the epistemological reliability of findings. In reality, any contradiction between accepted and new propositions immediately becomes apparent — especially when the system is more and more axiomatized, thereby permitting choices to be made clearly. (We can then determine how great the 'convulsive' impact of the new findings is on the whole system.) On the one hand, a 'multiplication effect' is generated by means of the exact measurement of the generality of a proposition; and implied possible applications reveal themselves spontaneously.

Within this general framework of consideration, we must see the etiological imputation which the experimental sociology of architecture tries to realize between characteristics of created space and the enveloped face-to-face communication network and structure. Cohen and Nagel (1944: 246-247) says that science presupposes systematic variations and order, which it tries to specify and verify. Any concomitance defined in abstract and objective (external) terms is the simplest order which science can establish. A sophisticated type of concomitance is the asymmetric and temporarily directed order ($\vec{CE}$) which is also realized in the etiological succession. It can take part as an element in a very complex process in which, by extending the time period considered (ΔT), interactive effects can appear. Relationships between cause (C) and effect (E) can be further complicated by the fact that man is capable not only of adapting himself to the recognized causation process, but can use its form of transformation while inverting C and E, making from E a final cause.

Researchers in pragmatic history and in experimental medicine look for the etiological relationship within the framework of individual cases, and their approach can be defined as a systematic elimination of antecedents (C) which do not specifically affect aspects of the 'succeedings' considered as effect (E). This sentence does not give a definition of the etiological relationship, but specifies *how* it is researched. In order to investigate the possible effects (E) of a specific factor (C) – or even its effect within the individual context of a single case – or in order to find the various possible (indispensable, substitutive and/or suspending) causes of an effect; we must devise comparable cases. That is, we must devise events which are recurrent, with some differences. Experimentation is the method of systematically constructing series of comparable cases. For this reason, it is the ultimate of all empirical falsification procedures. Indeed, the demonstration of an etiological imputation demands an exhaustive scientific exposition of all antecedents relevant to the 'succeedings'. The two temporal stages of the events must be separable, and in addition the elements of the C and E stages must be isolable from one another according to heuristic principles (for this reason we said 'scientific exposition'). Elements which are present but irrelevant can be of finite or infinite number.

Although set theory and combination allow a more generalized approach in the construction of comparable cases, Nagel and other authors are critical of Stuart Mill's five methods of scientific induction, without, however, going further than a simple 'critical reedition' of them in their own work.

By investigating the etiological relation between C and E, we can combine them basically in four ways (see 0 in Figure 4.1). The truth table allows 16 combinations by eliminating one or the other as false (0) or admitting it (1) as nonexcluded – i.e., possibly true. Depending on heuristic considerations in relation to the data at hand, and available laboratory facilities, the experimenter can choose any of the 16 cases.

Regardless of which of the 16 cases is chosen, the results cannot conclusively prove the existence of a particular casual structure; but they can eliminate (falsify) specific hypotheses of causation (Pagès 1974: 315-316, 274; Cohen and Nagel 1944; 265).

Systematic observation and inferences 447

0.

	E	Ē
C	CE	CĒ
C̄	C̄E	C̄Ē

or

11	10
01	00

C.... Antecedent.
E.... Effect.
C̄.... Absence of C.
(Hilbert's nomenclature).
n > 0.

The 4 possible relations between C and E.

1.

CE	
11	1
10	1
01	0
00	1

E.g.

50	20
	30

Falsification.

	n

Method of difference.

2.

CE	
11	1
10	1
01	0
00	1

E.g.

30	
20	50

Falsification.

0	

or

	n

Method of agreement.

3.

CE	
11	1
10	1
01	0
00	1

E.g.

50	
	50

Falsification.

0	

or

n	

or

	n

Combination of 1 and 2.

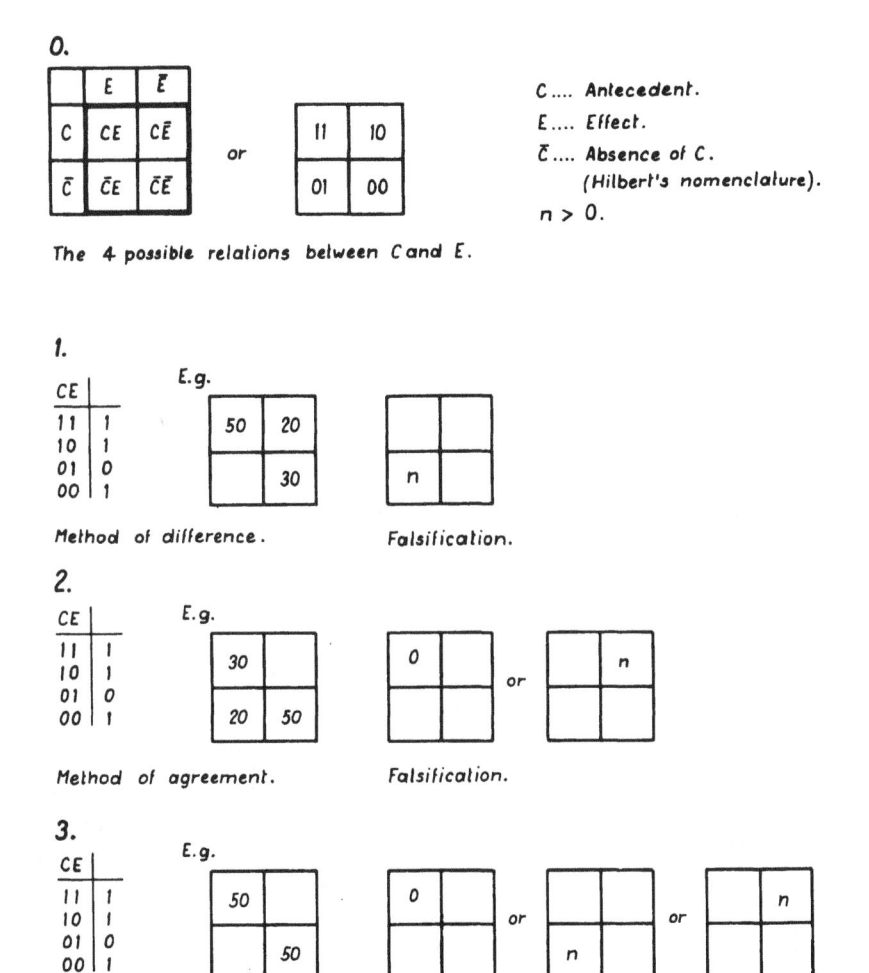

Figure 4.1. *Etiological inferences.*

In the structure of etiological relations we can distinguish three basic types of relevance and their combinations.

(1) Disjunction or alternation. In Fortran IV: .OR. In logic: (∨). It is shown in terms of Boolean or switching algebra in 1 in Figure 4.2. C_1 and C_2 show individually sufficient causes. Replaceability (substitutability).

(2) Conjunction. In Fortran IV: .AND. In logic: (∧). It is shown in switching algebra in 2 in Figure 4.2. C_1 and C_2 are both necessary. Indispensability.

448 Studying space effects by experimentation

(3) By using relays in a complex switching model we can also represent negation (or denial), the case of suspending cause (see 3 in Figure 4.2).

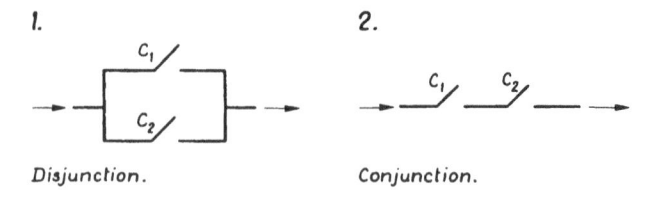

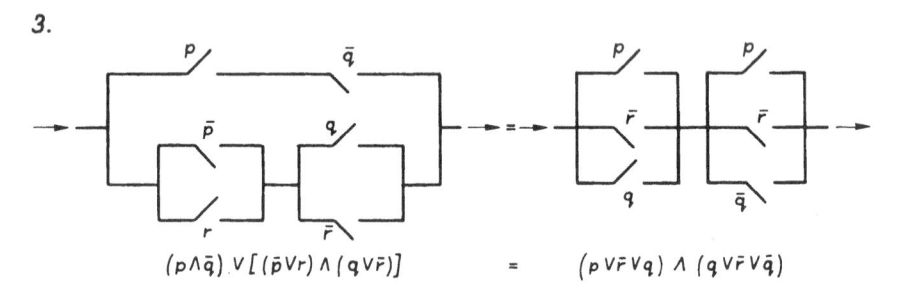

1.

2.

Disjunction.   Conjunction.

3.

$(p \wedge \bar{q}) \vee [(\bar{p} \vee r) \wedge (q \vee \bar{r})]$ = $(p \vee \bar{r} \vee q) \wedge (q \vee \bar{r} \vee \bar{q})$

Negation.

Figure 4.2. *Relevant logical relations in terms of Boolean algebra.*

In stochastic terms, etiological relation is indicated by the fact that in the distribution in the quadrate shown in Figure 4.1 (CE, $\bar{C}E$, $C\bar{E}$, $\bar{C}\bar{E}$) only one square is filled. This indicates logical implication (this is the method of difference, i.e., the second case in Mill's enumeration). An example is shown in 1 in Figure 4.1. (In human science experimentation using control groups, the groups are represented by the cases 01 and 00 noted on Figure 4.1.) The values introduced in the numeric example are, of course, arbitrary. To falsify a presumed necessary etiological relation, it is sufficient to fulfill *one* criterion — i.e., that the square $\bar{C}E$ remains empty.

The case of inverse implication indicates a sufficient cause corresponding to Mill's first case, the method of agreement (Cohen and Nagel 1944: 249 and Mill 1900: 451, 452, 458). An example is shown in 2 in Figure 4.1. The falsification of a hypothesis involving the case of sufficient cause can be made in two ways: either the CE square must be empty or $C\bar{E}$ must not be. (The sufficient cause characterizes more the general nature and power of a factor or X variable, rather than specifying aspects of the Y variable.)

The strict implication (iff; biconditional) or converse relation signifies sufficient and necessary etiological relation at the same time. It is Mill's third case which is in fact the combination of cases one and two. An example is shown in 3 in Figure 4.1. This relation can be falsified in three different ways (see 3 in Figure 4.1): either CE is not empty, or $C\bar{E}$ is, or $\bar{C}E$ is empty. In practice, it is always easier to refute an enunciation rich in information than one with less information. (That is, a general statement may more easily be refuted than a particular one.)

We stated that experimentation makes possible the falsification of enunciation expressed in abstract terms, and therefore generalizable by studying a discretionary number of comparable cases. Indeed, we can control the validity of a hypothesis, if it is formulated in terms meeting the criteria of abstract relevance and operationalism (Blalock 1970: 102). The experimenter can manipulate and produce, in the desired combination and dosage (Blalock 1970: 102), the X variables at a given moment (time) and place. These latter conditions are necessary for a reliable recording of the effects on the Y variables. Furthermore, if other factors intervene, they must be controlled (parasitic factors; Blalock 1970: 95, 41; Chapanis 1967: 561), either by holding them constant or by neutralizing their effects. The production *and* observation of a sequence of events in the most desired form and circumstances following a design, a program, a well-established scenario with its expectations (hypotheses), is the promise of the experimentation. Experimentation is a constructed, controlled procedure, and one which can be described because it is recordable. The replication of comparable events: repetition, reiteration, and reprise *at will*, are necessary for any demonstration by induction which involves an irrefutability beyond a given degree of probability (Blalock 1970: 34-35) as well as quantitative precision (Francès 1966: 113). A hypothesis becomes a thesis if it was formulated in terms which could be tested empirically and resisted the procedure of falsification.

This exposition of the essential characteristics of the experimental method, which are by definition closely related to the inductive production of knowledge as well as to the theoretical and scientific relevance of the enunciations, shows implicitly why the experimental method is superior to any other method of empirical research – to nonexperimental approaches such as comparative statistics or parallel groups (Hovland et al. 1953), or to quasi-experimental approaches. The presentation also shows how the experimental method has only a contingent relationship to its most common technique and setting: the laboratory.

Setup of Experiments

Experiments consist of a design and a physical setup. Because the idea of experimentation is so closely tied in most people's minds to the laboratory – with all its advantages and drawbacks – and because this is a crucial aspect of the experimental sociology of architecture, let us discuss this question immediately.

The experimental setup is a constructed world where all perceptible elements are defined in abstract terms within the scope of the theoretical problem under study. (Indeed, the experimental setup is neither necessarily the scene of everyday life nor a mental simulation in order to make precise the structure of a hypothesis: mental experiment, Pagès 1974: 325.) The setup for experimentation follows a strict epistemological order and by its very construction — like a built-in trap — sets in motion the X variables, controls the process, and measures the effects. The setup creates a situation where the variation of the X and Y variables can be isolated and the imputation studied. It is that which ensures the internal validity of the experimentation, and thus the generalization of the conclusions for all repetitions of the same situation as existed during the experiment. The internal validity of the experimentation is a *sine qua non* for any generalizable conclusions generated by empirical research. It cannot be shirked without epistemological consequences. This question is naively overlooked by many amateur researchers, particularly those in the fashionable field of environmental research. Indeed, internal validity and external validity are not in competition but complement one another.

In addition, to return to the question of factor isolation, it cannot be produced exclusively by means of sophisticated statistical treatment of well-classified variables. The proper use of statistical techniques — the statistical clearing of the data — is a common concern of all empirical (or inductive) research, including experimental research. Indeed, as we indicated, factor isolation (among other things) makes necessary a particular experimental setup — but factor isolation cannot always be achieved solely by elimination of the nonstudied factors in the setup. Sophisticated statistical methods permit those factors standing in an experimental design's way to be dealt with. Some factors, such as a cluster (Blalock 1970: 102), are inseparable and do not allow a free combination (e.g., a Chinese with blue eyes). And other factors may be present and even relevant but remain unidentifiable.

The task of an experimental setup is to come as close as possible to creating a situation where all observed differences can be imputed to the action of the manipulated factor. This is realized as far as the experimenter can isolate the system under study (*in vitro*, Zimmermann 1972: 44), which assures the requirement for *ceteris paribus* in a controlled manner (Blalock 1970: 95). This provides an analytically defined situation permitting comparisons which are not purely intuitive or 'implicit'. For this purpose, variables fall, from an epistemological viewpoint, into four classes:

(1) Variables under study (X and Y variables).
(2) Potentially interfering factors which are under control (e.g., randomized).

(3) Parasitic factors.
(4) Hidden factors — i.e., those with unknown effects (Blalock 1970: 98, 41).

Methodological efforts made partly by an ingenious setup, and partly by sophisticated statistical treatment, try first of all to eliminate the class 4 factors, or at least to reintegrate 3 and 4 into class 2.

The experimental design establishes a strictly defined and programmed sequence of operations. In order to make analytical comparison of the change induced by the independent variable for an authentic experimentation, the researcher has two different possibilities:

(1) To measure the dependent variable before and after the introduction of the independent variable on the subjects (as the hypothesized causes) in which case no control group is needed as a standard for comparison.
(2) To use both an experimental group and a control group, and to measure each only once (e.g., subjects in the control group receive a placebo.)

In human science, the second method is more often used. In this way, relevant factors which are not introduced as independent variables are randomized. These relevant factors can also be neutralized by other techniques such as matching, screening, or physical elimination by experimental setup.

Before discussing experimentation in sociology in particular, let us touch on the external or ecological validity of the experimental results (Brunswick 1956; Chapanis 1967; Orne 1973). Indeed, there are only two possible serious challenges to the epistemological superiority of the experimental method: an impossibility to realize the conditions prescribed by the experimental design, or irrelevance of the results to situations outside the laboratory or experimental setup, viz., lack of ecological validity. Many authors use these arguments to 'prove' the inappropriateness of the experimental method to the human sciences; which is to overlook the fact that these problems are not only present in the human sciences, but also occur in some natural sciences (e.g., the applicability of soil mechanics in a geological milieu). Therefore the problems must be both considered and solved within a broader framework of the sciences, rather than within the epistemology specific to the human sciences. If the experimental design does not require the separated variation of each independent variable, the practical significance of the conclusions increases, because the experiment more closely simulates the real universe. Indeed, before its use in scientific experimentation the 'randomized block design' had long been applied in agriculture, where as a rule more than one factor varies simultaneously. The factorial experiment, in which more than one experimental variable is used and the results are submitted to an analysis of variance (ANOVA), knocks holes in any 'ecological' objection to the experimental method in the human sciences.

Experimentation in Sociology and Peculiarities of the Sociology of Architecture

Which are the particular problems in applying the experimental method to human science? How can we reduce these problems?

Common knowledge has it that no one learns from history and that history repeats itself; but in the scholarly German tradition established by Windelband and Rickert the topics of all human sciences are considered nonrecurrent, irreproducible, and unique with unmatchable complexity. Many authors (Ankerl 1972a: 13-31; Machlup 1963: 160, 172; cf. Burgers 1975) recognize that the prediction of geological events using laws established by experimental physics is in principle a problem of similar subtlety as the application of experimental methods in sociology, particularly in microsociology. Indeed, the problem particular to human science is not the historical character of human events but human reflection and the resultant *anticipation* (Ankerl 1972a: 23; Machlup 1963: 173). Therefore an essential task for the proper application of experimentation in human science is to prevent imperceptible, uncontrolled infiltration of effects upon the dependent variables caused by the subjects' anticipations. This is especially relevant to experimental setups in the laboratory. In what way can we expect the sociology of architecture to solve the problem?

Let us examine how the experimental sociology of architecture relates to the main aspects of experiments:

(1) The stimulus chosen as experimental variable (Kameron 1973: 167).
(2) The experimental subjects which react.
(3) Other relevant factors which are not physically eliminated but neutralized, or whose effects are estimated.
(4) The act of observation — mechanical (instrumental) or human.

In exceptional cases of natural situations which lend themselves to experimentation, there is no need for manipulation of the original stimulus or X variable by the experimenter (nature's experiment). The subject, therefore, has nothing to anticipate and such an experiment is *eo ipso* 'without reactive bias' (Webb et al. 1971: 69-70). Usually, however, in order to obtain the stimulus at a given time and place, the experimenter must manipulate it, or at least intervene by its introduction (Sherif 1954; Chombart de Lauwe et al. 1967). Apart from the elimination of interfering factors, this manipulation by the experimenter is the only constructed aspect of such an experiment. A prime effect caused by an experimenter, which renders results dubious, comes from his behavior if he introduces the X variable and, being full of expectations, does not succeed in producing the stimulus according to the standard (even though he may not actually play the role of *agent provocateur*).

In this way the independent variable *itself* is altered. This kind of experimental bias, present in pure sociology, is eliminated in ecological sociology by definition, because the X variable is a physical factor the effect of which is under study. This is a first privilege inherent to the sociology of architecture.

Human response can also be modified by the sensation of artificiality, strangeness, or abnormality of the situation in a laboratory. But the sociology of architecture studies the effect of the architectural space itself. The constructed nature of the space is accepted as normal, since this is an essential of architecture; the artifactual nature of the architectural space is not additive to the architectural space's 'natural' occurrences, distorting it as an operant X variable. (Therefore it is sufficient if the experimenter choose the type of room usually assigned to a given type of sojourn – e.g., for a longitudinal experiment, an institution where the sojourn is of long duration.)

In fact, experiments are often conducted in laboratories with unnaturally sparse furnishings – furnishings carefully chosen and inventoried in the experimenter's effort to keep down and control the effects of relevant factors. This emptiness however, itself arouses suspicion. In the case of sociology of architecture, the response to the space itself is under study, and realizing that space situations originate from an architect is an effect which is not detrimental to the validity of results.

The same can be said of variation in the space's characteristics. In order to construct a theory, the experimental design must program variation of the spaces; this is relatively easily devised by the initial architectural design (modifiable rooms), and is accepted as taking part of the architectural message.

Finally, the fact of being observed in itself or simply being in the presence of others can modify the subject's reponse (reactivity – Webb et al. 1971). This is not a problem peculiar to the sociology of architecture but to *all* empirical human science. Even animals react – and humans still more so – if congeners are present. Should the congener turn out to be a scientific investigator, a detective, or a supervisor, the subject begins to behave in a manner designed to create a certain impression of himself. Opportunities to disguise the fact of observation are not necessarily better in a natural than in a laboratory setting. Of course, a mechanical recording is preferable, not only from this viewpoint but also because of the reliability of the data obtained compared to that from a human observer. In sociology of architecture the installation of various recording devices is easy because they can be hidden 'in the X variable' – within the envelope of the 'devised space' itself. By definition it is easy to bring the subject near to the recording device, since for the sociology of architecture only those events are relevant which occur within the rooms. This convenient situation from a recording standpoint makes possible highly reliable results which permit comparison and replication

– particularly when compared to other snapshot methods such as hidden cameras in the hands of *'paparazzi'* of the social sciences (Curry and Clarke 1977).

We can say that in all considered respects, sociology of architecture lends itself to experimentation, and is a privileged field to become the first chapter within experimental sociology.

The crucial problem in experiments with living beings in general, and humans in particular, is that the reliability of the data increases if we can use unobtrusive methods which do not destroy the authenticity of the response even before it is measured (in an effect of anticipation). This problem is especially delicate if the experimental design requires successive measurements on the same subjects. Because it is always difficult to be certain about the presence of the effect of anticipation, human science applies the experimental design involving control groups. In this way we can avoid the inconvenience of successive measurement as well as learn the presence of anticipation effects (if any) in quantitative terms. Despite objections of expensive maximalism and some practical objections, simple designs such as those with three and four groups remain the most advisable among the orthodox experimental designs.

The intent in this chapter was not so much to discuss the experimental method itself as to demonstrate why sociology of architecture opens up new possibilities for applying it to the human sciences in general, and to sociology in particular.

21

Traceable Elements for a Model in Experimental Sociology of Architecture

> 'It is the relation between people's experience of their environment and the objective structure of the physical world that is of interest for physical planning, because planning tries to accomplish better experiences for people, not by changing man, but by rearranging the objective structures.'
>
> G. Lindberg and J. Hellbert, 'Strategic Decision in Research Design'. In Michelson 1975: 17.

In order to arrive at a suitable experimental design and setup, it is necessary to develop a model which takes into account not only the X and Y variables selected for study, but also all other factors which might influence or bias the results.

The first step, however, is to specify the set of independent and dependent variables the research will focus on. Part III identified the independent variable of concern — the space system designed by the architect, insofar as the shape and volume of spaces, and the syntactical arrangement of their system, are perceptible to the people placed within them. The dependent variables, discussed in Part II, are the characteristics of the various social gatherings which take place in the space system specified.

As in any study, the subject of interest is extrinsically motivated — either by the topic's importance for further development of the science or by pragmatic concern. The topic need not be defended in epistemological terms; we are, however, accountable for the *way* we handle it because the validity of the results will depend on it. For this very reason our interest will not extend to topics considered by the general public, or even by an initiated audience, as of primary interest, if such subjects cannot be dealt with in strictly empirical terms operant in experimentation. In so defining the field of interest, our intent is to present methods leading to solid knowledge. The communication process, with its various sensory aspects and sequential characteristics — network and structure — lends itself to this approach. We can arrive at isolable and objectively measurable results concerning precisely those aspects of the dependent variable (i.e., social-gathering characteristics) which seem *a priori* to be most strongly affected by variations in the independent variable (i.e., architectural space).

Let us relate the variables described above to the prevailing sociological categories. Broadly speaking, we might say that the experimental sociology of architecture studies how changes in the architectural scene (F. Pogany) influence social gathering. Such studies can be carried out in two different ways: by comparing analogous gatherings which occur in different spaces, or by studying constancies in the patterns of different gatherings which occur in the same space. In either case, a certain degree of selectivity is required in regard to the dependent variable, with observations being made only upon those aspects of the social gathering which are affected by variations in the properties of the enclosing architectural space.

COMMUNICATION PATTERN AS THE DEPENDENT OR *Y* VARIABLE

This reasoning leads us to consider those aspects of the sociological variables which consist of physical meeting, since it is in precisely this respect that the physical and perceptible nature of the architectural space takes on significance as an independent variable. (It is characteristic, however, that the vocabulary developed by sociologists using culturalist approaches is poor in regard to terms which can be used to describe this phenomenon.) To be in a face-to-face communication network defined by mutual positions, where direct communication can occur, is a basic social fact, with a pattern that can be described. The network can be described by the mutual positions; and the structure at the primary level can be described by its substratum, the perceptible polysensory communication flow. The network should be related to specific properties of architectural space — described in terms of how the first fills the second — as should the aspects of the message-bearing emissions (such as the frequency, duration, and intensity, simultaneously, for each sensory channel).

The communicative nature of an emission is confirmed by the response. Emissions can thus be recorded at two points in the network: at the communicator's position, or at that of each receiver. As we have already argued (Ankerl 1972a: 73ff), a fundamental problem arises from two facts. First, sociological formations are defined on a higher level of abstraction than that of interpersonal relationship. And second, those formations which have a duration lasting over generations or population changes have been defined in the special literature in *nominal* terms — usually relying on legal fiction as a crutch (e.g., 'a village', 'a country') — without any precise and explicit reference to objective patterns (Lachenmeyer 1971: 85ff, 101). It is very difficult to bridge this gap without becoming mired either in the field of interpersonal relationship — mistaking it for the object of sociology — or in symbolic interaction, which is also less than vaguely related to the physical aspects of social phenomena. Rather than studying events in properly behavioral terms, symbolic interactionism studies them in attitudinal terms and in those of conduct — if not exclusively in terms of verbal expression — and thus leads even further away from the specific effects which architecture has on the observable, sensory aspects of the communication process (cf. Gutman).

Let us survey once more (Ankerl 1972a) the layers of sociological abstraction.

A chance gathering in an airport waiting room, where those present in all likelihood will not meet again, represents one level of sociological abstraction. Here the mapping of constant pattern in the communication process permits a fairly easy formulation of hypotheses about specific effects of the space.

On the interpersonal level, a given group of persons might have frequent gatherings (such as every week) in the same space. J. Altman (in J. E. Rasmussen 1973: 262-263) writes: 'Members of well-developed groups often have unique and idiosyncratic communication systems . . .' and 'different behavior repertoire. . . . Unique modes of communication reflect the state of their general relationship.' Indeed, we can record patterns of their communication process and establish constancies and trends. When the group changes its meeting place, the rupture observed in the trends, and the modification in the constant aspects of the pattern, can help in formulating hypotheses about effects of the architectural spaces.

The identification of sociological entities (as dependent variable) becomes more abstract if we admit that a social formation can exist without being composed of the same population. The sociologist can base his affirmation of the existence of a formation on either of two different phenomena: either the group maintains the same denomination, or they have a distinctive communication pattern. For the first case, a social club might 'die out' and later be revived following the same charter. An example of the second case is a secret society which is identified because of its distinctive communication pattern (e.g., if the Italian police recognizes that the Red Brigade and Lutta Continua share the same communication pattern — including network and structure in face-to-face communication as well as in telecommunication — then the police learn that they are merely two different denominations for one and the same sociological unit). A sociology which will be submitted to proper experimental control can identify units only if they can be defined in explicit terms of patterns of perceptible interactions. *Grosso modo*, we can say that a completely developed model for sociology of architecture will have a communication pattern at hand which, first, identifies a social formation as such; and which, second, tries to isolate effects on this pattern stemming from the fact that at different meetings, different members with their varying personal histories participate; and which, finally, takes the study of the modulation caused by a change in meeting rooms as its proper task.

A word must also be said about social institutions. Indeed, this is a very ambiguous expression. At a less empirical level of abstraction, we find generic terms which at best have a legal definition like 'family', 'social club', or 'nonprofit organization'. Such ideal typic legal concepts must not be confused with properly sociological ones, which consist of the functioning of a set of families of a given lineage; or the study of associations which not only bear the same name but have, at some level, communication between them (e.g., Rotary Clubs). If *all* families do not have some permanent pattern of interaction which distinguishes itself from friendship, etc., then the term 'family' must be banned from sociology or used only for such purposes as characterizing the legal system. Much sterile debate comes from the vague use of terms invited by the similarly vague concept of 'social institution' (family versus housemates and households, Ankerl 1978: 84.)

In the attempt in the coming pages to develop experimental methods useful for the sociology of architecture we will not consider 'associations', 'institutions', etc., which cannot at present be defined and identified in explicit terms of social interactions. We will have dependent variables which do not refer to softer and less observable concepts than the independent variable does. The behavioral pattern will stand on its own without implicit reference to attitude.

ARCHITECTURAL SPACE AS THE INDEPENDENT OR X VARIABLE

We indicated earlier that architectural space — as a physically well-defined object perceived in the unequivocal categories volume and shape — is a model for other variables. This is what makes the field of sociology of architecture especially attractive for experimental investigations. Now, however, we must recall that architectural space itself cannot be used in experimentation before some epistemological problems are solved.

The sociology of architecture will study the effects upon face-to-face communication specifically caused by the created space. However, only those effects of the created space can be studied which are related to its objective, perceptible characteristics and which exist before any name is attached as a label.

Names are already present in the program which an architect receives — usually in denotative terms as a functional denomination, to which the 'resourceful' architect adds others in order to make the space seem more valuable, prestigious, and desirable. This is the stage of *architecture parlée*, comparable to a cook's transforming the terms of a recipe into those of a menu, an art especially developed in French cuisine. A final, *a posteriori* stage sometimes comes as well, if an event which happened in the past in the space inspires the public to attach a new name to the roomraum (often an amusing one). In this case, occupancy and space become confused.

The whole process of labeling occurs on the emic level and hinders a space's objective, etic aspect in exerting its proper influence (Michelson 1975: 286, 290). So it is necessary to devise methods which attempt to identify, isolate, and eliminate the effects of labeling. The complexity of the problem is increased by the fact that verbal denotations and connotations are often underscored by objective means. Functional denotations are given by furnishings, fittings, equipment — and by even more integrated architectural characteristics such as cold flooring, which is not only effective for a haptic space impression but also suggests a washable surface and therefore a kitchen or an 'industrial' use of the space. A connotative label is enhanced by the luxurious or ostentatious nature of the materials used, as well as by the whole setup (e.g., *'Salle Louis XV'* as opposed to, say, a *'Rathskeller'*).

Finally, the location of a space in the syntactical arrangement of a space system does not only give an identity to each room and thus influence the impression of the space's volume and shape, but also invites the beholder to guess at the space's purpuse and connotative value.

How can we eliminate the connotation by a null hypothesis? The experimental design must take it into account in a way such as the following. The experimenter can present to various subject classes two rooms of identical shape and volume, and also having a completely symmetrical location in the space system's syntactical arrangements — e.g., two opposite doors in a corridor. The experimenter, however, can vary the names of the two rooms, or the furniture, without varying any aspects (e.g., color) directly affecting the space impression on the sensory level. The experimenter can then look for systematic bias. If the 'Louis XV room' is always perceived as larger than the 'saloon' of the same volume, the null hypothesis can be rejected (Zajonc 1966: 111, 113). Furthermore, by making the 'saloon' larger and larger, the bias attributable to labeling can even be quantitatively measured.

DIMENSIONS OF VARIABLES TO MEASURE

The X variable — also called the independent variable — has been discussed in detail in Part III. Here is a brief summary of the X variable's dimensions.

Each autonomous sensory space has a geometrical shape (sh) and volume (V), and acoustical, optical, and haptic-hermetic physical qualities (q).

Three autonomous spaces can be distinguished: acoustic, optic, and haptic. Since these sensory spaces can, by definition, be noncoextensive, when multiplied with the three types of characteristics, the Cartesian product (AS, OS, HS) · (sh, V, q) gives nine possible data types.

Furthermore, in the case of noncoextension, relative location must be added. This data is proper to the multisensory intricacy of the compound architectural word. It can best be specified in relation to a beholder's position as focal point or origin. Remember that multisensory intricacy can double the complexity of the architectural word already manifested on the unisensory level; this complexity occurs when the space is bound, isolating the component spaces from one another in only one direction.

An architectural creation exerts its sociological influence through the space impression generated in the group present in the space; and directly as the situational field which determines the face-to-face communication network as well as the communication flow. Therefore the aspects just enumerated of architectural spaces as the X variable of the sociology of architecture must be considered on two different levels.

First, the manner in which the objective characteristics of the space affect the transmission of face-to-face communication must be considered. And second, the space must be considered as an architectural expression which takes part in the architectural communication (process) from designer to recipients, and which operates through the space impression. Indeed, the group members participating in the face-to-face communication process within the space are influenced in their communication by the space impression.

The Y variable or dependent variable is measured first in terms of the face-to-face communication network and its transformation. For instance, if a group which meets regularly changes its room, and in so doing changes the configuration of its network expressed in relative spatial positions, this can be studied as a function of the space characteristics.

The other level on which the Y variable is considered and measured is the communication flow or structure. In physical terms, the communication flow has a time sequence — the same dimension as the time budget, which has amount, frequency, and pattern (Michelson 1975: 181, 287); and a quality — hylic characteristics proper to the sensory modalities such as the intensity of sound emitted and received.

In light of the culturalist postwar sociological tradition (Michelson 1975: 12, 280) — in which the application of interview and questionnaire methods for studying social reality increased enormously — why the communication structure at this level of substratum should be considered a variable in its own right must be justified (Ankerl 1973: 37). Today's sociologist, educated in the *verstehende* [interpretive] tradition – sometimes in the phenomenological one – feels comfortable decoding linguistically articulated verbal messages; and feels very handicapped indeed when confronted with communication phenomena where linguistic elements are absent. And even with the most carefully designed structuralist research, at some final level of interpretation data is evaluated in a manner which is based on an understanding of the language (see Moscovici's research; emics versus etics; cf. Harris 1964: 148).

What kinds of results can one obtain by distinguishing a level of analysis of the communication structure where significance is completely disregarded?

The answer lies in epistemological considerations in the search for operant concepts and hard knowledge, as well as in considerations specific to the experimental sociology of architecture.

As a subject of investigation, significance is dubious indeed. There is no empirical means of establishing the nature of an expression's message as accepted in general social use even at a given point in time. Furthermore, Spiegel and Machotka correctly point out (1974) the absence of an isomorphic or invariant relationship between expressed behavior and internal motive. They note (1974: 73) '... subjectivity involved in relating an internal variable to its mode of expression' and (1974: 74) 'the necessity of validating statements about the inside *independently*.' Internal variables can always be verified directly by the subject within himself (this is the basis of a private science), and extrapolated to apply to other subjects (human and other living beings) due to a supposed analogy between them. While not denying the pertinence of these efforts *a priori*, the epistemological utility of keeping separate the data on communication structure obtained first at the level of its physical substratum must be emphasized.

In fact, sociology has here an opportunity to become more objective than experimental psychology (Piéron 1968: 50), and by inference a harder science than the latter.

Psychology tried to become a harder science by reverting from the mental and cognitive levels to physiological interpretation (ϕ or phenomenal level versus p or physiological level). Yet sociology, studying inter- or superindividual phenomena, can hold the entire internal – mental or physiological – processing of external stimuli completely in a 'black box'. This progress in sociology, without losing its topic of investigation, would be especially easy to achieve – and especially welcome – in environmental sociology in general, and in the experimental sociology of architecture in particular, which is the first chapter of environmental sociology.

There is considerable debate about the importance of the influence of the physical environment – and architecture in particular – on social reality. Some speak of architectural determinism, while others would replace it altogether with an organizational theory. Still others qualify the influence of physical factors by terming them merely 'catalytic', 'permissive', 'supportive', or 'restrictive'.

One need not, however, debate here the relative importance of architecture as an independent variable in the etiological process of social reality, nor the primordial importance of the architectural creation which affects, of course, the social prestige of its professionals. Rather, the focus here is upon the question of what specific effects architecture has on the social communication process, and where these effects are the most pronounced. The only assumption made – and it may be verified – is that if architecture has specific sociological effects, these are the most explicit on the face-to-face communication network, on the transformation of this network, and on the communication structure as it is manifested at its substratum level (its time dimension and hylic aspects). This is nonlinguistic, face-to-face communication, and verbal communication at its prosodic level.

There are two ways in experimental design to render the effects of architectural space more easily measurable. First, in the setup, the experimenter can try to 'thin out' furniture and other elements which do not belong to the architectural space as such and which have a tendency to impart to the space a label other than the purely physical one – i.e., a functional or other connotation. The second device is a methodological one. Among the methods of controlling extraneous variables which interfere with the etiological relation being studied, preference should be given wherever possible to the matching technique, because it is especially adapted to studying etiological relations even where the factors in the overall process have only secondary importance. Matching is, however, a very demanding method, and cannot always be applied. Indeed, its use requires that the experimenter construct a comprehensive model in which virtually all operant factors are enumerated.

RECORDING VARIABLES, THEIR RELATIONS, AND TECHNIQUES OF RECORDING

The architectural space as X variable affects the face-to-face communication process directly by its physical dimensions, volume and shape, and by the hylic characteristics of its envelope, and on one other level by the impression of its volume and shape attributable to any sensory spaces. However, these two levels do not affect all characteristics of the Y variable – i.e., the face-to-face communication network, its transformation, and the communication structure.

Indeed, each sensory space by its physical characteristics determines the communication network of the same sensory channel directly by the reflection conditions prevailing in the space in question (e.g., $AS \to ac$.) It is the communication network which determines how a given emitted message is transmitted and received.

The network transformation as well as the communication flow depend upon the participants' decision: therefore the effect of the architectural space is mediated through its impression generated in the communicator and the receiver. Indeed, the communicator before sending a message — in choosing a channel and intensity — forms an idea about the network. In precise terms the experienced space (cf. Lindberg in Michelson, 1975: 17) is not yet the *espace vécu*, connoting the space with various memories and feelings, but the space impression which consists of evaluating the space's volume, shape, and position. This is a very important point, because it ensures an X variable still expressed in objective categories. Indeed, responses to questions concerning a space's physical dimensions are not equivalent in operational terms to responses to questions about *espace vécu* — i.e., only the latter must share the phenomenologist's concern (subjectivism), and need extensive epistemological (mainly conceptual) filtering before any scientific use.

The important aspect of the influence of the space impression is that the effect is not limited to bijective relations going from a sensory space to the same sensory communication channel; cross effects must also be admitted, and this complicates the model and the recording process. The impression of any unisensory space, and its relation to other sensory spaces perhaps simultaneously present, can affect any sensory aspects of the polysensory expression used by the communicator in the space. (See Figure 4.3.)

We see that the physical space exerts its influence chiefly through the shaping of the communication transmission between emission and reception. In contrast, the space impression already exerts its influence on the communicator; and since the receiver's response, by confirming the reception, completes — in terms of objective sociology — the event as a truly communicative one, the influence of the space impression so far, as measured by the receiver's reception, also reveals the influence exerted by the space impression on the receiver himself.

This requires clearly that the communication flow must be recorded at *two* points: at the point of emission and at the point of reception. For recording the emission, the more sensitive the recording device can be, the better. However, for recording the received communication, this rule needs qualification. Indeed, only perceptible messages are effective in the communication process (cf. Harris 1964: 28); therefore in order to simulate the data reception, the sensor must be calibrated to correspond to human sensitivity for each sense. This is not without problems. Indeed, at first glance we might imagine what it is enough to ask the subject about the smallest perceptible stimulus — i.e., the absolute threshold. However, a considerable body of research shows that stimuli are often received without the subject himself noticing at all. Numerous authors note the effects of 'subvisual' (Hall 1969: 55) and other 'subperceptible' impressions (e.g., 'micromomentary' facial expressions reported in van Koolwijk and Wieken-Mayser 1974: 72; Michelson 1975: 284).

A final consideration in the strategy of variable recording is the fact that very few expressions address themselves to only one sensory organ. In order to give uniform and complete coverage to the communication flow, we will now consider all its sensory facsimiles one by one; visible, audible, and tangible; and finally the recording of synchronization in the reception of polysensory messages.

Optical Imprinting (Facsimiles) of Communicative Expression: Videotape

Internal physiological or mental processes, which we do not attempt to define here, generate external changes which often become perceptible. If an expression can be reconstructed in a time sequence as a consequence of some previous change occurring in either the physical or the social environment, it is a response. The reaction to a human expression, which is perceptible and becomes an impression, is a communicative event. This section will consider only expressions which are optically manifest – i.e., visible – or those which at least can be recorded by optical means. We call the latter 'optical facsimile'. The difference between an overt response and an implicit response or expression is that the latter is either too rapid or too small to be perceived by another human being occupying a given communication network position.

On the subjective side – viz., the communicator's side – the expression can be either voluntary or involuntary, as well as perceptible by the communicator or not at all. On the receiver's side, most expressions can also be perceived by more than one sense organ – e.g., lipreading of a verbal message. Here, however, we are concerned only with the optical vector, and its visible component.

Although a distinction must be made between optical facsimile and visible impression – in the latter case the receiver realizes the existence of the message through visual means – it would be arbitrary to exclude those optical messages to which the receiver responds after having received the visual message unknowingly. In order to advance research in this field, we suggest recording all expressions that appear as optical facsimile without considering human reception (Winston 1975). We would, therefore, record palpation in the dark with infrared photography, or use ultrarapid camera techniques and zoom lenses to record otherwise imperceptible expressions (Franck 1957; Metz 1971).

A systematic handling of the optical vectors which enter into the face-to-face communication flow necessitates grouping the expressions. Visible human expressions are either glandular or motor in origin.

Expressions of glandular origin involve tears, perspiration, and color changes such as blushing or turning pale.

The amplitude and rapidity of expressions of motor origin depend on the part of the body involved. The trunk moves with exhaling and inhaling. Exhaling is used in sighing, inhaling in laughing, and both are used in sobbing. The second group of visible expressions originates in the limbs. One's gait, for instance, is expressed primarily by the legs. The arms gesticulate, the hands point, and fingers gesture on a smaller scale. The limbs can also tremble. On the body's surface, the skin can produce still finer, pilimotor movements such as gooseflesh and hair standing on end. The head as a whole nods, shakes, and turns, and the face smiles and grimaces. On a still more specific level there are the ocular, periocular, oral, and perioral (including lingual) expressions (Schuele 1976).

There are two main problems in optical recording. The first is how to conceal the observer or camera without disturbing the authenticity of the event to be recorded, yet without shirking on the requirement that all aspects of the expressions be recorded. A glance at photographs made by the anthropologist Sorenson (1974: 1,080-1,081) shows that the mother and child pay more attention to the cameraman than to each other.

A second problem is how to process the data obtained by mechanical recording. Automatic recording indiscriminately collects data both relevant and irrelevant to the communicative events which are the target. Many researchers try to solve the problem by using preestablished categories, which then introduces bias. Some aspects of the problem can be solved by videotape connected to a computer programmed for systematic and automatic sampling. In the face of abundant data, the choice and classification of relevant data is a *sine qua non* prerequisite to any scientific use: to indexing the data, to collecting data with the aim of selective retrieval, to recognizing patterns in the data. This implies the acceptance — explicit or implicit — of a taxonomy. But hereby all data collected becomes dependent on the taxonomy. There is, however, a modern approach which permits 'open-ended' data collection (Sorenson 1974: 1,080-1,081).

Optical recording of face-to-face communication can be done by observer's notation, camera, or videotape.

Serious scientific research does not, however, accept an observer's notation as a sufficiently rigorous data source. Von Cranach (1977) treats the problem of observing 'looking behavior' (which is obviously the most delicate problem but far from unique). Disregarding the observer's effect on the observation target, the recording itself is a mine of subjectivity (in the selection of which facts to record, and in the lack of a constant level of attention). For this reason, even if a researcher settles on a convenient coding system in advance, such as the labanotation of ballet (Hutchinson 1954) or the 'microkinetic transcription system' (Birdwhistell 1970: 147), this could only be applied in a reliable manner using filmed material.

Comparing film with videotape, the advantages lie overwhelmingly with videotape (Weick 1968), especially if the events can be recorded from a fixed position — which is the case in an architectural space if more than one video camera is used. The batteries required for videotape also weigh less (van Koolwijk and Wieken-Mayser 1974: 98; Sorenson 1974: 1,079).

Videotape makes recording possible in an unobtrusive manner by using one-way glass. Furthermore, videotape can be connected to a computer which, following an accepted pictographic transcription (e.g., that of Birdwhistell) performs an automatic sequence analysis. An even more sophisticated use of videotape/computer data generating is when a computer program is used which is capable of itself recognizing the code-category schemata prevailing in the data series, which prevents bias coming from preestablished concepts and categories (e.g., by following too limited a repertoire of visible expression).

Finally, videotape can be conveniently synchronized with recorders of other facsimiles of expression — e.g., tape recorders — making possible the study of polysensory organization of expressions (coordination, complementarity, compensation; 'human ethogram'). Complex models can also be developed along these lines. To these major advantages of videotape in data collecting must be added an economic advantage, since videotape can be erased and reused.

Because the amplitude and speed of expressions vary widely — e.g., eye movements are minute events, of the order of a few milliseconds in duration (Schluesser; Sperling) — some problems concerning the recording of various types of expressions must be resolved. Let us examine some recording examples.

Ekman et al. (1969: 297-312) developed code-category schemata: SCAN (System for Classification and Analysis of Nonverbal behavior). The schemata make it possible to analyze the sequence of expressions, in order to discover recurrences and coordination of simultaneous movements. Ekman's equipment makes possible automatic discovery of crystalized expression patterns. The equipment used permits a 'digital treatment' of the data of face-to-face communication, and even an automatic study of correlation between the data and the characteristics of the space where the communicative events take place. Furthermore, the equipment can include an information display and retrieval system, VID-R, which allows direct interpretation by the spectator as well as didactic use.

Unfortunately, Ekman's schematization does not stay on the objective, pictographic level throughout the whole treatment of the data, but becomes dependent upon subjective, often arbitrary semantic interpretation of psychiatric inspiration. Even the application of Birdwhistell's system — which is not 'open-ended' — would ensure the accumulation of information which can be useful beyond its association with any particular doctrine.

Scheflen's system concentrates on recording and treating data coming from postural movements, postural kinetic makers (gross-body movement, Jones and Hanson 1961).

Loeb (1968) records the fisting by camera. Krout (1954) studies the spontaneous movement of the hands. Freedman and Hoffman (1967) try to develop an objective approach to the study of movements. Research on hand movement is generally very paralinguistically inspired. Freedman and Hoffman record hand movements of the mentally ill during interviews, and apply a binary classification: movement is either object- or body-oriented. The population and recording circumstances are too specific, however, as well as too psychotherapeutically oriented, to permit general inferences.

The recording of miniature and very ephemeral or rapid expressions, such as those of the face, or of the ocular region in particular, presents the greatest challenge. Such recording demands a very sophisticated technique, particularly if the basic, epistemological requirement of remaining unobtrusive is to be observed. Zoom lenses, teleobjectives, and prismatic mirrors installed on cameras or videotapes (Eibl-Eibesfeld), permit recording in deviated directions as well as simultaneous multiple photographs (Birdwhistell), which can be subsequently presented using a split-screen technique. In order to increase the range of possibilities, some researchers use interrupted-light photography (Jones and Narva 1955) and others use special lighting (glow lamp). These techniques are not, however, unobtrusive (van Koolwijk and Wieken-Mayser 1974: 85).

The analysis of facial expressions with their miniature, ephemeral, and rapid character, also raises particular problems. Indeed, it is a danger that details may be perceived by the interlocutor but missed in analysis of the recorded data. It is necessary that the recording make possible a later enlargement, as well as a slow-motion playback, for analysis. We use the term Micro-Momentary Expression (MME). Haggard and Isaacs (1966) show that expressions which contain in normal vision 5 to 27 elements can be broken down into 38 to 91 discernable elements. (Seaford distinguished 19 elements among the oral muscle movements alone.) Slow-motion projection first made us aware of the fact that the difference between the expressions labeled as grimace and smile consists in rapidity. The smile is a slowed-down grimace (cf. Osgood 1966). A very good summary of research conducted before 1965 can be found in Ewert 1965. He correctly stresses that Ekman's statement about the universality of the 'facial language' is unsubstantiated, and that his categories – generated from the study of particular mimicry and the art of mime – cannot claim to be general.

The most delicate and most important field in visible communication is the oculo-ocular. It can only be recorded for scientific analysis by optical facsimile. (Yet as we saw in Part II, even among opticians the terminology for the different facets of vision is not standardized.) It is, for obvious reasons, difficult to devise techniques for unobtrusive mechanical recording of oculo-ocular communication. On the one hand, rapid micromovements must be recorded; and on the other hand, due to the possibility of head rotation, this fine recording must be done in a very large range of positions.

Recording in this field thus remains at a very amateur level – it employs observer's notation or obtrusive techniques which disturb the authenticity of the recorded phenomena. A survey of the literature shows that directions of looking, various eye movements (monocular, binocular; convergence; etc.), frequency, and duration, as well as the diameter of pupil openings, have been recorded. A basic problem is that sociologically the interaction of the partners' eyes is significant – the oculo-ocular process – yet a human observer cannot record synchronization in any reliable manner. Recent studies are well summarized in Argyle's work (1967), and methodological issues are debated in his discussion with Stephenson (1970).

As we noted, reporting of subtle and detailed phenomena of oculo-ocular communication involved human observation and reactive research. Ellring (1970) points out that if the observer is near, he disturbs the relation; and if he is far, the recording becomes less and less reliable (e.g., point of fixation). Exline and Winters (1965) describe a typical setup in great detail. Politz Media Studies (1959) observed the locations of eyes in relation to commercial posters, but the camera, although automatically activated, was visible to the persons observed. Watson (1970) made his observations from behind one-way glass but without using mechanical recording. We can find further discussion of these questions in J. J. Gibson and Pick (1963); in Krueger and Hueckstedt (1969); and in Boring (1953).

The reliable recording of ocular expression can make further progress by employing new means in a clever way. Glass walls, for example, are often placed between client and cashier, and can be conveniently used for installing invisible sensors to record the eye's expression from an even nearer point than that from which the partner sees it.

R. Davis, founder of the Environmental Analysis Group Lts. (TEAG), as well as V. Ayers (in Michelson 1975: 236) have reason to say that photographic recording of visible aspects of behavior has meaning only if it is done within a precise conceptual framework and subjected to a rigorous structure of testing and analysis. Indeed, as already said, recordings all too often take place only in the context of interviews. The limitation of observation to these situations often reflects the researcher's predilection for handling all visible expressions — even those which bear more affective than informative/discursive content — within the confines of paralinguistics where all expressions — even pantomine — are considered as a complement of some kind of verbal expression or its substitute. Of course, this tendency is enforced by the fact that recording in a seated interview position is also easiest.

Acoustical Imprintings (Facsimiles) of Communicative Expression: Audiotape

An acoustical phenomenon becomes an auditory element of the direct (or face-to-face) communication structure if the sound both originates from and is received by man. The recording must be made directly at the point of emission — mouth, hand, etc. — as well as at the ears of the receiver. Indeed, the direction of the sound emission, the distance and the acoustical space characteristics make the difference between the sound at the place of emission and that at the place of reception.

The communication structure consists of the received message sequence. As indicated in Part II, this structure is considered on the prosodic level, which is measured in terms of the temporal sequence of the sound's waves and amplitudes as well as their simultaneity. The properly communicative and sociological aspect appears when we record the alternation between speaker and listener in the presence of the group.

Considered as Y variable, the multisensory space characteristics influence the sound emission; and the interlocutors' chosen position in the communication network and the acoustical space characteristics influence the sound perceptible at the place of reception. The receiver has an impression about the duration of the sound emission, its intensity, and its frequency. And if there is simultaneously more than one emission, the receiver has an impression about their superposition (overtones). The impression of loudness (measured in sone or phon) and pitch (measured in mel) both depend upon the intensity and frequency — loudness primarily upon intensity, and pitch primarily upon frequency. In this case, intensity and frequency are measured at the place of reception (at the ears). On this objective level, the acoustical space exerts its influence upon the audible communication through the difference between the transmitted sound (the intensity and frequency) in the given space and in an anechoic chamber. But sound reception is a psycho-acoustical phenomenon, and it therefore depends on the listener's disposition as well — which in turn reflects the influence of spaces other than the acoustical one.

Furthermore, the exchange through the acoustical channel of communication is not only 'inserted' in the multisensory space in general and in the acoustical in particular: it is also inserted in the polysensory communication flow. In order to simplify the experimental design by isolating the audible component, the study of communication in the dark or among blind persons can be very instructive.

Basic problems in recording the audible communication flow

The recording of sound in an analyzable form is a fairly developed art. Unobtrusive recording is especially feasible if the subjects are in fixed positions. Furthermore the recorded can be calibrated in a manner which eliminates unwanted sounds — e.g., for psycholinguistic research, incomprehensible sounds can be eliminated by a low pass content filter (see research conducted at MIT by A. J. Friedhoff and P. F. Ostwald). The recorded sound can also be reconstructed by a synthesizer in its original composition, and an electroacoustical recording apparatus also allows spectrographic display (Crystal and Quirk 1964; Lieberman 1967; van Koolwijk and Wieken-Mayser 1974: 124; Chao 1968: 174-190). In the case of our research, good recording is assured by the fact that the experimenter chooses a room with given acoustical properties (P. D. Dénes).

However, even if we assume that only the intensity, frequency, composition in overtones, and duration can change, very complex sound patterns can appear (e.g., polyphony; irregular wave forms of speech composed of up to 30 components). The production of software facilitating the mathematical description of the recorded patterns is a very difficult task (Fourier analysis reduces complex wave forms to partials). In order to orient the research heuristically in promising directions, conceptual problems must be carefully resolved at the onset. Indeed, elocutions, musical configurations, and the like, are often defined without any empirically identifiable reference (P. B. Dénes in van Koolwijk and Wieken-Mayser 1974: 124).

In order to solve the problems step by step, let us begin with a discussion on the audible communication structure's simplest aspect: its duration. Duration is, more precisely, the alternation of sound emission and silence. Studies in duration began with psychological research carried out by E. Chapple and his colleagues.

Their research stems from the 1930s. Their objective was not sociological at all: indeed, Chapple tried to verify the hypothesis that every person has his own rhythm deriving from a personal equation which also dictates the alternation between silence and sound emission in a monologue. They studied the question chiefly in interview situations in a well-isolated acoustical space. Indeed, in a dyad the interlocutors must accommodate their personal rhythms to one another.

In mathematical terms, the temporal distribution of silence and sound emission can be studied like any other linear distribution, using such aspects as the average duration of emissions; the consecutive emission/silence ratio; and the vectorial evolution in time (dynamics). If we consider silence exclusively as an interruption of a fluency in sonic emission, breathing pauses (cf. Mahl: respiratory rates [RR]) and pauses caused by the phonetics of the language are not differentiated.

On the other hand, the establishment of minimal units (Hargreaves 1960) which will be considered as *a* silence makes it possible to eliminate certain types of pauses. Kasl et al. (1956) fix this time threshold at 500 msec. Cassotta et al. (1964) fix it at 300 msec., and stipulate that a recorded sound emission must have at least 3.3 Hz as a frequency. Data recorded within this framework is interpreted in the research of Ramsey, as well as of Goldman-Eisler (in Salzinger and Salzinger 1967: 269-280), as evidence that the sound emission/silence ratio most strongly expresses the interlocutor's personal equation among aspects of the audible communication structure. Mahl uses the silence quotient of silence/global time. Chapple himself uses both, and reaffirms (1971: 160): 'I stated in 1940 that frequency distributions of durations of actions and silences could be best fitted by a negative exponential J-shaped curve.'

We discussed these studies to show how the duration vector can be used to express communication structure. Our interest is purely methodological. Personal equations for research on the influence of architectural space on face-to-face communication as a sociological phenomenon are factors which must be neutralized.

Sound variation as a variable The emission-silence sequence is a binary system. Even after elimination of noise considered parasitic by a filter (an Allison filter or the Kay Sonograph of K. N. Stevens), the analysis of the other aspects of the communication structure — frequency, intensity, and superposition in complex wave form of sonic expressions, on the one hand, and their impression or reception in terms of loudness, pitch, and timbre (timbre is associated with overtones), on the other — remains an awkward and complicated task; and yet it can and must be done because they are not less significant aspects of the audible communication structure. The pioneering research carried out by P. D. Dénes and others in the Bell Telephone Laboratories in Murray Hill, New Jersey, shows that manner of speech ('*Sprechweise*', in van Koolwijk and Wieken-Mayser 1974: 124) had not yet been related to the objective data of audible communication just enumerated. The content of speech affects basically the manner of speech but not the quality of speech — which consists in pitch and timbre. According to Friedhoff, Ostwald, and others, the emotional aspect of a message is reflected in the quality of speech rather than in the manner of speech ('*Sprechweise* vs. *Sprechqualitaet*') — especially in the lower range of octave; therefore these characteristics can be recorded even if a low pass content filter eliminates high-frequency sounds (Starkweather). Further discussion of recording of relative quality (prosodic aspect related to pitch) and of absolute quality (related to timbre) of verbal expression is found in Markel's work (1965) and in Höffe's work in Germany — where the strong tradition of phenomenological psychology hindered the deeper discussion of the problems and techniques of empirical measurement.

The audible structure of group communication It is already difficult to analyze the synchronization of interaction in a dyadic situation. With any increase in the number of participants the number of relationships increases very rapidly $\binom{n}{2}$.

The two basic problems in group communication are:

(1) How can one objectively disentangle a communication situation from a continuum of exchanges of responses without content analysis?
(2) How can one determine the addressee?

Jones and Gerard (1967) and other authors reproach Skinner for supposing that an exchange takes place between pigeons — i.e., a ping-pong match — without disproving the possibility that two monologues are taking place (reactive pseudocontingency). Indeed, even in conversation there is no strict sequential organization of the statements and responses of speaker A and speaker B. (The overly organized exchange of dialogue in a play can deprive the conversation of all authenticity.) Assuming that the interlocutors A and B can be distinguished by the timbre of their voices, we have (if we account for the possibility of simultaneous speaking too) four cases in the dyad 10, 01, 00, 11 (Duncan, Chapple). Chapple and other researchers use the concept of episode to distinguish a continuous exchange. A new sequence of exchange needs an initiative. Episodes are separated from one another by a complete silence of minimal duration.

The identification of the addressee solely by auditory data is a very delicate task. If the addressee is not identified by name, then the transformation of the network position by turning the head or by changing the distance gives solid cues. The 'respondent' also gives a posterior cue. Argyle et al. (1968: 4, 13-15) and Kasl et al. (1956) show that the timing — i.e., synchronization — of an exchange, as well as identification of the addressee, is controlled by the visual component of face-to-face communication. (Cook, Argyle, and Lalljee show that if visual cues are absent, more repetition occurs in auditory communication.) Matarazzo (1964) had the privilege of studying exhaustively a chain of conversation of long duration which took place in an identified architectural space: the oral communication between astronauts and ground control personnel. He found that a long question is usually answered by a response of similar length.

The audible communication structure can serve to map group structure: leadership as a function of the quantity (volume) of verbal emissions (Bavelas et al. 1965); cliques, factions, isolation, and so on. A major problem is the development of a program which allows an automatic analysis of the sonic data with its many aspects and attributes. Lashbrooke (1967, 1969) developed the program PROANA 5 at Michigan State University to evaluate the verbal communication structure of a group of five, by computer. Lashbrooke had been inspired by the Collins-Gutzkow decision-making model (1964).

Study on the effects of space as the X variable

We have already indicated that the acoustical space can influence the audible communication structure in two ways:

(1) Objectively, in the way the emitted voice is modified at the place of reception by reverberation.
(2) Subjectively, in the way the space impression causes the speaker to change his position in the network or to change the quality of his voice. In addition, the space impression can also cause the listener to transform his network position, or to perceive the same sound intensity and frequency as different in loudness and pitch (we do not know of any research on this point within environmental sociology or sociology of architecture).

In 1948 Black carried out a study in environmental psychology from which we can learn some methods. Black (1950) used in the School of Aviation Medicine in Pensacola, Florida, eight rectangular and drum-shaped rooms. He varied their reverberation times (0.8-1.0 and 0.2-0.3) by their volumetric magnitude (150 and 1600 cubic feet). The Y variable was the intensity of the voice's vibration during the delivery as well as the duration of the reading of twelve four-word sentences. Measurements were taken using both directional and nondirectional microphones situated two meters from the speaker.

By varying the shape without affecting the reverberation time, neither the intensity nor the duration of the speaker's pronunciation was effected. In contrast, a change of volume and reverberation time influenced both aspects of the Y variable. Except for the relationship between reverberation time and duration, which was positive, the relationship between the X and Y variables was negative. Repeating the experiment in dead and live rooms showed that the negative correlation between volume and the intensity of voices was especially strong in the case of very voluminous live rooms. We can also conclude that the acoustical component of the polysensory space, which is present in a live room, is primarily relevant for the effect of space impression upon aspects of the audible expression.

Mechanical Imprinting (Facsimiles) of Communicative Expression

In order to bring together the various ways that communicative expressions can be received by somesthesis and kinesthesis, we used in Part III the term introduced by Géza Révész and also used by W. M. Austin and other authors (e.g., Gibson): the haptic. Now we will look at how this 'most consequential of all sensations' (Cohen) can be recorded by a mechanical 'sensor'.

In calibrating the instrument, the basic problem once again is that it is difficult to determine the lower threshold, because some haptic senstations may not be consciously received but nevertheless evoke a response in the receiver (cf. Piéron 1967: 133).

Another problem comes from the fact that the tactual sense is a proximo-receptor, and it is therefore difficult to intercept the actual communication flow, especially in an unobtrusive manner. Indeed, it is conceptually difficult to articulate components of the haptic exchange, and to separate expressions from responses. This calls to mind the research of Masters and Johnson, which runs the risk of altering the process itself by obtrusion of the recording instruments.

Recording of positioning

Despite some basic difficulties, we can begin this section on an optimistic note concerning recording the zones of the face-to-face communication network and its transformation by walking through its mechanical facsimile (imprinting). There are no major theoretical difficulties and a well-established praxis already exists.

We have seen that the polysensory face-to-face communication network is composed of zones commanded by predominant sensory channels. On the other hand, within the 'haptic zone' we can distinguish three subzones. The first subzone is related to shaking the hand; the second to using one's extremities to touch any part of the other's body; and the third to network positions whereby any part of the partner (or of partners, if more than one person communicate by the haptic channel) can be touched without hands.

We see the mechanical recording of paths is not a recording of the communication structure but of the network with its inherent haptic communication possibilities. If the subzones are established, the network position recording and the recording of its transformation can be made conveniently — i.e., with precision and in an unobtrusive manner — in a permanent, analyzable form.

'Approaching-avoiding behavior' (Levinger and Gunner 1967; Willis 1966; van Koolwijk and Wieken-Mayser 1974: 86-89) can be analyzed using the subzones as categories introduced into the software of a computer, which in turn commands the recording process itself. Furthermore, there is in principle nothing to prevent working out a more sophisticated program which relates the data on the 'waltzing about' of group members on the floor to the coordinates of the enveloping space — and even analyzes the 'ballet' data as a function of the haptic space as the X variable.

March and Steadman speak (1971: 7) of 'space-filling polygons' — proximity as a function of the axial density in the space (Ankerl 1974: 578). They used a mapped floor and plotted movement against the plan. Weight can identify the individuals (e.g., adults vs. children), and the continuous path maintains an individual's identity throughout the recorded events.

Let us now briefly examine previous experiments in recording pedal pressures in an unobtrusive manner.

Before any experimental studies were made at all, anthropologists studied the paleolithic era. Differing degrees of erosion in pathways and stairsteps are an indication of the frequency of use, i.e., frequentation (Webb et al. 1971: 44). Modern techniques introduce registration instruments beneath the floor tiles which are connected to a computer which, under direction of its program, determines what data to record (e.g., anything above a specified minimal weight, or beyond a given duration of stay). Programs can also follow individuals on their paths, recording the speed and directional changes. In his pioneering work Bechtel (1967) employed a hodometer. Winkel also uses this technique to study the frequentation of exhibits. The Teledeltos recording system (Blount 1967; Bauer et al. 1969: pp. 157-159) used by Held's team first at Brandeis University and later at MIT, makes possible not only the registration of the data but also automatic handling of the data by computer. Finally, the US Immigration Service, following military experience in Vietnam, used electronic equipment connected to a geophone (cf. Indian's ears) to track *grosso modo* human movement in a natural setting — along the Mexican-American border.

Actometry, kinesimetry

A next step in the measurement of locomotion as haptic expression was odometry. An odometer placed on the subject's neck measures his 'pedestrial data' based on his movements. These data can check those obtained by recording under the floor tiles. However, this 'necklace' can be unobtrusively employed only with children.

The actometer measures the total level of activity. Schulman and Reisman (1959) placed actometers on children's arms in an unobtrusive manner. These measurements correspond to those of oxygen consumption, which also reflects the total activity level (Webb et al. 1971: 43; Bungard and Lueck 1974: 113). Dittman and Llewellyn (1969) also measured the total level of muscular activity by accelerometer.

Other researchers use instruments to measure the amplitude, duration, and frequency of specific components of motor expressions: skeletal, postural, gestural, facial, brachial, and visceral expressions. The measurement of kinesic expressions of various body parts is studied by Birdwhistell (1970), Frey and von Cranach (1971), Watson and Graves (1966) and Mehrabian (1969). Electrography is the technique generally used. However, the basic issue is not solved, because these expressions are palpable but are not observed and recorded as taking part in the haptic exchange: they are conveyed by the visual channel of communication. Furthermore these precise measurements of motor activities are applied in an obtrusive manner.

Let us enumerate the most important measurements. The electrodermography of psychogalvanic reactions measures the glandular activities such as the sudoriferous on the palmar and plantar regions. The galvanic skin reflex (GSR) measures the electrodermal reactions, the electromyograph (EMG) the muscular expressions (J. F. Davis 1959). In fact, the GSR could be accompanied by dynamometric and myometric measurements. Sainesbury (1955) studies gestural movements by electromyograph, but he records only the movements' frequency and not their form. McGuigan and Pavek (1972) used an electromyograph for studying movements in two of seven bodily regions. Neuro- and vago-activities are also measured by electrography. Eyelid movements, mechanical brow movements, and periocular movements in general can be measured by mechanical means (R. G. Coss in Hutt and Hutt 1970: 122, 136). Eyeball movements can be measured by electronystagmography. Electrooculography (EOG) allows perfect vectographic recomposition of glances (F. Lhermitte and F. Chain in Dubois et al. 1971: 315; M. Jeannerod in Dubois et al. 1971; 85-108 and V. Gabersek's dissertation.)

The electromagnetic movement meter is used for recording gross-body movements (Kreitsinger 1959; Lyle 1953). Kreitsinger's research with this instrument gave results which are 'objective, essentially linear and completely removed from the subject's awareness'. He applied the instrument to the arms of chairs in a dark movie theater. Unfortunately, most instruments which give precise measurements cannot be applied in obscurity — where the haptic expression cannot be addressed through the visual channel but only through the haptic.

Other electrographic measurements concern movements unrelated to communicative behavior.

Recording of Polysensorily Coordinated Communication Flow

We have now discussed the three main sensory flows of face-to-face communication as they are recorded to detect regularities as the Y variable of the architectural space. However, some structures do not appear on any one of these sensory flows, because these flows are only facets of a polysensory stream where all three are coordinated in their simultaneity. Let us now see how this synchronization can be recorded for analysis.

The polysensory coordination of the exchange occurs on the side of the communicator as well as on that of the receiver. The communicator's coordination occurs at the level of motor activities. By anticipating the possible polysensory reception of his expression, he articulates his polysensory communication flow in relation to the addressee's relative position in the network.

In analyzing polysensorily coordinated communication, a first level of coordination is related to the double aspect of kinesics: body movement — especially gross-body movement — must be recorded in terms of network transformation (positioning); as well as in terms of perceptible expression ('posturing'). Data obtained must be capable of analysis on both levels.

Even posturing can be addressed to more than one sense: it can be both visible and palpable. This question can be fully developed when the recording tries to simulate the reception. But the communicator expresses himself primarily through more than one channel (cf. the multicanal model of Scherer in van Koolwijk and Wieken-Mayser 1974: 68). Motions considered in terms of kinemes are coordinated with phonemes as well as with ocular expressions. Considerable literature exists on this subject, but it is centered chiefly on the process of how the speaker (with more or less awareness) qualifies his speech with 'postular' or 'postular-kinesic' markers (Scheflen 1964, 1969, 1976), or other paralinguistic features. As we have done throughout this book, we attempt to confine our analysis to a level where subjectivism has minimal impact — on the level of data collection at the least.

As a matter of fact, the technique of analyzing some simultaneous expressions where the verbal or entire audible facet is only a secondary phenomenon accompanying other (e.g., ocular) expressions remains unresolved.

On the other hand, data recording must be centered not on the analysis of conscious coordination, but on the factual synchronous or simultaneous nature of the communicator's output. This makes the registration independent from prevailing doctrines centered on 'cephalic and verbal' aspects (Spiegel and Machotka 1974: 64) and, furthermore, makes it possible to integrate in the analysis unconscious expressions — e.g., vascular — of which the communicator himself is fully aware neither during nor after the emission.

We can speak about polysensory coordination on the side of the receiver. Because we consider the receiver's internal processing as a black box, the structure of his reception can be detected using his responses. His responses can follow messages received through any one of the various channels.

Sociologically speaking, the communication structure within a group in a given architectural situation can in the end only be analyzed by recording and tabulating the communicative initiative and response taken through *all* sensory channels. We must enlarge Chapple's sequential analysis to consider all channels and all group gearings, which also integrate the analysis of crossmodal exchanges. Spiegel and Machotka on the level of corporal movement consider syntropism (1974: 131) and synkinetic intervals (1974: 136). Eibl-Eibesfeld's 'human ethogramme' (1971) could replace Chapple's 'episode', if we free its categories and the segmentation of actions it employs from a civilization-centered, emic bias. From the viewpoint of data collection and methodology for analyzing sequences and synchronization of multichannel communication, using categories uncontaminated by subjective taxonomy, a combination of Ekman's VID-R and SCAN with PRONA 5 seems the most promising.

It is worth reiterating that the recording and analysis of some of the unisensory communication structure itself is still in a very rudimentary stage. Therefore this discussion of polysensory analysis concerns quite distant goals. Yet without keeping distant goals in mind, the various research efforts will not be truly constructive and cumulative. In experimental sociology of architecture, the problem is still more complicated because not only is the Y variable polysensory in its nature, but the X variable — i.e., the architectural space — also has multisensory intricacy. In order to make a heuristic elimination in the research strategy, experimental verification of the null hypothesis makes it possible to avoid blind alleys and fruitless effort in investigation.

22

Prospects for Future Research

Research strategy is always determined, on the one hand, historically, by the impetus of past findings; and on the other hand, by the systematic choice within the framework of the scientific field, as well as by the 'epistemological format' of the knowledge sought as determined by the accepted falsification procedure — e.g., experimental, speculative, introspective — which largely determines the method to employ.

The experimental sociology of architecture has been defined as a study of the one-way communication going from the designer to the beholder by the sole means of architecture, as well as the study of how the face-to-face communication structure is influenced by enveloping architectural spaces. In order to create an objective science — external sociology — where findings are independent from 'emic' understanding (*verstehen*) and semantic connotation, results are formulated in behavioral terms — as the word is used in chemistry. Within this perspective we might also admit meanings of verbal expressions in the field where the subject's language — i.e., the object-language — could not be tainted with connotation, — as the language of sociology (as scientific metalanguage) should not be. This is the case in Part III, where the experimenter asks a subject about the difference in volume or shape between two spaces, and the response is a binary, clearly denotative one (cf. Studer 1966: 290-296, Lindburg in Michelson 1975: 17). From this viewpoint an 'attitudinal' concept appears only as a composed behavioral pattern of a higher order. Interpersonal attractiveness is formulated in terms of types, frequency, and intensity of interaction, or in our case, esthetic preference for architectural space in terms of the frequency of visits, and so on.

On the practical level, the usefulness of such findings can be and has been questioned. Such results are often considered an artificially truncated knowledge. It is clear that these scientific products are not extremely expressive; yet this very restraint brings about the solidity of the findings as well as determining the extent of the universe where they can be applied. Is not a physician more helpless in diagnosing the illness of a nonhuman being than a veterinary surgeon in diagnosing that of a human being?

The usefulness of the findings of the experimental sociology of architecture depends on the designers or decision-makers in general learning to formulate or translate their expectation in terms which meet the requirements of scientific prediction. For instance, which behavior does the architect want to bring about in a given room — more talkative cooperation, or more silent coaction, as in a library — insofar as he can do so by prefiguration of the possible set of face-to-face communication networks in the room. Of course, formulating objectives in physically measurable terms is difficult. But the great advantage lies in the possibility of verification of the design's efficacy by the designer himself as well as by his client.

RESEARCH STRATEGY AND PAST TRENDS

The prospects for future studies are affected by research made in the following areas:

(a) space perception;
(b) the face-to-face communication process;
(c) special subjects within general environmental sociology and psychology, even if the physical environment was not an architectural one.

Research which most nearly concerns sociology of architecture is generally in a very discouraging state. Much of it proceeds in an anecdotic, fragmentary manner without a well-reasoned conceptual framework and a well-established taxonomy. At the same time, particularly in view of publications where the same articles are reproduced over and over again mixed with a few new ones (cf. Proshansky's book), the literature increases in vertiginous proportions. Despite these efforts, basic paradigms, a core knowledge, and even findings which might be compared to one another are not developed because of their dubious epistemological status. The most important work of future research is not, therefore, to find a spot still untouched by past efforts, but to look for sound foundations from which a constructive and cumulative process can be successfully begun which does not bloat the field but, rather, works in a 'vertical' direction.

Against this research appeal for a solid theoretical and conceptual framework, some argue for a purely pragmatic approach. The argument is enforced by an epistemological pessimism which assumes that social phenomena in general have the peculiarity of being unique — idiosyncratic — to such a degree that any search for abstract statements based on a general theory and well-constructed sampling is beyond one's grasp (Altman in Rasmussen 1973: 262). In view of the historical science, we refuted this superficial argument in the first chapter of a past work (Ankerl 1972a). As applied to the sociology of architecture, the proposition is that the approach must be a purely methodological one. It has been suggested (cf. Ankerl 1973) that this science only develop methods to simulate the process of space utilization, in order that the designer can anticipate effects in any concrete case with a very good probability. There are two basic objections to this approach. A good simulation is practicable only on a model in natural size which, at least in the case of major space, is unrealizable. (At the same time, such simulations are the most expensive, making mistakes the most costly.) Architecture in its most important embodiments is not an ephemeral construction, or a simple improvisation (or a simple staging for an improvization); rather, numerous generations of beholders may use it. In order that the behavior in the simulated space produces conclusions valid for all the potential user generations, any sampling must be theoretically founded. Finally, a case-by-case approach is not only epistemologically dubious but uneconomical: indeed, the 'high general costs' involved in basic experiments designed for theory construction are rapidly paid off by the large range of application. The fundamental task of the sociology of architecture is to develop a solid conceptual framework; to find 'exemplary situations' as samples (specimen; R. G. Barker) for representative experimentation (Rasmussen 1973: 196), which make it possible to produce knowledge which, as a function of specific parameters (Rasmussen 1973: 272) can be applied to each task of a designer by external or ecological validation. But before discussing this further, we must depict those tendencies prevalent in past research, in order to show the difficulties involved.

As far as choice of topics goes, the tradition of space perception research (Held) is anchored too strongly in research about objects *in* the space, instead of the perception of the space itself. Although Kameron recognizes that space perception — which he calls room perception — is related to the basic unit of architectural design, even researchers like Aubrée who explore concave space (rooms) are influenced by the tendency to equate space perception with object localization.

As regards our topic itself, the visuocentric consideration of architectural space is another handicap. Analytical experimental research is concentrated on the optical space. Due to this lack of recognition of the possible multisensory intricacy of the architectural space, research in natural settings — these studies are more 'feasibility studies' than basic ones (e.g., for astronauts) — are either exclusively concerned with polysensory spaces — where the different sensory spaces are coextensive — or arbitrarily neglect differences in multisensory composition. The results are, accordingly, warped.

Geographers' contributions to the field bring other problems (cf. the series *Timing Space and Spacing Time,* Halsted, New York; — Lindburg in Michelson 1975: 38). On the one hand, by their very profession, geographers study the atmospheric space which we call the contextual space for architectural spaces. This is a very different situation from studying the effects of a roomraum which has precise volumetric magnitude and delimited shape. T. F. Saarinen even studies the planetary universe which, of course, is unrelated to any architectural space.

On the other hand, architectural space can be and is by definition manipulated — as the X variable in an experiment is, too. Geographic space, in constrast, usually is not. Yet geographers could develop research which would be relevant to our subject, by studying the effects of natural cavities which are near to architectural spaces. Natural cavities are not manipulated as architectural spaces, and precisely this aspect permits conclusions to be drawn about the net space effect without any intervention on the part of the subject to decipher the architect's intentions.

The matters just discussed represent a detour from our research: but it is an even more pernicious tendency for research to press on investigating attitudes about space without knowing about space impression — i.e., how space is connotated without knowing how it is denoted in terms of volumetric magnitude and shape. It is often inspired by psychiatrists' clinical concern, or by the *verstehende* tendencies (cf. interpretive method) in sociology — lying in the *kulturwissenschaftliche* (Weber) ('culturalist') tradition or in the tradition of phenomenological and introspective psychology. It is symptomatic that such research proceeds by preference through interviews and questionnaires, by content analysis of verbal responses instead of observing other external behavior in the space. (Man is considered an animal with language: Moscovici.) On the other hand, we do not say that all opinion research is without any justifiable object, but that it is placing the cart before the horse to ask, for example, about the beauty of ugliness of a space as connoting verbal labels before the subject's impression of the space's physical characteristics (as its denotation) is known (motivational research versus perception).

Finally, studies about the proper object of our investigation — the effect of architectural spaces upon face-to-face communication — are so sparse in the field of environmental sociology that we can speak about neither a developed methodology nor a generally accepted body of knowledge.

We have already discussed Black's studies on the effects of acoustical space. These studies fall within the field of environmental psychology, and Black himself says that the reliability of his conclusions suffers from the fact that the experimental design was not sufficiently sophisticated to ensure the 'authenticity' of the subjects' reactions.

Concerning the osmo-haptic — hermetic — space, Grifitt (1970) found that people underestimate the mutual distances between themselves if the temperature increases. This means that people perceive the face-to-face communication network as physically smaller and therefore, e.g., they might whisper.

Then, too, we know that the transmission of perceptible voice is also directly influenced by the room's temperature. Ostwald also reported that he cannot refute as a null hypothesis a tendency for a very obtrusive odor concentration to influence the variation of vocal intensity, particularly in the inferior range of the octave (motans).

These studies illustrate that the effects of all components of multisensory architectural space on the communication flow can be investigated; but the developing of studies in the field of environmental sociology with reliable results demands very complicated experimental designs. We will attempt in the following pages to make some suggestions for longitudinal experiments where the very setting of the experiments helps satisfy design requirements.

OPPORTUNITIES FOR EXPERIMENTS AND SAMPLING: 'NORMAL' CONFINEMENTS AS EXPERIMENTAL FIELD LABORATORIES

At the beginning of this part we saw that the removal of phenomena for study from their normal setting into a laboratory setting does not necessarily provide the same advantages for the science of the behavior of living beings — especially human beings — as it does for physics, which is the paragon of exact science (von Bertalanffy 1968: 13). The advantages of easy manipulation of the X variable and of the elimination of parasitic effects can be obliterated by an animated subject's reaction, anticipation, and recollection. More specifically speaking, the subject reacts to the fact that he is watched, the spatial isolation can be perceived as artificial, and the temporal restriction of the subject's presence in the laboratory deprives the experimenter of any opportunity to obtain data about long-range effects, maturation, and learning. For this reason, before any general conclusion can be drawn from an observed event and any prediction made about its future occurrence under specific circumstances, the first problem which must be solved is the sampling in time.

We spoke earlier about the case of a meeting of a branch of an association. In order to draw conclusions about the effects of the transfer of the meeting place from one room into another, we must neutralize factors such as trends in the personal lives of members, as well as trends of the 'local', branch, chapter, or whole association as organization (e.g., shrinking membership, new charter). The latter factors (coming from pure sociology) can be neutralized by comparing more than one branch of the association (Ankerl 1972a: 23). Personal factors can be assessed by the study of the time budget in terms of the communicative activity sequence as well as in terms of passage from one space to another. However, in everyday life, even if the circuit of all individuals is very limited (cf. the 'private city'), it is inconceivable that any investigator could follow individuals' activities — including intimate ones — for a sufficiently long period of time without the individuals taking notice; thus the research becomes reactive and obtrusive with all the epistemological consequences.

Now in order to go beyond Mills' epistemological pessimism concerning the building of an experimental social science (Pagès 1974: 311), R. Emerson (in Burgess and Bushell 1969: 405) notes that longitudinal experimentation must be among the sociologist's main tools because social structures are developmental entities.

How can one perform longitudinal experiments? Which opportunities actually exist?

We know that experimentation can be divorced from a laboratory setup. It must be understood rather as a given research design — which, however, in its strict sense necessarily involves an institutional and physical setting which permits specific control and offers reliable observation conditions.

In the case of human science, despite the mobile nature of the subjects, the experimenter must lure them without any coercion into his greenhouse. One such compound where longitudinal experiments can be carried out is an artic station or similar refuge city, compounds to which entry is highly desired due to the inclemency of the surrounding atmospheric space. The subjects become familiarized with the place (Haggard 1964; Rasmussen 1973: 72). This setup is especially useful for longitudinal experiments in sociology of architecture where the spaces are manipulated. In such a confined habitat as total institution we find a whole society in a capsule (Sells in Rasmussen 1973: 286). The experimenter can manipulate the space system as X variable, record the whole environment with its changes, and in general register all events which — according to the experimental design — are relevant to the research. In order to become a normal setup for learning of space effects of all kinds of spaces — systematically — which can be constructed in the future, it is desirable that the experimenter be involved in the original architectural design process of the space systems used for experimentation.

Usually, all new proposals only replace an old problem with new ones which seem less loaded with unrealizable epistemological requisites, or which promise more complementary information compared to the previous methodological solution. As far as the setup goes, a zoological garden cannot completely simulate the virgin forest as environment. Or, for sociology, social isolates can only approximate the isolation of the individual migrant worker in his ghetto. Further, institutions of confinement preselect the individuals admitted (social deviants, sick people, etc.). Results cannot, therefore, be generalized before reevaluating them in light of the particularity of each type of institution as a parameter insofar as it is susceptible to bias. Comparing findings made in institutions of different types permits progress to be made in widening the applicability of the findings to the universe of normal people in everyday settings.

Some researchers focused their attention on learning specifically about one or another type of confinement with a population of given characteristics. Therefore they had to identify exactly and eliminate adaptation effects, which made the subjects' reactions normal again. (Zuckerman 1969; Zubeck in Rasmussen 1973: 67, 30). Even though these studies were conducted to learn more about the particularities and particular effects of types of institutions, they can also be useful to us in our desire to learn how to normalize reactions in institutional settings, and how to neutralize the factors which are not under study.

CIRCUMSTANTIAL PARAMETERS OF TOTAL INSTITUTIONS

Let us now see, in a systematic manner, the various types of isolates where activities can be observed for a long period in a relatively natural setting. We will then be better placed to weigh the relative advantages and disadvantages of each type of institution from the viewpoint of the epistemology of experimental science, and to choose the type most preferable to experimental sociology of architecture.

Obviously compounds which shelter a population of sufficiently various composition, but have limited extent as well as limited fluctuation in a limited number of stimuli (Sells in Rasmussen 1973: 294, 281-282; Rasmussen 1973: 31), allow convenient conditions for planning the experimental manipulation of the X variable, controlling other factors, and observing events with enough exhaustivity and reliability. These advantages for experimentation must be weighed against the normality — or rather the abnormality — of life in the compounds as perceived by the inmates. Long-distance vessels without frequent port calls, submarines, and spaceships are good examples. (The Mormon or Maoist 'long marches' are not very good 'isolates' for longitudinal experimentation due to the always-changing physical environments.) An appropriate compromise must be sought between the limitedness of the surrounding circumstances desired by the experimenter and the variety of stimuli necessary for normal functioning — the number of which increases with the duration of the isolation. Indeed, at first the lack of familiarity with the environment predominates, but a learning process occurs which modifies the behavior pattern: with time, adaptation grows; however, with a longer period of time, the temptation of escape and evasion (cf. Midnight Express) shows the critical moment in the confinement. An optimal compromise is realized in the setting if the extent of the frequented social and physical milieus becomes larger and larger with the passage of time and bears a resemblance to the pattern observed in normal life (with its daily, weekly, seasonal, yearly, and once-in-a-lifetime frequentation cycles: Ankerl 1974: 580).

On the other hand, we find experimentation where the effects of extreme sensory and perceptual deprivation has been studied. As already mentioned, in these experiments, of course, the purpose is exactly opposed to ours: to construct the environment with the most possible artificiality – e.g., a situation without any external stimulus, which is practically impossible to construct. Haggard (1964) developed as a heuristic working hypothesis a three-component theory. Zubeck (in Rasmussen 1973: 72) summarized it as follows: a theory

> ... according to which the onset of and magnitude of the various isolation effects is postulated to be related primarily to the extent and duration of the disparity existing between subject's normal environment and the experimental environment that he is exposed to.

For the authenticity of an inmate's reaction it is a basic criterion that he at least does not perceive his situation in the compound as that of a guinea pig – i.e., knowing that a variable is manipulated – which would develop either resistance or overzealousness in the reaction to the X variable. (The limitedness of the compound must be accepted for institutional reasons other than experimentation.) A further step toward the 'normalization' of responses (Sells in Rasmussen 1973: 293) must assure that the limits of the compound are accepted by the inmates themselves. This means that they do not feel socially cut off from the rest of society; or, alternately, that being cut off is precisely their goal, so that the inmates never physically 'experience' the barrier (Sells in Rasmussen 1973: 282). This is a question of the institutional setting and acceptance of the *vase clos*. The difference is immediately obvious if we compare an exclusive neighborhood of people who do not wish to associate with the remainder of society, with a ghetto imposed as a measure of policy, or a prison with the function of excluding its inmates from the rest of society. The criterion is from which side the lock is operated. This question touches on the external or ecological validity of the experimental findings, their generalizability and applicability.

What total institutions are accepted by our society? What are their particular characteristics?

Ellenberger, a historian of psychiatry and professor of criminology (1971: 200), defines the confined milieu as a world with barriers separating the internal from the external which are difficult or impossible to cross over. He gives also an enumeration: monasteries, general hospitals, special hospitals (psychiatric hospitals, sanatoriums), institutions of tutelage like children's homes, orphanages, nursing homes, homes for sensorily handicapped, prisoners-of-war (POW) camps, concentration camps, prisons, penitentiaries (cf. Sells in Rasmussen 1973: 294). Fraser (Rasmussen 1973: 222-223) defines confinement 'as a physical and temporal limitation on the activities and translational motions of an individual or group.' Gurvitch (1964: 92) also briefly mentions these institutions.

Whether or not the confinement is voluntary we always find — according to Haggard's three-component theory — three aspects but in varying proportions. It is our task now to qualify each institution from the viewpoint of its appropriateness for our studies. Indeed, all institutions will show — as compounds:

(1) Some kind of physical confinement: the world which was round becomes a disk with a *perimeter*.
(2) In normal, everyday life, if we count both face-to-face encounters and telecommunication, everyone has a countless and nearly inexhaustible number of individuals with whom he can have contact in a lifetime (Pool 1973). In confinement this perceived infinity becomes limited, and even relations of long standing will be interrupted. The situation is called social isolation (SI) (Zubeck in Rasmussen 1973: 67).
(3) Finally, compared to normal everyday life, the confinement causes some sensory deprivation. In punitive, interrogatory, and experimental situations, sensory deprivation is deliberately created.

The Three Components

1. Sensory deprivation

In the familiar milieu of everyday life, individuals receive a certain number of stimuli by simultaneous and sequential variations of their physical and social environment. Daily and seasonal cycles are natural phenomena on the earth, other variations are obtained by displacement and by the procession of other people, as when one looks through a window onto Main Street or sits at a sidewalk café. Sensory deprivation divests us of our time giver, and distortions as well as compensatory mechanisms step in — e.g., internal stimuli such as breathing or pulse are perceived with excessive attention.

Here are some findings about the actual and long-range effects of sensory deprivation under extreme conditions in more or less long-term confinement imposed by experimental psychologists.

On the level of visual perception, Hebb's team at McGill University in Montreal made interesting findings. After two to three days of deprivation from light, color perception is modified, especially perception of the desaturated hues. In the same context we must note that ophthalmologists established that Siffre (1964), who passed two months in the darkness of a cavern, confused green with blue (temporary dichromatism), showed myopia, and suffered an alteration of his binocular vision. As adaptation proceeds in both directions — the perceptive capacity shows an adaptation to deprived milieu and can also readapt to a normal one — the effects of deprivation on Siffre disappeared after one month spent in a normal environment. Concerning depth perception, Hebb sees no effect of eight days of sensory deprivation on the subjects' depth perception (cf. Fraisse in Piaget 1967: iv-181; Zubeck in Rasmussen 1973; pp. 30-43, Enoch et al. 1979).

The ubiquitous — and continuously developing — telecommunication makes it possible to dissociate physical confinement from sensory deprivation. Indeed, visual and especially auditory stimuli of an inanimate or social nature can penetrate even the space of totally paralized or strictly confined patients (e.g., patients in iron lungs; Sells in Rasmussen 1973: 281). For the experimenter this fact gives rise to a dilemma: he has the choice of either making the experimental compound very normal by allowing this audiovisual penetration, or excluding it, thereby rendering the situation more artificial. In the first case the recording can be made in an unobtrusive manner, but the inconvenience is that the stimuli are much too numerous for a well-mastered experimental design. Nevertheless, for the experimental sociology of architecture the fact that the architectural space does not change for a long period, but other physical stimuli penetrate — *in camera* situations like those which happen in Sartre's *Huis Clos* — can be interesting — i.e., the experimenter can test the null hypothesis concerning the relative effect of the absence of variation of the architectural space, the effect of which is thus isolated in comparison to those of other physical stimuli.

2. Social isolation

There are still more experimental studies about extreme cases of social isolation — i.e., individual confinement: individuals in trapped situations, convicts, monks. Because our study has for its Y variable the face-to-face communication as sociological effect, these studies are only marginally relevant. It is far more interesting to study relative social isolation: a minimal social situation continued for a long period of time. It is interesting to study, for instance, how two people's communication structure is influenced by the dimensions of the room where they are confined. Confinement of people chosen at random — e.g., in a semiprivate double room — brings about effects of being cut off from the previous network of relations, as well as in the long run an adaptation by resocialization. Since sociology of architecture studies the effect of space, it must give preference to situations where either the roommates have known each other for a long period of time and the effect of moving them from one room to another can be studied, or to situations with people who did not know each other at the onset but whose relation stabilized on a level of communication flow, at least from the standpoint of resocialization, and thus the space change's effect can be more easily isolated.

A very extended discussion exists about the separability of social isolation from the other two components present in confinement, sensory deprivation and physical confinement (Zubeck in Rasmussen 1973: 67). However, it is fairly easy to devise situations where they are clearly distinct (Ankerl 1974), even if the objective observability of these situations is not always straightforward. (For instance, all closed but migrant groups, like the Mormons mentioned earlier, or nomads, are in certain respect socially isolated without sensory deprivation and physical confinement.)

As far as the method of past studies goes, social isolation has rarely been investigated other than as a residual effect in respect to the two other components (Haythorn in Rasmussen 1973: 225). Persky et al. (1966) studied, for example, the psychoendocrine effect as a relative measure of stress. One reason for this relative neglect comes from the difficulty inherent in the numerous ramifications of social isolation, which render it difficult to pin down with a precise and operational definition. We can only say that complete 'privacy' — being without human contact of any kind, either face-to-face or telecommunication — for a determined span of time is the only clear-cut situation. Otherwise social isolation is graded in two respects: how many people are enclosed and whether or not they are former acquaintances; of course, duration is always a basic parameter. The analytical study of social isolation as a social phenomenon can be conveniently begun by the observation of dyads. Altman reports (Rasmussen 1973: 247-248) that the social isolation of a dyad of strangers accelerates their interpersonal penetration toward intimacy. Miyakawa (1960) studied the effects of nonacquaintance on communication in relatively short-term isolation.

3. Physical confinement

A restricted nature is the most important characteristic of a compound where successful longitudinal experimentation will be carried out. Here the researcher can manipulate the X variable in a planned manner and can also record the resulting events unobtrusively and exhaustively. We have already mentioned that the 'normality' of the reactions — and thus the generalizability and ecological or external validity of the conclusions — depends largely on the acceptance of confinement by the subjects as a 'natural' social institution.

Two basic parameters permit us to specify the appropriateness of the situation of physical confinement for our experimental purposes. One is the physical perimeter. The other is whether the compound is closed from the interior or to the exterior — i.e., whether the confinement is voluntary (e.g., the monk as God's slave) or enforced (e.g., the prisoner).

The perimeter is limiting insofar as the barriers cut the subjects off from their usual routes. Indeed, the astronomically and socially regulated daily, weekly, and seasonal displacement of subjects is limited, at the very least, by the walking capacity of the subject, the means of transport, and the means of finance. The artificial limitation caused by confinement is manifested by running against the barrier.

As the actual length of the everyday routes depends upon the concentration of the variety of perceptible objects, if the compound has a less varying environment, the inmates 'run' more often against the barriers (physical confinement in relation to sensory deprivation).

Let us consider variety from the standpoint of the X variable. Variety then means variedness of architectural spaces; variedness of volume and shapes; intricacy in the spaces' multisensory composition; sophistication in the construction of space systems; and presence of the atmospheric space (open air) as contextual space, with its astronomical variations.

Of course, the variety of spaces brings about normal reactions and attenuates distortions resulting from the physical confinement. And if this variety is high in regard to the X variable, the experimental design model becomes complicated. Indeed, there are already many hypotheses which posit that the architectural space's effect on the social — i.e., communicative — behavior is minimal, even negligible in quantitative terms. We know that according to Stevens scientific measurement can be made on four different levels: nominal, ordinal, in interval, and in ratio (Newman in *Sensation and Measurement* 1974: 137). If the researcher wishes to discover specific effects attributable to variation of the characteristics of architectural spaces, he has an interest in magnifying quantitatively the effects of these architectural variables. A simple way to do this is to deprive the subjects of normal architectural stimuli by sharply limiting the number and variety of spaces.

An attempt at separating the effects of sensory deprivation and physical confinement has seldom been made in the laboratory. Zuckerman et al. (1968) tried to analyze effects of sensory deprivation, social isolation, and physical confinement *per se,* in their experimental setup with the subjects studied, they conclude that certain effects, such as the slowing of EEG activity and cognitive deficits, can be imputable to physical confinement *per se.* Zubeck et al. (1969) also try to quantify the share each of the components has in the effects, and conclude that sensory deprivation and physical confinement each contribute 50 percent (the effect of social isolation was negligible).

We have already referred to Zuckerman's study (1969) of the effects of adaptation. He notes that not only is the duration of the isolation an important parameter, but also the period in the subject's life cycle when he arrives at the institution. The variation of the response as a function of time will be different, as well as the change of variation: $y' = f(t)$. For our purposes, the experimental results are more conclusive if experimentation proceeds in a stationary situation $y' = C$, where a resocialization has already occurred — where the subjects have regained their composure (Sommer 1974: 89, 95). Rasmussen (1973: 218) will, within the compound, 'engineer a complete human existence, an ecologically balanced "mini-world" with the potential of keeping groups socially and emotionally viable in social isolation for indefinite periods of time.'

An interesting aspect of the time dimension as a parameter of confinement is that the temptation to escape is not necessarily limited to institutions, but is present in everyday life as well. An example is tourism. For the exact same reasons as those which give rise to a 'tourism' kind of escape in everyday life, physical confinement which has reached its state of equilibrium can still produce escape temptations on a cyclical, annual, or biannual basis.

Attributes of Various Enclosed Institutions

In order to experiment for a limited length of time on human beings without their awareness, the experimenter can use various pretexts to bring subjects to — and keep them in — the laboratory or other setup. With longitudinal experiments, however, the researcher cannot use simple tricks for invitation: he must either confess his intent of experimenting, which involves the well-known negative effects on the authenticity of the reactions; or he must work with enclosed institutions. These institutions have, however, their own purposes in society which determine their regulations, conditions of admission, and physical setting. The experimenter must respect the rules of the institution itself as well as accept its selected population. Indeed, many researchers resent the conflict of interest between experimental and clinical goals. Chapple experienced it in psychiatric institutions, and Zubek in a penitentiary. In order to achieve generalizable results, findings must be reinterpreted, first, in light of the peculiarity of the situation as a function of all aspects of the three components — sensory deprivation, social isolation, physical confinement — prevailing in the institution. And second, findings must be reinterpreted in light of the specific population sample present in the compound.

Correcting for the population sample is a very complicated matter. The basic problem is that an enclosed population chosen at random is an exception. One of these exceptions is the jury in the American judiciary system; but here all recording is prohibited by law, and scientific curiosity has only occasionally transgressed this rule (before becoming Attorney General, professor Levy of Chicago bugged jury rooms for academic purposes; cf. also Strodtbeck and Nook 1961).

It is of course insufficient to select a sample at random within an institution, because the generalization does not extend beyond the given type of institution. This bias can be partially corrected by cluster sampling (Blalock 1970: 80) in enclosed institutions of various kinds. However, the problem is far from resolved: almost all enclosed institutions have a marginal population of one or another sort (Bodenheimer 1967: 36-37, 41-42). This marginality does not automatically imply a negative selection; it can be a positive one, in the direction of selection by excellence. Enclosed institutions admit not only the handicapped – as do psychiatric institutions, nursing homes, institutes for the blind, and homes for the aged – but also adventurers such as astronauts, saints in monasteries, and so on.

Many practical and theoretical difficulties of experimentation in enclosed institutions can be solved or attenuated. Some proceedings of the institution itself often coincide with the proceedings desired by the experimenter. This makes it possible to reach at least an internal validity of the experimental results: the experimental results can be hatched out like a cuckoo egg along with the realization of the institution's custodial or therapeutical tasks. Experimental goals can be grafted onto the original goals of the institution. Indeed, especially in modern institutions, discrete electronic monitoring – which is unobtrusive – is preferable, for all purposes, to explicit barriers.

Many difficulties of ecological validation of results of longitudinal experimentation come from the fact that too many experiments have been carried out exclusively in psychiatric institutions and penitentiaries, and the financing is generally related to specific applications and does not allow cluster sampling – where for the same experiment, more than one type of institution must be involved.

Of course, for the study of the effects of architectural spaces, the population of an asylum for various sensorily handicapped persons has a value analogous to that of identical twins for the researcher in genetics.

Another very useful population for our study is sick people who do not leave their beds.

In all of these cases it is necessary to test the ways in which the enclosed population's selection exerts significant bias for the generalization of the results beyond the type of institution involved. If this has been done, particularly by means of cross-institutional studies, the advantages of the increased internal validity obtained by longitudinal experiments can be realized without any loss of ecological validity.

Indeed, it is worth repeating that longitudinal experiments have the advantage of isolating effects coming from the learning process, of making possible the manipulation of the X variable without arousing suspicion, of making possible the forming of control groups in a convenient manner (e.g., building block A versus block B) and of giving the opportunity of recording all relevant events in an unobtrusive manner.

23

Epistemological Qualifiers of Hardness (in Soft Sciences)

> '... no study can become scientific ... until it provides itself with a suitable technical nomenclature, whose every term has a single meaning ... and whose vocables have no such sweetness or charms as might tempt loose writers to abuse them ...'
>
> C. S. Peirce

There are certain conditions which permit conclusions to be called scientific. The conclusions must be formulated in an unequivocal manner (concerning definition of concepts and rules of syntax). A procedure of falsification must be explicitly stated (in operational terms). And the conclusions must not be an isolated statement, but fitted together with other compatible statements within the framework of a theory, which allows a systematic accumulation of a durable (not volatile) body of knowledge.

Insofar as sociology will become an exacting and method-observant discipline, and produce not only potentially useful information but also scientific knowledge, the conditions just given must be respected (Park 1969; Lachenmeyer 1971; Ankerl 1972a: 277). The sociology of architecture construed as an experimental and objective (external) sociology readily lends itself to this undertaking. It must be not only a practical (or applied) sociology but also part of the theory. Viewing science while it is still being constructed, propositions of different epistemological status exist simultaneously — e.g., unfinished products, viz., hypotheses, finished results, and refutations (about internal validity see Serrus 1945: chapter 8). This variety in the epistemological hardness of theses is also of primary importance in their application, by alerting the designer to their applicability. Moreover, scientific statements can help decision making only if objectives are expressed in operational terms; in the particular case of the experimental sociology of architecture, propositions must be formulated in terms of physical metrics used by

Epistemological qualifiers of hardness 495

the designer, and, on the other hand, the designers must also program their expectations in positive terms whose realization can later be checked by the external behavior of the users (e.g., frequentation, frequency of actual communication; Zeisel 1975: 20; Ankerl 1973). Further, because the designer's decision must be made within a time limit, he cannot refuse to use theses which have a different epistemological status; but he must be forewarned. For this very practical reason – besides the more fundamental reason of theory construction – all propositions of a science must be accompanied by a qualifier which clearly specifies the epistemological status or relative epistemological hardness (i.e., the probability of the proposition's truth).

Furthermore, the designer must evaluate not only the external or ecological validity – we could say 'applicability' – of various scientific statements, but he must also fill up the zones where science cannot commit itself to any valid statement, by using intuition or informed guessing. (Some authors speak of the ignorance of the comparative value and relevance of information at a designer's disposal, and the paucity of design-relevant information.)

Indeed, the actual results of environmental sociology remain largely apart from the potentiality inherent in this field and the help which the designer might expect from the application of this science. The accumulation of knowledge in environmental sociology is heterogeneous in more than one respect. Results differ in their formulation – the nomenclature, concepts used, and so on – as well as in the applicable falsification procedure. Environmental sociology as it stands today encompasses experimental findings which have at least solid internal validity, as well as casual, anecdotal observations. If environmental sociology itself cannot establish a hierarchical order in the degree of confidence which can be placed in its findings as a function of their epistemological format, the designer cannot be expected to do so, because his abilities lie elsewhere.

Michelson's book (1970b) gives a very significant sample of this 'dumping' of amalgamated findings without the proper epistemological qualification which would make them commensurable. (In other respects, this volume, as well as many others, such as that of Proshansky and Ittelson 1970, is merely a reproduction of 20-year-old articles. Gutman's book (1972) is a rare and welcome exception.)

We can illustrate the problem by discussing some of the 24 findings presented by Michelson (1970b: 93-95).

1. Intense, frequent association with a wide range of relatives thrives in areas in which many people have easy physical access to each other, while the same people find that this style of life diminishes involuntarily in the areas of low density....
6. Direct access to the outside maximizes control in child raising under conventional parent-child relationships....

13. Completely random placement of working class residents among middle class neighbors results in the isolation of the former rather than in any intended, positive results.

These theses have been chosen from the 24 because they are the more solidly assessed, in not referring to verbally expressed attitudes. Nevertheless, we see at a glance the vagueness of their formulation (the absence of any qualification), which prevents verification as well as application by the designer who must work with physical magnitudes. Furthermore, Michelson himself admits that it is impossible to specify the relative epistemological value of his findings (1970b: 197).

To our knowledge, the urbanist Spivack (1972) is the only researcher in the field who has tried to attach a 'credibility rating' to his findings (personal communication). In order to give an idea of the various criteria envisaged by him, let us look at the system which he applied.

Credibility rating:

(I) Systematic research strongly supports finding X. Recommendation of X' (statement of statistical probability).
(II) Unsystematic and/or qualitative research supports testable hypotheses.
   (1) Extrapolation of theory X suggests hypothesis X'.
   (2) Field observations suggest hypothesis X'.
   (3) Survey of the literature suggests hypothesis X'.
(III) Speculation or informal observation which may or may not be testable.
   (1) Expert opinion without systematic research (an individual, educated guess.
   (2) Repeated experience and casual observation of phenomenon – no systematic research.
   (3) Casual observation of or by others, or subjective observation.
   (4) Intuitive hunch.

The questions which arise are the following: is this credibility rating based on the fundamental categories which must be involved in any epistemological evaluation or rating of scientific findings? From the point of view of constructing a science, does this rating fulfill the heuristic function of promoting the accumulation of scientific knowledge? And finally, does the rating facilitate the practical application of the results?

Indeed, if we look at the systematization of the criteria, we immediately see that they come too directly from the design practitioner's concern without any deeper epistemological reasoning. Properly epistemological criteria are in fact given under point I, but without sufficient breakdown (e.g., experimental results, quasi-experimental results, and so on). In contrast, other aspects of the findings – which are confined primarily to statements of possible hypothetical values and are therefore in the 'antechamber' of science – are detailed in a disproportionately extended manner.

Epistemological qualifiers of hardness 497

In reality, statements with scientific claim could be evaluated in the light of gnoseological criteria if we consider the following aspects:

— Objective identifiability of the proposition's elements (taxonomy and concepts; definition of technical terms by the actual sphere of concepts; class of spatio-temporal entities as referent).
— Amplitude, substantial content of lexis with its quantifier of generality (we use the term 'lexis' as it is employed in logic and not in linguistics).
— Modal neatness of the copula in the logical syntax (prediction of a 'predicable proposition').
— Falsification procedure actually applied.

The first point refers to the empirical relevance of the elements, the second to the 'wealth' of the posited information, the third to the syntactic formulation, and the fourth chiefly to the verification of propositions by systematic, controlled observation.

It is the theoretical framework which places individual propositions in perspective and makes it possible to examine their mutual compatibility. A tabular (synoptic) presentation of propositions ordered according to their content facilitates such control (laterally or in hierarchical order by inference).

We see in 2 in Figure 4.3, all propositions must be given Roman and Arabic numerals such as II.2 or I.II.1.2 (see 'Multisensory Space' in Part III). We must note that a statement's content is already fully expressed by the formulation by lexis, where the predicate can still remain in 'infinitive' (predicate vs. predication). In contrast, this formulation does not yet allow any confirmation or negation of the statement by falsification (Lalande 1962: 557, 636). It must also be noted that the quantifier which provides the proposition with its amplitude — i.e., by saying how general the statement is — is not a logical characteristic of it as some authors pretend, because it refers to the content (e.g., a proposition can be a general statement including all cases, or it can refer to the average or median value of the class under consideration). In a strict sense the logical characteristic of an individual proposition is related only to its copula, which can be affirmative or negative. The exact and formalizable nature of this predication is a *sine qua non* not only of an actual falsification, but even of the possibility of falsification itself (Morgenstern 1966: 316; Wonnacott and Wonnacott 1969: 3). It must be added that negative statements are always less rich in content than affirmative ones.

EPISTEMOLOGICAL MODALITIES AND ETIOLOGICAL RELATIONS

The sociology of architecture, insofar as it studies the effects of constructed sensorial spaces on the objective structure of polysensory face-to-face

498 Studying space effects by experimentation

1.

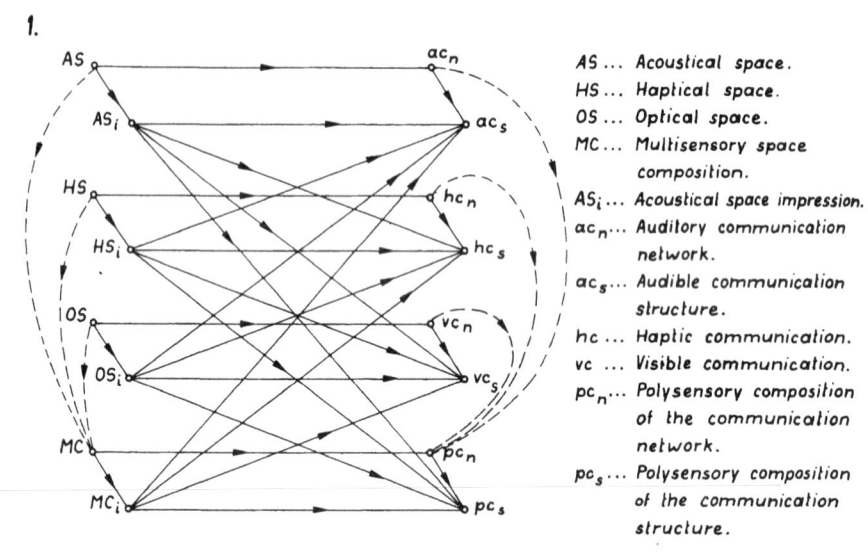

AS ... Acoustical space.
HS ... Haptical space.
OS ... Optical space.
MC ... Multisensory space composition.
AS_i ... Acoustical space impression.
ac_n ... Auditory communication network.
ac_s ... Audible communication structure.
hc ... Haptic communication.
vc ... Visible communication.
pc_n ... Polysensory composition of the communication network.
pc_s ... Polysensory composition of the communication structure.

Elementary model concerning space effects on face-to-face communication structure.

2.

Dimensions of Y variable.	Dimensions of X variable.				
	I. AS / AS_i	II. HS / HS_i	III. OS / OS_i	IV. MC / MC_i	V. Syntax. Impression
1. ac_s					
2. hc_s					
3. vc_s					
4. pc_s					

Tabulation of propositions.

Figure 4.3. *Schematic presentation of etiological relations.*

communication, is concerned with etiological relations. These statements fall in the category of relational propositions. Etiological relations are, more precisely — from a logical viewpoint — hypothetical relations between propositions. In the case of the null hypothesis — i.e., if independence or non-dependence is posited — the relation is a categorial one. Disjunctive relation, as a formulation of an exhaustive enumeration of alternatives (e.g., alternative explanations; a system of substitution) is, though nearly unrealizable, a significant ideal model used in the elaboration of experimental designs.

In this section we are not concerned with the modality of the substantial propositions themselves but with a higher semantic degree $(n + 1)$, which frames the original propositions by attributing an epistemological value to them. This value indicates the value of the logical operator in the original statement (e.g., telling if the proposition is possible, necessary, or whatever). Kant clearly states that the function of modality is not to contribute to the content of a proposition in any way; modality is concerned with the copula's relation to the thought in general.

What procedure would permit us to assign to propositions of our science an epistemological modality?

Propositions which are susceptible to falsification by empirical means belong in the category of so-called 'problematical' (or contingent) modality, and not in the category of apodictical modality. Their 'portion of truth' can be calculated using probability; the cipher reaches unity as the upper limit for the assertoric (existential) certainty.

FALSIFICATION PROCEDURES

Constructed in deductive order, the corpus of an empirical science admits new knowledge if its validity is established in one of these ways:

(1) Propositions which are formulated in theory-relevant terms (Machlup 1963: 167: 'exactness'), and whose validity is established by a protocol of empirical observation.
(2) Assumptions which are posited as 'evidence' or axiom *a priori*. If explicitly stated as such, no verification is required, but the formulation must follow a format which meets the standard of formulation prevailing in the science.
(3) Postulates of empirical thought (Kant), the rational categories which are the general conditions of the construction of the science, and which cannot be verified within the framework of external observation carried out by the science in question.

At any stage in its development, a science is composed not only of unimpeachable bits of knowledge — theses which have not been falsified despite repeated testing — but also of hypotheses which are testable but yet not systematically tested propositions. Hypotheses occupy science's antechamber. On the other hand, we find in the 'archives' propositions which have been falsified. The conservation of such propositions is important to prevent their resurgence in the labyrinths of the science.

Thus all propositions have an epistemological control label. Among all these various propositions we are now exclusively concerned with those which can be verified in the framework of the experimental sociology of architecture. We see that propositions which 'may not be testable'(cf. Spivack 1972: chap. 3) have no place in the scientific construction, even have no heuristic function in its antechamber, excepting, of course, axioms and postulates. They are in fact likely to distract from serious scientific research and to spread confusion. For this very reason, hypotheses must be formulated — as mentioned earlier — in analytical and objective (external) terms, refering ultimately to a class of observable spatio-temporal entities. (Lachenmeyer 1971: 58: 'Sociologists use vague, ambiguous, opaque, and contradictory definitions.')

This condition is prime and general. Not only is it irrational to tackle by sophisticated mathematical means propositions which are formulated in empirically unverifiable terms, but it is detrimental to the development of the science. Indeed, any sociology which admits sentences formulated in empirically inoperant terms can serve pernicious ideological purposes. It is a subterfuge for ideological rhetoric — i.e., the presence of propositions in a 'science' insinuates their real existence, though they have only imaginary values (e.g., alienation, natural law).

Empirical falsification itself has three phases:

(1) The reliable recording of a simple fact which is valid because it occurred in a controlled situation (Opp 1970: 51-52).
(2) Recording of repeated cases (Blalock), which repetition increases the probability of possible falsification and in the absence of actual falsification thereby provides the inductive proof. Of course, (1) is a *sine qua non* condition for the procedure (2) (retest by replication).
(3) Successful use of a proposition in application in contexts varying radically from the original, experimental one in which its internal validity was established. This provides the proposition with a probable external or ecological validity, and delineates its practical significance. The practical inapplicability of a proposition (its 'external invalidity') is irrelevant for its internal validity. Indeed, the relation between internal and external validities is not mutual; internal validity is a precondition for external validity, but the inverse is not true. However, if an experimental finding is inapplicable, this fact can be considered an *a posteriori* notice to repeat the experiments under more

controlled circumstances, which often makes it possible to discover supplementary specifications for determining the field of validity.

Addendum to (1): concerning the data, each data item must be reliable; scientific observation must be exact, objective, and circumstantial (detailed). Hard data is obtained in controlled experimental situations. Furthermore, in human science, we must be careful that the data is genuine, as it will be if in the framework of an experimental design, a homology exists between the object of study and the object of observation (Chapanis 1967: 566-567). By nonreactive measuring we must prevent the subject's anticipation from disturbing the results. As indicated in the previous section, the mechanical recording appropriate for our study ensures a nondisturbed response as well as objective measurement (Webb et al. 1971: 155). (If the measurement is not an individual one but a series of replications, sometimes it is impossible to repeat the same experiments on the same subjects, because they anticipate the experimentation. This is, however, to a certain extent a problem shared with natural science, where it is often impossible to take a measurement without destroying the sample measured.)

During the construction of a theory, nonexperimental data cannot simply be added to experimental data because nonexperimental data has a different degree of hardness. And if at the beginning of theory construction hard data is lacking, this deficit cannot be compensated for by a sophisticated treatment of whatever data do exist. It is preferable to begin the data collection again.

Addendum to (2): results cannot be applied to a universe unless a carefully constructed experimental design makes the data commensurable (Bénézé 1967: 2). When such a design is absent, we cannot attribute any degree of certainty to an inductive proof obtained by repeated observations.

Addendum to (3): it would be ill-advised to imagine that a proposition whose validity is proven as universal can be applied in any ecological context. The inductive proof of any propositions in human science as well as in natural science predicts only the applicability of the proposition in a universe defined by the experimental design — i.e., in cases analogous to the circumstances where the inductive proof was produced (Machlup 1963: 171-177). (This planned application already represents a step forward from the findings produced by the traditional trial-and-error method, where any reapplication is impossible.) Indeed, in the experimental setting the researcher recreates a real situation relevant to the theory being tested, but this reproduction involves the greatest possible neutralization of all relevant factors — except the X and Y variables (Scheuch and Rueschenmeyer 1966: 353 n. 15). Of course, because of the dependency of the external validity on the internal validity, the careful study of this neutralization process (e.g., using matching) also gives 'insight' about the ecological context in which the proposition might be applied with more likelihood of success, but this insight is only a by-product of the scientific research itself. It is not an alternative or shorter way of producing useful scientific knowledge which can bypass the experimental proof. Any leapfrog approach which bypasses the question of internal validity cannot pretend to be scientific. It can produce only intuitive insights. (Even sciences which are far from physics, such as astronomy and even the modern science of history, cannot renounce reference to experimentation in the strict sense of the word.)

PRIORITY AND HIERARCHICAL ORDER IN EPISTEMOLOGICAL CERTAINTY: CRITERIOLOGY

The construction of scientific theory works through induction, but the propositions which constitute the body of the science are arranged in deductive order. The deductive presentation creates a compact arrangement where all consequences of the rejection (falsification) of one proposition become almost immediately apparent. This internal 'cleaning' of the system can be made (in an axiomatized system) by computer without inventing any original algorithm; however, this 'costless' internal productivity of the deductive system also has its negative side: in reality, all production of knowledge which does not use induction based on individual observations can create 'affirmative propositions' by negating negative ones, and can only replace general propositions with more limited individual ones.

Our problem is more complex: we look for criteria telling us which statements must be given preference if they are in contradiction, and they show, at the same time, different epistemological deficiencies.

Let us try to summarize the applicable rules, and to denounce any confused compromises as traps which are often presented as reasonable solutions.

The accumulation of scientific knowledge follows a well-established order where weakness in the foundation cannot be corrected in a later stage.

Concerning data, hard and experimental data give first and foremost the factual basis for theory-relevant empirical research. Multilevel (and multidimensional) analysis refers to the complementarity of research instruments; however, this must not be used to obscure the principle that any amount of soft data, no matter how large, cannot replace or refute a result based on a hard data sample (cf. Campbell and Fiske 1959: 81-105). Any certification of soft data in this way is also inadmissable.

Concerning inductive and deductive procedures, experimental falsification cannot usefully be applied if the hypothesis is not already formulated in a manner which meets the requirements of the grammar of scientific language or if the terms do not refer to hard data. Without satisfying these preconditions, it is not worthwhile later to employ highly sophisticated, formalized operations in theory construction (Festinger et al. 1950: 344). In any deductive system no proposition can have more certainty or an epistemologically higher modality than the weakest proposition. A principle of primariness applies to the computation of errors in this field. Indeed, a correct algorithm in the research strategy requires that as soon as a deficiency in the foundation is discovered, the whole construction process must come to a standstill until it is corrected — or, if this is impossible, the whole process must begin all over again.

In the controversy concerning the relation between internal validity and external (or ecological) validity, the order of precedence is also clear and irreversible. It is a fundamentally erroneous endeavor to try to 'compensate' for a lack of internal validity with a stress on the external kind. Seeking a so-called 'optimal compromise' between the two validities reveals insufficient grounding in epistemology. The abandonment of experimental rigor cannot be compensated for by any means and it improves neither prediction nor technical application; rather, it creates a confused situation where any calculation of certainty and of scientific validity of results is impossible.

In contrast, a judiciously chosen, ingenious research strategy allows steady and fairly rapid progress. It must also begin with the crucial point in the scope of the problem and with an appropriate choice of the experimental setting. Sociology of architecture is a field which offers a privileged springboard for the construction of an experimental sociology on a par with the other exact sciences.

Despite this epistemological optimism, design professionals should realize that *no* future stage of the development of sciences can provide complete knowledge which will ever obviate the need for other information which has no scientific base (intuition, informed guessing, etc.) in order to make technical decisions.

Bibliography

Abbreviations

AIA	.....	*American Institute of Architects*
AJS	.....	*American Journal of Sociology*
Am.	.....	*American*
ASR	.....	*American Sociological Review*
CSTB	.....	*Centre Scientifique et Technique du Bâtiment*
EB	.....	*Environment and Behavior*
EDRA	.....	*Environmental Design Research Association*
J.	.....	*Journal*
MES	.....	*Man-Environment System*
RIBA	.....	*Royal Institute of British Architects*

Abraham, R., and Schapiro, G. (1969). 'Hyperspace: Gallery Installation'. *Architectural Design*, 383-384.
Acking, C. A., and Kuller, B. (1973). 'Presentation and Judgement of Planned Environment and the Hypothesis of Arousal'. In *EDRA*, 4th edition, W. Preiser (ed.). Stroudsburg, Pa.
Ackoff, R. L. (1962). *Optimizing Applied Research Decisions*. New York.
Adolfson, J. (1974). *Human Performance and Behaviour in Hyperbaric Environments*. New York.
Agoston, G. A. A. (1979). *Color Theory and Its Application in Art and Design*. New York.
Aicher, O., and Krampen, M. (1977). *Zeichensysteme der visuellen Kommunikation*. Stuttgart.
Alain (pseud.) (1963). *Système des beaux-arts*. Paris.
Albrecht, M., et al. (eds.) (1970). *The Sociology of Art and Literature*. New York.
Alexander, C. (1959). 'Perception and Modular Coordination'. *RIBA Journal*, 425-429.
_____ (1964). *Notes on the Synthesis of Form*. Cambridge, Mass.
_____ (1967). 'The City as a Mechanism for Sustaining Human Contact'. In Ewald 1967.
_____, Ishikawa, S. and Silverstein, M. (1977). *A Pattern Language*. New York.
Alleton, V. (1970). *L'écriture chinoise*. Paris.
Alluisi, N. (1960). 'On the Use of Information Measures in Studies of Form Perception'. *Perceptual and Motor Skills*, 195-203.
Alsleben, K. (1962). *Aesthetische Redundanz*. Hamburg.
Altman, I. (1975). *The Environment and Social Behavior*. New York.
_____, and Wohlwill, F. (eds.) (1976-1977). *Human Behavior and Environment*, 2 volumes. New York.

American Society for Testing and Materials. Annual Books. Philadelphia.
Amir, N., and Kugelmass, S. (1959). 'The Kinesthetic Estimation of Distance in Relation to the Body in Normal Persons'. *Acta Psychologica*, 235-244.
Anastasi, A. (1936). 'The Estimation of Areas'. *J. of General Psychology*, 201-225.
Anderson, J. (1971). 'Space-Time Budgets and Activity Studies in Urban Geography and Planning'. *Environment and Planning*, 353-368.
Anderson, R. T. (1972). 'Recent Trends in Ethnoscience: 1966-70', *The Annals*, 143-153.
Anker, V. (1976). 'Les liens entre la sculpture et l'architecture'. *Werk*, 507-508.
Ankerl, G. (1958). *Babel in Brussels.* Vienna.
_____(1965). *L'Epanouissement de l'Homme dans les Perspectives de la Politique Economique: Concept de l'Investissement dans la Personne comme Aspect de la Politique de Répartition.* Paris.
_____(1970). *Communauté et Société: Appartenance et Association Contractuelle.* Montreal.
_____(1971a). 'L'Environnement et ses Architectes'. *Architecture Concept*, 24-26.
_____(1971b). 'Face au Synchronocentrisme, la sociology est-elle l'histoire immediate de l'ère audio-visuelle?' *Quality and Quantity*, 209-223.
_____(1972a). *Sociologues allemands: Etudes de cas en sociologie historique et non-historique avec le dictionnaire de "l'Ethique Protestante et l'Esprit du Capitalisme" de Max Weber.* Neuchâtel.
_____(1972b). 'From Intuitive to Formal Book Critique: A Semiotic Approach'. *Heuristics*, 35-43.
_____(1973). 'Sociologie spatial, thème de l'architecture: méthodes, concepts objectifs dans les récentes recherches américaines'. *Architecture, Mouvement, Continuité*, 37-40.
_____(1974). 'Spezifische Faktoren in stadtsoziologischen Analysen: Ueberlegungen zur systematischen Analysen der Stadt als eines Netzes und einer Struktur unmittelbaren Kommunikation', *Kölner Zeitschrift für Soziologie*, 568-587.
_____(1977). 'Reply to Th. Kando'. *Contemporary Sociology*, 284-285.
_____(1978). *Beyond Monopoly Capitalism and Monopoly Socialism: Distributive Justice in a Competitive Society*, Cambridge, Mass.
_____, and Pereboom, D. (1974). 'Scientific Methods in Ethology'. *Science*, 814-815.
Apt, C. M. (ed.) (1977). *Flavor: Its Chimical, Behavioral and Commercial Aspects.* (Proceedings of a Symposium.) Cambridge, Mass.
Apter, M. J. (1970). *The Computer Simulation of Behavior.* New York.
Appleyard, D., et al. (1964). *The View from the Road.* Cambridge, Mass.
Arens, F. (1927-1928). 'Zur Soziologie und Kulturpsychologie der Baukunst'. *Ethos*, 133-150, 297-460.
Argyle, M. (1967). *The Psychology of Interpersonal Behavior.* Harmondsworth, U.K.
_____(1970). 'Eye Contact and Distance: A Reply to Stephanson and Rutter'. *British J. of Psychology*, 395-396.
_____(1975). *Bodily Communication.* New York.
_____, and Cook, M. (1976). *Gaze and Mutual Gaze.* New York.
_____, and Dean J. (1965). 'Eye Contact, Distance, and Affiliation'. *Sociometry*, 289-304.
_____, and Kendon, A. (1967). 'The Experimental Analysis of Social Performance'. In *Advances in Experimental Social Psychology*, L. Berkowitz (ed.), 55-98. New York.
_____, Lalljee, M., and Cook, M. (1968). 'The Effects of Visibility on Interaction in a Dyad'. *Human Relations*, 3-17.

Arnheim, R. (1954). *Art and Visual Perception.* Berkeley, Calif.
_____(1966). 'Inside and Outside in Architecture: A Symposium'. *J. of Aesthetics and Art Criticism,* 3-7.
_____(1978). *Dynamics of Architectural Forms.* Berkeley, Calif.
Ashihara, Y. (1970). *Exterior Design in Architecture.* New York.
Asimov, I. (1957). *Naked Sun.* Garden City, N.Y.
Athanasiou, R., and Yoshioka, G. (1973). 'The Spatial Character of Friendship Formation'. *EB,* 43-65.
Atteslander, P. (1975). *Dichte and Mischung der Bevoelkerung.* Berlin.
_____, and Hamm, B. (eds.) (1974). *Materialien zur Siedlungssoziologie.* Cologne.
Attneave, F. (1950). 'Dimensions of Similarity'. *Am. J. of Psychology,* 516-556.
_____(1954). 'Some Informational Aspects of Visual Perception'. *Psychological Review,* 183-193.
_____(1959). 'Stochastic Composition Processes'. *J. of Aesthetics and Art Criticism,* 501-503.
_____, and Reynolds, M. (1950) 'A Visual Beat Phenomenon'. *Am. J. of Psychology,* 107-110.
Aubrée, A. (1968). 'La perception de l'espace', *Cahiers du CSTB,* 2-5.
'Die Aussage der Architektur' (1971). *Werk* 242-272, 384-399, and 682-703.
Bachelard, G. (1952). 'Nouvelle construction de l'espace'. *XX siècle, Nouvelle Série,* 2.
_____(1969). *Poetics of Space,* Boston, Mass.
Backo, M., et al. (1977). *Techniques douces, habitat et société.* Paris.
Bahrdt, H. P. (1974). *Umwelterfahrung.* Munich.
Baird, J. C. (1970). *Psychological Analysis of Visual Space.* Oxford, U. K.
Baldassare, M. (1979). *Residential Crowding in Urban America.* Berkeley, Calif.
Balint, M. (1945). 'Friendly Expanses – Horrid Empty Space'. *International J. of Psychoanalysis.*
Ball, D. W. (1973). 'Microecology: Social Situations and Intimate Space'. Unpublished doctoral thesis, University of Indiana, Indianapolis.
Banham, R. (1967). *Theory and Design in the First Machine Age.* New York.
_____(1973). *Architecture of the Well-Tempered Environment.* Chicago.
Baranek, L. L. (1972). *Music Acoustics and Architecture.* New York.
Barden, H. P. (1927). 'Ueber die Schaetzung von Winkel bei Knaben und Maedchen verschiedener Alterstufen'. *Archiv der gesamten Psychologie,* 81-94.
Bardet, G. (1963). *L'urbanism.* Paris.
Barker, R. G. (1965). 'Explorations in Ecological Psychology'. *A. Psychologist,* 1-14.
_____ (1968). *Ecological Psychology: Concepts and Methods for Studying the Environment of Human Behavior.* Stanford, Calif.
Barker, R. G. (ed.) (1978). *Habitat, Environments, and Human Behavior: Studies in Ecological Psychology and Eco-Behavioral Science from the Midwest Psychological Field Station: 1947-72.* San Francisco.
Barnes, R. D. (1963). 'Thermography of Human Body'. *Science,* May 24, 870-877.
Barnett, J. H. (1959). 'The Sociology of Art'. In *Sociology Today,* R. K. Merton (ed.). New York.
Barnlund, D. S., and Harland, C. (1963). 'Propinquity and Prestige as Determinants of Communication Networks'. *Sociometry,* 467-479.
Barthès, E. (1957). 'Etudes expérimentales pour la mise au point d'une méthode de calcul du point de couleur de la lumière recu par le plan utile dans un local à parois colorés'. *Bulletin de la Société Francaise de l'Eclairage,* 7, 8.

Barthès, E. (1957). 'Jeux de lumière sur les revêtements colorés'. *Couleur*, 1-2.
Barthes, R. (1965). *La Tour Eiffel*. Paris.
_____(1970). 'Semiologie et urbanisme'. *Architecture d'Aujourd'hui*, 11-13.
_____(1977a). *Elements of Semiology*. New York.
_____(1977b). *Writing Degree Zero*. New York.
Barthley, S. H. (1958). *Principles of Perception*. New York.
Bass, B. M., and Klubeck, S. (1952). 'Effects of Seating Arrangements on Leaderless Group Discussion'. *J. of Abnormal and Social Psychology*, 724-727.
Basso, K. H., and Anderson, N. (1973). 'A Western Apache Writing System'. *Science*, 1013-1022.
Batchelder, W. H. (1975). 'Applications of Formalism'. *Science*, 374-375.
Baudrillard, J. (1968). *Le système des objets*. Paris.
Bauer, J. A., Jr., Wood, G. D., and Held, R. (1969). 'A Device for Rapid Recording of Positioning Responses in Two Dimensions'. *Behavior Research Methods and Instrumentation*, 157-159.
Baum, A., and Epstein, Y. M. (eds.) (1978). *Human Response to Crowding*. New York.
Baum, A., and Valins, S. (1978). *Architecture and Social Behavior*. New York.
Baum, A., et al. (1974). 'Architectural Variants of Reaction to Spatial Invasion'. *EB*, 91-100.
Baum, G., and Stroke, G. W. (1975). 'Optical Holographic Three-Dimensional Ultrasonography'. *Science*, 994-995.
Bauml, B. J., and Bauml, F. H. (1975). *A Dictionary of Gestures*. Metuchen, N. J.
Bavelas, A., et al. (1965). 'Experiments on the Alternation of Group Structure'. *J. of Experimental Social Psychology*, 55-70.
Bearse, P., et al. (eds.) (1976). *American Values and Habitat: A Research Agenda*. American Association for the Advancement of Science. Washington, D.C.
Bechtel, R. (1967). *Footsteps as a Measure of Human Performance*. Topeka, Kans.
_____(1977). *Enclosing Behavior*. Stroudsburg, Pa.
_____, and Strivastava, R. (1966). 'Human Movement and Architectural Environment'. *Milieu*, 7-8.
Beck, Jacob (1972). *Surface Color Perception*. Ithaca, N. Y.
Becker, F. D., and Mayo, C. (1971). 'Delineating Personal Distance and Territoriality'. *EB*, 375-384.
Becker, N. (1959). 'Space Analysis in Architecture', *J. of AIA*, 40-43.
Bedickek, R. (1960). *The Sense of Smell*. New York.
Bénézé, G. (1967). *La méthode expérimentale*. Paris.
Bense, M. (1971). *Zeichen und Design*. Baden-Baden.
_____, and Walther, E. (1973). *Woerterbuch der Semiotik*. Cologne.
Benson, R. V. (1966). *Euclidean Geometry and Convexity*. New York.
Benthall, J., and Polhemus, T. (eds.) (1976). *Body as a Medium of Expression*. New York.
Berenson, B. (1967). 'Sensory Architecture'. *Landscape*, 19-21.
Berge, C. (1966 [1963]). *Theory of Graphs and Its Applications*. (3rd reprint.) London. (French edition 1963.)
_____(1971). *Principles of Combinatorics*. New York.
Berger, J., et al. (eds.) (1962). *Types of Formalization in Small-Group Research*. Boston.
Bergson, H. (1967). *Essai sur les données immédiates de la conscience*. Paris.
Berlin, B. (1970). 'A Universalist-Evolutionary Approach in Ethnographic Semantics'. In *Current Directions in Anthropology*, A. Fisher, (ed.). *American Anthropological Association Bulletin* 3.
_____, and Kay, P. (1969). *Basic Color Terms*. Berkeley, Calif.

Berlyne, D. E. (1966). 'Les mesures de la préfetence esthétique'. *Science de l'art*, 9-22.
_____(ed.) (1974). *Experimental Aesthetics: Steps toward an Objective Psychology of Aesthetic Appreciation.* New York.
Bernardino, J. R. (1970). 'Architecture for Blind Persons'. *New Outlook for Blind*, 262-265.
Best, G. (1970). 'Direction Finding in Large Buildings'. In Canter 1970.
Bettini, S. (1968). 'Critica semantica continuità storica dell' architettura europea' *Zodiac*, 2.
Bidault, J., and Giraud, P. (1946). *L'homme et la tente.* Paris.
Birch, M. C. (ed.) (1974). *Pheromones.* New York.
Birdwhistell, R. L. (1970). *Kinesics and Context: Essays on Body Motion Communication.* Philadelphia, Pa.
Birren, F. (1961a). *Creative Colors*, New York.
_____(1961b). *Color, Form, and Space.* New York.
_____(1969). *Light, Color, and Environment.* New York.
_____(1977). *Principles of Color: A Review of Past Traditions and Modern Theories.* New York.
Black, J. W. (1950). 'The Effect of Room Characteristics upon Vocal Intensity and Rate'. *J. of the American Acoustical Society*, 174-176.
Blackwell, H. R. (1963). 'Visual Benefits of Polarized Light'. *J. of AIA*, 87-92.
Blake, R. R., et al. (1956). 'Housing Architecture and Social Interaction'. *Sociometry*, 133-139.
Blalock, H., Jr. (1970). *An Introduction to Social Research.* Englewood Cliffs, N. J.
Blanc, C. (1860). *Grammaire des ãrts et du dessin.* Paris.
Blank, A. A. (1953). 'The Luneburg Theory of Binocular Visual Space'. *J. of Optical Society of America*, 717-727.
Blasdel, H. (1969). *Semantics vs. Measurements of Acoustic, Luminous, and Thermal Environments: Current Research.* Berkeley, Calif.
Bleiker, A. H. (1972). 'The Proximity Model of Urban Social Relations', *Urban Anthropology*, 151-175.
Blount, F. I. (1967). 'Design of a Low Cost Computer Graphical Input Device'. Unpublished ms., M.I.T. Eng. Library, Cambridge, Mass.
Blumer, H. (1954). What is wrong with social theory? *ASR*, 3-10.
Bochenski, I. M. (1965). *The Methods of Contemporary Thought.* Boston.
Bocquet, C., et al. (eds.) (1977). *Les problèmes de l'espace dans le règne animal*, volume 2. Mémoire No. 2 de la Société Zoologique de France. Paris.
Bodenheimer, A. R. (1967). *Versuch ueber die Elemente der Beziehung.* Basel.
Bongardus, E. S. (1959). *Social Distance.* Yellow Springs, Ohio.
Boring, E. G. (1943). 'The Moon Illusion'. *Am. J. of Physics*, 55-60.
_____(1953). 'The Role of Theory in Experimental Psychology'. *Am. J. of Psychology*, 169-184.
_____(1954). 'The Nature of Experimental Control'. *Am. J. of Psychology*, 573-589.
_____(1969). 'Perspective: Artifact and Control'. In Rosenthal 1969, 1-11.
Borissavliévitch, M. (1954). *Traité de l'esthétique scientifique de l'architecture.* Paris. (English ed.: *The Golden Number and the Scientific Aesthetics of Architecture.* London, 1958.)
Bosma, J. F. (ed.) (1966). *Symposium on Oral Sensation.* New York.
Booth, A. (1976). *Urban Crowding and Its Consequences.* New York.
Boudon, P. (1971). *Sur l'espace architectural.* Paris.
_____(1972). *Lived-In Architecture: LeCorbusier's Pessac Revisited.* Cambridge, Mass.

Boudon, P. (1978). *Richlieu, ville nouvelle: essai d'architecturologie*. Paris.
Boudon, R. (1967). *L'analyse mathématique des faits sociaux*. Paris.
Bouissac, P. (1973). *La mesure des gestes: Prolegomènes à la sémiotique gestuelle*. The Hague.
Bouma, P. J. (1971). *Physical Aspects of Colour*. New York.
Bourdieu, P. (1970). *Zur Soziologie der symbolischen Formen*. Frankfurt.
Boursin, J. L. (1966). *Les structures du hasard*. Paris.
Bouveresse, R. (1976). 'Le nombre d'or'. *Psychologie*, 57-61.
Boynton, R. M. (1960). 'Spatial Vision'. *Annual Review of Psychology*, 171-200.
____ (1964). *Psychophysics of Vision*. Proceedings of the International Congress on Technology and Blindness, volume 2, 5-20. (Quoted from Haber 1970, 8-25.)
Brannigan, C., and Humphries, D. (1969). 'I See what you Mean'. *New Scientist*, 406-408.
Brecher, R., and Brecher, E. (eds.) (1974). *Analysis of Human Sexual Response*. New York.
Breheny, M. (1974). 'Towards Measures of Spatial Opportunity'. *Progress in Planning*, 2.
Brereton, J. L. (1971). 'Inter-Animal Control of Space'. In Esser 1971.
Briggs, R. (1972). 'On Relation between Cognitive and Objective Distance'. In *EDRA 4*, W. Preisser (ed.), 186-192. Stroudsburg, Pa.
Brillat-Savarin, J.-A. (1975). *Physiologie du goût*. Paris.
Broadbent, G. (1969). 'Meaning into Architecture'. In Jencks 1969, 51-75.
____(1978). *Design in Architecture: Architecture and the Human Science*. New York.
Broady, M. (1966). 'Social Theory in Architectural Design'. *Arena*, 149-153.
Brookfield, H. C. (1970). 'On the Environment as Perceived'. In *Progress in Geography* 1, C. Board et al. (eds.), 51-80.
Brown, D. R., and Losasso, J. S. (1967). 'Pattern Degradation, Discrimination Difficulty, and Quantified Stimulus Attributes'. *Psychonomic Science*, 351-352.
Brown, E. L. and Deffenbacher, K. (1979). *Perception and the Senses*. New York.
Bruhn, J. G. (1971). 'Ecological Responsibility in Sociology'. *Sociological Quarterly*, 77-82.
Brunner, J. S., et al. (eds.) (1956). *Study of Thinking*. New York.
Brunner, J. S., and Taguiri, R. (1954). 'The Perception of People'. In *Handbook of Social Psychology*. Cambridge, Mass.
Brunswick, E. (1956). *Perception and Representative Design of Psychological Experiments*. Berkeley, Calif.
Buchwald, Art (1974). 'Twenty Years Later'. *International Herald Tribune*, 448.
Bucksch, H. (1976). *Woerterbuch fuer Architektur, Hochbau und Baustoffe*, volumes I-IV (German-English and German-French and vice versa). Wiesbaden.
Buechel, A. (1969). 'System Engineering', *Industrielle Organisation*, 2.
Bungard, W., and Lueck, H. E. (1974). *Forschungsartefakte und nicht-reaktive Messverfahren*. Stuttgart.
Bunge, W. (1966). *Theoretical Geography*. Lund.
Burgers, J. M. (1975). 'Causality and Anticipation'. *Science*, 194-198.
Burgess, R. L., and Bushell, D., Jr. (eds.) (1969). *Behavioral Sociology: The Experimental Analysis of Social Process*. New York.
Burgess, R. L., and Nielsen, J. M. (1974). 'An Experimental Analysis of Some Structural Determinants of Equitable and Inequitable Exchange'. *ASR*, 427-443.
Burton, J., et al. (1978). *The Environment as Hazard*. New York.
Buschke, H. (1974). 'Spontaneous Remembering after Recall Failure'. *Science*, 579-581.
Busnel, R. G., et al. (1962). 'Un cas de langue sifflée utilisée dans les Pyrennées francaises'. *Logos*, 76-91.

Buswell, G. T. (1935). *How People Look at Pictures.* Chicago.
Buttimer, A. (1969). 'Social Space in Interdisciplinary Perspective'. *Geographical Review,* 417–426.
Buytendick, F. (1959). 'Perception de l'espace.' *Acta Psychologica,* 276–277.
Byrne, D. (1961). 'The Influence of Propinquity and Opportunities for Interaction on Classroom Relationships'. *Human Relations,* 63–69.
Cadwell, P. K. (1970). *Mathematical Reflexions.* Cambridge, U. K.
Cagnacci-Schwicker, A. (ed.) (1961). *International Dictionary of Building Construction* (English-German-French-Italian). Paris.
Cain, W. S. (1977). Differential Sensitivity for Smell. *Science,* 796–798.
Calhoun, J. B. (1966). 'The Role of Space in Animal Sociology'. *J. of Social Issues,* 46–58.
_____(1970). 'Space and Strategy of Life'. In Esser 1970, 329–387.
Calsat, J. H., and Sydler, J. P. (eds.) (1970). *International Dictionary of Town Planning and Architecture* (French-German-English). Paris.
Campbell, D. T. (1969). 'Perspective: Artifact and Control'. In Rosenthal 1969, 351–382.
_____, and Fiske, D. W. (1959). 'Convergent and discriminant validation by the multitrait-multimethod matrix'. *Psychological Bulletin*: 81–105.
_____, and Stanley, J. C. (1966). 'Experimental and Quasi-Experimental Design for Research'. In *Handbook of Research on Teaching,* N. L. Gage (ed.). Chicago.
Canestrari, R., and Minguzzi, G. F. (1959). 'Contributions experimentales à l'interprétation de quelques-unes des démonstrations de Ames dans la perception'. *Acta Psychologica,* 237–297.
Canter, D. V. (1968). 'Office Size: An Example of Psychological Research in Architecture'. *Architects' J.,* 881–888.
_____(1970). *Architectural Psychology.* London.
_____(1971). *Architectural Psychology: Bibliography.* Royal Institute of British Architects. London.
_____(1975). *Psychology for Architects.* New York.
_____(1976). *Environmental Interaction.* New York.
_____(1977). *The Psychology of Place.* New York.
_____(ed.) (1969). *Papers Presented at the Conference on Environmental Psychology,* Dalandhui University, Strathclyde, 28 Feb.-2 Mar.
_____, and Lee, T. (eds.) (1974). *Psychology and the Built Environment.* London.
Carmon, C. et al. (1969). 'Threshold for Pressure and Sharpness in the Right and Left Hands.' *Cortex,* 27–35.
Carpenter, E., and McLuhan, M. (eds.) (1960). *Exploration in Communication.* Boston.
Carrington, R. A. (1970). 'Analysis of Mobility and Change in a Longitudinal Sample'. *Ekistics,* 183–186.
Cassotta, L., et al. (1964). 'AVTA: A Device for Automatic Vocal Transaction Analysis'. *J. of Experimental Analytical Behavior,* 99–104.
Castell, R. (1970). 'Physical Distance and Visual Attention as Measures of Social Interaction between Child and Adult'. In Hutt and Hutt 1970.
Castells, M. (1967). 'Y a-t-il une sociologie urbaine? Notes critiques'. *Sociologie du Travail.*
Catton, W. R., Jr., and Dunlap, R. E. (1978). 'Environmental Sociology: A New Paradigm'. *Am. Sociologist,* 41–49.
Cazeneuve, J. (1964). 'Perception archaïque des étendues'. *Cahiers Internationaux de Sociologie,* 107–117.
Ceccato, S. (1968). *Corso di Linguistica Operativa.* Milan.

Cesarec, Z. (1963). 'Figure–Ground Reversal as Related to Stimulus Exposure, Observation Time, and Some Personality Dimensions'. *Psychological Research Bulletin* 5. Lund.

─── , and Nilsson, L. (1963). 'Level of Activation and Figure–Ground Reversal: Inter-Individual Comparison'. *Psychological Research Bulletin* 6 and 7.

Chamboredon, J. C., and Lemaire, S. (1970). 'Distance sociale et proximité spatial dans les grandes ensembles'. *Revue Francaise de Sociologie* 1.

Chance, M. R. A. (1967). 'Attention Structure as the Basis of Primate Rank Order'. *Man*, 503–518.

Chang, K. C. (ed.) (1968). *Settlement Archeology*. Palo Alto, Calif.

Chao, Yuen-Ren (1968). *Language and Symbolic Systems*. Cambridge, U. K. (French edition 1970.)

Chapanis, A. (1967). 'The Relevance of Laboratory Studies to Practical Situations'. *Ergonomics*, 557–577.

─── , et al. (1949). *Applied Experimental Psychology*. New York.

Chapin, F. S. (1955). *Experimental Design in Sociological Research*. New York.

Chapple, E. D. (1970). 'Experimental Production of Transients in Human Interaction'. *Nature*, 630–633.

─── (1971). 'Toward a Mathematical Model of Interaction'. In *Explorations in Mathematical Anthropology*, P. Kay (ed.). Cambridge, Mass.

─── , and Kline, N. S. (1965). 'Territoriality of Patients on a Research Ward'. In *Recent Advances in Biological Psychology*, J. Wortis (ed.). New York.

Chase, S. (1959). *The Tyranny of Words*. New York.

Chauchard, P. (1965). *Les messages de nos sens*. Paris.

Chermayeff, S., and Alexander, C. (1963). *Community and Privacy*. New York.

Choay, F. (1969). 'Urbanism and Semiology'. In Jencks 1969, 11–26.

─── (1980). *La Règle et le modèle: Sur la théorie de l'architecture et de l'urbanisme*. Paris.

Chombart de Lauwe, P. -H., et al. (1967). *Famille et habitation*, volume 2. Paris.

Chomsky, N. (1965). *Aspects of the Theory of Syntax*. Cambridge, Mass.

─── (1972). *Language and Mind* (enlarged edition). New York. (French edition 1970.)

Churchman, C. W., and Ratoosh, P. (eds.) (1959). *Measurement: Definitions and Theories*. New York.

Clark, D. L. (1968). *Analytical Archeology*. London.

Cline, M. G. (1967). 'The Perception of where a Person is Looking,' *Am. J. of Psychology*, 41–50.

Clouten, N. H. (1970). 'On the Visual Perception and Representation of Space'. *Architectural Science Review*, 121–127.

Cohen, J. (1969). *Sensation and Perception: II. Audition and the Minor Senses*. Chicago.

Cohen, M. R., and Nagel, E. (1944). *Introduction to Logic and Scientific Method*. Madison, Wisc.

Collins, B. E., and Gutzkow, H. (1964). *A Social Psychology of Group Processes for Decision-Making*. New York.

Collins, J. B. (1970). 'Perceptual Dimensions of Architectural Space Validated Against Behavioral Criteria'. *MES*, S.24.

Comfort, A. (1971). 'Communication May Be Odorous'. *New Scientists and Science J.*, 412–414.

Computerunterstuetztes Entwerfen, Entwickeln, Messen und Bewerten von Grundrissen (1975). Stuttgart.

Conway, D. (1976). *Architectural Design and Social Sciences*. Washington, D.C.

Cook, M. (1970). 'Experiments on Orientation and Proxemics'. *Human Relations*, 61-76.
Cook, P. (1970). *Experimental Architecture*. London.
Cornsweet, T. (1970). *Visual Perception*. New York.
Coulon, D., and Kayser, D. (1969). 'Un exemple de reconnaissance de forme à l'aide d'ordonnateur'. *L'Onde Electrique*, 103-112.
Cournot, A. A. (1911). *Traité d'enchaînement des idées fondamentales dans les sciences et dans l'histoire*. Paris.
Cousin, J. (1970). *Topological Organization of Architectural Spaces*. Montreal.
Cox, G. H., and Marley, E. (1959). 'The Estimation of Motility During Rest or Sleep'. *J. of Neurology, Neurochirurgy and Psychiatry*, 57-60.
Craik, K. H., and Zube, E. H. (eds.) (1976). *Perceiving Environmental Quality*. New York.
Critchley, M. (1975). *Silent Language*. Woburn, Mass.
Critchlow, K. (1969). *Order in Space: A Design Source Book*. London.
Crystal, D., and Quirk, R. (1964). *Systems of Prosodic and Paralinguistic Features in English*. The Hague.
Cullen, G. (1968). *Notation*. London.
Curry, T. J., and Clarke, A. C. (1977). *Introducing Visual Sociology*. Dubuque, Iowa.
Cuvillier, A. (1970). *Manuel de sociologie*, volumes 1-3. Paris.
Cyprian, G. (1978). *Sozialisation in Wohngemeinschaft: Eine empirische Untersuchung ihrer strukturellen Bedingungen*. Stuttgart.
David, E. E., Jr., and Dénes, P. B. (1972). *Human Communication: An Unified View*. New York.
Davis, D. -E. (1974). *Behavior as an Ecological Factor*. Stroudsburg, Pa.
Davis, J. F. (1959). *Manual of Surface Electromyography*. WADC Tech. Rep. 59-184. Wright Air Development Center.
Davis, M. (1972). *Understanding Body Movement: An Annotated Bibliography*. New York.
Davitz, J. R. (ed.) (1964). *The Communication of Emotional Meaning*. New York.
Dawson, M. E., and Grings, W. W. (1978). *Emotions and Bodily Responses: A Psychophysical Approach*. New York.
Day, B. F., Ford, R. D., and Lord, P. (1969). *Building Acoustics*. New York.
Day, H. (1965). 'Brief Note on the Berlyne-Heuckhausen Controversy'. *Psychological Report*, 225-226.
de Buccar, M. (1953). 'Les couleurs changeant avec la lumière'. *Finitions*, 1-3.
de Fusco, R. (1972). *Architektur als Massmedium: Anmerkungen zu einer Semiotik der gebauten Formen*. Wiesbaden. (Original Italian edition published 1967.)
DeJonge, D. (1967). 'Applied Hodology'. *Landscape*, 10-11.
de Keyser, E. (1970). *Art et mesure de l'espace*. Paris.
Della Valle, L. T., Andrews, G., and Ross, S. (1956). 'Perceptual Thresholds of Curvilinearity and Angularity as Function of Line Length'. *J. of Experimental Psychology*, 343-347.
DeLong, A. J. (1971). 'Content vs. Structure: The Transformation of the Continuous into the Discrete'. *MES* 1.
Dénes, P. B., and Pinson, E. N. (1963). *The Speech Claim: The Physics and Biology of Spoken Language*. Murray Hill, N. J.
Denis-Prinzhorn, M. (1960). 'Perception des distances et constance des grandeurs'. *Archives de Psychologie*, 181-309.
Déribéré, M. (1959). *La couleur dans les activités humaines*. Paris.
———(1964). *La couleur*. Paris.

de Saussure, F. (1967). *Cours de linguistique générale (de 1915)*. Paris. (Revised edition 1977.)
Desportes, J. -P. (1976). *Les effets de la présence de l'experimentateur dans les sciences de comportement*. Paris.
_____, Duflos, A., and Provansal, B. (1972). 'Effet de la dominance des sujets sur la réponse physiologique à la proximité de congénères chez la souris mâle'. *Revue du Comportement Animal*, 1-12.
_____, Duclos, A., and Zaleska, M. (1972). 'L'étude des effets de la présence physique de congénères chez les hommes: Mode d'approche et perspectives de recherches'. In *Modèles animaux du comportement humain*. Paris.
Deutsch, F. (1952). 'Analytic Posturology'. *Psychoanalytic Quarterly*, 196-214.
Deutsch, K. W. (1971). 'On Social Communication and Metropolis'. In *Internal Structure of the City*, L. S. Bourne (ed.), 222-230. New York.
de Zurko, E. R. (1957). *Origins of Functionalist Theory*. New York.
Dittman, A. T., and Llewellyn, L. G. (1969). 'Movement and Speech Rhythm in Social Conversation'. *J. of Personality and Social Psychology*, 98-106.
Dixon, N. F. (1971). *Subliminal Perception: The Nature of a Controversy*. New York.
Dodd, G. G. and Rosel, L. (eds.) (1979). *Computer Vision and Sensor-Based Robots*. New York.
Doelle, L. L. (1972). *Environmental Acoustics*. New York.
Dorfles, G. (1952). *Discorso tecnico delle arte*. Pisa.
_____(1969). 'Structuralism and Semiology in Architecture'. In Jencks 1969.
Dourgnon, J., and Krossaw, R. J. (1949). 'Couleur et reflexion mutuelle'. *Cahiers du CSTB*, 1-22.
Downs, R. M., and Stea, D. (eds.) (1973). *Image and Environment: Cognitive Mapping and Spatial Behavior*. Chicago.
Drever, J. (1968). *Dictionary of Psychology*. Harmondsworth, U. K.
Drimmick, F. L. (1948). 'Vision'. In *Foundations of Psychology*, E. G. Boring et al, (eds.)., ch. 12.
Drouillard, T. F., and Laner, F. J. (1979). *Acoustic Emission: A Bibliography with Abstracts*. New York.
Dubois, A., et al. (eds.) (1971). *La fonction du regard*. Paris.
Duncan, S. D., Jr. (1969). 'Nonverbal Communication'. *Psychological Bulletin*, 118-137.
_____ (1970). 'Towards a Grammar for Floor Apportionment: A System Approach to Face-to-Face Interaction'. In *EDRA 2*, J. Archea and C. Estman (eds.), 225-235. Pittsburgh, Pa.
_____ , and Fiske, D. W. (1977). *Face-to-Face Interaction: Research, Methods, and Theory*.
Dungen, F. H. (1934). *Acoustique des salles*. Paris.
Dunlap, R. E. (1976). *A Sociological and Social-Psychological Perspective on Environmental Issues: A Bibliography*. Monticello, Ill.
Duverger, M. (1964). *Méthodes des sciences sociales*. Paris.
Duvignaud, J. (1967). *Sociologie de l'art*. Paris.
Easterman, C. M., and Harper, J. (1967). 'A Study of Proxemic Behavior; Towards a Predictive Model'. *EB*, 418-437.
Eco, U. (1968). *La Struttura Assente*. Milan.
_____(1971). 'Architecture et sémiologie'. *Werk*, 682-686.
_____(1978). *A Theory of Semiotics*. Bloomington, Ind.
Edwards, A. L. (1963). *Experimental Design in Psychological Research*. New York.

Efron, J. S. (1968). 'Looking for Approval: Effects on Visual Behavior of Approbation from Persons Differing in Importance'. *J. of Personality and Social Psychology*, 21-25.

Efstathiou, et al. (1967). 'Altered Reaching Following Adaptation to Optical Displacement of the Hand'. *J. of Experimental Psychology*, 113-120.

Ehrenkrantz, E. (1956). *The Modular Number Pattern: Flexibility through Standardization*. London.

Eibl-Eibesfeld, I. (1967). *Grundriss der vergleichenden Verhaltensforschung*. Munich.

———(1971). 'The Human Ethological Film Archive of the Max Planck Association'. *Homo*, 252.

Eiserman, P. (1969). 'Syntactics in Architecture'. Mimeographed. Rotch Library, M. I. T.

Ekambi-Schmidt, J. (1972). *La perception de l'habitat*. Paris.

Ekman, G., and Junge, K. (1962). 'Psychophysical Relations in Visual Perception of Length, Area and Volume'. *Scandinavian J. of Psychology* 2.

Ekman, P. (1972). 'Universals and Cultural Differences in Facial Expressions of Emotion'. In *Nebraska Symposium on Motivation*. J. Cole (ed.). Lincoln, Neb.

———(1976). 'Les visages parlent le même langage'. *Psychologie*, 11-15.

———(ed.) (1973). *Darwin and Facial Expression: A Century of Research in Review*. New York.

———, et al. (1969). 'Pan-Cultural Elements in Facial Displays of Emotion'. *Science*, 86-88.

———, and Friesen, W. V. (1969). 'The Repertoire of Non-Verbal Behavior: Origins, Usage, Coding and Categories'. *Semantica* I, 49-98.

———, Friesen, W. V., and Ellsworth, P. (1972). *Emotion in the Human Face: Guidelines for Research and an Integration of Findings*. New York.

———, Friesen, W. V., and Taussig, T. G. (1969). 'VID-R and SCAN: Tools and Methods for the Automated Analysis of Visual Records'. In *Content Analysis*, G. Gerber (ed.), 297-312. New York.

Elkin, L. (1964). 'The Behavioral Use of Space'. Unpublished Master's Thesis, University of Saskatchewan.

Ellenberger, H. F. (1971). 'Behavior Under Involuntary Confinement'. In Esser 1971.

Ellring, J. H. (1970). 'Die Bedeutung des Blickes auf Punkte innerhalb des Gesichtes'. *Zeitschrift für Experimentelle und Angewandte Psychologie*, 600-607.

Ellis, N. R., and Pryer, R. S. (1959). 'Quantification of Gross Bodily Activity in Children with Severe Neuropathology'. *Am. J. of Mental Deficiency*, 1034-1037.

Ellsworth, P. C., et al. (1972). 'The Stare as a Stimulus to Flight in Human Subjects: A Field Study'. *J. of Personality and Social Psychology*, 302-311.

Emmerich, D. G. (1969). 'Architectes sans Architecture'. *Architecture d'Aujourd'hui*, LXII.

English, P., and Mayfield, R. C. (eds.) (1972). *Man, Space, and Environment*. New York.

Enoch, J. M., et al. (1979). 'Monocular Light Exclusion for a Period of Days Reduces Directional Sensitivity of the Human Retina'. *Science*, 705-707.

Environment: A Bibliography of Social Science and Related Literature (1974). Washington, D.C.

L'Epistémologie de l'espace. (1964). Paris.

Esser, A. H. (ed.) (1971). *Behavior and Environment: The Use of Space by Animals and Men*. New York.

Evans, R. M. (1974). *The Perception of Color*. New York.

Ewald, W. R. (ed.) (1967). *Environment for Man*. Bloomington, Ind.

Ewert, O. M. (1965). 'Sematologie des Ausdrucks'. In *Ausdruckspsychologie*, volume 5, R. Kirchhoff (ed.), 220-254. Göttingen.
Exline, R. V., and Winters, L. C. (1965). 'Affective Relations and Mutual Glances in Dyads'. In *Affect, Cognition, and Personality*, S. S. Tomkins and C. W. Izard (eds.), 319-350. New York.
Faber, C. (1963). *Candela: The Shell Builder*. London.
Fast, J. (1970). *Body Language*. New York. (German edition 1971.)
Fauques, R. (1973). 'Pour une nouvelle approche sémiologique de la ville'. *Espace et Société*, 9.
Faure, E. (1964). *L'esprit des formes*, volume 2. Paris.
Feigenberg, I. M. (1972). *Funktionelle Verbindungen der sensorischen System*. Stuttgart.
Fejes, Toth (1964). *Regular Figures*. Oxford, U. K.
Feldman, A. S., and Tilly, C. (1960). 'The Interaction of Social and Physical Space'. *ASR*, 877-884.
Festinger, L. (1966). 'The Relevance of Mathematics to Controlled Experimentation in Sociology'. In *Logik des Sozialwissenschaften*, E. Topitsch (ed.), 335-344. Cologne. (First English publication 1954 in *International Social Science Bulletin*, 622-627.)
_____, et al. (1950). *Social Pressure in Informal Groups: A Study of Human Factors in Housing*. Palo Alto, Calif.
Finsterbusch, G. (1976). *Man and Earth: Their Changing Relationship*. Indianapolis, Ind.
Fitch, J. M. (1972). *American Buildings 2: The Environmental Forces that Shape It*. Boston.
Flament, C. (1965a). *Réseaux de communication et structure de group*. Paris.
_____(1965b). 'Les procès de communication'. In *Traité de psychologie experimentale*, volume 9, P. Fraisse and J. Piaget (eds.), 171-216. Paris.
Ford, L. R. (1956). *Network Flow Theory*. Santa Monica, Calif.
Forrester, J. W. (1969). *Urban Dynamics*. Cambridge, Mass.
Foshee, J. G. (1958). 'Studies in Activity Level: I. Simple and Complex Task Performances in Defectives'. *Am. J. of Mental Deficiency*, 882-886.
Foulke, E. (1969). 'The Development and Testing of the Caster Cane'. *New Outlook for Blind*, 10.
Fraenkel, G. S., and Gunn, D. L. (1961). *The Orientation of Animals*. New York.
Fralberg, S. (1977). *Insights from the Blind*. New York.
Francastel, P. (1960). 'Problèmes de la sociologie de l'art'. In *Traité de sociologie*. volume 2, G. Gurvitch (ed.), 278-296. Paris.
_____(1970). *Etudes de sociologie de l'art*. Paris.
Francès, R. (1966). *Perception*. Paris.
_____(1968). *Psychologie de l'esthétique*. Paris.
Franck, L. K. (1957). 'Tactile Communication in Genetic Psychology'. *Psychological Monographs*, 209-255.
_____ (1966). 'The World as a Communication Network'. In *Sign, Image, and Symbol*, G. Kepes (ed.), 1-14. New York.
Frankl, P. (1968). *Principles of Architectural History*. Cambridge, Mass. (Original German edition published 1914.)
Freedman, J. (ed.) (1975). *Crowding and Behavior*. San Francisco, Calif.
Freedman, N., and Hoffman, S. (1967). 'Kinetic Behavior in Altered Clinical States: Approach to Objective Analysis of Motor Behavior During Interview'. *Perceptual and Motor Skills*, 527-539.
Freides, D. (1974). 'Human Information Processing and Sensory Modality: Cross-Modal Functions, Information Complexity, Memory and Deficit'. *Psychological Bulletin*, 284-310.

Freisitzer, K. (1966). *Sociologische Elemente in der Raumordnung.* Graz.
Frey, S., and Cranach, M. von (1971). 'Verfahren zur Messung motorischer Aktivitaet'. *Zeitschrift fuer Experimentelle und Angewandte Psychologie,* 392–410.
Fried, R. (1964). 'Monocular and Binocular Comparison of Apparent Size'. *Am. J. of Psychology,* 476–479.
Friedhoff, A. J., et al. (1964). 'Infra-Content Channel of Vocal Communication'. In *Disorders of Communication,* D. McRioch and E. A. Weinstein (eds.), T42. Baltimore, Md.
Friedman, S., and Juhasz, J. (1973). *Environments: Notes and Selections on Objects, Spaces and Behaviors.* Monterey, Calif.
Friedman, Y. (1970). *L'architecture mobile.* Paris.
_____ (1975). *Toward a Scientific Architecture.* Cambridge, Mass. (Original French edition published 1971.)
Fuller, R. Buckminster (1975). *Synergetics.* New York.
Furth, H. G. (1966). *Thinking without Language.* New York.
Gabor, D. (1948). *Holography.* New York.
Gaerling, T. (1969-1970). 'Studies in Visual Perception of Architectural Spaces and Rooms'. *Scandinavian J. of Psychology,* 1969: 250–256, 257–268; 1970: 124–131.
Gaito, J. (1959). 'Visual Discrimination of Straight and Curved Lines'. *Am. J. of Psychology,* 236–242.
Gandelsonas, M. (1972). 'On Reading Architecture: Eiserman and Graves'. *Progressive Architecture,* 68–87.
Gardi, R. (1974). *Architecture sans architecte.* Bern.
Gardner, M. (1963). *More Mathematical Puzzles and Inversions from Scientific American.* London.
Garner, W. R., and Clement, D. E. (1963). 'Goodness of Pattern and Pattern Uncertainty'. *J. of Verbal Learning and Verbal Behavior,* 446–452.
Gatz, K., and Achtenberg, G. (1966). *Color and Architecture.* New York. (Original German edition published 1956.)
Geldard, F. A. (1953). *The Human Senses.* New York.
_____ (ed.) (1973). *Conference on Cutaneous Communication Systems and Devices.* Austin, Texas.
Gerard, R. M. (1958). 'Differential Effects of Colored Lights on Psychophysical Function'. Unpublished dissertation, University of California, Los Angeles.
Gheorghiu, A., and Dragomir, V. (eds.) (1978). *Geometry and Structural Forms.* Philadelphia, Pa. (French edition 1972.)
Gibson, J. J. (1950). *The Perception of the Visual World.* Boston.
_____ (1961). 'Ecological Optics'. *Visual Research,* 253–262.
_____ (1962). 'Observations on Active Touch'. *Psychological Review,* 477–491.
_____ (1966). *The Senses Considered as Perceptual Systems.* Boston.
_____ (1970). 'On Theories for Visual Space Perception: A Reply to Johansson'. *Scandinavian J. of Psychology,* 75–79.
_____, and Bergman, R. (1954). 'The Effect of Training on Absolute Estimation of Distance over the Ground'. *J. of Experimental Psychology,* 473–482.
_____, and Pick, D. (1963). 'Perception of Another Person's Looking Behavior'. *Am. J. of Psychology,* 86–94.
_____, et al. (1955). 'A Method of Controlling Stimulation for the Study of Space Perception: The Optical Tunnel'. *J. of Experimental Psychology,* 1–14.
Gibson, Michael (1973). 'Art in Paris'. *International Herald Tribune,* Oct. 24.
Giedion, S. (1963). *Space, Time and Architecture.* Cambridge, Mass.

Giedion, S. (1971). *Architecture and the Phenomena of Transition: The Three Space Conceptions in Architecture.* Cambridge, Mass.
Gilchrist, A. L. (1977). 'Perceived Lightness Depends on Perceived Spatial Arrangement'. *Science*, 185-187.
Gilinsky, A. S. (1951). 'Perceived Size and Distance in Visual Space'. *Psychological Review*, 460-482.
Gillod, J. (1957). 'La métrique des couleurs'. *Couleurs*, 3.
Glossary of Terms Frequently Used in Optics and Spectroscopy (1960). American Institute of Physics. New York.
Goddard, J. B., and Morris, D. (1976). 'The Communication Factor in Office Decentralization'. *Progress in Planning*, 1. Oxford, U. K.
Goffman, E. (1963). *Stigma.* Englewood Cliffs, N. J.
Goldberg, G. N., et al. (1969). 'Visual Behavior and Face-to-Face Distance During Interaction'. *Sociometry*, 43-53.
Goldfinger, E. (1941a). 'The Sensation of Space'. *Architectural Review*, 129-131.
_____(1941b). 'Urbanism and Social Order'. *Architectural Review*, 163-166.
_____(1942). 'The Elements of Enclosed Space'. *Architectural Review*, 5-9.
Goldmann-Eisler, F. (1961a). 'The Distribution of Pause Duration in Speech'. *Language and Speech*, 132-137.
_____ (1961b). 'A Comparative Study of Two Hesitation Phenomena'. *Language and Speech*, 18-26.
Goldmeier, E. (1972). *Similarity in Visually Perceived Forms.* New York.
Goldstein, H. (1979). *The Design and Analysis of Longitudinal Studies.* New York.
Gonzalez, R. C., and Thomason, M. G. (1978). *Syntactic Pattern Recognition.* New York.
Goodenough, W. H. (1970). *Description and Comparison in Cultural Anthropology.* Chicago.
Goodey, B. (1969). 'Message in Space'. *North Dakota Quarterly*, 34-49.
Goodrick, C. L. (1962). 'A Psychophysical Analysis of the Perception of Difference in Random Shapes'. *Am. Psychologist*, 351.
Gosztonyi, A. (1957). 'Das Raumproblem'. *Studium Generale*, 532-541.
_____(1976). *Der Raum: Geschichte seiner Problem im Philosophie und Wissenschaften.* Freiburg.
Gould, J. L. (1975). 'Honey Bee Recruitment: The Dance-Language Controversy'. *Science*, 685-693.
Gould, P. R., and White, P. R. (1974). *Mental Maps.* Harmondsworth, U. K.
Gove, W. R. (1979). 'The Review Process and its Consequences in the Major Sociological Journals'. *Contemporary Sociology*, 799-804.
_____, and Hughes, M. (1980). The Effects of Crowding Found in the Toronto Study: Some Methodological and Empirical Questions. ASR, 864-870.
Gray, D. J. (1980). ' "Errorless" Sociology'. *Contemporary Sociology*, 330-331.
Greimas, A. J. (1966). *Sémantique structurelle.* Paris.
_____, and Courtes, J. (1979). *Sémiotique: Dictionnaire raisonné de la théorie du langage.* Paris.
Grifitt, W. (1970). 'Ambient Effective Temperature and Attraction'. *J. of Personality and Social Psychology*, 240-244.
Gruber, E. H. (1954). 'The Relation of Perceived Size to Perceived Distance'. *Am. J. of Psychology*, 411-426.
_____(1956). 'The Size-Distance Paradox: A Reply to Gilinsky'. *Am. J. of Psychology*, 469-476.
Gruber, J. S. (1967). 'Look and See'. *Language*, 937-947.

Guilford, J. P. (1954). *Psychometrics Methods.* New York.
Guiraud, P. (1956). *Les Caractères statistiques du vocabulaire.* Paris.
_____(1966). *La sémantique.* Paris.
_____(1967). *La grammaire.* Paris.
_____(1968). *Les mots savants.* Paris.
_____(1971). *La sémiologie.* Paris.
Gundlach, C., and Macoubry, C. (1931). 'The Effect of Color on Apparent Size'. *Am. J. of Psychology,* 109-111.
Gürkaynak, M. R., and LaCompte, W. A. (1979). *Human Consequences of Crowding.* New York.
Gurvitch, G. (1964). 'Perceptions collectives des étendues'. *Cahiers Internationaux de Sociologie,* 79-106.
Gutman, R. (1966). 'City Planning and Social Behavior'. *J. of Social Issues,* 103-115.
_____(ed.) (1972). *People and Buildings.* New York.
Haber, R. N. (1970). *Contemporary Theory and Research in Visual Perception.* London.
Haggard, E. A. (1964). In 'Personality Change.' In P. Worchel and D. Byrne (eds.), 443-469. New York.
_____, and Isaacs, K. S. (1966). 'Micromomentary Facial Expressions as Indicators of Ego Mechanisms in Psychotherapy'. In *Methods of Research in Psychotherapy,* L. A. Gottschalk and A. H. Auerbach (eds.), 154-165. New York.
Haggett, P., and Chorley, R. J. (1970). *Network Analysis in Geography.* New York.
Halasz, I., and Bush-Brown, A. (1959). 'Notes Toward a Basis for Criticism'. *Architectural Record,* 183-194.
Hall, E. T. (1961). 'The Language of Space'. *AIA J.,* 71-74.
_____(1969). *The Hidden Dimension.* Garden City, N. Y.
Halldane, J. F. (1968a). *Architecture and Visual Perception.* Berkeley, Calif.
_____(1968b). *Psychophysical Synthesis of Environmental Systems.* Berkeley, Calif.
Halmos, P. (1953). *Solitude and Privacy.* New York.
Halprin, L. (1965). 'Notation'. *Progressive Architecture,* 126-133.
Hammond, A. L. (1973). 'Mathematical Groups'. *Science,* 146-147.
Handel, S., and Buffardi, L. (1968). 'Pattern Perception: Integrating Information Presented in Two Modalities'. *Science,* 1,026-1,028.
Hardy, R., and Legge, D. (1968). 'Cross-Modal Induction of Changes in Sensory Thresholds, I'. *Quarterly J. of Experimental Psychology.*
Hare, A. P., and Bales, R. F. (1963). 'Seating Position and Small Group Interaction'. *Sociometry,* 480-486.
Hareven, Tamara K. (1970). 'Family Time and Historical Time'. *Daedalus,* 106: 57-70.
Hargreaves, W. A. (1960). 'A Model for Speech Unit Duration'. *Language and Speech,* 164-173.
_____, and Starkweather, J. A. (1959). 'Collection of Temporal Data with Duration Recorder'. *J. of Experimental Analysis of Behavior,* 179-183.
Harris, M. (1964). *The Nature of Cultural Things.* New York.
Harris, Zelling S. (1952). 'Discourse Analysis'. *Language,* 1-30.
_____(1963). *Discourse Analysis.* The Hague.
_____(1968). *Mathematical Structure of Language.* New York.
Harrison, R. (1973). 'Nonverbal Communication'. In Pool 1973, 93-115.
Hass, H. (1970). *The Human Animal.* London.
Hastorf, C., Osgood, E., and Ono, H. (1966). 'The Semantics of Facial Expressions and the Prediction of the Meanings of Stereoscopically Fused Facial Expressions'. *Scandinavian J. of Psychology,* 179-188.

Haumont, N. (1967). 'Architecture et sociology'. *Architecture, Mouvement, Continuité*, 162.
Haynes, R. M. (1969). 'Behavior Space and Perception Space: A Reconnaissance'. *Papers in Geography* 3.
Haynes, V. (1973). 'The Calico Site: Artifacts or Geofacts?' *Science*, 305-309.
Hayward, S. C., and Franklin, S. S. (1974). 'Perceived Openness-Enclosure of Architectural Space'. *EB*, 34-52.
Hazard, J. N. (1962). 'Furniture Arrangement as a Symbol of Judicial Roles'. *ETC*, 181-188.
Hearn, G. (1957). 'Leadership and Spatial Factor in Small Groups'. *J. of Abnormal and Social Psychology*, 269-272.
Hebb, D. O. (1949). *Organization of Behaviour: A Neuropsychological Theory*. London.
____(1972). *A Textbook of Psychology*. Philadelphia, Pa.
Hecht, K. (ed.) (1972). *Zur Funktion des Organismus-Umwelt-Verhaltens: Eine Modellvorstellung*. Jena.
Heckhausen, H. (1964). 'Complexity in Perception: Phenomenal Criteria and Information Theoretical Calculus – A Note on D. E. Berlyne's "Complexity Effects" '. *Canadian J. of Psychology*, 168-173.
Heider, F. (1958). *The Psychology of Interpersonal Relations*. New York.
Hein, A., et al. (1979). 'Eye Movements Initiate Visual-Motor Development in the Cat'. *Science*, 1321-1322.
Held, R. (1968). 'Dissociation of Visual Functions by Deprivation and Rearrangement'. *Psychologische Forschung*, 338-348.
____(1970). 'Two Modes of Processing Spatially Distributed Visual Stimulation'. In *The Neurosciences*, F. O. Schmitt (ed.), 317-324. New York.
____(1971). *Perception*. In A. Dubois et al. 1971.
____(ed.) (1972). *Perception Mechanisms and Models*. San Francisco, Calif.
____(1974). *Image, Object, and Illusion*. San Francisco, Calif.
____(1976). *Recent Progress in Perception*. San Francisco, Calif.
____, Efstathiou, A., and Greene, M. (1966). 'Adaptation to Displaced and Delayed Visual Feedback from the Hand'. *J. of Experimental Psychology*, 887-891.
____, and Hein, A. (1967). 'On the Modifiability of Form Perception'. In *Models for the Perception of Speech and Visual Form*, W. Walthen-Dunn (ed.), 296-303. Cambridge, Mass.
____, and Rekosh, J. (1963). 'Motor-Sensory Feedback and Geometry of Visual Space'. *Science*, 722-723.
Henning, H. (1926). 'Psychologische Studien am Geruchsinn'. In *Handbuch der biologischen Arbeitsmethoden*, N. Urban et al. (eds.). Berlin.
Henri, P. (1962). *La vie des aveugles*. Paris.
Henschel, R. L. (1971). 'Sociology and Prediction'. *Am. Sociologist*, 213-220.
Herron, J. (1979). *Sinistral Mind*. New York.
Hershberger, R. G. (1974). 'Predicting the Meaning of Architecture'. In Lang 1974, 149s.
Hess, E. H. (1965). 'Attitude and Pupil Size'. *Scientific American*, 46-54.
____, and Polt, J. M. (1960). 'Pupil Size as Related to Interest Value of Visual Stimuli'. *Science*, 349-350.
Hesselgren, S. (1967). *Language of Architecture*. Lund.
____(1973). 'Architectural Semiotics'. In Kuller 1973.
Heyman, M. (1969). 'Space and Behavior: A Selected Bibliography'. *Landscape*, 4-10.
Higgins, P. C. (1980). *Outsiders on a Hearing World: A Sociology of Deafness*. Beverly Hills, Calif.

Hilbert, D., and Cohn-Vossen, S. (1952). *Geometry and Imagination*. New York. (Original German edition *Anschauliche Geometrie*. Leipzig, 1932.)
Hillier, B., et al. (1976). 'Space Syntax'. *Environment and Planning, B*, 147–185.
Hillier, B., and Leaman, A. (1973). 'The Man: Environment Paradigm and its Paradoxes'. *Architectural Design*.
Himes, H. W. (1965). 'Space as a Component of Environment'. In *School Environments Research: Environmental Evaluation*, 53–72. Ann Arbor, Mich.
Hinde, R. A. (ed.) (1972). *Non-Verbal Communication*. Cambridge, U. K.
Hitchcock, L., Jr., et al. (1962). 'Stimulus Complexity and the Judgment of Relative Size'. *Perceptual and Motor Skills*, 210.
Hjelmslev, L. (1961). *Prolegomena to a Theory of Language*. Madison, Wisc.
Hochberg, C. B., and Hochberg, J. G. (1952). 'Familiar Size and the Perception of Depth'. *Journal of Psychology*, 107–114.
Hodder, I. (ed.) (1978). *The Spatial Organization of Culture*. Pittsburgh, Pa.
Hoeffe, W. (1966). *Sprachlicher Ausdrucksgehalt und akustische Struktur*. Ratingen.
Holahan, C. J. (1978). *Environment and Behavior: A Dynamic Prespective*. New York.
Holland, J., and Stener, M. D. (1969). *Mathematical Sociology: A Selected Annotated Bibliography*. London.
Holmberg, L. (1963). 'The Distribution of Certain Colour Vision Data as Measured by the Pickford-Nicolson Anomaloscope'. *Psychological Research Bulletin* 4.
_____ (1964). 'Psychophysical Experiments on Colour Saturation'. *Psychological Research Bulletin* 4.
_____ (1965). 'Discontinuity in the Subjective Scale of Colour Saturation as a Result of a Shift of Instruction'. *Psychological Research Bulletin* 3.
_____, et al. (1966). 'The Perception of Volume Content of Rectangular Rooms as a Function of the Ratio Between Depth and Width'. *Psychological Research Bulletin*, 1–10.
_____ (1967). 'The Perception of Volume Content of Rectangular Rooms'. *Psychological Research Bulletin*, 1–13.
Honkavaara, S. (1961). 'The Psychology of Expression'. *British J. of Psychology*, Monographs Supplement 32.
Hoog, M. (1964). *Peintres célèbres*. Paris.
Horowitz, M., et al. (1970). 'The Body-Buffer Zone: An Exploration of Personal Space'. In Proshansky, 214–220.
Hovland, et al. (1953). *Communication and Persuasion*. New Haven, Conn.
Howard, I. P., and Templeton, W. B. (1966). *Human Spatial Orientation*. London.
Howells, L. T., and Becker, S. W. (1962). 'Seating Arrangement and Leader Emergence'. *J. of Abnormal and Social Psychology*, 148–150.
Hublin, A. (1971). 'L'espace architectural est-il combinatoire?' *Neuf*, 3–18.
Huszar, L., and Grove, D. (1964). *The Towns of Ghana*. Accra.
Hutchison, A. (1954). *Labanotation: The System for Recording Movement*. New York.
Hutt, S. J., and Hutt, C. (eds.) (1970). *Behaviour Studies in Psychiatry*. Oxford, U. K.
Hutt, C., and Ounstead, C. (1966). 'The Biological Significance of Gaze Aversion with Particular Reference to the Syndrome of Infantile Autism'. *Behavioral Science*, 346–356.
Hutt, G., and Vaizey, M. (1966). 'Differential Effects of Group Density on Social Behaviour'. *Nature*, 1371–1372.
Ittelson, W. H. (1960). *Visual Space*. New York.
_____ (ed.) (1973). *Environment and Cognition*. New York.
Itten, J. (1975). *Design and Form: The Basic Course at the Bauhaus*, 2nd ed. Florence, Ky.

Jackson, C. V. (1953). 'Visual Factors in Auditory Localization'. *Quarterly J. of Experimental Psychology*, 52-65.
James, E. O. (1965). *From Cave to Cathedral*. New York.
James, J. (1951). 'A Preliminary Study of the Size Determinant in Small Group Interaction'. *ASR*, 474-477.
James & James (1968). *Mathematics Dictionary*. New York.
Jampolsky, P. (1940). 'De la vue et du sens statique'. *Année Psychologique*.
Jeannière, A., and Antoine, P. (1970). *Espace mobile et temps incertain*. Paris.
Jeanpierre, C. (1968). 'La perception de l'espace et les dimensions des locaux d'habitation'. *Cahiers du CSTB*, 6-11.
Jencks, C. (1972). 'Rhetoric and Architecture'. *Architectural Association Quarterly*, 4-17.
———(1978). *The Language of Post-Modern Architecture*. New York.
———, and Baird, G. (eds.) (1969). *Meaning in Architecture*. London.
Jenkin, N., and Hyman, R. (1959). 'Attitude and Distance Estimation as Variables in Size Matching'. *Am. J. of Psychology*, 68-76.
Jennings, B. H. (1978). *The Thermal Environment: Conditioning and Control*. New York.
Joedicke, J. (1979). *Moderne Architektur, 1945-1980*. Stuttgart.
Johansson, G. (1970). 'Theories for Visual Space Perception: A Letter to Gibson'. *Scandinavian J. of Psychology*, 67-74.
Jonas, F. (1968). *Geschichte der Soziologie*, volume 4. Hamburg.
Jones, F. P., and Hanson, J. A. (1961). 'Time-Space Pattern in Gross Body Movement'. *Perceptual and Motor Skills*, 35-41.
Jones, F. P., and Narva, M. (1955). 'Interrupted Light Photography to Record the Effect of Changes in the Poise of the Head upon Pattern of Movement and Posture in Man'. *J. of Psychology*, 125-131.
Jones, E. E., and Gerard, H. B. (1967). *Foundations of Social Psychology*. New York.
Joos, M. (1967). *Five Clocks*. New York.
Julesz, B. (1972). 'Texture and Visual Perception'. In Held 1972, 183-194.
Kalmus, H. (1958). 'The Chemical Senses'. *Scientific American*, 97-106.
Kameron, J. (1973). 'Experimental Studies of Environmental Perception'. In Ittelson 1973, 157-179.
Kaminski, G., and Osterkamp, U. (1962). 'Untersuchungen ueber die Topologie sozialer Handlugsfelder'. *Zeitschrift fuer Experimentelle und Angewandte Psychologie*, 417-451.
Kasl, E., et al. (1956). 'A Simple Device for Obtaining Certain Verbal Activity Measures During Interview'. *J. of Abnormal and Social Psychology*, 388-390.
Kasmar, J. V. (1970). 'The Development of a Usable Lexicon of Environmental Descriptors'. *EB*, 153-169.
Kates, R. W. (1970). 'Comment l'homme perçoit son environnement'. *Revue Internationale des Sciences Sociales*, 707-720.
Kaufman, L. (1979). *Perception: The World Transformed*. New York.
Kaufmann, A. (1968). *Introduction à la combinatorique en vue des applications*. Paris.
Kaufmann, P. (1967). *Expérience émotionnelle de l'espace*. Paris.
Kay, P. (1970). 'Some Theoretical Implications of Ethnographic Semantics'. In *Current Directions*, A. Fisher (ed.). *Anthropological Association Bulletin* 3.
Kelley, H. H. and Thibaut, J. W. (1978). *Interpersonal Relation*. New York.
Kendon, A. (1967). 'Some Functions of Gaze-Direction in Social Interaction'. *Acta Psychologica*, 22-63.

Kendon, A. (1970). 'Movement Coordination in Social Interaction'. *Acta Psychologica*, 100–125.
____(1973). 'The Role of Visible Behavior in the Organization of Social Interaction'. In von Cranach and Vine 1973.
____(ed.) (1975). *Organization of Behavior in Face-to-Face Interaction*. The Hague.
Kenner, H. (1973). *Bucky: A Guided Tour of Buckminster Fuller*. New York.
Kenshalo, D. R. (ed.) (1968). *The Skin Senses*. Springfield, Ill.
Key, M. R. (1975). *Paralanguage and Kinesics; Nonverbal Communication with Bibliography*. Metuchen, N. J.
Keyes, R. (1980). *The Height of your Life*. Boston.
Kish, L. (1959). 'Some Statistical Problems in Research Design'. *ASR*, 328–338.
Kilpartick, F. P., and Ittelson, W. H. (1953). 'The Size-Distance Invariance'. *Psychological Review*, 223–231.
Klaus, G. (1968). *Woerterbuch des Kybernetik*. East Berlin.
____(1969). *Semiotik und Erkenntnistheorie*. East Berlin. (2nd ed.)
Kleck, R. (1968). 'Physical Stigma and Non-Verbal Cues Emitted in Face-to-Face Interaction'. *Human Relations*, 19–28.
____, and Nuessle, W. (1968). 'Congruence between Indicative and Communicative Functions of Eye Contact in Interpersonal Relations'. *British J. of Social and Clinical Psychology*, 241–246.
Knowles, E. S. (1972). 'Boundaries Around Social Space: Dyadic Responses to an Invader'. *EB*, 437–445.
Knudsen, V. O., and Harris, C. H. (1950). *Acoustical Design in Architecture*. New York.
Koelega, H. S., and Koester, E. P. (1974). 'Some Experiments on Sex Difference in Odor Perception'. *Annals of the New York Academy of Science*.
Koenig, G. K. (1970). *Architettura e Communicazione*. Florence.
____(1971). 'Zur architektonischen Semiotik'. In 'Die Aussage' 1971, 386–390.
Kohler, I. (1962). 'Experiments with Goggles'. *Scientific American*.
____(1964). *Formation and Transformation of the Perceptual World*. New York.
Kohler, W. (1974). *Gestalt Psychology*. New York. (French edition 1964.)
Kolata, G. B. (1974). 'Combinatorics: Steps toward a Unified Theory'. *Science*, 839–840 and 883.
Kolers, P. A., et al. (1979). *Processing of Visible Language*, volume 1. New York.
Konau, E. (1977). *Raum and soziales Handeln: Studien zu einer vernachlaessigten Dimension soziologischer Theoriebildung*. Stuttgart.
Kowalsiski, P. (1978). *Vision et mesure de la couleur*. Paris.
Kraehenbuehl, D., and Coons, E. (1959). 'Information as Measure of the Experience of Music'. *J. of Aesthetics and Art Criticism*, 510–522.
Krames, L., et al. (eds.) (1974). *Nonverbal Communication*. New York.
Krampen, M. (1971). 'Das Messen von Bedeutung in Architektur, Stadtplanung und Design'. *Werk*, 1–2.
Krantz, D. H., et al. (eds.) (1974). *Contemporary Developments in Mathematical Psychology*, volume 2: *Measurement, Psychophysics and Neural Information Processing*. San Francisco.
Krebs, J. R., and Davies, N. B. (eds.) (1978). *Behavioral Ecology*. Sunderland, Mass.
Kreitsinger, E. A. (1959). 'An Experimental Study of Restiveness in Preschool Educational Television Audience'. *Speech Monographs*, 72–77.
Kroell, F. (1974). *Bauhaus 1919-1933: Kuenstler zwischen Isolation und kollektiver Praxis*. Duesseldorf.

Krout, M. (1954). 'An Experimental Attempt to Determine the Significance of Unconscious Manual Symbolic Movements'. *J. of General Psychology*, 121-152.
Krueger, K., and Hueckstedt, B. (1969). 'Die Bedeutung von Blickrichtungen'. *Zeitschrift fuer Experimentelle und Angewandte Psychologie*, 452-472.
Kuennapas, T. M. (1957). 'The Vertical Horizontal Illusion and the Visual Field'. *J. of Experimental Psychology*, 405-407.
―――(1959). 'The Vertical Horizontal Illusion in Artificial Visual Field'. *J. of Experimental Psychology*, 41-48.
―――(1960). 'Scaling for Subjective Distance'. *Scandinavian J. of Psychology*, 187-192.
―――(1968). 'Distance Perception as Function of Available Visual Cue'. *J. of Experimental Psychology*, 523-529.
Kullenberg, J., and Bergström, (1975). 'Communications chimiques entre êtres vivants'. *Endeavour*, 59-66.
Kuller, R. (ed.) (1974). *Architectural Psychology.* Stroudsburg, Pa.
Kummer, H. (1971). 'Spacing Mechanism in Social Behavior'. In *Man and Beast: Comparative Social Behavior*, J. F. Eisenberg and W. S. Dillon (eds.). Washington, D.C.
Kund, T. (1964). 'Grammaire, lexicologie et sémantique'. *Cahiers de Lexicologie*, 3-7.
Kuratowski, K. (1930). 'Sur le problème des courbes gauches en topologie'. In *Fundamenta Mathematicae.*
La Barre, W. (1964). 'Paralinguistics, Kinesics and Cultural Anthropology'. In Sebeok (ed.) 1964.
Lachenmeyer, C. (1971). *The Language of Sociology.* New York.
Lalande, A. (1962). *Vocabulaire technique et critique de la philosophie.* Paris.
Lalo, C. (1951). 'Esquisse d'une classification structurale des Beaux-Arts'. *Journal de Psychologie.* (Special issue: 'Formes de l'art – formes de l'esprit'.)
Lam, W. M. C. (1977). *Perception and Lighting: Formgivings for Architecture.* New York.
Lamoral, R. (1975). *Acoustique et architecture.* Paris.
Laner, S., Morris, P., and Oldfield, R. C. (1957). 'A Random Pattern Screen'. *Quarterly J. of Experimental Psychology*, 105-108.
Lang, J. (ed.) (1974). *Designing for Human Behavior: Architecture and the Behavioral Sciences.* Stroudsburg, Pa.
Langer, S. (1953). *Feelings and Form: A Theory of Art.* London.
―――(1966). 'The Social Influence of Design'. In *Who Designs America?* L. B. Holland (ed.), 35-50. Garden City, N. Y.
Largey, G. P., and Watson, D. R. (1972). 'The Sociology of Odors'. *AJS*, 1021-1034.
Lashbrooke, W. B. (1967). 'PROANA 5: A Computerized Technique for the Analysis of Small Group Interaction'. In *Report 3-67*, Speech Research Laboratory, Michigan State University. East Lansing, Mich.
―――(1969). 'PROANA 5: A Venture in Computer Assisted Instruction in Small Group Communication'. *Computer Studies in the Humanities and Verbal Behavior*, 98-101.
Lawlor, M. (1955). 'Cultural Influence on Preference for Designs'. *J. of Abnormal Social Psychology*, 690-692.
Lawrence, A. (1969). 'The Architect and his Client's Ears'. *AIA J.*, 54-56.
Lawrence, D. H. (1938). *Kangaroo.* Paris.
Leathers, D. (1976). *Nonverbal Communication Systems*, Boston.
Leblanc, M., et al. (1958). *L'éclairage et l'installation électrique dans le bâtiment.* Paris.
Leclercq, J. (1963). *Introduction à la sociologie*, 3rd edition. Paris.
Le Corbusier (pseud.) (1927). *Toward a New Architecture.* New York.
―――(1954). *Modulor: A Harmonious Measure to the Human Scale Universally Applicable to Architecture and Mechanics*, volume 1. Cambridge, Mass.

Le Corbusier (1974). *Oeuvres Completes: 1910-1967*, 8 volumes. New York.
Lee, T. R. (1969). 'The Psychology of Spatial Orientation'. *Architectural Association Quarterly*, 11-15.
―――― (1971a). 'Psychology and Architectural Determinism, Part 2'. *Architects' J.*, 475-483.
―――― (1971b). 'Architecture and Environmental Determinism, Part 3'. *Architects' J.*, 651-659.
Leeuwenberg, E. L. J. (1968). 'Structural Information of Visual Patterns: An Efficient Coding System'. In *Perception*. The Hague.
――――, and Buffart, H. F. J. M. (eds.) (1978). *Formal Theories of Visual Perception*. New York.
Lefebvre, H. (1968). *Droit à la ville*. Paris.
――――(1974). *La production de l'espace*. Paris.
Leff, H. L. (1978). *Experience, Environment, and Human Potentials*. New York.
Leger, F. (1956). 'La couleur'. *Esthétique Industrielle* 5.
Le Grand, Y. (1956). *Optique physiologique*. volume II: *L'espace visuel*. Paris.
――――(1967). *Form and Space Vision*. Bloomington, Ind.
Lehman, R. (1961). *L'acoustique des bâtiments*. Paris.
――――(1969). *Elements de physiologie et de psychoacoustique*. Paris.
Leibman, M. (1970). 'The Effects of Sex and Race Norms on Personal Space'. *EB*, 217-242.
Le Magnen, J. (1948). *Odeur et parfum*. Paris.
――――(1952).\'Phéromènes olfacto-sexuels chez l'homme'. *Archives de Psychologie*.
Lénard, J. S. (1977). *Les processus de la communication parlée*. Paris.
Lenihan, J., and Fetcher, W. W. (1978). *Man and Environment*, volumes 7 and 8. New York.
Leonov, A., and Lebedev, V. (1971). *Space and Time Perception by the Cosmonaut*. Moscow.
Leroy, C., et al. (1970). *Représentation de l'espace architectural*. Rémy-les-Chevreuse.
Lerup, L. (1977). *Building the Unfinished: Architecture and Human Action*. Beverly Hills, Calif.
Leventhal, H., and Sharp, E. (1965). 'Facial Expressions as Indicators of Distress'. In *Affect, Cognition, and Personality*, S. S. Tomkins and C. E. Izard (eds.), 296--318. New York.
Levin, H. (1967). *Why Is Literary Criticism Not an Exact Science?* Cambridge, Mass.
Levinger, G., and Gunner, J. (1967). 'Interpersonal Grid, I'. *Psychonomic Science*, 173-174.
Lewin, K. (1969). *Principles of Topological Psychology*. New York.
Lhermitte, F. (1971). 'Contribution'. In Dubois et al. 1971.
Libby, W. L. (1970). 'Eye Contact and Direction of Looking as Stable Individual Differences'. *J. of Experimental Research and Personality*, 303-312.
Lieberman, P. (1967). *Intonation, Perception and Language*. Cambridge, Mass.
Linton, R. (1945). *The Cultural Background of Personality*. New York.
Loeb, F. F., Jr. (1968). 'The Fist: The Microscopic Film Analysis of Function of a Recurrent Behavioral Pattern in Psychotherapeutic Session'. *J. of Nervous and Mental Disease*, 605-618.
Loo, C. -M (ed.) (1974). *Crowding and Behavior*. New York.
Loveless, N. E., et al. (1973). 'Bisensory Presentation of Information'. *Psychological Bulletin*, 161-210.
Lowenthal, D. (1962). 'Not Every Prospect Pleases: What is our Criterion of Scenic Beauty'. *Landscape*, 19-26.

Lowenthal, D., and Riel, M. (1972). *Environmental Structures: Semantic and Experiential Components.* New York.
Luneburg, R. K. (1947). *Mathematical Analysis of Binocular Vision.* Princeton, N. J.
Luning Prak, N. (1968). *The Language of Architecture: A Contribution to Architectural Theory.* The Hague.
Luria, S. M., and Kinney, J. A. S. (1970). 'Underwater Vision'. *Science,* 1454-1461.
Lyle, H. M. (1953). 'An Experimental Study of Certain Aspects of the Electromagnetic Movement Meter as a Criterion to Audience Attention'. *Speech Monographs.*
Lyman, S. M., and Scott, M. B. (1967). 'Territoriality: A Neglected Sociological Dimension'. *Social Problems,* 236-249.
Lynch, K. (1960). *The Image of the City.* Cambridge, Mass.
____(1976). *What Time is this Place?* Cambridge, Mass.
____, and Rodwin, L. (1970). 'A Theory of Urban Form'. In Proshansky and Ittelson 1970, 84-100.
Lythgoe, J. N. (1979). *The Ecology of Vision.* New York.
Lyunsternik, L. A. (1966). *Convex Figures and Polyhedra.* New York.
McCardle, E. S. (1974). *Nonverbal Communication.* New York.
McCartney, E. J. (1976). *Optics of the Atmosphere.* New York.
McGinnis, R. (1958). 'Randomization and Inference in Sociological Research'. *ASR.*
McGuigan, F. J., and Pavek, G. V. (1972). 'On Psychophysical Identification of Covert Nonoral Language Processes'. *J. of Experimental Psychology,* 237-245.
McGuire, W. J. (1969). 'Theoretical and Substantive Biases in Sociological Research'. In *Interdisciplinary Relationship in the Social Sciences,* M. Sherif and C. W. Sherif (eds.), 21-51. New York.
McIntyre, D. A., and Griffiths, I. D. (1972). 'Subjective Response to Radiant and Convective Environments'. *Environmental Research,* 471-482.
____(1974). 'The Thermal Environment'. In Canter and Lee 1974, 14-18.
MacKay, D. M. (1950). 'Quantal Aspects of Scientific Information'. *Philosophical Magazine,* 289-301.
McKenchie, G. E. (1973). *Manual for the Environmental Response Inventory.* Palo Alto, Calif.
Mackenzie, B. D. (1977). *Behaviourism and the Limits of Scientific Method.* Atlantic Highlands, N. J.
MacLeod, R. B., and Pick, H. L., Jr. (eds.) (1974). *Perception.* Ithaca, N. Y.
McQuail, D. (1975). *Communication.* London.
Machlup, F. (1963). 'Are the Social Sciences Really Inferior?' In *Philosophy of the Social Sciences,* M. Matanson (ed.), 158-180. New York.
Mahl, G. F. (1956). 'Normal Disturbance in Spontaneous Speech'. *Am. Psychologist,* 390.
Mahoney, E. R. (1974). 'Compensatory Reaction to Spatial Immediacy'. *Sociometry,* 423-431.
'Maîtriser l'environnement de l'homme (1970). *Revue Internationale des Sciences Sociales* 4.
Major, M. (1967). *The Specificity of Architecture.* Budapest.
Maki, W. S. (1979). 'Discrimination Learning Without Short-Term Memory: Dissociation of Memory Process in Pigeons'. *Science,* 83-85.
Mansvelt, E. (1928). Over het schatten van de grotte van figuren van verschillenden vorm. *Meded. u. h. Psychol. Lab. d. Rijksuniv. t. Urecht,* 134-137.
Manz, W. (1974). 'Die Beobachtung verbaler Kommunikation in Labo'. In van Koolwijk and Wieken-Mayser 1974.
March, L., and Martin, L. (1972). *Urban Space and Structure.* Cambridge, U. K.

March, L., and Steadman, P. (1971). *The Geometry of Environment.* London. (2nd edition 1974.)
Markel, N. N. (1965). 'The Reliability of Coding Paralanguage: Pitch, Loudness, and Tempo'. *J. of Verbal Learning and Verbal Behavior,* 306-308.
Marks, R. W. (1966). *The Dymaxion World of Buckminster Fuller.* Carbondale, Ill.
Martin, B. (1969). 'The Smallest Building: The Genesis of the Mark 8 Telephone Boxes'. *RIBA Journal,* 320-325.
Martindale, C., and Hines, D. (1975). 'Dimensions of Olfactory Quality'. *Science,* 74-75.
Martinet, A. (1966). *Elements of General Linguistics,* Chicago.
Maser, S. (1971). *Grundlagen der allgemeinen Kommunikationstheorie.* Stuttgart.
Matarazzo, J. D., et al. (1964). 'Speech Durations of Astronaut and Ground Communication'. *Science,* 148-150.
Matoré, G. (1976). *L'espace humain.* Paris.
Maudet, C. (1973). *Méthodes scientifiques, modèles et simulation en architecture.* Paris.
Maugé, G. (1955). 'Représentation du mouvement et schématisation'. *J. de Psychologie,* 243-252.
Maugh, T. H., II (1973). 'Medium-Size Computers: Bringing Computers into the Laboratory'. *Science,* 270-272.
Mehrabian, A. (1969). 'Some Reference and Measures of Nonverbal Behavior'. *Behavioral Research and Instrumentation,* 203-207.
____(1971). *Silent Messages,* Hartford, Conn.
____(1972). *Nonverbal Communication.* Chicago, Ill.
____(1976). *Public Places and Private Spaces.* New York.
____, and Russell, J. A. (1974). *An Approach to Environmental Psychology.* Cambridge, Mass.
Meier, R. L. (1962). *Communications Theory and Urban Growth.* Cambridge, Mass.
Meisser, M. (1978). *La pratique acoustique dans le bâtiment.* Paris.
Menchikoff, A. (1975). 'La perception des volumes'. *Psychologie,* 48-51.
Merlin, P. (1973). *Méthodes quantitatives et espace urbain.* Paris.
Merton, R. K. (1948). 'The Social Psychology of Housing'. In *Current Trends in Social Psychology,* W. Dennis (ed.), 163-217. Pittsburgh, Pa.
Merveldt, D. (1971). *Grossstaedtische Kommunikationsmuster.* Cologne.
Metz, C. (1971). *Langage et cinéma.* Paris.
Metzger, W. (1975). *Gesetze des Sehens.* Darmstadt.
Meyer-Eppler, W. (1969). *Grundlagen und Anwendung der Informationstheorie* (2nd edition). Berlin.
Michelis, P. A. (1963). *Esthétique de l'architecture du béton armé.* Paris.
____(1977). *Aisthetikos: Essays in Art, Architecture and Aesthetics.* Detroit, Mich.
Michelson, W. (1968). 'Most People Do Not Want What Architects Want'. *Transaction.*
____(1970a). 'Selected Aspects of Environmental Research in Scandinavia'. *MES,* P/2.
____(1970b). *Man and His Urban Environment: A Sociological Approach.* Reading, Mass. (Revised edition 1976.)
____(1977). *Environmental Choice, Human Behavior and Residential Satisfaction.* New York.
____(ed.) (1975). *Behavioral Research Methods in Environmental Design.* Stroudsburg, Pa.
Michotte, A. (1946). *La perception de la causalité.* Paris.
Mill, John Stuart (1900). *A System of Logic, Ratiocinative and Inductive, Being Connected View of the Principles of Evidence and the Method of Scientific Investigation.* 8th edition. London.

Miller, G. A. (1956). 'The Magic Number 7, Plus or Minus'. *Psychological Review*, 81-97. (Reprint in *Sensation*, 1974.)
_____, et al. (1960). *Plans and the Structure of Behavior*. New York.
Milton, G. D., and Clark, L. L. (1968). 'Trends of the Research and Development Process on the Sensory Impaired'. *New Outlook for the Blind*, 265-269.
Missenard, A. (1941). *Chauffage des habitations*. Paris.
_____(1969). *La chaleur animale*. Paris.
Mitchell, M. J., and Gregson, R. A. M. (1971). 'Between-Subject Variation and Within-Subject Consistency of Olfactory Intensity Scaling'. *J. of Experimental Psychology*, 314-318.
Miyakawa, T. (1960). 'On the Familiarity of Behavioral Space: II. Social Interaction of Strangers'. *Japanese J. of Educational Psychology*, 38-47.
Moholy-Nagy, L. (1947). *Vision in Motion*. Chicago.
Moles, A. (1966). *Information Theory and Esthetic Perception*. Urbana, Ill.
_____, and Rohmer, E. (1978). *Psychologie de l'espace* (2nd edition). Paris.
Montagu, A. (1971). *Touching: The Human Significance of the Skin*. New York.
Monty, R. A., and Boynton, R. M. (1962). 'Stimulation Overlap and Form Similarity under Suprathreshold Conditions'. *Perceptual and Motor Skills*, 487-498.
Moos, R. H. (1976). *The Human Context: Environmental Determinants of Behavior*. New York.
Morgenstern, O. (1966). 'Logistik und Sozialwissenschaften'. In *Logik der Sozialwissenschaften*, E. Topitsch (ed.), 315-336. Cologne.
Morris, C. W. (1938). *Foundations of the Theory of Signs: Foundations of the Unity of Science*. Chicago.
_____(1946). *Signs, Language and Behavior*. New York.
Morrison, J., and Hall, J. (1978). *Environmental Studies: A Field Laboratory Approach*. New York.
Moscovici, S., and Plon, M. (1966). 'Les situations colloques – observations théoriques et experimentales, *Bulletin de Psychology*, 702-722.
Moskowitz, H. R., et al. (1974). 'Sugar Sweetness and Pleasantness'. *Science*, 583-585.
Moss, H. E. (1974). *Behaviour and Perception in Strange Environments*. London.
Moulin, R., et al. (1973). *Les architectes: Métamorphose d'une profession libérale*. Paris.
Mounier, G. (1959). Les systèmes de communication non-linguistiques et leur place dans la vie du XXe siècle. *Société de Linguistique de Paris*, 176-200.
Mounin, G. (1974). *Dictionnaire de la linguistique*. Paris.
Mucchielli, R. (1972). *Introduction to Structural Psychology*. New York.
Muench, W. (1971). *Datensammlung in den Sozialwissenschaften*. Stuttgart.
Muller, C. (1968). *Initiation à la statistique linguistique*. Paris.
Mumford, L. (1963). *Technics and Civilization*. New York.
Murch, G. M. (1973). *Visual and Auditory Perception*. Indianapolis.
Murphy, E. B. (1971). 'A Theory of the Influence of Architecture in Casual Social Contacts'. Unpublished dissertation, Princeton University. Microfilm, 3892-A, Ann Arbor, Mich.
Nédoncelles, M. (1960). *Introduction à l'esthétique*. Paris.
Negroponte, N. (1970). *The Architecture Machine*. Cambridge, Mass.
_____(1974). *Soft Architecture Machine*. Cambridge, Mass.
_____(ed.) (1975). *Computer Aids to Design and Architecture*. New York.
Nesselroade, J. R. and Baltes, P. B. (1979). *Longitudinal Research in the Study of Behavior and Development*. New York.

Newhall, S. M., et al. (1943). 'Final Report of the Optical Society of American Subcommittee on the Spacing of the Munsell Colors'. *J. of Optical Society of America*, 385-422.
Nielsen, G. (1962). *Studies in Self Confrontation.* Copenhagen.
Nieman, T. J., and Viohl, R. C. (1976). *The Description of, Classification, and Assessment of Visual Landscape Quality: An Annotated Bibliography.* Monticello, Ill.
Nilles, J. M. (1976). *The Telecommunication-Transportation Tradeoff: Options for Tomorrow.* New York.
Nitschke, G., and Thiel, P. (1968). 'Anatomie des gelebten Raumes'. *Bauen und Wohnen*, 9-12.
Norberg-Schulz, C. (1966). *Intentions in Architecture.* Cambridge, Mass.
_____(1971). *Existence, Space and Architecture.* New York.
_____(1975). *Meaning in Western Architecture.* New York.
Northwood, T. D. (ed.) (1977). *Architectural Acoustics.* Stroudsburg, Pa.
Noton, D., and Stark, L. (1971). 'Eye Movements and Visual Perception'. *Scientific American*, 34-43.
O'Farrell, P. N., and Markham, J. (1975). 'The Journey to Work: A Behavioral Analysis'. *Progress in Planning* 3.
Ogle, K. N. (1950). *Research in Binocular Vision.* Philadelphia, Pa.
_____(1962). 'Spatial Localization According to Direction'. In *The Eye*, H. Davson (ed.), volume 4, 220-221. New York.
Oleron, P. (1978). *Eléments de répertoire du langage gestuel des sourds-muets.* Paris.
Olver, R., and Hornsby, J. (1972). 'On Equivalence'. In *Language and Thought*, P. Adams (ed.), 306-320. Harmondsworth, U. K.
Opp, K. D. (1970). 'The Experimental Method in the Social Sciences: Some Problems and Proposals for its More Effective Use'. *Quantity and Quality*, 39-54.
Ono, H., et al. (1970). 'Underwater Distance Distortion Within the Manual Work Space'. *Human Factors*, 473-480.
Ore, O. (1963). *Graphs and Their Uses.* New York.
Orne, M. T. (1973). 'Communication by the Total Experimental Situation: Why It Is Important, How It Is Evaluated and Its Significance for the Ecological Validity of Findings'. In *Communication and Affect*, P. Pliner (ed.). New York.
Osgood, C. E. (1953). *Method and Theory in Experimental Psychology.* New York.
_____ (1966). 'Dimensionality of the Semantic Space for Communication Via Facial Expressions'. *Scandinavian J. of Psychology*, 1-30.
Osmond, H. (1965). 'The Psychological Dimension of Architectural Space'. *Progressive Architecture*, 159-167.
Ostwald, P. F. (1963). *Soundmaking: The Acoustic Communication of Emotion.* Springfield, Ill.
Pagès, R. (1974). 'Das Experiment in der Soziologie'. In *Grundlagende Methoden und Techniken der empirischen Sozialforschung*, R. Koenig (ed.). volume 3a, PII, 273-333.
Panofsky, E. (1948). *A Gothic Architecture and Scholasticism.* Latrobe, Pa. (French edition 1967)
Pantle, A., and Picciano, L. (1976). 'A Multistable Movement Display: Evidence for Two Separate Motion Systems in Human Vision'. *Science*, 500-502.
Paris, J. (1965). *L'espace et le regard.* Paris.
Park, P. (1969). *Sociology Tomorrow: An Evaluation of Sociological Theories in Terms of Science.* New York.
Parkes, A. S., and Bruce, H. M. (1961). 'Olfactory Stimuli in Mammalian Reproduction'. *Science*, 1,049-1,054.

Parry, J. (1967). *Psychology of Human Communication.* London.
Parsons, H. M. (1974). 'What Happened at Hawthorne?' *Science,* 922s.
Parthey, H., and Wahl, D. (1966). *Die experimentelle Methode in Nature und Gesellschaftswissenschaften.* East Berlin.
Pastalan, L. A., and Carson, D. H. (eds.) (1970). *Spatial Behavior of Older People.* Ann Arbor, Mich.
Patterson, A. H. (1977). 'Environment'. *Contemporary Sociology,* 186-187.
Patterson, M. (1968). 'Spatial Factors in Social Interaction'. *Human Relations,* 351-361.
Pawles, M. (1971). *Architecture versus Housing.* New York.
Payne, I. (1970). 'Complexity as a Fundamental Dimension of the Visual Environment: A Pupillary Study'. *MES,* S/26.
Peeples, D. R., and Teller, D. Y. (1975). 'Color Vision and Brightness Discrimination in Two-Month-Old Human Infants'. *Science,* 1102-1103.
Pei, M. (1966). *Glossary of Linguistic Terminology.* New York.
Peirce, C. S. (1934). 'Pragmatism and Pragmaticism'. In *Collected Papers,* volume 5. Cambridge, Mass.
Pellegrini, R. J., and Empey, J. (1970). 'Interpersonal Spatial Orientation in Dyads'. *J. of Psychology,* 67-70.
Pelpel, L., Moulin, R., and Lautman, J. (1978). 'La profession d'architecte'. *Cahiers de Recherche Architecturale,* 1-55.
Peluzzi, G. (1970). *Forme et couleur dans l'intérieur moderne.* Paris.
Pennartz, P. J. (1969). *Answer to a Space: An Inquiry on Basic Patterns in Adapting to a Square Space.* Wageningen, The Netherlands.
'Perception de l'espace' (1959). *Acta Psychologica.*
Perin, C. (1972). *With Man in Mind: An Interdisciplinary Prospectus for Environmental Design.* Cambridge, Mass.
Persky et al. (1966). 'Psychoendocrine Effects of Perceptual and Social Isolation'. *Arch. Gen. Psychiatry,* 499-505.
Peter, R. (1976). *Playing with Infinity.* New York.
Pevsner, N., Fleming, J., and Honour, H. (1977). *A Dictionary of Architecture.* Harmondsworth, U. K.
Pfeiffer, H. (1966). *L'harmonie des couleurs.* Paris.
Phillips, B. S. (1970). *Empirische Sozialforschung, Strategie und Taktik.* Vienna.
Piaget, J. (1960). *Les mécanismes perceptifs.* Paris.
_____, et al. (1967). *Traité de psychologie experimentale,* volume VI: *Perception.* Paris.
_____(1973). *Dictionary of Terms,* A. M. Bettro (ed.). New York.
_____, and Imfeld, B. (1967). *Child's Conception of Space.* New York.
_____ and Morf, A. (1954). 'L'action des facteurs spatiaux et temporels de centration dans l'estimation visuelle des longueurs'. *Archives de Psychologie,* 243-288.
Pierce, J. R. (1961). *Symbols, Signs and Noise: The Nature and Process of Communication.* New York.
Piéron, P. (1967). *La sensation.* Paris.
_____(1968). *Vocabulaire de la psychologie.* Paris.
Pike, K. (1954). *Language in Relation to a Unified Theory of the Structure of Human Behavior.* Glendale, Calif.
Pizzey, E. (1977). *Scream Quietly or the Neighbors Will Hear.* Short Hills, N. J.
Politz Media Studies. (1959). *A Study of Outside Transit Poster Exposure.* New York.
Polya, G., and Szegoe, G. (1951). *Isoperimetric Inequality in Mathematical Physics.* Princeton, N. J.
Pool, I. de Sole (ed.) (1973). *Handbook of Communication.* Cambridge, Mass.
_____(1977). *The Social Impact of the Telephone.* Cambridge, Mass.

Portas, N. (1967). 'Définition et évaluation des normes du logement'. *Cahiers du CSTB*, 1-16.
Porter, E., et al. (1970). 'What is Signalled by Proximity?' *Perceptual and Motor Skills*, 39-42.
Pouillon, F. (1968). *Mémoires d'un architecte*. Paris.
Poyner, B. (1967). *The Atoms of Environmental Structure*. London.
Pratt, M. B. (1926). 'The Visual Estimation of Angles'. *J. of Experimental Psychology*, 132-140.
Preziosi, D. (1979). *Architecture, Language, and Meaning*. The Hague.
Priest, R. F., and Sawyer, J. (1967). 'Proximity and Peership'. *AJS*, 633-649.
Prieto, L. J. (1975). *Etudes de linguistique et de sémiologie générales*. Geneva.
Prihar, Z. (1956). 'Topological Properties of Telecommunication Network'. *Proceedings of the Institute of Radio Engineers*, volume 44, 929-933.
Prokasy, W. F., and Raskin, D. C. (eds.) (1974). *Electrodermal Activity in Psychological Research*. New York.
Proshansky, H. M., and Ittelson, W. H. (eds.) (1970). *Environmental Psychology: Man and his Physical Setting*. New York.
Pujolle, J. (1971). *Lexique-guide d'acoustique*. Paris.
Purdy, W. C. (1958). 'The Hypothesis of Psychophysical Correspondence in Space Perception'. Unpublished dissertation, Cornell University. Microfilm, 58-5594, Ann Arbor, Mich.
——, and Gibson, J. J. (1955). 'Distance Judgments by Methods of Fraction'. *J. of Experimental Psychology*, 374-380.
Purkis, H. J. (1966). *Building Physics: Acoustics*. New York.
Pyron, B. (1972). 'Form and Space Diversity in Human Habitat: Perceptual Responses'. *EB*, 87-120.
Ramsey, R. S. (1968). 'Speech Pattern and Personality'. *Language and Speech*, 54-63.
Rapoport, A. (1968). 'The Design Professions and the Behavioural Sciences'. *Architectural Association Quarterly*, 20-24.
——(1969). *House Form and Culture*. Englewood Cliffs, N. J.
——(1970). 'Observations Regarding Man-Environment Studies'. *MES*, P/1.
——(1973). 'Some Thought on the Methodology of Man-Environment Studies'. *International J. of Environmental Studies*, 135-140.
——(1975). 'Toward a Redefinition of Density'. *EB*, 133-158.
——(1977). *Human Aspects of Urban Form*. New York.
——(ed.) (1977). *The Mutual Interaction of People and Their Built Environment*. The Hague.
——, and Horowitz, H. (1960). 'The Sapir-Whorf-Korzybski Hypothesis – A Report and a Reply'. *ETC* 17.
——, et al. (1967). 'Complexity and Ambiguity in Environmental Design'. *J. of Am. Institute of Planners*, 210-221.
Rapp, F. (ed.) (1974) *Contributions to a Philosophy of Technology*. Dordrecht, The Netherlands.
Rasmussen, J. E. (ed.) (1973). *Man in Isolation and Confinement*, Chicago.
Rasmussen, S. E. (1959). *Experiencing Architecture*. London.
Raush, H. L. (1969). 'Method and Clinical Approach'. In *Naturalistic Viewpoints in Psychological Research*, E. P. Willems and H. L. Raush (eds.), 122-146. New York.
Raven, J. (1967). 'Sociological Evidence on the House'. *Architectural Review*, 68-72 and 236-240.
Raymond, H. (1968). 'Analyse du contenu et entretien non-directif: Application au symbolisme de l'habitat'. *Revue Francaise de Sociologie*, 167-179.

Raymond, H. (1974). 'Habitat, modèles culturels et architecture'. *Architecture d'Aujourd'hui*, 174.

———, and Segault, M. (1970). *Analyse de l'espace architectural. LeCorbusier*. Rémy-les-Chevreuse.

Read, H. (1960). 'Von der Universalitaet der Architektur'. *Werk*, 261-263.

Reese, E. S. (1975). 'Filming of Behavior'. *Science*, 414.

Reimann, H. (1968). *Kommunikations-Systeme: Umrisse einer Soziologie der Vermittlungs- und Mitteilungsprocesse*. Tuebingen.

Révész, G. (1938). *Die Formwelt des Tastsinnes*, volumes 1 and 2. The Hague.

———(1950). *Psychology and Art of the Blind*. London.

———(1953). *Revision der Gestaltpsychologie*. Berlin.

Riesen, A. H., and Mellinger, J. C. (1956). 'Interocular Transfer of Habits in Cats after Alternating Monocular Visual Experience'. *J. of Comparative and Physiological Psychology*, 516-520.

Robinson, J. T. (1973). *Early Hominid Posture and Locomotion*. Chicago.

Rock, I., and Harris, C. S. (1967). 'Vision and Touch'. *Scientific American*, 96-104.

Rock, I., and Victor, J. (1964). 'Vision and Touch: An Experimentally Created Conflict Between the Two Senses'. *Science*, 594-596.

Rodieck, R. W. (1977). 'Metric of Color Borders'. *Science*, 1,195-1,196.

Roesch, S. (ed.) (1973). *Die grosse Farbordnung*. Ravensburg.

Rommetveit, R. (1974). *On Message or the Study of Language and Communication*. Chichester, U. K.

Rosenberg, B. G., and Langer, J. (1965). 'A Study of Postural-Gestural Communication'. *J. of Personality and Social Psychology*, 593-597.

Rosenblith, W. A. (ed.) (1961). *Sensory Communication*. New York.

Rosenthal, R. (1976). *Experimenter Effects in Behavioral Research* (2nd edition). New York.

———, and Rossow, R. L. (eds.) (1969). *Artifact in Behavioral Research*. New York.

Rosow, L. (1961). 'Social Effects of the Physical Environment'. *J. of the Am. Institute of Planners*, 127-133.

Ross, H. E. (1974). *Behaviour and Perception in Strange Environments*. London.

Ross, M., et al. (1973). 'Affect, Facial Regard and Reactions to Crowding'. *J. of Personality and Social Psychology*, 69-76.

Rousseau, P. (1942). *La lumière*. Paris.

Rudofsky, B. (1969). *Architecture without Architects*. New York.

Rushton, G. (1969). 'Analysis of Spatial Behavior by Revealed Space Preference'. *Annals of the Association of Am. Geographers*, 391-400.

Sabatier, J. (1968). 'Le mur vivant'. *Architecture Francaise*, 98.

Sachs, L. (1972). *Statistische Methoden*. Berlin.

Sackeim, H. A., et al. (1978). 'Emotions are Expressed More Intensely on the Left Side of the Face'. *Science*, 343-345.

Saddy, P. (1973). 'Radiateur et code classique'. *Architecture, Mouvement, Continuité*, 41-47.

Saegert, S. (1976). *Crowding in Real Environments*. Beverly Hills, Calif.

Sainesbury, P. (1955). 'Gestural Movement During Psychiatric Interview'. *Psychosomatic Medicine*, 458-469.

Salzinger, K., and Salzinger, S. (eds.) (1967). *Research in Verbal Behavior and Some Neurophysiological Implications*. New York.

Sandstroem, C. -I. (1951). *Orientation in the Present Space*. Stockholm.

Sanoff, H., and Burgwyn, H. (1970). *Social Implications of the Physical Emphasis on Housing and Neighborhood Characteristics: An Annotated Bibliography*. Monticello, Ill.

Santarcangeli, P. (1967). *Il Libro dei Labirinti: Storia di un Mito e di un Simbolo.* Florence. (French edition published 1974.)
Sartori, A. (1932) *Gli Elementi dell' Architettura Funzionale.* Milan.
Savary, N. (1975). 'Gardons nos distances'. *Psychologie,* 8-12.
Scagnelli, P. (1969). *Relationships among Visual Imagery, Language and Haptics in Spatial Perception.* Unpublished doctoral dissertation. Duke University, Durham, N. C.
Scalvini, M. L. (1975). *Architettura Come Semiotica Connotative.* Milan.
Scheflen, A. E. (1964). 'The Significance of Posture in Communication Systems'. *Psychiatry,* 316-331.
_____(1968). 'Human Communication'. *Behavioral Science,* 42-55.
_____(1969). *Stream and Structure of Communication Behavior.* Bloomington, Ind.
_____(1976). *Human Territories: How We Behave in Space-Time.* Englewood Cliffs, N. J.
Scheuch, E. K., and Rueschemeyer, D. (1966). 'Soziologie und Statistik: Ueber den Einfluss der modernen Wissenschaftslehre auf ihr gegenseitiges Verhaeltnis'. In *Logik der Sozialwissenschaften,* E. Topitsch (ed.), 345-363. Cologne.
Schnaiberg, A. (1980). *The Environment.* New York.
Schneider, G. E. (1967). 'Contrasting Visuomotor Function of Tectum and Cortex in the Golden Hamster'. *Psychologische Forschung,* 52-62.
Scholfield, P. H. (1958). *The Theory of Proposition in Architecture.* Cambridge, U. K.
Scholtz, D. A. (1957). 'Die Grundsaetze der Gestaltwahrnehmung in der Haptik'. *Acta Psychologica.*
Schuele, W. (1976). *Ausdruckswahrnehmung des Gesichts: Experimentelle Untersuchungen.* Bern.
Schuessler, K. F. (ed.) (1977). *Sociological Methodology.* San Francisco.
Schulman, J. L., and Reisman, J. M. (1959). 'An Objective Measure of Hyperactivity'. *Am. J. of Mental Deficiency,* 455-456.
Schulze-Fielitz, E. (1971). *Stadtsysteme I, Urban Systems I.* Stuttgart, New York.
Schwann, P. C. (1958). *La peinture chinoise.* Paris.
Schwartz, B. (1968). 'The Social Psychology of Privacy'. *AJS,* 741-752.
Scott, A. J. (1971). *Combinatorial Programming, Spatial Analysis and Planning.* London.
Sebeok, T. A. (1975). *Zoosemiotics: At Intersection of Nature and Culture.* New York.
_____(1976). *Contributions to the Doctrine of Signs.* Bloomington, Ind.
_____(1977). *How Do Animals Communicate?* Bloomington, Ind.
_____(1978). *Semiosis in Nature and Culture.* New York.
_____(ed.) (1964). *Approach to Semiotics.* London. (Revised edition 1972, The Hague.)
_____, and Ramsay, A. (eds.) (1969). *Approaches to Animal Communication.* The Hague.
_____, and Umiker-Sebeok, D. J. (eds.) (1976). *Speech Surrogates: Drum and Whistle Systems.* The Hague.
Segal, S. J., and Fusella, V. (1971). 'Effects of Images in 6 Sense Modalities on Detection of Visual Signal from Noise'. *Psychonomic Science,* 55-56.
Segall, N., Marshall, H., and Campbell, D. T. (1963). 'Cultural Differences in the Perception of Geometrical Illusion'. *Science,* 769-771.
Seiler, D. A., and Zusne, L. (1967). 'Judged Complexity of Tachistoscopically Viewed Random Shapes'. *Perceptual and Motor Skills,* 884-886.
Sennett, R. (1970). *The Uses of Disorder.* New York.
_____(1980). *Authority.* New York.
Sensation and Measurement: Papers in Honor of S. S. Stevens (1974). Boston.
Serrus, C. (1945). *Traité de Logique.* Paris.
Shannon, C. E., and Weaver. W. (1949). *The Mathematical Theory of Communication.* Urban, Ill.
Sharp, D. (1972). *A Visual History of Twentieth Century Architecture.* Waltham, Mass.

Shaw, M. E. (1964). 'Communication Networks'. In *Advances in Experimental Social Psychology*, volume I, L. Berkowitz (ed.), 111–147. New York.
Sheldon, W. (1970). *Atlas of Men: A Guide for Somatyping the Adult Male of All Ages.* New York.
Shepard, R. N. (1963). 'Analysis of Proximities as a Technique for Study of Information Processing'. *Human Factors*, 33–48.
Sherif, M. (1954). 'Integrating Field Work and Laboratory in Small Group Research'. *ASR*, 759–771.
Shorey, H. H. (1976). *Animal Communication by Pheromones.* New York.
Short, W., et al. (eds.) (1976). *The Social Psychology of Telecommunications.* New York.
Shucard, D. W. (1977). 'Auditory Evoked Potentials as Probes of Hemispheric Differences in Cognitive Processing'. *Science*, 12, 95–97.
Siebel, W. (1965). *Die Logik des Experiments in den Sozialwissenschaften.* Berlin.
Siegman, A. W., and Pope, B. (eds.) (1972). *Studies in Dyadic Communication.* New York.
———, and Feldstein, S. (1979). *On Speech and Time: Temporal Speech Patterns in Interpersonal Contexts.* Hillsdale, N. J.
Sieverts, T. (1969). 'Spontaneous Architecture'. *Architectural Association Quarterly*, 36–43.
Siffre, M. (1964). *Beyond Time.* New York.
Silverstein, C. H., and Stang, D. J. (1976). 'Seating Position and Interaction in Triad: A Field Study'. *Sociometry*, 166–170.
Simmel, G. (1906). 'Soziologie des Raumes'. *Schmollers Jahrbuch fuer Gesetzgebung*, XXIIs.
———(1921). 'Sociology of the Senses'. In *Introduction to the Science of Sociology*, R. E. Park and E. Burgess (eds.). 1969. Chicago.
———(1950). *Sociology of Georg Simmel*, 320–324, 330–376, 409–424. Glencoe, Ill.
Simon, H. A. (1969). *The Science of the Artificial.* Cambridge, Mass.
Simondon, G. (1965). 'La perception'. *Bulletin de Psychology.*
Sims, J. H., and Baumann, D. D. (eds.) (1974). *Human Behavior and the Environment.* Chicago.
Siqueiros, D. A. (1976). *Art and Revolution: The Work and Techniques of D. Siqueiros.* Brooklyn Heights, N. Y.
Sire, M. (1960). *La vie sociale des animaux.* Paris.
Sleight, R. B., and Duvoisin, G. (1952). *An Annotated Bibliography of Form Perception.* Office of Naval Research, Washington, D. C.
Smith, J. P. (1964). 'The Effects of Figural Shape on the Perception of Area'. Unpublished dissertation, Fordham University. Microfilm, 3712, Ann Arbor, Mich.
Smith, O. W. (1958). 'Distance Constancy'. *J. of Experimental Psychology*, 388–389.
Smith, P. F. (1972). 'The Pros and Cons of Subliminal Perception'. *Ekistics*, 367–369.
Snelfield, and Russell, J. A. (eds.) (1976). *Behavioral Basis of Design.* Stroudsburg, Pa.
Sokol, R. R., et al. (1961). 'Factor Analytical Procedures in a Biological Model'. *University of Kansas Science Bulletin*, 1099–1121.
Solomon, R. (1949). 'An Extension of Control Group Design'. *Psychological Bulletin*, 137–150.
Sommer, R. (1966). 'Leadership and Group Geography'. *Sociometry*, 99–110.
———(1967). 'Small Group Ecology'. *Psychological Bulletin*, 145–152.
———(1968). 'Howthorn Dogma'. *Psychological Bulletin*, 592–595.
———(1969). *Personal Space.* New York.
———(1974). *Tight Spaces.* Englewood, N. J.

Sonnefeld, J. (1966). 'Variable Values in Space Landscape: An Inquiry into the Nature of Environmental Necessity'. *J. of Social Issues*, 71-82.
Sorenson, E. R. (1974). 'Anthropological Film'. *Science*, 1,079-1,085.
Souriau, E. (1957). 'Les limites de l'esthétique'. In *Atti del III. Congresso Internazionale di Estetica in Venezia (1956)*, 26-32. Turin.
'Space Perception: A Symposium' (1959). *Acta Psychologica* 15.
Speer, D. C. (ed.) (1974). *Nonverbal Communication.* Beverly Hills, Calif.
Speier, M. (1973). *How to Observe Face-to-Face Communication: A Sociological Introduction.* Santa Monica, Calif.
Spencer, B. G. (1972). *Laws of Form.* New York.
Spiegel, J. P., and Machotka, P. (1974). *Messages of the Body.* New York.
Spivack, M. (1972). A Place to Eat. MH 15314. Mimeographed. Cambridge, Mass.
Spreiregen, P. D. (1965). *The Architecture of Towns and Cities.* New York.
Starkweather, J. A. (1960). 'A Speechrate Meter for Vocal Behavior Analysis'. *J. of Experimental Analysis of Behavior*, 111-114.
Stea, D. (1967). 'Mediating the Medium'. *AIA J.*, 67-70.
_____ (ed.) (1973). *Image and Environment: Cognitive Mapping and Spatial Behavior.* Chicago.
_____, and Dawns, R. M. (1970). 'From the Outside Looking In at the Inside Looking Out', *EB*, 3-12.
Steele, F. I. (1969). 'Problem Solving in the Spatial Behavior'. *MES*, S/15.
Steinbach, M. J. (1969). 'Eye Tracking of Self-Moved Targets: The Role of Efference'. *J. of Experimental Psychology*, 366-376.
Steinhaus, H. (1969). *Mathematical Snapshots.* New York.
Steinzor, B. (1950). 'The Spatial Factor in Face-to-Face Discussion Groups'. *J. of Abnormal and Social Psychology*, 552-555.
Stephenson, G. M., and Rutter, D. R. (1970). 'Eye Contact, Distance and Affiliation: A Reevaluation'. *British J. of Psychology*, 385-393.
Stern, P. C. (1979). *Evaluating Social Science Research.* New York.
Stevens, S. S. (1957). 'On the Psychophysical Law'. *Psychological Review*, 153-181.
_____(1966). 'Operations or Words?' *Psychological Monographs*, 33-38.
Stewart, K. (1975). *Pygmies and Dream Giants.* New York.
Stokols, D. (1972). 'A Social–Psychological Model of Human Crowding Phenomena', *J. of the American Institute of Planners*, 72-83.
_____(ed.) (1976). *Perspectives on Environment and Behavior.* New York.
Studer, R. G. (1966). 'On Environmental Programming'. *Arena.*
_____ (1969). 'The Dynamics of Behavior-Contingent Physical Systems'. In *Design Methods in Architecture*, G. Broadbent and A. Ward (eds.), 55-72. London.
_____, and Stea, D. (1966). 'Architectural Programming and Human Behavior'. *J. of Social Issues*, 127-136.
Strodtbeck, F. L. (1973). 'Communication in Small Groups'. In Pool 1973, 646-665.
_____, and Nook, L. H. (1961). 'The Social Dimension of a Twelve-Man Jury Table'. *Sociometry*, 397-415.
Summerson, J. (1957). 'The Case for a Theory of Modern Architecture'. *British Architects' J.*, 307-311.
Sury, K. (1967). *Woerterbuch der Psychologie und ihre Grenzgebiete.* Basel.
Sweeny, D. R., et al. (1970). 'Dimensions of Affective Expression in Four Expressive Modes'. *Behavioral Science*, 393-407.
Sweets, J. A. (1973). 'The Relative Operation Characteristic in Psychology'. *Science*, 990-1,000.

Tabor, P. (1971). *Traffic in Buildings 1: Pedestrian Circulation in Offices.* Cambridge, U. K.
Tafuri, M. (1971). 'Architecture et sémiologie', *Werk,* 690.
──── (1976). *Architecture and Utopia: Design and Capitalist Development.* Cambridge, Mass.
Takagi, K. (1926). 'On Visual Estimation of Length of Various Curves'. *Japanese J. of Psychology,* 476-498.
Talbot, R. E., and Humphrey, D. R. (eds.) (1979). *Posture and Movement.* New York.
Tansley, B. W., and Boynton, R. M. (1976). 'A Line, Not a Space, Represents Visual Distinctness of Borders Formed by Different Colors'. *Science,* 954-957.
──── (1977). 'Metric of Color Borders'. *Science,* 1,196.
Tarry, G. (1895). 'Le problème des labyrinths'. In *Nouvelles Annales de Mathématiques,* vol. 14.
Taut, B. (1958). *Houses and People in Japan.* Tokyo.
Tavolga, N. T. (1974). 'Application of Concept of Levels of Organization to the Study of Animal Communication'. In Krames et al. 1974, 51-76.
Taylor, S., Alexander, A. G., and Glass, R. (1953). 'Failure of the New Densities'. *Architectural Review,* 355-362.
Taghtsoonian, M. (1965). 'The Judgment of Size'. *Am. J. of Psychology,* 392-402.
Theodorson, G. A., and Theodorson, A. G. (1970). *Modern Dictionary of Sociology.* New York.
Thibaut, J. W., and Kelley, H. H. (1959). *The Social Psychology of Groups.* New York.
Thiel, P. (1969). 'La notation de l'espace, du mouvement et de l'orientation', *Architecture d'Aujourd'hui,* 49-58. (Originally 'A Sequence-Experience Notation for Architectural and Urban Spaces'. *Town Planning Review* (1961), 33-52.)
Thompson, D. L. (1969). 'New Concept of Subjective Distance: Store Impressions Affect Estimates of Travel Time'. In *Analytical Human Geography,* P. J. Ambrose (ed.), 197-203. London.
────, and Metzler, L. (1964). 'Communicating Emotional Intent by Facial Expression'. *J. of Abnormal and Social Psychology,* 129-135.
Thompson, d'Arcy W. (1942). *On Growth and Form.* New York.
Tien, H. C. (1978). *Videology: Theory and Techniques.* New York.
Tiger, L., and Fox, R. (1966). 'The Zoological Perspective in Social Science'. *Man* I.
Toennies, F. (1969). *Gemeinschaft und Gesellschaft.* Darmstadt. (Partial translation 1972: *Pure, Applied and Empirical Sociology: Selected Writings of F. Toennies.* Chicago.)
Towsend, J. C. (1953). *Introduction to Experimental Method.* New York.
Trager, G. L. (1958). 'Paralanguage: A First Approximation'. *Linguistics,* 1-12.
Turner, J. F. C., and Fichter, R. (eds.) (1972). *Freedom to Build: Housing for and by People.* London.
Unruh, D. R. (1970). *Space and Environment: An Annotated Bibliography.* Monticello, Ill.
Utudjian, E. (1964). *L'urbanisme souterrain.* Paris.
Valentine, C. W. (1962). *The Experimental Psychology of Beauty.* London.
van Bergeijk, W. A., Pierce, J. R., and David, E. E. (1960). *Waves and the Ear.* New York.
Van der Kellen, D., and Van der Kellen, H. (1970). *International Documentation of Architecture: English, German, French, and Netherlandish,* volume 3. Anvers, Belgium.
Van der Meer, F. (1970). 'The Basilica'. In *The Sociology of Art and Literature.* C. M. Albrecht et al. (eds.), 90-104. New York.

van Hout, G. (1969). *Mathématique moderne, langage du futur.* Brussels.
van Koolwijk, J., and Wieken-Mayser, M. (eds.) (1974). *Techniken der empirischen Sozialforschung*, volume 3: *Erhebungsmethoden: Beobachtung und Analyse von Kommunikation.* Munich.
van Lier, H. (1959). *Les arts de l'espace: Peinture, sculpture, architecture, arts décoratifs.* Tournai.
―――(1971). 'Architecture et sémiologie'. *Werk*, 244-245.
Vasarhely, V. (1970). *Plasti-cité.* Tournai.
Venturi, R. (1966). *Complexity and Contradiction in Architecture.* New York.
Vernon, M. D. (1952). *Further Study of Visual Perception.* New York.
Villey, P. (1914). *Le monde des aveugles.* Paris.
Vitruvius (1960). *The Ten Books on Architecture.* New York.
von Bertalanffy, L. (1968). *General System Theory.* New York.
von Hornbostel, E. (1966). Das räumliche Hören. In *Handbuch der Psychologie*, Metzger, W. (ed.), Göttingen: 518-555.
von Cranach, M. (ed.) (1977). *Methods of Inference from Animal to Human Behavior.* The Hague.
―――, and Vine, I. (eds.) (1973). *Social Communication and Movement: Studies of Interaction and Expression in Man and Chimpanzee.* New York.
von Frisch, K. (1976). *Animal Architecture.* New York.
von Holst, E. (1954). 'Relations Between the Central Nervous System and the Peripheral Organs'. *British J. of Animal Behaviour*, 89-94.
von Meiss, P., and Schaffner, L. (1972). 'Laboratoires d'expérimentation avec les espaces architecturaux'. *Bulletin Technique de la Suisse Romande*, 293-298.
von Senden, M. (1960). *The Perception of Space and Shape in Congenitally Blind Before and After Operation.* London.
von Uexkuell, J. J. (1921). *Umwelt und Innenwelt der Tiere.* Berlin. (Translated into English 1964 as 'A Stroll Through the World of Animals and Men'. In *Instinctive Behavior*, C. H. Scholler [ed.]. New York.)
Vurpillot, E. (1956). 'Perception de la distance et de la grandeur des objets'. *Année Psychologique*, 437-452.
―――(1967). 'La perception de l'espace'. In Piaget et al. 1967, VI, 102-189.
―――(1975). *The Visual World of the Young Child.* New York.
Wachsmann, K. (1961). *The Turning Point of Building.* New York.
Wagner, E. (1931). 'Das Abschaetzen von Flaechen'. *Psychotechnische Zeitschrift*, 140-148.
Wagner, P. L. (1972). 'Cultural Landscape and Region: Aspects of Communication'. In English and Mayfield (eds.), 55-68.
Wagner, R. H. (1978). *Environment and Man*, 3rd edition. New York.
Walther, E. (1968). 'Abriss der Semiotik'. *Arch+, Studienhefte fuer architekturbezogene Umweltforschung* 8. Stuttgart.
Wapner, S., and Cohen, S. B. (eds.) (1976). *Experiencing the Environment.* New York.
Wapner, S., and Wapner, H. (1957). *Perceptual Development: An Investigation Within the Framework of Sensori-Tonic Field Theory.* Worcester, Mass.
Ward, C. D. (1968). 'Seating Arrangement and Leadership Emergence in Small Discussion Group'. *J. of Social Psychology*, 83-90.
Warren, J. M., and Pinneau, S. R. (1955). 'Influence of Form on Judgement of Apparent Area'. *Perceptual and Motor Skills*, 7-10.
Warusfel, A. (1966). *Dictionnaire raisonné de mathématique.* Paris.
―――(1969). *Les mathématiques modernes.* Paris.

Watson, M. (1970). *Proxemic Behavior.* Paris.
____, and Graves, T. D. (1966). 'Quantitative Research in Proxemic Behavior'. *Am. Anthropologist,* 971-985.
Webb, E. J., et al. (1971). *Unobtrusive Measures: Nonreactive Research in Social Science.* Chicago.
Webber, M. (1963). *Order in Density: Community Without Propinquity in Cities and Space.* Baltimore, Md.
Weber, M. (1966). *The City.* New York.
Weick, K. E. (1968). 'Systematic Observational Techniques'. In *Handbook of Social Psychology,* volume 2, G. Lindrey and E. Aronson (eds.), 357-451. Reading, Mass.
Weitz, S. (ed.) (1979). *Nonverbal Communication,* 2nd edition. New York.
Wellman, B., and Whitaker, M. (1972). *Community-Network-Communication: An Annotated Bibliography.* Monticello, Ill.
Weyl, H. (1967). *Symmetry.* Princeton, N. J.
Whebelle, C. F. J. (1969). 'Corridors: A Theory of Urban Systems'. *Am. Geographers,* 1-26.
White, H. C. (1970). *Chains of Opportunity: System Models of Mobility in Organizations.* Cambridge, Mass.
Whitehead, B., and Eldars, M. Z. (1964). 'An Approach to the Optimum Layout of Single-Storey Building'. *Architects' J.*
Whorf, B. L. (1956). *Language, Thought and Reality.* Cambridge, Mass.
Wickler, W. (1973). *Verhalten und Umwelt.* Hamburg.
Wiener, M, and Mehrabian, A. (1968). *Language Within Language: Immediacy, a Channel in Verbal Communication.* New York.
Wiggins, J. A. (1968). 'Hypothesis Validity and Experimental Laboratory Method'. In *Methodology in Social Resarch,* H. M. Blalock and A. B. Blalock (eds.), 390-427. New York.
Wiley, N. (1979). 'The Substitution of Method for Theory'. *Contemporary Sociology,* 793-799.
Willems, E. (1970). *Dictionnaire de sociologie.* Paris.
____(1973). 'Behavioral Ecology: An Experimental Analysis'. In *Life-Span in Developmental Psychology,* P. B. Baltes (ed.). New York.
Willis, F. N. (1966). 'Initial Speaking Distance as a Function of Speakers' Relationship'. *Psychonomic Science,* 221-222.
Willmott, P., and Cooney, E. (1963). 'Space Standard Research'. *J. of the American Institute of Planners.*
Winkel, G. H., and Sasnoff, R. (1966). *An Approach to an Objective Analysis of Behavior in Architectural Space.* University of Washington, Seattle.
Winston, P. H. (1975). *The Psychology of Computer Vision.* New York.
Wintermantel, M. (1973). *Soziale Genese von Sprechstilen: Diktionsdistanz.* Meisheim.
Wittelson, S. F. (1976). 'Sex and the Single Hemisphere: Specialization of the Right Hemisphere for Spatial Processing'. *Science,* 425-427.
Wittkower, R. (1960). 'The Changing Concept of Proportion'. *Daedalus,* 199-215.
____(1962). *Architectural Principles of the Age of Humanism.* London.
Wohlwill, J. F. (1976). 'Environmental Aesthetics: The Environment as a Source of Affect'. In Altman and Wohlwill 1976.
____, and Carson, D. H. (eds.) (1972). *Environment and the Social Sciences.* Washington, D. C.
Wolfe, M. (1975). 'Room Size, Group Size, and Density'. *EB,* 199-224.
Wonnacott, T. H., and Wonnacott, R. J. (1969). *Introductory Statistics.* New York.

Woodworth, R. S., and Schlosberg (eds.) (1954). *Experimental Psychology*. New York.
Worchel, P. (1960). 'Space Perception and Orientation in the Blind'. *Psychological Monographs* 15.
____, and Byrne, D. (eds.) (1964). *Personality Change*. New York.
Yaglom, I. M., and Boltyanski, V. G. (1961). *Convex Figures*. New York.
Yale, P. B. (1968). *Geometry and Symmetry*. San Francisco.
Yasuo, M. (1960). 'On the Semiotic'. *Zinbun*, 17-24.
Yi-Fu Tuan (1977). *Space and Place: The Perspective of Experience*. Minneapolis.
Zajackowska, A. (1958). 'Experimental Determination of Luneburg's Constants σ and K'. *Quarterly J. of Experimental Psychology*, 66-78.
Zajonc, R. B. (1966). *Social Psychology: An Experimental Approach*. Monterey, Calif.
Zeisel, J. (1970). 'Interior Designers Discover Behavioral Research'. *Design and Environment*.
____(1975). *Sociology and Architectural Design*. New York.
Zeitoun, J. (1971). 'Eléments de combinatoire'. *Environnement*, 36-41.
____(1977). *Trames Planes: Introduction à une étude architecturale des trames*. Paris.
Zelditch, M., Jr. (1968). 'Can you Really Study an Army in the Laboratory?' In *A Sociological Reader in Complex Organizations*, A. Etzioni (ed.). New York.
Zevi, B. (1957). *Architecture as Space*. New York.
____(1978). *The Modern Language of Architecture*. Seattle.
Zimmermann, E. (1972). *Das Experiment in den Sozialwissenschaften*. Stuttgart.
Zubeck, J. P., et al. (1969). 'Relative Effects of Prolonged Social Isolation and Confinement: Behavioral and Physiological Effects'. *J. of Abnormal Psychology*, 625-631.
Zuckerman, M. (1969). 'Variable Affecting Deprivation Results'. In *Sensory Deprivation: Fifteen Years' Research*, J. P. Zuber (ed.), 47-84. New York.
____, Persky, H., et al. (1968). 'Experimental and Subject Factors Determining Responses to Sensory Deprivation, Social Isolation and Confinement'. *J. of Abnormal Psychology*, 183-194.
Zusne, L. (1965). 'Moments of Area and of the Perimeter of Visual Form as Predictors of Discrimination Performance'. *J. of Experimental Psychology*, 213-220.
____(1970). *Visual Perception and Form*. New York.

Subject Index

A. *See* Architecture
(AH)S. 331, 333
(AHO)S. *See* Polysensory space
(AO)S. 331-333
Accessibility: *See also* Distance: direct, 378; indirect, 378; metric, 379; topological, 357, 360, 374, 378-381, *fig.* 3.30
Acousteme 318-320, 330. *See also* Impression of acoustical space, modifiers of
Acoustical space 200, 206, 208-210, 229--230, *fig.* 3.8
Actometry 476-477
Address of a space 369
Adjacency graph. *See* Syntagmatic graph
Air conditioning. *See* Osmotic space
Air house 298
Alias 181, 341, 366-368, *fig.* 3.27, 369--370, 398, 400, 410
Alignment of rectangular spaces: *fig.* 3.37
Ankerl's sociological theory of architecture x, 235, 479
Apartment. *See* Sentence, architectural
Aquatic space 299, 308-309
Arab architecture 383
Architect 69, 160-161, 273, 341, 357, 462, 503; alchemy of, 189, 195, 235--236, 320-321, 338, 411, 418, 424, 428-431, 437. *See also* Doctrine, architectural; as craftsman 1, 55-56; as connoisseur 398, 401, 437; expectation of, 50, 55, 162, 362, 407, 430, 480, 495; rhetoric of, 41. *See also* 'Architecture parlée'
Architectural competence 1-3, 8, 49, 157-159, 160, 171, 172, 373
Architectural critic 160
Architectural and geographical determinism 28, 29-31, 47, 159, 461-462, 490
Architectural imagination viii, 169, 178, 179-184, 190, 192, 198, 215-216, 230, 232, 233-234, 242-244, 246, 258, 274, 283, 298, 319-320, 322, 330, 370-371, 374, 382, 386, 389, 399, 406, 411, 416-417, 425, 430
Architectural science vii, 1-3, 49, 160, 213, 234-240, 243-245, 248, 254, 258, 262, 274, 311-312, 319, 322, 338, 359, 388, 405, 494-495, 503; and mathematics 371-374, 500
Architecture 15-16, 21, 24, 27, 55, 57, 69, 150-154, 156, 159, 164, 207, 338, 339, 373, 383, 386; defined as communication media 35-38, 40-42, 151, 154-157, 314, 384, 390, 406-408; defined as space system 15, 150, 157--158; as general paradigm of human creation 154, 159, 311; historiography of, 405-407; history of, 338, 406, 437; as machine 32, 150; monumentality of, 28-29, 384, 386, 481; and painting 37, 154, 236, 242, 245, 252, 259, 269, 303, 338; permanence of, 29-39, *fig.* 1.1, 56, 299, 354; representation of, viii, 26, 158-159, 182, 203, *fig.* 3.18, *fig.* 3.28, 326, 371-372, 377; and sculpture 28-29, 37-38, 42, 149, 303, 331; themes of, 6, 22, 32-33, 34, 36, 40, 42, 137, 152, 155, 170, 171--172, 311, 381; urban, *see* Space system, dense, Contextual space
'Architecture parlée' 2, 13, 41, 158-161, 459
Architecturology. *See* Architectural science
Artifact 22-23, 27, 59-60, 102
Atmospheric space. *See* Contextual space
Audible human expression, classification of, 110-112

Subject Index

Audiotape. *See* Facsimile, acoustical
Audition and vision 92, 106-107, 208, 211, 230, 326, 327
Auditorium, multipurpose, 223-234, 298, 352

Baroque 246, 263, 351
Bas-relief. *See* Space impression
Beeline. *See* Distance
Birth 84, 88-89
Bound form 25, 165-166, *fig.* 3.2, 294, 320, 330, 331, 358, 374. *See also* Space, architectural
Builder 56
Building. *See* Opus, architectural
Building trade 179, 182-183

Capacity of space 105. *See also* Density, Volumetric magnitude
Catacomb 384, 399
Cavern. *See* Space, geofactual
Centroid 199
Church 223, 248
Circulation 381, 382
City planning. *See* Urbanism
Class of substitution. *See* Repertory, architectural, item of
Classification of arts 150, 154. *See also* Architecture
Client 12, 35, 55, 428, 480
Cloister 394, 486
Color. *See* Optical space, spectrometric characteristics
Communication 68. *See also specific headings*; architectural, 6, 19-20, 47, 54-56, *fig.* 1.3, 67-68, 159-160, 253, 262, 341, 357, 361, 390, 400, 429-430; social, 55, *fig.* 1.3, 150, 152, 156
Communications theory 40, 71-72 142
Complex space 25, 44, 166, 221, 312, 356, 374
Composition 149, *fig.* 3.1, 383, 406, 411, 415, 418, 428-431. *See also* Multisensory composition of space, Complex space; multilayer nature of, 420, 423, 425, 426, 428, 533-534, 538; syntactic, 389, 397
Compound architectural morpheme 165, 166, *fig.* 3.29, 377

Computer application in sociology of architecture 175, 178, 180, 183, 202-203, 248, 261, 349, 371, 398, 430, 465, 466, 475, 478, 502
Concavity 5, 20-21, 180, 187
Concrete 298-299; ferro-, 28, 31, 182
Configuration. *See* Gestalt
Congener 91, 453
Connotation 37, 41-42, 225, 406-407, 459
Connotative label (of a locale) 459, 482
Constituent 371, 377; immediate, 357, 368, 438; ultimate, 356-357
Contextual space 7, 27-29, 150, 152, 155, 357, 377, 383, 384-386, 390, 408, 414, 484; envelope of, 241, 385, 429, 430-431
Continuous deformation of space envelope 175, 177
Control group 451, 454, 493
Convexity. *See* Concavity
Corridor. *See* Function space
Cross-modal face-to-face communication 142
Crowding 73, 87, 89
Crystallographic restriction 197, 411, 524-428, 438
Cube 205, 289, 292, 370, 425-426, 432-434
Cycles in everyday life 485, 487, 490, 491

Data 22
Dance 127, 299
Dead spot. *See* Impression of acoustical space, special cases
Decision-making process 29, 30-31, 55-56
Demi-degree. *See* Paradigmatic valence
Demography: and genealogy 89; and objective sociology 86-90
Demolition 30
Demology 80
Denotation 36, 41-42, 48, 67, 69, 154, 407; and space impression 225, 254
Density 132-133; concept of, 86-87; demographic, 81, 86; umbilical, 87-88; residential, 45, 87; social, 14, 29, 71
Developer 12, 55-56
Diagram of a graph. *See* Graph, isomorphism of

Direct communication. *See* Face-to-face communication
Discoteque 108
Distance 69, 70, 75, 81-82, 137, 379, 392; abathic, *fig.* 3.12, 258-259; ecological or functional, 359, 379, 393, 398; estimation of, *fig.* 3.12; social, 13-14; topological, 392, 397
Doctrine, architectural 2, 197
Domes, geodesic 195-197
Door 166, 172, 294, 298, 337, 343, 357, 361-362, 364, 368, 386. *See also* Paradigmatic valence
Dupinian surface: *fig.* 3.5, 186, 192, 195, 198
Dyad. *See* Elementary relation

Echo. *See* Impression of acoustical space, special cases
Egg 18, 188-189
Elementary relation 80-84, *fig.* 1.2, *fig.* 2.2, 99-102, 488; homologeous, 99, 101-102, 107, 127, 128; mutual, 80--81, 127; reciprocal, 80-82, 99, 127, 128
Elevator 320, 378, 382, 286, 417. *See also* Function space
Ellipsoid 179, 188, 199, 205, 266
Elliptic: point 186; surface 187-188
Emic description 143, 236, 459, 461, 478
Empty word in architecture. *See* Function space
Enantiomorphism and syntagmatic operation in architecture 366-367
Engineering (civil) 1-2, 158, 161, 166, 179, 182, 189-190, 191, 196, 234, 338, 358, 415
Environment 182; physical, 21, 58-60; social, 21, 60
Ephemeral space 30-31
Epistemological privilege of experimental sociology of architecture 4-5, 8, 443, 453, 461, 503
Epistemological qualifier of hardness in science 494-503
Epistemology of experimental science 480, 485
Equiaffine transformation. *See* Shape
Equiconcave mapping. *See* Symmetrization
Ergonomic activity 36

Esthetics 22, 34, 150, 151, 235, 311, 415, 430-431, 435, 437, 482; geographical, 22, 151, 435
Ethnoscience 236
Ethology 50, 117, 121, 143, 466, 478
Etic description 5, 143, 236, 459, 461
Etiological relation 443, 445-449, 462, 473-474, 497-499, *fig.* 4.3
Eulerian sequence. *See* Reading of architecture, perusal
Experiencing architecture. *See* Reading of architecture
Experiment 4, 6, 7, 50-51, 80, 319-320, 446, 449, 451, 481, 501, 502; longitudinal, 51-52, 453, 483-493
Experimental design 23, 36-37, 48, 50-51, 102, 163, 168, 204, 211, 224, 226--227, 237, 238, 249, 253-254, 258, 259, 261, 264-268, 275-276, 278--280, 304-306, 309, 311-312, 313--314, 317, 323, 325, 326, 327-330, 342, 347-349, 401-404, 449-451, 454, 456, 462, 470, 478, 482-484, 488-489, 490, 492, 499, 501
Experimental design and laboratory 51, 260, 353, 444, 449, 452-453, 483, 486
Exploration of space 226, 326, 339, 343--345, 399; dynamic, 335, 339-341, 345, 348, 353: with dynamic strategy 335, 340, 341, 346, 348; kinesthetic, 340-341, 346-348; static, 339, 341, 348; stationary, 335, 339-340, 348, 353
Exposition hall 389
Extension 16
External sociology. *See* Sociology, objective

Facade 5, 20-21, 28-29, 180, 248, 357, 383, 429, 430
Face-to-face communication 7, 78
Face-to-face communication channel. *See* Face-to-face communication network
Face-to-face communication flow. *See* Face-to-face communication structure
Face-to-face communication network 46, 59-60, *fig.* 1.2, 72-74, 81, 88, 89, 142, 151; intervals in auditory, 112-113; intervals in haptic, 126-128, 130-132, *fig.* 2.8, 474-475; intervals in osmatic,

544 Subject Index

Face-to-face communication network; intervals in osmatic (*contd.*), 119-120; sapid, 134-135; transformation of, 47, 59, 73, 76, 137, 145, 158, 355, 475, 477; intervals in visual, 95-98, 101, *fig.* 2.5; zones of, 73, 74-75, 88, 110, 136--143, *fig.* 2.10, 145

Face-to-face communication structure 46, 72-73, 88, 89, 142, *fig.* 2.11, 151, 477; audible, 472-473; haptic, 122--126, 128-133, *fig.* 2.8, 476, 477; osmatic, 117-119, 307-308; sapid, 134-135; visible, 465, 467;

Facsimiles of communicative expression 463-464; acoustical, 469-474; mechanical, 474-478; optical, 464-469

Falsification procedure 446, 449, 498--502

Fetal space. *See* Space, biofactual

Floor 105, 184, 185, 189, 192, 219, 285, 303, 305, 341, 342, 343, 349, 364, 368, 459

Flutter space. *See* Acoustical space, special cases

Formwork 179, 189, 195. *See also* Building trade

Free block 172, 368

Free form 25, 151, 165-166, 374. *See also* Space, architectural

Frequentation: of a space 50, 361-362, 475, 479, 495; of space system 378, 384, 392, 407, 408, 475, 485

Frequenter. *See* User

Function. *See* Purpose

Function space 347, 359, 360, 377, 381--382, 400, 403, 404, 415

Functionalism 32

Furniture. *See* Movables

Garage 40

Geography 179-180, 198-199, 203, 405, 481

Geometry 4, 24, 49, 157, 168-169, 373--374, 414; of concave shape 179-181, 183, 196; internal, 170, 171-174, 180, 341, 366; renewal of, 181-206

Gestalt 5, 180, 249, 254, 275-276, 294, 320, 323-324

Ghetto 484, 486

Golden section. *See* Regularities, planar

Gothic 246

Gradient of acuity of senses 136, 138-140

Grammatical: characteristics of architecture 386-389, 391, 408-411; unit of architecture. *See* Sentence, architectural

Graph 344, 373; dual of the planar, 380, 414-415, *fig.* 3.34, 426; isomorphism of, 380-381, 398, 409-410, *fig.* 3.32, 412, 423; multi-, 362, 379, *fig.* 3.30; planar, 343, 412-415, *fig.* 3.33, 417, 418; regular, 409; representing face-to-face communication network 72, *fig.* 2.2, 141; representing space exploration 340, 343-345, 389-399; representing space systems 357, 385, 389, 408-411

Graphic features. *See* Impression of optical space, modifiers of

Group 102-103, 131-132; macrosocial, 80-81, 84, *fig.* 2.8, 86-90, 104-105; microsocial, 80-81, 85, 103-104

(HO)S. 314, 330, 333

Hamiltonian sequence. *See* Reading of architecture, perusal

Hapteme 318-320, 328, 330-331. *See also* Peripheral variable of perceptible space

Haptic space 293, 296, 302, 341, 361; thermal aspect of 295, 296, 303, 305--306

Haptics and the other senses 122-124, 130, 131, 293, 294, 297, 300, 304--305, 326, 327-328, 346

Hermetic space 307-310

Hoisting by crane. *See* Syntactical operation

Homeomorphic surfaces 175, 177

Homogeneous graph. *See* Graph, regular

Homothetic transformation. *See* Shape

Homotopic transformation. *See* Continuous deformation

Hospice 389

Hospital 389, 404, 486

Hotel 389

House. *See* Opus, architectural

Housing 178, 179, 389

Hue. *See* Opteme

'Humanization of architecture' 411

Hylic 5, 38, 40-41, 155, 253, 312, 318--320, 329. *See also* Peripheral variables of perceptible space

Subject Index 545

Hyperbolic: point 186, 190; surface 189
Hyperbolic paraboloid 179, 189-190, 338

Identity of an architectural space 356, 368, 387, 400
Igloo 309
Illusion, sensory 28, 33, 41, 160, 163, 168, 211, 230, 249, 257, 258, 265, 274, 282, 313, 318-320, 325, 330--331, 348, 351, 353-354
Impression of acoustical space 213, 218, 224; modifiers of, 215-217; special cases of, *fig.* 3.8, 218-222, 249
Impression of haptic space 293, 297, 300--306, *fig.* 3.23, 339, 349-350
Impression of hermetic space 308-310, 482-483
Impression of optical space 227-229, 259--262, 280-281, 340, 350-351; modifiers of, 239, 240, 241-242, 246-262, *fig.* 3.11. 265-272, *fig.* 3.14; shape comparison in, 267, 275-283; volume estimate (rectangular parallelepipeds) in, 284, 286-288, *fig.* 3.16
Impression of polysensory space 310, 325, 326-329, 340, 351-353; and intersensory association 320-322, 325, 327
Impression of space system 361, 390, 391, 395, 400
Imprinting. *See* Facsimiles
Introduction 449, 500, 502
Information theory 33-34, 246, 282; in relation to architecture 261-262
Infrastructural graph. *See* Syntagmatic graph
Institutions, total. *See* Experiment, longitudinal
Interface 358, 359, 362, 366
Interior. *See* Space, architectural
Interrelatedness of morphological, syntagmatic and syntactic composition. *See* Composition, multilayer nature of
Intimacy 43, 96, 103, 150, 155, 228, 338
Intricacy. *See* Multisensory composition of space
Involution. *See* Reading of architecture, nonsense in
Iron structure 31
Irregularity 419-420. *See also* Shape of a space, complexity of

Isoconcave indicatrix 188, 199-206, 214. *See also* Shape, Geometry of concave shape; application of, 215, 297
Isoconcave mapping. *See* Symmetrization
Isolation. *See* Hylic, Peripheral variables of perceptible space, Bound form
Isometry. *See* Repertory, architectural, item of
Isomorphism between signifier and signified 35, 41, 153, 155
Iteration 390, 391, 392

Kinesics 75-77, 126-127. *See also* Face-to-face communication network, transformation of
Kinesimetry 476-477
Kitchen 12, 34, 311

Labyrinth 358, 392, 397, 399, 401
Landscape 28. *See also* Contextual space, envelope of, Esthetics, geographical
Language 35, 38, 41, 151, 155; and architectural communication 151, 152, 155, 311, 386; and face-to-face communication 35, 38, 41; levels of consideration of, 111, 151-152; and visual bias 294, 301, 304
Lateralization 402
Legibility. *See* Readability
Linguistics 38, 142, 168-170, 356
Lithosphere 5, 358, 383-384, 386, *fig.* 3.31
Locale 357, 369, 377, 391, 397, 400, 408-409
Localization 322; intersensory, 333
Location. *See* Relative location
Luminary 240-241

Major space 28, 163, 182, 195, 196, 216, 221-222, 274, 389, 392, 481
Man-made object. *See* Artifact
Marsupial pouch. *See* Space, biofactual
Matching technique 462, 501
Materials and isolation 182, 329-330, 331
Matrix, incidence 410, *fig.* 3.32
Message and meaning 40, 42
Metaphysical Space. *See* Space concept, origin of
Migration 88-89
Mirror. *See* Specular surface

Model for experimental sociology of architecture: *fig.* 1.3, 59, 462-464, *fig.* 4.3; archetypical, 19-20
Modeling in architectural laboratory 200--202, 215, 481
Modular coordination. *See* Regularities
Morpheme, architectural. *See* Space, architectural
Morphology, architectural 162-164, 171--172, 312, 356, 358, 387, 407
Morphology, social 71, 407
Movables 58-59, 387, 406
Multipurpose 31, 33, 223, 309, 387
Multisensory composition of space 5, 26, 44, 156, *fig.* 3.1, 165, 311, 315, 317, *fig.* 3.28, 374-377; cases of, 298, 329, *fig.* 3.29; shared parcel of, *fig.* 3.18.3, 375
Music 108, *fig.* 2.7, 112. *See also* Time and music

Nature 27-29, 30, 383
Network position value 46-47, 73, 74, 76, 80-82, 98-99, 119, 131, 136-137, 141-142. *See also* Face-to-face communication network
Nonbook vii
Notation. *See specific headings*
Null element. *See* Function space
Null hypothesis. *See* Falsification procedure

Oculo-ocular communication, findings in 100-102. *See also* Face-to-face communication structure, visible
O-data 51
Olfaction and the other senses 116, 117, 120, 307-308
Open region 164, 169, 171-172
'Open plan architecture'. *See* Multisensory composition of space, Acoustical space, Haptic space
Opera house 223
Operations. *See specific headings*
Opteme 263-264, 318-320. *See also* Impression of optical space, modifiers of
Optical space 227-228; in relation to acoustical space 229-230, 276; peripheral variables of, 234-235; spectrometric characteristics of the envelope of 236-237, 263

Opus, architectural 7, 357, 361, 377-378, 385-386, 408, 429
Orientation 401-402
Osmatic communication. *See* Face-to-face communication structure, osmatic
'Osmotic space' 307, 310, 482-483
Outdoor space. *See* Contextual space

Paired comparison 227, 254, 283, 288, 318, 329, 332. *See also* Repertory, architectural, construction of
Parabolic: point 186; surface 189
Paradigmatic transformation 152, 169, 356, 366, 369-370
Paradigmatic valence: *fig.* 3.2, *fig.* 3.21, 337, 342, *fig.* 3.22, 356, *fig.* 3.25, 366, *fig.* 3.30, 377, 378-379, 408; application of, 394-395
Paralinguistics 75-77, 110-111, 467, 469, 477-478
Path: *fig.* 3.2, 341-345, 357, 390-392
Pentagonal profile: *fig.* 2.10
'Perfect rectangle'. *See* Regularities, planar
Peripheral variables of perceptible space 167-168, *fig.* 3.3, 318, 325. *See also specific headings* Impression of
Photographing architecture, 5, 26-27, 260, 339, 382
Physical confinement 486, 489-491
Pictogram 35, 37, 41, 153
Pictorial feature. *See* Impression of optical space, modifiers of
Plane surface 192, 364, *fig.* 3.26. *See also* Floor
Pleasantness 6, 23, 33-34, 36-37, 167, 179, 203, 249, 263
Podium 105, *fig.* 2.5
Polyhedron 177, 187, 188, 192-196, 205, 278, 280, 281, 303; regular, 177, 182, 193-195, 205-206, 281, 418, 419
Polysensorily coordinated communication flow 142-144; recording of, 477-478
Polysensory space, 26, 44, *fig.* 3.1, 165, 167, 215, 308, 313-314, 317-318
Position. *See* Network position value
Posture 74, 83, 99, 477
Prefabrication 172, 174, 367-368, 369, 377, 418-419, 438-439
Presence 68-69, 86

Subject Index   547

Presentation 68. *See also* Representation, and Isomorphism between signifier and signified
Prismatic restriction. *See* Regularities, three-dimensional
Prison: *fig.* 3.2, 394, 399, 486
Proprioception and space exploration 130, 226, 322-323, 340, 345-346
Proxemics. *See* Network position value
Proximity. *See* Distance
Proximospace 302-303, 326, 329, 350
Pseudodoor 176, 362, *fig.* 3.25
Pseudospace 174, 176, 354
Public 12, 392-393, 398
Purpose of architectural space 357, 390, 397, 459; social, 5-6, 67-69. *See also* Architecture, themes of
Pyramid 149, 156, 338, 383

Readability 31, 33, 249, 258, 311
Reading of architecture 157, 314, 337, 340-343, 357, 359-362, 377, 378, 389-391, 400-401; dynamic, 340-341; nonsense in, 383, 430; by perusal, 357, 390-391, 393-396; represented by graph 340, 343-345, 389-399; by skimming 391-393, 396-399
Reception of communication 78, 79
Recording of (behavioral) variables 88, 456, 465, 470-471, 476, 501; automatic, 88, 211, 227-228, 238, 259, 261, 342, 454, 465, 468, 472, 475, 501; and data analysis 465, 466, 471, 473, 475
Regular 172, 188, 214, 282, 418; definition of, 193, 419-420
Regularities and rhythms in composition 245-246, 418-420, 438-439; planar, 411, *fig.* 3.36, *fig.* 3.38, 435-438; three-dimensional 197, 411, 425-428, 438
Relais 37, 38, 150, 153, 154
Relation (social), longitudinal dimension of, 89, 488-489
Relational field 80, 84-85, 86, 457
Relational space. *See* Functional space
Relative location of unisensory spaces: *fig.* 3.1, 313, *fig.* 3.18, 317, 333
Repertory, architectural 6, 35-37, 48, 152-153, 155, 160, 162-164, 168,

Repertory: architectural (*contd.*), 182-183, 192-193, 202, 211, 253, 279, 280, 292, 342, 356, 366; construction of, 254-255, 266, 276, 348, 366; items of, 181, 197-198, 204-206, 252, 276-277, 283, 368, 374; lexical aspects of, 169, 170, 198, 204, 356, 364-366, 374, 382; transitivity of, 170, 204, 283
Representation 38, 150, 153-154, 155
Representational 59-60, 68, 248
Research strategy 23, 36-37, 48, 53-54, 57, 61, 480-483. *See also* Experimental design
Resonance. *See* Impression of acoustical space
Reverberation time. *See* Impression of acoustical space
Rhythm. *See* Regularities
Rococo 222-223
Roof 21-22, 179, 190, 191
Roomraum 16, 152, 171. *See also* Space, architectural (concept of)
Route. *See* Path

Sampling: and population 491-492, 501; in time 483. *See also* Experiment, longitudinal
Sauna 306
Self-presentation 75
Semantics 39-40, 151, 152, 153
Semiology, architectural 39
Semiotics 40
Sensory deprivation 487-489
Sensory modalities 78, 142-143, 144, 320-322, 326-327; order of priority of, 78-79, 138-141, 142-143, 207-208, 230, 300, 314, 352
Sentence, architectural 16, 42, 152, 171, 355-357, 368, 377, *fig.* 3.31, 386-389
Shadow 240, 242, 266-267, 280
Shape of space 5, 155, 157, 162, 168-169, 180-181, 186, 197-198, 202, 255, 265, 275, 277, 281, 303, 317, 324, 366; indicatrixes of, 186, 198-200; complexity of, 282-283, 289-291
Similitude. *See* Shape
Simulating architectural experience. *See* Photographing architecture, Modeling architecture
Simultaneous reciprocity. *See* Elementary relation, homologous

548 Subject Index

Skeleton. *See* Submorphemic level
Sky. *See* Contextual space, envelope of
Skyscraper 28
Sleeping 31-32, 36, 87
Social fact 71-72, 152, 456-457, 461. *See also* Sociology, subject of
Social force. *See* Sociology, pure
Social isolation 487, 488-489
Sociology 50, 444, 456-458; allo-, 117; eco-, 43, 51, 71, 78, 87, 102, 443, 453, 461, 480; economic, *see* eco-; environmental, *see* eco-; experimental, 7-8, 50-52, 80, 102, 254, 443-445, 451--454, 458; of the habitat 11, 54; objective, 24, 35, 49-50, 69, 126, 159, 254, 407, 456-458, 460-461, 466--467, 479, 500; pure, 7, 43, 51, 71, 78, 80, 88, 102, 112, 453; spatial, 43, 49-50, 70-71, 80, 210; subject of, 34-35, 51, 67, 71-72, 456-457
Sociology as science vii, viii, 3-4, 8, 49, 311-312, 372, 444-445, 456-458
Sound foci. *See* Impression of acoustical space, special cases
Space 4-5, 15-20, 157, 300. *See also specific headings;* architectural, 4-5, 15, 42, 58, 151-152, 162, 164-166, *fig.* 3.3, 170, 171-172, 210, 294, 301, 329, 341, 373, 443; biofactual, 5, 16--20, 150, 294, 301, 336, 385; geofactual, 20-22, 149-150, 180, 383, 385, 482; objective, 36, 40-41, 208, 213, 261, 294, 312; as prime frame of reference 17, 28, 30, 31, 35, 51, 57, 58, 150, 159, 254, 260, 278, 286, 443. *See also* Environment, physical; unisensory, 25-26, 164-165, 167, 208-209, 307, 312, 315
'Space' concept, origin of, 16-20
Space envelope 48, 58, 171, *fig.* 3.4, 174--176, 183, 209, 212, 239, 296-297, 308, 318, 328; classification of, 184, 186-187; quasi-surface on the, 241; topological genus of, 175-178
Space filling (medium) 211-212, 227, 298-299, 307, 308-310
Space impression 23-27, 33, 37, 47-48, 154, 155, 168, 204, 227, 254, 312--314, 318, 323-324, 328, 339-341, 343-345, 361, 367, 382-383, 400. *See also specific headings* Impression of;

Space impression: (*contd.*) autonomous, 25, 167, 208-210, 312; denotative characteristics in, 225, 307; effects of, 47, 225, 306, 429, 463, 469, 473-474, *fig.* 4.3; and sentence stress 400-401.
'Space perception' 259-262, 276, 481; schoolmaster's, 261-262, 284-286
Space system 15-16, 44, 310, 357, 371--372, 378, 386, 405; aspects of, 407--408, 411, 420, 432-434; dense, 29-31, 44, 68, 415, 418; and multisensory intricacy 374-377, *fig.* 3.29; one level, 415-418, 421, 431; regular, 395; semiregular, 395; three-dimensional, 364, 378, 386, *fig.* 3.31, 395, 415-418
'Space, Time, and Architecture' ix, 237--238
Spacecraft 295, 302, 307, 349, 356, 385, 485
Spatiality 16, 19, 23-25
Specular surface 228, 230, 232, 239, 260, 268, 330
Sphere 164, 174, 175, 176, 178, 181, 185, 186, 187, 194-195, 200, 214, 264--265, 289-290, 297
Spherical surface 187-188
Stadium 28
Stairways 342, 382, 400, 417. *See also* Function space
Station in the face-to-face communication network 82, 127
Streetscape. *See* Contextual space, envelope of, Urbanism
Structural archeology and architecture 357, 387-389, 405-407
Style 389, 405-406, 411-415, 420, 428
Submorphemic level 42, 152, 330, 425, 437
Symmetrical. *See* Regular
Symmetrization 200-202, *fig.* 3.6, 295
Synagogue 224
Syntactic graph 337, 378, 383-384, 388--389, 397, 406, 408-411
Syntactic operation 362, 367-368, 369
Syntactic order 359, *fig.* 3.24, *fig.* 3.26, 366, *fig.* 3.28, 377, 381, 387, 395, 397, 400, 403; one level, 412-416, 420-425, *fig.* 3.36; regular, 380, 395, 409, 420; rules of, 410-411;

Syntactic order: (*contd.*) sociological significance of, 379; three-dimensional, 7, 380, 395, *fig.* 3.35, 415–418, 425, 428
Syntagmatic arrangement 152, 169-170, 192, 337, 356, 358, 359-360; geometrical implications of, 362, 364–365; regular, 370-371, 415, 420–425, *fig.* 3.36, 427–428, *fig.* 3.37, 431–434, 437–439
Syntagmatic graph 359-360, 377, 408, 417, 421, *fig.* 3.36, 425, 433–434
Syntagmatic operation 367, 368-369

T_R. *See* Reverberation time
Tattoo 60, 102
T-data 51
Teaching architectural design 21, 234
Telecommunication 7, 44, 56, 60, 68-69, 136, 224, 307, 488; and communication network 60, 136
Tent 298-299, 368, 378, 407
Text, architectural 357, 358, 359, 368, 378, 385, *fig.* 3.31, 409
Texture. *See* Impression of haptic space
Theater 207, 220, 222, 389; motion-picture, 224, 267, 268
Threshold difference and architectural repertory 36, 162-163
Time 4, 16, 23-25; and architecture 328-329, 337-341, 348, 351, 401, 402–404. *See also* Reading architecture; impression of, 487; and music 24, 339, 341
'Topart' 372-374
Topological characteristics: of space 164, 169, 171-172; of space envelope 171, *fig.* 3.4, 174-178, 204, 364-366; of space system 364-366, 373, 374
Topology and architecture 373-374
Torus: *fig.* 3.4, 175, 178, 205
Total institutions. *See* Experiment, longitudinal
Traffic engineering 158, 311, 374, 383
Transformation of telecommunication into face-to-face communication network 47, 76, 89, 158, 355
Transit space. *See* Function space
Transportation 44-45, 68
Triad. *See* Group, microsocial

U space. *See* Contextual space
U' space. *See* Contextual space
Underground architecture 20-21, 28, 31, 383, *fig.* 3.31.D, *fig.* 3.35, 417
Unifunction 31, 33
Unisensory space 5. *See also specific headings*
Universal space. *See* Contextual space
Unobtrusive measure 454, 466, 467, 474, 476, 477, 484, 489, 501
Urban sociology 11, 29
Urban space. *See* Contextual space
Urbanism 21, 27, 29, 46, 68, 157-158, 161, 232, 248, 299, 311, 374, 383, 385-386, 389, 405, 416
User 29, 30, 35, 55-56, 59, 162, 167, 311, 358, 362, 378, 390, 401, 407, 408, 430, 481, 495

Validity 8, 451, 495, 500-502; external or ecological, 450, 451, 453, 481, 486, 489, 492, 499, 500-502, 503; internal, 450, 451, 492, 494, 500-502, 503
Variables 450, 455-456, 473-474, *fig.* 4.3, 501; X or independent, 58, 61, 452-453, 459-460, 471; Y or dependent, 61, 456-458, 460-462, 469
Verification. *See* Falsification procedure
Vestibule 390, 408
Videotape 465-466
Vision and audition 92, 106-107, 208, 211, 230, 326, 327
Vision and proprioception 226, 260, 322–323, 346
Visitor. *See* Public
Visual sensitivity 92-95, *fig.* 2.4
Volumetric magnitude 5, 15, 155, 199–200, 209, 255. *See also* Capacity of space

Walking distance. *See* Distance, ecological
Wall 22, 42, 208, 209, 303, 307, 350; glass, 313, 314, 330
Wet chamber 297, 309
Window 294
Womb. *See* Space, biofactual
Word, architectural. *See* Space, architectural